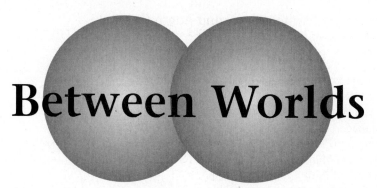

Between Worlds

A Reader, Rhetoric, and Handbook

Sixth Edition

Susan Bachmann

El Camino College

Melinda Barth

El Camino College

Longman

New York San Francisco Boston
London Toronto Sydney Tokyo Singapore Madrid
Mexico City Munich Paris Cape Town Hong Kong Montreal

Again, and again, to the men in our lives:
Ron, Dylan, and Evan Barth
and
Walter, Ryan, and Adam Gajewski

Senior Sponsoring Editor: Virginia L. Blanford
Assistant Editor: Rebecca Gilpin
Senior Marketing Manager: Sandra McGuire
Production Manager: Stacey Kulig
Project Coordination, Text Design, and Electronic Page Makeup: Pre-Press PMG
Senior Cover Design Manager/Cover Designer: Nancy Danahy
Cover Image: Dale Chihuly
Photo Researcher: Clare Maxwell
Manufacturing Buyer: Roy Pickering
Printer and Binder: Courier Corporation
Cover Printer: Courier Corporation

For permission to use copyrighted material, grateful acknowledgment is made to the copyright holders on pp. 619–622, which are hereby made part of this copyright page.

Library of Congress Cataloging-in-Publication Data
Between worlds : a reader, rhetoric, and handbook / Susan Bachmann,
Melinda Barth. -- 6th ed.
    p. cm.
 Includes biographical references and index.
 ISBN-13: 978-0-205-69302-3
 ISBN-10: 0-205-69302-4
1. College readers. 2. English language--Rhetoric--Handbooks, manuals, etc. 3. English language--Grammar--Handbooks, manuals, etc. 4. Report writing--Handbooks, manuals, etc. I. Bachmann, Susan. II. Barth, Melinda.
 PE1417.B43 2010
 808'.0427--dc22

                         2009001270

1 2 3 4 5 6 7 8 9 10—CRS—12 11 10 09

Longman
is an imprint of

www.pearsonhighered.com

ISBN 13: 987-0-205-69302-3
ISBN 10:   0-205-69302-4

Contents

Preface   xvi

PART I   THE READER   1

Getting the Most from Your Reading   2

   Active Reading   2

Thanksgiving *Ellen Goodman*   3

*At Thanksgiving, we realize that we are "a part of and apart from" our families—
"raised in families . . . to be individuals."*

   Discussion of Active Reading   5

   Active Reading as Prewriting   6

   Practicing Active Reading   6

Chapter 1   Between Generations   7

My Son, My Compass *Janna Malamud Smith*   8

*A son questions his family's diet, expounding on the "inhumanity of mass meat
consumption" until he finally convinces his parents of the "ethical, practical, and
ecological issues" involved in eating red meat.*

The Good Daughter *Caroline Hwang*   12

*Immigrant parents make many sacrifices for their daughter. Is she then "indentured"
to her parents, forced to "straddle two cultures"?*

The Color of Love *Danzy Senna*   16

*After an angry argument with her white grandmother, the narrator begins a more
honest relationship with her: "I was proudly black and young and political, and she
was who she was: subtly racist, terribly elitist, and awfully funny."*

Breaking Tradition *Janice Mirikitani*   21

*Having discovered "the lies my mother told me," the narrator longs to communicate
more openly with her daughter whose "secretive eyes are walls of smoke / and music
and telephones."*

On Teenagers and Tattoos *Andres Martin*   24

*Parents may see tattoos and piercings as "self-mutilation" rather than "bodily adorn-
ment," but a nonjudgmental awareness of teenagers' tattoos can be a useful way of
making contact with them.*

Under My Skin *Jon Bowen*   29
*The author explains the reasons that he and others may decide to get a tattoo and
then, years later, to have it removed: "To undo or not to undo—that's the question."*

The Only Child *John Leonard*   34
*"Speed kills slowly, and he fiddled too much with the oxygen flow to his brain," says
the author of his drug-addicted brother.*

Are Families Dangerous? *Barbara Ehrenreich*   37
*While the family can teach "the finest things human beings can learn from one an-
other," too often the family teaches "nasty things like hate and rage and shame."*

The Lanyard *Billy Collins*   41
*In this poignant yet humorous poem, Collins reflects on a childhood gift to his
mother who gave him "a breathing body and a beating heart / strong legs, bones
and teeth, / and two clear eyes to read the world . . .".*

Chapter 2 Between Genders   44

**Boy Friend: Between Those Two Words, A Guy Can
Get Crushed** *Libby Copeland*   45
*When one member in a platonic relationship wishes the friendship were romantic,
the discovery confirms that "the cruelest crush is one between friends."*

Modern Romance *Celeste Biever*   51
*"The Internet has pitched us into a new era of romance that offers greater
opportunities to meet the right partner and a better environment for intimate
and honest communication. But it also plays by different rules."*

Virtual Love *Meghan Daum*   56
*The author discovers that an email relationship is "intense" and "intoxicating," but
its remote nature maintains a "mystique" that can't survive in the physical world.*

Who's Cheap? *Adair Lara*   68
*Should men treat women as "precious" and pick up the check on dates, as they
did in the past?*

Peaches *Reginald McKnight*   71
*Rita's father rejects the "rich white boy" who attempts to win his daughter's affection
by traveling to Africa.*

Blue Spruce *Stephen Perry*   79
*When the town manicurist was pregnant with his child, the barber "bundled her out
of town." His family turned against him, but the writer remembers his music and
laughter.*

Watching My Back *Jeff Z. Klein*   82
*"I hadn't been in a punch-up since I was 10 and had no idea what to do in an actual
fight. But I had seen [my girlfriend] in class, whupping two heavily padded, mock attackers. I knew what she could do."*

Pigskin, Patriarchy, and Pain *Don Sabo*   85
*The former football player believes pain "stifles men's awareness of their bodies and
limits [their] emotional expression."*

When a Woman Says No *Ellen Goodman*   89
*The author focuses on a "change of public mind" as well as the confused messages
and the "yes-no-maybes" that sometimes occur in sexual relationships.*

Where Are You Going, Where Have You Been? *Joyce Carol Oates*   92
Connie felt her heart pound faster as she realized Arnold Friend "wasn't a kid, he was much older—thirty, maybe more."

Chapter 3   Between Cultures   108

Living in Two Worlds *Marcus Mabry*   109
A student travels "between the universes of poverty and affluence" as he moves between home and college life.

Conspiracy Against Assimilation *Robert J. Samuelson*   112
The author offers his own solutions to the immigration problem, contending that both the "guest worker" advocates and "cop school" proponents are, in reality, working against the necessary assimilation of immigrants.

Terra Firma—A Journey from Migrant Farm Labor
to Neurosurgery *Alfredo Quiñones-Hinojosa*   116
Although his cousin told him he would spend the rest of his life as a farm worker, this illegal immigrant went from a community college to the University of California at Berkeley and then on to Harvard Medical School.

Race Is a Four-Letter Word   *Teja Arboleda*   120
The author is "exhausted" from trying to easily describe his mixed heritage and culture and the international experiences that have been an integral part of his life.

An Identity Reduced to a Burka *Semeen Issa and Laila Al-Marayati*   124
"Stereotypical assumptions about Muslim women are as inaccurate as the assumption that all American women are personified by the bikini-clad cast of 'Baywatch.'"

Hidden in Plain Sight *Zaiba Malik*   129
The Muslim author, donning a full Islamic covering for the first time, feels "dissociated" from her mirrored reflection and then suffers discomfort and scorn when she wears the "niqab" in public.

Mr. Z *M. Carl Holman*   133
Distancing himself from his race, Mr. Z married someone who "had somewhere lost her Jewishness," and from there he climbed, "unclogged by ethnic weights."

The Red Convertible *Louise Erdrich*   135
Lyman and his brother Henry owned the first convertible on their reservation, and they owned it together until Henry's "boots filled with water on a windy night," and he bought out Lyman's share of the car.

Los Vendidos *Luis Valdez*   144
The governor's secretary is seeking "a Mexican type for the administration," but the model offered is not at all what she expected.

Chapter 4   Between Perceptions   157

Living under Circe's Spell *Matthew Soyster*   158
The author describes the decline into a "sitting life" in a wheelchair: "People see through me now, or over me. They don't see me at all."

The Difference Between Pity and Empathy *John A. Vaughn*   162
A physician recalls what he learned in med school—from a patient with AIDS: "He never saw the doctor that he helped me become, but every patient I have cared for since has benefited from the lesson he taught me."

The Fringe Benefits of Failure, and the Importance of Imagination *J. K. Rowling*   165

The author of Harry Potter narrates what she learned when she was "the biggest failure [she] knew," and she explains how she came to realize that failure and imagination are vital to creating a rich and meaningful life.

The Myth of the Latin Woman *Judith Ortiz Cofer*   172

A Puerto Rican female living in the United States resents the stereotypes that her Hispanic appearance evokes in many people she meets.

If the Genes Fit *Dan Neil*   178

Sexual orientation is genetically determined, and most people know—without indoctrination or someone else's agenda—"that they were born straight or gay."

Black Men and Public Space *Brent Staples*   181

The author contends with his "unwieldy inheritance . . . the ability to alter public space in ugly ways."

Who Shot Johnny? *Debra Dickerson*   186

Angry that her nephew has been paralyzed by "a brother," the writer reveals, "We've known and feared him all our lives. . . . He and his cancerous carbon copies eclipse the vast majority of us who are not sociopaths."

King Curtis's Echo *Max Thayer*   191

Appalled that he was "ready to go to fist city with a stranger," the author recalls how the gifted sax player King Curtis was stabbed to death when he confronted a stranger relieving himself in front of King's home.

Facing It *Yusef Komanyakaa*   195

The speaker looks at the Vietnam Veterans Memorial and confronts his feelings and memories as he examines the 58,022 names on the wall: "I'm stone. I'm flesh."

Discrimination at Large *Jennifer A. Coleman*   198

Jokes and attitudes against fat people "are as wrong and damaging as any racial or ethnic slur."

O.K., So I'm Fat *Neil Steinberg*   201

It is not the "social stigma," the "medical peril," or "discomfort of dragging all that excess weight around." The real problem with being fat is dealing with thin people.

"Diabesity," A Crisis in an Expanding Country *Jane E. Brody*   204

"Unless we change our eating and exercise habits and pay greater attention to this disease, more than one-third of whites, two-fifths of blacks and half of Hispanic people in this country will develop diabetes."

Bodily Harm *Pamela Erens*   208

Eating disorders—bingeing, excessive dieting, and excessive exercising—are rampant among college women. Shouldn't women's liberation have freed women from "bodily harm"?

Six Rules for Eating Wisely *Michael Pollan*   214

"Don't eat anything your great-great-great-grandmother wouldn't recognize as food," advises the author who poses five additional simple rules "for eating wisely."

Chapter 5 Between Points of View — 218

The Whole World is Watching *Thomas L. Friedman* — 219
Because nearly everyone "has a blog, a MySpace page, or Facebook entry," people are more exposed and "transparent"—an openness that creates paranoia but also opportunities to "outbehave your competition."

YouTube This! *Joe Queenan* — 222
The author refutes the assumption that "some future version of American society will actually hold people accountable for their bozo-like past behavior" and revelations on YouTube!

When the Patient Is a Googler *Scott Haig* — 225
An orthopedic surgeon turns away a suspicious and aggressive patient who Googles and talks more than she's willing to listen.

Is There a Doctor in the Mouse? *Rahul K. Parikh* — 229
Criticizing Scott Haig's "angst about the Internet" in the above essay, this author urges his fellow physicians to help their patients take advantage of the Internet's "vast potential of healthcare information . . . that informs, empowers, and helps patients be smarter and healthier."

Why Reality TV Is Good for Us *James Poniewozik* — 233
Reality shows leave viewers "feeling part of a communal experience" but hating that we feel "sucked into it."

When Reality TV Gets Too Real *Jeremy W. Peters* — 239
Recognizing that "people on the edge make for good television," the author explores the danger inherent in many reality television programs whose producers are not legally required to intervene.

Coke *Philip Dacey* — 243
"Coca-Cola was America / and my Dad drove its truck," boasts the boy, unaware of "the dark, sweet flood / of American sleep" engulfing him.

The Philosophy of Andy Warhol *Andy Warhol* — 246
"You can be watching TV and see Coca-Cola, and you can know that the president drinks Coke, Liz Taylor drinks Coke, and just think, you can drink Coke, too."

Makes Learning Fun *Clifford Stoll* — 247
"What good are glitzy gadgets to a child who can't pay attention in class, won't read more than a paragraph, and is unable to write analytically?"

From Learning as Torture to Learning as Fun *Don Tapscott* — 255
"Learning math should be an enjoyable, challenging, and, yes, entertaining activity just like learning a video game."

In Groups We Shrink *Carol Tavris* — 261
People in groups "do not behave badly because they are inherently bad"; their passivity "has more to do with the nature of groups than the nature of individuals."

Shooting an Elephant *George Orwell* — 264
Even a strong individual can be pressured to act against his own better judgment: "When the white man turns tyrant, it is his own freedom that he destroys."

The Rights of the Born *Anne Lamott*   271
Unable to silence the "insistent" voice of her conscience, the author—a "progressive Christian"—alienates many in her audience when she defends "the reproductive rights of all women."

Tilling a New World *Bill McKibben*   276
Our society is driven to achieve more, but "more" isn't "better" if the planet is doomed by increasing greenhouse gases that are created by the quest for "more."

Three Ways of Meeting Oppression *Martin Luther King Jr.*   279
People handle oppression in different ways, but there is only one practical and moral way to create a community.

Chapter 6   Between Screens   283

Film as Text   283
Between Worlds and Film Choices   285
Common Film Terms and Concepts   286
Active Viewing   286
Final Tips for Writing about Film   287

American Beauty   288
A satire of American culture as a middle-aged man becomes infatuated with his daughter's close friend.
Transcending the Suburbs *David Denby*   288
Dad's Dead, and He's Still a Funny Guy *Janet Maslin*   291
The Rose's Thorns *Kenneth Turan*   294

Crash   298
A series of vignettes exposes anxieties about urban life and conflicts exacerbated by racial and ethnic tension.

Angry People *David Denby*   299
"Crash" *Roger Ebert*   302
Bigotry as the Outer Side of Inner Angst *A. O. Scott*   304

An Inconvenient Truth   308
The truth about global warming may be "inconvenient," but if we acknowledge the scientific evidence we have, "the moral imperative to make big changes is inescapable."

Al Gore Warms Up to a Very Hot Topic *Kevin Crust*   308
Did Al Get the Science Right? *Katharine Mieszkowski*   310
Warnings of Calamities and Hoping for a Change *A. O. Scott*   316

Man on Wire   320
A thrilling account of Philippe Petit's death-defying walk between the towers of the World Trade Center—and the suspenseful preparations that led up to this feat.

Walking on Air Between the Towers *A. O. Scott*   321
"Man on Wire" *Kenneth Turan*   323

PART II   THE RHETORIC   328

Chapter 7   Getting Started . . . Now!   329
   Short Assignments   *Anne Lamott*   329
      Approach a writing assignment "bird by bird."
Prewriting as Discovery   333
   Individual Brainstorming   333
Freewriting   333
   Practicing Freewriting   334
Journal Writing   335
   Practicing Journal Writing   337
Clustering   337
   Practicing Clustering   338
Listing   339
   Practicing Pre-Reading Listing   340
   Practicing Post-Reading Listing   340
Active Reading   341
   Practicing Active Reading and Critical Thinking   342
Group Brainstorming—Collaborative Learning and Critical Thinking 342
   Practicing Brainstorming in Small Groups   343
Incubation   344
Considering Audience   345
   Practicing Style   347
Analyzing Audience Awareness   347
   EXAMPLE: CONVINCING AN AUDIENCE   347
   Why Stop Smoking? Let's Get Clinical   *William F. Harrison* 347
      "About 415,000 people die prematurely each year in the U.S. as a result of smoking—
      the equivalent of eighteen 747s crashing every week with no survivors."
   Practicing Audience Awareness   350

Chapter 8   Organizing and Drafting an Essay   351
From Prewriting to Purpose   351
Discovering the Claim—From General to Specific   353
   Practice Exercise: Recognizing a Thesis   354
   Practicing Thesis Writing   358
Supporting a Thesis   360
Writing an Outline   364
Writing a Paragraph   367
   Practicing Topic Sentences   368
   Practicing How to Recognize Irrelevant Details   370
Using Sources for Support   372
   Practicing the Sandwich   374

Paraphrasing   377
    Practicing Paraphrasing   377
    Practicing Combining Paraphrase and Quotation   379

Chapter 9   Revising an Essay   381

Rewriting and Rewriting   381
    EXAMPLE: DRAFT WITH INSTRUCTOR'S COMMENTS   382
    STUDENT EXAMPLE: FINAL ESSAY   387

    Dieting Daze: No In-Between *Rachel Krell*   387
       The media share blame for eating disorders.

Rewriting for Coherence   390
    Practicing Coherence   396
Writing Titles   397
Writing Introductions   398
Writing Conclusions   401
    Final Tips for Revising   403

Chapter 10   Writing to Persuade   404

Prevalence of Persuasion   404
Persuasion as Argument   405
The Doubting and Believing Games   405
When to Use Argument   406
Brainstorming for an Argument   406
Explicit and Implicit Arguments   407
Arguments and Proposals   409
Sound Reasoning: Balancing Logos, Pathos, and Ethos   409
Audience and Argument   410
Argument Introductions   410
Organizing and Developing An Argument   411
    Preparing Your Argument   411
Strategies for Writing An Argument Essay   412
    Illustrations from the Text   412
    Conceding and Refuting   414
Evaluating an Argument   415
    EXAMPLE: AN ARGUMENT ESSAY   415

    My Favorite School Class: Involuntary Servitude *Joe Goodwin*   416
       Mandatory community service in high school can extend learning
       beyond the classroom—fostering responsibility, civic concern, and understanding.

Avoiding Logical Fallacies   419
    Practicing Writing Argument Essays   421
Final Tips for Argument Essays   421

Chapter 11   Methods for Developing Essays — 422
Combining Multiple Methods — 422

Summary — 425
Organizing and Developing a Summary — 425
STUDENT EXAMPLE: A SUMMARY — 426

A Summary of "Three Ways of Meeting Oppression" *Chris Thomas* — 427
Dr. Martin Luther King argues that only a mass movement of nonviolent resistance will effectively fight oppression and unite people.

Summary as Part of a Larger Assignment — 429
Final Tips for a Summary — 429

Narration — 429
When to Use Narration — 429
Organizing and Developing a Narrative — 430
STUDENT EXAMPLE: A NARRATIVE — 433

Through the Cracks *Rebekah Hall-Naganuma* — 433
An unexpected hospitalization compels a family to stop trying to seem perfect.

Practicing Writing Essays with Narration — 437
Final Tips for a Narrative — 437

Evaluative Response — 438
When to Write an Evaluative Response Essay — 438
Organizing and Developing an Evaluative Response Essay — 438
STUDENT EXAMPLE: AN EVALUATIVE RESPONSE ESSAY — 439

Thanksgiving Beyond the Cleaver Family *Marin Kheng* — 439
Ellen Goodman's essay describes an ideal American Thanksgiving that doesn't represent reality for all families.

Practicing Writing an Evaluative Response Essay — 443
Final Tips for an Evaluative Response Essay — 444

Definition — 444
When to Use Definition — 444
Organizing and Developing a Definition Essay — 445
The Purpose of Defining — 445
EXAMPLE: AN ESSAY BASED ON DEFINITION — 446

You Call That Irony? *Jon Winokur* — 446
Readers who have often exclaimed, "That's ironic!" may rethink their use of the word because of Winokur's provocative examination of this term.

Practicing Writing Definition Essays — 449
Final Tips for a Definition Essay — 449

Cause and Effect   449
When to Use Cause-and-Effect Development   450
Organizing and Developing a Cause-and-Effect Essay   450
    EXAMPLE: A CAUSE-AND-EFFECT ESSAY   451

      I Confess Some Envy *Robert McKelvey*   451
        "It was our curious, sad fate to be blamed for a war we had not chosen to fight,
        when in reality we were among its victims."
    Practicing Writing Essays about Causes and Effects   453
    Final Tips for Cause-and-Effect Development   454

Comparison and Contrast   454
When to Use Comparison-Contrast Development   454
Organizing and Developing a Comparison-Contrast Essay   455
Which Method to Use: Block or Point by Point?   456
    EXAMPLE: A COMPARISON-CONTRAST ESSAY   456

      Reality Check *Alex Garcia*   456
        On a trip to Cuba, the author questions his most basic assumptions and values.
    Practicing Writing Essays That Use Comparison and Contrast   460
    Final Tips for Comparison and Contrast Essays   460

Chapter 12 Analysis   461

Analysis of a Process, Problem, or Subject   461
When to Use Analysis   461

Analysis of a Process   462
    Practicing Process Analysis in Small Groups   463
EXAMPLE: A PROCESS ANALYSIS ESSAY   463

      How to Get Better Gas Mileage *Katharine Mieszkowski*   463
        Providing "simple steps that every driver can take with an existing car, truck, or SUV
        to save fuel," the author proposes ways to save drivers "the equivalent of $1 a gallon"
        or nearly 33 percent of their fuel.
    Practicing Writing a Process Analysis Essay   467
    Final Tips for a Process Analysis Essay   468

Analysis of a Problem   468
    EXAMPLE: A PROBLEM ANALYSIS ESSAY   469

      Don't Let Stereotypes Warp Your Judgments   *Robert L. Heilbroner*   470
        The author focuses on stereotypes, "a kind of gossip about the world, a gossip that
        makes us prejudge people before we ever lay eyes on them."
    Practicing Writing a Problem Analysis Essay   473
    Final Tips for a Problem Analysis Essay   474

Analysis of a Subject   474
Poetry and Character Analysis   476
   What Is Poetry Analysis?   476
   EXAMPLE: ACTIVE READING OF A POEM   478

   Breaking Tradition *Janice Mirikitani*   478
   STUDENT EXAMPLE: POETRY ANALYSIS   480

   Breaking the Ties That Bind *Robert Sakatani*   480
     The mother who narrates Mirikitani's poem not only traces her own rebellious nature and desire to "break tradition," but she also recognizes a parallel between her daughter's life and her own past.
   Practicing Writing Poetry Analysis   484
   Final Tips for Poetry Analysis   485
   What Is Character Analysis?   485
   Character Analysis: Short Story   485
   STUDENT EXAMPLE: CHARACTER ANALYSIS ESSAY   489

   Who Were You, Connie, and Why Did You Go? *Marianela Enriquez*   489
     Oates's chilling story destroys the reader's sense that negative outcomes can be prevented.
   Practicing Writing a Character Analysis   493
   Character Analysis: Biography   493
   STUDENT EXAMPLE: BIOGRAPHY ESSAY   497

   The Earhart Appeal *Leselle Norville*   497
     Amelia Earhart was an intriguing blend of reserve and charm, of restlessness and determination, and of competence and complacency; however, it is her insecurity that accounted for her varied shades of character.
   Final Tips for Writing a Focused Biography   507

Chapter 13   Writing the Research Paper   509
Planning the Research Paper   509
Gathering Library Material   512
Beginning a Periodical Search—Head for the Databases   513
Beginning an Internet Search—Some Cautions   514
Refining an Internet Search   515

   Evaluation Criteria for Web Sources: "The Good, the Bad, and the Ugly" *Susan E. Beck*   517
   Practice Finding the Errors   519
Gathering Additional Information: The Interview   522
   STUDENT EXAMPLE: RESEARCH PAPER   523

   From Access to Acceptance: Enabling America's Largest Minority *Shannon Paaske*   524
     A well-documented research paper shows us that individuals must follow the steps taken by government, science, and the media to secure acceptance for the disabled.

Documenting the Research Paper: MLA Style   540
   Indicating Titles   540
   Writing Parenthetical Citations   540
   Preparing the Works Cited Page   544
   Sample MLA Entries   546
Documenting the Research Paper: APA Style   554
   Writing Parenthetical Citations   554
   Specific Examples of APA Form   555
   Preparing the References Page   556
   Sample APA Entries   556

PART III   THE HANDBOOK

PART III   THE HANDBOOK   560

Chapter 14   Understanding How Sentences Work

Chapter 14   Understanding How Sentences Work   561
Subjects   561
Objects   562
Verbs   563
Adjectives and Adverbs   564
Phrases   564
Clauses   566
Sentence Variation   567
   Practicing Sentence Variation   568

Chapter 15   Understanding Common Errors

Chapter 15   Understanding Common Errors   569
Fragments   569
Run-on or Fused Sentences   571
Pronoun Reference Agreement   574
Pronoun Case   576
Subject-Verb Agreement   577
Shifts   579
Mixed Sentences   581
Misplaced and Dangling Modifiers   583
Faulty Parallelism   584

Chapter 16   Understanding Punctuation

Chapter 16   Understanding Punctuation   586
The Comma   586
The Apostrophe   589
The Period, Question Mark, and Exclamation Point   593
The Semicolon   593
The Colon   594
The Dash   595
Quotation Marks   595

Italics 597
The Ellipsis 598
Parentheses 599
Brackets 600
The Slash 600
The Hyphen 601

Chapter 17 Understanding Faulty Word Choice 603
Clichés 603
Slang, Jargon, and Colloquial Words 603
Archaic Words, Euphemisms, and Pretentious Words 604
Redundancies 605
Sexist Language 606
Glossary of Usage: Commonly Confused Words 607
Credits 619
Author Index 623
Subject and Title Index 624

Editing Symbols chart appears opposite page 636.

Preface

The sixth edition of *Between Worlds* remains a Reader, Rhetoric, and Handbook—a three-in-one textbook, thereby saving students money and providing instructors all the essentials under one cover. The Reader features topics that students care about, ranging from dating and tattoos to ethnic stereotyping and YouTube—all designed to prompt lively discussions and spirited writing. Following the readings, a concise Rhetoric guides students through every aspect of the writing process with modeled writing assignments, including two student research papers. The Handbook is particularly student-friendly, providing succinct explanations to correct those common errors typically noted on students' essays. Although each part of this textbook can be used independently, both instructors and students value our instructive connections between readings and writing assignments.

Since the publication of the first edition, we have received overwhelming support for combining three texts within one cover, for our selection of lively readings, and for a voice that students find appealing. Instructors appreciate the meaningful discussion questions and writing topics for each reading—huge time savers for faculty and helpful prompts for students. We have connected each of the readings not only by theme but also by authors' strategies and intentions. Further, those same readings are analyzed in the Rhetoric to demonstrate writing strategies that students can emulate. The sixth edition retains our successes and includes some exciting changes and additions:

The Most Requested Addition: A New Chapter—Writing to Persuade　Realizing that nearly all college writing aims to persuade or convince a reader, we are providing an entire chapter focused on argument. Students will learn how to brainstorm for a topic to determine their own views and position on an issue. We encourage students to play Peter Elbow's "believing game—the disciplined practice" of welcoming unfamiliar ideas—as energetically as they play the doubting game—questioning and scrutinizing reasons and assumptions. We provide strategies for shaping an explicit or implicit argument, for anticipating a reader's objections, for developing a sound and convincing paper, and for avoiding logical fallacies. We urge students to consider alternative views of a subject in order to discover their own stance.

A New Chapter of Provocative Readings: Between Points of View　In this chapter, we have deliberately paired writers with contrasting views on subjects that students will want to discuss, debate, and write about—self-exposure on the Internet, Googling for information, reality TV programming, computers in the classroom, and the influence of the group on individual behavior. Other provocative readings argue for the rights of the born and against thoughtless consumption.

New Additions to the Rhetoric   In responding to our students and reviewers—and our colleagues who have used this book for nearly two decades—we have

- expanded our prewriting material.
- provided additional practice exercises.
- demonstrated pre-reading strategies.
- developed the section on thesis statements.
- offered more materials to help students strengthen their paragraphs.
- strengthened instruction on avoiding plagiarism.
- illustrated how to write effective titles.
- designed more interactive questions for revising an essay.
- developed a new chapter, Writing to Persuade.
- included new models for a definition and a process analysis essay.

New Guideline, Materials, and Essays Featuring the Internet   Recognizing the prevalence of the Internet in our academic and personal lives, we have integrated online materials throughout this edition:

- **An updated guideline about evaluating Internet sources:** "The Good, the Bad, and the Ugly" by Susan E. Beck
- **Recommended databases, web sites, and methods** for successful on-line searches
- **More illustrations and practice exercises to avoid plagiarism** both on-line and offline
- **Essays examining life and work on the Internet**: "Modern Romance," "Virtual Love," "When the Patient Is a Googler," "Is There a Doctor in the Mouse?" "The Whole World Is Watching," "YouTube This," "Makes Learning Fun," and "From Learning as Torture to Learning as Fun"

New Genre: Documentary Films   Two highly-acclaimed documentaries join our film chapter: *An Inconvenient Truth* and *Man on Wire*. Al Gore's film compels viewers to re-evaluate our country's policies and our own personal habits, and Philippe Petit's biographical film draws audiences into a life that is both awesome and terrifying. Both documentaries provide stirring subjects for the writing assignments on character analysis and focused biography. In fact, Philippe Petit's 2002 memoir, *To Reach the Clouds*, might be studied in conjunction with the film for a longer assignment based on biography. These films join our other best-picture offerings, *American Beauty* and *Crash*. Readily available at libraries or rental facilities, these provocative films provide energizing alternatives to traditional texts. Detailed study questions and writing assignments ensure that instructors do not have to undertake this work mid-semester and that students have focused instruction prior to viewing the films. Analytic essays by favorite American critics stimulate critical thinking, provoke class discussions, and serve as catalysts and models for writing assignments. Further, the study guides are provided in the familiar format: "Thinking about the Text," "Writing from the Text," and "Connecting with Other Texts," and all questions are discussed in greater detail in the *Instructor's Manual*.

New Readings and More Varied Topics New selections revitalize each of the existing chapters to reflect the conflicting realms—the "between worlds"—in which most of us live. Like us, the individuals in these readings are caught *between* balancing the burdens of work and school, *between* satisfying family obligations and meeting personal needs, and *between* defining self while relating with others. New readings show divergent views about love and dating, the individual in society, the nature of families, and gender and culture identification. Recognizing the value of wit in creating memorable writing (and keeping readers awake!), we have added more humorous selections as well as cartoons that complement our essays. In response to instructors' recommendations, we have also added many more provocative argument essays.

New Voices and Favorite Voices Esteemed writers *new* to this edition include Billy Collins, Thomas L. Friedman, Bill McKibben, Dan Neil, Jeremy W. Peters, Michael Pollan, James Poniewozik, Joe Queenan, Robert Samuelson, and Andy Warhol, and film reviewer Kevin Crust. This edition continues to include writers favored by students and instructors: Judith Ortiz Cofer, Meghan Daum, Barbara Ehrenreich, Louise Erdrich, Ellen Goodman, Jeff Z. Klein, Martin Luther King Jr., Yusef Komanyakaa, Anne Lamott, Joyce Carol Oates, George Orwell, Brent Staples, Neil Steinberg, Cliff Stoll, Carol Tavris, Luis Valdez, and popular reviewers David Denby, Janet Maslin, A. O. Scott, and Kenneth Turan.

New Reading Questions and Writing Assignments The "Thinking about the Text" questions have been revised to focus as much on audience and purpose as on content—to encourage students to examine the writer's strategies and to experiment with their own. The "Writing from the Text" sections provide students with varied writing prompts for each reading. In "Connecting with Other Texts," both the new and retained readings are linked by theme, technique, and purpose.

Diverse Forms, Styles, and Techniques Our varied genres include lively essays; film reviews, analyses, and interviews; editorials and commentaries;

paired arguments with contrasting positions; stirring narratives; and short stories, poems, biographies, memoirs, and a play. In addition, we include photos and cartoons which visually complement the writings and films.

New Materials on Research Chapter 13 includes the very latest MLA changes as well as APA guidelines and documentation forms. Because so much of the research process is now done online, we continue to offer a section on using, evaluating, and abusing electronic sources—"The Good, the Bad, and the Ugly"—as well as on documenting electronic sources.

New Handbook Entries Part III, a handbook designed to empower students but not overwhelm them, focuses on the most common errors—the "terrible ten"—that persist in student writing. To help students interpret their instructors' comments, a list of marginal symbols is included on the inside back cover.

New Instructor's Manual An updated *Instructor's Manual* features answers to "Thinking about the Text" questions, including extraordinarily detailed analyses of the five films, subthemes found in each chapter, cross-referencing of readings between chapters, and sample course syllabi.

Applause

This textbook could never have been written without the help of many people who have been particularly supportive and generous with their time as we worked on this book. Superb librarians and computer specialists assisted us in countless ways. We continue to be grateful to Ed Martinez, Claudia Striepe, and Moon Ichinaga from the El Camino College library, and librarian Eileen Wakiji and computer specialist Walter Gajewski, both from California State University at Long Beach. All of these knowledgeable individuals gave of their time and technological expertise to help us teach students and improve this book. Over the years, colleagues at El Camino College have readily and generously shared readings, strategies, and writing ideas that inspired many aspects of this book. We are indebted to these colleagues: Amanda Ackerman, Marilyn Anderson, Mimi Ansite, Nancy Armstrong, Sara Blake, Debra Breckheimer, Matt Cheung, Dana Crotwell, Nancy Currey, Paul Freeborn, Elise Geraghty, Julia Hackner, Greta Hendricks, Julia Hackner, Zahid Hossain, Dalia Juarez, Mandy Kronbeck, Debra Mochidome, Kareema Nasouf, Leah Pate, Kim Runkle, Cynthia Silverman, Eric Takamine, Cindy Tino-Sandoval, Evelyn Uyemura, Kathy Vertullo, and Steve Waterworth.

We are also grateful to our Humanities Division Associative Dean Barbara Jaffe and to our administrative staff member Charlotte Koyanagi for their support of our book. We are especially pleased to include the work of our fine students: Marianela Enriquez, Rebekah Hall-Naganuma, Marin Kheng, Leselle Norville, Shannon Paaske, Robert Sakatani, and Chris Thomas, all of whom exemplify the extraordinary commitment of so many college writers. These, and all of our students, have helped us select readings and develop instructional materials for each new edition. They merit hearty applause.

A number of fine academic reviewers brought insights from their teaching to improve this book: Glenda Conway, University of Montevallo; Ed Davis, Sinclair Community College; Jane Flesher, Chippewa Valley Technical College; Doug Friedlander, Hofstra University; Jim Hayes, Grand Rapids Community College; Carl Sennhenn, Rose State College; Roberta Tragarz, Santiago Canyon College.

We are grateful to our editor at Pearson Longman, Ginny Blanford, whose enthusiasm and support encouraged us to include visuals, to feature an entire chapter on film, and to expand our argument section into a complete chapter. We also thank our assistant editor Rebecca Gilpin for her prompt responses and dependable help. Special thanks must go to Ken Clark at Chihuly Studios for his persistent search through the archives for yet another photo for our cover. We are indebted to our permissions editor Caroline Gloodt for her tireless efforts contacting authors and to Kim Hansen and Daniel Nighting for their diligent reading and perceptive editing of our text. Artist Nancy Danahy, who has demonstrated her fine talents on several of our covers, deserves our thanks. We also appreciate Teresa Ward's flexibility with the schedule and her conscientious work on the *Instructor's Manual*.

Finally, we want to try to thank our families who have, for nearly two decades, lived *Between Worlds* with us. As the book has grown and changed its shape, our families, too, have metamorphosed, and one now has expanded to include two women, Tia and Delaiah, both English teachers. The children we once banished so we could write—Dylan, Evan, Ryan, and Adam—are now adults who use the book in their writing and teaching. We have come to count on their valuable suggestions. In addition to providing creative insights, Walter and Ron continue to support our book by resolving the technical emergencies and by handling the domestic spheres we have abandoned in order to write. Our family members and friends often send us relevant articles and now recommend significant films. As we revise and expand each edition, they often inquire when our work on the book will be done. We honestly and consistently reply, "Never!" Fortunately, they all believe our book is worth their being temporarily "displaced," and we applaud their willingness to live "between worlds" with us.

Susan Bachmann

Melinda Barth

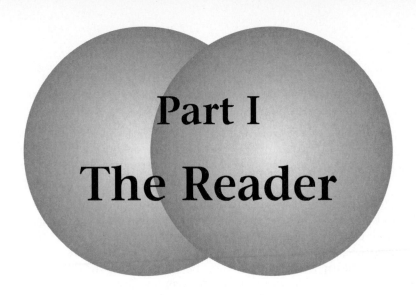

Part I

The Reader

The readings in this book have been chosen to reflect the interests of college students like you, who are juggling school and work as well as social lives and family expectations. The selections in Part I have been arranged into six chapters:

Chapter 1. *Between Generations:* Many of the authors in this chapter are caught between generations and, like you, may be trying to understand themselves in relation to parents and grandparents.

Chapter 2. *Between Genders:* Just as you may be examining the roles that define your gender, many authors in this chapter argue for a reexamination of the roles that limit the lives of people of both sexes.

Chapter 3. *Between Cultures:* Whether you are a newcomer to the United States, a second- or third-generation American, or a native whose roots go back for generations, you may find that the writers in this chapter describe experiences that you have had, living between cultures.

Chapter 4. *Between Perceptions:* Your self-perception is inevitably colored by the images that others have of you. Yet your desire to be perceived as an individual, rather than a stereotype, is also the experience of many college students and of the authors who write about being between perceptions.

Chapter 5. *Between Points of View:* Examining the contrasting ideas of the authors included in this chapter will help you to assess your own convictions, something that you may be doing more seriously since you started college.

Chapter 6. *Between Screens:* Each film discussed and reviewed in this chapter invites you to view the multiple worlds in which we live and the tensions that pull us between the realms of generations, genders, cultures, perceptions, and points of view.

We chose these readings and films to stimulate your thinking and to enable you to write meaningful essays—the goal of any composition course.

Each chapter contains readings, all arranged to illustrate parallels or contrasts with each other. Three sets of exercises follow each reading. The first, called "Thinking About the Text," consists of questions designed as a review prior to class and for small-group discussions during class. These questions are followed by "Writing from the Text," which are writing assignments drawn from the readings and from your own experience. Your instructor may assign these topics, or you may use them for practice writing in a journal. You will find help for writing these assignments in Part II, the rhetoric portion of this book. The last set of exercises, "Connecting with Other Texts," asks you to compare two or more readings in this book. Some assignments encourage you to find additional material in the library, which is useful if your instructor assigns a paper that requires research. You will find information on how to write research papers of various lengths in Part II.

Getting the Most from Your Reading

How often have you spent time reading something only to discover that you have no idea what you've just read? Worse still, have you ever found yourself supposedly reading but, instead, daydreaming about your last date, a great play-off game, or a conversation with friends? The hours that you waste in unproductive reading can be saved. Here's how.

Active Reading

Active reading is a strategy that helps you to remain focused on the text and retain what you have read. Useful in all of your courses, active reading enables you to perceive the author's thesis and key points, supporting details, and meaningful lines, as well as to discover your own thoughts about the material.

Active reading involves reading with a pen in your hand. Although highlighters are popular with many students, it is impossible to use them to write summary notes in the margin and too difficult to switch between highlighter and pen. If you are using your own book, you can make marks directly on your copy as you are reading. If you are using a library book, you will need to photocopy the pages you intend to read actively. With either method, you should do the following as you read:

- *Underline* the thesis (if it is explicitly stated), key points, and supporting details.
- *Mark* meaningful or quotable language.
- *Place checkmarks and asterisks* next to important lines.
- *Jot* brief summary or commentary notes in the margins. Infer the thesis and write it in the margin if it is not explicitly stated.
- *Circle* or *put a box around* unfamiliar words and references to look up later.
- *Ask* questions as you read.
- *Seek* answers to those questions.
- *Question* the writer's assumptions and assertions as well as your own.

Reading actively allows you to enter into a conversation with your authors—to examine and challenge their ideas. Active reading also helps you find important lines more easily so that you don't have to reread the entire work each time that you refer to it during class discussions or in your essays. Having the key points underlined means you can quickly review them for a quiz. If your instructor asks you to keep a journal of your responses to readings, you can use the meaningful lines you have marked or the marginal notes to begin your journal entry. Don't underline or highlight *everything,* however, or you will defeat your purpose of finding just the important points.

Let's now look at an active reading of Ellen Goodman's "Thanksgiving." What comments or questions can you add?

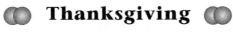

Thanksgiving

Ellen Goodman

A journalist who has worked for *Newsweek,* CBS, NBC, and a number of metropolitan newspapers, Ellen Goodman (b. 1941) has written a widely syndicated column from her home paper, the *Boston Globe,* since 1967. Goodman won the Pulitzer Prize in 1980 for distinguished commentary. She is author of *Paper Trails: Common Sense in Uncommon Times* (2004), coauthor with Patricia O'Brien of *I Know Just What You Mean: The Power of Friendship in Women's Lives* (2000), and the author of *Value Judgments,* a collection of newspaper columns (1993). Goodman asserts that it is "much more important to look at the underlying values by which this country exists . . . the vast social changes in the way men and women lead their lives and deal with each other, [and] about children" than to write about the "trivia," like politics, that other columnists write about. The essay included here, on the importance of family, was first published in the *Boston Globe* in 1980.

nice image!

1   Soon they will be together again, all the <u>people who travel between their own lives and each other's</u>. The package tour of the season will lure them this week to the family table. By Thursday, feast day, family day, Thanksgiving day, Americans who value individualism like no other people will collect around a million tables in a <u>ritual of belonging</u>.

Thanksgiving: "a ritual of belonging"

2   They will assemble their families the way they assemble dinner: each one bearing a <u>personality as different as cranberry sauce and pumpkin pie.</u> For one dinner they will cook for each other, fuss for each other, feed each other and argue with each other. They will nod at their <u>common heritage, the craziness and caring of other generations.</u> They will measure their <u>common legacy . . . the children.</u>

"craziness and caring"

3   All these complex cells, these men and women, old and young, with different dreams and disappointments will give homage again to the group they are <u>a part of</u> and <u>apart from</u>: their family. <u>Families and individuals.</u> The <u>"we" and the "I."</u> As good Americans we <u>all travel between these two ideals.</u> We take value trips from the great American notion of individualism to the great American vision of family. We wear out our tires driving back and forth, using speed to shorten the distance between these two principles.

thesis

2 ideals: families & individuals

"We" & "I"

4   There has always been some pavement between a person and a family. From the first moment we recognize that we are separate we begin to wrestle with aloneness and togetherness. Here and now these conflicts are especially acute. We are, after all, <u>raised in families . . . to be individuals.</u> This double message follows us through life. We are taught about the freedom of the "I" and the safety of the "we." The loneliness of the "I" and the intrusiveness of the "we." The selfishness of the "I" and the burdens of the "we."

ironic →

"we" & "I" again

5   We are taught what André Malraux said: "<u>Without a family, man, alone in the world, trembles with the cold.</u>" And taught what he said another day: "The denial of the supreme importance of the mind's development accounts for many revolts against the family." In theory, the <u>world rewards</u> "the supreme importance" of the individual, <u>the ego.</u> We think alone, inside our heads. We write music and literature with an enlarged sense of self. We are graded and paid, hired and fired, on our own merit. The ⬚rank⬚ individualism is both exciting and cruel. Here is where the fittest survive.

ideal quote for journal

world rewards the "ego"—meaning?

meaning?

6   The family, on the other hand, at its best, works very differently. <u>We don't have to achieve to be accepted by our families.</u> We just

true?

have to be. Our membership is not based on credentials but on birth. As Malraux put it, "A friend loves you for your intelligence, a mistress for your charm, but your family's love is unreasoning: You were born into it and of its flesh and blood."

7   The <u>family</u> is formed not for the <u>survival of the fittest</u> but for the <u>weakest</u>. It is not an economic unit but an emotional one. This is not the place where people ruthlessly compete with each other but where they work for each other. Its business is taking care, and <u>when it works</u>, it is <u>not callous but kind</u>.

family → where the weakest survive

8   There are fewer heroes, fewer stars in family life. While the world may glorify the self, the family asks us, at one time or another, to submerge it. While the <u>world may abandon</u> us, the family promises, at one time or another, to protect us. So we commute daily, weekly, yearly <u>between one world and another.</u> Between a life as a family member that can be nurturing or smothering. Between life as an individual that can free us or flatten us. We vacillate between two separate sets of demands and possibilities.

*
"world may abandon us" family should "protect us"*

meaning?

"between worlds" theme

9   The people who will gather around this table Thursday <u>live in both of these worlds, a part of</u> and <u>apart from</u> each other. With any luck the territory they travel from one to another can be a fertile one, rich with care and space. It can be a place where the "I" and the "we" interact. On this day at least, they will bring to each other something both special and <u>something to be shared: these separate selves.</u>

thesis restated (words varied)

Discussion of Active Reading

As we read Ellen Goodman's essay, we were on the lookout for key phrases, important concepts, unfamiliar words, and the thesis or focus of the essay. We immediately underlined her description of "people who travel between their own lives and each other's" and noted "nice image!" in the margin. As soon as we found memorable phrases such as the definition of Thanksgiving as "a ritual of belonging" or the simile comparing personalities of family members "as different as cranberry sauce and pumpkin pie," we underlined these as well and made relevant notations in the margin. We also underlined Goodman's description of people's "common heritage, the craziness and caring of other generations" and "their common legacy . . . the children," noting "craziness and caring" in the margin.

We boxed in two words—"rank" and "vacillate"—that we thought students might not be familiar with, and we wrote "meaning?" in the margin as a reminder to look them up in the dictionary. When we spotted what we thought was Goodman's thesis, we identified it in the margin: "All these complex cells, these men and women, old and young, with different dreams and disappointments will give homage again to the group they are a part of and apart from: their family." We continued to underline key phrases or meaningful lines and noted a brief response to each in the margin.

We also noted how Goodman begins her conclusion by repeating her thesis but in different words: "The people who will gather around this table Thursday live in both of these worlds, a part of and apart from each other." You will find another example of active reading on page 4 and advice for active viewing of a film on page 286.

Active Reading as Prewriting

Because active reading is a natural warm-up for writing, we encourage you, as we do our students, to keep a journal of meaningful lines from readings. It helps to copy each quotation at the top of a journal page as a prompt for your response. You can respond with your personal feelings about the ideas in the quoted line. These ideas might remind you of an experience from your childhood or comments made by a family member or friend.

Sometimes you may react vehemently to the author's tone or idea in the quoted line and write responses you wouldn't feel comfortable giving in class discussion. The journal responses to these quoted lines can become a part of future writing assignments or can just help you sort out your own ideas in an uncensored place.

PRACTICING ACTIVE READING

1. Select any reading in the first chapter, "Between Generations," or use the first reading assigned by your instructor to practice active reading. Follow the steps described above to interact with the text.

2. Actively read Robert L. Heilbroner's essay "Don't Let Stereotypes Warp Your Judgments" (p. 470), underlining meaningful lines and making summary notes in the margin. Look for his thesis and infer it if it is not explicitly stated.

3. Select a line from "Thanksgiving" that you find meaningful and copy it at the top of a page. Then write an uncensored response that expresses your feelings or your analysis of that quotation. If you keep your journal on a computer, you will be amazed by how much you have to express.

Chapter 1

Between Generations

In the essay that we used to demonstrate active reading (p. 3), author Ellen Goodman quotes André Malraux's belief that "without a family" the individual "alone in the world, trembles with the cold." The family often nurtures its members and tolerates differences and failings that friends and lovers cannot accept. Janna Malamud Smith describes a home environment that nourishes her son's individuality in diet and philosophy that eventually the entire family embraces. If you have, or have had, a strained bond with a grandparent, you will value Danzy Senna's acceptance of her strong-willed grandmother. If you and your parents are at odds over your decisions to change your body image, you will find Andres Martin's and Jon Bowen's views on tattoos instructive.

The differences between generations can be both illuminating and poignant, as you will see in Caroline Hwang's essay and Janice Mirikitani's and Billy Collins's poems. But as you may realize from your own experiences and observations, people also tremble with fear or anxiety even within the family unit. John Leonard illustrates in his essay that family members sometimes are forced to turn from one another, and, as Barbara Ehrenreich shows, the family can also be a place where love becomes insidious and can turn into something murderous. The writers in this chapter show the family as a source of both nurturing and anxiety.

Your awareness of gaps between generations, as well as a deeper sense of family connection, may inspire your own writing. The essays, short stories, and poems in this chapter attest to the will of the human spirit to mitigate family tension, to smile at some of the chaos, and to survive and thrive from one generation to the next.

"Mommy wants you to know where your food comes from."

 My Son, My Compass

Janna Malamud Smith

With an undergraduate degree from Harvard and a master's degree from Smith, Janna Malamud Smith (b. 1952) has been employed as a social worker in the department of psychiatry at Cambridge Hospital since 1979. Author of *A Potent Spell: Mother Love and the Power of Fear* (2003) and *Private Matters: In Defense of the Personal Life* (1997), Smith notes: "I have learned lately that I love research and winding it into writing. With language, less is more." A contributor to numerous professional journals and newspapers, Smith published the following essay in *OrganicStyle.com* in November 2004.

1   We stopped eating red meat in our house. Our younger, teenage son convinced us that it was something we had to do. He read aloud from books, shocked us with disgusting descriptions, and explained the ethical, practical, and ecological issues. He ordered large pictures of skinned cows' heads from People for the Ethical Treatment of Animals, found a friend willing to accompany him, and picketed a Burger King. He expounded on the inhumanity of mass meat production.

2   Weren't we big on humane? The square peg of our practices didn't fit into the round hole of our proffered worldview, the one we'd been belaboring him with since birth: "Pat the bunny," not "Eat the bunny." We felt cornered; for us, his force was startling. The cute, bottle-fed, nuzzling calf we'd kept warm near the stove was back—a grown bull busting its horns right through our screen door without slowing.

3   Not that we were philosophically opposed to his propositions; we were simply accustomed to eating cows, pigs, and sheep. In fact, we really enjoyed red meat: roasted spring lamb marinated with garlic and mustard à la Julia Child (bless her carnivorous soul); large grilled hamburgers with ketchup and sour pickles. My husband and I had long fancied ourselves gourmands and had spent years together preparing exacting recipes from French cookbooks. (You try convincing a pharmacist that the saltpeter—read: gunpowder ingredient—you wish to buy will be used to preserve a duck.) We were proud of our sense of culinary adventure.

4   Until you have raised a child, it is hard to comprehend how unsettling it is the first time you take moral direction from him. I'm not talking about instruction, such as how to skip tracks on the CD player or turn on the new computer. The feeling I describe is more fundamental. There is something about the momentous emotional occasion of giving birth to—or adopting—a child that creates a sweeping, elaborate frieze. You become the heroic protector holding off the attacking centaurs. However sturdy your fragile infant grows, you are still on that pediment: carved in stone, directing his view, your whole body and soul curved around him.

5   But somehow, in the middle of this tale, our boy departed from our story line. All at once, he led, and shouted to us to follow. He declared himself, voice trembling, a vegan, knowing we did not approve. He renounced not just meat, but fish, milk, cheese, eggs, honey, and leather products. He bought cloth sneakers and made a wallet out of duct tape. He started reading food labels, spotting hidden by-products such as ground-up cow udder in jars of tomato sauce.

6   I was beside myself—on one hand, feeling hassled by his assertions; on the other, fearful of his becoming malnourished or being put on some FBI domestic terrorism list. I felt I had fallen down a rabbit hole and landed in a world dominated by a tyrannical zealot who believed tempeh was food. He suffered, I said to my husband, from a left-wing, overprivileged-child eating disorder.

7   Or did he? I wondered, lying in bed, sleepless, worrying about protein deficiency. Could he be right? Or partly right? "Human beings have always eaten meat," I had challenged him. "Our bodies need animal protein."

8   "Mom, people needed any food they could get in the past. We don't. We have plenty of vegetable proteins, and vitamins and supplements. Half the

water used in this country goes for raising beef. And think of all the animal waste running into the rivers. It's not right. It's not right to bring animals into the world in crowded cages where they never walk or see daylight; to treat living creatures as if they were nothing more than industrial objects."

9   Trying to come to terms with my split feelings, I thought about a lecture on aging I'd heard by George Vaillant, a Harvard professor who studied adaptation. For decades, he had tracked and repeatedly interviewed hundreds of men, seeking to decipher who fared well or badly across time, and why. One trait the successful fellows held in common was that they allowed themselves to learn from their children.

10   "Easy for him to say," I grumbled. Yet, in spite of my grouchiness, the penny dropped. The years had repositioned me. At 12, I attended my first rally with Martin Luther King Jr. I marched against the Vietnam war and for women's rights. But time had reset the stage. At 50, mine had become the outdated worldview in need of reform. Not only was I being called upon to loosen my protective grip on my charge, I needed to reconsider my position in the universe. Like a skilled karate artist, our son took the very premises we'd espoused to him and pushed them further, until we toppled.

11   So ours is now a household, and a menu, in transition. My husband and I still eat fish and, occasionally, fowl, but our boy's efforts have fundamentally altered our thinking, and our diets. Most nights we cook vegan dishes. No tempeh yet, but red lentil soup; pinto bean, onion, salsa, and brown-rice burritos; baked winter squash stuffed with apples, raisins, and walnuts; pasta with spinach, sun-dried tomatoes, and artichokes. A fresh cornucopia.

12   I scan vegan cookbooks for recipes offering flavor and enough nutrition to appease the bones of a growing teenager. Some taste delicious. Others don't. Some evenings, walking around my neighborhood, the smell of meat grilling starts me hallucinating about flank steak marinated in garlic, soy sauce, and grated orange peel, seared medium rare, sliced on the bias, nicely salted. My husband and I sometimes whisper conspiratorially about sneaking away to, say, Italy for a delicate slice of prosciutto wrapped around a bit of perfectly ripened melon.

13   But the truth is, in spite of an occasional longing, I feel healthy consuming less animal protein—lighter, closer to the earth, in tune with an older Mediterranean diet. And I enjoy with my family a peaceable sense that by eating lower on the food chain, we're doing the right thing for the environment, and for livestock. It's gratifying to let a compelling argument alter your behavior. It gives you hope. If you can change, the world can. Every so often, I still annoy our son by lecturing him about some esoteric peril of vegan nutrition I've discovered on the Web. Every so often, he annoys me by proselytizing: "Couldn't you please stop eating dead birds, Mom?" But mostly, we are

all quietly satisfied to discover our family making its way together, finding our footing through two transitions: red meat to legumes, and sons to men.

THINKING ABOUT THE TEXT

1. The author might have saved the opening revelation—that her son convinced her and her husband to stop eating red meat—for the end of the essay. What are some advantages of *beginning* with this revelation? Explain each advantage.

2. In your own words, express the author's thesis so that her two-pronged themes of parenting and changing values are connected.

3. Why does the author allude to Harvard professor George Vaillant and his findings on adaptation? How does this reference sharpen and expand the author's focus beyond her son and red meat?

4. Explain and evaluate the son's reasons for renouncing all meat, fish, and animal by-products. Which reasons seem most or least convincing to you—and why?

5. Even though this is essentially a persuasive essay, discuss how and where the author uses narrative elements to enhance her argument.

6. Cite references where the author uses humor to lighten her tone and engage readers.

WRITING FROM THE TEXT

1. Write an analysis of how the narrative elements—first-person point of view, quoted remarks, and personal anecdotes about her family—enhance the author's argument and support her thesis.

2. Using details from Smith's essay—including her son's points and her own evaluation of the change—write an argument convincing your own household to stop eating red meat or at least to reduce red-meat consumption. Anticipate any objections they may have and counter them sufficiently to support your thesis.

3. Write an evaluative response essay critiquing the son's argument for renouncing all meat, fish, and animal by-products. Include quotations to support your evaluation. (See evaluative response, p. 438.)

4. Describe a change in your family that was initiated by the younger family members and resisted by the older ones. Let the reader see what prompted the change, how the family behaved beforehand, and whether the results were an improvement. Dramatize scenes that show the family interacting before and after the change.

5. Focusing on a time that you or your family attempted to change your diet or eating habits, write a comparison-contrast of your family's experience and the author's. Consider the reasons for the change, the difficulties sticking to the new diet, the sacrifices made, and any measures of success or failure.

CONNECTING WITH OTHER TEXTS

1. In this essay, Smith writes, "It's gratifying to let a compelling argument alter your behavior. It gives you hope. If you can change, the world can" (10). The essays of both Smith and Dan Neil ("If the Genes Fit," p. 178) use personal experience to indicate the possibility of change and acceptance on a wider scale. Analyze the "compelling argument" within each essay and evaluate whether both arguments seem equally persuasive and capable of effecting change in the larger society.

2. Read Caroline Hwang's "The Good Daughter." Compare and contrast the very different approaches illustrated by Hwang's narrator and Smith's son as they choose their own lifestyle and confront their parents' attitudes and behavior patterns. Write an essay analyzing the underlying reason for these differences. How significant is the role of gender and ethnic background in these essays? Support your thesis with specific statements from both essays and from your own experiences.

◖◗ The Good Daughter ◖◗
Caroline Hwang

Caroline Hwang (b. 1969) earned a B.A. in English from the University of Pennsylvania and has worked as an editor at *American Health*, *Mademoiselle*, *Glamour*, and *Redbook*. Hwang's novel *In Full Bloom* was published in 2003. Constantly juggling her varied projects as both a writer and an editor, Hwang observes, "I've often heard it said that the difference between being an editor and writer is that the editor has power and the writer gets the glory. I don't know that the difference is so clear-cut, but I can say that being on both sides has helped my writing and editing." The following essay was first published in *Newsweek* in 1998.

1   The moment I walked into the dry-cleaning store, I knew the woman behind the counter was from Korea, like my parents. To show her that we shared a heritage, and possibly get a fellow countryman's discount, I tilted my head forward, in shy imitation of a traditional bow.

2   "Name?" she asked, not noticing my attempted obeisance.

3   "Hwang," I answered.

4   "Hwang? Are you Chinese?"

5   Her question caught me off-guard. I was used to hearing such queries from non-Asians who think Asians all look alike, but never from one of my own people. Of course, the only Koreans I knew were my parents and their friends, people who've never asked me where I came from, since they knew better than I.

6   I ransacked my mind for the Korean words that would tell her who I was. It's always struck me as funny (in a mirthless sort of way) that I can more readily say "I am Korean" in Spanish, German and even Latin than I can in the language of my ancestry. In the end, I told her in English.

7   The dry-cleaning woman squinted as though trying to see past the glare of my strangeness, repeating my surname under her breath. "Oh, *Fxuang,*" she said, doubling over with laughter. "You don't know how to speak your name."

8   I flinched. Perhaps I was particularly sensitive at the time, having just dropped out of graduate school. I had torn up my map for the future, the one that said not only where I was going but who I was. My sense of identity was already disintegrating.

9   When I got home, I called my parents to ask why they had never bothered to correct me. "Big deal," my mother said, sounding more flippant than I knew she intended. (Like many people who learn English in a classroom, she uses idioms that don't always fit the occasion.) "So what if you can't pronounce your name? You are American," she said.

10   Though I didn't challenge her explanation, it left me unsatisfied. The fact is, my cultural identity is hardly that clear-cut.

11   My parents immigrated to this country 30 years ago, two years before I was born. They told me often, while I was growing up, that, if I wanted to, I could be president someday, that here my grasp would be as long as my reach.

12   To ensure that I reaped all the advantages of this country, my parents saw to it that I became fully assimilated. So, like any American of my generation, I whiled away my youth strolling malls and talking on the phone, rhapsodizing over Andrew McCarthy's blue eyes or analyzing the meaning of a certain upperclassman's offer of a ride to the Homecoming football game.

13   To my parents, I am all American, and the sacrifices they made in leaving Korea—including my mispronounced name—pale in comparison to the opportunities those sacrifices gave me. They do not see that I straddle two

cultures, nor that I feel displaced in the only country I know. I identify with Americans, but Americans do not identify with me. I've never known what it's like to belong to a community—neither one at large, nor of an extended family. I know more about Europe than the continent my ancestors unmistakably come from. I sometimes wonder, as I did that day in the dry cleaner's, if I would be a happier person had my parents stayed in Korea.

14   I first began to consider this thought around the time I decided to go to graduate school. It has been a compromise: my parents wanted me to go to law school; I wanted to skip the starched-collar track and be a writer— the hungrier the better. But after 20-some years of following their wishes and meeting all of their expectations, I couldn't bring myself to disobey or disappoint. A writing career is riskier than law, I remember thinking. If I'm a failure and my life is a washout, then what does that make my parents' lives?

15   I know that many of my friends had to choose between pleasing their parents and being true to themselves. But for the children of immigrants, the choice seems more complicated, a happy outcome impossible. By making the biggest move of their lives for me, my parents indentured me to the largest debt imaginable—I owe them the fulfillment of their hopes for me.

16   It tore me up inside to suppress my dream, but I went to school for a Ph.D. in English literature, thinking I had found the perfect compromise. I would be able to write at least about books while pursuing a graduate degree. Predictably, it didn't work out. How could I labor for five years in a program I had no passion for? When I finally left school, my parents were disappointed, but since it wasn't what they wanted me to do, they weren't devastated. I, on the other hand, felt I was staring at the bottom of the abyss. I had seen the flaw in my life of halfwayness, in my planned life of compromises.

17   I hadn't thought about my love life, but I had a vague plan to make concessions there, too. Though they raised me as an American, my parents expect me to marry someone Korean and give them grandchildren who look like them. This didn't seem like such a huge request when I was 14, but now I don't know what I'm going to do. I've never been in love with someone I dated, or dated someone I loved. (Since I can't bring myself even to entertain the thought of marrying the non-Korean men I'm attracted to, I've been dating only those I know I can stay clearheaded about.) And as I near that age when the question of marriage stalks every relationship, I can't help but wonder if my parents' expectations are responsible for the lack of passion in my life.

18   My parents didn't want their daughter to be Korean, but they don't want her fully American, either. Children of immigrants are living para-

doxes. We are the first generation and the last. We are in this country for its opportunities, yet filial duty binds us. When my parents boarded the plane, they knew they were embarking on a rough trip. I don't think they imagined the rocks in the path of their daughter who can't even pronounce her own name.

THINKING ABOUT THE TEXT

1. What might be Hwang's strategy for opening her essay with a brief narration of her encounter with the Korean dry-cleaning woman? What multiple issues does she introduce with this personal anecdote?

2. Explain how the dry cleaner's comment "You don't know how to speak your name" functions not simply as an observation but as a symbol throughout the essay.

3. What details does Hwang use to support the claim that "I straddle two cultures" and "I feel displaced in the only country I know"? (13).

4. Using your own words along with phrases from the essay, identify Hwang's *aim* or purpose in this essay as well as her key *claim* or thesis.

WRITING FROM THE TEXT

1. Including details from this essay and your own experiences and observations, write an evaluative response essay agreeing or disagreeing with Hwang's claim that "children of immigrants are living paradoxes" (14). Use examples from the essay to define "living paradoxes" and to support your key claim.

2. Incorporate specific details from Hwang's essay to write an analysis of the causes and effects of her parents' expectations.

CONNECTING WITH OTHER TEXTS

1. Focusing on "The Good Daughter" and "Breaking Tradition" (p. 21), write an essay analyzing the pressures and demands on children of immigrants.

2. Create a thesis about effective or ineffective parenting and write an essay incorporating support from any three of the following: "The Good Daughter," "My Son, My Compass" (p. 8), "Breaking Tradition" (p. 21), "Where Are You Going, Where Have You Been?" (p. 92), "Living in Two Worlds" (p. 109), and "Peaches" (p. 71). Include direct quotations and analyze them fully.

The Color of Love
Danzy Senna

The daughter of an African-Mexican father, author Carl Senna, and Irish American writer Fanny Howe, Danzy Senna (b. 1970) earned a B.A. from Stanford University and an M.F.A. from the University of California, Irvine. She won several awards for her best-selling novel *Caucasia* (1988), and in 2002 was honored with the Whiting Award, presented each year to ten outstanding writers who demonstrate ability and promise. She published the psychological thriller *Symptomatic* (2004) and is currently working on a screenplay and on a nonfiction book about her father's life. The following essay originally appeared in *O: The Oprah Magazine* in 2000.

1   We had this much in common: We were both women, and we were both writers. But we were as different as two people can be and still exist in the same family. She was ancient—as white and dusty as chalk—and spent her days seated in a velvet armchair, passing judgments on the world below. She still believed in noble bloodlines; my blood had been mixed at conception. I believed there was no such thing as nobility or class or lineage, only systems designed to keep some people up in the big house and others outside, in the cold.

2   She was my grandmother. She was Irish but from that country's Protestant elite, which meant she seemed more British than anything. She was an actress, a writer of plays and novels, and still unmarried in her thirties when she came to America to visit. One night while in Boston, she went to a dinner party, where she was seated next to a young lawyer with blood as blue as the ocean. Her pearl earring fell in his oyster soup—or so the story goes—and they fell in love. My grandmother married that lawyer and left her native Ireland for New England.

3   How she came to have black grandchildren is a story of opposites. It was 1968 in Boston when her daughter—my mother—a small, blonde Wasp poet, married my father, a tall and handsome black intellectual, in an act that was as rebellious as it was hopeful. The products of that unlikely union—my older sister, my younger brother, and I—grew up in urban chaos, in a home filled with artists and political activists. The old lady across the river in Cambridge seemed to me an endangered species. Her walls were covered with portraits of my ancestors, the pale and dead men who had conquered Africa and built Boston long before my time. When I visited, their eyes followed me from room to room with what I imagined to be an expression of scorn. Among the portraits sat my grandmother, a bird who had flown in to remind us all that there had indeed been a time when lineage and caste meant

something. To me, young and dark and full of energy, she was the missing link between the living and the dead.

4   But her blood flowed through me, whether I liked it or not. I grew up to be a writer, just like her. And as I struggled to tell my own stories—about race and class and post–civil rights America—I wondered who my grandmother had been before, in Dublin, when she was friend and confidante to literary giants such as William Butler Yeats and Samuel Beckett. Once, while snooping in her bedroom, I discovered her novels, the ones that had been published in Ireland when she was my age. I stared at her photograph on the jacket and wondered about the young woman who wore a mischievous smile. Had she ever worried about becoming so powerful that no man would want her? Did she now feel that she had sacrificed her career and wild Irishwoman dreams to become a wife and mother and proper Bostonian?

5   I longed to know her—to love her. But the differences between us were real and alive, and they threatened to squelch our fragile connection. She was an alcoholic. In the evening, after a few glasses of gin, she could turn vicious. Though she held antiquated racist views, my grandmother would still have preferred to see my mother married and was saddened when my parents split in the seventies. She believed that a woman without a man was pitiable. The first question she always asked me when she saw me: "Do you have a man?" The second question: "What is he?" That was her way of finding out his race and background. She looked visibly pleased if he was a Wasp, neutral if he was Jewish, and disappointed if he was black.

6   My mother ignored her hurtful comments but felt them just the same. She spent her visits to my grandmother's house slamming dishes in the kitchen, hissing her anger just out of hearing range, then raving, on the drive home, about what awful thing her mother had said this time. Like my mother, I knew the rule: I was not to disrespect elders. She was old and gray and would soon be gone. But I had inherited my grandmother's short temper. When I got angry, even as a child, I felt as if blood were rushing around in my head, red waves battering the shore. Words spilled from my mouth—cutting, vicious words that I regretted.

7   One autumn day in Cambridge, at my grandmother's place, I lost my temper. I was home from college for the holidays, staying in her guest room. I woke from a nap to the sound of her enraged voice shouting at what I could only imagine was the television.

8   "Idiot! You damn fool!" she bellowed. "You stupid, stupid woman!" It has to be *Jeopardy!*, I thought. She must be yelling at those tiny contestants on the screen. She knows the answers to those questions better than they do. But when the shouting went on for a beat too long, I went to the top of the stairs and looked down into the living room. She was speaking to a real person: her

cleaning lady, a Greek woman named Mary, who was on her hands and knees, nervously gathering the shards of a broken vase. My grandmother stood over her, hands on hips, cursing.

9   "You fool," my grandmother repeated. "How in bloody hell could you have done something so stupid?"

10   "Grandma." I didn't shout her name but said it loudly enough that she, though hard of hearing, glanced up.

11   "Oh, darling!" she piped, suddenly cheerful. "Would you like a cup of tea? You must be dreadfully tired."

12   Mary was on her feet again. She smiled nervously at me, then rushed into the kitchen with the pieces of the broken vase.

13   I told myself to be a good girl, to be polite. But something snapped. I marched down the stairs, and even she noticed something on my face that made her sit in her velvet chair.

14   "Don't you ever talk to her that way," I shouted. "Where do you think you are? Slavery was abolished long ago."

15   I stood over her, tall and long-limbed, daring her to speak. My grandmother shook her head. "It's about race, isn't it?"

16   "Race?" I said, baffled. "Mary's white. This is about respect—treating other human beings with respect."

17   She wasn't hearing me. All she saw was color. "The tragedy about you," she said soberly, "is that you are mixed." I felt those waves in my head: "Your tragedy is that you're old and ignorant," I spat. "You don't know the first thing about me."

18   She cried into her hands. She seemed diminished, a little old woman. She looked up only to say, "You are a cruel girl."

19   I left her apartment trembling yet feeling exhilarated by what I had done. But my elation soon turned to shame. I had taken on an old lady. And for what? Her intolerance was, at her age, deeply entrenched. My rebuttals couldn't change her.

20   Yet that fight marked the beginning of our relationship. I've since decided that when you cease to express anger toward those who have hurt you, you are essentially giving up on them. They are dead to you. But when you express anger, it is a sign that they still matter, that they are worth the fight.

21   After that argument, my grandmother and I began a conversation. She seemed to see me clearly for the first time, or perhaps she, a "cruel girl" herself, had simply met her match. And I no longer felt she was a relic. She was a living, breathing human being who deserved to be spoken to as an equal.

22   I began visiting her more. I would drive to Cambridge and sit with her, eating mixed nuts and sipping ginger ale, regaling her with tales of my latest love drama or writing project. In her presence, I was proudly black and

young and political, and she was who she was: subtly racist, terribly elitist, and awfully funny. She still said things that angered me: She bemoaned my mother's marriage to my father, she said that I should marry not for love but for money, and she told me that I needn't identify myself as black, since I didn't look it. I snapped back at her. But she, with senility creeping in, didn't seem to hear me; each time I came, she said the same things.

23   Last summer I went into hiding to work on my second novel at a writer's retreat in New Hampshire. The place was a kind of paradise for creative souls, a hideaway where every writer had his or her own cabin in the woods with no phone or television—no distractions to speak of. But I was miserable. I could not write. Even the flies outside my window seemed to whisper, "Go out and play. Forget the novel. Leave it till tomorrow."

24   I woke one morning at four, the light outside my window still blue. I felt panic and sadness, though I didn't know why. I got up, dressed, and went outside for a walk through the forest. But the panic persisted, and I began to cry. I assumed that my writer's block had seized me suddenly.

25   That night I ate dinner in the main house and received a call on the pay phone from my mother. She told me my grandmother had fallen and broken her leg. But that wasn't all; she had subsequently suffered a heart attack. Her other organs were failing. I had to hurry if I wanted to say good-bye.

26   I drove to Boston that night, not believing that we could be losing her. She would make it. I was certain. Sure, she was ninety-two, frail, unable to walk steadily. But she was lucid, and her tongue was as sharp as ever. Somehow I had imagined her as indestructible, made immortal by power and cruelty and wit.

27   The woman I found in the hospital bed was barely recognizable. My grandmother had always been fussy about her appearance. She never showed her face without makeup. Even in the day, when it was just she and the cleaning lady, she dressed as if she were ready for a cocktail party. At night she usually had cocktail parties; doddering old men hovered around her, sipping Scotch and bantering about theater and politics.

28   My grandmother's face had swollen to twice its normal size, and tubes came out of her nose. She had struggled so hard to pull them out that the nurses had tied her wrists to the bed rails. Her hair was gray and thin. Her body was withered and bruised, barely covered by the green hospital gown.

29   Her hazel eyes were all that was still recognizable, but the expression in them was different from any I had ever seen on her—terror. She was terrified to die. She tried to rise when she saw me, and her eyes pleaded with me to help her, to save her, to get her out of this mess. I stood over her, and I felt only one thing: overwhelming love. Not a trace of anger. That dark gray rage

I'd felt toward her was gone as I stroked her forehead and told her she would be okay, even knowing she would not.

30   For two days, my mother, her sisters, and I stood beside my grandmother, singing Irish ballads and reading passages to her from the works of her favorite novelist, James Joyce. For the first time, she could not talk. At one point, she gestured wildly for pen and paper. I brought her the pen and the paper and held them up for her, but she was too weak for even that. What came out was only a faint, incomprehensible line.

31   In death we are each reduced to our essence: the spirit we are when we are born. The trappings we hold on to our whole lives—our race, our money, our sex, our age, our politics—become irrelevant. My grandmother became a child in that hospital bed, a spirit about to embark on an unknown journey, terrified and alone, no matter how many of us were crowded around her. In the final hours, even her skin seemed to lose its wrinkles and take on a waxy glow. Then, finally, the machines around us went silent as she left us behind to squabble in the purgatory of the flesh.

Thinking about the Text

1. Compare and contrast Senna and her grandmother. Which differences most threaten their "fragile connection"?

2. Describe what provokes "the fight" between Senna and her grandmother and how both verbally attack each other.

3. Why is it important to Senna to "express anger"? In what ways does their fight ironically help their relationship?

4. How do both Senna's writer's block and her grandmother's deathbed scene bring a sense of resolution to this essay? What ultimately matters most to Senna and what are the "trappings" that seem irrelevant?

Writing from the Text

1. Focusing on your view of Senna's relationship with her grandmother, write an essay comparing and contrasting these two female writers. Include specific details to support your analysis and assessment of them. See comparison and contrast, pp. 454–456.

2. Based on details from this essay, write a character analysis of Senna's grandmother, and include specific characteristics and illustrations for support.

3. Write an essay about a conflict you have had with a relative or with someone who discriminated against you. Dramatize what led up to the conflict, how both of you interacted, and how the tension was resolved or intensified.

4. Considering Senna's realistic details of her grandmother dying, write an essay describing your own encounter with someone who was ill or dying. Focus on those details that support your thesis about how that person changed or how your view of him or her was altered by this experience.

CONNECTING WITH OTHER TEXTS

1. After reading "Race Is A Four-Letter Word" by Teja Arboleda (p. 120), write an essay showing how Senna's experience with her grandmother illustrates Arboleda's sense of the "barriers, pedestals, doors, and traps that form the boundaries that confine human beings to dominant and minority groups" (123). Include details from both essays to support your thesis.

2. In "Living in Two Worlds" (p. 109), Marcus Mabry discusses the guilt, helplessness, and embarrassment he often feels at leaving his family behind. Write an essay comparing and contrasting Senna's and Mabry's attitudes and experiences as they move between their new environments and the worlds of their families.

3. Read Heilbroner's "Don't Let Stereotypes Warp Your Judgments" (p. 470). Then write an essay showing specific examples of what Senna's grandmother could learn from Heilbroner's essay and how her judgment has been "warped" by stereotypes and prejudgments.

Breaking Tradition
Janice Mirikitani

A third-generation Japanese American, Janice Mirikitani (b. 1942) was interned at a relocation camp during World War II. Since then, she has emerged as both poet and proponent for social change. Serving as president of the Glide Foundation, she directs thirty-five programs that assist the homeless and poor in San Francisco. Mirikitani is also a founding member of Third World Communications, editing the works of other Japanese American writers. Her collections of poetry include *Awake in the River* (1978) and *We the Dangerous* (1995). Her works typically illustrate her opposition to oppression and her support for those seeking their own American identity rather than following traditional customs, as in this poem from *Shedding Silence* (1987).

for my daughter

My daughter denies she is like me,
Her secretive eyes avoid mine.

She reveals the hatreds of womanhood
already veiled behind music and smoke and telephones.

5   I want to tell her about the empty room of myself.
This room we lock ourselves in
where whispers live like fungus,
giggles about small breasts and cellulite,

10   where we confine ourselves to jealousies,
bedridden by menstruation.
This waiting room where we feel our hands
are useless, dead speechless clamps
that need hospitals and forceps and kitchens

15   and plugs and ironing boards to make them useful.
I deny I am like my mother. I remember why:
She kept her room neat with silence,
defiance smothered in requirements to be otonashii,
passion and loudness wrapped in an obi,

20   her steps confined to ceremony,
the weight of her sacrifice she carried like
a foetus. Guilt passed on in our bones.
I want to break tradition—unlock this room
where women dress in the dark.

25   Discover the lies my mother told me.
The lies that we are small and powerless.
that our possibilities must be compressed
to the size of pearls, displayed only as
passive chokers, charms around our neck.

30   Break Tradition.
I want to tell my daughter of this room of myself
filled with tears of violins,
the light in my hands,

35   poems about madness,
the music of yellow guitars—
sounds shaken from barbed wire and
goodbyes and miracles of survival.
This room of open window where daring ones escape.

40   My daughter denies she is like me
her secretive eyes are walls of smoke
and music and telephones,
her pouting ruby lips, her skirts
swaying to salsa, teena marie and the stones,

45   her thighs displayed in carnivals of color.
          I do not know the contents of her room.
    She mirrors my aging.
    She is breaking tradition.

THINKING ABOUT THE TEXT

1. The narrator repeats "room" numerous times throughout this poem in relation to herself, her mother, and her daughter. What are some reasons that she uses "room" and what might this word symbolize?

2. Early in the poem, how does the narrator describe "the empty room of myself"?

3. Analyze the images that the narrator uses to describe her mother's "room." What is the impact of these details on the narrator?

4. Later, after the narrator recognizes her own attempts to break tradition and to deny she is like her mother, she describes the room that she would now like to reveal to her daughter. Analyze specific images from this "room of myself." How does this new "room of myself" contrast with that earlier "empty room of myself"?

5. How does the narrator characterize her daughter? Examine specific images.

6. How do the last two lines of the poem signal a shift in the narrator's tone from the opening two lines? What might account for this change in attitude?

7. Analyze the author's extensive use of repetition, not only of "room" but also of the title and of both daughters' denial that they are like their mothers. Are these repetitions purposeful and effective? Support your views with details from the poem.

8. Speculate why the narrator includes the dedication "for my daughter" at the beginning of the poem? Did that phrase affect your reading of this work?

WRITING FROM THE TEXT

1. Considering your responses to exercises 1 and 7 above, analyze Mirikitani's use of repetition throughout the poem. Write an essay showing how the repetition of certain key words and phrases not only helps unify the poem but also develops the poem's themes.

2. In an analytic essay, evaluate whether the issues addressed in this poem are ones of universal concern or if any seem more limited to one particular

generation, gender, or culture. Use specific quotations to support your views.

3. Write an essay comparing and contrasting your own "room"—especially your views and values—with the "room" that best characterizes your mother or father. Describe the details in both "rooms" and explain any attempts made to "break tradition."

CONNECTING WITH OTHER TEXTS

1. Focusing on the narrator's mother in "Breaking Tradition" as well as the parents in "The Good Daughter" (p. 12), write an essay analyzing the parents' strategies, efforts, and results as they attempt to pass on certain traditions and expectations to their children.

2. Unlike the narrator's mother in "Breaking Tradition," some parents and grandparents may or may not understand the need for children to reject certain paths in order to find their own. Focusing on the narrator in "Breaking Tradition" as well as the parents in "My Son, My Compass" (p. 8) and "The Fringe Benefits of Failure, and the Importance of Imagination" (p. 165) or the grandmother in "The Color of Love" (p. 16), discuss why these individuals seem able to support and understand the need for change.

 # On Teenagers and Tattoos
Andres Martin

Professor of Child Psychiatry, Psychiatry Director of Medical Studies at the Yale Child Study Center and Medical Director of Children's Psychiatric Inpatient Service at the Yale-New Haven Children's Hospital, Andres Martin (b. 1966) is also Editor-in-Chief of the *Journal of the American Academy of Child and Adolescent Psychiatry*. He is widely published in professional journals of pediatric and adolescent psychology. The essay below was published in the *Journal of Child and Adolescent Psychiatry* (1997) and reprinted in *Reclaiming Children and Youth* (2000). You will notice that the in-text citations, in paragraphs 2 and 12, and the end "References" follow APA documentation form.

> The skeleton dimensions I shall now proceed to set down are copied verbatim from my right arm, where I had them tattooed: as in my wild wanderings at that period, there was no other secure way of preserving such valuable statistics.
>
> —MELVILLE, *Moby Dick*

1   Tattoos and piercing have become a part of our everyday landscape. They are ubiquitous, having entered the circles of glamour and the mainstream of fashion, and they have even become an increasingly common feature of our urban youth. Legislation in most states restricts professional tattooing to adults older than 18 years of age, so "high end" tattooing is rare in children and adolescents, but such tattoos are occasionally seen in older teenagers. Piercings, by comparison, as well as self-made or "jailhouse" type tattoos, are not at all rare among adolescents or even among school-age children. Like hairdo, makeup, or baggy jeans, tattoos and piercings can be subject to fad influence or peer pressure in an effort toward group affiliation. As with any other fashion statement, they can be construed as bodily aids in the inner struggle toward identity consolidation, serving as adjuncts to the defining and sculpting of the self by means of external manipulations. But unlike most other body decorations, tattoos and piercings are set apart by their irreversible and permanent nature, a quality at the core of their magnetic appeal to adolescents.

2   Adolescents and their parents are often at odds over the acquisition of bodily decorations. For the adolescent, piercing or tattoos may be seen as personal and beautifying statements, while parents may construe them as oppositional and enraging affronts to their authority. Distinguishing bodily adornment from self-mutilation may indeed prove challenging, particularly when a family is in disagreement over a teenager's motivations and a clinician is summoned as the final arbiter. At such times it may be most important to realize jointly that the skin can all too readily become but another battleground for the tensions of the age, arguments having less to do with tattoos and piercings than with core issues such as separation from the family matrix. Exploring the motivations and significance [underlying] tattoos (Grumet, 1983) and piercings can go a long way toward resolving such differences and can become a novel and additional way of getting to know teenagers. An interested and nonjudgmental appreciation of teenagers's surface presentations may become a way of making contact not only in their terms but on their turfs: quite literally on the territory of their skins.

3   The following three sections exemplify some of the complex psychological underpinnings of youth tattooing.

4   Tattoos and piercing can offer a concrete and readily available solution for many of the identity crises and conflicts normative to adolescent development. In using such decorations, and by marking out their bodily territories, adolescents can support their efforts at autonomy, privacy, and insulation. Seeking individuation, tattooed adolescents can become unambiguously demarcated from others and singled out as unique. The intense and often

disturbing reactions that are mobilized in viewers can help to effectively keep them at bay, becoming tantamount to the proverbial "Keep Out" sign hanging from a teenager's door.

5   Alternatively, feeling prey to a rapidly evolving body over which they have no say, self-made and openly visible decorations may restore adolescents' sense of normalcy and control, a way of turning a passive experience into an active identity. By indelibly marking their bodies, adolescents can strive to reclaim their bearings within an environment experienced as alien, estranged, or suffocating or to lay claim over their evolving and increasingly unrecognizable bodies. In either case, the net outcome can be a resolution to unwelcome impositions: external, familial, or societal in one case; internal and hormonal in the other. In the words of a 16-year-old girl with several facial piercings, and who could have been referring to her body just as well as to the position within her family: "If I don't fit in, it is because I say so."

6   Imagery of a religious, deathly, or skeletal nature, the likenesses of fierce animals or imagined creatures, and the simple inscription of names are some of the time-tested favorite contents for tattoos. In all instances, marks become not only memorials or recipients for dearly held persons or concepts: they strive for incorporation, with images and abstract symbols gaining substance on becoming a permanent part of the individual's skin. Thickly embedded in personally meaningful representations and object relations, tattoos can become not only the ongoing memento of a relationship, but at times even the only evidence that there ever was such a bond. They can quite literally become the relationship itself. The turbulence and impulsivity of early attachments and infatuations may become grounded, effectively bridging oblivion through the visible reality to tattoos.

7   Case Vignette: "A," a 13-year-old boy, proudly showed me his tattooed deltoid. The coarsely depicted roll of the dice marked the day and month of his birth. Rather disappointed, he then uncovered an immaculate back, going on to draw for me the great "piece" he envisioned for it. A menacing figure held a hand of cards: two aces, two eights, and a card with two sets of dates. "A's" father had belonged to Dead Man's Hand, a motorcycle gang named after the set of cards (aces and eights) that the legendary Wild Bill Hickock had held in the 1890s when shot dead over a poker table in Deadwood, South Dakota. "A" had only the vaguest memory of and sketchiest information about his father, but he knew he had died in a motorcycle accident: The fifth card marked the dates of his birth and death.

8   The case vignette also serves to illustrate how tattoos are often the culmination of a long process of imagination, fantasy, and planning that can start at an early age. Limited markings, or relatively reversible ones such as piercings, can at a later time scaffold toward the more radical commitment of a permanent tattoo.

9   The popularity of the anchor as a tattoo motif may historically have had to do less with guild identification among sailors than with an intense longing for rootedness and stability. In a similar vein, the recent increase in the popularity and acceptance of tattoos may be understood as an antidote or counterpoint to our urban and nomadic lifestyles. Within an increasingly mobile society, in which relationships are so often transient—as attested by the frequencies of divorce, abandonment, foster placement, and repeated moves, for example—tattoos can be a readily available source of grounding. Tattoos, unlike many relationships, can promise permanence and stability. A sense of constancy can be derived from unchanging marks that can be carried along no matter what the physical, temporal, or geographical vicissitudes at hand. Tattoos stay, while all else may change.

10   Case Vignette: A proud father at 17, "B" had had the smiling face of his 4-month-old baby girl tattooed on his chest. As we talked at a tattoo convention, he proudly introduced her to me, explaining how he would "always know how beautiful she is today" when years from then he saw her semblance etched on himself.

11   The quest for permanence may at other times prove misleading and offer premature closure to unresolved conflicts. At a time of normative uncertainties, adolescents may maladaptively and all too readily commit to a tattoo and its indefinite presence. A wish to hold on to a current certainty may lead the adolescent to lay down in ink what is valued and cherished one day but may not necessarily be in the future. The frequency of self-made tattoos among hospitalized, incarcerated, or gang-affiliated youths suggests such motivations: A sense of stability may be a particularly dire need under temporary, turbulent, or volatile conditions. In addition, through their designs teenagers may assert a sense of bonding and allegiance to a group larger than themselves. Tattoos may attest to powerful experiences, such as adolescence itself, lived and even survived together. As with Moby Dick's protagonist, Ishmael, they may bear witness to the "valuable statistics" of one's "wild wandering(s)": those of adolescent exhilaration and excitement on the one hand; of growing pains, shared misfortune, or even incarceration on the other.

12   Adolescents' bodily decorations, at times radical and dramatic in their presentation, can be seen in terms of figuration rather than disfigurement, of the natural body being through them transformed into a personalized body (Brain, 1979). They can often be understood as self-constructive and adorning efforts, rather than prematurely subsumed as mutilatory and destructive acts. If we bear all of this in mind, we may not only arrive at a position to pass more reasoned clinical judgment, but become sensitized through our patients' skins to another level of their internal reality.

References

Brain, R. (1979). *The decorated body.* New York: Harper & Row.
Grumet, G. W. (1983). Psychodynamic implications of tattoos. *American Journal of Orthopsychiatry,* 53, 482–92.

THINKING ABOUT THE TEXT

1. After acknowledging the prevalence and relative permanence of tattoos, Martin may surprise his readers with his argument for adults to accept teenagers' "bodily adornment." How does the wording of his thesis reflect his position? How does Martin's professional background possibly contribute to his position being accepted by his readers?

2. What three specific areas does Martin analyze to support his understanding and acceptance of tattoos? What appears to be the focus or assertion for each of Martin's three points?

3. How does Martin explain the symbols of the playing cards, anchor, and face tattooed on the subjects in his essay? What motif have you seen in tattoos that might also support Martin's analyses?

4. Martin discusses both the role of "limited markings, or relatively reversible ones" (26) as well as the tattoos that "promise permanence and stability" (27). How do you interpret these apparently contrasting types of tattoos?

5. Martin's original audience is readers of the *Journal of Child and Adolescent Psychiatry.* What does the author want his fellow psychiatrists to keep in mind as they work with patients who bear tattoos and body piercings?

6. How does the quotation from Melville's *Moby Dick* at the start of Martin's essay foreshadow the content of the essay? What is Martin's rhetorical strategy in returning to Melville's words at the end of his essay?

WRITING FROM THE TEXT

1. Using specific details from Martin's essay for support, write an essay that explains your decision to pierce or tattoo your body.

2. In light of Martin's analysis that tattoos "are often the culmination of a long process of imagination, fantasy, and planning" (26), write an essay analyzing one of your tattoos, or a tattoo you might design for yourself, or the specific tattoo of a friend. The case story of "A" might serve as inspiration for your essay.

3. If you regret a tattoo that you have, write an analysis of that tattoo that illustrates how your thinking about it has changed. Use explanations and

analysis from Martin's essay to present your evolution in understanding of your tattoo.

CONNECTING WITH OTHER TEXTS

1. Using the psychological explanations in Andres Martin's essay, write an analysis of Jon Bowen's decision (in "Under My Skin,") to get a tattoo, the design of his tattoo, and his plan to keep his tattoo.

2. Using both Martin's and Bowen's essays, write an argument against getting a tattoo.

3. Adopt the tone of Jennifer Coleman in "Discrimination at Large" (p. 198) to argue that our culture needs to stop seeing tattoos as "bodily mutilation" and to accept people's "bodily adornment" without discrimination. Use points made by both Martin and Bowen to support your argument.

 # Under My Skin

Jon Bowen

Working as a professional writer in Charlottesville, Virginia, Jon Bowen (b. 1965) has published articles in *The Washington Post, Salon.com, Garden Design,* and *Working Mother.* He earned a B.A. in English from George Mason University and an M.F.A. in Creative Writing from the University of Virginia. Bowen's story "Pulling Jane" was included in *A New Life: Stories and Photographs from the Suburban South* and another work appeared in *Howl: A Collection of the Best Contemporary Dog Wit.* The following essay was published in *Salon.com* on June 23, 1999.

1   Every tattoo tells a story. Mine tells a story about a story. I got it to commemorate my first fiction publication in a literary magazine—a minor milestone that, at the time, seemed so epic and momentous I wanted the occasion memorialized in my flesh for all eternity.

2   Flash Gordon was the name of my tattooist. He had an ordinary name—Robert or Richard Gordon, I think—but Flash was the name on his business card. (A quick hint for the uninitiated: The walls in tattoo studios are covered floor to ceiling with sheets of illustrations, and these sheets, which the prospective tattooee pores over to choose a design, are called "flash." Hence Mr. Gordon's nom de plume.)

3   You have 10 zillion designs to choose from. You have tribal tattoos; you have Celtic tattoos. You have biker babes with torpedo boobs straddling Harleys; you have Jesus Christ stranded on the cross. You have tigers, unicorns,

dragons and gargoyles; you have Jimi Hendrix and Yosemite Sam, Bruce Lee and Betty Boop—all creatures of the incarnate and cartoon worlds are available for inscription in your epidermis.

4   I chose the theater symbol of comedy and tragedy—those two masks, one laughing hysterically, the other sad-eyed and pouting. They say you choose a particular tattoo design as an advertisement for your self-definition. I chose mine because I saw it as an external mark of the private interplay of joy and melancholy that's de rigueur for all tortured writer types, and because the drama symbol seemed related to literature, if only tangentially—and because I thought the design looked, you know, cool.

5   Tattooists will put your tattoo wherever you say, pretty much, though some charge extra to work on your butt, and the more discriminating artists won't work above your neck or below your wrists—those taboo territories known as "public skin." Anyway, my tattoo went on my deltoid. No mystery there: The upper arm is one of the fleshier—and therefore less excruciating—places you can put a tattoo.

6   The tattooist shaves the peach fuzz from the tattoo area and dabs your skin with antiseptic. He traces your chosen design from the flash sheet, then uses an acetate stencil to transfer the sketch onto you. Finally he mixes the inks to get the desired colors. Applying the tattoo is a two-handed job. The tattooist stretches your skin taut with one hand and manipulates the machine with the other. The machine is a drill-like apparatus equipped with stainless steel needles that stab thousands of tiny holes in your skin and deposit the ink in the holes.

7   So you walk out of the studio with your brand-new tattoo. You feel good. You feel nonconformist. Years pass. You get married, you get a house—maybe a kid's on the way. You begin to view life in the long term.

8   Unless you live your whole life among vampire zombies of the we-only-come-out-at-night school, having a tattooed body, sooner or later, presents some awkward social moments. You avoid pool parties hosted by your preppie neighbors. You're reluctant to strip down bare-chested. Getting dressed in hot weather, you face the daily dichotomy: conceal or display? Sometimes, you just want the damn thing to disappear.

9   Now this isn't another gloomy tale of Mr. Grown-Up's Regret—some namby-pamby urge to dispose of the blemishes of youth's indiscretions. But there do come certain moments in adult life, in the long lull of Sunday afternoons, when your mind wanders toward themes of restoration and renewal. If you're tattooed, you may experience a sudden desire to start over fresh. To make of your flesh a tabula rasa. To be reborn in your untainted birthday suit. These are the underpinnings of my rationale, my vague motives, when I decide to investigate tattoo removal.

10   Unlike the process of getting a tattoo, removing one is a high-tech, highly clinical procedure. The machine used for tattoo removal is called a Q-switched Ruby Laser. It's a boxy monolith the size of a Xerox copier, with an LED panel and a dizzying array of buttons and switches. The machine has a hinged arm fixed onto a turret, like a dental drill, and at the business end of the arm is the tattoo-blaster itself—the tube-shaped thingamajig that produces the laser beam. The laser, shooting pulses of radiated light into your epidermis at nanosecond intervals, explodes the tattoo ink into a zillion tiny particles. Your body absorbs the particles, and they wash away in your bloodstream.

11   When it comes to tattoo removal, it's the laser technicians—like dental hygienists and labor nurses—who do most of the dirty work, while the doctors get all the glory. So the techs are the ones best able to answer questions like this one: How bad will it hurt?

12   "It's painful," says Linda Griffin, a registered nurse who performs tattoo removals at the Center for Dermatologic Laser Surgery in Washington. "It feels like a huge rubber band snapping against your skin. Then it feels like sunburn for about an hour afterward."

   "Topically, it is painful," says Larry Sumlin, a medical assistant at Central Medical Clinic in Clearwater, Fla. "Most patients claim that it feels like flecks of bacon grease spattering on their skin."

13   A topical anesthetic is applied to the tattooed area, but if you're worried about the pain you can usually get sedation. A professional tattoo may require anywhere from three to ten laser sessions, each session spaced about a month apart, with the exact number of treatments depending on the type and amount of inks used in your tattoo. Black, blue and red are the easiest to remove. Orange and purple are harder, green and yellow harder still. The total cost can range from a few hundred dollars to a few thousand, depending on the inks, size and intricacy of your tattoo.

14   So why do patients endure the pain and spend the boatload of cash to get their tattoos zapped? In most cases, it's because they want to rid themselves of the past. "They say, 'I was young and stupid.' It's something that embarrasses them now," Sumlin says. "It's like painting your house pink. It seems like a good idea at the time, but later you change your mind. Hindsight is 20/20."

15   "They got it done when they were young, and now they're professionals," says Griffin. "You see girls with ankle tattoos, and now they have to wear pantyhose to work. They're sick of it."

16   Lost love is another prime motivator. "We remove a lot of girlfriend names, boyfriend names," says Christi Smith, laser supervisor at the Laser Institute of Georgia. It's an old, familiar story: Dick tattoos Jane's name

across his chest, but then the romance falls apart—"and they want it off right away," says Smith. "They've had it. But a lot of people don't know there's a way to get tattoos removed."

17   In fact, there's more than one way. The old-school methods of tattoo removal include surgical excision (cutting the tattoo out), dermabrasion (scrubbing away the tattooed skin layers), salabrasion (using salt to scrape the tattoo area) and chemical peels (using acid to burn away layers of skin). But all these techniques hurt like the devil and, in place of the tattoos, leave ugly scars.

18   Laser surgery is far and away the preferred method. Doctors and laser technicians say there are absolutely no health dangers, side effects or lasting scars from the procedure. "It's the safest way to have a tattoo removed," Smith says. "And it does not leave scarring. You may see some lightening or darkening of the skin, but it corrects itself over time."

19   Does the tattoo completely disappear? "It depends on the [ink] colors," Griffin says. "Sometimes it looks like a little bruise, but you'd never guess a tattoo used to be there. It becomes unrecognizable to the casual observer."

20   Sumlin says, "Lighter-skinned people may have some ink residue. But generally you get 99 percent disappearance."

21   Most laser surgery centers offer potential customers a personal consultation that can range in cost anywhere from "complimentary" to about $100. You go in, get your tattoo assessed, and receive an estimate on the cost of removal.

22   To undo, or not to undo—that's the question. It's been nine years since Flash Gordon marked up my schoolboy flesh, and looking back—pondering the laser's purifying beam, weighing the pros and cons—I wonder: Does the tattooist remember you? Or do you fade into the inky mix, another nameless patch of skin on the long road of epidermis he doodles down? And years later, if you consider ditching your tattoo, does the tattooist—the creator, wherever he is—experience a psychic premonition of loss and send telepathic messengers ghosting through the ether to purr in your ear, "Don't."

23   I won't, Flash Gordon, I won't. I'm saying no thanks to the laser beam. Starting over fresh is famously refreshing, but there's something to be said, too, for preserving the past. I'll keep my tattoo and wear it as a shield against forgetfulness, because, after all, it's the mark on me of a landmark thrill in life's uneven landscape—a success story written in flesh.

THINKING ABOUT THE TEXT

1. Although this essay provides general information about acquiring and removing tattoos, Bowen begins and ends with personal narration about his own tattoo experience. How do his anecdotes about himself and his tattoo artist ("Flash Gordon") enrich this essay?

2. Bowen deliberately shifts from first person ("I") to second person ("you") as he describes the process of getting a tattoo and reconsidering the tattoo. Find examples of the second-person perspective as you evaluate this strategy. Why might using "you" be more effective than "I/me"?

3. Find examples of Bowen's use of humor, catchy phrases, and a lively tone to keep this informative essay from becoming tedious or predictable. You may need to look up or question others about allusions such as "under my skin," "Flash Gordon," "tabula rasa," and "to undo or not to undo—that's the question."

4. Explain the important aspects of the "preferred" laser method for tattoo removal. Then contrast its results with the "old-school methods."

5. Evaluate Bowen's inclusion of direct quotations from tattoo technicians and medical specialists to describe the reasons for removal, the degree of pain, and the results. How does Bowen keep this research from making his essay too technical or inaccessible for readers?

WRITING FROM THE TEXT

1. Focusing on Bowen's use of personal experience, direct quotations, humor, and allusions, write an evaluative response to "Under My Skin." You may include your own experience with or observations about tattoos, but personal experience with tattoos is not necessary to write this essay. See pp. 438–444 for additional suggestions about evaluative response essays.

2. If you have ever decided to get a tattoo, piercing, or other cosmetic procedure, write a narrative essay dramatizing your actual experience and explaining your motives, considerations, and the results. You may choose to compare and contrast your experience with Bowen's or include details from his essay to support your own points.

3. Write an essay about a costly regret such as making a commitment that you have outgrown or find unhealthy, getting rid of something and then trying to retrieve or replace it, saying or doing something that continues to haunt you, or investing in a product or business that brings nothing but problems. Fully describe the initial appeal, the actual experience, and the difficulty undoing the deed or decision. This assignment can be treated humorously or more seriously, depending on your subject and stance.

CONNECTING WITH OTHER TEXTS

1. Using details from Bowen's essay and from "On Teenagers and Tattoos" (p. 24), write an essay arguing either that teenagers should be able to make their own decisions to get a tattoo or that teenagers should more

seriously reconsider their reasons and should research removal options before they get a tattoo.

2. Write an essay comparing and contrasting the purpose, thesis, style, and intended audience of "Under My Skin" and "On Teenagers and Tattoos" (p. 24). Focus your thesis on a specific assertion that you can support about their differences and not simply on the fact that they are both similar and different.

3. After reading Bowen's essay and Tavris's "In Group We Shrink" (p. 261), write an essay arguing against impulsively getting a tattoo when others are getting them or because it helps teens fit in and feel cool. Include support from Bowen and Tavris to convince readers to better understand their own motives and the long-term consequences before they commit to a tattoo.

The Only Child

John Leonard

After studying at Harvard and Berkeley, where he received his B.A. in 1962, John Leonard (1939–2008) worked as a book reviewer, a producer of dramas and literature programs, a publicity writer, a staff writer for the *New York Times*, and a cultural critic for *Variety, Nation,* and *CBS This Morning.* He is the author of *Smoke and Mirrors: Violence, Television, and Other American Cultures* (1997), *When the Kissing Had to Stop* (1999), a collection of previously published pieces, and *Lonesome Rangers: Homeless Minds, Promised Lands, Fugitive Cultures* (2002). Leonard intends his writing to ask moral questions: How do you want your children to grow up? What do you think is decent and fair? Who are your friends, and why? The work included here, from *Private Lives in the Imperial City* (1976), probes family tensions and concerns.

1   He is big. He always has been, over six feet, with that slump of the shoulders and tuck in the neck big men in the country often affect, as if to apologize for being above the democratic norm in size. (In high school and at college he played varsity basketball. In high school he was senior class president.) And he looks healthy enough, blue-eyed behind his beard, like a trapper or a mountain man, acquainted with silences. He also grins a lot.

2   Odd, then, to have noticed earlier—at the house, when he took off his shabby coat to play Ping-Pong—that the white arms were unmuscled. The coat may have been a comment. This, after all, is southern California, where every man is an artist, an advertiser of himself; where every surface is painted and every object potted; where even the statues seem to wear socks. The entire population ambles, in polyesters, toward a Taco Bell. To wear a brown shabby cloth coat in southern California is to admit something.

3   So he hasn't been getting much exercise. Nor would the children have elected him president of any class. At the house they avoided him. Or, since he was too big to be avoided entirely, they treated his presence as a kind of odor to pass through hurriedly, to be safe on the other side. They behaved like cats. Of course, he ignored them. But I think they were up to more than just protecting themselves from his lack of curiosity. Children are expert readers of grins.

4   His grin is intermittent. The dimples twitch on and off; between them, teeth are bared; above them, the blue eyes disappear in a wince. This grin isn't connected to any humor the children know about. It may be a tic. It could also be a function of some metronome made on Mars. It registers inappropriate intervals. We aren't listening to the same music.

5   This is the man who introduced me to the mysteries of mathematical science, the man I could never beat at chess, the man who wrote haiku and played with computers. Now there is static in his head, as though the mind had drifted off its signal during sleep. He has an attention span of about thirty seconds.

6   I am to take him back to where he lives, in the car I have rented in order to pretend to be a Californian. We are headed for a rooming house in one of the beach cities along a coast of off-ramps and oil wells. It is a rooming house that thinks of itself as Spanish. The ruined-hacienda look requires a patio, a palm tree and several miles of corrugated tile. He does not expect me to come up to his room, but I insist. I have brought along a six-pack of beer.

7   The room is a slum, and it stinks. It is wall-to-wall beer cans, hundreds of them, under a film of ash. He lights cigarettes and leaves them burning on the windowsill or the edge of the dresser or the lip of the sink, while he thinks of something else—Gupta sculpture, maybe, or the Sephiroth Tree of the Kabbalah. The sink is filthy, and so is the toilet. Holes have been burnt in the sheet on the bed, where he sits. He likes to crush the beer cans after he has emptied them, then toss them aside.

8   He tells me that he is making a statement, that this room is a statement, that the landlord will understand the meaning of his statement. In a week or so, according to the pattern, they will evict him, and someone will find him another room, which he will turn into another statement, with the help of the welfare checks he receives on account of his disability, which is the static in his head.

9   There are no books, no newspapers or magazines, no pictures on the wall. There is a television set, which he watches all day long while drinking beer and smoking cigarettes. I am sufficiently familiar with the literature on schizophrenia to realize that this room is a statement he is making about

himself. I am also sufficiently familiar with his history to understand that, along with his contempt for himself, there is an abiding arrogance. He refuses medication. They can't make him take it, any more than they can keep him in a hospital. He has harmed no one. One night, in one of these rooms, he will set himself on fire.

10 He talks. Or blurts: scraps from Oriental philosophers—Lao-tzu, I think— puns, incantations, obscenities, names from the past. There are conspiracies; I am part of one of them. He grins, winces, slumps, is suddenly tired, wants me to get out almost as much as I want to get out, seems to have lapsed in a permanent parenthesis. Anyway, I have a busy schedule.

11 Well, speed kills slowly, and he fiddled too much with the oxygen flow to his brain. He wanted ecstasy and revelation, the way we grew up wanting a bicycle, a car, a girlfriend. These belonged to us by right, as middle-class Americans. So, then, did salvation belong to us by right. I would like to thank Timothy Leary and all the other sports of the 1960s who helped make this bad trip possible. I wish R. D. Laing would explain to me, once again and slowly, how madness is a proof of grace. "The greatest magician," said Novalis, "would be the one who would cast over himself a spell so complete that he would take his own phantasmagorias as autonomous appearances."

12 One goes back to the rented car and pretending to be a Californian as, perhaps, one had been pretending to be a brother. It is odd, at my age, suddenly to have become an only child.

Thinking about the Text

1. Discuss how each "telling detail" about Leonard's brother provides a glimpse of his early promise. Then explain how these same details now underscore his sad transformation.

2. Why does Leonard's brother feel that his lifestyle and room are "making a statement"? What type of "statement" does the author feel his brother is making?

3. In this autobiographical essay, Leonard, a New Yorker, can only "pretend to be a Californian." Find details that illustrate what California represents for him.

4. Who or what does Leonard seem to blame for his brother's experimentation with drugs? Why? What is Leonard's implied thesis?

5. Discuss all possible meanings of the title. Why does Leonard wait until the end to focus on it?

WRITING FROM THE TEXT

1. Write an essay contrasting Leonard's recollection of his brother before taking drugs with his perception of him now.

2. If drug addiction or mental illness has plagued any members of your own family, write an essay that illustrates an important insight you have learned from this experience.

3. Find a photograph that shows you with one of your relatives—a sibling, a parent, a cousin, or grandfather. Write an analysis of your relationship with that relative based on the dynamics that you perceive in the photograph.

CONNECTING WITH OTHER TEXTS

1. Read "Living in Two Worlds" (p. 109) and write an essay that shows how both Marcus Mabry and John Leonard live between worlds because of their families.

2. Using "The Only Child," "Thanksgiving" (p. 34; p. 3), or "The Color of Love" (p. 16), write an essay describing and analyzing the positive and negative aspects of family members reuniting and discovering how they have changed.

Are Families Dangerous?
Barbara Ehrenreich

Long known as a journalist and social critic, Barbara Ehrenreich (b. 1941) has written extensively as an advocate for women and for the poor. In addition to her frequent articles in the popular press—the *New York Times Magazine, Ms., Esquire, Vogue, Atlantic Monthly,* and *Mother Jones*—Ehrenreich is also known for *Witches, Midwives, and Nurses: A History of Women Healers* (1972), *The Sexual Politics of Sickness* (1973), *The Hearts of Men: American Dreams and the Flight from Commitment* (1983), *The Worst Years of Our Lives: Irreverent Notes from a Decade of Greed* (1990), *Nickel and Dimed: On (Not) Getting By in America* (2001), *Global Women: Nannies, Maids, and Sex Workers in the New Economy* (2003), and *Bait and Switch: The (Futile) Pursuit of the American Dream* (2005). Ehrenreich is a contributing writer to *Time* magazine. You can read her current views on politics and culture at *Barbara's Blog* (Ehrenreich.blogs.com). The essay that follows was first published in *Time* in 1994 and reflects Ehrenreich's concern for an institution—here the American family—and the social consequences of ignoring some of its problems.

1   A disturbing subtext runs through our recent media fixations. Parents abuse sons—allegedly at least, in the Menendez case—who in turn rise up and

kill them. A husband torments a wife, who retaliates with a kitchen knife. Love turns into obsession, between the Simpsons anyway, and then perhaps into murderous rage: the family, in other words, becomes personal hell.

2   This accounts for at least part of our fascination with the Bobbitts and the Simpsons and the rest of them. We live in a culture that fetishes the family as the ideal unit of human community, the perfect container for our lusts and loves. Politicians of both parties are aggressively "pro-family"; even abortion-rights bumper stickers proudly link "pro-family" and "pro-choice." Only with the occasional celebrity crime do we allow ourselves to think the nearly unthinkable: that the family may not be the ideal and perfect living arrangement after all—that it can be a nest of pathology and a cradle of gruesome violence.

3   It's a scary thought, because the family is at the same time our "haven in a heartless world." Theoretically, and sometimes actually, the family nurtures warm, loving feelings, uncontaminated by greed or power hunger. Within the family, and often only within the family, individuals are loved "for themselves," whether or not they are infirm, incontinent, infantile or eccentric. The strong (adults and especially males) lie down peaceably with the small and weak.

4   But consider the matter of wife battery. We managed to dodge it in the Bobbitt case and downplay it as a force in Tonya Harding's life. Thanks to O. J., though, we're caught up now in a mass consciousness-raising session, grimly absorbing the fact that in some areas domestic violence sends as many women to emergency rooms as any other form of illness, injury or assault.

5   Still, we shrink from the obvious inference: for a woman, home is, statistically speaking, the most dangerous place to be. Her worst enemies and potential killers are not strangers but lovers, husbands and those who claimed to love her once. Similarly, for every child like Polly Klaas who is killed by a deranged criminal on parole, dozens are abused and murdered by their own relatives. Home is all too often where the small and weak fear to lie down and shut their eyes.

6   At some deep, queasy, Freudian level, we all know this. Even in the ostensibly "functional," nonviolent family, where no one is killed or maimed, feelings are routinely bruised and often twisted out of shape. There is the slap or put-down that violates a child's shaky sense of self, the cold, distracted stare that drives a spouse to tears, the little digs and rivalries. At best, the family teaches the finest things human beings can learn from one another—generosity and love. But it is also, all too often, where we learn nasty things like hate and rage and shame.

7   Americans act out their ambivalence about the family without ever owning up to it. Millions adhere to creeds that are militantly "pro-family." But at the same time millions flock to therapy groups that offer to heal the "inner child" from damage inflicted by family life. Legions of women band together to revive the self-esteem they lost in supposedly loving relationships and to learn to love a little less. We are all, it is often said, "in recovery." And from what? Our families, in most cases.

8   There is a long and honorable tradition of "anti-family" thought. The French philosopher Charles Fourier taught that the family was a barrier to human progress; early feminists saw a degrading parallel between marriage and prostitution. More recently, the renowned British anthropologist Edmund Leach stated that "far from being the basis of the good society, the family, with its narrow privacy and tawdry secrets, is the source of all discontents."

9   Communes proved harder to sustain than plain old couples, and the conservatism of the '80s crushed the last vestiges of life-style experimentation. Today even gays and lesbians are eager to get married and take up family life. Feminists have learned to couch their concerns as "family issues," and public figures would sooner advocate free cocaine on demand than criticize the family. Hence our unseemly interest in O. J. and Erik, Lyle and Lorena: they allow us, however gingerly, to break the silence on the hellish side of family life.

10   But the discussion needs to become a lot more open and forthright. We may be stuck with the family—at least until someone invents a sustainable alternative—but the family, with its deep, impacted tensions and longings, can hardly be expected to be the moral foundation of everything else. In fact, many families could use a lot more outside interference in the form of counseling and policing, and some are so dangerously dysfunctional that they ought to be encouraged to disband right away. Even healthy families need outside sources of moral guidance to keep the internal tensions from imploding—and this means, at the very least, a public philosophy of gender equality and concern for child welfare. When, instead, the larger culture aggrandizes wife beaters, degrades women or nods approvingly at child slappers, the family gets a little more dangerous for everyone, and so, inevitably, does the larger world.

THINKING ABOUT THE TEXT

1. Ehrenreich suggests that beyond their notoriety, we are fascinated with the "subtext" revealed in recent highly publicized criminal and civil trials. What is the collective view or "subtext" that underlies the Menendez

brothers' murder of their parents, Lorena Bobbitt's attack on her husband, and O. J. Simpson's relationship with his former wife?

2. How are the theoretical and popular concepts of family life in marked contrast to what these trials reveal about families?

3. What is the "obvious inference" that Ehrenreich wants her readers to draw? Which of her specific statistics and examples support the inference?

4. Ehrenreich acknowledges the virtues family life can teach. What are they? But she also refers to the nonphysical, yet violent abuses inflicted on people in a family. What are they?

5. After acknowledging that "anti-family" ideas are not new, what specific suggestions does Ehrenreich make for working on the problems that exist in families?

WRITING FROM THE TEXT

1. Write an analysis of family life that demonstrates how "the finest things human beings can learn from one another" (p. 38) are evident in the specific examples you use to illustrate your position.

2. In an analysis of family life, show how even in functional and nonviolent families, "feelings are routinely bruised and often twisted out of shape," and how "nasty things like hate and rage and shame" are learned (p. 38). Use specific examples from families that you know to support your position. Is there a solution to the problems of these families that you can propose in your conclusion?

3. Take one or two examples from families that you know well and write an essay illustrating how outside help—moral guidance, education, or counseling—helped these particular families survive.

CONNECTING WITH OTHER TEXTS

1. Read "The Good Daughter" (p. 12) and consider Ehrenreich's idea that even in functional, nonviolent families "feelings are bruised" and the "slap or put-down" threatens self-esteem. Write an analysis of Caroline Hwang's life that suggests Ehrenreich may be right.

2. How do the families described in "My Son, My Compass" (p. 8) and "Who Shot Johnny?" (p. 186) illustrate that a family can teach "the finest things human beings can learn from one another—generosity and love"? Use the theoretical goodness noted by Ehrenreich to analyze how Smith's and Dickerson's families exemplify those specific virtues.

3. Using "Thanksgiving" (p. 3), "The Good Daughter?" (p. 12), and "Are Families Dangerous?" (p. 37), argue that even nonviolent families can bruise egos and create unhealthy individuals within the family unit.

 # The Lanyard

Billy Collins

Named U.S. Poet Laureate in 2001, Billy Collins (b.1941) has been awarded numerous honors, as well as fellowships from the New York Foundation for the Arts, the National Endowment for the Arts, and the Guggenheim Foundation. He has conducted summer poetry workshops in Ireland at University College Galway, and taught at Columbia University, Sara Lawrence, and Lehman College, City University of New York. Popular with readers of all ages, Collins typically engages students with humor and surprise. The poet Stephen Dunn has said that Collins "doesn't hide things from us, as I think lesser poets do. He allows us to overhear, clearly, what he himself has discovered." His books of poetry include *She Was Just Seventeen* (2006), *Nine Horses* (2002), *Sailing Alone Around the Room: New and Selected Poems* (2001), *Picnic, Lightning* (1998), *The Art of Drowning* (1995), and *Questions About Angels* (1991). The following poem was published in *The Trouble With Poetry* in 2005.

> The other day I was ricocheting slowly
> off the blue walls of this room,
> moving as if underwater from typewriter to piano,
> from bookshelf to an envelope lying on the floor,
> 5 when I found myself in the L section of the dictionary
> where my eyes fell upon the word *lanyard*.
>
> No cookie nibbled by a French novelist
> could send one into the past more suddenly—
> a past where I sat at a workbench at a camp
> 10 by a deep Adirondack lake
> learning how to braid long thin plastic strips
> into a lanyard, a gift for my mother.
>
> I had never seen anyone use a lanyard
> or wear one, if that's what you did with them,
> 15 but that did not keep me from crossing
> strand over strand again and again
> until I had made a boxy
> red and white lanyard for my mother.

She gave me life and milk from her breasts,
20   and I gave her a lanyard.
She nursed me in many a sick room,
lifted spoons of medicine to my lips,
laid cold face-cloths on my forehead,
and then led me out into the airy light

25   and taught me to walk and swim,
and I, in turn, presented her with a lanyard.
Here are thousands of meals, she said,
and here is clothing and a good education.
And here is your lanyard, I replied,
30   which I made with a little help from a counselor.

Here is a breathing body and a beating heart,
strong legs, bones and teeth,
and two clear eyes to read the world, she whispered,
and here, I said, is the lanyard I made at camp.
35   And here, I wish to say to her now,
is a smaller gift—not the worn truth

that you can never repay your mother,
but the rueful admission that when she took
the two-tone lanyard from my hand,
40   I was as sure as a boy could be
that this useless, worthless thing I wove
out of boredom would be enough to make us even.

THINKING ABOUT THE TEXT

1. What is the effect of the poet beginning this work with a casual reference to "the other day" and then mentioning ordinary objects before his "eyes fell" on the word "lanyard" in the dictionary? What is a lanyard?

2. When the narrator recalls the lanyard that he made for his mother years ago at camp, he playfully alludes to Marcel Proust's madeleine cookie that prompted Proust's seven-volume novel, *Remembrance of Things Past*. Why is this allusion effective?

3. What are the various "gifts" that the narrator's mother has given him?

4. How does the narrator undercut the value of his own gift to his mother?

5. What is the narrator's revelation at the end of his poem? Why is this admission ironic?

WRITING FROM THE TEXT

1. Focusing on a childhood action or belief that you perceived so differently years ago, write an essay that contrasts your perception then with your view now. Using sights, sounds, and sensations, dramatize your past and present views.

2. Write an analysis of "The Lanyard" that shows how this poem manages to be both moving and light at the same time.

CONNECTING WITH OTHER TEXTS

1. Focusing on "The Lanyard" and "Coke" (p. 243), write an essay comparing and contrasting each narrator's reflections on the past. What do they have in common and how are they distinct?

2. After reading "You Call That Irony?" (p. 446), write an essay analyzing the use of irony in the following poems: "The Lanyard," "Coke" (p. 243), "Blue Spruce" (p. 79) and "Mr. Z" (p. 133).

Chapter 2

Between Genders

As the selections in this chapter reveal, women and men still live with gender-related issues, but the tensions of even a decade ago seem remarkably reduced. The women's and men's movements of the past decades have helped to identify, address, and correct problems that previous generations ignored. Yet both genders still experience challenges in trying to move beyond traditional male and female roles while developing relationships and becoming allies. You and your friends may be in the process of exploring or resolving some of the same gender issues that the writers in this chapter discuss.

Some of the writers show how traditional dating patterns and problems have persisted, as in Adair Lara's essay about who pays for the date and Stephen Perry's depiction of his grandfather's womanizing. Reginald McKnight dramatizes flawed communication between the genders. And although Libby Copeland shows how a platonic relationship can evolve into a romance, she notes that the intense feelings are often only one-sided. Most recently, dating and mating rituals have changed in unexpected ways as both Celeste Biever and Meghan Daum illustrate in their narrations of Internet matches.

Ellen Goodman and Joyce Carol Oates explore, in an analytical essay and a short story, a problem affecting both genders—violence against women. Don Sabo further shows how a patriarchal system that encourages violent and self-destructive competition between men also fosters violence against women. More positively, Jeff Z. Klein applauds his girlfriend as an ally and respects her ability to defend them in a street attack.

You most likely have found that gender issues are everywhere, showing up in such diverse places as pop music lyrics, films, magazine articles, and the Internet. In this chapter, our writers question stereotypes, explore alternatives, deplore injustice and violence against both men and women, and celebrate improved alliances between the genders.

Boy Friend: Between Those Two Words, a Guy Can Get Crushed
Libby Copeland

After completing an English major at the University of Pennsylvania, Libby Copeland (b. 1976) interned with the *Washington Post* and has remained on their staff as a political and feature writer. In 2005, Copeland was the winner of the Feature Specialty Reporting competition held by the American Association of Sunday and Feature Editors. The article below was published in the *Post* in 2004.

1   The worst kind of temptation, as Tantalus found out, is the sort that's closest, the fruit that's barely out of reach. This holds true for infatuation, which is why the cruelest crush is one between friends.

2   We call this the friend-crush, and it happens when one member of a platonic relationship secretly harbors a desire for something more. The friend-crush survives through crying jags and significant others and drunken walks home. And when it ends, it often goes out with a humiliating fizzle, accompanied by something like, "I can't date you, Jason/Bobby/Steven/Mike. I value our friendship too much."

3   Apparently, no one talks about the friend-crush, about the fact that it's quite common, that it usually seems to be the guy doing the crushing, and that it is endemic to high schools and college campuses. Last autumn a college kid named Matt Brochu wrote about it in his school newspaper, and it was as if he'd just translated the Rosetta Stone of adolescent longing.

4   When Brochu's column ran in the University of Massachusetts paper in November, a cry of recognition arose from the young people of this nation. At last, someone had given voice to their silent suffering. Through instant messaging, the column spread from Amherst, Mass., to Boston to Austin to Muncie to Berkeley. It spread to England and Belgium and to a Navy enlistee in the middle of the Pacific Ocean and to a woman in eastern Canada who "almost cried" when she read it.

5   The Web site for the Massachusetts Daily Collegian, where Brochu's column was posted, was flooded. A typical column gets at most 1,000 readers in one month. Brochu's got 570,000 hits from November to March.

6   The column was an anatomy of Brochu's real-life crush, embellished by past experiences and by a sprinkling of imagination. Brochu, now a 21-year-old senior, fell into infatuation last summer, after he became friends with a girl from his home town of East Longmeadow, Mass. She was three years younger, an incoming freshman at UMass and—the way Brochu tells it—burdened by a boyfriend who wasn't good enough for her. (They never are.) She was flirtatious and beautiful and had an air of innocence. She and Matt wound up in psychology class together, where they chatted through each seminar and Brochu's roommate took notes for both of them. Then she broke up with her boyfriend.

7   Brochu started writing. When he finished, the column was effusive and tragic the way love paeans usually are. It was called "What she doesn't know will kill you," and it was written in the second person and filled with references specific to his slice of generation. You met her a few months ago, and somehow she managed to seep into your subconscious like that "Suga how you get so fly" song. . . . She's gorgeous, but gorgeous is an understatement. More like you're startled every time you see her because you notice something new in a "Where's Waldo" sort of way.

8   It described how a crush works on memory, causing the desirer to remember everything ever told to him by the object of his desire. It talked about the guy's everyday indecisions, such as what to get the girl for her birthday and whether to instant-message her at any given moment. It talked of "that cute little scar on her shoulder," and her love for calzones, and her utter obliviousness to his ardor. It talked of her boyfriend, the "tool," who didn't appreciate her.

9   Collegian Web site readers are allowed to write responses to articles. Most columns get three or four. Brochu's column got over 500, nearly all in gratitude and praise. Eventually, the exhausted editor running the feedback section told readers they couldn't write in any more. But the old messages are still up there, steeped in the drama of young love.

10   "Thank you for showing me that I'm not alone on this in this crazy world," wrote someone under the name "Hobbes."

11   "By the time I finished it, I was speechless and light-headed from the truthfulness of it all," wrote "Abel."

12   "i laughed when i saw resemblances of myself, yet inside i was really crying," wrote "Krunk."

13   Readers were inspired by the end of Brochu's column, a romantic call to arms that included a blank space where each reader could write the name of his beloved. The last lines are these:

14   Now cut this out, fill in her name, and give it to her, coward. Just let me know how it works out.

15   "Damn, I wish I could be so eloquent," wrote "P. Che." "Maybe it really is worth a shot no?"

16   Brochu thought so. He'd made up his mind to tell the girl.

17   Unlike the infatuation from afar, the friend-crush is especially powerful because the romance seems so almost possible. By its very nature, the friend-crush encourages Talmudic dissections of the beloved's psyche, hashing and rehashing of missed opportunities, optimistic interpretations of neutral behavior.

18   There's Brad Clark, 17, of Glen Burnie, who years ago became friends with a girl he had a crush on and tried to ask her out via a passed note. She wrote back, "I think you're really cool so we can be friends but I have a boyfriend."

19   For a week, Clark listened to moody Dashboard Confessional songs and analyzed the note over and over. He considered the phrase, But I have a boyfriend.

20   "Have. That's not a very strong word there," he thought.

21   There's Carl M. Schwarzenbach, a 17-year-old high school junior in Southwick, Mass., who had a crush on a certain girl since the first moment he saw her, 2 1/2 years ago, on the first day of school. It was the beginning of fifth period, choir class, at 12:03 P.M., as he recalls. He was a freshman. She was a senior. She was blond and beautiful and wearing a black tank top and jeans. They became close. Schwarzenbach says they kissed a few times, but they stayed just friends.

22   "She always had this mind-set that she was afraid of commitment and she didn't want to commit to anything 'cause she was afraid she would hurt me," Schwarzenbach says.

23   When Brochu's column came out, Schwarzenbach e-mailed it to the girl, with her name filled out in the blank. She's in college now, and they haven't seen each other much. She e-mailed him back, in pink, as always.

24   "She just said, uh, that it was really, really sweet and it made her smile," Schwarzenbach says. "I think it might have brought us a little closer."

25   The friend-crush is largely a phenomenon of adolescence, when hope is more persuasive then experience. Though it happens in high school, it blossoms in college, when a new culture shakes everything up. College is when you consider important questions like: Is there such a thing as a platonic back rub? Is there such a thing as a long-distance boyfriend?

26   It might have to do with the coed dorm setting, where near-strangers are thrust into an intimacy previously reserved for family. (Suitemates pass by in towels.) It might be the fluidity of college dating, in which nothing is defined, and in any case, no one knows what the definitions mean. Are you friends? Are you taking it slow? One person's "seeing each other" is another person's "dating each other," which is another person's "hanging out," which is another person's "friends with benefits."

27   Consider the experience that countless college guys have had. At a party, a certain girl—one you thought was taken—seems to be flirting with you. She takes your arm when you walk her home. The next day, when you instant-message her with the vaguely suggestive "I had a nice time last night," she says, "Me, too," and then mentions her boyfriend. What could it possibly mean?

28   Brian Murphy, a freshman at Robert Morris University in Pittsburgh, met a girl from his dorm on move-in day, and they became best friends. They walked to class together, ate lunch and dinner together, went to parties together. After parties, they had a ritual where they would go back to her room and cuddle. Murphy fell for her, hard. He says it was the kind of situation where—forced to choose between going out with guy friends and staying in with her to watch a chick flick—he'd watch the chick flick.

29   But she had a boyfriend of three years.

30   Murphy and the girl shared one guilty kiss, then they went home for Christmas break. During the break, Murphy read Brochu's column, and inspired by it, resolved to tell the girl how he felt. He made a scrapbook filled with pictures of the two of them. When they came back to school, he gave her the scrapbook and confessed his feelings.

31   "Get over me," she said. She said she had realized how much she loved her boyfriend.

32   Murphy was crushed.

33   "It's definitely the first time that I ever fell in love," he says.

34   Love is like wealth, or the world food supply. Some people hog it; others get nothing at all. To scroll down the feedback column below Matt Brochu's article is to realize how much love goes unrevealed, unrecognized and unrequited. If only there were some mechanism for spreading love around, everybody could get enough.

35   Instead, the postings sit static in cyberspace, declarations of love to people who may never read them.

36   "I've seen the sun rise over the mountains of Vermont and seen it set over the Caribbean. I've swam with tropical fish and seen the view from the top of Katahdin. But none of that even begins to compare to how beautiful she is."

37 "Katie Norris—if you ever read this, you know how I felt about you during that first month when I was in Mexico . . . look me up sometime. . . . I'd still like to try again."

38 "Shandie although i only just met you it seems like u are the one . . . dang girl ur perfect"

39 Some female readers, impressed by Brochu's way with words, try to woo the author himself.

40 "As a woman that constantly prays for a man with those sensitive values and beautiful words, you definitely took the right approach with this lucky lady. And as a little side note . . . if she didn't think she was as lucky as everyone thought she was; I would love to hear back from you."

41 A reader incensed by the number of girls praising Brochu writes:

42 "Girls, stop saying you hope to find someone like the guy who wrote this . . . you already have but you call them your best friend and what you don't know is that they are In Love with you."

43 The feedback column is a strange sort of conversation, taking place among 500 strangers over the course of months. Readers post responses that reference other posts and debate the efficacy of Brochu's just-tell-her approach. All the theories on love present themselves. There are the cynics. They write that if romance hasn't happened yet, it isn't meant to. They suggest that women want jerks more than "nice guys," and they question whether it's even possible to move from friendship to love. They offer cautionary tales.

44 "I guess all good stories aren't supposed to have a happy ending and all heroes are not supposed to win," writes a fellow named "Ryan," who posts a harrowing account of running two miles in the rain to a woman's house to declare his love. The woman listened, then told him they were better off as friends. "It was a long walk home that day, the rain. . . . laughing at me in a steady and harsh flow."

45 But there are more romantics than cynics. A girl writes in to reconsider the "dateability" of guys who are "right under my nose." Another writes in to say she knows a guy has a crush on her and she thinks she feels the same way, but she needs to take it slow. Some confess their love to the people they like, and contacted later, two guys say it actually worked out.

46 Someone named "Kate" writes:

47 "As heard one thousand times before . . . amazing article. But, answer us all one question, because we're all dying to know . . . did you get the girl?!"

48   The answer is: After the story ran, Brochu sent the link over instant messaging to his crush. She wrote back, asking who the column was about. He sent her a cautious, rambling set-up, which he saved, along with her responses, so that he could analyze them later. His set-up started like this:

49   "First off, I'm not really obsessed with this girl, I'm just interested, and I have been since the day I met her, and she doesn't have to worry about letting me down easy, b/c I'm not the type of person to let things get awkward and let it ruin the friendship we already have, b/c she's gotta realize. . . ."

50   It went on like this for a while. Then: "So yeah, it's you, sorry I had to make things all weird."

51   She called it the "sweetest thing" she'd ever read and the "nicest thing" that had ever happened to her, and they agreed to sleep on it and talk the next day.

52   She called him.

53   "You never know whether to believe it or not, whether she was letting me down nicely," Brochu says. She talked about her long relationship with her ex-boyfriend, and how she didn't want to get into something serious, and how she felt she'd get too serious with Brochu.

54   "She said that she could only hang out with people in that way that she couldn't see herself getting to like," Brochu says.

55   It hurt, but the strange thing is, it hurt only for two days and then Brochu was over it. He says it was as if a light switch inside of him was turned off. He wonders now how much of the crush was just him enjoying the chase, the thrill of the unattainable.

56   "I think it goes to show that my crush was just building upon itself from me not knowing," he says. "It was completely constructed."

57   They're still friends, and Brochu says he's totally over her.

58   Anyway, he's dating someone now. Or, seeing someone. He doesn't quite know what to call it. At the very least, they're hanging out.

THINKING ABOUT THE TEXT

1. Copeland refers to the Greek myth of Tantalus, who is punished by the gods who deny him the ability to reach water to quench his thirst or to pick succulent fruit that hangs just beyond his grasp. What comparison does Copeland intend in her opening allusion?

2. How does Copeland support her view that although no one talks about "the friend-crush," it is actually quite common?

3. Copeland believes that it is usually the male in the friendship who is "crushed." Why do you think that males are more apt to be the "victims" in a friend-crush?

4. How does Matt Brochu's crush story end? How does the columnist finally come to an understanding of his crush?

WRITING FROM THE TEXT

1. Write an analysis of one of your relationships or those of a friend that supports Copeland's view that much love goes "unrevealed, unrecognized and unrequited" (48).

2. Write an essay analyzing one infatuation between friends to show how "the thrill of the unattainable" is a driving motivation in the "crush."

CONNECTING WITH OTHER TEXTS

1. Read "Modern Romance" to compare and contrast the experiences couples have meeting online with the relationships college students have in a friend-crush.

2. Write an analysis contrasting and/or comparing Meghan Daum's romance with PFSlider and Pete ("Virtual Love," p. 56) with the relationship of a student in a friend-crush.

Modern Romance
Celeste Biever

Serving as biomedical editor for *New Scientist* magazine, Celeste Biever (b. 1978) has been on staff for several years as a technology reporter and technology editor for this global weekly science magazine published in the United States and Great Britain. Biever has her masters in chemistry from the University of Oxford and a diploma in journalism from City University, London. The following article originally appeared in the special issue on "Love" in *New Scientist* on April 28, 2006.

1   He was a strapping 28-year-old with a mane of brown hair, she a dazzling redhead in a white strapless vest and tight trousers. Garth Fairlight of London, UK, and Pituca Chang of Irvine, California, first met watching

fireworks and eating burgers at a Fourth of July party in 2003. It wasn't quite love at first sight, but after protesting against high taxes together, the chemistry became obvious. Two months later she moved in, and by November they were married.

2   It sounds like a fairy-tale romance, but it actually happened—in the online fantasy world of Second Life, that is. Garth and Pituca are actually screen names, and the pair is at least 20 years older than they look inside the game, where players appear as cartoon versions of themselves—called avatars—and communicate by typing messages.

3   If the idea of a cyber-romance doesn't turn you on, perhaps you should take a closer look. The couple insists the feelings they have for each other are real and that they were madly in love long before they met face to face. "The love part happened in the game," says Pituca, but she and Garth are now engaged to be married in real life. Catherine Smith, marketing director at Linden Lab in San Francisco, California, which produces Second Life, says the pair are just one of many couples who have got married inside the game. Others say that getting hitched in real life is rarer, but it happens.

4   While love in virtual worlds may still be unusual, less intense online relationships have become commonplace. A study completed last month by the non-profit Pew Internet & American Life Project based in Washington DC found that 74 per cent of single internet users in the U.S. have taken part in at least one online dating-related activity, including sites specifically devoted to finding a match, while 15 per cent of American adults (that's 30 million people) say they know someone who has been in a long-term relationship with a partner they met online. So what's the big attraction?

5   The Internet has some clear advantages over the real world as a place to meet people, says Dan Ariely, who studies online dating at the Massachusetts Institute of Technology's Media Lab. "The problem of meeting people in modern life is very real. Online relationships are a way to experiment cheaply and in a non-dangerous way with romantic life." Moreover, you can meet far more people online than you could ever hope to in a bar or in the office. And because online games and chat rooms often have a theme, they allow users to "hone" in on people with whom they share interests. Some online dating sites, including Match.com and eHarmony, apply algorithms that their creators claim can pick out couples most likely to be a successful match.

6   However, it is the nature of online interactions themselves that intrigues psychologists and sociologists. There is growing evidence that communicating

online is more conducive to openness than a face-to-face rendezvous. "We tend to interact differently online," says Ron Reynolds, a virtual-world consultant based in the UK. "We tend to be more honest, more intimate with people."

7   This is known as the "hyperpersonal" effect, a term coined in 1996 by Joe Walther of Cornell University in New York (*Communication Research*, vol 23, p 3). Walther says that communicating by typed message gives people time to construct their responses. It also frees them from worrying about how they look and sound, so they can focus exclusively on what they're saying. Without the cues that we rely on to form impressions during face-to-face encounters, such as facial expressions and mannerisms, people can build more positive impressions of each other without being confronted with a jarring reality that might put them off.

8   Nick Yee of Stanford University, California, studies how the hyperpersonal effect operates in virtual worlds, where people get to know each other "from the inside out." "In real life we judge a person by their physical appearance and then we get to know their character and values. In a massively multiplayer online role-playing game, the reverse is true," he writes on the virtual-worlds blog Terra Nova. This is an experience that Erika, who is in her early 20s and moved to the UK from the US after meeting her husband Damien inside Second Life, has also enjoyed. "In real life you are usually first attracted to someone by their looks," she says. "However, online you can't touch or look. All you can see is their personality."

9   Online communication can also encourage people to take risks because there is always the opportunity to simply disappear if things become awkward or embarrassing. And while it is certainly easy to lie online, it turns out it's even easier to tell the truth. In a 2002 study, Walther showed that people communicating online were much more likely to disclose personal details about themselves (*Human Communication Research*, vol 28, p 317). Experts believe that this is because people are shielded from disapproving facial expressions and awkward consequences.

10   So what happens when online couples finally meet in the flesh? Katelyn McKenna of Israel's Ben Gurion University suggested in 2002 that an attraction sparked online that might not have taken off in real life can be strong enough to survive even when the relationship moves offline. Her research shows that meeting someone "inside out" might, in some cases, be preferable to meeting them the right way round. When Pituca decided to meet Garth in London, exactly one year after they had first met in the game, things went swimmingly. "I'm there at Heathrow, and when I saw her come out, I immediately knew it was her," says Garth. "It felt like she had been on a business trip but that we had been together our whole life."

11   However, it seems the hyperpersonal effect also has a flip side. Although it brings greater intimacy and self-disclosure, it also encourages a hyperactive imagination that can result in dashed hopes. "You have less information and therefore individuals fill in the gaps with what they would like to believe," says Nicole Ellison, who is based at Michigan State University in East Lansing and studies self-disclosure in online dating sites.

12   The Internet has pitched us into a new era of romance that offers greater opportunities to meet the right partner and a better environment for intimate and honest communication. But it also plays by different rules. Plenty of people who have tried to make online relationships work in real life have been disappointed. For some, it's best to enjoy cyberromance for what it is. Whether or not it's love, it can certainly be life-changing.

13   "We tend to interact differently online, to be more honest, more intimate with people."

THINKING ABOUT THE TEXT

1. Why might Biever have chosen to open this essay with a description of "Garth" and "Pituca"? What details do we discover about their relationship and how are these facts relevant to this essay?

2. What is surprising about the statistics from the study by Pew Internet & American Life Project?

3. According to Dan Ariely at the MIT Media Lab, what are some clear advantages of getting acquainted with people on the Internet before meeting them in person?

4. Describe the "hyperpersonal" effect of Internet relationships. What are the positive and negative aspects of the hyperpersonal effect? Why are online relationships sometimes impossible to sustain offline?

WRITING FROM THE TEXT

1. Focusing on the difficulties or risks involved in dating—asking someone out or accepting a date, affording the costs of dating, or getting to know your date—write a narrative supporting your thesis on one of these topics drawn from Biever's essay.

2. Biever claims that "the Internet has pitched us into a new era of romance that offers greater opportunities to meet the right partner and a better environment for intimate and honest communication" (54). If you have ever

tried to begin a relationship online, write an evaluative response of the above claim, using your own experiences to defend your stance. Include specific details from Biever's essay as you analyze her support. (See evaluative response, p. 438.)

3. If you have had experience meeting people online, write an essay comparing and contrasting your online and offline relationships. Include specific points from Biever's essay as you support or counter each.

CONNECTING WITH OTHER TEXTS

1. Write an evaluative response of Biever's essay, using details from Meghan Daum's "Virtual Romance" (p. 56) to support or refute Biever's claims.

2. Using details from Biever's essay and from Libby Copeland's "Boy Friend: Between Those Two Words, A Guy Can Get Crushed" (p. 45), write an argument demonstrating that the modern options of e-mail, MySpace, and online match services are making it easier or more difficult to determine if a relationship is romantic or platonic. Illustrate and support all claims with specific examples.

"I can't wait to see what you're like online."

Virtual Love

Meghan Daum

A graduate of Vassar with a B.A. in English, Meghan Daum (b. 1970) earned an M.F.A. in writing from Columbia University. Her work has appeared in such popular magazines as the *New Yorker, Harper's, G.Q., Harper's Bazaar,* and *Vogue.* Currently on staff at the *Los Angeles Times* where her columns regularly appear, Daum also has been a columnist at *Self* and has contributed commentaries and stories to public radio programs such as *Morning Edition, This American Life,* and *The Savvy Traveler.* Her novel, *The Quality of Life Report,* was published in 2003. On writing, Meghan Daum has this advice: "Whether the form is fiction or nonfiction, I have always believed that the subject is only as interesting as the larger themes that fuel it. The reason I am such a fan of the essay form is that it allows room for a variety of literary approaches—personal narrative, reportage, satire, to name just a few—and the form encourages both the writer and the reader to explore intellectual and even controversial ideas in a way that is also engaging and entertaining." The following essay was first published in the *New Yorker* and is part of a collection of Daum's essays entitled *My Misspent Youth* (2001).

1   It started in cold weather; fall was drifting away into an intolerable chill. I was on the tail end of twenty-six, living in New York City, and trying to support myself as a writer. One morning I logged on to my America Online account to find a message under the heading "is this the real meghan daum?" It came from someone with the screen name PFSlider. The body of the message consisted of five sentences, written entirely in lowercase letters, of perfectly turned flattery, something about PFSlider's admiration of some newspaper and magazine articles I had published over the last year and a half, something else about his resulting infatuation with me, and something about his being a sportswriter in California.

2   I was charmed for a moment or so, engaged for the thirty seconds that it took me to read the message and fashion a reply. Though it felt strange to be in the position of confirming that I was indeed "the real meghan daum," I managed to say, "Yes, it's me. Thank you for writing." I clicked the "Send Now" icon and shot my words into the void, where I forgot about PFSlider until the next day when I received another message, this one entitled "eureka." "wow, it is you," he wrote, still in lowercase. He chronicled the various conditions under which he'd read my few and far between articles: a boardwalk in Laguna Beach, the spring training pressroom for the baseball team he covered for a Los Angeles newspaper. He confessed to having a "crazy crush" on me. He referred to me as "princess daum." He said he wanted to propose marriage or at least have lunch with me during one of his two annual trips to New York. He managed to do all of this without sounding like a schmuck.

As I read the note, I smiled the kind of smile one tries to suppress, the kind of smile that arises during a sappy movie one never even admits to seeing. The letter was outrageous and endearingly pathetic, possibly the practical joke of a friend trying to rouse me out of a temporary writer's block. But the kindness pouring forth from my computer screen was unprecedented and bizarrely exhilarating. I logged off and thought about it for a few hours before writing back to express how flattered and touched—this was probably the first time I had ever used the word "touched" in earnest—I was by his message.

3   I had received e-mail messages from strangers before, most of them kind and friendly and courteous—all of those qualities that generally get checked with the coats at the cocktail parties that comprise what the information age has now forced us to call the "three-dimensional world." I am always warmed by an unsolicited gesture of admiration or encouragement, amazed that anyone would bother, shocked that communication from a stranger could be fueled by anything other than an attempt to get a job or make what the professional world has come to call "a connection."

4   I am not what most people would call a "computer person." I have utterly no interest in chat rooms, news groups, or most Web sites. I derive a palpable thrill from sticking an actual letter in the U.S. mail. But e-mail, though at that time I generally only sent and received a few messages a week, proves a useful forum for my particular communication anxieties. I have a constant, low-grade fear of the telephone. I often call people with the intention of getting their answering machines. There is something about the live voice that has become startling, unnervingly organic, as volatile as incendiary talk radio. PFSlider and I tossed a few innocuous, smart-assed notes back and forth over the week following his first message. His name was Pete. He was twenty-nine and single. I revealed very little about myself, relying instead on the ironic commentary and forced witticisms that are the conceit of most e-mail messages. But I quickly developed an oblique affection for PFSlider. I was excited when there was a message from him, mildly depressed when there wasn't. After a few weeks, he gave me his phone number. I did not give him mine but he looked me up anyway and called me one Friday night. I was home. I picked up the phone. His voice was jarring yet not unpleasant. He held up more than his end of the conversation for an hour, and when he asked permission to call me again, I accepted as though we were in a previous century.

5   Pete, as I was forced to call him on the phone—I could never wrap my mind around his actual name, privately referring to him as PFSlider, "e-mail guy," or even "baseball boy"—began calling me two or three times a week. He asked if he could meet me in person and I said that would be okay. Christmas was a few weeks away and he would be returning east to see his family.

From there, he would take the short flight to New York and have lunch with me. "It is my off-season mission to meet you," he said. "There will probably be a snowstorm," I said. "I'll take a team of sled dogs," he answered. We talked about our work and our families, about baseball and Bill Clinton and Howard Stern and sex, about his hatred for Los Angeles and how much he wanted a new job. Other times we would find each other logged on to America Online at the same time and type back and forth for hours. For me, this was far superior to the phone. Through typos and misspellings, he flirted maniacally. "I have an absurd crush on you," he said. "If I like you in person you must promise to marry me." I was coy and conceited, telling him to get a life, baiting him into complimenting me further, teasing him in a way I would never have dared in the real world or even on the phone. I would stay up until 3 A.M. typing with him, smiling at the screen, getting so giddy that I couldn't fall asleep. I was having difficulty recalling what I used to do at night. My phone was tied up for hours at a time. No one in the real world could reach me, and I didn't really care.

6   In off moments, I heard echoes of things I'd said just weeks earlier: "The Internet is destroying the world. Human communication will be rendered obsolete. We will all develop carpal tunnel syndrome and die." But curiously, the Internet, at least in the limited form in which I was using it, was having the opposite effect. My interaction with PFSlider was more human than much of what I experienced in the daylight realm of live beings. I was certainly putting more energy into the relationship than I had put into any before, giving him attention that was by definition undivided, relishing the safety of the distance by opting to be truthful rather than doling out the white lies that have become the staple of real life. The outside world—the place where I walked around on the concrete, avoiding people I didn't want to deal with, peppering the ground with half-truths, and applying my motto of "let the machine take it" to almost any scenario—was sliding into the periphery of my mind. I was a better person with PFSlider. I was someone I could live with.

7   This borrowed identity is, of course, the primary convention of Internet relationships. The false comfort of the cyberspace persona has been identified as one of the maladies of our time, another avenue for the remoteness that so famously plagues contemporary life. But the better person that I was to PFSlider was not a result of being a different person to him. It was simply that I was a desired person, the object of a blind man's gaze. I may not have known my suitor, but for the first time in my life, I knew the deal. I knew when I'd hear from him and how I'd hear from him. I knew he wanted me because he said he wanted me, because the distance and facelessness and lack of gravity of it all allowed him to be sweeter to me than most real-life

people had ever managed. For the first time in my life, I was involved in a ritualized courtship. Never before had I realized how much that kind of structure was missing from my everyday life.

8   And so PFSlider became my everyday life. All the tangible stuff—the trees outside, my friends, the weather—fell away. I could physically feel my brain. My body did not exist. I had no skin, no hair, no bones; all desire had converted itself into a cerebral current that reached nothing but my frontal lobe. Lust was something not felt but thought. My brain was devouring all of my other organs and gaining speed with each swallow. There was no outdoors, the sky and wind were irrelevant. There was only the computer screen and the phone, my chair and maybe a glass of water. Pete started calling every day, sometimes twice, even three times. Most mornings I would wake up to find a message from PFSlider, composed in Pacific time while I slept in the wee hours. "I had a date last night," he wrote, "and I am not ashamed to say it was doomed from the start because I couldn't stop thinking about you." Then, a few days later, "If you stood before me now, I would plant the warmest kiss on your cheek that I could muster."

9   I fired back a message slapping his hand. "We must be careful where we tread," I said. This was true but not sincere. I wanted it, all of it. I wanted the deepest bow down before me. I wanted my ego not merely massaged but kneaded. I wanted unfettered affection, soul mating, true romance. In the weeks that had elapsed since I picked up "is this the real meghan daum?" the real me underwent some kind of meltdown, a systemic rejection of all the savvy and independence I had worn for years like a grown-up Girl Scout badge. Since graduating from college, I had spent three years in a serious relationship and two years in a state of neither looking for a boyfriend nor particularly avoiding one. I had had the requisite number of false starts and five-night stands, dates that I wasn't sure were dates, emphatically casual affairs that buckled under their own inertia even before dawn broke through the iron-guarded windows of stale, one-room city apartments. Even though I was heading into my late twenties, I was still a child, ignorant of dance steps or health insurance, a prisoner of credit-card debt and student loans and the nagging feeling that I didn't want anyone to find me until I had pulled myself into some semblance of an adult. I was a true believer in the urban dream—in years of struggle succumbing to brilliant success, in getting a break, in making it. Like most of my friends, I was selfish by design. To want was more virtuous than to need. I wanted someone to love me but I certainly didn't need it. I didn't want to be alone, but as long as I was, I had no choice but to wear my solitude as though it were haute couture. The worst sin imaginable was not cruelty or bitchiness or even professional failure but

vulnerability. To admit to loneliness was to slap the face of progress. It was to betray the times in which we lived.

10   But PFSlider derailed me. He gave me all of what I'd never realized I wanted. He called not only when he said he would, but unexpectedly, just to say hello. His guard was not merely down but nonexistent. He let his phone bill grow to towering proportions. He thought about me all the time and admitted it. He talked about me with his friends and admitted it. He arranged his holiday schedule around our impending date. He managed to charm me with sports analogies. He courted and wooed and romanced me. He didn't hesitate. He was unblinking and unapologetic, all nerviness and balls to the wall. He wasn't cheap. He went out of his way. I'd never seen anything like it.

11   Of all the troubling details of this story, the one that bothers me the most is the way I slurped up his attention like some kind of dying animal. My addiction to PFSlider's messages indicated a monstrous narcissism. But it also revealed a subtler desire that I didn't fully understand at the time. My need to experience an old-fashioned kind of courtship was stronger than I had ever imagined. The epistolary quality of our relationship put our communication closer to the eighteenth century than the uncertain millennium. For the first time in my life, I was not involved in a protracted "hang out" that would lead to a quasi-romance. I was involved in a well-defined structure, a neat little space in which we were both safe to express the panic and intrigue of our mutual affection. Our interaction was refreshingly orderly, noble in its vigor, dignified despite its shamelessness. It was far removed from the randomness of real-life relationships. We had an intimacy that seemed custom-made for our strange, lonely times. It seemed custom-made for me.

12   The day of our date was frigid and sunny. Pete was sitting at the bar of the restaurant when I arrived. We shook hands. For a split second he leaned toward me with his chin as if to kiss me. He was shorter than I had imagined, though he was not short. He registered to me as neither handsome nor unhandsome. He had very nice hands. He wore a very nice shirt. We were seated at a very nice table. I scanned the restaurant for people I knew, saw no one and couldn't decide how I felt about that.

13   He talked and I heard nothing he said. He talked and talked and talked. I stared at his profile and tried to figure out if I liked him. He seemed to be saying nothing in particular, though it went on forever. Later we went to the Museum of Natural History and watched a science film about the physics of storms. We walked around looking for the dinosaurs and he talked so much that I wanted to cry. Outside, walking along Central Park West at dusk, through the leaves, past the horse-drawn carriages and yellow cabs and splendid lights of Manhattan at Christmas, he grabbed my hand to kiss me and

I didn't let him. I felt as if my brain had been stuffed with cotton. Then, for some reason, I invited him back to my apartment, gave him a few beers, and finally let him kiss me on the lumpy futon in my bedroom. The radiator clanked. The phone rang and the machine picked up. A car alarm blared outside. A key turned in the door as one of my roommates came home. I had no sensation at all, only the dull déjà vu of being back in some college dorm room, making out in a generic fashion on an Indian throw rug while Cat Stevens'*Geatest Hits* played on the portable stereo. I wanted Pete out of my apartment. I wanted to hand him his coat, close the door behind him, and fight the ensuing emptiness by turning on the computer and taking comfort in PFSlider.

14   When Pete finally did leave, I sulked. The ax had fallen. He'd talked way too much. He was hyper. He hadn't let me talk, although I hadn't tried very hard. I berated myself from every angle, for not kissing him on Central Park West, for letting him kiss me at all, for not liking him, for wanting to like him more than I had wanted anything in such a long time. I was horrified by the realization that I had invested so heavily in a made-up character, a character in whose creation I'd had a greater hand than even Pete himself. How could I, a person so self-congratulatingly reasonable, have gotten sucked into a scenario that was more akin to a television talk show than the relatively full and sophisticated life I was so convinced I led? How could I have received a fan letter and allowed it to go this far? Then a huge bouquet of FTD flowers arrived from him. No one had ever sent me flowers before. I was sick with sadness. I hated either the world or myself, and probably both.

15   No one had ever forced me to forgive them before. But for some reason, I forgave Pete. I cut him more slack than I ever had anyone. I granted him an official pardon, excused his failure for not living up to PFSlider. Instead of blaming him, I blamed the Earth itself, the invasion of tangible things into the immaculate communication PFSlider and I had created. With its roommates and ringing phones and subzero temperatures, the physical world came barreling in with all the obstreperousness of a major weather system, and I ignored it. As human beings with actual flesh and hand gestures and Gap clothing, Pete and I were utterly incompatible, but I pretended otherwise. In the weeks that followed I pictured him and saw the image of a plane lifting off over an overcast city. PFSlider was otherworldly, more a concept than a person. His romance lay in the notion of flight, the physics of gravity defiance. So when he offered to send me a plane ticket to spend the weekend with him in Los Angeles, I took it as an extension of our blissful remoteness, a three-dimensional e-mail message lasting an entire weekend. I pretended it was a good idea.

16   The temperature on the runway at JFK was seven degrees Fahrenheit. We sat for three hours waiting for deicing. Finally we took off over the frozen city,

the DC-10 hurling itself against the wind. The ground below shrank into a drawing of itself. Laptop computers were plopped onto tray tables. The air re-circulated and dried out my contact lenses. I watched movies without the sound and thought to myself that they were probably better that way. Some-thing about the plastic interior of the fuselage and the plastic forks and the din of the air and the engines was soothing and strangely sexy, as fabricated and seductive as PFSlider. I thought about Pete and wondered if I could ever turn him into an actual human being, if I could ever even want to. I knew so many people in real life, people to whom I spoke face-to-face, people who made me laugh or made me frustrated or happy or bored. But I'd never given any of them as much as I'd given PFSlider. I'd never forgiven their spasms and their speeches, never tied up my phone for hours in order to talk to them. I'd never bestowed such senseless tenderness on anyone.

17   We descended into LAX. We hit the tarmac and the seat belt signs blinked off. I hadn't moved my body in eight hours, and now, I was walking through the tunnel to the gate, my clothes wrinkled, my hair matted, my hands shak-ing. When I saw Pete in the terminal, his face registered to me as blank and impossible to process as the first time I'd met him. He kissed me chastely. On the way out to the parking lot, he told me that he was being seriously consid-ered for a job in New York. He was flying back there next week. If he got the job he'd be moving within the month. I looked at him in astonishment. Something silent and invisible seemed to fall on us. Outside, the wind was warm and the Avis and Hertz buses ambled alongside the curb of Terminal 5. The palm trees shook and the air seemed as heavy and earthly as Pete's hand, which held mine for a few seconds before dropping it to get his car keys out of his pocket. The leaves on the trees were unmanageably real. He stood before me, all flesh and preoccupation. The physical world had invaded our space. For this I could not forgive him.

18   Everything now was for the touching. Everything was buildings and bushes, parking meters and screen doors and sofas. Gone was the computer; the erotic darkness of the telephone; the clean, single dimension of Pete's voice at 1 A.M. It was nighttime, yet the combination of sight and sound was blinding. We went to a restaurant and ate outside on the sidewalk. We were strained for conversa-tion. I tried not to care. We drove to his apartment and stood under the ceiling light not really looking at each other. Something was happening that we needed to snap out of. Any moment now, I thought. Any moment and we'll be all right. These moments were crowded with elements, with carpet fibers and direct light and the smells of everything that has a smell. They left marks as they passed. It was all wrong. Gravity was all there was.

19   For three days, we crawled along the ground and tried to pull ourselves up. We talked about things that I can no longer remember. We read the

Los Angeles Times over breakfast. We drove north past Santa Barbara to tour the wine country. I stomped around in my clunky shoes and black leather jacket, a killer of ants and earthworms and any hope in our abilities to speak and be understood. Not until studying myself in the bathroom mirror of a highway rest stop did I fully realize the preposterousness of my uniform. I felt like the shot in a human shot put, an object that could not be lifted, something that secretly weighed more than the world itself. We ate an expensive dinner. We checked into a hotel and watched television. Pete talked at me and through me and past me. I tried to listen. I tried to talk. But I bored myself and irritated him. Our conversation was a needle that could not be threaded. Still, we played nice. We tried to care and pretended to keep trying long after we had given up. In the car on the way home, he told me I was cynical, and I didn't have the presence of mind to ask him just how many cynics he had met who would travel three thousand miles to see someone they barely knew. Just for a chance. Just because the depths of my hope exceeded the thickness of my leather jacket and the thickness of my skin. And at that moment, I released myself into the sharp knowledge that communication had once again eliminated itself as a possibility.

20   Pete drove me to the airport at 7 A.M. so I could make my eight o'clock flight home. He kissed me goodbye, another chaste peck I recognized from countless dinner parties and dud dates from real life. He said he'd call me in a few days when he got to New York for his job interview, which we had discussed only in passing and with no reference to the fact that New York was where I happened to live. I returned home to the frozen January. A few days later, he came to New York and we didn't see each other. He called me from the plane back to Los Angeles to tell me, through the static, that he had gotten the job. He was moving to my city.

21   PFSlider was dead. Pete had killed him. I had killed him. I'd killed my own persona too, the girl on the phone and online, the character created by some writer who'd captured him one morning long ago as he read the newspaper. There would be no meeting him in distant hotel lobbies during the baseball season. There would be no more phone calls or e-mail messages. In a single moment, Pete had completed his journey out of our mating dance and officially stepped into the regular world, the world that gnawed at me daily, the world that fed those five-night stands, the world where romance could not be sustained because we simply did not know how to do it. Here, we were all chitchat and leather jackets, bold proclaimers of all that we did not need. But what struck me most about this affair was the unpredictable nature of our demise. Unlike most cyber romances, which seem to come fully equipped with the inevitable set of misrepresentations and false expectations, PFSlider and I had played it fairly straight. Neither of us had lied.

We'd done the best we could. We were dead from natural causes rather than virtual ones.

22   Within a two-week period after I returned from Los Angeles, at least seven people confessed to me the vagaries of their own e-mail affairs. This topic arose, unprompted, over the course of normal conversation. Four of these people had gotten on planes and met their correspondents, traveling from New Haven to Baltimore, New York to Montana, Texas to Virginia, and New York to Johannesburg. These were normal people, writers and lawyers and scientists, whom I knew from the real world. They were all smart, attractive, and more than a little sheepish about admitting just how deep they had been sucked in. Very few had met in chat rooms. Instead, the messages had started after chance meetings at parties and on planes; some, like me, had received notes in response to things they'd written online or elsewhere. Two of these people had fallen in love, the others chalked it up to a strange, uniquely postmodern experience. They all did things they would never do in the real world: they sent flowers, they took chances, they forgave. I heard most of these stories in the close confines of smoky bars and crowded restaurants and we would all shake our heads in bewilderment as we told our tales, our eyes focused on some distant point that could never be reigned in to the surface of the Earth. Mostly it was the courtship ritual that had drawn us in. We had finally wooed and been wooed, given an old-fashioned structure through which to attempt the process of romance. E-mail had become an electronic epistle, a yearned-for rule book. The black and white of the type, the welcome respite from the distractions of smells and weather and other people, had, in effect, allowed us to be vulnerable and passionate enough to actually care about something. It allowed us to do what was necessary to experience love. It was not the Internet that contributed to our remote, fragmented lives. The problem was life itself.

23   The story of PFSlider still makes me sad. Not so much because we no longer have anything to do with one another, but because it forces me to grapple with all three dimensions of daily life with greater awareness than I used to. After it became clear that our relationship would never transcend the screen and the phone, after the painful realization that our face-to-face knowledge of each other had in fact permanently contaminated the screen and the phone, I hit the pavement again, went through the motions of real life, said "hello" and "goodbye" to people in the regular way. In darker moments, I remain mortified by everything that happened with PFSlider. It terrifies me to admit to a firsthand understanding of the way the heart and the ego are entwined. Like diseased trees that have folded in on one another, our need to worship fuses with our need to be worshipped. Love eventually becomes only about how much mystique can be maintained. It upsets me

even more to see how this entanglement is made so much more intense, so unhampered and intoxicating, by way of a remote access like e-mail. But I'm also thankful that I was forced to unpack the raw truth of my need and stare at it for a while. This was a dare I wouldn't have taken in three dimensions.

24   The last time I saw Pete he was in New York, thousands of miles away from what had been his home and a million miles away from PFSlider. In a final gesture of decency, in what I later realized was the most ordinary kind of closure, he took me out to dinner. We talked about nothing. He paid the bill. He drove me home in his rental car, the smell and sound of which was as arbitrary and impersonal as what we now were to each other. Then he disappeared forever. He became part of the muddy earth, as unmysterious as anything located next door. I stood on my stoop and felt that familiar rush of indifference. Pete had joined the angry and exhausted living. He drifted into my chaos, and joined me down in reality where, even if we met on the street, we'd never see each other again, our faces obscured by the branches and bodies and falling debris that make up the ether of the physical world.

Thinking about the Text

1. What are the elements of the first e-mail message the author received from "PFSlider" that prompted her to send a short reply? What "touched" her in the second message?

2. Daum admits to not being a "computer person" and to not liking the telephone. Yet, in the course of a few weeks, she and PFSlider wrote a number of "smart-assed notes back and forth" and frequently spoke by phone. How do you explain this change in her habits?

3. Although the author once believed that "human communication will be rendered obsolete" by the Internet, she reports that her e-mailing with PFSlider "was more human than much of what [she] experienced in the daylight realm of live beings" (58). What does Daum mean by this? What was "more human" about her e-mail relationship than her real-life relationships? In what ways does this acknowledgment foretell the conclusion of her essay?

4. What is the "ritualized courtship" (59) that Daum relished in her relationship with PFSlider? Cite specific examples of this courtship.

5. What does the author mean when she confesses that she was "still a child" (p. 59) when she became "derailed" by PFSlider (60)? Why does she use the metaphoric word "derailed"? What self-awareness did the

author come to when she analyzed the attraction she had to her e-mailing correspondent?

6. Analyze what happened when PFSlider and the author met. What is revealed by the author when she writes that she wanted Pete to leave her apartment so that she could turn on the computer and find comfort in PFSlider? What is the realization that the author has about her relationship with Pete as contrasted with PFSlider? Why do you think she accepted the invitation to spend a weekend with him in Los Angeles, a continent away from her home in New York City?

7. In describing their three days together, the author writes that "the physical world had invaded our space" (62). Explain that statement and the author's metaphors that their "conversation was a needle that could not be threaded," and that "PFSlider was dead. Pete had killed him. I had killed him. I'd killed my own persona too" (63). In what way is the author right when she describes these deaths as "from natural causes rather than virtual ones" (64)?

8. What is significant about the author's revelation that seven of her friends—writers, lawyers, and scientists who are all smart and attractive—have engaged in e-mail affairs? What is Daum's strategy in ending her essay by moving away from her own experience? The author admits that the story of PFSlider still makes her sad, and she concludes with the idea that "love eventually becomes only about how much mystique can be maintained" (64). Analyze her statement and explain how that idea is central to the experience she has had.

WRITING FROM THE TEXT

1. Write a character analysis of Meghan Daum. Analyze her as a person who has admitted certain preferences and who has revealed herself in candid and metaphoric language. Your analysis should be supported with specific details from the text. Review how to write a character analysis (pp. 485–493) for help with this assignment.

2. Describe a time when you enjoyed a "ritualized courtship" (59) or perhaps longed for a relationship that might make you a "better person." Analyze what happened or describe what the ideal courtship—in the physical or virtual world—would be. Relate your analysis to Daum's experience if you can.

3. Work from Daum's assertion that the "borrowed identity is . . . the primary convention of Internet relationships" (58). Describe experiences you

or your friends have had connecting with others on the Internet. Were those experiences "truthful" or more of the "white lies that have become the staple of real life" (58)? What conclusions do you draw from your experiences and observations?

CONNECTING WITH OTHER TEXTS

1. Write an essay contrasting Daum's doomed experience with the successful Internet pairings described by Celeste Biever in "Modern Romance" (p. 51).

2. In "Makes Learning Fun" (p. 247), Clifford Stoll observes that real learning takes work, discipline, commitment, and responsibility, and that these qualities are not available in an on-line education. Could the same claim be made that a virtual romance can't provide the qualities and tests of a conventional dating relationship? Connect Stoll's essay with Daum's, and write an analysis of what is missing in a virtual romance.

"She's texting me, but I think she's also subtexting me."

Who's Cheap?
Adair Lara

A columnist for the *San Francisco Chronicle*, Adair Lara (b. 1952) is also a teacher of writing and the author of *Welcome to Earth, Mom: Tales of a Single Mother* (1992), *Slowing Down in a Speeded-Up World,* (1994), *The Best of Adair Lara* (1999), and *Hold Me Close, Let Me Go: A Mother, A Daughter, and an Adolescence Survived* (2001). The essay included here originally appeared in the *San Francisco Chronicle*.

1   It was our second date, and we had driven one hundred miles up the coast in my car to go abalone-diving. When I stopped to fill the tank at the only gas station in sight, Craig scowled and said, "You shouldn't get gas here. It's a rip-off."

2   But he didn't offer to help pay. And that night, after dinner in a restaurant, he leaned over and whispered intimately, "You get the next one." Though he was sensitive and smart, and looked unnervingly good, Craig was as cheap as a two-dollar watch.

3   This is not an ethical dilemma, you're all shouting. *Lose the guy,* and fast.

4   Lose the guy? Is this fair? My friend Jill is always heading for the john when the check comes, but I don't hear anybody telling me to lose *her.* And she's far from the only cheap woman I know. A lot of us make decent money these days, yet I haven't seen women knocking over tables in fights for the lunch tab. In fact, many women with 20/20 vision seem to have trouble distinguishing the check from the salt, pepper and other tabletop items. But if a guy forgets to chip in for gas or gloats too long over the deal he got on his Nikes, he's had it.

5   Why is this double standard so enduring? One reason is that, while neither sex has a monopoly on imperfection, there *are* such things as flaws that are much more distasteful in one sex than in the other. Women seem especially unpleasant when they get drunk, swear or even insist on pursuing an argument they'll never win. And men seem beneath contempt when they're cheap.

6   These judgments are a holdover from the days when women stayed home and men earned the money. Though that old order has passed, we still associate men with paying for things. And besides, there's just something appealing about generosity. Buying something for someone is, in a sense, taking care of her. The gesture says, "I like you, I want to give you something." If it comes from a man to whom we are about to entrust our hearts, this is a comforting message. We miss it when it's not forthcoming.

7   Then why *not* dump on cheap men?

8   Some men are just skinflints and that's it. My friend Skye broke up with her boyfriend because when they went to the movies he doled out M&Ms to her one at a time. Craig, my date back at the gas station, liked to talk about how he'd bought his car—which in California, where I live, is like buying shoes—as a special present to himself.

9   This kind of cheapness is ingrained; you'll never change it. That guy who parks two miles away to avoid the parking lot fee was once a little boy who saved his birthday money without being told to. Now he's a man who studies the menu and sputters, "Ten dollars for *pasta?*" His stinginess will always grate on you, since he is likely to dole out his feelings as parsimoniously as his dollars.

10   On the other hand, I know a wonderful man, crippled with debts from a former marriage, who had to break up with a woman because she never paid her share, and he was simply running out of money. Though she earned a lot more than he did, she couldn't expand her definition of masculinity to include "sometimes needs to go Dutch treat."

11   To men, such women seem grasping. One friend of mine, who spends a lot of money on concerts and theater and sailing but not on restaurants he considers overpriced, has evolved a strategy for women who are annoyed at the bohemian places he favors. If his date complains, he offers to donate to the charity of her choice the cost of an evening at her favorite spot. "Some women have bad values," he says, "And if the idea of spending money on a good cause, but not on her, makes her livid, I know she's one of them."

12   I had a bracing encounter with my own values when I told my friend Danny the humorous (I thought) story of a recent date who asked if I wanted a drink after a concert, then led me to the nearest water fountain.

13   Danny gave one of his wry looks. "Let's get this straight," he said, laughing. "As a woman, you are so genetically precious that you deserve attention just because you grace the planet. So, of course, he should buy you drinks. He should also drive the car, open the door, ask you to dance, coax you to bed. And then when you feel properly pampered, you can let out that little whine about how he doesn't treat you as an equal."

14   On second thought, I guess I'd rather buy my own drink.

15   So here's the deal. Before dumping a guy for ordering the sundowner dinner or the house white, better first make sure that you aren't burdening the relationship with outdated ideas of how the sexes should behave. Speaking for myself, I know that if a man looks up from the check and says, "Your share is eleven dollars," part of me remembers that, according to my mother, *my* share was to look charming in my flowered blouse.

16   Wanting the man to pay dies hard. What many of us do now is *offer* to split the check, then let our purses continue to dangle from the chair as we give him time to realize that the only proper response is to whip out his own wallet.

17   Is this a game worth playing? It's up to you, but consider that offering to help pay implies that the check is his responsibility. And this attitude can work both ways. My sister gets angry when her husband offers to help clean the house. "Like it's *my* house!" she snorts.

18   Like it's *his* check.

Thinking about the Text

1. Authors may use humor to engage an audience—even when their intention is to argue a serious point. Is Lara's main purpose in this essay mostly to entertain or to persuade her audience?

2. Does Lara have a claim? If so, what is it? Does she have support?

3. What does Lara mean when she writes that some flaws seem "much more distasteful in one sex than in the other" (p. 68)? *Are* women more unpleasant than men when they "get drunk, swear or even insist on pursuing an argument they'll never win" (p. 68) or are these the author's sexist generalizations? (If they are generalizations, what is her goal in using them?)

4. In what way is the point of Lara's essay embedded in Danny's response to Lara's anecdote about the after-concert drink? Why does Lara manipulate her essay so that its central wisdom appears in Danny's words? What is the author's strategy?

5. What conventional and sexist ideas are challenged in this essay?

Writing from the Text

1. Lara cites a number of specific ways that people save money—avoiding commercial parking lots, eating the "sundowner" or "early bird" dinner, and drinking the house wine. Make a list of all of the ways that you save money. How many of your habits would be regarded by a date or friends as "cheap"? Develop your list into supporting examples for a thesis of your own.

2. Describe the habits of your dates and friends when it comes to ignoring a bill or saving money. The focus of your essay can be to laud or deplore your friends' habits.

3. Using Lara's essay for support, write an essay arguing that the double standard Lara describes hurts both men and women.

Connecting with Other Texts

1. After reading "In Groups We Shrink" (p. 261), write an essay analyzing how pressure from others and within social groups can condition our behavior on a date. Incorporate the ideas of both Tavris and Lara as you focus on group conventions and individual expectations.

2. Using Lara's essay and Jeff Z. Klein's "Watching My Back" (p. 82), write an essay that illustrates how couples might redefine romantic relationships free from stereotypical role playing.

 Peaches

Reginald McKnight

The Hamilton Holmes professor of English at the University of Georgia in Athens, Reginald McKnight (b. 1956) received a B.A. from Colorado College and an M.A. from the University of Denver in 1987. He has taught English and creative writing in Senegal as well as at the Metropolitan State University in Denver.

McKnight is the author of *Moustapha's Eclipse* (1988), *I Get on the Bus* (1990), *The Kind of Light That Shines on Texas: Stories* (1992), *White Boys* (1998), and *He Sleeps* (2001). He also is the editor of *African-American Wisdom* (1994) and *Wisdom of the African World* (1996). In addition, his work has been published in literary magazines such as *Leviathan*, *Prairie Schooner*, *Kenyon Review*, and the *Black American Literature Forum*. McKnight has said that his work generally "deals with the deracinated African-Americans who came of age after the civil rights struggle. These are people who are at the front lines of the current struggle for human rights." The following story is from *Moustapha's Eclipse*.

1   J.C. crosses the sun-faded carpet looking truculent and surly. He looks at me with his woman-get-out-my-seat-face. His tail points straight up to the ceiling. He lets out with his most irate meow, stomps back and forth in front of me in that stiff-legged strut that drives me crazy. He always does this when I sit in "his" chair. "Looks like everybody's mad at me today," I say, crossing my arms and legs at the same time. Momma doesn't say a word so I know what's up with her. Daddy drops the paper to his lap, and sits up in his chair. Its old, arthritic wood creaks. "Ain't nobody mad, Baby Sister," he says, removing his glasses. "Ain't nobody disappointed, hurt, upset—'cept that little pea-brain cat of yours. Mystery to me why you even sit in that chair after he done rubbed all his hair off in it."

2   "Have you heard from Marc lately, Rita?" asks Momma, not looking up from her puzzle.

3   "Good Lord Almighty have I heard from him. Tuesday I got four letters. Four separate letters. In four separate envelopes."

4   "What's all this 'Lord Almighty' business, girl," says Daddy. "I ain't sending you to no twenty-thousand-dollar-a-year college to hear you talk like a imitation me. You gonna be a scientist. Let me hear my money's worth."

5   "Your money?" Momma says, "You mean Uncle Sam's money."

6   "I'll take his money too if it help put Baby Sis through school. I ain't proud."

7   "You ain't rich neither," Momma says, snapping a puzzle piece into place.

8   J.C. leaps up into my lap. His purring irritates me so I get up and move to the other side of the room.

9   "We got a postcard from him a couple of days before you got here, Rita," my mother says, still not looking up from the table. "Didn't say much though."

10   "Why didn't you tell me when I got home, Momma?"

11   "Moody as you was? No ma'am. I got better things to do than listen to you bawl from sunup to sundown. Anyway, we already talked about your plans before you got here. Now if I'd been bringing up his name all the time you might have thought I was trying to push you into sending him that. . . the—"

12   "How 'bout 'Dear John,' Lucille."

13   "James!"

14   "Daddy—"

15   "Well, that's the truth. I'm calling a spade a spade. Just like he did."

16   "James! Now I am not going to have you—"

17   "All right now, I'm just playing. But I don't care how much ass that boy kiss. And I don't care how long he stay in Africa to sensitize hisself. Cain't no rich white boy call my child no nigger and—"

18   "Maybe not, but she grown, James. It's her life. Her decision. You and I got nothing to say whatsoever about what Rita decide. Now you promised me you'd leave the poor girl alone. Can't you see she upset as it is?" Momma snaps another piece into the puzzle, pushes her glasses up on her nose and looks up at Daddy. Daddy picks up the newspaper, crosses his legs, clears his throat. "You right," he grunts, then clears his throat again. "Yeah, you right. But if you ask me, you an apple, he an orange." I can tell from his eyes that he is staring at but not reading the paper. The room is as silent as the moon. Dust motes swim through the lamplight around Daddy's head. He looks hurt and I'd like to tell him he needn't be, because I myself am not hurting. I am numb. I don't know what to think or feel or do. I veer toward anger, then careen toward love, then roll toward regret and guilt. But as has been the case since the fight, I end up weightless and static like one of those motes around Daddy's head.

19   Daddy tosses the paper to the floor and in the silence it sounds like firecrackers. J.C. springs up from the chair and scoots under the couch. The room again falls silent, the brief flurry of sound and action is swallowed up like stones tossed into the ocean.

20   After awhile Daddy's chair squeaks and cracks. He inhales deep and slow, then slips on his glasses. "I believe," he says, "I could use a little help outside picking some peaches for old Mrs. Li's sweet and sour sauce. She says she gonna make some extry for you to take back to school with you. Come on."

21   The fog has not yet lifted, but the air feels dryer than usual. Mr. Givens's dog yaps at us from behind the gray cedar fence. In the thirteen years my

parents and I and my two sisters have lived here, I've never seen the old dog and I don't know its name. Each evening, when chastising the dog, when telling it to shut up, when calling it in, Mr. Givens calls it, "Git-yer-dumb-ass-outta-that-garden, Shut-the-hell-up-ya-stupid-mutt, and Giddin-here-ya-damn-dog." As far as I can tell the dog seldom obeys. In the evenings Mr. Givens can often be heard bellowing, "OK, then don't eat, ya stupid!"

22   When the dog has barked long enough, my father picks up the usual peach pit, zings it in the area of Mr. Givens's garden, and finally we hear: "How many times I gotta tell ya to keep yer dumb ass outta that garden?" Silence. My father and I are alone in the backyard which is redolent with the smell of peaches, the sight of peaches. We feel peach pits beneath our feet.

23   "Grab that raggedy-looking box over next to the fence, Baby Sis," Daddy says. "Half them bushel baskets old Givens give me cain't hold air."

24   "This one?"

25   "Um hmm."

26   "Do we need a stepladder?"

27   "Well, they should be plenty of good ones on the ground. And if we shake us a branch or two we won't need a ladder." He kneels and begins sorting peaches, asks me a few questions about how school is going. I answer him in monosyllables, hoping the conversation won't drift toward anything that will upset us both. The afternoon air becomes cool all of a sudden. Goose-bumps erupt on my arms and neck. "Daddy, I'll be right back," I say, "I need a jacket."

28   In my room I stand before the closet door, looking at my reflection in the full-length mirror. I look at myself, forgetting for several moments why I have come into the room. There I stand in baggy white pants and what Marcus calls my "favorite Dinty Moore shirt." He never told me he disliked the way I dress, but when I was clad in my flannels and baggies his eyes often glanced around—toward the bookshelf, "Hey, a new one by Mishima?" or my stereo, "Let's listen to some Marvin Gaye," or the Dali prints, "When did you say that one was painted?" He, like most men, wants to see women dress in anything tight enough to keep the blood static. He always told me he wasn't particu-larly a breast man, or a leg man—"I'm not an anything man," he'd say. "I'm an everything man. Legs, ass, brains, conscience." But he only seemed to tell me that kind of thing when I was wearing flannels and baggies.

29   "What does he see in me?" I think as I peruse the frizzy, uncombable black hair, the burdensome breasts, the face that he insisted no guy on cam-pus could forget, the legs he insisted are not birdlike. "And look at my legs," he'd say, indicating with both hands, "They look like a couple of Venus number twos." He told me never to change a thing about myself. "I'm the one who needs to change," he'd say. And I'd tell him, in the beginning, he

didn't need to change. That he was fine the way he was. But he would always sneer, "Simmons, you don't know the half of it." He kept saying things like that, becoming more strident, histrionic, and distant. "I'm no goddamned good," he'd say over and over. And soon enough, I began to feel as though his kisses were trying to smother something, that the walls of his apartment enfolded secret passages and chambers, that his conversation, numinous and trivial, full of New Age jargon, spoke around rather than of something. There was always something fleeting about him. Something just out the corner of my eye, something just out of reach. I imagined that an invisible incubus paced between us when we were together, thumbing its invisible nose at us, flipping us the invisible finger. I felt its presence so acutely sometimes, that I could almost see it burst forth in hyperactive, muscled flesh. Sometimes it made me fear him. Sometimes I think it made me love him more.

30   The more I loved him, the less I understood him, the farther I slipped from him. And when he started punching walls, calling me at two in the morning to apologize for no reason at all, threatening to slash his wrists every time I told him I was busy, I sensed how ripe he was for procreation.

31   "You never have time anymore, Rita. What's the matter, you mad at me?"

32   "Why should I be mad at you? I'm mad at me. I've got to really get going on my thesis."

33   "I know, I understand. I just want to see you. Why are you hiding from me all of a sudden?"

34   I'd say nothing.

35   "What's wrong, Rita? I just want to see you for one hour."

36   "Marc, I just haven't got the time."

37   He never let up. He'd set his heels and push. And push.

38   "Is it something I said to you? Is it my beliefs? When we first met, you always said I was too rarefied for you. You said I strut around 'up there' acting fey while you're 'down here' accepting life for what it is. 'Fey,' you said. Jesus Christ, Rita, I got no problem with your science. Why can't you give me what's mine?"

39   "I know, Marc. I know. I should. I do. It's got nothing to do with your beliefs. Really. I'm just preoccupied. I've got two midterms tomorrow. I've got that lousy seminar. We can talk about this tomorrow, at dinner."

40   And push.

41   "It's because you think I got no soul or some crap like that, isn't it? I just can't give you what a black guy can give you, right? That's what you think, isn't it? Well if it is, Rita, then you're wrong. It's all an illusion. It's maya. If anything, I can give you more because my world is so different from yours."

42   "Marc, there's only this world—"

43   "Look, Rita, I've been through this before. I've had relationships with Black women and Hispanic women, and Asian women. You can tell me. I think I'd understand. You probably think I don't take you seriously. You think I'm just using you."

44   He'd ask me if it was his disapproving family, his derisive friends, his age, his intellect, or that he was an undergraduate English major and I was a semester away from a master's degree in chemistry. It often left us very little to talk about at dinner. He'd ask if his beard looked silly, or if he dressed poorly, or if my family really hadn't liked him but had simply been Oscarwinning polite, or if he was too easily depressed, irascible, antisocial, untruthful, or was I sure-really-sure "it's not because I'm white?" I'd always say no.

45   I'd say no because it was easy to say no. Easier than unleashing untenable fears, easier, after awhile, than holding him close, feeling his diffuse heat. He'd push, and it was as if he'd started pushing too deeply inside himself, rummaging and scraping, uncovering things that I'm not sure were ever there. "What's wrong with me?" he'd demand. "Tell me. Just tell me something. Do you still love me? Do I offend you in some way?" I couldn't tell him. I knew I'd just have to wait, then I'd see, he'd know. I'd tried to tell him once or twice, but everything would lock up inside me when I'd try to explain. And then it finally just slid out from him, loud and ugly. The word. The beast-incubus word, the inevitable issue of the "yin-yang" relationship. His phrase, "yin-yang relationship." Had I drawn it from him, headfirst screaming, kicking into the world? Or did he plant it in me, water it with his tears, incubate it in the heat of my womblike reticence? I don't know.

46   All I could say that night was, "That, Marc. That's just what I was afraid of. Wasn't but a matter of time, was it?"

47   How would things have gone if I had just told him of my fears and talked it out with him? I never did because to do so would have implied that he had transcended nothing. I flat would have been calling him a liar, or blind. And he was neither. He had transcended something, somehow. Or what if I had just buried myself in his auburn beard, his ginseng breath, the bend and curve of his body, and listened to his nonsense about the Ghosts of Lemuria, the Light of Atlantis, the Race of Tan just for the sake of hearing his voice. His voice was so nice to listen to, a little raspy, a little flutelike. Sometimes it seemed he told his stories in song. Sweet nonsense. And when I actually heard him say the word I was so sure he would eventually say, I was shocked. Shocked both because it always shocks you when someone calls you nigger and because the word fell from his mouth so awkwardly—as if he had never heard it before, said it before, imagined saying it before.

48   So he bought a ticket to Liberia. I didn't know what to feel. He told me he wouldn't come back till he knew, till he really, really understood what blackness

was. I didn't know what to say. He hugged me, kissed me longer than I could stand, said goodbye, promised he'd change, we'd get it straight, he'd return reborn, we'd marry and raise fat, tan, unrarefied babies. He got on the plane. He called me from Denver. He called me from New York. He called me from Dakar. He called me from Monrovia. I got his first letter in two weeks. By six weeks I'd received eight more. In three months over forty letters, bombarded by missives of love, the seed of self-discovery. They came daily, weekly. Tidings of hope, love, joy. Peace Profound. Images of beautiful babies, beautiful ocean, sleek, cat-black men, women in rich Day-glo rags. The taste of this. The smell of that. The size, shape, volume of his ever-expanding, ever-pregnant African love. But I just didn't. His seed fell on unsettled dust, a haze of motes never coming to rest.

49   "It won't lie still," I say aloud, suddenly remembering why I've come up to my room. I grab something warm-looking and bluish, then run back outside.

50   I stand on the stoop and watch Daddy kneeling in the grass, peach in hand. He sniffs, squeezes, removes his glasses and inspects it, then tosses it aside. His face is grave, almost sullen. I cross the yard and kneel beside him, trying to imitate the way he inspects the peaches, but I'm not really sure what he's looking for.

51   I've always loved the way my father throws himself into the task at hand. Whether it be selecting peaches for Mrs. Li's sauce, adjusting a bicycle seat, or expounding to three enraptured daughters at the dinner table just what it is that makes a grocery clerk's job so much more dangerous than a San Francisco cop's, there is no one I know with the intensity, the undivided surrender to the action, the moment.

52   While we sort through hard, woody peaches and soft, muddy peaches, peaches bruised and scarred, peaches clear-complected, he tells me the secret of Mrs. Li's sauce: "She take a whisk broom to J.C.'s chair and use all them cat hairs and cookie crumbs y'all leave in it." And he hints at the secret secret to his peach cobbler, which he says he extracted, through torture, from a Japanese POW. "If I told you, you wouldn't eat it." He tells me it once rained peaches in San Francisco when I was "just a baby, and couldn't possibly remember." And that old Moses told God that no way on earth would he sign those "commandoes or commandants, or whatever you call em, till you take peaches off the list." He tells me he never would have looked twice at Momma had she never stuffed peaches under her sweater back in '47, that peaches, at one time, contained an explosive substance instead of sugar, and the last recorded use of the exploding peach was in the Boer War. "That was before your time," he is quick to add. He tells me about the Peach Bowl of 1968 (LSU won because they ate more peaches. "Well, why you think they call it Peach Bowl?").

53   "Paul Robeson couldn't sing note one 'less he had two, three quarts of peach wine in him," he says. And he tells me about the peachy-keen people

he had ever known (me, Juanita, and Theresa May, "and sometimes that hard-head mother of yours"). He tells me how Big Daddy used to push his cart around the streets of Alabaster, Alabama, hollering, "Waaaatermelon? Strawberries and Peeeeachez! Cold, sweet Peeeeachez! Peaches and cream, peach ice cream, peacherinoes and peacherines, peach yogurt, peach popsicles, peach lipstick, peach pie, jam, and jelly. Cold, sweet peeeeachez!"

54   The box is full of what he assures me are the finest peaches that soil could possibly produce. I offer him a peach from the brimming box; he frowns and says, "Shooot, naw, Baby Sister, I cain't eat them things." We laugh for a long time, leaning away from each other, folding toward each other, like jazz dancers. And then I start to cry. I cry so hard I can scarcely breathe. Daddy holds me, saying nothing. He doesn't even try to shush me, just holds me till I stop. Then he reaches in the box, takes out a peach, examines it, sniffs it, throws it aside. He takes another one and does the same thing. Then another, and another, and another.

55   Finally, he turns the whole box over. Peaches tumble across the lawn. He inspects every last one. His long fingers caress each, every one. His nose and eye, inspecting, seed-deep, each, every one. And then he finds what he is looking for. It is very large, the color of a sunrise, flows into a sunset, flows into the color of Mrs. Li's blush. He rubs it on his sleeve, holds it out to me in the palm of his hand. I wipe my nose with a finger, regard the peach for a long, long time. Till Daddy's arm trembles a bit. "Naw," I say, "I can't eat 'em." He drops the fruit and it cracks on the green grass. He takes my hand, and we walk inside.

Thinking about the Text

1. What is the effect of beginning and ending the story with Rita interacting with her family? Give details that characterize Rita and her parents, and that show their sensitivity toward each other.

2. Consider McKnight's strategy to have Rita escape to her room and to use the "mirror device." From her descriptions, speech, and behaviors, what do we learn about Rita when she is in her room and reflecting on her relationship with Marc?

3. To prepare for a character analysis, write a list of observations about Rita in one column and, in another column next to it, write the corresponding inferences that you have drawn from each observation. Then write another two columns of observations and inferences about Marc. (See p. 486 for an example of listing for a character analysis.)

4. Rita claims that Marc's conversation "full of New Age jargon, spoke around rather than of something" (74). Look up some of the terms he uses—"incubus," "fey," "maya," "yin-yang," "Ghosts of Lemuria," "Light of

Atlantis"—and explain what Marc's language and his use of this particular vocabulary reveal about him.

5. Describe the different "worlds" that Rita and Marc inhabit. What has contributed to the gulf between them and how likely is it that they will marry and resolve their differences?

6. Referring to the title and closing scene, what are some possible meanings of "peaches" that relate to this story? Consider the father's litany of references to peaches and his search for one that "is very large, the color of a sunrise, flows into a sunset, flows into the color of Mrs. Li's blush" (77). Analyze this quotation in terms of the story and explore what the peach might symbolize.

7. What is ironic about the revelation that neither Rita nor her father can eat peaches? How might this revelation relate to the story and particularly to the central conflict between Rita and Marc? How does it contribute to the resolution of the story?

Writing from the Text

1. Using your lists for exercise 3 above, write a character analysis of either Rita or Marc. Focus on a strong assertion about your chosen character and include supporting details and direct quotations to illustrate your points. (See character analysis, pp. 485–488.)

2. Working from your responses to exercise 5, above, write an analysis of the factors contributing to the conflict between Rita and Marc. Assess which factors seem more difficult to resolve and whether a more lasting relationship between Marc and Rita seems likely. Support your assessment with specific details from the story.

3. Write an analysis of the multiple meanings of "peaches" in this story and show how this symbolism relates to the characters and central conflict.

4. If you have ever had someone call you an offensive name or if you have ever blurted out a racial or ethnic slur, write an essay explaining and dramatizing what prompted this name calling, what effect it had at the moment, how the incident ended, and what lasting effect it has had on you.

Connecting with Other Texts

1. Read "Living in Two Worlds" (p. 109) and examine Mabry's contrasting worlds—home and university—in terms of Rita's. Write an essay comparing their "between worlds" experiences and their ways of managing an attachment to family and a commitment to their own goals.

2. In "Race is a Four-Letter Word" (p. 120), Arboleda argues that one's race should not ultimately matter, that his identity cannot be defined in terms of

race. But Marc seems focused on race and on his experience dating women of diverse ethnicity and cultures. Write an essay contrasting these two positions as you show how Marc is limited in ways that Arboleda is not.

Blue Spruce

Stephen Perry

While teaching creative writing—at Long Beach City College, University of California at Irvine, and the UCLA Extension Writers' Program—Stephen Perry (b. 1950) has published more than sixty-five poems in anthologies and in journals such as the *New Yorker, Yale Review, Virginia Quarterly Review, Kenyon Review, Antioch Review,* and *Salmagundi.* Perry has also served as poetry consultant to the Disney Corporation—the only such consultant in the company's history. He is currently seeking a publisher for his collection of poems, *Homecoming.* Perry shares a "co-dependent" Web site with his author wife, Susan Perry, and invites readers to visit and interact with them at www.bunnyape.com.

Referring to "Blue Spruce," Perry reveals, "When I read this poem at poetry readings, I usually tell people that everything in the poem is true, except for the title. There were no blue spruces (that I know of) in the little town in Missouri where I set the poem. I just like the double pun on 'blue' and 'spruce.' " The poem was published in the *New Yorker* in 1991.

My grandfather worked in a barbershop
smelling of lotions he'd slap on your face,
hair and talc. The black razor strop

hung like the penis of an ox. He'd draw
5   the sharp blade in quick strokes over
the smooth-rough hide, and then carefully

over your face. The tiny hairs would gather
on the blade, a congregation singing
under blue spruce in winter,

10   a bandstand in the center of town
bright with instruments, alto sax, tenor
sax, tuba or sousaphone—the bright

oompah-pahs shaving the town somehow,
a bright cloth shaking the air
15   into flakes of silvering hair

floating down past the houses, the horses
pulling carriages past the town fountain,
which had frozen into a coiffure

of curly glass. My grandfather had an affair
20   with the girl who did their nails
bright pink, bright red, never blue,

perhaps as the horses clip-clopped on ice
outside his shop, his kisses
smelling of lather and new skin—

25   when she grew too big and round
with his child, with his oompah love,
with his bandstand love, with his brassy love,

and the town dropped its grace notes
of gossip and whispered hiss,
30   he bundled her out of town

with the savings which should have gone
to my mom. But how could you hate him?
My mother did, my father did,

and my grandmother, who bore his neglect.
35   When she was covered in sheets
at her last death,

he flirted with the nurses, bright
as winter birds in spruces
above a bandstand—

40   I'll always remember him in snow, a deep lather
of laughter, the picture
where he took me from my mother

and raised me high, a baby, into the bell
of his sousaphone, as if I were a note
45   he'd play into light—

THINKING ABOUT THE TEXT

1. List all the images that Perry uses to characterize the grandfather, then describe the resulting "portrait."

2. Discuss the narrator's perception of his grandfather and compare and contrast it with the views of family members and the townspeople.

3. Look up both "blue" and "spruce" in the dictionary. Which definitions relate to this poem? Discuss possible meanings of the title.

4. Cluster (see p. 337) all the references to music or anything musical in the poem. Why might the poet have chosen to connect the grandfather with music and, specifically, with the sousaphone? How do these references add to your understanding of his character?

5. How does the winter setting contribute to the poem? What is the significance of the reference to "light" at the end and of the repetitions of the word "bright" throughout?

WRITING FROM THE TEXT

1. Referring to the images you listed in exercise 1 of "Thinking About the Text," write a character analysis of the grandfather from his grandson's perspective.

2. Working from the clustering you did for exercise 4, write an analysis of the poet's use of music to help characterize the grandfather and the town.

3. With supporting details from this poem, write an essay analyzing Perry's depiction of life in a small town and its effect on the individual. Does he seem at all critical of the small town or of the grandfather?

CONNECTING WITH OTHER TEXTS

1. Using details from this poem and focusing on a character from at least one other work—the schizophrenic brother in "The Only Child" (p. 34), the narrator in "Black Men and Public Space" (p. 181), and the father in *American Beauty* (p. 288), write a paper analyzing the pressures of "fitting into" a particular society and the individual's varying responses to such pressures.

2. Consider the images used to describe the grandparents in "Blue Spruce" and in "Breaking Tradition" (p. 21). With these images in mind, write a paper contrasting these two portraits.

3. Visit Perry's Web site at www. bunnyape.com and read some of his other poems. Write an essay focusing on a recurring image or theme in Perry's writing as exhibited in "Blue Spruce" and any of his other works.

Watching My Back
Jeff Z. Klein

Employed as staff editor of the *New York Times* since 1996, Jeff Z. Klein previously was sports editor of the *Village Voice* for five years and has been an avid ice hockey fan. He is the author of *Mario Lemieux: Ice Hockey Star* (1995) and *Messier* (2005), which "takes readers behind the headlines and statistics for a revealing look at a hockey legend." Klein is also coauthor of *The Coolest Guys on Ice* (1996), *The Death of Hockey* (1998), and two editions of *The Hockey Compendium*. The following essay was first published in the *New York Times Magazine* in 2001.

1   He charged at me, shouting something in Czech. It was the middle of the night in Prague. My girlfriend and I were there for New Year's, and as we strolled through a deserted business district, two young men came bounding out of a pedestrian underpass. Loud, menacing and drunk, one ran up and shoved me, then missed with a liquor-slow karate kick. I shoved back. We squared off, staring.

2   Here I should say that my girlfriend had just completed an advanced self-defense course. She was standing to my left. I couldn't see her, but I could hear her firmly addressing the attacker—"Back off! Go away!"—as she had been taught. I hadn't been in a punch-up since I was 10 and had no idea what to do in an actual fight. But I had seen her in class, whupping two heavily padded mock attackers. I knew what she could do.

3   As my assailant and I faced each other, another couple, a big man and a woman, walked unaware onto the scene. My assailant suddenly went after the big guy, who simply threw him to the ground. That was plenty for me. "He's got it," I said to my girlfriend. "Let's go." We backed away, but after a few steps, she stopped and said: "Wait. We should go back. They may need our help." I wasn't keen on the idea, but back we went. We saw the big guy standing over the assailant, who was down and out. It was over. Everyone dispersed.

4   My girlfriend and I walked down into Wenceslas Square to an all-night cash machine. "I've got your back," she assured me jokingly as I went into the bank. As we waited for a cab, I admitted that I was still pretty wired. "I'm not," she said. "I was ready to fight, but I'm fine now. Of course, I wasn't the one the guy tried to start a fight with."

5   Once we were back where we were staying, I asked my girlfriend how she would have handled it if he had attacked her. "Let's say I'm the guy, and I try to kick you like this," I said.

6   She demonstrated, pantomiming a series of blocks and strikes. "But something worries me," she said as I stood there, utterly blown away. "I'm

afraid I'd make a mistake." I thought she meant she was afraid she would forget what to do in the heat of action. But that wasn't it.

7   "We're trained to start fighting as soon as an attacker throws a punch and to keep going until he can't get up again," she said. "But you got out of it without fighting, even though he actually came at you. So I'm worried that I'd start fighting and really hurt the guy—or maim him, or even kill him—when it could've ended without anyone getting hurt at all."

8   Now I was really blown away. Months earlier, while she was taking the basic self-defense course for women, she told me about a man who approached her on a train. "He was kind of creepy," she said, "but I figured it was O.K. because I knew I could beat him up." At the time, I was impressed by how quickly she had absorbed the confidence that the course was supposed to impart, but I wasn't convinced. I was now. Fully.

9   I tried to fall asleep, but I couldn't. So I went to find her. There she was, supercool, soaking her feet in the tub, reading *Bridget Jones's Diary*.

10   The next night, we were out having a drink, still rehashing what happened. "I've got to tell you something," I said. "I know this might sound weird, but do you know how attractive it is that you can do this?"

11   She looked somewhat astonished, because obviously she hadn't learned how to fight to titillate me or anyone else. "I never thought of it in those terms," she said. "I just like knowing that in a situation like the one last night, I can be of help."

12   At that point, I resolved to take the men's course. It turned out, several weeks later, that half the men were in the class precisely because their wives or girlfriends had taken it, and they were dazzled by how capable the women were. Since then I've taken a couple of other courses, both in the company of my girlfriend. Some of the mystery, I must admit, is gone, but I still love the way she moves, and I love the idea that she knows exactly what to do to defend herself.

13   The day after we got back to New York, she offered to do some of my laundry. "I can't let you," I said. "It's too, I don't know, *traditional*."

14   "Look," she said. "A few days ago, I was willing to beat some guy up for you. So, come on, I can do your laundry."

15   I happened to be facing away from her as I spoke. "Do you really think," I asked, "you would've done a better job beating up that guy than I would have?"

16   "Not a *better* job," she said. "But I would've been much less likely to get hurt doing it. Especially if he wasn't drunk and had been thinking clearly."

17   I turned and looked at her. "I think you're right," I said, and I leaned in to kiss her. It's nice to have a girlfriend who's got your back.

THINKING ABOUT THE TEXT

1. Explain Klein's strategy in opening his essay in the middle of the action—specifically, this unexpected street assault.

2. How does the narrator's initial reaction to the attacker contrast with his girlfriend's immediate response? What are some reasons for this difference?

3. Explain what still worries the narrator's girlfriend about this incident. Why is the narrator "blown away" by her explanation?

4. Rather than being intimidated or embarrassed by his girlfriend's ability to defend them, what does the narrator initially admit about her skill? What is her response? How does her training later influence his behavior?

5. From the title of his essay to his concluding line, analyze the author's attitude toward the changing roles of males and females in a romantic relationship.

6. How does the girlfriend's attitude and behavior resist any attempt to reduce her to a stereotype? Include examples from the essay to show how multifaceted she appears.

WRITING FROM THE TEXT

1. Using details from this essay and from your own experience, write an essay arguing that the changing roles and expectations of men and women today are or are not contributing to healthier romantic relationships. (See evaluative response, pp. 438–444).

2. Write an analysis showing how Klein's dramatizing techniques—choice actions, characterization, and dialogue—work to illustrate any one of the important insights drawn from this essay.

CONNECTING WITH OTHER TEXTS

1. After reading "Pigskin, Patriarchy, and Pain" (p. 85), write an essay contrasting Sabo's previous expectations for the roles of men and women with Klein's views. Include details from both essays as you develop a point-by-point comparison-contrast (see p. 454).

2. Using specific details from this work and from "Virtual Love" (p. 56), write an essay defining the elements of a healthy romantic relationship.

3. After reading "Who's Cheap?" (p. 68), write an essay contrasting Lara's depiction of women's roles with Klein's view of women.

Pigskin, Patriarchy, and Pain
Don Sabo

A professor of social science at D'Youville College in Buffalo, New York, Don Sabo (b. 1947) has lectured and written on men's issues. Sabo is a fitness enthusiast and a former NCAA Division I defensive football captain. He is the coauthor of *Jock: Sports and Male Identity, Humanism in Sociology, Sport, Men, and the Gender Order: Critical Feminist Perspectives,* and 1994's *Sex, Violence and Power in Sports,* where the following essay first appeared.

1   I am sitting down to write as I've done thousands of times over the last decade. But today there's something very different. I'm not in pain.

2   A half year ago I underwent back surgery. My physician removed two disks from the lumbar region of my spine and fused three vertebrae using bone scrapings from my right hip. The surgery is called a "spinal fusion." For seventy-two hours I was completely immobilized. On the fifth day, I took a few faltering first steps with one of those aluminum walkers that are usually associated with the elderly in nursing homes. I progressed rapidly and left the hospital after nine days completely free of pain for the first time in years.

3   How did I, a well-intending and reasonably gentle boy from western Pennsylvania, ever get into so much pain? At a simple level, I ended up in pain because I played a sport that brutalizes men's (and now sometimes women's) bodies. *Why* I played football and bit the bullet of pain, however, is more complicated. Like a young child who learns to dance or sing for a piece of candy, I played for rewards and payoffs. Winning at sport meant winning friends and carving a place for myself within the male pecking order. Success at the "game" would make me less like myself and more like the older boys and my hero, Dick Butkus. Pictures of his hulking and snarling form filled my head and hung over my bed, beckoning me forward like a mythic Siren. If I could be like Butkus, I told myself, people would adore me as much as I adored him. I might even adore myself. As an adolescent I hoped sport would get me attention from the girls. Later, I became more practical-minded and I worried more about my future. What kind of work would I do for a living? Football became my ticket to a college scholarship which, in western Pennsylvania during the early 'sixties, meant a career instead of getting stuck in the steelmills.

4   My bout with pain and spinal "pathology" began with a decision I made in 1955 when I was 8 years old. I "went out" for football. At the time, I felt uncomfortable inside my body—too fat, too short, too weak. Freckles and glasses, too! I wanted to change my image, and I felt that changing my body was one place to begin. My parents bought me a set of weights, and one of the older boys in the neighborhood was solicited to demonstrate their use.

I can still remember the ease with which he lifted the barbell, the veins popping through his bulging biceps in the summer sun, and the sated look of strength and accomplishment on his face. This was to be the image of my future.

5   That fall I made a dinner-table announcement that I was going out for football. What followed was a rather inauspicious beginning. First, the initiation rites. Pricking the flesh with thorns until blood was drawn and having hot peppers rubbed in my eyes. Getting punched in the gut again and again. Being forced to wear a jockstrap around my nose and not knowing what was funny. Then came what was to be an endless series of proving myself: calisthenics until my arms ached; hitting hard and fast and knocking the other guy down; getting hit in the groin and not crying. I learned that pain and injury are "part of the game."

6   I "played" through grade school, co-captained my high school team, and went on to become an inside linebacker and defensive captain at the NCAA Division I level. I learned to be an animal. Coaches took notice of animals. Animals made first team. Being an animal meant being fanatically aggressive and ruthlessly competitive. If I saw an arm in front of me, I trampled it. Whenever blood was spilled, I nodded approval. Broken bones (not mine of course) were secretly seen as little victories within the bigger struggle. The coaches taught me to "punish the other man," but little did I suspect that I was devastating my own body at the same time. There were broken noses, ribs, fingers, toes and teeth, torn muscles and ligaments, bruises, bad knees, and busted lips, and the gradual pulverizing of my spinal column that, by the time my jock career was long over at age 30, had resulted in seven years of near-constant pain. It was a long road to the surgeon's office.

7   Now surgically freed from its grip, my understanding of pain has changed. Pain had gnawed away at my insides. Pain turned my awareness inward. I blamed myself for my predicament; I thought that I was solely responsible for every twinge and sleepless night. But this view was an illusion. My pain, each individual's pain, is really an expression of a linkage to an outer world of people, events, and forces. The origins of our pain are rooted *outside*, not inside, our skins.

8   Sport is just one of the many areas in our culture where pain is more important than pleasure. Boys are taught that to endure pain is courageous, to survive pain is manly. The principle that pain is "good" and pleasure is "bad" is crudely evident in the "no pain, no gain" philosophy of so many coaches and athletes. The "pain principle" weaves its way into the lives and psyches of male athletes in two fundamental ways. It stifles men's awareness of their bodies and limits our emotional expression. We learn to ignore

personal hurts and injuries because they interfere with the "efficiency" and "goals" of the "team." We become adept at taking the feelings that boil up inside us—feelings of insecurity and stress from striving so hard for success—and channeling them in a bundle of rage which is directed at opponents and enemies. This posture toward oneself and the world is not limited to "jocks." It is evident in the lives of many nonathletic men who, as tough guys, deny their authentic physical or emotional needs and develop health problems as a result.

9   Today, I no longer perceive myself as an *individual* ripped off by athletic injury. Rather, I see myself as just *one more man among many men* who got swallowed up by a social system predicated on male domination. Patriarchy has two structural aspects. First, it is a hierarchical system in which men dominate women in crude and debased, slick and subtle ways. Feminists have made great progress exposing and analyzing this dimension of the edifice of sexism. But it is also a system of *intermale dominance,* in which a minority of men dominates the masses of men. This intermale dominance hierarchy exploits the majority of those it beckons to climb its heights. Patriarchy's mythos of heroism and its morality of power-worship implant visions of ecstasy and masculine excellence in the minds of the boys who ultimately will defend its inequities and ridicule its victims. It is inside this institutional framework that I have begun to explore the essence and scope of "the pain principle."

10   Patriarchy is a form of social hierarchy. Hierarchy breeds inequity and inequity breeds pain. To remain stable, the hierarchy must either justify the pain or explain it away. In a patriarchy, women and the masses of men are fed the cultural message that pain is inevitable and that pain enhances one's character and moral worth. This principle is expressed in Judeo-Christian beliefs. The Judeo-Christian god inflicts or permits pain, yet "the Father" is still revered and loved. Likewise, a chief disciplinarian in the patriarchal family, the father has the right to inflict pain. The "pain principle" also echoes throughout traditional Western sexual morality; it is better to experience the pain of *not* having sexual pleasure than it is to have sexual pleasure.

11   Most men learned to heed these cultural messages and take their "cues for survival" from the patriarchy. The Willie Lomans of the economy pander to the profit and the American Dream. Soldiers, young and old, salute their neo-Hun generals. Right-wing Christians genuflect before the idols of righteousness, affluence, and conformity. And male athletes adopt the visions and values that coaches are offering: to take orders, to take pain, to "take out" opponents, to take the game seriously, to take women, and to take their place on the team. And if they can't "take it," then the rewards of athletic camaraderie, prestige, scholarship, pro contracts, and community recognitions are not forthcoming.

12   Becoming a football player fosters conformity to male-chauvinistic values and self-abusing lifestyles. It contributes to the legitimacy of a social structure based on patriarchal power. Male competition for prestige and status in sport and elsewhere leads to identification with the relatively few males who control resources and are able to bestow rewards and inflict punishment. Male supremacists are not born, they are made, and traditional athletic socialization is a fundamental contribution to this complex social-psychological and political process. Through sport, many males, indeed, learn to "take it"—that is, to internalize patriarchal values which, in turn, become part of their gender identity and conception of women and society.

13   My high school coach once evoked the pain principle during a pregame peptalk. For what seemed like an eternity, he paced frenetically and silently before us with fists clenched and head bowed. He suddenly stopped and faced us with a smile. It was as though he had approached a podium to begin a long-awaited lecture. "Boys," he began, "people who say that football is a 'contact sport' are dead wrong. Dancing is a contact sport. Football is a game of pain and violence! Now get the hell out of here and kick some ass." We practically ran through the wall of the locker room, surging in unison to fight the coach's war. I see now that the coach was right but for all the wrong reasons. I should have taken him at his word and never played the game!

THINKING ABOUT THE TEXT

1. Why did the author decide, as a child, to play football? What were the specific rewards he gained by engaging in the sport? Can you relate Sabo's decision to one you have made in your own life?

2. What were the initiation rites that preceded his involvement with the football team? What do you imagine is the purpose of these rites?

3. Sabo relates that he became "an animal" inflicting pain on others and also incurring his own body injuries and pain. Why do boys (and increasingly girls) accept the pain of the game?

4. Sabo concludes that men suffer more than physical injury playing football. They suffer because they stifle their awareness of their bodies and they limit their emotional expression by directing their feelings, instead, to the team and its goals. School counselors often recommend that children play team sports to learn cooperation and willingness to apply themselves to a group goal. How might Sabo respond to this advice?

5. Today, Sabo sees himself as "one more man among many men who got swallowed up by a social system predicated on male domination" (106).

What is the hierarchical system the author perceives and how does playing football support this system?

6. What is Sabo's strategy in examining the verb "to take"? In how many ways does he use the verb? What is the strategy of his title?

7. What does the author conclude are the serious social and psychological results of participation in football?

WRITING FROM THE TEXT

1. Sabo writes that "male supremacists are not born, they are made, and traditional athletic socialization is a fundamental contribution to this complex social-psychological and political process" (88). Show your agreement or disagreement with this assertion in an essay that uses specific examples from your involvement with or observations of team sports.

2. Write an essay that reveals how your ability "to take it" in some athletic activity helped you achieve a goal in your life outside of athletics.

3. Describe a time when you engaged in a socially approved activity because you wanted the rewards of friendship or public adoration. Review the strategies on how to write a narrative (pp. 430–437) after you have done some freewriting on the topic.

4. Write an essay that analyzes activities other than football that foster "conformity to male-chauvinistic values and self-abusing lifestyles." You might try using humor or irony in your essay.

CONNECTING WITH OTHER TEXTS

1. Read "King Curtis's Echo" (p. 191) and write an analysis of how the messages that males learn playing football may interfere with Thayer's notion of self-restraint.

2. Write an essay contrasting Sabo's early view of masculinity with the male image Jeff Z. Klein represents in "Watching My Back" (p. 82).

When a Woman Says No
Ellen Goodman

A widely syndicated columnist whose home paper is the *Boston Globe*, Ellen Goodman (b. 1941) has won a Pulitzer Prize for her outstanding journalism. Goodman believes that she writes about issues more important than politics, like the "underlying values by which this country exists . . . the vast social changes in the way men and women lead their lives and deal with each other." The essay included here, first published in the *Boston Globe* in 1984, is indicative of Goodman's concerns.

Another essay by Goodman and additional biographical information appears on page 3.

1   There are a few times when, if you watch closely, you can actually see a change of public mind. This is one of those times.

2   For as long as I can remember, a conviction for rape depended as much on the character of the woman involved as on the action of the man. Most often the job of the defense lawyer was to prove that the woman had provoked or consented to the act, to prove that it was sex, not assault.

3   In the normal course of events the smallest blemish, misjudgment, misstep by the woman became proof that she had invited the man's attentions. Did she wear a tight sweater? Was she a "loose" woman? Was she in the wrong part of town at the wrong hour? A woman could waive her right to say no in an astonishing number of ways.

4   But in the past few weeks, in Massachusetts, three cases of multiple rape have come into court and three sets of convictions have come out of juries. These verdicts point to a sea change in attitudes. A simple definition seems to have seeped into the public consciousness. If she says no, it's rape.

5   The most famous of these cases is the New Bedford barroom rape. There, in two separate trials, juries cut through complicated testimony to decide the central issue within hours. Had the woman been drinking? Had she lied about that in testimony? Had she kissed one of the men? In the end none of these points were relevant. What mattered to the juries that found four of these six men guilty was that they had forced her. If she said no, it was rape.

6   The second of these cases involved a young woman soldier from Ft. Devens who accepted a ride with members of a rock band, the Grand Slamm. She was raped in the bus and left in a field hours later. Had she flirted with the band members? Had she told a friend that she intended to seduce one of the men? Had she boarded the bus willingly? The judge sentencing three of the men to jail said, "No longer will society accept the fact that a woman, even if she may initially act in a seductive or compromising manner, has waived her right to say no at any further time." If she said no, it was rape.

7   The third of these cases was in some ways the most notable. An Abington woman was driven from a bar to a parking lot where she was raped by four men, scratched with a knife, had her hair singed with a cigarette lighter and was left half-naked in the snow. The trial testimony showed that she previously had sex with three of the men, and with two of them in a group setting. Still, the jury was able to agree with the district attorney: "Sexual consent

between a woman and a man on one occasion does not mean the man has access to her whenever it strikes his fancy." If she said no, it was rape.

8 Not every community, courtroom or jury today accepts this simple standard of justice. But ten years ago, five years ago, even three years ago these women might not have even dared press charges.

9 It was the change of climate that enabled, even encouraged, the women to come forward. It was the change of attitude that framed the arguments in the courtroom. It was the change of consciousness that infiltrated the jury chambers.

10 The question now is whether that change of consciousness has become part of our own day-to-day lives. In some ways rape is the brutal, repugnant extension of an ancient ritual of pursuit and capture. It isn't just rapists who refuse to take no for an answer. It isn't just rapists who believe that a woman says one thing and means another.

11 In the confusion of adolescence, in the chase of young adulthood, the sexes were often set up to persist and to resist. Many young men were taught that "no" means "try again." Many young women were allowed to excuse their sexuality only when they were "swept away," overwhelmed.

12 The confused messages, the yes-no-maybes, the overpowered heroines and overwhelming heroes, are still common to supermarket gothic novels and *Hustler* magazine. It isn't just X-rated movies that star a resistant woman who falls in love with her sexual aggressor. It isn't just pornographic cable-TV that features the woman who really "wanted it." In as spritely a sitcom as *Cheers,* Sam blithely locked a coyly ambivalent Diane into his apartment.

13 I know how many steps it is from that hint of sexual pressure to the brutality of rape. I know how far it is from lessons of sexual power plays to the violence of rape. But it's time that the verdict of those juries was fully transmitted to the culture from which violence emerges. If she says no, it means no.

THINKING ABOUT THE TEXT

1. In this essay, Goodman gives a brief history of social response to rape. In the past, how did lawyers defend alleged rapists? What seems to be the present attitude toward a charge of rape?

2. Goodman recounts three different rape trials. What is the logic of her arrangement of the three examples to support her thesis?

3. Beyond the assertion in the title of Goodman's essay, what is the important point she makes?

WRITING FROM THE TEXT

1. Describe a time when the "confused messages, the yes-no-maybes" resulted in an incomplete or erroneous understanding of a point you were trying to make.

2. Write a response to Goodman's allegation that "many young men were taught that 'no' means 'try again'" (91). Argue that she is correct or incorrect. Use specific examples to support your view.

CONNECTING WITH OTHER TEXTS

1. Use "Who's Cheap?" (p. 68) and "When a Woman Says No" to write an analytical essay about the "confused messages" that women may give men in a dating situation.

2. Read recent periodical accounts of rape trials. Is Goodman accurate in her essay that there has been a "sea change" in public consciousness about rape?

Where Are You Going, Where Have You Been?

Joyce Carol Oates

A novelist, poet, playwright, editor, and critic, Joyce Carol Oates (b. 1938) also teaches creative writing at Princeton. Since her first collection of short stories appeared when she was 25, Oates has been averaging almost two books a year. Although she writes in a variety of genres and literary styles, Oates may be best known for her ability to write suspenseful tales and to create a sense of terror in an apparently ordinary situation, as the story included here illustrates. Oates has responded to critics' comments about the terror that permeates her work: "Uplifting endings and resolutely cheery world views are appropriate to television commercials but insulting elsewhere. It is not only wicked to pretend otherwise, it is futile." Some of Oates's book titles—*The Crosswicks Horror, Will You Always Love Me?* and *Zombie*—suggest the kinds of terror and anxieties embedded in her work. Recent books include *Middle Age: A Romance* (2001), *Beasts* (2002), *I'll Take You There* (2002), *Rape: A Love Story* and *The Tattooed Girl* (2003), *The Falls: A Novel* (2004), and *Missing Man* (2006). The story included here, from *The Wheel of Love*, has been widely anthologized since its first publication in 1965.

For Bob Dylan

1   Her name was Connie. She was fifteen and she had a quick nervous giggling habit of craning her neck to glance into mirrors or checking other

people's faces to make sure her own was all right. Her mother, who noticed everything and knew everything and who hadn't much reason any longer to look at her own face, always scolded Connie about it. "Stop gawking at yourself, who are you? You think you're so pretty?" she would say. Connie would raise her eyebrows at these familiar complaints and look right through her mother, into a shadowy vision of herself as she was right at that moment: she knew she was pretty and that was everything. Her mother had been pretty once too, if you could believe those old snapshots in the album, but now her looks were gone and that was why she was always after Connie.

2   "Why don't you keep your room clean like your sister? How've you got your hair fixed—what the hell stinks? Hair spray? You don't see your sister using that junk."

3   Her sister June was twenty-four and still lived at home. She was a secretary in the high school Connie attended, and if that wasn't bad enough—with her in the same building—she was so plain and chunky and steady that Connie had to hear her praised all the time by her mother and her mother's sisters. June did this, June did that, she saved money and helped clean the house and cooked and Connie couldn't do a thing, her mind was all filled with trashy daydreams. Their father was away at work most of the time and when he came home he wanted supper and he read the newspaper at supper and after supper he went to bed. He didn't bother talking much to them, but around his bent head Connie's mother kept picking at her until Connie wished her mother were dead and she herself were dead and it were all over. "She makes me want to throw up sometimes," she complained to her friends. She had a high, breathless, amused voice which made everything she said sound a little forced, whether it was sincere or not.

4   There was one good thing: June went places with girlfriends of hers, girls who were just as plain and steady as she, and so when Connie wanted to do that her mother had no objections. The father of Connie's best girlfriend drove the girls the three miles to town and left them off at a shopping plaza, so that they could walk through the stores or go to a movie, and when he came to pick them up again at eleven he never bothered to ask what they had done.

5   They must have been familiar sights, walking around that shopping plaza in their shorts and flat ballerina slippers that always scuffed the sidewalk, with charm bracelets jingling on their thin wrists: they would lean together to whisper and laugh secretly if someone passed by who amused or interested them. Connie had long dark blond hair that drew anyone's eye to it, and she wore part of it pulled up on her head and puffed out and the rest of it she let fall down her back. She wore a pullover jersey blouse that looked one way when she was at home and another way when she was away from

home. Everything about her had two sides to it, one for home and one for anywhere that was not home: her walk that could be childlike and bobbing, or languid enough to make anyone think she was hearing music in her head, her mouth which was pale and smirking most of the time, but bright and pink on these evenings out, her laugh which was cynical and drawling at home—"Ha, ha, very funny"—but high-pitched and nervous anywhere else, like the jingling of the charms on her bracelet.

6   Sometimes they did go shopping or to a movie, but sometimes they went across the highway, ducking fast across the busy road, to a drive-in restaurant where older kids hung out. The restaurant was shaped like a big bottle, though squatter than a real bottle, and on its cap was a revolving figure of a grinning boy who held a hamburger aloft. One night in mid-summer they ran across, breathless with daring, and right away someone leaned out a car window and invited them over, but it was just a boy from high school they didn't like. It made them feel good to be able to ignore him. They went up through the maze of parked and cruising cars to the bright-lit, fly-infested restaurant, their faces pleased and expectant as if they were entering a sacred building that loomed out of the night to give them what haven and what blessing they yearned for. They sat at the counter and crossed their legs at the ankles, their thin shoulders rigid with excitement, and listened to the music that made everything so good: the music was always in the background like music at a church service, it was something to depend upon.

7   A boy named Eddie came in to talk with them. He sat backward on his stool, turning himself jerkily around in semicircles and then stopping and turning again, and after a while he asked Connie if she would like something to eat. She said she did and so she tapped her friend's arm on her way out—her friend pulled her face up into a brave droll look—and Connie said she would meet her at eleven, across the way. "I just hate to leave her like that," Connie said earnestly, but the boy said that she wouldn't be alone for long. So they went out to his car and on the way Connie couldn't help but let her eyes wander over the windshields and faces all around her, her face gleaming with a joy that had nothing to do with Eddie or even this place; it might have been the music. She drew her shoulders up and sucked in her breath with the pure pleasure of being alive, and just at that moment she happened to glance at a face just a few feet from hers. It was a boy with shaggy black hair, in a convertible jalopy painted gold. He stared at her and then his lips widened into a grin. Connie slit her eyes at him and turned away, but she couldn't help glancing back and there he was still watching her. He wagged a finger and laughed and said, "Gonna get you, baby," and Connie turned away again without Eddie noticing anything.

8   She spent three hours with him, at the restaurant where they ate hamburgers and drank Cokes in wax cups that were always sweating, and then down an alley a mile or so away, and when he left her off at five to eleven only the movie house was still open at the plaza. Her girlfriend was there, talking with a boy. When Connie came up the two girls smiled at each other and Connie said, "How was the movie?" and the girl said, "*You* should know." They rode off with the girl's father, sleepy and pleased, and Connie couldn't help but look at the darkened shopping plaza with its big empty parking lot and its signs that were faded and ghostly now, and over at the drive-in restaurant where cars were still circling tirelessly. She couldn't hear the music at this distance.

9   Next morning June asked her how the movie was and Connie said, "So-so."

10   She and that girl and occasionally another girl went out several times a week that way, and the rest of the time Connie spent around the house—it was summer vacation—getting in her mother's way and thinking, dreaming, about the boys she met. But all the boys fell back and dissolved into a single face that was not even a face, but an idea, a feeling, mixed up with the urgent insistent pounding of the music and the humid night air of July. Connie's mother kept dragging her back to the daylight by finding things for her to do or saying, suddenly, "What's this about the Pettinger girl?"

11   And Connie would say nervously, "Oh, her. That dope." She always drew thick clear lines between herself and such girls, and her mother was simple and kindly enough to believe her. Her mother was so simple, Connie thought, that it was maybe cruel to fool her so much. Her mother went scuffling around the house in old bedroom slippers and complained over the telephone to one sister about the other, then the other called up and the two of them complained about the third one. If June's name was mentioned her mother's tone was approving, and if Connie's name was mentioned it was disapproving. This did not really mean she disliked Connie and actually Connie thought that her mother preferred her to June because she was prettier, but the two of them kept up a pretense of exasperation, a sense that they were tugging and struggling over something of little value to either of them. Sometimes, over coffee, they were almost friends, but something would come up—some vexation that was like a fly buzzing suddenly around their heads—and their faces went hard with contempt.

12   One Sunday Connie got up at eleven—none of them bothered with church—and washed her hair so that it could dry all day long, in the sun. Her parents and sister were going to a barbecue at an aunt's house and Connie said no, she wasn't interested, rolling her eyes to let her mother know just what she thought of it. "Stay home alone then," her mother said sharply.

Connie sat out back in a lawn chair and watched them drive away, her father quiet and bald, hunched around so that he could back the car out, her mother with a look that was still angry and not at all softened through the windshield, and in the back seat poor old June all dressed up as if she didn't know what a barbecue was, with all the running yelling kids and the flies. Connie sat with her eyes closed in the sun, dreaming and dazed with the warmth about her as if this were a kind of love, the caresses of love, and her mind slipped over onto thoughts of the boy she had been with the night before and how nice he had been, how sweet it always was, not the way someone like June would suppose but sweet, gentle, the way it was in movies and promised in songs; and when she opened her eyes she hardly knew where she was, the back yard ran off into weeds and a fence line of trees and behind it the sky was perfectly blue and still. The asbestos "ranch house" that was now three years old startled her—it looked small. She shook her head as if to get awake.

13   It was too hot. She went inside the house and turned on the radio to drown out the quiet. She sat on the edge of her bed, barefoot, and listened for an hour and a half to a program called *XYZ Sunday Jamboree,* record after record of hard, fast, shrieking songs she sang along with, interspersed by exclamations from "Bobby King": "An' look here you girls at Napoleon's—Son and Charley want you to pay real close attention to this song coming up!"

14   And Connie paid close attention herself, bathed in a glow of slow-pulsed joy that seemed to rise mysteriously out of the music itself and lay languidly about the airless little room, breathed in and breathed out with each gentle rise and fall of her chest.

15   After a while she heard a car coming up the drive. She sat up at once, startled, because it couldn't be her father so soon. The gravel kept crunching all the way in from the road—the driveway was long—and Connie ran to the window. It was a car she didn't know. It was an open jalopy, painted a bright gold that caught the sunlight opaquely. Her heart began to pound and her fingers snatched at her hair, checking it, and she whispered "Christ, Christ," wondering how bad she looked. The car came to a stop at the side door and the horn sounded four short taps as if this were a signal Connie knew.

16   She went into the kitchen and approached the door slowly, then hung out the screen door, her bare toes curling down off the step. There were two boys in the car and now she recognized the driver: he had shaggy, shabby black hair that looked crazy as a wig and he was grinning at her.

17   "I ain't late, am I?" he said.

18   "Who the hell do you think you are?" Connie said.

19   "Toldja I'd be out, didn't I?"

20   "I don't even know who you are."

21   She spoke sullenly, careful to show no interest or pleasure, and he spoke in a fast bright monotone. Connie looked past him to the other boy, taking her time. He had fair brown hair, with a lock that fell onto his forehead. His sideburns gave him a fierce, embarrassed look, but so far he hadn't even bothered to glance at her. Both boys wore sunglasses. The driver's glasses were metallic and mirrored everything in miniature.

22   "You wanta come for a ride?" he said.

23   Connie smirked and let her hair fall loose over one shoulder.

24   "Don'tcha like my car? New paint job," he said. "Hey."

25   "What?"

26   "You're cute."

27   She pretended to fidget, chasing flies away from the door.

28   "Don'tcha believe me, or what?" he said.

29   "Look, I don't even know who you are," Connie said in disgust.

30   "Hey, Ellie's got a radio, see. Mine's broke down." He lifted his friend's arm and showed her the little transistor the boy was holding, and now Connie began to hear the music. It was the same program that was playing inside the house.

31   "Bobby King?" she said.

32   "I listen to him all the time. I think he's great."

33   "He's kind of great," Connie said reluctantly.

34   "Listen, that guy's *great*. He knows where the action is."

35   Connie blushed a little, because the glasses made it impossible for her to see just what this boy was looking at. She couldn't decide if she liked him or if he was just a jerk, and so she dawdled in the doorway and wouldn't come down or go back inside. She said, "What's all that stuff painted on your car?"

36   "Can'tcha read it?" He opened the door very carefully, as if he was afraid it might fall off. He slid out just as carefully, planting his feet firmly on the ground, the tiny metallic world in his glasses slowing down like gelatine hardening and in the midst of it Connie's bright green blouse. "This here is my name, to begin with," he said. ARNOLD FRIEND was written in tarlike black letters on the side, with a drawing of a round grinning face that reminded Connie of a pumpkin, except it wore sunglasses. "I wanta introduce myself, I'm Arnold Friend and that's my real name and I'm gonna be your friend, honey, and inside the car's Ellie Oscar, he's kinda shy." Ellie brought his transistor radio up to his shoulder and balanced it there. "Now these numbers are a secret code, honey," Arnold Friend explained. He read off the numbers, 33, 19, 17 and raised his eyebrows at her to see what she thought of that, but she didn't think much of it. The left rear fender had been smashed and around it was written, on the gleaming gold background: DONE BY CRAZY WOMAN DRIVER. Connie had to laugh at that. Arnold Friend was pleased at her laughter and

looked up at her. "Around the other side's a lot more—you wanta come and see them?"

37 "No."

38 "Why not?"

39 "Why should I?"

40 "Don'tcha wanta see what's on the car? Don'tcha wanta go for a ride?"

41 "I don't know."

42 "Why not?"

43 "I got things to do."

44 "Like what?"

45 "Things."

46 He laughed as if she had said something funny. He slapped his thighs. He was standing in a strange way, leaning back against the car as if he were balancing himself. He wasn't tall, only an inch or so taller than she would be if she came down to him. Connie liked the way he was dressed, which was the way all of them dressed: tight faded jeans stuffed into black, scuffed boots, a belt that pulled his waist in and showed how lean he was, and a white pullover shirt that was a little soiled and showed the hard small muscles of his arms and shoulders. He looked as if he probably did hard work, lifting and carrying things. Even his neck looked muscular. And his face was a familiar face, somehow: the jaw and chin and cheeks slightly darkened, because he hadn't shaved for a day or two, and the nose long and hawklike, sniffing as if she were a treat he was going to gobble up and it was all a joke.

47 "Connie, you ain't telling the truth. This is your day set aside for a ride with me and you know it," he said, still laughing. The way he straightened and recovered from his fit of laughing showed that it had been all fake.

48 "How do you know what my name is?" she said suspiciously.

49 "It's Connie."

50 "Maybe and maybe not."

51 "I know my Connie," he said, wagging his finger. Now she remembered him even better, back at the restaurant, and her cheeks warmed at the thought of how she sucked in her breath just at the moment she passed him—how she must have looked at him. And he had remembered her. "Ellie and I come out here especially for you," he said. "Ellie can sit in back. How about it?"

52 "Where?"

53 "Where what?"

54 "Where're we going?"

55 He looked at her. He took off the sunglasses and she saw how pale the skin around his eyes was, like holes that were not in shadow but instead in

light. His eyes were like chips of broken glass that catch the light in an amiable way. He smiled. It was as if the idea of going for a ride somewhere, to some place, was a new idea to him.

56 "Just for a ride, Connie sweetheart."

57 "I never said my name was Connie," she said.

58 "But I know what it is. I know your name and all about you, lots of things," Arnold Friend said. He had not moved yet but stood still leaning back against the side of his jalopy. "I took a special interest in you, such a pretty girl, and found out all about you like I know your parents and sister are gone somewheres and I know where and how long they're going to be gone, and I know who you were with last night, and your best girlfriend's name is Betty. Right?"

59 He spoke in a simple lilting voice, exactly as if he were reciting the words to a song. His smile assured her that everything was fine. In the car Ellie turned up the volume on his radio and did not bother to look around at them.

60 "Ellie can sit in the back seat," Arnold Friend said. He indicated his friend with a casual jerk of his chin, as if Ellie did not count and she should not bother with him.

61 "How'd you find out all that stuff?" Connie said.

62 "Listen: Betty Schultz and Tony Fitch and Jimmy Pettinger and Nancy Pettinger," he said, in a chant. "Raymond Stanley and Bob Hutter—"

63 "Do you know all those kids?"

64 "I know everybody."

65 "Look, you're kidding. You're not from around here."

66 "Sure."

67 "But—how come we never saw you before?"

68 "Sure you saw me before," he said. He looked down at his boots, as if he were a little offended. "You just don't remember."

69 "I guess I'd remember you," Connie said.

70 "Yeah?" he looked up at this, beaming. He was pleased. He began to mark time with the music from Ellie's radio, tapping his fists lightly together. Connie looked away from his smile to the car, which was painted so bright it almost hurt her eyes to look at it. She looked at that name. ARNOLD FRIEND. And up at the front fender was an expression that was familiar—MAN THE FLYING SAUCERS. It was an expression kids had used the year before, but didn't use this year. She looked at it for a while as if the words meant something to her that she did not yet know.

71 "What're you thinking about? Huh?" Arnold Friend demanded. "Not worried about your hair blowing around in the car, are you?"

72 "No."

73 "Think I maybe can't drive good?"

74 "How do I know?"

75   "You're a hard girl to handle. How come?" he said. "Don't you know I'm your friend? Didn't you see me put my sign in the air when you walked by?"

76   "What sign?"

77   "My sign." And he drew an X in the air, leaning out toward her. They were maybe ten feet apart. After his hand fell back to his side the X was still in the air, almost visible. Connie let the screen door close and stood perfectly still inside it, listening to the music from her radio and the boy's blend together. She stared at Arnold Friend. He stood there so stiffly relaxed, pretending to be relaxed, with one hand idly on the door handle as if he were keeping himself up that way and had no intention of ever moving again. She recognized most things about him, the tight jeans that showed his thighs and buttocks and the greasy leather boots and the tight shirt, and even that slippery friendly smile of his, that sleepy dreamy smile that all the boys used to get across ideas they didn't want to put into words. She recognized all this and also the singsong way he talked, slightly mocking, kidding, but serious and a little melancholy, and she recognized the way he tapped one fist against the other in homage of the perpetual music behind him. But all these things did not come together.

78   She said suddenly, "Hey, how old are you?"

79   His smile faded. She could see then that he wasn't a kid, he was much older—thirty, maybe more. At this knowledge her heart began to pound faster.

80   "That's a crazy thing to ask. Can'tcha see I'm your own age?"

81   "Like hell you are."

82   "Or maybe a coupla years older, I'm eighteen."

83   "Eighteen?" she said doubtfully.

84   He grinned to reassure her and lines appeared at the corners of his mouth. His teeth were big and white. He grinned so broadly his eyes became slits and she saw how thick the lashes were, thick and black as if painted with a black tarlike material. Then he seemed to become embarrassed, abruptly, and looked over his shoulder at Ellie. "*Him*, he's crazy," he said. "Ain't he a riot, he's a nut, a real character." Ellie was still listening to the music. His sunglasses told nothing about what he was thinking. He wore a bright orange shirt unbuttoned halfway to show his chest, which was a pale, bluish chest and not muscular like Arnold Friend's. His shirt collar was turned up all around and the very tips of the collar pointed out past his chin as if they were protecting him. He was pressing the transistor radio up against his ear and sat there in a kind of daze, right in the sun.

85   "He's kinda strange," Connie said.

86   "Hey, she says you're kinda strange! Kinda strange!" Arnold Friend cried. He pounded on the car to get Ellie's attention. Ellie turned for the first time

and Connie saw with shock that he wasn't a kid either—he had a fair, hairless face, cheeks reddened slightly as if the veins grew too close to the surface of his skin, the face of a forty-year-old baby. Connie felt a wave of dizziness rise in her at this sight and she stared at him as if waiting for something to change the shock of the moment, make it all right again. Ellie's lips kept shaping words, mumbling along with the words blasting in his ear.

87 "Maybe you two better go away," Connie said faintly.

88 "What? How come?" Arnold Friend cried. "We come out here to take you for a ride. It's Sunday." He had the voice of the man on the radio now. It was the same voice, Connie thought. "Don'tcha know it's Sunday all day and honey, no matter who you were with last night today you're with Arnold Friend and don't you forget it!—Maybe you better step out here," he said, and this last was in a different voice. It was a little flatter, as if the heat was finally getting to him.

89 "No. I got things to do."

90 "Hey."

91 "You two better leave."

92 "We ain't leaving until you come with us."

93 "Like hell I am—"

94 "Connie, don't fool around with me. I mean, I mean, don't fool *around*," he said, shaking his head. He laughed incredulously. He placed his sunglasses on top of his head, carefully, as if he were indeed wearing a wig, and brought the stems down behind his ears. Connie stared at him, another wave of dizziness and fear rising in her so that for a moment he wasn't even in focus but was just a blur, standing there against his gold car, and she had the idea that he had driven up the driveway all right but had come from nowhere before that and belonged nowhere and that everything about him and even about the music that was so familiar to her was only half real.

95 "If my father comes and sees you—"

96 "He ain't coming. He's at a barbecue."

97 "How do you know that?"

98 "Aunt Tillie's. Right now they're—uh—they're drinking. Sitting around," he said vaguely, squinting as if he were staring all the way to town and over to Aunt Tillie's back yard. Then the vision seemed to get clear and he nodded energetically. "Yeah. Sitting around. There's your sister in a blue dress, huh? And high heels, the poor sad bitch—nothing like you, sweetheart! And your mother's helping some fat woman with the corn, they're cleaning the corn—husking the corn—"

99 "What fat woman?" Connie cried.

100 "How do I know what fat woman, I don't know every goddam fat woman in the world!" Arnold laughed.

101   "Oh, that's Mrs. Hornby . . . Who invited her?" Connie said. She felt a little light-headed. Her breath was coming quickly.

102   "She's too fat. I don't like them fat. I like them the way you are, honey,"
he said, smiling sleepily at her. They stared at each other for a while, through
the screen door. He said softly, "Now what you're going to do is this: you're
going to come out that door. You're going to sit up front with me and Ellie's
going to sit in the back, the hell with Ellie, right? This isn't Ellie's date. You're
my date. I'm your lover, honey."

103   "What? You're crazy—"

104   "Yes, I'm your lover. You don't know what that is, but you will," he said.
"I know that too. I know all about you. But look: it's real nice and you couldn't
ask for nobody better than me, or more polite. I always keep my word. I'll tell
you how it is. I'm always nice at first, the first time. I'll hold you so tight you
won't think you have to try to get away or pretend anything because you'll
know you can't. And I'll come inside you where it's all secret and you'll give
in to me and you'll love me—"

105   "Shut up! You're crazy!" Connie said. She backed away from the door.
She put her hands against her ears as if she'd heard something terrible,
something not meant for her. "People don't talk like that, you're crazy," she
muttered. Her heart was almost too big now for her chest and its pumping
made sweat break out all over her. She looked out to see Arnold Friend pause
and then take a step toward the porch lurching. He almost fell. But, like a
clever drunken man, he managed to catch his balance. He wobbled in his
high boots and grabbed hold of one of the porch posts.

106   "Honey?" he said. "You still listening?"

107   "Get the hell out of here!"

108   "Be nice, honey. Listen."

109   "I'm going to call the police—"

110   He wobbled again and out of the side of his mouth came a fast spat
curse, an aside not meant for her to hear. But even this "Christ!" sounded
forced. Then he began to smile again. She watched this smile come, awkward
as if he were smiling from inside a mask. His whole face was a mask, she
thought wildly, tanned down onto his throat but then running out as if he
had plastered makeup on his face but had forgotten about his throat.

111   "Honey—? Listen, here's how it is. I always tell the truth and I promise
you this: I ain't coming in that house after you."

112   "You better not! I'm going to call the police if you—if you don't—"

113   "Honey," he said, talking right through her voice, "honey, I'm not
coming in there but you are coming out here. You know why?"

114   She was panting. The kitchen looked like a place she had never seen
before, some room she had run inside but which wasn't good enough, wasn't

going to help her. The kitchen window had never had a curtain, after three years, and there were dishes in the sink for her to do—probably—and if you ran your hand across the table you'd probably feel something sticky there.

115 "You listening, honey? Hey?"

116 "—going to call the police—"

117 "Soon as you touch the phone I don't need to keep my promise and can come inside. You won't want that."

118 She rushed forward and tried to lock the door. Her fingers were shaking. "But why lock it," Arnold Friend said gently, talking right into her face. "It's just a screen door. It's just nothing." One of his boots was at a strange angle, as if his foot wasn't in it. It pointed out to the left, bent at the ankle. "I mean, anybody can break through a screen door and glass and wood and iron or anything else if he needs to, anybody at all and specially Arnold Friend. If the place got lit up with a fire honey you'd come runnin' out into my arms, right into my arms an' safe at home—like you knew I was your lover and'd stopped fooling around. I don't mind a nice shy girl but I don't like no fooling around." Part of those words were spoken with a slight rhythmic lilt, and Connie somehow recognized them—the echo of a song from last year, about a girl rushing into her boyfriend's arms and coming home again—

119 Connie stood barefoot on the linoleum floor, staring at him. "What do you want?" she whispered.

120 "I want you," he said.

121 "What?"

122 "Seen you that night and thought, that's the one, yes sir. I never needed to look anymore."

123 "But my father's coming back. He's coming to get me. I had to wash my hair first—" She spoke in a dry, rapid voice, hardly raising it for him to hear.

124 "No, your Daddy is not coming and yes, you had to wash your hair and you washed it for me. It's nice and shining and all for me. I thank you, sweetheart," he said, with a mock bow, but again he almost lost his balance. He had to bend and adjust his boots. Evidently his feet did not go all the way down; the boots must have been stuffed with something so that he would seem taller. Connie stared out at him and behind him Ellie in the car, who seemed to be looking off toward Connie's right into nothing. This Ellie said, pulling the words out of the air one after another as if he were just discovering them, "You want me to pull out the phone?"

125 "Shut your mouth and keep it shut," Arnold Friend said, his face red from bending over or maybe from embarrassment because Connie had seen his boots. "This ain't none of your business."

126 "What—what are you doing? What do you want?" Connie said. "If I call the police they'll get you, they'll arrest you—"

127   "Promise was not to come in unless you touch that phone, and I'll keep that promise," he said. He resumed his erect position and tried to force his shoulders back. He sounded like a hero in a movie, declaring something important. He spoke too loudly and it was as if he were speaking to someone behind Connie. "I ain't made plans for coming in that house where I don't belong but just for you to come out to me, the way you should. Don't you know who I am?"

128   "You're crazy," she whispered. She backed away from the door but did not want to go into another part of the house, as if this would give him permission to come through the door. "What do you . . .You're crazy, you . . ."

129   "Huh? What're you saying, honey?"

130   Her eyes darted everywhere in the kitchen. She could not remember what it was, this room.

131   "This is how it is, honey; you come out and we'll drive away, have a nice ride. But if you don't come out we're gonna wait till your people come home and then they're all going to get it."

132   "You want that telephone pulled out?" Ellie said. He held the radio away from his ear and grimaced, as if without the radio the air was too much for him.

133   "I toldja shut up, Ellie," Arnold Friend said, "you're deaf, get a hearing aid, right? Fix yourself up. This little girl's no trouble and's gonna be nice to me, so Ellie keep to yourself, this ain't your date—right? Don't hem in on me. Don't hog. Don't crush. Don't bird dog. Don't trail me," he said in a rapid meaningless voice, as if he were running through all the expressions he'd learned but was no longer sure which one of them was in style, then rushing on to new ones, making them up with his eyes closed, "Don't crawl under my fence, don't squeeze in my chipmunk hole, don't sniff my glue, suck my popsicle, keep your own greasy fingers on yourself!" He shaded his eyes and peered in at Connie, who was backed against the kitchen table. "Don't mind him honey he's just a creep. He's a dope. Right? I'm the boy for you and like I said you come out here nice like a lady and give me your hand, and nobody else gets hurt, I mean, your nice old bald-headed daddy and your mummy and your sister in her high heels. Because listen: why bring them in this?"

134   "Leave me alone," Connie whispered.

135   "Hey, you know that old woman down the road, the one with the chickens and stuff—you know her?"

136   "She's dead!"

137   "Dead? What? You know her?" Arnold Friend said.

138   "She's dead—"

139   "Don't you like her?"

140   "She's dead—she's—she isn't there anymore—"

141   "But don't you like her, I mean, you got something against her? Some grudge or something?" Then his voice dipped as if he were conscious of a rudeness. He touched the sunglasses perched on top of his head as if to make sure they were still there. "Now you be a good girl."

142   "What are you going to do?"

143   "Just two things, or maybe three," Arnold Friend said. "But I promise it won't last long and you'll like me the way you get to like people you're close to. You will. It's all over for you here, so come on out. You don't want your people in any trouble, do you?"

144   She turned and bumped against a chair or something, hurting her leg, but she ran into the back room and picked up the telephone. Something roared in her ear, a tiny roaring, and she was so sick with fear that she could do nothing but listen to it—the telephone was clammy and very heavy and her fingers groped down to the dial but were too weak to touch it. She began to scream into the phone, into the roaring. She cried out, she cried for her mother, she felt her breath start jerking back and forth in her lungs as if it were something Arnold Friend were stabbing her with again and again with no tenderness. A noisy sorrowful wailing rose all about her and she was locked inside it the way she was locked inside this house.

145   After a while she could hear again. She was sitting on the floor with her wet back against the wall.

146   Arnold Friend was saying from the door, "That's a good girl. Put the phone back."

147   She kicked the phone away from her.

148   "No, honey. Pick it up. Put it back right."

149   She picked it up and put it back. The dial tone stopped.

150   "That's a good girl. Now you come outside."

151   She was hollow with what had been fear, but what was now just an emptiness. All that screaming had blasted it out of her. She sat, one leg cramped under her, and deep inside her brain was something like a pinpoint of light that kept going and would not let her relax. She thought, I'm not going to see my mother again. She thought, I'm not going to sleep in my bed again. Her bright green blouse was all wet.

152   Arnold Friend said, in a gentle-loud voice that was like a stage voice, "The place where you came from ain't there any more, and where you had in mind to go is canceled out. This place you are now—inside your daddy's house—is nothing but a cardboard box I can knock down any time. You know that and always did know it. You hear me?"

153   She thought, I have got to think. I have to know what to do.

154   "We'll go out in a nice field, out in the country here where it smells so nice and it's sunny," Arnold Friend said. "I'll have my arms tight around you

so you won't need to try to get away and I'll show you what love is like, what it does. The hell with this house! It looks solid all right," he said. He ran a fingernail down the screen and the noise did not make Connie shiver, as it would have the day before. "Now put your hand on your heart, honey. Feel that? That feels solid too, but we know better, be nice to me, be sweet like you can because what else is there for a girl like you but to be sweet and pretty and give in?—and get away before her people come back?"

155   She felt her pounding heart. Her hand seemed to enclose it. She thought for the first time in her life that it was nothing that was hers, that belonged to her, but just a pounding, living thing inside this body that wasn't really hers either.

156   "You don't want them to get hurt," Arnold Friend went on. "Now get up, honey. Get up all by yourself."

157   She stood.

158   "Now turn this way. That's right. Come over here to me—Ellie, put that away, didn't I tell you? You dope. You miserable creepy dope," Arnold Friend said. His words were not angry but only part of an incantation. The incantation was kindly. "Now come out through the kitchen to me honey, and let's see a smile, try it, you're a brave sweet little girl and now they're eating corn and hot dogs cooked to bursting over an outdoor fire, and they don't know one thing about you and never did and honey you're better than them because not a one of them would have done this for you."

159   Connie felt the linoleum under her feet; it was cool. She brushed her hair back out of her eyes. Arnold Friend let go of the post tentatively and opened his arms for her, his elbows pointing in toward each other and his wrists limp, to show that this was an embarrassed embrace and a little mocking, he didn't want to make her self-conscious.

160   She put out her hand against the screen. She watched herself push the door slowly open as if she were safe back somewhere in the other doorway, watching this body and this head of long hair moving out into the sunlight where Arnold Friend waited.

161   "My sweet little blue-eyed girl," he said, in a half-sung sigh that had nothing to do with her brown eyes but was taken up just the same by the vast sunlit reaches of the land behind him and on all sides of him, so much land that Connie had never seen before and did not recognize except to know that she was going to it.

THINKING ABOUT THE TEXT

1. Identify Connie's character traits and illustrate each. How is she a rather typical 15-year-old, and how is she unique?

2. List the various ways that Arnold Friend initially appeals to Connie.

3. Identify the numerous intimidation tactics that Friend uses to manipulate Connie.

4. Study Ellie's role in this story. How does Oates use him to illuminate Arnold Friend's character, temperament, and motives?

5. Although the ending is ambiguous, Oates has revealed that this story was based on details from actual rapes and murders committed by Charles Schmid and his accomplice John Saunders in Tucson, Arizona, during the 1960s. How do various details in the story and, particularly, in the ending suggest that a crime was committed?

6. Without reducing this story to simple morals, discuss the insights (about subjects such as adolescence, parenting, role playing, manipulation, and intimidation) that we can draw from this story.

WRITING FROM THE TEXT

1. Write a character analysis (pp. 485–493) of Arnold Friend, demonstrating how he knows and preys upon the insecurities and fantasies of a 15-year-old girl. Include details from the story to support your thesis.

2. In an essay, argue that Connie does or does not *choose* to go with Arnold Friend at the end. Could she have resisted more than she did? Cite specific evidence from the story to support your thesis.

3. Considering Connie's character and lifestyle, is Oates suggesting that Connie is to be blamed for what happened to her, or does the blame fall on Arnold Friend for taking advantage of a vulnerable 15-year-old? Write an essay to support your argument.

CONNECTING WITH OTHER TEXTS

1. Read "When a Woman Says No" (p. 89) and write an essay applying Ellen Goodman's comments to Connie's experience.

2. Find and read the article in *Life* magazine (March 4, 1966) about the Charles Schmid case. Then write an essay comparing the actual details of his rapes and murders with this story.

3. Joyce Chopra's 1985 feature film *Smooth Talk,* based on Oates's story, is available on video, and Oates is reported to have been pleased with this adaptation. Note the differences between the video and the story versions, and write an essay analyzing the changes made in the film.

Chapter 3

Between
Cultures

E very year, more than a million people from different countries come to
live in the United States. Your classrooms no doubt reflect this diversity—
and your life after class probably does, too. You may find yourself
enjoying sushi, falafel, or tacos, digesting cultural diversity as easily as you
munch a Big Mac. Or you may find yourself perplexed by cultural pluralism,
unsure of its merits. The readings in this chapter illustrate the joys and
stresses of living with cultural differences. As you will discover, assimilation
and rejection are issues not only for immigrants, but also for longtime residents of the United States who experience the psychological, political, and
economic realities of living between cultures.

This chapter begins with an essay by someone like yourself, a college student, who describes the contrasts between his home and college environments. Marcus Mabry, an African American from New Jersey, writes of the
discomfort he experiences traveling "between the two worlds" of poverty at
home and affluence at Stanford. This discomfort may be felt by Muslim
women living abroad, as in the case of Zaiba Malik, or in the United States, as
both Laila Al-Marayati and Semeen Issa attest in their study of bias against
the burka. Even if you have not lived in a foreign country, you sometimes may
feel like you are living in a foreign environment. For example, you may have
grown up in the tranquil suburbs but now attend a busy city university surrounded by street vendors and honking horns. Thus you can find yourself between cultures even in your own country.

Cultural characteristics may be important because they suggest who we
are, but they can also lead to misunderstanding and stereotyping. Certainly it

would be a mistake to stereotype the illegal, migrant farmworker Quiñones-Hinojosa, whose extraordinary achievement defies any bias. Immigrant achievement is the focus of Robert J. Samuelson's essay arguing for assimilation and acceptance of immigrants with guidelines for practical controls.

Teja Arboleda cautions against sorting people according to race or ethnicity. In a short story, Louis Erdrich shows one character's drive to rise above the stereotypes prevalent in Erdrich's own Native American culture. M. Carl Holman's poem satirizes people's efforts to deny race and culture in order to create an artificial persona, and Luis Valdez's short play satirizes the use and abuse of Latinos.

Most people would agree that the United States has been enriched by multiculturalism. American art, music, literature, food, sports, dance, clothing—and so much more—all reflect the contributions of a diverse society. This chapter celebrates those contributions without ignoring the controversies.

Living in Two Worlds
Marcus Mabry

After completing his B.A. in English and French literature at Stanford, Marcus Mabry (b. 1967) also earned a B.A. in international relations and an M.A. in English, all within the four years of his scholarship agreement. He has served as a correspondent for *Newsweek* at the State Department and in Paris and Johannesburg. In addition to freelance writing for *Emerge* and *Black Collegiate*, Mabry also conceived, wrote, produced, and narrated a documentary on African-American families for French television. His 1995 memoir, *White Bucks and Black-Eyed Peas: Coming of Age Black in White America*, examines Mabry's decision to live in the white world where he decides he is "more comfortable" because "it demanded less role-playing" of him. In "No Father, and No Answers," an essay appearing in *Newsweek* in 1992, Mabry addresses the concerns he has had in trying both to understand and to establish a relationship with the father he only recently met (who twenty years earlier left Mabry's unwed mother to raise her son without emotional or economic support). Mabry is currently at work on a biography of Condoleezza Rice. The selection included here also appeared in *Newsweek on Campus*.

1   A round, green cardboard sign hangs from a string proclaiming, "We built a proud new feeling," the slogan of a local supermarket. It is a souvenir from one of my brother's last jobs. In addition to being a bagger, he's worked at a fast-food restaurant, a gas station, a garage and a textile factory. Now, in the icy clutches of the Northeastern winter, he is unemployed. He will soon be a father. He is 19 years old.

2   In mid-December I was at Stanford, among the palm trees and weighty chores of academe. And all I wanted to do was get out. I joined the rest of the

undergrads in a chorus of excitement, singing the praises of Christmas break. No classes, no midterms, no finals . . . and no freshmen! (I'm a resident assistant.) Awesome! I was looking forward to escaping. I never gave a thought to what I was escaping to.

3   Once I got home to New Jersey, reality returned. My dreaded freshmen had been replaced by unemployed relatives; badgering professors had been replaced by hard-working single mothers, and cold classrooms by dilapidated bedrooms and kitchens. The room in which the "proud new feeling" sign hung contained the belongings of myself, my mom and my brother. But for these two weeks it was mine. They slept downstairs on couches.

4   Most students who travel between the universes of poverty and affluence during breaks experience similar conditions, as well as the guilt, the helplessness and, sometimes, the embarrassment associated with them. Our friends are willing to listen, but most of them are unable to imagine the pain of the impoverished lives that we see every six months. Each time I return home I feel further away from the realities of poverty in America and more ashamed that they are allowed to persist. What frightens me most is not that the American socioeconomic system permits poverty to continue, but that by participating in that system I share some of the blame.

5   Last year I lived in an on-campus apartment, with a (relatively) modern bathroom, kitchen and two bedrooms. Using summer earnings, I added some expensive prints, a potted palm and some other plants, making the place look like the more-than-humble abode of a New York City Yuppie. I gave dinner parties, even a *soirée française*.

6   For my roommate, a doctor's son, this kind of life was nothing extraordinary. But my mom was struggling to provide a life for herself and my brother. In addition to working 24-hour-a-day cases as a practical nurse, she was trying to ensure that my brother would graduate from high school and have a decent life. She knew that she had to compete for his attention with drugs and other potentially dangerous things that can look attractive to a young man when he sees no better future.

7   Living in my grandmother's house this Christmas break restored all the forgotten, and the never acknowledged, guilt. I had gone to boarding school on a full scholarship since the ninth grade, so being away from poverty was not new. But my own growing affluence has increased my distance. My friends say that I should not feel guilty: what could I do substantially for my family at this age, they ask. Even though I know that education is the right thing to do, I can't help but feel, sometimes, that I have it too good. There is no reason that I deserve security and warmth, while my brother has to cope with potential unemployment and prejudice. I, too, encounter prejudice, but it is softened by my status as a student in an affluent and intellectual community.

8   More than my sense of guilt, my sense of helplessness increases each time I return home. As my success leads me further away for longer periods of time, poverty becomes harder to conceptualize and feels that much more oppressive when I visit with it. The first night of break, I lay in our bedroom, on a couch that let out into a bed that took up the whole room, except for a space heater. It was a little hard to sleep because the springs from the couch stuck through at inconvenient spots. But it would have been impossible to sleep anyway because of the groans coming from my grandmother's room next door. Only in her early sixties, she suffers from many chronic diseases and couldn't help but moan, then pray aloud, then moan, then pray aloud.

9   This wrenching of my heart was interrupted by the 3 A.M. entry of a relative who had been allowed to stay at the house despite rowdy behavior and threats toward the family in the past. As he came into the house, he slammed the door, and his heavy steps shook the second floor as he stomped into my grandmother's room to take his place, at the foot of her bed. There he slept, without blankets on a bare mattress. This was the first night. Later in the vacation, a Christmas turkey and a Christmas ham were stolen from my aunt's refrigerator on Christmas Eve. We think the thief was a relative. My mom and I decided not to exchange gifts that year because it just didn't seem festive.

10   A few days after New Year's I returned to California. The Northeast was soon hit by a blizzard. They were there, and I was here. That was the way it had to be, for now. I haven't forgotten; the ache of knowing their suffering is always there. It has to be kept deep down, or I can't find the logic in studying and partying while people, my people, are being killed by poverty. Ironically, success drives me away from those I most want to help by getting an education.

11   Somewhere in the midst of all that misery, my family has built, within me, "a proud feeling." As I travel between the two worlds it becomes harder to remember just how proud I should be—not just because of where I have come from and where I am going, but because of where they are. The fact that they survive in the world in which they live is something to be very proud of, indeed. It inspires within me a sense of tenacity and accomplishment that I hope every college graduate will someday possess.

THINKING ABOUT THE TEXT

1. Describe Mabry's university world and his role in it. Then contrast the university world with details from his family's home.

2. Mabry describes living "between the universes of poverty and affluence" (129). Detail the emotional toll this takes.

3. What happens during Christmas break to restore his sense of guilt?

4. How is the supermarket sign, hanging in the bedroom, both ironic and deeply symbolic of Mabry's life between worlds?

WRITING FROM THE TEXT

1. Using details from the story, compare and contrast Mabry's "worlds." What is ironic about the impact of success on his life?

2. For Mabry, attending college has secured him a spot in a new world vastly different from his past. Focus on your own between-worlds experience— college and home life, school and work worlds, high school and college relationships. Help the reader see each world as vividly as Mabry does; include your emotional responses, too.

3. Write about a time when you tried to escape one world and exchange it for another. How successful were you? What was your emotional toll?

CONNECTING WITH OTHER TEXTS

1. Analyze the between-worlds experiences of Zaiba Malik in "Hidden in Plain Sight" (p. 129) and of Mabry. How do they compare? What conclusions can you draw about the "cultural tug of war"?

2. Compare and contrast the home and college environments of Rita Simmons in "Peaches" (p. 71) with those of Mabry. Use specific details from each essay to support your points.

3. Write an essay contrasting the high achievements of Marcus Mabry, Alfredo Quiñones-Hinojosa (p. 116), and Brent Staples (p. 181) with their family's and peers' low expectations for them.

4. Write a research paper examining your college's admissions and recruiting policies, scholarship programs, dropout rate, and success record for minority students. You may want to focus your paper on what your research indicates has been the most serious obstacle or most successful accomplishment for affirmative action on your campus.

 # Conspiracy Against Assimilation
Robert J. Samuelson

A contributing editor of both *Newsweek* and the *Washington Post*, Robert J. Samuelson (b. 1945) typically explains economic, political, and social problems with extensive facts and figures. He earned his B.A. from Harvard where he majored in government, and he has won numerous journalism awards. His articles have appeared in *The Boston Globe*, the *Los Angeles Times*, *The New Republic*, and the *Columbia Journalism Review*. Samuelson has also published two books: *The Good Life and Its Discontents: The American Dream in the Age of Entitlement* (1995) and *Untruth: When the Conventional Wisdom Is (Almost Always) Wrong* (2001). This essay initially appeared in the *Washington Post* in 2006.

1   It's all about assimilation—or should be. One of America's glories is that it has assimilated many waves of immigrants. Outsiders have become insiders. But it hasn't been easy. Every new group has struggled: Germans, Irish, Jews and Italians. All have encountered economic hardship, prejudice and discrimination. The story of U.S. immigration is often ugly. If today's immigration does not end in assimilation, it will be a failure. By this standard, I think the major contending sides in the present bitter debate are leading us astray. Their proposals, if adopted, would frustrate assimilation.

2   On the one hand, we have the "cop" school. It adamantly opposes amnesty and would make being here illegally a felony rather than a lesser crime. It toughens a variety of penalties against illegal immigrants. Somehow, elevating the seriousness of the crime would deprive them of jobs, and then illegal immigrants would return to Mexico, El Salvador or wherever. This is a pipe dream; the numbers are simply too large.

3   But it is a pipe dream that, if pursued, would inflict enormous social damage. The mere threat of a crackdown stigmatizes much of the Hispanic population—whether they're legal or illegal immigrants; or whether they've been here for generations. (In 2004 there were 40 million Hispanics, says the Pew Hispanic Center; about 55 percent were estimated to be native-born, 25 percent legal immigrants and 20 percent illegal immigrants.) People feel threatened and insulted. Who wouldn't?

4   On the other hand, we have the "guest worker" advocates. They want 400,000 or more new foreign workers annually. This would supposedly curtail illegal immigration—people who now sneak into the country could get work permits—and also cure "shortages" of unskilled American workers. Everyone wins.

5   Not really.

6   For starters, the term guest worker is a misnomer. Whatever the rules, most guest workers would not leave. The pull of U.S. wages (on average, almost five times what can be earned in Mexico) is too great. Moreover, there's no general shortage of unskilled workers. In March, the unemployment rate of high-school dropouts 25 years and older was 7 percent; since 1996, it has been below 6 percent in only two months. By contrast, the unemployment rate of college graduates in March was 2.2 percent. Given the glut of unskilled workers relative to demand, their wages often lag behind inflation.

From 2002 to 2004, consumer prices rose 5.5 percent. Median wages rose 4.8 percent for janitors, 4.3 percent for landscapers and not at all for waitresses.

7   Guest worker advocates don't acknowledge that poor, unskilled immigrants—whether legal or illegal—create huge social costs. Every year the Census Bureau issues a report on "Income, Poverty and Health Insurance Coverage." Here's what the 2004 report shows:

- Since 1990 the number of Hispanics with incomes below the government's poverty line has risen 52 percent; that's almost all (92 percent) of the increase in poor people.
- Among children, disparities are greater. Over the same period, 43 percent more Hispanic children are living in poverty while the numbers of black and non-Hispanic white children in poverty declined 16.9 percent and 18.5 percent, respectively.
- Hispanics account for most (61 percent) of the increase of Americans without health insurance since 1990. The overall increase was 11.1 million; Hispanics, 6.7 million.

8   By most studies, poor immigrants pay less in taxes than they use in government services. As these social costs have risen, so has the backlash. Already, there's a coalition of Mayors and Executives for Immigration Reform. It includes 63 cities, counties and towns, headed by Republicans and Democrats, ranging from Cook County, IL (population: 5.3 million) to Gilliam County, OR (population: 1,817). Coalition members want the federal government to reimburse their extra costs.

9   We have a conspiracy against assimilation. One side would offend and ostracize much of the Hispanic community. The other would encourage mounting social and economic costs. The result either way is a more polarized society.

10   On immigration, I am an optimist. We are basically a decent, open and tolerant nation. Americans respect hard work and achievement. That's why assimilation has triumphed. But I am not a foolish optimist. Assimilation requires time and the right conditions. It cannot succeed if we constantly flood the country with new, poor immigrants or embark on a vendetta against those already here.

11   I have argued that our policies should recognize these realities. Curb illegal immigration with true border barriers. Provide legal status (call it amnesty or whatever)—first, work permits, then citizenship—for most illegal immigrants already here. Remove the job lure by imposing harsh fines against employers who hire *new* illegal immigrants. Reject big guest worker programs.

12   It's sometimes said that today's Hispanics will resemble yesterday's Italians. Although they won't advance as rapidly as some other groups of more

skilled immigrants, they'll still move into the mainstream. Many have—and will. But the overall analogy is a stretch, according to a new study, "Italians Then, Mexicans Now," by sociologist Joel Perlmann of Bard College. Since 1970, wages of Mexican immigrants compared with those of native whites have declined. By contrast, wages of Italians and Poles who arrived early in the last century rose over time. For the children of immigrants, gaps are also wide. Second-generation Italians and Poles typically earned 90 percent or more compared to native whites. For second-generation Mexican Americans, the similar figure is 75 percent.

13   One big difference between then and now: Immigration slowly halted during and after World War I. The Italians and Poles came mainly between 1890 and 1915. Older immigrants didn't always have to compete with new-comers who beat down their wages. There was time for outsiders and insiders to adapt to each other. We should heed history's lesson.

THINKING ABOUT THE TEXT

1. Why does Samuelson open his essay by confirming that he supports the assimilation of immigrants—the acceptance and integration of them into the national culture? What does he fear about the current immigration proposals?

2. Explain the position of the two contending sides: the "cop" school and the "guest worker" advocates. What does each side propose?

3. How does Samuelson support his contention that the "cop" school is a "pipe dream" that would actually "inflict enormous social damage"?

4. According to Samuelson, why is the term "guest worker" a "misnomer"— and how does he support this claim? What are the "huge social costs" that guest worker advocates seem to ignore?

5. What is Samuelson's proposition and what, does he argue, are its strengths?

6. How are today's Hispanic immigrants different from yesterday's European immigrants? What can we learn from the assimilation of European immigrants who arrived before World War I?

WRITING FROM THE TEXT

1. Write an evaluative response of Samuelson's argument and his support. Your thesis should clarify your view of his proposition by analyzing specific quotations and points. You may include your own experience with immigrants and immigration, if it is relevant to Samuelson's essay, but

stay focused on his essay. See pp. 438–444 for suggestions and an example of an evaluative response essay.

2. Samuelson notes that all immigrants "have encountered economic hardship, prejudice, and discrimination" (113). If you have experience as an immigrant or living with immigrants, write an essay supporting or countering Samuelson's claim. Include specific illustrations to support your thesis.

3. Write an essay illustrating or refuting Samuelson's claim that there is a "conspiracy against assimilation." You may certainly add to his reasons or counter his reasons with examples of your own. You may want to consider whether immigrants themselves sometimes resist assimilation or may feel that others discourage them from assimilating fully.

CONNECTING WITH OTHER TEXTS

1. Write an essay using details from "Terra Firma" to support Samuelson's argument as well as his criticism of both the "cop" school and the "guest worker" advocates. Include direct quotations from both essays throughout your work.

2. Write an essay about the difficulties of fully assimilating immigrants into a nation's culture. In addition to Samuelson's essay, you should include details from at least two of the following works: "The Good Daughter" (p. 12), "Breaking Tradition" (p. 21), "Race Is a Four-Letter Word" (p. 120), "An Identity Reduced to a Burka" (p. 124), "Hidden in Plain Sight" (p. 129), and *Los Vendidos* (p. 144).

Terra Firma—A Journey from Migrant Farm Labor to Neurosurgery
Alfredo Quiñones-Hinojosa

An illegal immigrant when he crossed into the United States in the mid-1980s, Alfredo Quiñones-Hinojosa (b. 1966) is an assistant professor of neurosurgery and oncology, director of the brain-tumor stem-cell laboratory at Johns Hopkins School of Medicine, and director of the brain-tumor program at the Johns Hopkins Bayview campus. In an interview which you can hear at www.nejm.org, Quiñones-Hinojosa discusses his concerns about how immigrants today face discrimination and often feel unwelcome in emergency rooms, where they may come too late for appropriate medical treatment. Quiñones-Hinojosa's inspiring personal narrative below appeared in the *New England Journal of Medicine* on August 9, 2007.

1   "You will spend the rest of your life working in the fields," my cousin told me when I arrived in the United States in the mid-1980s. This fate indeed appeared likely: a 19-year-old illegal migrant farm worker, I had no English language skills and no dependable means of support. I had grown up in a small Mexican farming community, where I began working at my father's gas station at the age of 5. Our family was poor, and we were subject to the diseases of poverty: my earliest memory is of my infant sister's death from diarrhea when I was 3 years old. But my parents worked long hours and had always made enough money to feed us, until an economic crisis hit our country in the 1970s. Then they could no longer support the family, and although I trained to be a teacher, I could not put enough food on the table either.

2   Desperate for a livable income, I packed my few belongings and, with $65 in my pocket, crossed the U.S. border illegally. The first time I hopped the fence into California, I was caught and sent back to Mexico, but I tried again and succeeded. I am not condoning illegal immigration; honestly, at the time, the law was far from the front of my mind. I was merely responding to the dream of a better life, the hope of escaping poverty so that one day I could return home triumphant. Reality, however, posed a stark contrast to the dream. I spent long days in the fields picking fruits and vegetables, sleeping under leaky camper shells, eating anything I could get, with hands bloodied from pulling weeds—the very same hands that today perform brain surgery.

3   My days as a farm worker taught me a great deal about economics, politics, and society. I learned that being illegal and poor in a foreign country could be more painful than any poverty I had previously experienced. I learned that our society sometimes treats us differently depending on the places we have been and the education we have obtained. When my cousin told me I would never escape that life of poverty, I became determined to prove him wrong. I took night jobs as a janitor and subsequently as a welder that allowed me to attend a community college where I could learn English.

4   In 1989, while I was working for a railroad company as a welder and high-pressure valve specialist, I had an accident that caused me to reevaluate my life once again. I fell into a tank car that was used to carry liquefied petroleum gas. My father was working at the same company. Hearing a coworker's cry for help, he tried to get into the tank; fortunately, someone stopped him. It was my brother-in-law, Ramon, who climbed in and saved my life. He was taken out of the tank unconscious but regained consciousness quickly. By the time I was rescued, my heart rate had slowed almost to zero, but I was resuscitated in time. When I awoke, I saw a person dressed all in white and was flooded with a sense of security, confidence, and protection, knowing that a doctor was taking care of me. Although it was clear to me

that our poverty and inability to speak English usually translated into suboptimal health care for my community, the moment I saw this physician at my bedside, I felt I had reached terra firma, that I had a guardian.

5   After community college, I was accepted at the University of California, Berkeley, where a combination of excellent mentorship, scholarships, and my own passion for math and science led me to research in the neurosciences. One of my mentors there convinced me, despite my skepticism, that I could go anywhere I wanted for medical school. Thanks to such support and encouragement, I eventually went to Harvard Medical School. As I pursued my own education, I became increasingly aware of the need and responsibility we have to educate our country's poor.

6   It is no secret that minority communities have the highest dropout rates and the lowest educational achievement levels in the country. The pathway to higher education and professional training programs is not "primed" for minority students. In 1994, when I started medical school, members of minority groups made up about 18% of the U.S. population but accounted for only 3.7% of the faculty in U.S. medical schools. I was very fortunate to find outstanding minority role models, but though their quality was high, their numbers were low.

7   Given my background, perhaps it is not surprising that I did not discover the field of neurosurgery until I was a medical student. I vividly remember when, in my third year of medical school, I first witnessed neurosurgeons peeling back the dura and exposing a real, live, throbbing human brain. I recall feeling absolute awe and humility—and an immediate and deep recognition of the intimacy between a patient and a doctor.

8   That year, one of my professors strongly encouraged me to go into primary care, arguing that it was the best way for me to serve my Hispanic immigrant community. Although I had initially intended to return to Mexico triumphant, I had since fallen in love with this country, and I soon found myself immersed in and committed to the betterment of U.S. society. With my sights set on neurosurgery after medical school, I followed my heart and instincts and have tried to contribute to my community and the larger society in my own way. I see a career in academic medicine as an opportunity not only to improve our understanding and treatment of human diseases but also to provide leadership within medicine and support to future scientists, medical students, and physician scientists from minority and nonminority groups alike.

10   My grandmother was the medicine woman in the small town in rural Mexico where I grew up. As I have gotten older, I have come to recognize the crucial role she played not only in instilling in me the value of healing but also in determining the fate and future of others. She was my first role model,

and throughout my life I have depended on the help of my mentors in pursuing my dreams. Like many other illegal immigrants, I arrived in the United States able only to contemplate those dreams—I was not at that point on solid ground. From the fields of the San Joaquin Valley in California to the field of neurosurgery, it has been quite a journey. Today, as a neurosurgeon and researcher, I am taking part in the larger journey of medicine, both caring for patients and conducting clinical and translational research on brain cancer that I hope will lead to innovative ways of fighting devastating disease. And as a citizen of the United States, I am also participating in the great journey of this country. For immigrants like me, this voyage still means the pursuit of a better life—and the opportunity to give back to society.

THINKING ABOUT THE TEXT

1. What specific details of Quiñones-Hinojosa's account are most characteristic of an illegal immigrant's life?

2. What features of his life contributed to his eventually becoming a medical doctor and professor of neurosurgery and oncology?

3. This narration of an amazing personal history does not have an explicit thesis. What position is implicit in Quiñones-Hinojosa's inspiring account?

4. What does the title "Terra Firma" mean? In what ways does the term have significance in the author's life story?

WRITING FROM THE TEXT

1. Write an essay to encourage someone to come to the United States. Use details of Quiñones-Hinojosa's life story to inspire your reader.

2. Using specific examples from Quiñones-Hinojosa's narration, write an essay arguing for increased mentoring for immigrant college students.

3. Write a response to Alfredo Quiñones-Hinojosa to tell him your feelings and ideas after reading of his triumphant, inspiring success. You might want to hear an interview with Dr. Quiñones-Hinojosa at www.nejm.org.

CONNECTING WITH OTHER TEXTS

1. After reading Robert J. Samuelson's essay "Conspiracy Against Assimilation" (p. 112), write an essay to illustrate the forces that thwart immigrant assimilation. Use details from both Samuelson's and Quiñones-Hinojosa's works in your analysis.

2. In "Race Is a Four-Letter Word" (p. 120), Teja Arboleda offers himself "as a case study in transcending the complex maze of barriers, pedestals, doors, and traps that form the boundaries that confine human beings to dominant and minority groups" (123). Write an analysis of Quiñones-Hinojosa's life story that supports Arboleda's self-impression.

 Race Is a Four-Letter Word

Teja Arboleda

Assistant Professor at The New England Institute of Art in Brookline, Massachusetts, where he teaches media production as well as race and ethnic relations courses, Teja Arboleda founded Entertaining Diversity, Inc. in 1992 with the intention of teaching through entertainment about race, cultural diversity, and human potential. He has earned degrees in film-making and sociology, and an M.Ed. in Education and Media. Having worked as a television producer, director, writer, and entertainer, Arboleda directed a series on cultural diversity on PBS in 2001. Arboleda has appeared before the Senate Committee on Racial Classifications where he testified for changes in federal racial and ethnic categories. His father is African American/Native American and Filipino Chinese, and his mother is German Danish, a personal history that informs Arboleda's work, including the essay below from his book *In the Shadow of Race* (1998).

1   I've been called *nigger* and a neighbor set the dogs on us in Queens, New York.

2   I've been called *spic* and was frisked in a plush neighborhood of Los Angeles.

3   I've been called *Jap* and was blamed for America's weaknesses.

4   I've been called *Nazi* and the neighborhood G.I. Joes had me every time.

5   I've been called *Turk* and was sneered at in Germany.

6   I've been called *Stupid Yankee* and was threatened in Japan.

7   I've been called *Afghanistani* and was spit on by a Boston cab driver.

8   I've been called *Iraqi* and Desert Storm was America's pride.

9   I've been called *mulatto, criollo, mestizo, simarron, Hapahaoli, masala, exotic, alternative, mixed-up, messed-up, half-breed,* and *in between.* I've been mistaken for Moroccan, Algerian, Egyptian, Lebanese, Iranian, Turkish, Brazilian, Argentinean, Puerto Rican, Cuban, Mexican, Indonesian, Nepalese, Greek, Italian, Pakistani, Indian, Black, White, Hispanic, Asian, and being a Brooklynite. I've been mistaken for Michael Jackson and Billy Crystal on the same day.

10   I've been ordered to get glasses of water for neighboring restaurant patrons. I've been told to be careful mopping the floors at the television station

where I was directing a show. Even with my U.S. passport, I've been escorted to the "aliens only" line at Kennedy International Airport. I've been told I'm not dark enough. I've been told I'm not White enough. I've been told I talk American real good. I've been told, "Take your hummus and your pita bread and go back to Mexico!" I've been ordered to "Go back to where you belong, we don't like *your* kind here!"

11   I spent too much time and energy as a budding adult abbreviating my identity and rehearsing its explanation. I would practice quietly by myself, reciting what my father always told me: "Filipino-German." He never smiled when he said this.

12   My father's dark skin told many stories that his stern face and anger-filled tension couldn't translate. My mother's light skin could never spell empathy—even suntanning only made her turn bright red. My brother Miguel and I became curiosity factors when we appeared in public with her. During the past 34 years, my skin has lightened, somewhat, but then in the summers (even in New England where summers happen suddenly, and disappear just as quickly), I can darken several degrees in a matter of hours. This phenomenon seems a peculiar paradigm to which people's perceptions of my culture or race alter with the wanning and waxing of my skin tone. I can almost design others' perceptions by counting my minutes in the sun. My years in Japan, the United States, Germany, and the numerous countries, cities, and towns through which I've traveled, have proven that my flesh is irrelevant to the language I speak, to the way I walk and talk, or the way I jog or mow my lawn or to the fact that I often use chopsticks to eat. It is irrelevant to *who* or *what* I married, my political viewpoints, my career, my hopes, desires and fears.

13   I don't remember being taught by my parents never to *question* skin color, yet when I compare the back of my hand to these pages, I cannot help myself—I must know. Like a sickness coursing through my veins with the very blood that makes me who I am, I ask: What color am I? And, what color was I yesterday? Tomorrow? There is also that pesky, familiar feeling I get when, in the corner of my eye, I catch passing strangers with judgments written on their brows. Maybe paranoia, maybe vanity, but the experiences and memories of too often being "different" or "undefinable" have left me with a weary sense of instant verdict on my part. And sometimes I study their thousands of faces, hoping somehow to connect. I know that they ask themselves the same questions, as they are plagued by the same epidemic, asking and reasking themselves, ourselves, "Who and what are we?"

14   Overadapting to new environments has become second nature to me, as my father and my mother eagerly fed me culture. As a child I felt like I was

being dragged to different corners of the planet with my parents, filling their need for exploration and contact, and teaching us the value and beauty of difference. Between packing suitcases and wandering through unfamiliar territory, all I had ever wanted was to be "the same."

15   The United States is going through growing pains. The immigrants coming to the United States and becoming citizens are no longer primarily of European origin. But let's not fool ourselves into thinking that America is only now becoming multicultural.

16   In 1992, *Time* magazine produced a special issue entitled, "The New Face of America" with the subtitle, "How immigrants are shaping the world's first multicultural society." The cover featured a picture of a woman's face. Next to the face was a paragraph that suggested her image was the result of a computerized average of faces of people of several different races.

17   The operative words on the cover are "races," "culture," and "first." Race and culture are very different words. Race in America is predominantly determined by skin color. Culture is determined by our experiences and our interactions within a society, large or small.

18   Then there is this idea of being "first." Are we to say that this continent was never populated by a mix of people? Are we to say that the Locata and Iroquois were of exactly the same culture? What about the different Europeans who settled here later on? Of course, African slaves were not all from the same tribe, and they certainly were not of the same culture as the slave traders.

19   In the middle of the magazine, there was a compilation, more like a chart of photographs of people from all over the world. The editor and computer artist scanned all the pictures into a computer. Then, by having the computer average the faces together, they produced a variety of facial combinations. Remember, however, they said on the cover, "People from different *races* . . . to form the world's first *multicultural* society." But in the body of the article and its accompanying pictures, many people were not identified by their *race*, but rather by their *nationalities*—such as Italian and Chinese—in other words *citizenship*, a very different word.

20   Through it all, *Time* was trying to educate us, but at the same time, we're miseducated. The world—not just this country—has always been and always will be a multicultural environment. So what is it about the words *multicultural* or *diversity* that is confusing or overwhelming?

21   In the next 20 years, the average American will no longer be technically White. This will have to be reflected in the media, in the workplace, and in the schools, not out of charitable interest, but out of necessity. More people are designating themselves as multiracial or multicultural. People continue

to marry across religious, cultural, and ethnic barriers. A definition for "mainstream society" is harder to find.

22   My mother's father, Opa, died a year after Oma passed away. The day after the funeral in Germany, my mother's relatives told her, for the first time, that her father was not really her father (i.e., biologically). All the people who knew the true identity of her father have long since passed away. So, if my mother's biological father was, let's say, Italian or Russian, does that make her German-Italian or German-Russian? She says no. German, only German, because that's how she was raised.

23   My brother, Miguel, married a Brazilian. (*Pause.*) Do you have an image in your head of what she looks like? I did when he first told me about her over the phone. Well, she is Brazilian by culture and citizenship, but her parents are Japanese nationals who moved to Brazil in their early 20s to escape poverty in Japan after World War II. So she *looks stereotypically* Japanese. But she speaks Portuguese and doesn't interact socially like most Japanese do.

24   I offer myself as a case study in transcending the complex maze of barriers, pedestals, doors, and traps that form the boundaries that confine human beings to dominant and minority groups.

25   I am tired. I am exhausted. I am always looking for new and improved definitions for my identity. My very-mixed heritage, culture, and international experiences seem like a blur sometimes, and I long for a resting place. A place where I can breathe like I did in my mother's womb: without having to open my mouth.

THINKING ABOUT THE TEXT

1. What is Teja Arboleda's racial ethnic identity? What seems to be his cultural identity and what are the distinctions he makes between the terms?

2. Why does Arboleda open with conflicting and negative impressions of how he has been perceived? What tone of voice do you hear in the rest of Arboleda's essay? What does he mean when he describes himself as "exhausted"?

3. Arboleda describes, in great detail, a 1992 *Time Magazine* issue on "The New Face of America." How does the author use the images and text from *Time* to support his points?

4. How is Arboleda's account of his brother's marriage to a Brazilian relevant to his essay? Why the "(pause)"?

5. Why does Arboleda devote two paragraphs to describing his and his parents' skin color? What conclusion does he ultimately come to through his analysis of skin tone?

6. Arboleda does not have an explicit thesis, a strong assertion that serves as a controlling idea for his essay. Try to write what you think might serve as Teja Arboleda's thesis.

WRITING FROM THE TEXT

1. Arboleda writes: "My flesh is irrelevant to the language I speak, to the way I walk and talk, or the way I jog or mow my lawn or the fact that I often use chopsticks to eat" (p. 121). Write an essay analyzing your behavior or that of some of your multicultural friends to illustrate that you or they can not easily be categorized by a racial designation.

2. Write a narrative describing a time when you were misperceived as being of a race, ethnicity or culture that you don't feel was accurate. What conclusions can you draw from this experience?

CONNECTING WITH OTHER TEXTS

1. After reading "The Myth of the Latin Woman" (p. 172), write an essay comparing Arboleda's experiences with those of Judith Ortiz Cofer. Use examples from both essays and try to draw some conclusions about race and culture based on the author's narrations.

2. Using examples from the film *Crash* and the ideas expressed in "Don't Let Stereotypes Warp Your Judgments" (p. 470), write an essay arguing that "race" is a delimiting and often derogatory word based more on stereotypes than accurate observations.

An Identity Reduced to a Burka
Semeen Issa and Laila Al-Marayati

Born in Tanzania in 1962, Semeen Issa is a teacher and also the president of the Muslim Women's League. She came to the United States in 1970 and graduated with both undergraduate and graduate degrees in education from the University of Southern California. Issa believes that "it is important in this country of great diversity that we take advantage of what others have to offer and that we stop judging people by how they look."

A practicing gynecologist as well as a writer, Laila Al-Marayati (b. 1962) is the author of articles on women's rights, women's sexuality, and female circumcision. She was born in the United States to a Palestinian father and a mother of French, German, and Native American heritage. The following article originally appeared in the *Los Angeles Times* on January 20, 2002, and was written because of the authors' growing frustration with the media's reductive perception of Muslim women.

1   A few years ago, someone from the Feminist Majority Foundation called the Muslim Women's League to ask if she could "borrow a burka" for a photo shoot the organization was doing to draw attention to the plight of women in Afghanistan under the Taliban. When we told her that we didn't have one, and that none of our Afghan friends did either, she expressed surprise, as if she'd assumed that all Muslim women keep *burkas* in their closets in case a militant Islamist comes to dinner. She didn't seem to understand that her assumption was the equivalent of assuming that every Latino has a Mexican sombrero in their closet.

2   We don't mean to make light of the suffering of our sisters in Afghanistan, but the *burka* was—and is—not their major focus of concern. Their priorities are more basic, like feeding their children, becoming literate and living free from violence. Nevertheless, recent articles in the Western media suggest the *burka* means everything to Muslim women, because they routinely express bewilderment at the fact that all Afghan women didn't cast off their *burkas* when the Taliban was defeated. The Western press' obsession with the dress of Muslim women is not surprising, however, since the press tends to view Muslims, in general, simplistically.

3   Headlines in the mainstream media have reduced Muslim female identity to an article of clothing—"the veil." One is hard-pressed to find an article, book or film about women in Islam that doesn't have "veil" in the title: "Behind the Veil," "Beyond the Veil," "At the Drop of a Veil" and more. The use of the term borders on the absurd: Perhaps next will come "What Color is Your Veil?" or "Rebel Without a Veil" or "Whose Veil Is It, Anyway?"

4   The word "veil" does not even have a universal meaning. In some cultures, it refers to a face-covering known as a *niqab*; in others, to a simple head scarf, known as *hijab*. Other manifestations of "the veil" include all-encompassing outer garments like the ankle-length *abaya* from the Persian Gulf states, the *chador* in Iran or the *burka* in Afghanistan.

5   Like the differences in our clothing from one region to another, Muslim women are diverse. Stereotypical assumptions about Muslim women are as inaccurate as the assumption that all American women are personified by the bikini-clad cast of "Baywatch." Anyone who has spent time interacting with Muslims knows that, despite numerous obstacles, Muslim women are active, assertive and engaged in society. In Qatar, women make up the majority of graduate-school students. The Iranian parliament has more women members than the U.S. Senate. Throughout the world, many Muslim women are educated and professionally trained; they participate in public debates, are often catalysts for reform and champions for their own rights. At the same time, there is no denying that in many Muslim countries, dress has been used as a tool to wield power over women.

6   What doesn't penetrate Western consciousness, however, is that forced uncovering is also a tool of oppression. During the reign of Shah Mohammad Reza Pahlavi in Iran, wearing the veil was prohibited. As an expression of their opposition to his repressive regime, women who supported the 1979 Islamic Revolution marched in the street clothed in *chadors*. Many of them did not expect to have this "dress code" institutionalized by those who led the revolution and then took power in the new government.

7   In Turkey, the secular regime considers the head scarf a symbol of extremist elements that want to overthrow the government. Accordingly, women who wear any type of head-covering are banned from public office, government jobs and academia, including graduate school. Turkish women who believe the head-covering is a religious obligation are unfairly forced to give up public life or opportunities for higher education and career advancement.

8   Dress should not bar Muslim women from exercising their Islam-guaranteed rights, like the right to be educated, to earn a living, and to move about safely in society. Unfortunately, some governments impose a strict dress code along with other restrictions, like limiting education for women, to appear "authentically Islamic." Such laws, in fact, are inconsistent with Islam. Nevertheless, these associations lead to the general perception that "behind the veil" lurk other, more insidious examples of the repression of women, and that wearing the veil somehow causes the social ills that plague Muslim women around the world.

9   Many Muslim men and women alike are subjugated by despotic, dictatorial regimes. Their lot in life is worsened by extreme poverty and illiteracy, two conditions that are not caused by Islam but are sometimes exploited in the name of religion. Helping Muslim women overcome their misery is a major task. The reconstruction of Muslim Afghanistan will be a test case for the Afghan people and for the international community dedicated to making Afghan society work for everyone. To some, Islam is the root cause of the problems faced by women in Afghanistan. But what is truly at fault is a misguided, narrow interpretation of Islam designed to serve a rigid patriarchal system.

10   Traditional Muslim populations will be more receptive to change that is based on Islamic principles of justice, as expressed in the Koran, than they will be to change that abandons religion altogether or confines it to private life. Muslim scholars and leaders who emphasize Islamic principles that support women's rights to education, health care, marriage and divorce, equal pay for equal work and participation in public life could fill the vacuum now occupied by those who impose a vision of Islam that infringes on the rights of women.

11   Given the opportunity, Muslim women, like women everywhere, will become educated, pursue careers, strive to do what is best for their families and
contribute positively according to their abilities. How they dress is irrelevant.
It should be obvious that the critical element Muslim women need is freedom,
especially the freedom to make choices that enable them to be independent
agents of positive change. Choosing to dress modestly, including wearing a
head scarf, should be as respected as choosing not to cover. Accusations that
modestly dressed Muslim women are caving in to male-dominated
understandings of Islam neglect the reality that most Muslim women who
cover by choice do so out of subservience to God, not to any human being.

12   The worth of a woman—any woman—should not be determined by the
length of her skirt, but by the dedication, knowledge and skills she brings to
the task at hand.

THINKING ABOUT THE TEXT

1. What is the authors' strategy in opening their essay with a narrative? How
   does the anecdote embody the authors' point of view?

2. What do you infer is the authors' thesis? Despite the seriousness of their
   claim, the authors' tone is humorous throughout. What is their strategy in
   employing humor? What is their aim?

3. What did you learn about the "veil" in different Muslim countries? How
   do the differences in styles and purposes for covering relate to the authors'
   point about Muslim women?

4. The authors insist that enforced dress codes are not the major problem
   facing most Islamic women, and their religion is not the delimiting factor
   in their lives. What are the problems facing these women? How do the authors' points help non-Muslim readers perceive the situation of Muslim
   women?

WRITING FROM THE TEXT

1. Remember a time when a clothing code was imposed on you—for school,
   work, or for a social event within your peer group or family. Describe how
   you felt about the requirement, and whether you rebelled or conformed.
   Are identities reduced or enhanced by clothing regulations?

2. The authors observe that we tend to see Muslim women "simplistically"
   or stereotypically, in part because of our fixation on the *burka*. Write an
   essay that examines other nationalities and cultures that have been stereotyped by dress and analyze the consequences of such stereotyping.

3. Imagine yourself a traditional Muslim woman from an Afghan village who is transported to a city in the United States. You start to observe Western dress styles for women and now, in an essay, must show your approval or disapproval of American women's choices.

4. After this essay appeared in the *Los Angeles Times,* one letter to the editor pointed out that how women dress is not irrelevant, and that women who wear *burkas* would not become surgeons, for example, because veiling of any kind would not be possible in an operating room. Make a list of other activities or professions that you imagine could not reasonably be done by someone wearing a head covering. Write an essay that comes to some conclusion about whether the way women dress is relevant.

CONNECTING WITH OTHER TEXTS

1. The authors write that "in many Muslim countries, dress has been used as a tool to wield power over women," and they note that "forced uncovering

is also a tool of oppression" (126). Write an essay that analyzes how cloth-ing codes have wielded power over women and men in many cultures. You might consider styles of clothing in affluent nations, as well as com-pulsory garments or uniforms throughout the world.

2. Write an essay comparing the experience of Zaiba Malik with the observa-tions of Issa and Al-Marayati. Focus your essay on the reasons for and consequences of women wearing a veil.

3. Interview two Muslim women you know or can meet on your campus, one who wears a head covering of some kind and one who does not. In your prepared questions for the interview, you might consider asking why each has chosen "to veil or not to veil" and what experiences each has had as a result of her decision, including how she is perceived in the Muslim and non-Muslim cultures. In your comparative essay, come to some conclu-sion about the nature of "the veil."

Hidden in Plain Sight

Zaiba Malik

A former pupil of the Girls Grammar School of Bradford, England, British broadcaster and freelance journalist Zaiba Malik was once incarcerated in Bangladesh where she was de-tained while filming a documentary for Britain's Channel 4 about Islamic militants and links to terror organizations. As her narrative here reveals, Malik is clearly exploring what it means to be a Muslim woman today. The essay below appeared in the *Los Angles Times* in 2006.

1   There's a poster on the wall of an Islamic dress shop in East London showing a young woman in a black *hijab*. Above her is the word "Pure." The saleswoman who is helping me also has a scarf covering her head.

2   I'm here to buy a *hijab* too—but that's not all. I'm here for the full Islamic covering, the complete three-piece suit: the *hijab* that I will wrap around my head, the shapeless robe known as an *abaya*, and the now-terribly-controversial *niqab*—a square of material that goes over one's face with a slit of about five inches for my eyes.

3   I buy it for $73 and take it all home, but I don't put it on until the next morning. When I do, I see myself for the first time in full Islamic dress—and I'm horrified. I have disappeared, and somebody I don't recognize is looking back at me. I cannot tell how old she is, how much she weighs, whether she has a kind face or a sad face. Even my own mother couldn't recognize me.

4   I've seen this shrouded figure in news reports from the mountains of Afghanistan and the cities of Saudi Arabia, but she looks out of place here in my bedroom in West London. In fact, I feel so dissociated from my own reflection that it takes me over an hour to pluck up the courage to leave the house.

5   I've never worn the *niqab* before. Growing up in a Muslim household in Bradford, a city in the north of England, in the 1970s and '80s, I dressed modestly. But my hair was only covered in the presence of the imam and while I was reading the Koran. Today, however, things have changed. I see second- and third-generation British Muslims concealed in black. They say they wear the *niqab* voluntarily, to demonstrate their dedication to Allah and to protect them from male eyes.

6   In recent weeks, this dress code has become the focus of an intense debate that has gripped Britain. It began when Jack Straw, a former British foreign secretary and member of Parliament for Blackburn (a town with a high percentage of Muslims) started the ball rolling. He revealed that he asks Muslim women to remove their veils when they visit him because it makes him feel uncomfortable. These comments were, needless to say, incendiary, and Prime Minister Tony Blair added to the controversy when he described the item of clothing as a "mark of separation."

7   As I head onto the street, it takes just seconds for me to become the object of attention. I quickly discover that there are different categories of stares. The one favored by elderly people is to glare directly; women wait until you've passed and then turn around when they think you can't see; men look out of the corner of their eyes, and children just stare, point and laugh blatantly.

8   I'm having coffee with a friend. I'm finding it hard to breathe. There is no inlet for air (although the material itself is somewhat porous), and I can feel the heat of every breath I exhale. Plus the slit for my eyes keeps slipping down, so I can barely see a thing. My peripheral vision is obscured, as if I were stuck in a car that is completely buried in snow with only a tiny sliver of clean windscreen. I can't fathom a way of drinking my cappuccino, and when I become aware that everybody in the coffee shop is staring at me, wondering how I'm going to do it, I give up.

9   At the supermarket, a baby no more than 2 years old takes one look at me and bursts into tears.

10   After a few hours, I get used to the gaping and the sniggering. But what does surprise me is what happens when I head into central London. I have arranged to meet a friend at the National Portrait Gallery. In the 15-minute walk from the bus stop to the gallery, two things happen. A man in his 30s stops in front of me and asks: "Can I see your face?"

11   "Why do you want to see my face?" I ask.

12   "Because I want to see if you are pretty. Are you pretty?"

13   Before I can reply, he shouts: "You—ing tease!"

14   I'm completely taken aback.

15   Just as I'm thinking about this, I hear the impatient beeping of a horn. A middle-aged man is behind the wheel of a van, leering at me. "Watch where you're going, you stupid Paki!" he screams. This time I'm a bit faster.

16   "How did you know I'm Pakistani, underneath all of this?" I shout at him. He responds by driving so close past me that when he yells "Terrorist!" I can feel his breath on my veil.

17   Things don't get much better at the National Portrait Gallery. Art lovers pay as much attention to me as they do to the paintings. I might as well be one of the exhibits. Maybe they're trying to come to grips with the irony of a faceless woman staring at faces.

18   I float from room to room, like some apparition, looking at paintings of Queen Anne and Mary II. They're in extravagant ermines and taffetas, and their ample bosoms are on display. All I can think is that if all women dressed in the *niqab*, how sad and how strange this place would be.

19   I miss seeing my own face, my own shape. Yet at the same time I feel completely naked. The women I have met who have taken to wearing the *niqab* tell me that it gives them confidence, but I find that it saps mine.

20   Nobody has forced me to wear it, but I feel as though I have oppressed myself and isolated myself.

21   Maybe I'd feel more comfortable being so covered if I were among women who dress in a similar fashion? I head to the Central Mosque in Regents Park.

22   Hundreds of women are seated on the floor. I look up and down the lines of worshipers. Of course the women here have their heads covered, but I am the only person wearing the *niqab*. Everyone else's face is visible. The woman next to me explains that the *niqab* is seen as "extreme."

23   "Allah gave us faces, and we should not hide them," she says.

24   I'm reassured by her words. I think deep down my anxiety about having to wear the *niqab*, even for a day, was based on guilt—that I am not a true Muslim unless I cover myself from head to toe. But the Koran says: "Allah has given you clothes to cover your shameful parts, and garments pleasing to the eye. But the finest of all these is the robe of piety."

25   I don't understand the need of women to wear something as severe as the *niqab*. But for that tiny number that do, I will shake their gloved hands for bearing this endurance task—the staring, the swearing and the discomfort. On the streets of London, the black veil does nothing to distract attention—and everything to attract it.

THINKING ABOUT THE TEXT

1. What distinctions among the Islamic women's dress—the *hijab*, the *abaya*, and the *niqab*—does Malik make?

2. What is the author's initial reaction to seeing herself in "full Islamic dress"? Why is wearing the *niqab* particularly discomforting to her?

3. The writer cites numerous specific responses to her complete coverings. Who are the people who respond or comment on her dress and what is the tone of their remarks and reactions? How does Malik feel about these responses to her attire? Compare the comments of the former British foreign secretary and former Prime Minister of England to the general public's response to Malik.

4. In the National Portrait Gallery in London, as Malik looks at paintings of famous women in extravagant gowns displaying their "ample bosoms," she has a moment of awareness and realization of irony. Explain her perceptions.

5. How do the women at the author's mosque respond to her wearing the *niqab*? What is Malik's ultimate awareness of herself, the Koran, and women who typically wear the *niqab*?

6. Analyze the meanings of Malik's title.

WRITING FROM THE TEXT

1. Write an analysis of Islamic women's coverings that supports or refutes former Prime Minister Tony Blair's perception that the Islamic "dress-code" is "a mark of separation" (130).

2. Write a descriptive account of a time when your choice of clothing created attention that you did not intend to draw. Can you compare some of your feelings with the intense descriptions of anxiety, self-consciousness, and even guilt that Malik describes?

3. Write an evaluative response of Malik's essay. (See pp. 438–444 for a review of this kind of essay.) In your writing, consider Malik's self-observations, the responses of people on the street, and her concluding awareness after her visit to the mosque.

4. Write an essay describing and then analyzing the significance of three or four traditional items or codes of dress chosen by a religious group or a specific culture. Come to some conclusion about each group's intention in adhering to the characteristic garb.

5. Interview two of the Muslim women on your campus, one who wears some form of traditional Islamic covering and one who does not. Write an analysis contrasting their appearances, their experiences with non-Muslims on campus, and their beliefs about suitable dress for Muslim women.

CONNECTING WITH OTHER TEXTS

1. Read "An Identity Reduced to a Burka" (p. 124) and write an essay that uses Issa and Al-Marayati's views, as well as Malik's, to analyze whether how Muslim women dress "is irrelevant" (127). Do Malik's experiences support Issa and Al-Marayati's stance?

2. Read "The Myth of the Latin Woman" (p. 172) and write an essay comparing and contrasting the stereotyping and public embarrassment experienced by Cofer and Malik.

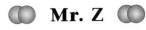

Mr. Z

M. Carl Holman

A poet, professor, and civil rights activist, M. Carl Holman (1919–1988) taught at Clark College in Atlanta, Georgia, from 1949 to 1962. He also worked as an editor on the *Atlanta Inquirer* and was on the U.S. Commission for Civil Rights. He served as president of the National Urban Coalition from 1971 until his death in 1988. Throughout his life, he won numerous awards for public service and for his poetry. The following poem, written in 1967, demonstrates his ability to meld his two passions—poetry and civil rights.

    Taught early that his mother's skin was the sign of error,
    He dressed and spoke the perfect part of honor;
    Won scholarships, attended the best schools.
    Disclaimed kinship with jazz and spirituals;
5   Chose prudent, raceless views for each situation.
    Or when he could not cleanly skirt dissension
    Faced up to the dilemma, firmly seized
    Whatever ground was Anglo-Saxonized.

    In diet, too, his practice was exemplary;
10   Of pork in its profane forms he was wary;
    Expert in vintage wines, sauces and salads.
    His palate shrank from cornbread, yams and collards.

    He was as careful whom he chose to kiss;
    His bride had somewhere lost her Jewishness.
15   But kept her blue eyes; an Episcopalian
    Prelate proclaimed them matched chameleon.
    Choosing the right addresses, here, abroad,
    They shunned those places where they might be barred;

Even less anxious to be asked to dine
20   Where hosts catered to kosher accent or exotic skin.
And so he climbed, unclogged by ethnic weights,
An airborne plant, flourishing without roots.
Not one false note was struck—until he died;
His subtly grieving widow could have flayed
25   The obit writers, ringing crude changes on a clumsy phrase:
"One of the most distinguished members of his race."

THINKING ABOUT THE TEXT

1. The opening line reveals that Mr. Z was "taught early that his mother's skin was the sign of error" (1), as if it were a mistake, something to correct or avoid. Why does the poet emphasize that he was "taught" this? How can the reader be sure what "his mother's skin" symbolizes? What does he shun?

2. List all the details that support the poet's claim that Mr. Z "dressed and spoke the perfect part of honor" (2). What does "perfect part" imply? What other words are used to show that every decision is calculated?

3. How does Mr. Z's bride seem ideal for him? What is she denying and avoiding? Why are they described as "matched chameleon"? What is telling about the contrast in the emotion that she exhibits over his death and the emotion that she feels for the "obit writers" who change his obituary?

4. Explain the significance of these lines: "And so he climbed, unclogged by ethnic weights, / An airborne plant, flourishing without roots" (20–21).

5. How is this poem a satire and what is the poet satirizing?

6. Irony is key to this poem. The poem reads like a list of praises, but what is the attitude of the poet toward Mr. Z? How can the reader be sure? Explain the irony in the last line.

7. What are possible meanings related to the name, "Mr. Z"? How is this name ironic?

WRITING FROM THE TEXT

1. Write an analysis of the use of irony in "Mr. Z." Include specific images for support and analyze them fully. (See poetry analysis, pp. 476–485.)

2. Focusing on "Mr. Z," write an essay about any experiences that you or someone close to you has had denying his or her heritage. Were the successes worth the sacrifices? Can you infer Holman's view?

CONNECTING WITH OTHER TEXTS

1. Read "The Myth of the Latin Woman" (p. 172) and contrast the author's self-concept and values with those of Mr. Z. In your essay try to account for these differences.

2. Read "Black Men and Public Space" (p. 181) and compare Brent Staples's "solution" to being misperceived by others with the choices that Mr. Z makes. Compare and contrast their motives and their acceptance of their identity.

 # The Red Convertible

Louise Erdrich

The daughter of a Chippewa mother and a German American father, Louise Erdrich (b. 1954) explores Native American themes in her writing, and her characters often represent both sides of her heritage. Erdrich's novels include *Love Medicine* (1984), *The Beet Queen* (1986), *Tracks* (1988), *The Bingo Palace* (1994), *Tales of Burning Love* (1996), *The Painted Drum* (2005), *The Plague of Doves* (2008), and, with her late husband Michael Dorris, *The Crown of Columbus* (1991). Erdrich has also published poetry, a memoir, *The Blue Jay's Dance: A Birth Year* (1995), and a children's book, *Grandmother's Pigeon* (1996). Erdrich attributes her interest in writing to her childhood and heritage where people sit and tell stories. Her father, in fact, used to give her a nickel for every story she wrote. The short story included here is from Erdrich's first novel, *Love Medicine*, and is told in the voice of one of the characters living on a reservation near Erdrich's fictional town of Argus, North Dakota.

1   I was the first one to drive a convertible on my reservation. And of course it was red, a red Olds. I owned that car along with my brother Henry Junior. We owned it together until his boots filled with water on a windy night and he bought out my share. Now Henry owns the whole car, and his youngest brother Lyman (that's myself), Lyman walks everywhere he goes.

2   How did I earn enough money to buy my share in the first place? My own talent was I could always make money. I had a touch for it, unusual in a Chippewa. From the first I was different that way, and everyone recognized it. I was the only kid they let in the American Legion Hall to shine shoes, for example, and one Christmas I sold spiritual bouquets for the mission door to door. The nuns let me keep a percentage. Once I started, it seemed the more money I made the easier the money came. Everyone encouraged it. When I was fifteen I got a job washing dishes at the Joliet Café, and that was where my first big break happened.

3   It wasn't long before I was promoted to bussing tables, and then the short-order cook quit and I was hired to take her place. No sooner than you know it I was managing the Joliet. The rest is history. I went on managing. I soon became part owner, and of course there was no stopping me then. It wasn't long before the whole thing was mine.

4   After I'd owned the Joliet for one year, it blew over in the worst tornado ever seen around here. The whole operation was smashed to bits. A total loss. The fryalator was up in a tree, the grill torn in half like it was paper. I was only sixteen. I had it all in my mother's name, and I lost it quick, but before I lost it I had every one of my relatives, and their relatives, to dinner, and I also bought that red Olds I mentioned, along with Henry.

5   The first time we saw it! I'll tell you when we first saw it. We had gotten a ride up to Winnipeg, and both of us had money. Don't ask me why, because we never mentioned a car or anything, we just had all our money. Mine was cash, a big bankroll from the Joliet's insurance. Henry had two checks—a week's extra pay for being laid off, and his regular check from the Jewel Bearing Plant.

6   We were walking down Portage anyway, seeing the sights, when we saw it. There it was, parked, large as life. Really as *if* it was alive. I thought of the word *repose,* because the car wasn't simply stopped, parked, or whatever. That car reposed, calm and gleaming, a FOR SALE sign in its left front window. Then, before we had thought it over at all, the car belonged to us and our pockets were empty. We had just enough money for gas back home.

7   We went places in that car, me and Henry. We took off driving all one whole summer. We started off toward the Little Knife River and Mandaree in Fort Berthold and then we found ourselves down in Wakpala somehow, and then suddenly we were over in Montana on the Rocky Boys, and yet the summer was not even half over. Some people hang on to details when they travel, but we didn't let them bother us and just lived our everyday lives here to there.

8   I do remember this one place with willows. I remember I laid under those trees and it was comfortable. So comfortable. The branches bent down all around me like a tent or a stable. And quiet, it was quiet, even though there was a powwow close enough so I could see it going on. The air was not too still, not too windy either. When the dust rises up and hangs in the air around the dancers like that, I feel good. Henry was asleep with his arms thrown wide. Later on, he woke up and we started driving again. We were somewhere in Montana, or maybe on the Blood Reserve—it could have been anywhere. Anyway it was where we met the girl.

9   All her hair was in buns around her ears, that's the first thing I noticed about her. She was posed alongside the road with her arm out, so we stopped. That girl was short, so short her lumber shirt looked comical on her, like a

nightgown. She had jeans on and fancy moccasins and she carried a little suitcase.

10   "Hop on in," says Henry. So she climbs in between us.

11   "We'll take you home," I says. "Where do you live?"

12   "Chicken," she says.

13   "Where the hell's that?" I ask her.

14   "Alaska."

15   "Okay," says Henry, and we drive.

16   We got up there and never wanted to leave. The sun doesn't truly set there in summer, and the night is more a soft dusk. You might doze off, sometimes, but before you know it you're up again, like an animal in nature. You never feel like you have to sleep hard or put away the world. And things would grow up there. One day just dirt or moss, the next day flowers and long grass. The girl's name was Susy. Her family really took to us. They fed us and put us up. We had our own tent to live in by their house, and the kids would be in and out of there all day and night. They couldn't get over me and Henry being brothers, we looked so different. We told them we knew we had the same mother, anyway.

17   One night Susy came in to visit us. We sat around in the tent talking of this thing and that. The season was changing. It was getting darker by that time, and the cold was even getting just a little mean. I told her it was time for us to go. She stood up on a chair.

18   "You never seen my hair," Susy said.

19   That was true. She was standing on a chair, but still, when she unclipped her buns the hair reached all the way to the ground. Our eyes opened. You couldn't tell how much hair she had when it was rolled up so neatly. Then my brother Henry did something funny. He went up to the chair and said, "Jump on my shoulders." So she did that, and her hair reached down past his waist, and he started twirling, this way and that, so her hair was flung out from side to side.

20   "I always wondered what it was like to have long pretty hair," Henry says. Well we laughed. It was a funny sight, the way he did it. The next morning we got up and took leave of those people.

21   On to greener pastures, as they say. It was down through Spokane and across Idaho then Montana and very soon we were racing the weather right along under the Canadian border through Columbus, Des Lacs, and then we were in Bottineau County and soon home. We'd made most of the trip, that summer, without putting up the car hood at all. We got home just in time, it turned out, for the army to remember Henry had signed up to join it.

22   I don't wonder that the army was so glad to get my brother that they turned him into a Marine. He was built like a brick outhouse anyway. We

liked to tease him that they really wanted him for his Indian nose. He had a nose big and sharp as a hatchet, like the nose on Red Tomahawk, the Indian who killed Sitting Bull, whose profile is on signs all along the North Dakota highways. Henry went off to training camp, came home once during Christmas, then the next thing you know we got an overseas letter from him. It was 1970, and he said he was stationed up in the northern hill country. Whereabouts I did not know. He wasn't such a hot letter writer, and only got off two before the enemy caught him. I could never keep it straight, which direction those good Vietnam soldiers were from.

23   I wrote him back several times, even though I didn't know if those letters would get through. I kept him informed all about the car. Most of the time I had it up on blocks in the yard or half taken apart, because that long trip did a hard job on it under the hood.

24   I always had good luck with numbers, and never worried about the draft myself. I never even had to think about what my number was. But Henry was never lucky in the same way as me. It was at least three years before Henry came home. By then I guess the whole war was solved in the government's mind, but for him it would keep on going. In those years I'd put his car into almost perfect shape. I always thought of it as his car while he was gone, even though when he left he said, "Now it's yours," and threw me his key.

25   "Thanks for the extra key," I'd said. "I'll put it up in your drawer just in case I need it." He laughed.

26   When he came home, though, Henry was very different, and I'll say this: the change was no good. You could hardly expect him to change for the better, I know. But he was quiet, so quiet, and never comfortable sitting still anywhere but always up and moving around. I thought back to times we'd sat still for whole afternoons, never moving a muscle, just shifting our weight along the ground, talking to whoever sat with us, watching things. He'd always had a joke, then, too, and now you couldn't get him to laugh, or when he did it was more the sound of a man choking, a sound that stopped up the throats of other people around him. They got to leaving him alone most of the time, and I didn't blame them. It was a fact: Henry was jumpy and mean.

27   I'd bought a color TV set for my mom and the rest of us while Henry was away. Money still came very easy. I was sorry I'd ever bought it though, because of Henry. I was also sorry I'd bought color, because with black-and-white the pictures seem older and farther away. But what are you going to do? He sat in front of it, watching it, and that was the only time he was completely still. But it was the kind of stillness that you see in a rabbit when it freezes and before it will bolt. He was not easy. He sat in his chair gripping the armrests with all his might, as if the chair itself was moving at a high speed and if he let go at all he would rocket forward and maybe crash right through the set.

28   Once I was in the room watching TV with Henry and I heard his teeth click at something. I looked over, and he'd bitten through his lip. Blood was going down his chin. I tell you right then I wanted to smash that tube to pieces. I went over to it but Henry must have known what I was up to. He rushed from his chair and shoved me out of the way, against the wall. I told myself he didn't know what he was doing.

29   My mom came in, turned the set off real quiet, and told us she had made something for supper. So we went and sat down. There was still blood going down Henry's chin, but he didn't notice it and no one said anything, even though every time he took a bit of his bread his blood fell onto it until he was eating his own blood mixed in with the food.

30   While Henry was not around we talked about what was going to happen to him. There were no Indian doctors on the reservation, and my mom was afraid of trusting Old Man Pillager because he courted her long ago and was jealous of her husbands. He might take revenge through her son. We were afraid that if we brought Henry to a regular hospital they would keep him.

31   "They don't fix them in those places," Mom said; "they just give them drugs."

32   "We wouldn't get him there in the first place," I agreed, "so let's just forget about it."

33   Then I thought about the car.

34   Henry had not even looked at the car since he'd gotten home, though like I said, it was in tip-top condition and ready to drive. I thought the car might bring the old Henry back somehow. So I bided my time and waited for my chance to interest him in the vehicle.

35   One night Henry was off somewhere. I took myself a hammer. I went out to that car and I did a number on its underside. Whacked it up. Bent the tail pipe double. Ripped the muffler loose. By the time I was done with the car it looked worse than any typical Indian car that has been driven all its life on reservation roads, which they always say are like government promises—full of holes. It just about hurt me, I'll tell you that! I threw dirt in the carburetor and I ripped all the electric tape off the seats. I made it look just as beat up as I could. Then I sat back and waited for Henry to find it.

36   Still, it took him over a month. That was all right, because it was just getting warm enough, not melting, but warm enough to work outside.

37   "Lyman," he says, walking in one day, "that red car looks like shit."

38   "Well it's old," I says. "You got to expect that."

39   "No way!" says Henry. "That car's a classic! But you went and ran the piss right out of it, Lyman, and you know it don't deserve that. I kept that car in A-one shape. You don't remember. You're too young. But when I left, that

car was running like a watch. Now I don't even know if I can get it to start again, let alone get it anywhere near its old condition."

40   "Well you try," I said, like I was getting mad, "but I say it's a piece of junk."

41   Then I walked out before he could realize I knew he'd strung together more than six words at once.

42   After that I thought he'd freeze himself to death working on that car. He was out there all day, and at night he rigged up a little lamp, ran a cord out the window, and had himself some light to see by while he worked. He was better than he had been before, but that's still not saying much. It was easier for him to do the things the rest of us did. He ate more slowly and didn't jump up and down during the meal to get this or that or look out the window. I put my hand in the back of the TV set, I admit, and fiddled around with it good, so that it was almost impossible now to get a clear picture. He didn't look at it very often anyway. He was always out with that car or going off to get parts for it. By the time it was really melting outside, he had it fixed.

43   I had been feeling down in the dumps about Henry around this time. We had always been together before. Henry and Lyman. But he was such a loner now that I didn't know how to take it. So I jumped at the chance one day when Henry seemed friendly. It's not that he smiled or anything. He just said, "Let's take that old shitbox for a spin." Just the way he said it made me think he could be coming around.

44   We went out to the car. It was spring. The sun was shining very bright. My only sister, Bonita, who was just eleven years old, came out and made us stand together for a picture. Henry leaned his elbow on the red car's windshield, and he took his other arm and put it over my shoulder, very carefully, as though it was heavy for him to lift and he didn't want to bring the weight down all at once.

45   "Smile," Bonita said, and he did.

46   That picture. I never look at it anymore. A few months ago, I don't know why, I got his picture out and tacked it on the wall. I felt good about Henry at the time, close to him. I felt good having his picture on the wall, until one night when I was looking at television. I was a little drunk and stoned. I looked up at the wall and Henry was staring at me. I don't know what it was, but his smile had changed, or maybe it was gone. All I know is I couldn't stay in the same room with that picture. I was shaking. I got up, closed the door, and went into the kitchen. A little later my friend Ray came over and we both went back into that room. We put the picture in a brown bag, folded the bag over and over tightly, then put it way back in a closet.

47   I still see that picture now, as if it tugs at me, whenever I pass that closet door. The picture is very clear in my mind. It was so sunny that day Henry

had to squint against the glare. Or maybe the camera Bonita held flashed like a mirror, blinding him, before she snapped the picture. My face is right out in the sun, big and round. But he might have drawn back, because the shadows on his face are deep as holes. There are two shadows curved like little hooks around the ends of his smile, as if to frame it and try to keep it there—that one, first smile that looked like it might have hurt his face. He has his field jacket on and the worn-in clothes he'd come back in and kept wearing ever since. After Bonita took the picture, she went into the house and we got into the car. There was a full cooler in the trunk. We started off, east, toward Pembina and the Red River because Henry said he wanted to see the high water.

48   The trip over there was beautiful. When everything starts changing, drying up, clearing off, you feel like your whole life is starting. Henry felt it, too. The top was down and the car hummed like a top. He'd really put it back in shape, even the tape on the seats was very carefully put down and glued back in layers. It's not that he smiled again or even joked, but his face looked to me as if it was clear, more peaceful. It looked as though he wasn't thinking of anything in particular except the bare fields and windbreaks and houses we were passing.

49   The river was high and full of winter trash when we got there. The sun was still out, but it was colder by the river. There were still little clumps of dirty snow here and there on the banks. The water hadn't gone over the banks yet, but it would, you could tell. It was just at its limit, hard swollen glossy like an old gray scar. We made ourselves a fire, and we sat down and watched the current go. As I watched it I felt something squeezing inside me and tightening and trying to let go all at the same time. I knew I was not just feeling it myself; I knew I was feeling what Henry was going through at that moment. Except that I couldn't stand it, the closing and opening. I jumped to my feet. I took Henry by the shoulders and I started shaking him. "Wake up," I says, "wake up, wake up, wake up!" I didn't know what had come over me. I sat down beside him again.

50   His face was totally white and hard. Then it broke, like stones break all of a sudden when water boils up inside them.

51   "I know it," he says. "I know it. I can't help it. It's no use."

52   We start talking. He said he knew what I'd done with the car. It was obvious it had been whacked out of shape and not just neglected. He said he wanted to give the car to me for good now, it was no use. He said he'd fixed it just to give it back and I should take it.

53   "No way," I says, "I don't want it."

54   "That's okay," he says, "you take it."

55   "I don't want it, though," I says back to him, and then to emphasize, just to emphasize, you understand, I touch his shoulder. He slaps my hand off.

56   "Take that car," he says.

57   "No," I say, "make me," I say, and then he grabs my jacket and rips the arm loose. That jacket is a class act, suede with tags and zippers. I push Henry backwards, off the log. He jumps up and bowls me over. We go down in a clinch and come up swinging hard, for all we're worth, with our fists. He socks my jaw so hard I feel like it swings loose. Then I'm at his ribcage and land a good one under his chin so his head snaps back. He's dazzled. He looks at me and I look at him and then his eyes are full of tears and blood and at first I think he's crying. But no, he's laughing. "Ha! Ha!" he says. "Ha! Ha! Take good care of it."

58   "Okay," I says, "okay, no problem. Ha! Ha!"

59   I can't help it, and I start laughing, too. My face feels fat and strange, and after a while I get a beer from the cooler in the trunk, and when I hand it to Henry he takes his shirt and wipes my germs off. "Hoof-and-mouth disease," he says. For some reason this cracks me up, and so we're really laughing for a while, and then we drink all the rest of the beers one by one and throw them in the river and see how far, how fast, the current takes them before they fill up and sink.

60   "You want to go on back?" I ask after a while. "Maybe we could snag a couple nice Kashpaw girls."

61   He says nothing. But I can tell his mood is turning again.

62   "They're all crazy, the girls up here, every damn one of them."

63   "You're crazy too," I say, to jolly him up. "Crazy Lamartine boys!"

64   He looks as though he will take this wrong at first. His face twists, then clears, and he jumps up on his feet. "That's right!" he says. "Crazier 'n hell. Crazy Indians!"

65   I think it's the old Henry again. He throws off his jacket and starts swinging his legs out from the knees like a fancy dancer. He's down doing something between a grouse dance and a bunny hop, no kind of dance I ever saw before, but neither has anyone else on all this green growing earth. He's wild. He wants to pitch whoopee! He's up and at me and all over. All this time I'm laughing so hard, so hard my belly is getting tied up in a knot.

66   "Got to cool me off!" he shouts all of a sudden. Then he runs over to the river and jumps in.

67   There's boards and other things in the current. It's so high. No sound comes from the river after the splash he makes, so I run right over. I look around. It's getting dark. I see he's halfway across the water already, and I

know he didn't swim there but the current took him. It's far. I hear his voice, though, very clearly across it.

68   "My boots are filling," he says.

69   He says this in a normal voice, like he just noticed and he doesn't know what to think of it. Then he's gone. A branch comes by. Another branch. And I go in.

70   By the time I get out of the river, off the snag I pulled myself onto, the sun is down. I walk back to the car, turn on the high beams, and drive it up the bank. I put it in first gear and then I take my foot off the clutch. I get out, close the door, and watch it plow softly into the water. The headlights reach in as they go down, searching, still lighted even after the water swirls over the back end. I wait. The wires short out. It is all finally dark. And then there is only the water, the sound of it going and running and going and running and running.

THINKING ABOUT THE TEXT

1. Who is the narrator of "The Red Convertible"? What does the narrator specifically tell the reader about himself and what can we infer based on the information that he gives and the way he tells the story?

2. Every story needs conflict or there is no story, but sometimes the conflicts are not easy to identify. What is the plot of the "The Red Convertible" and what are the conflicts within this story?

3. In what specific ways does the setting—time and place—contribute to this short story?

4. What is Erdrich's intention in adding Susy to the brothers' story? How do the parts of the story with Susy contribute to the reader's understanding of Henry and Lyman?

5. The red convertible is central to the brothers' relationship and functions literally as a vehicle for their trips. List specific ways the car also works symbolically.

6. What happens at the end of the story? Why does it happen? How has the opening paragraph of the story foreshadowed its conclusion?

WRITING FROM THE TEXT

1. Write an analysis of Lyman's character—his values, motivations, and sensitivities—based on inferences you can draw from all parts of the short story. (See the character analysis section, pp. 485–493.)

2. Write an analysis of how the red convertible functions in this story. Pay close attention to the way the car's description, from the first image of it when it "reposed, calm and gleaming" (p. 136) to the end of the story when its headlights short out. Include examples of Erdrich's language as you work to analyze the scenes with the car.

3. On their last outing in the red convertible, Lyman describes the feelings he has of "squeezing" and "tightening" and "trying to let go" (p. 141), and he knows that Henry is going through these feeling at the same time. Write an essay that analyzes the brothers' relationship. Show how this scene and others express Lyman's empathy for Henry throughout the story.

CONNECTING WITH OTHER TEXTS

1. Use this short story, the essay "I Confess Some Envy" (p. 451), and the poem "Facing It" (p. 195) to write an analysis of the effects of the Vietnam War on the people who did not go to the war as well as the soldiers who returned. What insights do you gain from these works?

2. Read "The Only Child" (p. 34) and write an analysis of Leonard's and Lyman's brothers and the narrators' relationships with them. You might choose to use comparison or contrast development for your essay. (See pp. 454–460 for help with this mode of development.)

3. Both "The Red Convertible" and the film *American Beauty* open with fore-shadowing that is explicit in the film, when the narrator announces he'll be dead within a year, and more subtle in the short story, when Lyman states that he owned the car with his brother until Henry's "boots filled with water." Compare the effects of foreshadowing on the reader or audience. How are the ultimate tragic dimensions of each work influenced by these opening statements? (See pp. 288–298 for material on the film *American Beauty*.)

Los Vendidos[1]

Luis Valdez

Director, actor, and playwright, Luis Valdez (b. 1940) is acclaimed in the worlds of stage and film. The son of migrant farmworkers, Valdez earned his B.A. in English from San Jose State University and worked as a lecturer at the University of California at Berkeley and at Santa Cruz. In 1965, he founded El Teatro Campesino to support the grape boycott and farmworkers' strike. His major plays include *Zoot Suit* (1978), which was made into a film in 1982, and *I Don't Have to Show You No Stinking Badges* (1986). In 1987 he directed

---

[1]The Sellouts

La Bamba, a film about Chicano pop musician Ritchie Valens, and in 1994 he wrote and directed the television screenplay *The Cisco Kid. Mummified Deer and Other Plays* was published in 2005. In his theatrical works Valdez created the *acto*—a drama written in both English and Spanish intended to educate and entertain farmworkers as well as urban audiences. *Los Vendidos,* first produced in 1967, is an example of this form.

CHARACTERS

HONEST SANCHO

SECRETARY

FARMWORKER

JOHNNY

REVOLUCIONARIO

MEXICAN AMERICAN

[Scene: Honest Sancho's Used Mexican Lot and Mexican Curio Shop. Three models are on display in Honest Sancho's shop: to the right, there is a Revolucionario, complete with sombrero, carrilleras,² and carabina 30-30. At center, on the floor, there is the Farmworker, under a broad straw sombrero. At stage left is the Pachuco,³ filero⁴ in hand.]

[Honest Sancho is moving among his models, dusting them off and preparing for another day of business.]

SANCHO: Bueno, bueno, mis monos, vamos a ver a quien vendemos ahora, ¿no? [*To audience.*] ¡Quihubo!⁵ I'm Honest Sancho and this is my shop. Antes fui contratista pero ahora logré tener mi negocito.⁶ All I need now is a customer. [*A bell rings offstage.*] Ay, a customer!

SECRETARY: [*entering*] Good morning, I'm Miss Jimenez from—

SANCHO: ¡Ah, una chicana! Welcome, welcome Señorita Jiménez.

SECRETARY: [*Anglo pronunciation*] JIM-enez.

SANCHO: ¿Qué?

SECRETARY: My name is Miss JIM-enez. Don't you speak English? What's wrong with you?

SANCHO: Oh, nothing, Señorita *Jim*-enez. I'm here to help you.

SECRETARY: That's better. As I was starting to say, I'm a secretary from the state office building, and we're looking for a Mexican type for the administration.

---

²Cartridge belts.
³Chicano youths of the 1940s and 1950s who belonged to street gangs.
⁴Knife (*pachuco* slang)
⁵Okay, okay, my darlings, let's see which one of you we're going to sell now—right? What's up?
⁶I used to be a labor contractor, but now I have my own little business.

SANCHO: Well, you come to the right place, lady. This is Honest Sancho's Used Mexican Lot, and we got all types here. Any particular type you want?

SECRETARY: Yes, we were looking for somebody suave—

SANCHO: Suave.

SECRETARY: Debonair.

SANCHO: De buen aire.

SECRETARY: Dark.

SANCHO: Prieto.

SECRETARY: But of course not too dark.

SANCHO: No muy prieto.

SECRETARY: Perhaps, beige.

SANCHO: Beige, just the tone. Así como cafecito con leche, ¿no?[7]

SECRETARY: One more thing. He must be hardworking.

SANCHO: That could only be one model. Step right over here to the center of the shop lady. (*They cross to the Farmworker.*) This is our standard farmworker model. Take special notice of his four-ply Goodyear huaraches, made from the rain tire. This wide-brimmed sombrero is an extra added feature—keeps off the sun, rain, and dust.

SECRETARY: Yes, it does look durable.

SANCHO: And our farmworker model is friendly. Muy amable.[8] Watch. (*Snaps his fingers.*)

FARMWORKER: (*lifts up head*) Buenos días, señorita. (*His head drops.*)

SECRETARY: My, he's friendly.

SANCHO: Didn't I tell you? Loves his patrones![9] But his most attractive feature is that he's hardworking. Let me show you. (*Snaps fingers. Farmworker stands.*)

FARMWORKER: ¡El jale![10] (*He begins to work.*)

SANCHO: As you can see, he is cutting grapes.

SECRETARY: Oh, I wouldn't know.

SANCHO: He also picks cotton. (*Snap. Farmworker begins to pick cotton.*)

SECRETARY: Versatile, isn't he?

SANCHO: He also picks melons. (*Snap. Farmworker picks melons.*) That's his slow speed for late in the season. Here's his fast speed. (*Snap. Farmworker picks faster.*)

SECRETARY: Chihuahua . . . I mean, goodness, he sure is a hard worker.

---

[7]Somewhat like the color of coffee with milk—right?
[8]Very friendly.
[9]Bosses
[10]Work! (*pachuco* slang)

SANCHO: *(pulls the Farmworker to his feet)* And that isn't the half of it. Do you see these little holes on his arms that appear to be pores? During those hot sluggish days in the field when the vines or the branches get so entangled it's almost impossible to move, these holes emit a certain grease that allows our model to slip and slide right through the crop with no trouble at all.

SECRETARY: Wonderful. But is he economical?

SANCHO: Economical? Señorita, you are looking at the Volkswagen of Mexicans. Pennies a day is all it takes. One plate of beans and tortillas will keep him going all day. That, and chile. Plenty of chile. Chile jalapeños, chile verde, chile colorado. But, of course, if you do give him chile *(Snap. Farmworker turns left face. Snap. Farmworker bends over.)*, then you have to change his oil filter once a week.

SECRETARY: What about storage?

SANCHO: No problem. You know the farm labor camps our Honorable Governor Reagan has built out by Parlier or Raisin City? They were designed with our model in mind. Five, six, seven, even ten in one of those shacks will give you no trouble at all. You can also put him in old barns, old cars, riverbanks. You can even leave him out in the field overnight with no worry!

SECRETARY: Remarkable.

SANCHO: And here's an added feature: every year at the end of the season, this model moves on and doesn't return until next spring.

SECRETARY: How about that. But tell me, does he speak English?

SANCHO: Another outstanding feature is that last year this model was programmed to go out on *strike!* *(Snap.)*

FARMWORKER: ¡HUELGA! ¡HUELGA! Hermanos, sálganse de esos files.[11] *(Snap. He stops.)*

SECRETARY: No! Oh no, we can't strike in the state capital.

SANCHO: Well, he also scabs. *(Snap.)*

FARMWORKER: Me vendo barato, ¿y qué?[12] *(Snap.)*

SECRETARY: That's much better but you didn't answer my question. Does he speak English?

SANCHO: Bueno . . . no, pero[13] he has other—

SECRETARY: No.

SANCHO: Other features.

SECRETARY: *No!* He just won't do!

---

[11]STRIKE! STRIKE! Get out of those fields, brothers.
[12]I sell myself cheap—so what?
[13]Well . . . no, but

SANCHO: Okay, okay pues.[14] We have other models.

SECRETARY: I hope so. What we need is something a little more sophisticated.

SANCHO: Sophisti—¿qué?

SECRETARY: An urban model.

SANCHO: Ah, from the city! Step right back. Over here in this corner of the shop is exactly what you're looking for. Introducing our new Johnny Pachuco model! This is our fastback model. Streamlined. Built for speed, low-riding, city life. Take a look at some of these features. Mag shoes, dual exhausts, jet black paint-job, dark-tint windshield, a little poof on top. Let me just turn him on. *(Snap. Johnny walks to stage center with a pachuco bounce.)*

SECRETARY: What was that?

SANCHO: That, señorita, was the Chicano shuffle.

SECRETARY: Okay, what does he do?

SANCHO: Anything and everything necessary for city life. For instance, survival: he knife-fights. *(Snap. Johnny pulls out switchblade and swings at Secretary.)*

[Secretary screams.]

SANCHO: He dances. *(Snap.)*

[Johnny sings and dances. Sancho snaps his fingers.]

SANCHO: And here's a feature no city model can be without. He gets arrested, but not without resisting, of course. *(Snap.)*

JOHNNY: I didn't do it! I didn't do it! *(Johnny turns and stands up against an imaginary wall, legs spread out, arms behind his back.)*

SECRETARY: Oh no, we can't have arrests! We must maintain law and order.

SANCHO: But he's bilingual!

SECRETARY: Bilingual?

SANCHO: Simón que yes.[15] He speaks English! Johnny, give us some English. *(Snap.)*

JOHNNY: *(comes downstage)* Down with whites! Brown power!

SECRETARY: *(gasps)* Oh! He can't say that!

SANCHO: Well, he learned it in your school.

SECRETARY: I don't care where he learned it.

SANCHO: But he's economical!

SECRETARY: Economical?

SANCHO: Nickels and dimes. You can keep Johnny running on hamburgers, Taco Bell tacos, Lucky Lager beer, Thunderbird wine, yesca—

SECRETARY: ¿Yesca?

---

[14]then

[15]Yes indeedy. *(pachuco slang)*

SANCHO: Mota.

SECRETARY: ¿Mota?

SANCHO: Leños . . . *Marijuana. (Snap. Johnny inhales on an imaginary joint.)*

SECRETARY: That's against the law!

JOHNNY: *(big smile, holding his breath)* Yeah.

SANCHO: He also snorts coke. *(Snap. Johnny snorts coke. Big smile.)*

JOHNNY: That's too much, ése.[16]

SECRETARY: No, Mr. Sancho, I don't think this—

SANCHO: Wait a minute, he has other qualities I know you'll love. For example, an inferiority complex. *(Snap.)*

JOHNNY: *(to Sancho)* You think you're better than me, huh, ése? *(Swings switch-blade.)*

SANCHO: He can also be beaten and he bruises; cut him and he bleeds; kick him and he—*(He beats, bruises, and kicks Johnny.)* Would you like to try it?

SECRETARY: Oh, I couldn't.

SANCHO: Be my guest. He's a great scapegoat.

SECRETARY: No really.

SANCHO: Please.

SECRETARY: Well, all right. Just once. *(She kicks Johnny.)* Oh, he's so soft.

SANCHO: Wasn't that good? Try again.

SECRETARY: *(kicks Johnny)* Oh, he's so wonderful! *(She kicks him again.)*

SANCHO: Okay, that's enough, lady. You ruin the merchandise. Yes, our Johnny Pachuco model can give you many hours of pleasure. Why, one police department just bought twenty of these to train their rookie cops on. And talk about maintenance. Señorita, you are look-ing at an entirely self-supporting machine. You're never going to find our Johnny Pachuco model on the relief rolls. No, sir, this model knows how to liberate.

SECRETARY: Liberate?

SANCHO: He steals. *(Snap. Johnny rushes the secretary and steals her purse.)*

JOHNNY: ¡Dame esa bolsa, vieja![17] *(He grabs the purse and runs. Snap by Sancho. He stops.)*

[Secretary runs after Johnny and grabs purse away from him, kicking him as she goes.]

SECRETARY: No, no, no! We can't have any more thieves in our state adminis-tration. Put him back.

SANCHO: Okay, we still got other models. Come on, Johnny, we'll sell you to some old lady. *(Sancho takes Johnny back to his place.)*

---

[16]Man (*pachuco* slang)

[17]Gimme that purse, lady!

SECRETARY: Mr. Sancho, I don't think you quite understand what we need. What we need is something that will attract the women voters. Something more traditional, more romantic.

SANCHO: Ah, a lover. *(He smiles meaningfully.)* Step right over here, señorita. Introducing our standard Revolucionario and/or Early California Bandit type. As you can see, he is well built, sturdy, durable. This is the International Harvestor of Mexicans.

SECRETARY: What does he do?

SANCHO: You name it, he does it. He rides horses, stays in the mountains, crosses deserts, plains, rivers, leads revolutions, follows revolutions, kills, can be killed, serves as a martyr, hero, movie star—did I say movie star? Did you ever see *Viva Zapata? Viva Villa, Villa Rides, Pancho Villa Returns, Pancho Villa Goes Back, Pancho Villa Meets Abbott and Costello . . .*

SECRETARY: I've never seen any of those.

SANCHO: Well, he was in all of them. Listen to this. *(Snap.)*

REVOLUCIONARIO: *(scream)* ¡VIVA VILLAAAAA!

SECRETARY: That's awfully loud.

SANCHO: He has a volume control. *(He adjusts volume. Snap.)*

REVOLUCIONARIO: *(mousy voice)* Viva Villa.

SECRETARY: That's better.

SANCHO: And even if you didn't see him in the movies, perhaps you saw him on TV. He makes commercials. *(Snap.)*

REVOLUCIONARIO: Is there a Frito Bandito in your house?

SECRETARY: Oh yes, I've seen that one!

SANCHO: Another feature about this one is that he is economical. He runs on raw horsemeat and tequila!

SECRETARY: Isn't that rather savage?

SANCHO: Al contrario,[18] it makes him a lover. *(Snap.)*

REVOLUCIONARIO: *(to Secretary)* ¡Ay, mamasota, cochota, ven pa'cá![19] *(He grabs Secretary and folds her back, Latin-lover style.)*

SANCHO: *(Snap. Revolucionario goes back upright.)* Now wasn't that nice?

SECRETARY: Well, it was rather nice.

SANCHO: And finally, there is one outstanding feature about this model I *know* the ladies are going to love: he's a *genuine* antique! He was made in Mexico in 1910!

SECRETARY: Made in Mexico?

SANCHO: That's right. Once in Tijuana, twice in Guadalajara, three times in Cuernavaca.

---

[18]On the contrary
[19]Oh mama, you cute thing, come over here!

SECRETARY: Mr. Sancho, I thought he was an American product.

SANCHO: No, but—

SECRETARY: No, I'm sorry. We can't buy anything but American made products. He just won't do.

SANCHO: But, he's an antique!

SECRETARY: I don't care. You still don't understand what we need. It's true we need Mexican models such as these, but it's more important that he be *American.*

SANCHO: American?

SECRETARY: That's right, and judging from what you've shown me, I don't think you have what we want. Well, my lunch hour's almost over, I better—

SANCHO: Wait a minute! Mexican but American?

SECRETARY: That's correct.

SANCHO: Mexican but . . . *(A sudden flash) American!* Yeah, I think we've got exactly what you want. He just came in today! Give me a minute. *(He exits. Talks from backstage.)* Here he is in the shop. Let me just get some papers off. There. Introducing our new Mexican American! Ta-ra-ra-ra-ra-RA-RAAA!

[Sancho brings out the Mexican American model, a clean-shaven middle-class type in a business suit, with glasses.]

SECRETARY: *(impressed)* Where have you been hiding this one?

SANCHO: He just came in this morning. Ain't he a beauty? Feast your eyes on him! Sturdy U.S. steel frame, streamlined, modern. As a matter of fact, he is built exactly like our Anglo models except that he comes in a variety of darker shades: Naugahyde, leather, or leatherette.

SECRETARY: Naugahyde.

SANCHO: Well, we'll just write that down. Yes, señorita, this model represents the apex of American engineering! He is bilingual, college-educated, ambitious! Say the word *acculturate* and he accelerates. He is intelligent, well-mannered, clean—did I say clean? *(Snap. Mexican American raises his arm.)* Smell.

SECRETARY: *(smells)* Old Sobaco,[20] my favorite.

SANCHO: *(Snap. Mexican American turns toward Sancho.)* Eric? *(To Secretary)* We call him Eric García. *(To Eric)* I want you to meet Miss *Jim*-enez, Eric.

MEXICAN AMERICAN: Miss *Jim*-enez, I am delighted to make your acquaintance. *(He kisses her hand.)*

SECRETARY: Oh, my, how charming!

---

[20]Old Armpit

SANCHO: Did you feel the suction? He has seven especially engineered suction cups right behind his lips. He's a charmer, all right!

SECRETARY: How about boards—does he function on boards?

SANCHO: You name them, he is on them. Parole boards, draft boards, school boards, taco quality control boards, surfboards, two-by-fours.

SECRETARY: Does he function in politics?

SANCHO: Señorita, you are looking at a political *machine*. Have you ever heard of the OEO, EEOC, COD, War on Poverty? That's our model! Not only that, he makes political speeches.

SECRETARY: May I hear one?

SANCHO: With pleasure. *(Snap.)* Eric, give us a speech

MEXICAN AMERICAN: Mr. Congressman, Mr. Chairman, members of the board, honored guests, ladies and gentlemen. *(Sancho and Secretary applaud.)* Please, please. I come before you as a Mexican American to tell you about the problems of the Mexican. The problems of the Mexican stem from one thing and one thing alone: he's stupid. He's uneducated. He needs to stay in school. He needs to be ambitious, forward-looking, harder-working. He needs to think American, American, American, AMERICAN, AMERICAN, AMERICAN. GOD BLESS AMERICA! GOD BLESS AMERICA! GOD BLESS AMERICA!! *(He goes out of control.)*

[Sancho snaps frantically and the Mexican American finally slumps forward, bending at the waist.]

SECRETARY: Oh my, he's patriotic too!

SANCHO: Sí, señorita, he loves his country. Let me just make a little adjustment here. *(Stands Mexican American up.)*

SECRETARY: What about upkeep? Is he economical?

SANCHO: Well, no, I won't lie to you. The Mexican American costs a little bit more, but you get what you pay for. He's worth every extra cent. You can keep him running on dry Martinis and steaks.

SECRETARY: Apple pie?

SANCHO: Only Mom's. Of course, he's also programmed to eat Mexican food at ceremonial functions, but I must warn you: an overdose of beans will plug up his exhaust.

SECRETARY: Fine! There's just one more question: *How much do you want for him?*

SANCHO: Well, I tell you what I'm gonna do. Today and today only, because you've been so sweet, I'm gonna let you steal this model from me! I'm gonna let you drive him off the lot for the simple price of—let's see, taxes and license included—fifteen thousand dollars.

SECRETARY: Fifteen thousand *dollars?* For a *Mexican?*

SANCHO: Mexican? What are you talking, lady? This is a Mexican *American!* We had to melt down two pachucos, a farmworker, and three gaba-chos[21] to make this model! You want quality, but you gotta pay for it! This is no cheap runabout. He's got class!

SECRETARY: Okay, I'll take him.

SANCHO: You will?

SECRETARY: Here's your money.

SANCHO: You mind if I count it?

SECRETARY: Go right ahead.

SANCHO: Well, you'll get your pink slip in the mail. Oh, do you want me to wrap him up for you? We have a box in the back.

SECRETARY: No, thank you. The Governor is having a luncheon this afternoon, and we need a brown face in the crowd. How do I drive him?

SANCHO: Just snap your fingers. He'll do anything you want.

[Secretary snaps. Mexican American steps forward.]

MEXICAN AMERICAN: ¡RAZA QUERIDA, VAMOS LEVANTANDO ARMAS PARA LIBERARNOS DE ESTOS DESGRACIADOS GABACHOS QUE NOS EXPLOTAN! VAMOS—[22]

SECRETARY: What did he say?

SANCHO: Something about lifting arms, killing white people, and so on.

SECRETARY: But he's not supposed to say that!

SANCHO: Look, lady, don't blame me for bugs from the factory. He's your Mexican American, you bought him, now drive him off the lot!

SECRETARY: But he's broken!

SANCHO: Try snapping another finger.

[Secretary snaps. Mexican American comes to life again.]

MEXICAN AMERICAN: ¡ESTA GRAN HUMANIDAD HA DICHO BASTA! ¡Y SE HA PUESTO EN MARCHA! ¡BASTA! ¡BASTA! ¡VIVA LA RAZA! ¡VIVA LA CAUSA! ¡VIVA LA HUELGA! ¡VIVAN LOS BROWN BERETS! ¡VIVAN LOS ESTUDIANTES![23] CHICANO POWER!

[The Mexican American turns toward the Secretary, who gasps and backs up. He keeps turning toward the Pachuco, Farmworker, and Revolucionario, snapping his fingers and turning each of them on, one by one.]

---

[21]Anglos

[22]Beloved Chicano people, let us take up arms to liberate ourselves from these despicable Anglos that exploit us! Let us—

[23]This great mass of humanity has said, Enough! And it begins to march! Enough! Enough! Long live the Chicano people! Long live La Causa! Long live the strike! Long live the Brown Berets! Long live the students!

PACHUCO: *(Snap. To Secretary)* I'm going to get you, baby! Viva la Raza!

FARMWORKER: *(Snap. To Secretary)* ¡Viva la huelga! ¡Viva la huelga! ¡VIVA LA HUELGA!

REVOLUCIONARIO: *(Snap. To Secretary)* ¡Viva la revolucion! ¡VIVA LA REVOLUCION!

[The three models join together and advance toward the Secretary, who backs up and runs out of the shop screaming. Sancho is at the other end of the shop holding his money in his hand. All freeze. After a few seconds of silence, the Pachuco moves and stretches, shaking his arms and loosening up. The Farmworker and Revolucionario do the same. Sancho stays where he is, frozen to his spot.]

JOHNNY: Man, that was a long one, ése. *(Others agree with him.)*

FARMWORKER: How did we do?

JOHNNY: Perty good, look all that lana,[24] man! *(He goes over to Sancho and removes the money from his hand. Sancho stays where he is.)*

REVOLUCIONARIO: En la madre, look at all the money.

JOHNNY: We keep this up, we're going to be rich.

FARMWORKER: They think we're machines.

REVOLUCIONARIO: Burros.

JOHNNY: Puppets.

MEXICAN AMERICAN: The only thing I don't like is, how come I always got to play the Mexican American?

JOHNNY: That's what you get for finishing high school.

FARMWORKER: How about our wages, ése?

JOHNNY: Here it comes right now. Three thousand dollars for you, three thousand for you, three thousand for you, and three thousand for me. The rest we put back into the business.

MEXICAN AMERICAN: Too much, man. Hey, where you vatos[25] going tonight?

FARMWORKER: I'm going over to Concha's. There's a party.

JOHNNY: Wait a minute, vatos. What about our salesman? I think he needs an oil job.

REVOLUCIONARIO: Leave him to me.

[The Pachuco, Farmworker, and Mexican American exit, talking loudly about their plans for the night. The Revolucionario goes over to Sancho, removes his derby hat and cigar, lifts him up and throws him over his shoulder. Sancho hangs loose, lifeless.]

REVOLUCIONARIO: *(to audience)* He's the best model we got! ¡Ajua! *(Exit.)*

---

[24]Money (colloquial).

[25]Guys; dudes *(pachuco* slang)

THINKING ABOUT THE TEXT

1. What is Valdez's strategy of setting this play in "Honest Sancho's Used Mexican Lot and Mexican Curio Shop"? How does this setting establish the tone and theme of this play?

2. How does Valdez depict the secretary and how does she see herself? Use specific quotations to support your interpretations.

3. Identify the stereotypes that Valdez uses and analyze his purpose in doing so.

4. What is ironic about "Honest Sancho" and how do you explain the twist at the end? What is Valdez suggesting in this ending?

5. What is the significance of the title, "The Sellouts"? According to Valdez, who are the sellouts and why?

6. Why does Valdez use both English and Spanish in this play? How do you feel about this mixing of languages? If you don't understand Spanish, would you have been able to follow the play without translations in the footnotes? Why?

7. Examine this play as a satire: a literary work that uses humor, ridicule, and exaggeration to expose or criticize certain values, beliefs, myths, practices, or institutions. What are the targets of Valdez's satire and what is he criticizing about each?

WRITING FROM THE TEXT

1. Focusing on the mixture of English and Spanish in *Los Vendidos,* write an essay arguing that the mixing of languages adds to or detracts from an understanding of the play. Include specific quotations from the play to illustrate your claims.

2. In an essay on stereotypes, analyze how Valdez's use of Mexican stereotypes underscores the themes of this play.

3. If you have experienced stereotyping or exploitation because of your culture, write an evaluative response essay relating your experiences to specific conflicts or attitudes in this play.

4. Using materials gathered for exercise 7, write an analytic essay examining the targets of Valdez's satire. Explain what he is exposing and criticizing throughout this play.

CONNECTING WITH OTHER TEXTS

1. Read "Don't Let Stereotypes Warp Your Judgments" (p. 470) and write an essay using examples from Valdez's play to support and illustrate Heilbroner's points and cautions.

2. Read "The Myth of the Latin Woman" (p. 172), and write an essay showing how Cofer's experiences reflect those Luis Valdez satirizes. You may include your own observations to create an amusing essay.

3. Focusing on the purposes and strategies involved in satire, write an essay examining the aspects of American society satirized in both "Coke" (p. 243) and *Los Vendidos*. You may want to focus your thesis on common targets of satire.

4. Write an essay contrasting the attitudes, values, and experiences of the fictional characters in Luis Valdez's play with the actual experiences of Alfredo Quiñones-Hinojosa (p. 116).

Chapter 4

Between Perceptions

How we perceive ourselves is intrinsically related to our racial and ethnic roots, as well as to our gender. Our sense of self, however, goes beyond any definition of male or female, race or culture. Self-perception is often conditioned by the roles we assume—as students, workers, family members—but our self-image and how others see us may be distinct from the roles we play. You regard yourself as a college student, but when you are at home you might be the "baby" in the family, or the one diapering the baby. You know that by working extra hours you can earn much-needed overtime pay, but your perception of yourself as an "A" student prompts you to cut back on hours instead. A woman who is physically disabled may not define herself as "handicapped," and a man who qualifies for financial assistance may not see himself as "disadvantaged." Perceiving oneself beyond labels or stereotypes is an essential process, as the readings in this chapter indicate

However, others' images of you do influence your self-perception. If you feel that you are constantly trying to exist among worlds that perceive you differently, you will relate to the tensions described in the essays by Matthew Soyster and Jennifer Coleman as they resist others' limited perceptions of them. Their essays express the frustrations of productive individuals whose self-acceptance is threatened by the delimiting views of others.

Self-perception can be altered in a moment of intense reflection, as we see in the epiphanies narrated by John Vaughn and Max Thayer. Focusing on her own life epiphanies, J. K. Rowling, the creator of the *Harry Potter* series, encourages readers to perceive the benefit of "failure" and the "crucial importance of imagination" in our lives.

Sometimes negative perceptions may prompt people to make unwise choices that threaten their health. In "Bodily Harm," Pamela Erens chronicles the problems of many women who have eating disorders and who struggle toward self-understanding and acceptance rather than perpetuating destructive behavior. Neil Steinberg humorously accepts the fact that he's fat even as he regrets the attitudes of some thin people around him. In contrast, Jane E. Brody and Michael Pollan want to change people's complacent perception of obesity and improve everyone's eating habits. Dan Neil wants to alter his readers' judgmental perceptions of homosexuality, arguing that sexual orientation is as innate in homosexuals as it is in heterosexuals.

To be perceived as an individual rather than as a racial or ethnic stereotype may be a challenge for you or some of your friends. Fighting stereotypes can be life-threatening, as Brent Staples and Debra Dickerson reveal in their essays, or irritating, as Judith Ortiz Cofer shows in hers. In his poem "Facing It," Yusef Komanyakaa shows that painful life experiences can also obscure perceptions of self. Balancing how others see us with who we think we are is the condition of being between perceptions—and the basis of the writings in this chapter.

◖◗ Living Under Circe's Spell ◖◗

Matthew Soyster

A freelance writer, editor, and college instructor, Matthew Soyster (b. 1954) earned a B.A. in French and Italian literature from Stanford and an M.A. in English and Norwegian literature from the University of California at Berkeley. His work has appeared in *Newsweek, Stanford Magazine*, the *San Francisco Examiner*, and numerous other publications. Soyster has been associate editor of *Change Magazine* and a repeated guest on KPFA-FM radio, discussing images of the disabled—"Monster/Victim/Hero"—in Western film literature and popular culture. In 1989 he organized a $10,000 benefit concert for the Multiple Sclerosis Society, and in 1991 he wrote and performed "Shape Shifter," a monologue for the premiere of the Contemporary Dance Company at a Berkeley theater. The following article appeared in *Newsweek* in 1993.

1   "Life is brief, time's a thief." This ribbon of pop lyricism keens from an apartment-house radio into the hot afternoon air. Across the street I am sprawled in the gutter behind my minivan, bits of glass and scrap metal chewing at my knees and elbows, a cut on my hand beginning to well crimson.

2   There has been no assailant, no wound except to my psyche. I'm just a clumsy cripple whose legs buckled before he reached his wheelchair. A moment ago I yanked it from my tailgate, as I've done a thousand times.

But when it spun off at a crazy angle I missed the seat and slumped to the ground.

3   Now the spasms start, shooting outward from the small of my back, forcing me prone, grinding my cheek into the asphalt. What will I look like to the first casual passerby before he catches sight of the telltale chair? A wine-soaked rummy? A hit-and-run victim? Maybe an amateur mechanic checking the rear suspension, wrong side up.

4   I'm too young and vital looking to be this helpless. I shrink from the inevitable clucking and concern. Then again, this isn't the best neighborhood. The first person to come along may simply kick me and take my wallet. No wonder I'm ambivalent about rescue, needing but not wanting to be discovered. With detachment I savor the hush of this deserted street, the symphony of birdsong in the treetops.

5   I am trying to remember T. S. Eliot's line about waiting without hope, because hope would be hope for the wrong thing. Instead, that idiot TV commercial for the medical alarm-pager keeps ringing through my brain: "Help me. I've fallen and I can't get up."

6   It was only a matter of time. I've known for months that my hair's-breadth maneuvering would eventually fail me. For years, in fact. When I first learned that I had multiple sclerosis I was a marathon runner and white-water-rafting guide, a cyclist and skier, the quintessential California golden boy. Cardiovascular fitness had long since become our state religion. I lived for and through my legs.

7   But that's only the ad-slick surface of the California dream, the sunshine without the shadow. The town I live in is also the mecca of the disabled, the home of the Independent Living Movement, the place where broken people come to patch together their dignity and their dreams.

8   Yin and yang. In Berkeley, there are wheelchair users on every corner. Propped in sagging hospital-issue chairs. Space-age sports chairs. Motor-driven dreadnoughts. When I could still walk, I crossed the street to avoid them. What an odd tribe they seemed, with their spindly, agitated limbs, always hurtling down the avenue on some manic errand.

9   How could I imagine my own swift decline? A few months or years passed. Soon I was relying on a cane, then crutches, and finally—after many thigh-bruising falls and a numbness so intense it turned my legs to driftwood—a wheelchair. My response to these limitations was compensation and denial. I thought I could become a disabled Olympian: wheelchair racing, tennis, rugby. I thought I could go on as before.

10   Wrong again. To paraphrase Tolstoy, all able-bodied people are alike, but each disabled person is crippled in his own way. MS not only played havoc with my upper-body strength and agility; it clouded my mind and sapped my

energy. I could totter a few steps supported at both wrists, but my days in the winter surf, high peaks and desert canyons were over.

11   So what is it like to spend your life forked at the waist, face-level with children? The syndrome has been amply described. People see through me now, or over me. They don't see me at all. Or they fix me with that plangent, aching stare: sympathy.

12   They offer too much assistance, scurrying to open doors, scrambling out of my way with unnecessary apologies, or they leave me no space at all, barking their shins on my foot pedals. My spirit rallies in the face of such humiliations; they have their comic aspect. What disturbs me most is not how others see me, but how I've lost my vision of myself.

13   Growing crippled is a bitch. First your body undergoes a strange enchantment: Circe's spell. Then your identity gives way. You become someone or something other, but for a long time you're not sure what that other is.

14   Along the way, I've had to give up activities and passions that define me, my safe position in society, my very sense of manhood. In our species, the pecking order is distinctly vertical. True for women. Doubly true for men. A man stands tall, stands firm, stands up for things. These are more than metaphors. The very act of sitting implies demotion. Anyone who's witnessed boardroom politics knows this much. Have a seat, barks the boss. It's not an invitation, it's an order.

15   All of this brings me back to the gutter, where I lie listening to birdsong, recognizing but not apologizing for the obstinacy that landed me here. For months my friends and family have watched my legs grow weaker. They've prodded me relentlessly to refit my van with a wheelchair lift in order to avoid just this disaster. But I've refused.

16   Twice a day at least, I've dragged my reluctant legs from beneath the steering column, hauled myself erect beside the driver's seat, inched my way down the roof rail to the rear stowage. And removed the chair by hand, standing.

17   Why have I clung to this ritual, knowing it's dangerous and futile? It's the only task I rise for anymore, in a sitting life. For a moment in the driver's doorway, I'm in control, unreliant on technology or assistance, upright. Or so I've told myself. But that moment is so fragile, the control so illusory.

18   When the time comes to change, I've said, I'll know.

19   Now I know.

20   I feel the lesson, sharp as the rap of a Zen master's stick. Lying in the hot gutter, I take a deep breath and my whole body relaxes. Tuning in to Rod Stewart's tinny wisdom from the window. Listening for a passing car or pedestrian.

21   Waiting.

THINKING ABOUT THE TEXT

1. This essay opens with the writer "sprawled in the gutter" and ends with him still "waiting" for a passing car or pedestrian to help. Analyze the effect of creating such a scene to prompt his discussion and of using the present tense (even though this event happened in the past).

2. Describe, in detail, the writer's life and his attitude about the disabled before he himself became "a clumsy cripple."

3. Soyster explains, "What disturbs me most is not how others see me, but how I've lost my vision of myself" (160). What does he mean by this, and how does his threatened self-image relate to his refusal to refit his van with a wheelchair lift?

4. Throughout this essay Soyster includes a number of *allusions*—indirect references to sources outside the work: pop lyrics, singer Rod Stewart, poet T. S. Eliot, novelist Leo Tolstoy, the myth of Circe, the Zen religion, and yin and yang. Look up these allusions in a dictionary, reader's encyclopedia, or online and explain how each contributes to your understanding of the writer and his perspective.

WRITING FROM THE TEXT

1. Using the information you gathered for exercise 4, write an essay explaining how the allusions in this essay are essential to helping us see the writer as a unique and intriguing individual and not just "a clumsy cripple."

2. Write about an event in your life that caused you to lose a vision of yourself. Dramatize your life before this crisis or event and contrast it with your current life.

CONNECTING WITH OTHER TEXTS

1. Matthew Soyster and Shannon Paaske (p. 542) both examine the attitudes that many harbor toward the disabled. Using details from these works, write an essay supporting your own thesis about how and why people feel uneasy around the disabled—and what can be done about it.

2. Matthew Soyster, Brent Staples (p. 181), and Jennifer Coleman (p. 198) describe how others have incorrectly stereotyped and humiliated them. Using details from any of these narratives and from "Don't Let Stereotypes Warp Your Judgments" (p. 470), write an analysis of the causes and effects of such stereotyping on the stereotyped person and on the one doing the stereotyping.

The Difference Between Pity and Empathy

John A. Vaughn

Serving as both physician and senior editor for Health Care Multi-Media Communications at the Ohio State University Student Health Services, John A. Vaughn (b. 1971) has been able to combine his talents as a doctor and a writer. In addition to practicing medicine, Vaughn has written numerous reviews of medical books as well as guest columns and articles for publications such as the *Los Angeles Times,* The *San Francisco Chronicle,* and *The Cleveland Plain Dealer.* Vaughn offers this advice for student writers: "Read as much and as widely as possible. Revise, revise, revise. Always remember that no matter how fantastic the situation, it is the personal element of a story that connects to your reader." The following essay first appeared in the *Los Angeles Times,* March 28, 2005, and clearly shows that Vaughn follows his own advice.

1   He was the first patient I cared for in medical school. At first glance, he looked pretty good. He sat on the covers of his hospital bed in a button-down shirt that was tucked neatly into creased khakis. His shoes gleamed from polish.

But I quickly saw that the fastidious clothes were a disguise. His skin looked like old china: yellowed and glassy with a damp patina. His dyed blond hair was matted down in a wide part and his precisely trimmed mustache was covered by a fine mist of sweat.

2   He had AIDS. Pneumocystis pneumonia clogged his lungs, cytomegalovirus retinitis clouded his eyes and Kaposi's sarcoma ulcerated his esophagus. He was dying an agonizing death. And he was only 30. I stumbled through my painfully thorough evaluation, pulling reflex hammers, flashlights and tuning forks out of my lab coat like a bad magician.

3   I did a rectal exam to check for internal bleeding and gamely tried to explain the mechanics of the exam—only to be met with a statement that he was gay, followed by a humorless joke about his sexual practices.

4   Despite my inexperience, I knew that men often deflect their embarrassment at this exam with locker room humor. But his comment still caught me off guard. I awkwardly laughed at the joke and pulled gloves onto my shaking hands.

Apparently this wasn't the response he was looking for, because as he dropped his pants he continued, this time with a comment about romance.

5   He wasn't simply deflecting his embarrassment; he was throwing it back at me with as much resentment as he could muster. My first instinct was to

retaliate. To say "Hey, pal, don't blame me. You got yourself in this mess. I'm just trying to help." Instead, I finished the exam in silence and left the room as quickly as possible. We were both so furious and afraid; he at being eaten away by this horrible disease, and me at feeling like an inadequate idiot because I had no idea how to help him.

6   I went to visit him the next day, determined that things would go better. His room revealed no signs of a life beyond its walls: not a single get-well card tacked to the bulletin board, not one little fold-up tent card on the bed-side table notifying him of a missed call from a friend. I had never seen someone so alone. I asked him what he did for a living. He told me that he worked in computer networking and was hoping to finish his design for a new audiovisual coupling technique before he died.

7   He said it was his last chance to make a mark on the world. This seemed to sadden him more than his physical suffering; it wasn't that his life was ending, but that he would have so little to show for it.

I asked him about his family. Unlike many gay AIDS victims, his parents were tolerant of his lifestyle and even offered to care for him during his illness. I offered to call them but he adamantly refused. He said it would be too hard on his mom.

8   The familiarity with which he said this caught my breath. The outside world flooded into the room, and I suddenly saw this man not as a patient, but as someone's son. I finally got a taste of the anguish he was trying to make me feel the day before. His condition worsened precipitously the next night and I finally convinced him to let me call his parents. They said they would leave as soon as they could but they lived in New Jersey, nine hours away.

9   He died during rounds the following morning. As his pupils dilated and his breathing became a rhythmic, mechanical gasp, his nurse reached out and held his hand. I grabbed his other wrist as if to check for a pulse, hoping the gesture appeared sufficiently clinical to my attending physician.

10   An hour later, his parents called from a rest stop in Pennsylvania about four hours away. I thought his mother would be more upset, but I got the feeling, that she expected things to end this way. He had underestimated her; she had been strong enough to respect his need to spare her suffering, even though she knew it meant that she might never see him again. He had underestimated himself too. He never saw the doctor that he helped me become, but every patient I have cared for since has benefited from the lesson he taught me.

11   I had leaned into our conversations with all the sympathetic voice inflections and reassuring touches I could muster from my doctor-patient

relationship class. But I had looked at him with pity, not empathy, and he saw right through me. It wasn't until he made me see him as a person that I was able to effectively treat him as my patient. The mark he made on the world extended further than he'd imagined.

THINKING ABOUT THE TEXT

1. How does Vaughn's detailed description of his patient both prepare readers for his patient's illness and yet shock readers as they discover that the patient is only 30 and yet "dying an agonizing death"? What are his AIDS-related ailments?

2. Why are both doctor and patient "furious and afraid"? What seems to sadden the patient more than his physical suffering and imminent death?

3. What prompts the new doctor to see his patient differently? Explain the doctor's before-and-after perceptions of his patient.

4. What lasting legacy has the patient left this world? Explain Vaughn's distinction between pity and empathy.

WRITING FROM THE TEXT

1. Using illustrations from Vaughn's work, write an essay contrasting "pity" and "empathy" in order to support the author's argument that the latter is essential for the best patient care. You may include illustrations of doctors whom you've known to support Vaughn's claims.

2. Write an essay describing a situation when you initially felt pity for another or were pitied by someone—and then later when that emotion changed to empathy. Let the reader see what prompted the change and how it affected the way you reacted.

CONNECTING WITH OTHER TEXTS

1. Using Vaughn's essay, Quiñones-Hinojosa's "Terra Firma" (p. 116), and Soyster's "Living Under Circe's Spell" (p. 158), write an essay demonstrating the importance of empathy, rather than pity, in the treatment of those with an illness.

2. Including details from Vaughn's essay, "The Color of Love" (p. 16), and "The Only Child" (p. 34), write an essay analyzing the barriers to empathizing with others, as well as ways to overcome these barriers.

The Fringe Benefits of Failure, and the Importance of Imagination

J. K. Rowling

The author of the world-famous *Harry Potter* fantasies that have sold nearly 400 million copies, Joanne "Jo" Rowling (b. 1965), who writes under the name J. K. Rowling, is a graduate of Exeter University and a teacher. She is almost as famous for her rise to millionaire status from being an unemployed single parent on welfare as she is for her popular books. Rowling's fortune, estimated at $1.1 billion, is philanthropically used to support such charities as Comic Relief, One Parent Families and the Multiple Sclerosis Society of Great Britain. Noting her social, moral, and political commitments, in 2007 *Time Magazine* named her a runner-up for its Person of the Year Award. Rowling's humanity and wisdom are evident in the text of her June 2008 Harvard University Commencement Address, reprinted here.

1   President Faust, members of the Harvard Corporation and the Board of Overseers, members of the faculty, proud parents, and, above all, graduates.

2   The first thing I would like to say is 'thank you.' Not only has Harvard given me an extraordinary honour, but the weeks of fear and nausea I've experienced at the thought of giving this commencement address have made me lose weight. A win-win situation! Now all I have to do is take deep breaths, squint at the red banners and fool myself into believing I am at the world's best-educated Harry Potter convention.

3   Delivering a commencement address is a great responsibility; or so I thought until I cast my mind back to my own graduation. The commencement speaker that day was the distinguished British philosopher Baroness Mary Warnock. Reflecting on her speech has helped me enormously in writing this one, because it turns out that I can't remember a single word she said. This liberating discovery enables me to proceed without any fear that I might inadvertently influence you to abandon promising careers in business, law or politics for the giddy delights of becoming a gay wizard.

4   You see? If all you remember in years to come is the 'gay wizard' joke, I've still come out ahead of Baroness Mary Warnock. Achievable goals: the first step towards personal improvement.

5   Actually, I have wracked my mind and heart for what I ought to say to you today. I have asked myself what I wish I had known at my own graduation, and what important lessons I have learned in the 21 years that has expired between that day and this.

6   I have come up with two answers. On this wonderful day when we are gathered together to celebrate your academic success, I have decided to talk to you about the benefits of failure. And as you stand on the threshold of

what is sometimes called 'real life,' I want to extol the crucial importance of imagination.

7   These might seem quixotic or paradoxical choices, but please bear with me.

8   Looking back at the 21-year-old that I was at graduation, is a slightly uncomfortable experience for the 42-year-old that she has become. Half my lifetime ago, I was striking an uneasy balance between the ambition I had for myself, and what those closest to me expected of me.

9   I was convinced that the only thing I wanted to do, ever, was to write novels. However, my parents, both of whom came from improverished backgrounds and neither of whom had been to college, took the view that my overactive imagination was an amusing personal quirk that could never pay a mortgage, or secure a pension.

10   They had hoped that I would take a vocational degree; I wanted to study English Literature. A compromise was reached that in retrospect satisfied nobody, and I went up to study Modern Languages. Hardly had my parents' car rounded the corner at the end of the road than I ditched German and scuttled off down the Classics corridor.

11   I cannot remember telling my parents that I was studying Classics; they might well have found out for the first time on graduation day. Of all subjects on this planet, I think they would have been hard put to name one less useful than Greek mythology when it came to securing the keys to an executive bathroom.

12   I would like to make it clear, in parenthesis, that I do not blame my parents for their point of view. There is an expiry date on blaming your parents for steering you in the wrong direction; the moment you are old enough to take the wheel, responsibility lies with you. What is more, I cannot criticise my parents for hoping that I would never experience poverty. They had been poor themselves, and I have since been poor, and I quite agree with them that it is not an ennobling experience. Poverty entails fear, and stress, and sometimes depression; it means a thousand petty humiliations and hardships. Climbing out of poverty by your own efforts, that is indeed something on which to pride yourself, but poverty itself is romanticised only by fools.

13   What I feared most for myself at your age was not poverty, but failure.

14   At your age, in spite of a distinct lack of motivation at university, where I had spent far too long in the coffee bar writing stories, and far too little time at lectures, I had a knack for passing examinations, and that, for years, had been the measure of success in my life and that of my peers.

15   I am not dull enough to suppose that because you are young, gifted and well-educated, you have never known hardship or heartbreak. Talent and intelligence never yet inoculated anyone against the caprice of the Fates, and

I do not for a moment suppose that everyone here has enjoyed an existence of unruffled privilege and contentment.

16   However, the fact that you are graduating from Harvard suggests that you are not very well-acquainted with failure. You might be driven by a fear of failure quite as much as a desire for success. Indeed, your conception of failure might not be too far from the average person's idea of success, so high have you already flown academically.

17   Ultimately, we all have to decide for ourselves what constitutes failure, but the world is quite eager to give you a set of criteria if you let it. So I think it fair to say that by any conventional measure, a mere seven years after my graduation day, I had failed on an epic scale. An exceptionally short-lived marriage had imploded, and I was jobless, a lone parent, and as poor as it is possible to be in modern Britain, without being homeless. The fears my parents had had for me, and that I had had for myself, had both come to pass, and by every usual standard, I was the biggest failure I knew.

18   Now, I am not going to stand here and tell you that failure is fun. That period of my life was a dark one, and I had no idea that there was going to be what the press has since represented as a kind of fairy tale resolution. I had no idea how far the tunnel extended, and for a long time, any light at the end of it was a hope rather than a reality.

19   So why do I talk about the benefits of failure? Simply because failure meant a stripping away of the inessential. I stopped pretending to myself that I was anything other than what I was, and began to direct all my energy into finishing the only work that mattered to me. Had I really succeeded at anything else, I might never have found the determination to succeed in the one arena I believed I truly belonged. I was set free, because my greatest fear had already been realised, and I was still alive, and I still had a daughter whom I adored, and I had an old typewriter and a big idea. And so rock bottom became the solid foundation on which I rebuilt my life.

20   You might never fail on the scale I did, but some failure in life is inevitable. It is impossible to live without failing at something, unless you live so cautiously that you might as well not have lived at all—in which case, you fail by default.

21   Failure gave me an inner security that I had never attained by passing examinations. Failure taught me things about myself that I could have learned no other way. I discovered that I had a strong will, and more discipline than I had suspected; I also found out that I had friends whose value was truly above rubies.

22   The knowledge that you have emerged wiser and stronger from setbacks means that you are, ever after, secure in your ability to survive. You will never truly know yourself, or the strength of your relationships, until both

have been tested by adversity. Such knowledge is a true gift, for all that it is painfully won, and it has been worth more to me than any qualification I ever earned.

23   Given a time machine or a Time Turner, I would tell my 21-year-old self that personal happiness lies in knowing that life is not a check-list of acquisition or achievement. Your qualifications, your CV, are not your life, though you will meet many people of my age and older who confuse the two. Life is difficult, and complicated, and beyond anyone's total control, and the humility to know that will enable you to survive its vicissitudes.

24   You might think that I chose my second theme, the importance of imagination, because of the part it played in rebuilding my life, but that is not wholly so. Though I will defend the value of bedtime stories to my last gasp, I have learned to value imagination in a much broader sense. Imagination is not only the uniquely human capacity to envision that which is not, and therefore the fount of all invention and innovation. In its arguably most transformative and revelatory capacity, it is the power that enables us to empathise with humans whose experiences we have never shared.

25   One of the greatest formative experiences of my life preceded Harry Potter, though it informed much of what I subsequently wrote in those books. This revelation came in the form of one of my earliest day jobs. Though I was sloping off to write stories during my lunch hours, I paid the rent in my early 20s by working in the research department at Amnesty International's headquarters in London.

26   There in my little office I read hastily scribbled letters smuggled out of totalitarian regimes by men and women who were risking imprisonment to inform the outside world of what was happening to them. I saw photographs of those who had disappeared without trace, sent to Amnesty by their desperate families and friends. I read the testimony of torture victims and saw pictures of their injuries. I opened handwritten, eye-witness accounts of summary trials and executions, of kidnappings and rapes.

27   Many of my co-workers were ex-political prisoners, people who had been displaced from their homes, or fled into exile, because they had the temerity to think independently of their government. Visitors to our office included those who had come to give information, or to try and find out what had happened to those they had been forced to leave behind.

28   I shall never forget the African torture victim, a young man no older than I was at the time, who had become mentally ill after all he had endured in his homeland. He trembled uncontrollably as he spoke into a video camera about the brutality inflicted upon him. He was a foot taller than I was, and seemed as fragile as a child. I was given the job of escorting him to the Underground Station afterwards, and this man whose life had been shattered

by cruelty took my hand with exquisite courtesy, and wished me future happiness.

29 And as long as I live I shall remember walking along an empty corridor and suddenly hearing, from behind a closed door, a scream of pain and horror such as I have never heard since. The door opened, and the researcher poked out her head and told me to run and make a hot drink for the young man sitting with her. She had just given him the news that in retaliation for his own outspokenness against his country's regime, his mother had been seized and executed.

30 Every day of my working week in my early 20s I was reminded how incredibly fortunate I was, to live in a country with a democratically elected government, where legal representation and a public trial were the rights of everyone.

31 Every day, I saw more evidence about the evils humankind will inflict on their fellow humans, to gain or maintain power. I began to have nightmares, literal nightmares, about some of the things I saw, heard and read.

32 And yet I also learned more about human goodness at Amnesty International than I had ever known before.

33 Amnesty mobilises thousands of people who have never been tortured or imprisoned for their beliefs to act on behalf of those who have. The power of human empathy, leading to collective action, saves lives, and frees prisoners. Ordinary people, whose personal well-being and security are assured, join together in huge numbers to save people they do not know, and will never meet. My small participation in that process was one of the most humbling and inspiring experiences of my life.

34 Unlike any other creature on this planet, humans can learn and understand, without having experienced. They can think themselves into other people's minds, imagine themselves into other people's places.

35 Of course, this is a power, like my brand of fictional magic, that is morally neutral. One might use such an ability to manipulate, or control, just as much as to understand or sympathise.

36 And many prefer not to exercise their imaginations at all. They choose to remain comfortably within the bounds of their own experience, never troubling to wonder how it would feel to have been born other than they are. They can refuse to hear screams or to peer inside cages; they can close their minds and hearts to any suffering that does not touch them personally; they can refuse to know.

37 I might be tempted to envy people who can live that way, except that I do not think they have any fewer nightmares than I do. Choosing to live in narrow spaces can lead to a form of mental agoraphobia, and that brings its own terrors. I think the wilfully unimaginative see more monsters. They are often more afraid.

38   What is more, those who choose not to empathise may enable real monsters. For without ever committing an act of outright evil ourselves, we collude with it, through our own apathy.

39   One of the many things I learned at the end of that Classics corridor down which I ventured at the age of 18, in search of something I could not then define, was this, written by the Greek author Plutarch: What we achieve inwardly will change outer reality.

40   That is an astonishing statement and yet proven a thousand times every day of our lives. It expresses, in part, our inescapable connection with the outside world, the fact that we touch other people's lives simply by existing.

41   But how much more are you, Harvard graduates of 2008, likely to touch other people's lives? Your intelligence, your capacity for hard work, the education you have earned and received, give you unique status, and unique responsibilities. Even your nationality sets you apart. The great majority of you belong to the world's only remaining superpower. The way you vote, the way you live, the way you protest, the pressure you bring to bear on your government, has an impact way beyond your borders. That is your privilege, and your burden.

42   If you choose to use your status and influence to raise your voice on behalf of those who have no voice; if you choose to identify not only with the powerful, but with the powerless; if you retain the ability to imagine yourself into the lives of those who do not have your advantages, then it will not only be your proud families who celebrate your existence, but thousands and millions of people whose reality you have helped transform for the better. We do not need magic to change the world, we carry all the power we need inside ourselves already: we have the power to imagine better.

43   I am nearly finished. I have one last hope for you, which is something that I already had at 21. The friends with whom I sat on graduation day have been my friends for life. They are my children's godparents, the people to whom I've been able to turn in times of trouble, friends who have been kind enough not to sue me when I've used their names for Death Eaters. At our graduation we were bound by enormous affection, by our shared experience of a time that could never come again, and, of course, by the knowledge that we held certain photographic evidence that would be exceptionally valuable if any of us ran for Prime Minister.

44   So today, I can wish you nothing better than similar friendships. And tomorrow, I hope that even if you remember not a single word of mine, you remember those of Seneca, another of those old Romans I met when I fled down the Classics corridor, in retreat from career ladders, in search of ancient wisdom: As is a tale, so is life: not how long it is, but how good it is, is what matters. I wish you all very good lives. Thank you very much.

THINKING ABOUT THE TEXT

1. What specific techniques does Rowling use to engage her audience? What qualities of her original audience—graduates of Harvard University—does she seem aware of and play to in her speech?

2. What two important lessons does Rowling wish she had known at her own university graduation that she wishes to impart to her audience?

3. How did her parents' impoverished backgrounds affect Rowling's personal and academic goals? Why does she not blame her parents for what might be seen as their negative impact on her decisions?

4. Acknowledging that Harvard graduates may not be as experienced in knowing failure as the average person, Rowling describes her own "epic scale" failure and its subsequent benefits. How does she describe the values of being at "rock bottom"? In what way does she believe some failure is essential?

5. What does Rowling believe personal happiness is *not*, and how is that belief a valuable insight for a university graduate?

6. What are the values of imagination, according to Rowling?

7. What awareness did Rowling gain from her work with Amnesty International? Which specific narratives from her job resonate with you? How does her work experience contribute to the person she is and the writing she does?

8. How does Rowling perceive people who lack the imagination or will to imagine the suffering of others?

9. How does Rowling connect her wisdom about the benefits of failure and the value of imagination to create a directive for the college graduates she addresses?

10. How does Rowling's concluding reference to a quotation from Seneca reinforce her views on the benefits of both failure and imagination?

WRITING FROM THE TEXT

1. Using Rowling's acknowledged "epic scale" failures as inspiration for your own revelations, describe a period of failure in your life. Then recount in your essay what you did to create a solid foundation from the "rock bottom" where you temporarily resided. Incorporate some of Rowling's language as you write your own account.

2. Define "failure" by analyzing the specific life choices and values of people you know. Perceive a way to categorize the examples of failure in order to organize your presentation.

3. Write an analysis of others' expectations for you that conflict with or support your personal notion of success and achieving a good life.

CONNECTING WITH OTHER TEXTS

1. After reading "The Good Daughter" (p. 12), write an analysis that shows both comparison and contrast between Hwang's and Rowling's history and choices. What conclusions can you draw as you contrast the reasoning and decisions of these authors?

2. Read "The Difference Between Pity and Empathy" (p. 162) to compare Vaughn's understanding of empathy with what Rowling perceives as the value of imagination. Using both works, write an essay that illustrates how imagination is vital to achieving a life of goodness.

3. Do an internet investigation of Amnesty International in order to write a descriptive analysis of the organization for someone who does not know its philosophy, procedures, and ability to help others.

The Myth of the Latin Woman
Judith Ortiz Cofer

Born in Puerto Rico in 1952, poet, essayist, and novelist Judith Ortiz Cofer has written extensively on being reared with her parents' traditional island culture while growing up in New Jersey. In an interview, Cofer described the contradictions in her cultural identity: "I write in English, yet I write obsessively about my Puerto Rican experience.... I am a composite of two worlds." A professor of English at the University of Georgia, Cofer has published essays, poems, and fiction. Her work includes *Woman in Front of the Sun: On Becoming a Writer* (2000), *The Meaning of Consuelo* (2003), *A Love Story Beginning in Spanish: Poems* (2005), and *Call Me Maria*, a young adult novel. The piece included here is from *The Latin Deli*, published in 1993.

1   On a bus trip to London from Oxford University where I was earning some graduate credits one summer, a young man, obviously fresh from a pub, spotted me and as if struck by inspiration went down on his knees in the aisle. With both hands over his heart, he broke into an Irish tenor's rendition of "Maria" from *West Side Story*. My politely amused fellow passengers gave his lovely voice the round of gentle applause it deserved. Though I was not quite as amused, I managed my version of an English smile: no show of teeth, no extreme contortions of the facial muscles—I was at this time of my life practicing reserve and cool. Oh, that British control, how I coveted it. But "Maria" had followed me to London, reminding me of a prime fact of

my life: you can leave the island, master the English language, and travel as far as you can, but if you are a Latina, especially one like me who so obviously belongs to Rita Moreno's gene pool, the island travels with you.

2   This is sometimes a very good thing—it may win you that extra minute of someone's attention. But with some people, the same things can make *you* an island—not a tropical paradise but an Alcatraz, a place nobody wants to visit. As a Puerto Rican girl living in the United States and wanting like most children to "belong," I resented the stereotype that my Hispanic appearance called forth from many people I met.

3   Growing up in a large urban center in New Jersey during the 1960s, I suffered from what I think of as "cultural schizophrenia." Our life was designed by my parents as a microcosm of their *casas* on the island. We spoke in Spanish, ate Puerto Rican food bought at the *bodega,* and practiced strict Catholicism at a church that allotted us a one-hour slot each week for mass, performed in Spanish by a Chinese priest trained as a missionary for Latin America.

4   As a girl I was kept under strict surveillance by my parents, since my virtue and modesty were, by their cultural equation, the same as their honor. As a teenager I was lectured constantly on how to behave as a proper *senorita.* But it was a conflicting message I received, since the Puerto Rican mothers also encouraged their daughters to look and act like women and to dress in clothes our Anglo friends and their mothers found too "mature" and flashy. The difference was, and is, cultural; yet I often felt humiliated when I appeared at an American friend's party wearing a dress more suitable to a semiformal than to a playroom birthday celebration. At Puerto Rican festivities, neither the music nor the colors we wore could be too loud.

5   I remember Career Day in our high school, when teachers told us to come dressed as if for a job interview. It quickly became obvious that to the Puerto Rican girls "dressing up" meant wearing their mother's ornate jewelry and clothing, more appropriate (by mainstream standards) for the company Christmas party than as daily office attire. That morning I had agonized in front of my closet, trying to figure out what a "career girl" would wear. I knew how to dress for school (at the Catholic school I attended, we all wore uniforms), I knew how to dress for Sunday mass, and I knew what dresses to wear for parties at my relatives' homes. Though I do not recall the precise details of my Career Day outfit, it must have been a composite of these choices. But I remember a comment my friend (an Italian American) made in later years that coalesced my impressions of the day. She said that at the business school she was attending, the Puerto Rican girls always stood out for wearing "everything at once." She meant, of course, too much jewelry, too many accessories. On that day at school we were simply made the

negative models by the nuns, who were themselves not credible fashion experts to any of us. But it was painfully obvious to me that to the others, in their tailored skirts and silk blouses, we must have seemed "hopeless" and "vulgar." Though I now know that most adolescents feel out of step much of the time, I also know that for the Puerto Rican girls of my generation that sense was intensified. The way our teachers and classmates looked at us that day in school was just a taste of the cultural clash that awaited us in the real world, where prospective employers and men on the street would often misinterpret our tight skirts and jingling bracelets as a "come-on."

6   Mixed cultural signals have perpetuated certain stereotypes—for example, that of the Hispanic woman as the "hot tamale" or sexual firebrand. It is a one-dimensional view that the media have found easy to promote. In their special vocabulary, advertisers have designated "sizzling" and "smoldering" as the adjectives of choice for describing not only the foods but also the women of Latin America. From conversations in my house I recall hearing about the harassment that Puerto Rican women endured in factories where the "bossmen" talked to them as if sexual innuendo was all they understood, and worse, often gave them the choice of submitting to their advances or being fired.

7   It is custom, however, not chromosomes, that leads us to choose scarlet over pale pink. As young girls, it was our mothers who influenced our decisions about clothes and colors—mothers who had grown up on a tropical island where the natural environment was a riot of primary colors, where showing your skin was one way to keep cool as well as to look sexy. Most important of all, on the island, women perhaps felt freer to dress and move more provocatively since, in most cases, they were protected by the traditions, mores, and laws of a Spanish/Catholic system of morality and machismo whose main rule was: *You may look at my sister, but if you touch her I will kill you.* The extended family and church structure could provide a young woman with a circle of safety in her small pueblo on the island; if a man "wronged" a girl, everyone would close in to save her family honor.

8   My mother has told me about dressing in her best party clothes on Saturday nights and going to the town's plaza to promenade with her girlfriends in front of the boys they liked. The males were thus given an opportunity to admire the women and to express their admiration in the form of *piropos:* erotically charged street poems they composed on the spot. (I have myself been subjected to a few *piropos* while visiting the island, and they can be outrageous, although custom dictates that they must never cross into obscenity.) This ritual, as I understand it, also entails a show of studied indifference on the woman's part; if she is "decent," she must not acknowledge the man's impassioned words. So I do understand how things can be lost in translation.

When a Puerto Rican girl, dressed in her idea of what is attractive, meets a man from the mainstream culture who has been trained to react to certain types of clothing as a sexual signal, a clash is likely to take place. I remember the boy who took me to my first formal dance leaning over to plant a sloppy, over-eager kiss painfully on my mouth; when I didn't respond with sufficient passion, he remarked resentfully: "I thought you Latin girls were supposed to mature early," as if I were expected to *ripen* like a fruit or vegetable, not just grow into womanhood like other girls.

9   It is surprising to my professional friends that even today some people, including those who should know better, still put others "in their place." It happened to me most recently during a stay at a classy metropolitan hotel favored by young professional couples for weddings. Late one evening after the theater, as I walked toward my room with a colleague (a woman with whom I was coordinating an arts program), a middle-aged man in a tuxedo, with a young girl in satin and lace on his arm, stepped directly into our path. With his champagne glass extended toward me, he exclaimed "Evita!"

10   Our way blocked, my companion and I listened as the man half-recited, half-bellowed "Don't Cry for Me, Argentina." When he finished, the young girl said: "How about a round of applause for my daddy?" We complied, hoping this would bring the silly spectacle to a close. I was becoming aware that our little group was attracting the attention of the other guests. "Daddy" must have perceived this too, and he once more barred the way as we tried to walk past him. He began to shout-sing a ditty to the tune of "La Bamba"—except the lyrics were about a girl named Maria whose exploits rhymed with her name and gonorrhea. The girl kept saying "Oh, Daddy" and looking at me with pleading eyes. She wanted me to laugh along with the others. My companion and I stood silently waiting for the man to end his offensive song. When he finished, I looked not at him but at his daughter. I advised her calmly never to ask her father what he had done in the army. Then I walked between them and to my room. My friend complimented me on my cool handling of the situation, but I confessed that I had really wanted to push the jerk into the swimming pool. This same man—probably a corporate executive, well-educated, even worldly by most standards—would not have been likely to regale an Anglo woman with a dirty song in public. He might have checked his impulse by assuming that she could be somebody's wife or mother, or at least *somebody* who might take offense. But, to him, I was just an Evita or a Maria: merely a character in his cartoon-populated universe.

11   Another facet of the myth of the Latin woman in the United States is the menial, the domestic—Maria the housemaid or countergirl. It's true that work as domestics, as waitresses, and in factories is all that's available to

women with little English and few skills. But the myth of the Hispanic menial—the funny maid, mispronouncing words and cooking up a spicy storm in a shiny California kitchen—has been perpetuated by the media in the same way that "Mammy" from *Gone with the Wind* became America's idea of the black woman for generations. Since I do not wear my diplomas around my neck for all to see, I have on occasion been sent to that "kitchen" where some think I obviously belong.

12   One incident has stayed with me, though I recognize it as a minor offense. My first public poetry reading took place in Miami, at a restaurant where a luncheon was being held before the event. I was nervous and excited as I walked in with notebook in hand. An older woman motioned me to her table, and thinking (foolish me) that she wanted me to autograph a copy of my newly published slender volume of verse, I went over. She ordered a cup of coffee from me, assuming that I was a waitress. (Easy enough to mistake my poems for menus, I suppose.) I know it wasn't an intentional act of cruelty. Yet of all the good things that happened later, I remember that scene most clearly, because it reminded me of what I had to overcome before anyone would take me seriously. In retrospect I understand that my anger gave my reading fire. In fact, I have almost always taken any doubt in my abilities as a challenge, the result most often being the satisfaction of winning a convert, of seeing the cold, appraising eyes warm to my words, the body language change, the smile that indicates I have opened some avenue for communication. So that day as I read, I looked directly at that woman. Her lowered eyes told me she was embarrassed at her faux pas, and when I willed her to look up at me, she graciously allowed me to punish her with my full attention. We shook hands at the end of the reading and I never saw her again. She has probably forgotten the entire incident, but maybe not.

13   Yet I am one of the lucky ones. There are thousands of Latinas without the privilege of an education or the entrees into society that I have. For them life is a constant struggle against the misconceptions perpetuated by the myth of the Latina. My goal is to try to replace the old stereotypes with a much more interesting set of realities. Every time I give a reading, I hope the stories I tell, the dreams and fears I examine in my work, can achieve some universal truth that will get my audience past the particulars of my skin color, my accent, or my clothes.

14   I once wrote a poem in which I called all Latinas "God's brown daughters." This poem is really a prayer of sorts, offered upward, but also, through the human-to-human channel of art, outward. It is a prayer for communication and for respect. In it, Latin women pray "in Spanish to an Anglo God/with a Jewish heritage," and they are "fervently hoping/that if not omnipotent,/at least He be bilingual."

THINKING ABOUT THE TEXT

1. What is the author's strategy in opening her essay with the anecdote about the bus passenger singing to her? What does the author mean when she claims that "you can leave the island" and travel to distant places, "but if you are Latina . . . the island travels with you" (173)? Do you think her awareness reflects the experience of members of other ethnicities as well?

2. Cofer describes the "cultural schizophrenia" of growing up in New Jersey but living in a home that reflected her family's Puerto Rican heritage. In which specific areas did this between-worlds schizophrenia appear?

3. The author is aware that most adolescents feel "out of step much of the time" (174), but how did the codes of her Puerto Rican family intensify the separation she felt from the Anglo culture she lived in?

4. The author writes that "mixed cultural signals have perpetuated certain stereotypes" (174) about the Hispanic woman. What are those stereotypes and how can they be perceived as dangerous as well as irritating? Why are the dress styles and behavior patterns of mothers who grew up on a tropical island not easily transported to a northern, urban society?

5. In addition to being identified with the Maria of *West Side Story* and Evita Peron, the author has also been assumed to be Maria the domestic. In her essay's conclusion, in what specific ways does Cofer use the anecdote about being presumed the waitress?

WRITING FROM THE TEXT

1. Write about a time when you or a friend were stereotyped because of how you looked, perhaps by your "gene pool" that travels with you. Were you amused, irritated, frightened? In your narrative, show how you were treated and how you felt. Review how to write a narrative (pp. 429–437) for help in writing this essay.

2. Describe particular customs that you have observed in your family or the families of friends that seem to keep you or your friends "out of step" in the United States. Is a compromise in style possible or desirable, or is "cultural schizophrenia" inevitable? Perhaps that awareness will be a part of your conclusion.

3. Describe the myths that are attached to particular ethnicities, in a way similar to Cofer's observations of how Latinas are stereotyped as "sexual firebrands" or "domestics." In your analysis, speculate on the origins of the myths connected to certain groups, and in your conclusion speculate on the consequences of such stereotyping.

CONNECTING WITH OTHER TEXTS

1. Cofer's essay and the essays of Zaiba Malik (p. 129) and Brent Staples (p. 181) deal with the problems of being perceived as other than one actually is. Write an essay that illustrates how frustrating and potentially dangerous it is to be stereotyped based on appearance. Use the specific experiences of the authors, as well as your own observations, to support your points.

2. Use films such as *Mississippi Massala, East Is East,* and *My Big Fat Greek Wedding,* as well as others that you know, to write about the "cultural schizophrenia" described by Judith Ortiz Cofer. Include specific statements from Cofer as well as detailed descriptions and analyses of scenes from the films.

3. In an essay, argue that immigrant parents work against their children's assimilation and personal happiness by adhering to values and customs that don't transport to a different country. Use "The Good Daughter" (p. 12) and "The Myth of the Latin Woman" to support your point.

If the Genes Fit
Dan Neil

Journalist and writer of feature articles for publications such as *Men's Vogue*, Dan Neil (b. 1960) is a *Los Angeles Times* regular columnist and feature writer. In 2004, Neil won a Pulitzer Prize for his original approach to car reviews, an example of which can be seen in his description of driving a Ferrari: "I have one weekend and a $185,000 Italian sports car so sexy it appears to have been forged from metal bra clasps and garter belt snaps, so fast it can blow the foam off lattes outside of any Starbucks it passes." The essay below, published in the *Los Angeles Times* in June, 2005, reflects Neil's characteristic style even as it argues a critical point.

1   I didn't decide to be straight, never came to a sexually orienting fork in the road to choose the road more traveled. I was never indoctrinated by anyone advancing a heterosexual agenda. Talk about coals to Newcastle.

2   And it's the same for every gay person I've ever talked to. From the earliest stirrings of sexual proclivity, they were somehow aware that they belonged in the same-sex sandbox. This was the case with Brad, one of my best friends. But perhaps, I ventured, something environmental, something learned, accounted for his sexual orientation? "Yeah, right," he said, "I read a book on it when I was 3 years old."

3   Just in time for Gay Pride Month—and in time to be rushed to the battlefields of the culture wars—comes "When I Knew," edited by fashion photographer

Robert Trachtenberg, a collection of stories from gays and lesbians, famous and not so famous, describing their Eureka! moments. Of course, writes contributor Brian Leitch, you know, then you know-know, then you really, *really* know. 'Nuf said.

4   This is a funny, sad, wonderful little book, full of mordant vignettes of self-discovery and disclosure. When comic Michele Balan told her grandmother that she was a lesbian, her grandmother replied: "No you're not, you're Romanian. On your father's side!" For political fundraiser Barry Karas, it happened when he was 8 years old. After watching the boy skip around, playing hopscotch, a family friend leaned over to Karas' father and said, "Ben, I think you got a problem."

5   These childhood annunciations occur in strange ways. Makeup artist Jeff Judd remembers edging under the TV to look up the loincloth of Ron Ely, who played Tarzan. Composer Marc Shaiman had a crush on Dick Gautier, who played Hymie the robot on "Get Smart." As a child, "Will & Grace" producer Jon Kinnally became obsessed with the man's naked back on a box of Doan's pills.

6   What is striking is that they had such revelations to begin with. It never dawned on me that I was straight. I just was. For gays and lesbians, it seems, there is always a moment when they realize that what they want isn't officially sanctioned. A cognitive moment that marks a cleaving away from the larger heterosexual world, the opening of an otherness, like jets peeling off in the missing-man formation.

7   Also conveniently timed, a June 3 article in the biology journal Cell that describes a gene-modifying experiment in which scientists switched fruit flies' sexual orientation from straight to gay. In the words of the study's authors: "The splicing of a single neuronal gene thus specifies essentially all aspects of a complex innate behavior." At least for *Drosophila melanogaster,* sexual orientation is genetic.

8   A month ago, researchers in Sweden released the results of a brain-scanning study suggesting the existence of human pheromones—scent chemicals that govern sexual behavior in many species—and demonstrating that gay males react to male sweat pheromones the same way heterosexual women do. There was no mention of socks.

9   Sexuality is bewildering and complex and fantastically varied—on this, I think, all sides agree—and yet there is a growing body of evidence suggesting that sexual orientation has a biological foundation, and that homosexuality is not "unnatural" in the sense of not occurring in nature. Biologist Bruce Bagemihl's book *Biological Exuberance* (1999) documents hundreds of examples of homosexual behavior in the animal kingdom.

10   The common shorthand for all this is the "gay gene," a term popularized by geneticist Dean Hamer and journalist Peter Copeland's book *The Science of Desire* (1994).

11   The notion of a gay gene, or anything like it, is anathema to organizations such as the rabidly anti-gay Focus on the Family. If homosexuality is a natural variation in the human genome, homosexuals are not guilty of anything except being human. If it is established that homosexuality is genetically, or at least biologically, rooted—regardless of how such feelings are behaviorally shaded—then the campaign to marginalize and criminalize gays is revealed as the bigoted pogrom that it is.

12   How bad do Christian fundamentalists want to refute this idea? Watergate con and prison minister Charles Colson, in a piece last month responding to a *New York Times* op-ed article by Harvard cognitive scientist Steven Pinker, argues that "of course" homosexuality is "evolutionarily maladaptive," according to the tenets of natural selection. It took homophobia to rehabilitate Darwin in the eyes of fundamentalists.

13   In the long run, this is a fight homophobes cannot hope to win, simply because the fear they traffic in—that somehow America's children will be seduced into the homosexual lifestyle—is so at odds with common experience. Most people know, at the core of their self-conception, that they were born straight or gay, and no amount of indoctrinating, no agenda from either side, could change that.

THINKING ABOUT THE TEXT

1. Describe Dan Neil's purpose in writing and his position in this essay. How does he support his views?

2. The author acknowledges a contrast between his lack of a defining moment in perceiving himself as a heterosexual and the experiences of homosexuals who can and do relate a "cognitive moment that marks a cleaving away from the larger heterosexual world" (179). Why do you think homosexuals have this moment of "you know, then you know-know, then you really *really* know" (179)?

3. Dan Neil uses material from *When I Knew*, an edited collection of narrations from gays and lesbians relating their moments of sexual self-discovery. The author also relates findings from the biology journal *Cell*, the results of a study on scent chemicals and their relationship to sexual behavior, and he cites two books on biology and genetics. What is the author's intention in referring to so many sources in this short essay?

4. What is the author's strategy in twice referring to himself as a male who never questioned his sexual orientation, one who never decided to be straight?

5. Describe how the wordplay in Dan Neil's title establishes his writer's voice and implied thesis.

WRITING FROM THE TEXT

1. Write an account of your own awareness of sexual orientation to illustrate Dan Neil's point that "most people know, at the core of their self-conception, that they were born straight or gay" (180). You might write an analysis of early crushes or middle-school romantic feelings to show how you developed an awareness of yourself as a sexual person.

2. Using the points made in Dan Neil's piece, write an essay that argues for improved high school counseling and school clubs based on homosexual orientation.

CONNECTING WITH OTHER TEXTS

1. After reading "Don't Let Stereotypes Warp Your Judgments" (p. 470), write an essay that shows your awareness of how stereotyping can influence young people's views and lack of acceptance of homosexuals. Propose a solution to the problem.

2. Read Marcus Mabry's essay "Living in Two Worlds" (p. 109) and then write an essay showing how Mabry's and Neil's essays illustrate the guilt, helplessness, and embarrassment experienced by individuals traveling between majority and minority worlds, whether racial or sexual.

 Black Men and Public Space

Brent Staples

After earning his Ph.D. in psychology from the University of Chicago, Brent Staples (b. 1951) worked at the *Chicago Sun-Times* and wrote for other periodicals. He became an assistant metropolitan editor of the *New York Times* in 1985, and he is presently on that paper's editorial board. In his book *Parallel Time: Growing Up in Black and White* (1994), Staples writes about his poor childhood and his present position at the *New York Times*. Staples "despises" the expression "the black experience," and insists that "black people's lives in this country are too varied to be reduced to a single term." He says that he is writing about "universal themes—family and leaving home and developing your own identity. . . . Being black enriches my experience; it doesn't define me." Staples has co-authored *An American Love Story* (1999). The essay included here was first published in the September 1986 issue of *Ms.* magazine as one article in a section on men's perspectives.

1   My first victim was a woman—white, well dressed, probably in her early twenties. I came upon her late one evening on a deserted street in Hyde Park, a relatively affluent neighborhood in an otherwise mean, impoverished section of Chicago. As I swung onto the avenue behind her, there seemed to be a discreet, uninflammatory distance between us. Not so. She cast back a worried glance. To her, the youngish black man—a broad six feet two inches with a beard and billowing hair, both hands shoved into the pockets of a bulky military jacket—seemed menacingly close. After a few more quick glimpses, she picked up her pace and was soon running in earnest. Within seconds she disappeared into a cross street.

2   That was more than a decade ago. I was twenty-two years old, a graduate student newly arrived at the University of Chicago. It was in the echo of that terrified woman's footfalls that I first began to know the unwieldy inheritance I'd come into—the ability to alter public space in ugly ways. It was clear that she thought herself the quarry of a mugger, a rapist, or worse. Suffering a bout of insomnia, however, I was stalking sleep, not defenseless wayfarers. As a softy who is scarcely able to take a knife to a raw chicken—let alone hold it to a person's throat—I was surprised, embarrassed, and dismayed all at once. Her flight made me feel like an accomplice in tyranny. It also made it clear that I was indistinguishable from the muggers who occasionally seeped into the area from the surrounding ghetto. That first encounter, and those that followed, signified that a vast, unnerving gulf lay between nighttime pedestrians—particularly women—and me. And I soon gathered that being perceived as dangerous is a hazard in itself. I only needed to turn a corner into a dicey situation, or crowd some frightened, armed person in a foyer somewhere, or make an errant move after being pulled over by a policeman. Where fear and weapons meet—and they often do in urban America—there is always the possibility of death.

3   In that first year, my first away from my hometown, I was to become thoroughly familiar with the language of fear. At dark, shadowy intersections in Chicago, I could cross in front of a car stopped at a traffic light and elicit the *thunk, thunk, thunk, thunk* of the driver—black, white, male, or female—hammering down the door locks. On less traveled streets after dark, I grew accustomed to but never comfortable with people who crossed to the other side of the street rather than pass me. Then there were the standard unpleasantries with police, doormen, bouncers, cab drivers, and others whose business it is to screen out troublesome individuals *before* there is any nastiness.

4   I moved to New York nearly two years ago and I have remained an avid night walker. In central Manhattan, the near-constant crowd cover minimizes tense one-on-one street encounters. Elsewhere—visiting friends in SoHo, where sidewalks are narrow and tightly spaced buildings shut out the sky—things can get very taut indeed.

5   Black men have a firm place in New York mugging literature. Norman Podhoretz in his famed (or infamous) 1963 essay, "My Negro Problem—And Ours," recalls growing up in terror of black males, they "were tougher than we were, more ruthless," he writes—and as an adult on the Upper West Side of Manhattan, he continues, he cannot constrain his nervousness when he meets black men on certain streets. Similarly, a decade later, the essayist and novelist Edward Hoagland extols a New York where once "Negro bitterness bore down mainly on other Negroes." Where some see mere panhandlers, Hoagland sees "a mugger who is clearly screwing up his nerve to do more than just *ask* for money." But Hoagland has "the New Yorker's quick-hunch posture for broken-field maneuvering," and the bad guy swerves away.

6   I often witness that "hunch posture," from women after dark on the warrenlike streets of Brooklyn where I live. They seem to set their faces on neutral and, with their purse straps strung across their chests bandolier style, they forge ahead as though bracing themselves against being tackled. I understand, of course, that the danger they perceive is not a hallucination. Women are particularly vulnerable to street violence, and young black males are drastically overrepresented among the perpetrators of that violence. Yet these truths are no solace against the kind of alienation that comes of being ever the suspect, against being set apart, a fearsome entity with whom pedestrians avoid making eye contact.

7   It is not altogether clear to me how I reached the ripe old age of twenty-two without being conscious of the lethality nighttime pedestrians attributed to me. Perhaps it was because in Chester, Pennsylvania, the small, angry industrial town where I came of age in the 1960s, I was scarcely noticeable against a backdrop of gang warfare, street knifings, and murders. I grew up one of the good boys, had perhaps a half-dozen fist fights. In retrospect, my shyness of combat has clear sources.

8   Many things go into the making of a young thug. One of those things is the consummation of the male romance with the power to intimidate. An infant discovers that random flailings send the baby bottle flying out of the crib and crashing to the floor. Delighted, the joyful babe repeats those motions again and again, seeking to duplicate the feat. Just so, I recall the points at which some of my boyhood friends were finally seduced by the perception of themselves as tough guys. When a mark cowered and surrendered his money without resistance, myth and reality merged—and paid off. It is, after all,

only manly to embrace the power to frighten and intimidate. We, as men, are not supposed to give an inch of our lane on the highway; we are to seize the fighter's edge in work and in play and even in love; we are to be valiant in the face of hostile forces.

9   Unfortunately, poor and powerless young men seem to take all this non-sense literally. As a boy, I saw countless tough guys locked away; I have since buried several, too. They were babies, really—a teenage cousin, a brother of twenty-two, a childhood friend in his mid-twenties—all gone down in episodes of bravado played out in the streets. I came to doubt the virtues of intimidation early on. I chose, perhaps even unconsciously, to remain a shadow—timid, but a survivor.

10   The fearsomeness mistakenly attributed to me in public places often has a perilous flavor. The most frightening of these confusions occurred in the late 1970s and early 1980s when I worked as a journalist in Chicago. One day, rushing into the office of a magazine I was writing for with a deadline story in hand, I was mistaken for a burglar. The office manager called secu-rity and, with an ad hoc posse, pursued me through the labyrinthine halls, nearly to my editor's door. I had no way of proving who I was. I could only move briskly toward the company of someone who knew me.

11   Another time I was on assignment for a local paper and killing time be-fore an interview. I entered a jewelry store on the city's affluent Near North Side. The proprietor excused herself and returned with an enormous red Doberman pinscher straining at the end of a leash. She stood, the dog ex-tended toward me, silent to my questions, her eyes bulging nearly out of her head. I took a cursory look around, nodded, and bade her good night. Rela-tively speaking, however, I never fared as badly as another black male jour-nalist. He went to nearby Waukegan, Illinois, a couple of summers ago to work on a story about a murderer who was born there. Mistaking the reporter for the killer, police hauled him from his car at gunpoint and but for his press credentials would probably have tried to book him. Such episodes are not un-common. Black men trade tales like this all the time.

12   In "My Negro Problem—And Ours," Podhoretz writes that the hatred he feels for blacks makes itself known to him through a variety of avenues—one being his discomfort with that "special brand of paranoid touchiness" to which he says blacks are prone. No doubt he is speaking here of black men. In time, I learned to smother the rage I felt at so often being taken for a criminal. Not to do so would surely have led to madness—via that special "paranoid touchiness" that so annoyed Podhoretz at the time he wrote the essay.

13   I began to take precautions to make myself less threatening. I move about with care, particularly late in the evening. I give a wide berth to

nervous people on subway platforms during the wee hours, particularly when I have exchanged business clothes for jeans. If I happen to be entering a building behind some people who appear skittish, I may walk by, letting them clear the lobby before I return, so as not to seem to be following them. I have been calm and extremely congenial on those rare occasions when I've been pulled over by the police.

14   And on late-evening constitutionals along streets less traveled by, I employ what has proved to be an excellent tension-reducing measure: I whistle melodies from Beethoven and Vivaldi and the more popular classical composers. Even steely New Yorkers hunching toward nighttime destinations seem to relax, and occasionally they even join in the tune. Virtually everybody seems to sense that a mugger wouldn't be warbling bright, sunny selections from Vivaldi's *Four Seasons*. It is my equivalent of the cowbell that hikers wear when they know they are in bear country.

THINKING ABOUT THE TEXT

1. What is the effect on the reader of Staples's opening paragraph? How does it function to underscore the point of his essay?

2. In what places is Staples's effect on people related to his being black? Where is his maleness or stature a threat? Which aspect of his physiology does Staples believe is more threatening?

3. How has Staples adjusted his life to make himself less intimidating?

WRITING FROM THE TEXT

1. Write about a time when you unwittingly threatened someone. Describe the occasion using Staples's essay as a model, so that your reader can see and *hear* ("*thunk, thunk, thunk, thunk*") the scene.

2. Write an essay in which you describe the problems of being stereotyped as a member of a group that is perceived as threatening. What, if anything, have you done to counter or handle the dangerously charged or uncomfortable environment?

3. Write an essay describing the problem of being intimidated by a group or a member of a group. What have you done to avoid feeling intimidated or threatened?

CONNECTING WITH OTHER TEXTS

1. In what way is Staples "Living in Two Worlds"? After reading Marcus Mabry's essay (p. 109), write a comparison contrast essay that shows how

both of these authors have learned to straddle two distinct realms. (See comparison-contrast, pp. 454–460.)

2. After reading "Don't Let Stereotypes Warp Your Judgments" (p. 470), write an analysis of how people who discriminate against Staples "impoverish" themselves. Use specific details from both essays to support your thesis.

3. Find periodical articles that feature the stories of African or Hispanic Americans who have been stereotyped by the police, bouncers, or door-men as muggers, criminals, or gang members. Write an essay that uses the specific examples in the articles for support.

 # Who Shot Johnny?
Debra J. Dickerson

After serving for twelve years as an intelligence officer in the United States Air Force, Debra J. Dickerson (b. 1959) earned a B.A. in politics and government, an M.A. in international relations, and a J.D. from Harvard Law School. While at Harvard, she began writing a column for the Harvard Law Record and decided to pursue a full-time writing career instead of practicing law. Dickerson's work has appeared in *The Washington Post*, the *New York Times Magazine*, *Good Housekeeping*, *VIBE*, *Mother Jones*, *Slate*, *The Village Voice*, *Salon*, and many other publications. Dickerson has also published two books, *An American Story*, a memoir (2001), and *The End of Blackness: Returning the Souls of Black Folk to Their Rightful Owners* (2004). Initially published in *The New Republic* in 1996, the following essay was selected by Ian Frazier for *The Best American Essays 1997* and is credited by Dickerson for "jump-starting" her writing career.

1   Given my level of political awareness, it was inevitable that I would come to view the everyday events of my life through the prism of politics and the national discourse. I read *The Washington Post*, *The New Republic*, *The New Yorker*, *Harper's*, *The Atlantic Monthly*, *The Nation*, *National Review*, *Black Enterprise*, and *Essence* and wrote a weekly column for the Harvard Law School *Record* during my three years just ended there. I do this because I know that those of us who are not well-fed white guys in suits must not yield the debate to them, however well-intentioned or well-informed they may be. Accordingly, I am unrepentant and vocal about having gained admittance to Harvard through affirmative action; I am a feminist, stoic about my marriage chances as a well-educated, thirty-six-year-old black woman who won't pretend to need help taking care of herself. My strength flags, though, in the face of the latest role assigned to my family in the national drama. On July 27, 1995, my sixteen-year-old nephew was shot and paralyzed.

2   Talking with friends in front of his house, Johnny saw a car he thought he recognized. He waved boisterously—his trademark—throwing both arms in the air in a full-bodied, hip-hop Y. When he got no response, he and his friends sauntered down the walk to join a group loitering in front of an apartment building. The car followed. The driver got out, brandished a revolver, and fired into the air. Everyone scattered. Then he took aim and shot my running nephew in the back.

3   Johnny never lost consciousness. He lay in the road, trying to understand what had happened to him, why he couldn't get up. Emotionlessly, he told the story again and again on demand, remaining apologetically firm against all demands to divulge the missing details that would make sense of the shooting but obviously cast him in a bad light. Being black, male, and shot, he must apparently be involved with gangs or drugs. Probably both. Witnesses corroborate his version of events.

4   Nearly six months have passed since that phone call in the night and my nightmarish headlong drive from Boston to Charlotte. After twenty hours behind the wheel, I arrived haggard enough to reduce my mother to fresh tears and to find my nephew reassuring well-wishers with an eerie sang-froid.

5   I take the day shift in his hospital room; his mother and grandmother, a clerk and cafeteria worker, respectively, alternate nights there on a cot. They don their uniforms the next day, gaunt after hours spent listening to Johnny moan in his sleep. How often must his subconscious replay those events and curse its host for saying hello without permission, for being carefree and young while a would-be murderer hefted the weight of his uselessness and failure like Jacob Marley's chains? How often must he watch himself lying stubbornly immobile on the pavement of his nightmares while the sound of running feet syncopate his attacker's taunts?

6   I spend these days beating him at gin rummy and Scrabble, holding a basin while he coughs up phlegm and crying in the corridor while he catheterizes himself. There are children here much worse off than he. I should be grateful. The doctors can't, or won't, say whether he'll walk again.

7   I am at once repulsed and fascinated by the bullet, which remains lodged in his spine (having done all the damage it can do, the doctors say). The wound is undramatic—small, neat, and perfectly centered—an impossibly pink pit surrounded by an otherwise undisturbed expanse of mahogany. Johnny has asked me several times to describe it but politely declines to look in the mirror I hold for him.

8   Here on the pediatric rehab ward, Johnny speaks little, never cries, never complains, works diligently to become independent. He does whatever he is told; if two hours remain until the next pain pill, he waits quietly. Eyes bloodshot, hands gripping the bed rails. During the week of his intravenous

feeding, when he was tormented by the primal need to masticate, he never asked for food. He just listened while we counted down the days for him and planned his favorite meals. Now required to dress himself unassisted, he does so without demur, rolling himself back and forth valiantly on the bed and shivering afterward, exhausted. He "ma'am"s and "sir"s everyone politely. Before his "accident," a simple request to take out the trash could provoke a firestorm of teenage attitude. We, the women who have raised him, have changed as well; we've finally come to appreciate those boxer-baring, oversized pants we used to hate—it would be much more difficult to fit properly sized pants over his diaper.

9   He spends a lot of time tethered to rap music still loud enough to break my concentration as I read my many magazines. I hear him try to sound-lessly mouth the obligatory "mothafuckers" overlaying the funereal dirge of the music tracks. I do not normally tolerate disrespectful music in my or my mother's presence, but if it distracts him now . . .

10   "Johnny," I ask later, "do you still like gangster rap?" During the long pause I hear him think loudly, I'm paralyzed Auntie, not stupid. "I mostly just listen to hip-hop," he says evasively into his *Sports Illustrated*.

11   Miserable though it is, time passes quickly here. We always seem to be jerking awake in our chairs just in time for the next pill, his every-other-night bowel program, the doctor's rounds. Harvard feels a galaxy away—the world revolves around Family Members Living with Spinal Cord Injury class, Johnny's urine output, and strategizing with my sister to find affordable, accessible housing. There is always another long-distance uncle in need of an update, another church member wanting to pray with us, or Johnny's little brother in need of some attention.

12   We Dickerson women are so constant a presence the ward nurses and cleaning staff call us by name and join us for cafeteria meals and cigarette breaks. At Johnny's birthday pizza party, they crack jokes and make fun of each other's husbands (there are no men here). I pass slices around and try not to think, Seventeen with a bullet.

13   Oddly, we feel little curiosity or specific anger toward the man who shot him. We have to remind ourselves to check in with the police. Even so, it feels pro forma, like sending in those $2 rebate forms that come with new panty-hose: you know your request will fall into a deep, dark hole somewhere, but still, it's your duty to try. We push for an arrest because we owe it to Johnny and to ourselves as citizens. We don't think about it otherwise—our low expectations are too ingrained. A Harvard aunt notwithstanding, for people like Johnny, Marvin Gaye was right that only three things are sure: taxes, death, and trouble. At least it wasn't the second.

14   We rarely wonder about or discuss the brother who shot him because we already know everything about him. When the call came, my first thought was the same one I'd had when I'd heard about Rosa Parks's beating: a brother did it. A non-job-having, middle-of-the-day malt-liquor-drinking, crotch-clutching, loud-talking brother with many neglected children born of many forgotten women. He lives in his mother's basement with furniture rented at an astronomical interest rate, the exact amount of which he does not know. He has a car phone, an $80 monthly cable bill, and every possible phone feature but no savings. He steals Social Security numbers from unsuspecting relatives and assumes their identities to acquire large TV sets for which he will never pay. On the slim chance that he is brought to justice, he will have a colorful criminal history and no coherent explanation to offer for his act. His family will raucously defend him and cry cover-up. Some liberal lawyer just like me will help him plea-bargain his way to yet another short stay in a prison pesthouse that will serve only to add another layer to the brother's sociopathology and formless, mindless nihilism. We know him. We've known and feared him all our lives.

15   As a teenager, he called, "Hey, baby, gimme somma that boodie!" at us from car windows. Indignant at our lack of response, he followed up with, "Fuck you, then, 'ho!" He called me a "white-boy-lovin' nigger bitch oreo" for being in the gifted program and loving it. At twenty-seven, he got my seventeen-year-old sister pregnant with Johnny and lost interest without ever informing her that he was married. He snatched my widowed mother's purse as she waited in predawn darkness for the bus to work and then broke into our house while she soldered on an assembly line. He chased all the small entrepreneurs from our neighborhood with his violent thievery and put bars on our windows. He kept us from sitting on our own front porch after dark and laid the foundation for our periodic bouts of self-hating anger and racial embarrassment. He made our neighborhood a ghetto. He is the poster fool behind the maddening community knowledge that there are still some black mothers who raise their daughters but merely love their sons. He and his cancerous carbon copies eclipse the vast majority of us who are not sociopaths and render us invisible. He is the Siamese twin who has died but cannot be separated from his living, vibrant sibling; which of us must attract more notice? We despise and disown this anomalous loser, but for many he *is* black America. We know him, we know that he is outside the fold, and we know that he will only get worse. What we didn't know is that, because of him, my little sister would one day be the latest hysterical black mother wailing over a fallen child on TV.

16   Alone, lying in the road bleeding and paralyzed but hideously conscious, Johnny had lain helpless as he watched his would-be murderer come to stand over him and offer this prophecy: "Betch'ou won't be doin' nomo' wavin', mothafucker."

17   Fuck you, asshole. He's fine from the waist up. You just can't do anything right, can you?

THINKING ABOUT THE TEXT

1. How does the introductory paragraph both establish the author's persona and provide the compelling focus for her essay?

2. What are the shocking details that we initially are told about how Johnny was shot?

3. Why does the author not reveal, until the very end, what the shooter said to Johnny who was bleeding in the street? What is the effect of concluding with those words and with the author's response?

4. How is Johnny portrayed, both before he is shot and afterwards, while he is suffering in the hospital? Which details give the reader the most vivid picture of how his life has changed?

5. Without knowing the actual identity of Johnny's shooter, why does the author refer to him ironically as "a brother" and claim, "We already know everything about him"? What are the many details that she offers to characterize Johnny's shooter?

6. Is the author guilty of stereotyping Johnny's shooter in this essay—or do her life experiences and the fact that Johnny's shooting was cold-blooded and unprovoked justify Dickerson's assumptions about this "brother"?

WRITING FROM THE TEXT

1. If you or a family member has ever been the victim of a crime, write an essay dramatizing that experience as Dickerson has done. You may choose to compare and contrast your experience with Johnny's or to use Dickerson's essay as an example of how to focus on a strong thesis and to select vivid details for support.

2. Focusing on Johnny and including details from Dickerson's narration, write an essay about the emotional and physical difficulties—for both victim and family members—of surviving a crime.

3. Write an evaluative response of Dickerson's essay as you take a stance on her thesis, tone, and main points. (See evaluative response, p. 438.)

Connecting with Other Texts

1. After reading Brent Staples's essay "Black Men and Public Space" (p. 181), write an essay comparing and contrasting his thesis, focus, and style with Dickerson's. Although Staples's and Dickerson's personas and attitudes may seem quite different, be careful to show how their concerns, fears, and choices overlap, too.

2. Referring to Dickerson's essay and to works by Staples (p. 181) and Thayer (p. 191), write an argument convincing readers who may be tempted to use aggression or rage that their impulsive behavior could have deadly consequences for themselves and others. Include details from all three essays to illustrate your points.

3. Using details from Dickerson's essay and from the film *Crash,* write an analysis of the causes and the consequences (for both perpetrator and victim) of street crimes and attacks.

King Curtis's Echo
Max Thayer

After being drafted into the Army in 1966 and serving for three years, Max Thayer (b. 1946) decided to move to Los Angeles to break into the movies. With no acting training or Hollywood connections, he began studying plays and books on acting, and he performed with experimental and street theater groups. When he joined the Screen Actors Guild in 1972, he changed his name from Michael to Max, after a character in Harold Robbins's novel *The Carpetbaggers.* Thayer has performed on stage in New York and Los Angeles and has appeared in numerous action movies shot in Hollywood and around the world. Neither a stuntman or martial-artist, Thayer credits his love of sports and his childhood experiences with ice hockey, baseball, football, basketball, boxing, and swimming for helping him in his film work. In addition to numerous B-movies, Thayer has had small, background roles in *Pearl Harbor, The Man Who Wasn't There, Collateral Damage, American Gun, S.W.A.T.,* and *Terminator 3.* The following essay first appeared in the *Los Angeles Times Magazine* in 2005.

1   I don't know what made me do it, but I'm glad, in a strange way, that I did.

2   When I heard my neighbor call out "You can't park there," I knew what was going on. Someone had pulled into our single-lane driveway, which serves four apartments that sit atop a pawn shop and a Russian deli on Santa Monica Boulevard in West Hollywood. When I heard a muffled response and my neighbor's more urgent "No! Someone is coming. We need to keep that space clear," I jumped up to look out my window.

3   Despite the NO PARKING signs, deli customers routinely park in the mouth of the driveway, blocking exit or entrance, though most of the time a simple request to move is met with sheepish compliance. But today a man in his 30s, fit and full of himself, nonchalantly waved off the appeal and sauntered around the corner just as I leaned out the window and got off a "Hey!"

4   Maybe if I'd just kept my mouth shut I wouldn't have taken it personally. After all, just two minutes before, I had been sprawled out in my bedroom, windows wide open, enjoying a balmy Sunday morning leafing through the newspaper while monitoring the two football games in progress on TV. Absolute bliss.

5   My first bad move was slipping into a pair of flip-flops and trundling down to the landing to right this slight to my dignity. I wasn't going to yell, just walk up to him in the deli and murmur something along the lines of: "You were asked politely to move; would you please?"

6   When I turned the corner at the end of the driveway, Mr. Park Where I Want was striding away from the deli and toward me. Smugly self-assured and dressed in one of those velour warm-up suits, he was bouncing along as if he'd just won the lottery.

7   He smirked when we passed each other. I turned and retraced my steps as he approached his car. I pointed to the signs posted near the entrance. "In the future, no parking, OK?"

8   Our eyes met as he smirked again. "Caaalm down."

9   Calm down? "I'm calm, just don't park here."

10   At this point I should have kept on walking back to the funny papers and football.

11   "Caaalm down," he said again in a pat-on-the-head tone.

12   You know how annoying that is?

13   I gave him my best withering look. "It's real simple, no parking, *parksi nyetski,* right?"

14   He grinned as he slid into his car. He offered up an unoriginal obscenity, followed by "low-life."

15   I felt my anger surge into a raging boil.

16   I proffered my middle finger, cocked and ready to see what Mr. Big Shot in His Big Mercedes wanted to do about it.

17   More grinning as he slowly backed out of the driveway, returning the salute.

18   That's when I lost it, spewing every unprintable phrase that welled up in my febrile brain. I questioned his courage, his sexual proclivities, his family, his—you know the drill.

19   And that's when he braked in the middle of the street, grin gone and in its place an icy stare.

20   At that movement, a car barreling around the corner blared its horn and we lost eye contact. He maneuvered out of the way and drove off.

21   I was shaking when I went back inside. Where had this venom come from? I had been ready to go to fist city with a stranger, for what? I wanted everything the way it was 10 minutes ago, but the smudge of stupidity wouldn't wash out. As I paced and ranted with the incident churning through my mind like a Class V rapids, I shoved a stool piled high with vinyl LPs, a stack of shellac we used to call records. I had culled the essentials from my collection to download to my hard drive and now they were scattered across the floor in a hap-hazard display of rash behavior.

22   I was slumped over, gazing dejectedly at the LPs, when I saw him staring up at me with an almost baleful look.

23   King Curtis.

24   The album cover for "Blues at Montreux" was at my feet. Recorded live at the jazz festival in Switzerland, it's an unrehearsed, once-in-a-lifetime session of King Curtis and Champion Jack Dupree. King was a monster sax player of his time and Champion Jack was a pure blues barrelhouse piano player. Their chance meeting produced some of the most exuberant, joyous music you'll ever hear.

25   It snapped me out of my funk and sent me back to the early '70s, when I lived in New York. The way I heard it, one night some guy relieved himself in front of a brownstone that King Curtis owned in the upper 80s on the Westside. An argument led to a stabbing that led to King's death. Some jerk was making a mess on his property and King took offense. King ended up bleeding out, dead at 37.

26   That night, not yet aware of the tragedy, I was standing on the corner of 90th and Amsterdam, a few blocks from where the stabbing had happened. I was waiting for the light to change when I heard a saxophone wailing away with loose abandon. I crossed the street, turned a corner, went down and back up, tried the other corner and crossed the street again, but the player remained elusive.

27   I read about King the next day in the *Herald Tribune*, and these many years later the memory echoed. Do I want to die over a parking space? Do I want to live in a world where my response to a personal affront is going to land me in jail, an emergency room or the morgue?

28   I laughed and it set me free—finally. I won't choose to live that way, or worse.

29   Now, long after the anger over the driveway affront has dissipated, it's something I strive to remember when some idiot swerves into my lane without signaling or an eager shopper jostles me in the grocery store. The obscene waste of King Curtis's life and my memory of his jubilant horn give me pause

and, on a good day, a touch of grace. I have to thank the Russian deli customer for that.

THINKING ABOUT THE TEXT

1. How do Thayer's title and opening line capture reader interest? What other elements in his next two narrative paragraphs keep readers intrigued?

2. How does Thayer's description of himself before the confrontation contrast with his behavior when he "lost it"? How does this tirade affect "Mr. Park Where I Want"?

3. What aspect of Thayer's character surprises him and causes him to question, "Where had this venom come from? I had been ready to go to fist city with a stranger, for what?"(193).

4. What is relevant about Thayer's flashback to an earlier incident involving "monster sax player" King Curtis? What is significant about Thayer searching for the elusive sax player—and his "echo"?

5. Why is Thayer *thankful* for this encounter with the Russian deli customer, and what has he learned from it?

WRITING FROM THE TEXT

1. Write an essay analyzing how Thayer uses narration and its elements (dialogue, action, characterization, conflict, flashback, and symbolism) to present a strong argument against angry confrontations. Show how each story detail supports his thesis that insignificant squabbles can too easily escalate into deadly confrontations if they are not avoided.

2. Although Thayer's story is about deadly confrontations, write an essay arguing that it is as much about self-discovery as it is about dealing with other people. Use details from this story to support your claims.

3. Write a narrative about an experience that showed a surprising aspect of yourself that you hadn't expected or seen fully. Dramatize your typical behavior before that incident and then analyze what you learned about yourself and others through that encounter.

CONNECTING WITH OTHER TEXTS

1. After reading "Watching My Back" (p. 82), write an essay comparing and contrasting Klein's treatment of confrontations with Thayer's. Consider

their similar concerns as well as the differences in their theses, initial provocation, and conclusions.

2. Using Thayer's essay, Staples's "Black Men and Public Space" (p. 181), and Dickerson's "Who Shot Johnny?" (p. 186), write an essay analyzing what each author seems to be exploring and exposing about aggression and "bravado." Examine any solutions or answers that the authors offer.

Facing It

Yusef Komanyakaa

Scholar, professor, and prize-winning poet Yusef Komanyakaa (pronounced "koh-mun-yah-kuh") was born in 1947 in Bogalusa, Louisiana, the son of a carpenter. He has taught in the New Orleans schools and at Indiana University, Colorado State University, University of California at Berkeley, the University of Colorado, and New York University, where he presently teaches. Komanyakaa is the author of many poetry collections including

Coopacetic (1984), *I Apologize for the Eyes in My Head* (1986), *Magic City* (1992), *Neon Vernacular* (1993), which won the $50,000 Kingsley Tufts Poetry Award, *Pleasure Dome* (2001), *Talking Dirty to the Gods* (2001), *Taboo* (2004), and *Gilgamesh* (2006). His work is described by *New York Times* critic Bruce Weber as "fiercely autobiographical, poems that deal with the stains that experience leaves on a life, and they are often achingly suggestive without resolution." You might consider whether the poem below, published in *Dien Cai Dau* in 1988, offers a resolution. *Dien Cai Dau* (the title means "crazy" in Vietnamese and was a term used to describe American soldiers fighting in Vietnam) reflects the author's experiences as an information specialist and editor of the military newspaper *Southern Cross* from 1965 to 1967.

My black face fades,
hiding inside the black granite.
I said I wouldn't,

dammit: No tears.
5 I'm stone. I'm flesh.
My clouded reflection eyes me

like a bird of prey, the profile of night
slanted against morning. I turn
this way—the stone lets me go.

10 I turn that way—I'm inside
the Vietnam Veterans Memorial
again, depending on the light

to make a difference.
I go down the 58,022 names,
15 half-expecting to find

my own in letters like smoke.
I touch the name Andrew Johnson;
I see the booby trap's white flash.

Names shimmer on a woman's blouse
20 but when she walks away
the names stay on the wall.

Brushstrokes flash, a red bird's
wings cutting across my stare.
The sky. A plane in the sky.

25   A white vet's image floats
closer to me, then his pale eyes
look through mine. I'm a window.

He's lost his right arm
inside the stone. In the black mirror
30   a woman's trying to erase names:
No, she's brushing a boy's hair.

THINKING ABOUT THE TEXT

1. Who is the speaker in this poem and what is he doing?

2. How does the polished granite surface of the Vietnam Veterans Memorial influence what the speaker experiences as he visits this site? If you have been to this memorial, what were your observations about the wall and the mood at the site? How does this memorial differ from other commemorative war sites you may have visited?

3. Which of the reflections in the granite seem actual and which seem flashbacks to the speaker's war experience? Is it always clear which perceptions are actual and which recalled?

4. Explain the significance of the metaphors "I'm stone. I'm flesh." List all connotations of the words "stone" and "flesh."

5. What are the multiple dictionary definitions of the verb "to face"? How do these different meanings explain what the speaker is experiencing?

6. In the last three lines of the poem, the speaker expresses some confusion. He at first thinks a woman is erasing a name on the wall, but then decides she is "brushing a boy's hair." Why does the speaker confuse what he sees? Why do you think a woman at this site might actually be brushing a boy's hair? Why do you think the poet concludes his poem with a mistake and then corrected perception?

WRITING FROM THE TEXT

1. Write an analysis of the poem that shows how the multiple meanings of the verb "to face" and the noun "facing" contribute to the reader's understanding of the speaker's perceptions and the insights of the poem. (See pp. 476–485 for suggestions on how to write poetry analysis.)

2. Focusing on the images reflected—both off the granite and within the speaker's memory—write an analysis of "Facing It" that concludes with some insights that Yusef Komanyakaa provides his reader.

CONNECTING WITH OTHER TEXTS

1. Read "I Confess Some Envy" (p. 451) and write a paper to show how the experiences of Robert McKelvey help explain the perceptions expressed by the speaker in "Facing It."

2. Read "The Red Convertible" (p. 135) and compare and contrast Henry's condition after his return from Vietnam with the speaker's perceptions in "Facing It." What can you conclude about the effects of war on veterans and on family and friends who remain at home?

Discrimination at Large
Jennifer A. Coleman

A graduate of Boston College Law School, Jennifer A. Coleman (b. 1959) is a discrimination and civil rights lawyer in Buffalo, New York. Coleman wrote the essay printed here after seeing the film *Jurassic Park:* "The only bad person in the film is fat, and I'm tired of the stereotyping—which nobody objects to—that makes heavy people objects of ridicule and contempt." In addition to writing legal briefs, pleadings, letters, and a law review article, Coleman teaches constitutional law at Canisius College in Buffalo. The essay that follows first appeared in *Newsweek* in 1993.

1   Fat is the last preserve for unexamined bigotry. Fat people are lampooned without remorse or apology on television, by newspaper columnists, in cartoons, you name it. The overweight are viewed as suffering from moral turpitude and villainy, and since we are at fault for our condition, no tolerance is due. All fat people are "outed" by their appearance.

2   Weight-motivated assaults occur daily and are committed by people who would die before uttering anti-gay slogans or racial epithets. Yet these same people don't hesitate to scream "move your fat ass" when we cross in front of them.

3   Since the time I first ventured out to play with the neighborhood kids, I was told over and over that I was lazy and disgusting. Strangers, adults, classmates offered gratuitous comments with such frequency and urgency that I started to believe them. Much later I needed to prove it wasn't so. I began a regimen of swimming, cycling and jogging that put all but the most compulsive to shame. I ate only cottage cheese, brown rice, fake butter and steamed everything. I really believed I could infiltrate the ranks of the nonfat and thereby establish my worth.

4   I would prove that I was not just a slob, a blimp, a pig. I would finally escape the unsolicited remarks of strangers ranging from the "polite"—"You

would really be pretty if you lost weight"—to the hostile ("Lose weight, you fat slob"). Of course, sometimes more subtle commentary sufficed: oinking, mooing, staring, laughing and pointing. Simulating a fog-horn was also popular.

5   My acute exercise phase had many positive points. I was mingling with my obsessively athletic peers. My pulse was as low as anyone's, my cholesterol levels in the basement, my respiration barely detectable. I could swap stats from my last physical with anyone. Except for weight. No matter how hard I tried to run, swim or cycle away from it, my weight found me. Oh sure, I lost weight (never enough) and it inevitably tracked me down and adhered to me more tenaciously than ever. I lived and breathed "Eat to win," "Feel the burn." But in the end I was fit and still fat.

6   I learned that by societal, moral, ethical, soap-operatical, vegetable, political definition, it was impossible to be both fit and fat. Along the way to that knowledge, what I got for my trouble was to be hit with objects from moving cars because I dared to ride my bike in public, and to be mocked by diners at outdoor cafés who trumpeted like a herd of elephants as I jogged by. Incredibly, it was not uncommon for one of them to shout: "Lose some weight, you pig." Go figure.

7   It was confusing for a while. How was it I was still lazy, weak, despised, a slug and a cow if I exercised every waking minute? This confusion persisted until I finally realized: it didn't matter what I did. I was and always would be the object of sport, derision, antipathy and hostility so long as I stayed in my body. I immediately signed up for a body transplant. I am still waiting for a donor.

8   Until then, I am more settled because I have learned the hard way what thin people have known for years. There simply are some things that fat people must never do. Like: riding a bike ("Hey lady, where's the seat?"), eating in a public place ("No dessert for me, I don't want to look like her"). And the most unforgivable crime: wearing a bathing suit in public ("Whale on the beach!").

9   Things are less confusing now that I know that the nonfat are superior to me, regardless of their personal habits, health, personalities, cholesterol levels or the time they log on the couch. And, as obviously superior to me as they are, it is their destiny to remark on my inferiority regardless of who I'm with, whether they know me, whether it hurts my feelings. I finally understand that the thin have a divine mandate to steal self-esteem from fat people, who have no right to it in the first place.

10   Fat people aren't really jolly. Sometimes we act that way so you will leave us alone. We pay a price for this. But at least we get to hang on to what self-respect we smuggled out of grade school and adolescence.

11   Hating fat people is not inborn; it has to be nurtured and developed. Fortunately, it's taught from the moment most of us are able to walk and speak. We learn it through Saturday-morning cartoons, prime-time TV and movies. Have you ever seen a fat person in a movie who wasn't evil, disgusting, pathetic or lampooned? Santa Claus doesn't count.

12   Kids catch on early to be sensitive to the feelings of gay, black, disabled, elderly and speech-impaired people. At the same time, they learn that fat people are fair game. That we are always available for their personal amusement.

13   The media, legal system, parents, teachers and peers respond to most types of intolerance with outrage and protest. Kids hear that employers can be sued for discriminating, that political careers can be destroyed and baseball owners can lose their teams as a consequence of racism, sexism or almost any other "ism."

14   But the fat kid is taught that she deserves to be mocked. She is not OK. Only if she loses weight will she be OK. Other kids see the response and incorporate the message. Small wonder some (usually girls) get it into their heads that they can never be thin enough.

15   I know a lot about prejudice, even though I am a white, middle-class, professional woman. The worst discrimination I have suffered because of my gender is nothing compared to what I experience daily because of my weight. I am sick of it. The jokes and attitudes are as wrong and damaging as any racial or ethnic slur. The passive acceptance of this inexcusable behavior is sometimes worse than the initial assault. Some offensive remarks can be excused as the shortcomings of jackasses. But the tacit acceptance of their conduct by mainstream America tells the fat person that the intolerance is understandable and acceptable. Well it isn't.

Thinking about the Text

1. Jennifer Coleman's focus is evident from the first paragraph of her essay. After you have read the entire essay, what do you assume is her thesis or complete assertion?

2. What is the author's personal history, and how does knowing her background contribute to your understanding of her point?

3. *Are* the jokes and slurs about overweight people "as wrong and damaging as any racial or ethnic slur" (200)?

4. Examine Coleman's word choice in this essay. Which words and expressions specifically contribute to her making her point powerfully?

5. What are *your* feelings as you read the comments that people have made to and about Coleman?

WRITING FROM THE TEXT

1. Write an essay arguing that discrimination against the overweight is "as wrong and damaging as any racial or ethnic slur" (200). You will want to anticipate and counter the objection that people don't *have* to be overweight.

2. Describe the character traits, habits, and values of an overweight person you know. Let the description in your essay *show* what kinds of discrimination and problems your subject has faced.

CONNECTING WITH OTHER TEXTS

1. Body image is a particular preoccupation for many women and, according to Rachel Krell (p. 387), the world associates a thin body with beauty. Write an essay that argues that Jennifer Coleman has virtues that we admire even though she is not thin.

2. Write an essay contrasting the purpose and voice of Jennifer Coleman and Neil Steinberg, in the following essay. You might want to review the comparison-contrast method (pp. 454–460). See also What's Your Aim? (pp. 351–352).

3. Use Heilbroner's essay on stereotyping (p. 470) as a definitive starting point for a descriptive essay on the discrimination that overweight people experience. You might contrast specific stereotypical depictions of overweight people in films and on television with an overweight person you know.

O.K., So I'm Fat
Neil Steinberg

A graduate of Northwestern University, Neil Steinberg (b. 1960) writes a column for the *Chicago Sun-Times*. He is the author of *Complete and Utter Failure* (1994), and *If at All Possible, Involve a Cow: The Book of College Pranks* (1992), *Don't Give Up the Ship: Finding My Father While Lost at Sea* (2002), *Hatless Jack* (2004), and *Drunkard* (2008), a memoir of his struggle with alcoholism. His work has also appeared in *Rolling Stone, Esquire, Sports Illustrated, Eating Well*, and the *National Lampoon*, where he was a contributing editor. The following essay is the chapter "'F' Is For Fat" from Steinberg's book *The Alphabet of Modern Annoyances* (1996). Steinberg says he enjoys "writing about things people have trouble articulating—personal things, but not too personal."

1   Some people are no doubt fat because of glandular disorders or the wrath of an angry God. I am not one of those people. I am fat because I eat a lot.

2   Since fat people are held in such low regard, I should immediately point out that I am not *that* fat. Not fat in the Chinese Buddha, spilling-out-of-the-airplane-seat sense. The neighborhood kids don't skip behind me in the street, banging tin cans together and singing derisive songs.

3   Not yet, anyway.

4   But forget the social stigma of being fat. Ignore the medical peril, the sheer discomfort of dragging all that excess weight around. There is still a final ignominy almost too dire to mention: thin people.

5   All the drawbacks of being overweight could be shucked off—the fat are good at denial—were it not for the standing rebuke and constant insult that thin people offer, sometimes intentionally, sometimes simply by their very existence.

6   "Hey, big guy"—I get that a lot, from overly familiar office mates and, especially, from wiry panhandlers, as if it were a compliment that would inspire me to dig for change. Worse are those bent on my elevation to the sainted ranks of the thin: the sly references to fad diets, the inspirational tales of heroic weight loss. "Can I get you something?" a good friend I was visiting asked. "A Diet Coke, maybe?"

7   Others assume that thinness is forever beyond my grasp. I was once at a dinner party where the hostess was a wisp of a woman with legs like beef jerky. She prepared some intensely fattening dessert—Bananas Foster, thick slices of ripe bananas awash in butter and sugar and cinnamon and liqueur accompanied by ice cream. The concoction was set before us. I was halfway finished and already thinking about seconds when I noticed that she wasn't eating. I challenged her, nicely. "This is great. Aren't you having any?" She fluttered her eyes and demurred. Oh, no, she said, too sweet, too fattening. And she smiled. A halo didn't form over her head, but it might as well have. The smile said it all—smug superiority, gazing down from on high.

8   I wanted to take my Bananas Foster and grind her face in it. She wasn't having any because it was bad for her. Bad for her, but fine for her piggish guests to ruin themselves on. "Here's some poison I whipped up for you. Bon appetit!"

9   Thanks.

10   That moment of shame and surprise—cheeks packed hamster-full with Bananas Foster while numbly confronting the iron resolve of your moral betters—is the heart of the fat experience. The yin of the primal pleasure of satiation, lips closing happily down on the tip of a thick triangle of stuffed

Chicago pizza, balanced against the yang of stunned realization, as the mental fog parts for a moment and you catch sight of yourself in the mirror and see what's really there.

11   Small wonder we get mad at those who keep themselves in check. Envy-stoked anger is natural when dessert suddenly turns into a little lesson about restraint, a lesson I have endured for years but somehow never absorbed or profited by.

12   Surprisingly, I have less trouble with thin people who don't need to think about their weight. Those who are thin despite having eating habits that, if I practiced them, would quickly turn me into one of those elephantine men who periodically turn up on the news, dressed in sheets, removed from their homes through a hole in the wall, quickly weighed on a freight scale for the record, then placed under the personal care of Dick Gregory.

13   My wife's friend Larry, for instance, dresses in those tapered Italian suits and doesn't have enough fat on his body to make a butter pat. He actually keeps big bowls of candy scattered around his house. Not just for show. He'll casually dig his hand up to the wrist into one of the bowls, pull out a fistful of M & Ms and, tilting his head back, funnel them into his mouth.

14   Trim as a pencil. Yet, paradoxically, I find it easy to be around Larry. I'm comfortable, happy, never put off. Maybe it's because those who are effort-lessly thin seem to suggest that thinness is a fluke of capricious fate, and thus out of our control. Maybe it's because Larry doesn't exhibit any of the self-control that I, in my greedy-puppy-fat-person way, would egoistically interpret as a reproach.

15   Or maybe it's just because he has all that candy scattered around his house.

THINKING ABOUT THE TEXT

1. Reread the first paragraph and identify the specific ways that Steinberg establishes his stance toward the subject matter, his personal voice, and his purpose in writing the essay.

2. In spite of the humor in this essay, the author *is* making a point. What is it? What is the "final ignominy" that fat people must tolerate?

3. What are people's diverse responses to Steinberg's weight?

4. If Steinberg's tone and purpose were not to amuse, his thesis might be quite different. Create an angry or more intense thesis statement for this essay that Steinberg's specific examples would support.

WRITING FROM THE TEXT

1. In a letter context—perhaps you'll even mail this to a friend—describe four thin and possibly self-righteous people you know. Try to achieve the quality of one of Neil Steinberg's well-crafted images—for example, his description of the hostess "with legs like beef jerky" (202).

2. If you are heavy or overweight, make a list of responses you have heard from friends and strangers about your size. Then write an essay that focuses on the intentional or unintentional comments you have endured. Adopt a voice similar to Steinberg's or one of indignation—as you prefer.

3. If you are weight conscious or very thin, write an essay that addresses the indifference, gluttony, medical problems, or laziness that you perceive in overweight people. Consider your audience and purpose as you draft your essay.

CONNECTING WITH OTHER TEXTS

1. Compare and contrast the purpose and voice of Jennifer Coleman in "Discrimination at Large" (p. 198) and of Steinberg in this piece. Evaluate the two essays in your conclusion. See What's Your Aim? (pp. 351–352) for ideas.

2. Matthew Soyster (p. 158), Jennifer Coleman (p. 198), and Steinberg write about their perceptions of their bodies. Write an analysis of your understanding of their attitudes from a thesis that links these three writers and essays. Use details from the three texts to support your analysis.

3. Write a character analysis of Steinberg that draws supporting material from the text. You may stretch your imagination to infer character traits, but ground your analysis as much as possible in what the author reveals about himself in his essay and biographical material.

4. Read one of Steinberg's books cited in his biographical information (p. 201). Write an analysis of the kinds of humor apparent in his work.

 # "Diabesity," A Crisis in an Expanding Country

Jane E. Brody

Author of a widely syndicated newspaper column, "Personal Health," Jane E. Brody (b. 1941) has worked as a journalist for the *New York Times* since 1965. Initially majoring in biochemistry, Brody also enjoyed working as editor of her college literary magazine, so she decided to combine her two passions and become a science writer. Brody's best-selling books include *Jane Brody's The New York Times Guide to Personal Health* (1982), *Jane Brody's Good Food Book: Living the High Carbohydrate Way* (1985), and *Jane Brody's Nutrition Book*

(1987). Brody emphasizes that good nutrition doesn't need to be unpleasant: "I wrote *Jane Brody's Good Food Book* for the average American who likes to *eat* and likes to *live*. . . . I don't like to feel deprived any more than the next person." The following essay appeared in the *New York Times* on March 29, 2005.

1   I can't understand why we still don't have a national initiative to control what is fast emerging as the most serious and costly health problem in America: excess weight. Are our schools, our parents, our national leaders blind to what is happening—a health crisis that looms even larger than our former and current smoking habits?

2   Just look at the numbers, so graphically described in an eye-opening new book, *Diabesity: The Obesity-Diabetes Epidemic That Threatens America—and What We Must Do to Stop It* (Bantam), by Dr. Francine R. Kaufman, a pediatric endocrinologist, the director of the diabetes clinic at Children's Hospital Los Angeles and a past president of the American Diabetes Association. In just over a decade, she noted, the prevalence of diabetes nearly doubled in the American adult population: to 8.7 percent in 2002, from 4.9 percent in 1990. Furthermore, an estimated one-third of Americans with Type 2 diabetes don't even know they have it because the disease is hard to spot until it causes a medical crisis.

3   An estimated 18.2 million Americans now have diabetes, 90 percent of them the environmentally influenced type that used to be called adult-onset diabetes. But adults are no longer the only victims—a trend that prompted an official change in name in 1997 to Type 2 diabetes. More and more children are developing this health-robbing disease or its precursor, prediabetes. Counting children and adults together, some 41 million Americans have a higher-than-normal blood sugar level that typically precedes the development of full-blown diabetes.

4   And what is the reason for this runaway epidemic? Being overweight or obese, especially with the accumulation of large amounts of body fat around the abdomen. In Dr. Kaufman's first 15 years as a pediatric endocrinologist, 1978 to 1993, she wrote, "I never saw a young patient with Type 2 diabetes. But then everything changed." Teenagers now come into her clinic weighing 200, 300, even nearly 400 pounds with blood sugar levels that are off the charts. But, she adds, we cannot simply blame this problem on gluttony and laziness and "assume that the sole solution is individual change."

5   The major causes, Dr. Kaufman says, are "an economic structure that makes it cheaper to eat fries than fruit" and a food industry and mass media that lure children to eat the wrong foods and too much of them. "We have defined progress in terms of the quantity rather than the quality of our food," she wrote. Her views are supported by a 15-year study published in January

in *The Lancet*. A team headed by Dr. Mark A. Pereira of the University of Minnesota analyzed the eating habits of 3,031 young adults and found that weight gain and the development of prediabetes were directly related to unhealthful fast food.

6   Taking other factors into consideration, consuming fast food two or more times a week resulted, on average, in an extra weight gain of 10 pounds and doubled the risk of prediabetes over the 15-year period. Other important factors in the diabesity epidemic, Dr. Kaufman explained, are the failure of schools to set good examples by providing only healthful fare, a loss of required physical activity in schools and the inability of many children these days to walk or bike safely to school or to play outside later.

7   Genes play a role as well. Some people are more prone to developing Type 2 diabetes than others. The risk is 1.6 times as great for blacks as for whites of similar age. It is 1.5 times as great for Hispanic-Americans, and 2 times as great for Mexican-Americans and Native Americans. Unless we change our eating and exercise habits and pay greater attention to this disease, more than one-third of whites, two-fifths of blacks and half of Hispanic people in this country will develop diabetes.

8   It is also obvious from the disastrous patient histories recounted in Dr. Kaufman's book that the nation's medical structure is a factor as well. Many people do not have readily accessible medical care, and still many others have no coverage for preventive medicine. As a result, millions fall between the cracks until they are felled by heart attacks or strokes.

9   There is a tendency in some older people to think of diabetes as "just a little sugar," a common family problem. They fail to take it seriously and make the connection between it and the costly, crippling and often fatal diseases that can ensue. Diabetes, with its consequences of heart attack, stroke, kidney failure, amputations and blindness, among others, already ranks No. 1 in direct health care costs, consuming $1 of every $7 spent on health care. Nor is this epidemic confined to American borders. Internationally, "we are witnessing an epidemic that is the scourge of the 21st century," Dr. Kaufman wrote.

10   Unlike some other killer diseases, Type 2 diabetes issues an easily detected wake-up call: the accumulation of excess weight, especially around the abdomen. When the average fasting level of blood sugar (glucose) rises above 100 milligrams per deciliter, diabetes is looming. Abdominal fat is highly active. The chemical output of its cells increases blood levels of hormones like estrogen, providing the link between obesity and breast cancer, and decreases androgens, which can cause a decline in libido. As the cells in abdominal fat expand, they also release chemicals that increase fat accumulation, ensuring their own existence.

11   The result is an increasing cellular resistance to the effects of the hormone insulin, which enables cells to burn blood sugar for energy. As blood sugar rises with increasing insulin resistance, the pancreas puts out more and more insulin (promoting further fat storage) until this gland is exhausted. Then when your fasting blood sugar level reaches 126 milligrams, you have diabetes.

12   Two recent clinical trials showed that Type 2 diabetes could be prevented by changes in diet and exercise. The Diabetes Prevention Program Research Group involving 3,234 overweight adults showed that "intensive lifestyle intervention" was more effective than a drug that increases insulin sensitivity in preventing diabetes over three years. The intervention, lasting 24 weeks, trains people to choose low-calorie, low-fat diets; increase activity; and change their habits. Likewise, the randomized, controlled Finnish Diabetes Prevention Study of 522 obese patients showed that introducing a moderate exercise program of at least 150 minutes a week and weight loss of at least 5 percent reduced the incidence of diabetes by 58 percent.

13   Many changes are needed to combat this epidemic, starting with schools and parents. Perhaps the quickest changes can be made in the workplace, where people can be encouraged to use stairs instead of elevators; vending machines can be removed or dispense only healthful snacks; and cafeterias can offer attractive healthful fare. Lunchrooms equipped with refrigerators and microwaves will allow workers to bring healthful meals to work. Dr. Kaufman tells of a challenge to get fit and lose weight by Caesars Entertainment in which 4,600 workers who completed the program lost a total of 45,000 pounds in 90 days. Others could follow this example.

THINKING ABOUT THE TEXT

1. Cite the specific data that Brody includes from Kaufman's book on "diabesity" to support her claim that "excess weight" is "the most serious and costly health problem in America" (205).

2. What are the major causes and related factors that explain the current "diabesity" epidemic?

3. What is "Type 2 diabetes" and how can it be prevented?

4. List some of the changes in diet and guidelines for exercise that Brody recommends to combat and prevent this epidemic.

WRITING FROM THE TEXT

1. Using data and details from Brody's essay, write an essay directed to your school district's board of education assessing your high school's nutrition and physical education policies and recommending changes.

2. Write an analysis essay that examines Brody's thesis, tone, main points, and support. Whom is she identifying as her audience and how effective are her strategies and appeal?

3. Focusing on Brody's information, write an essay fully defining "Type 2 diabetes," including both the causes and effects as well as those individuals most prone to developing this disease. (See definition essay, pp. 444–449.)

CONNECTING WITH OTHER TEXTS

1. Read "Why Stop Smoking?" (p. 347) and write a comparison-contrast of Harrison's and Brody's approaches and strategies for getting people to understand the dangers of their addictions and to make significant changes in their lives. (See comparison-contrast, pp. 454–460.) Explain whether either author seems to appeal more to you and your peers—and why.

2. Read "O.K., So I'm Fat" (p. 201) and write an essay including details from Brody's article that address Steinberg's complacency.

3. After reading "Bodily Harm" (below) and "Dieting Daze: No In-Between" (p. 387), write an essay contrasting the causes and effects of the major eating disorders, anorexia and bulimia, with those of "diabesity," as described in Brody's essay.

Bodily Harm

Pamela Erens

A 1985 graduate of Yale, Pamela Erens (b. 1963) has worked as an editor and staff writer for *Connecticut Magazine* and *Glamour* magazine. Her reviews and articles have appeared in many magazines and newspapers, and she has also published a novel, *The Understory*

(2007). The essay included here was first published in *Ms.* in 1985, when Erens interned there the summer after her graduation.

1   "Before I'd even heard of bulimia," said Gloria, "I happened to read an article in *People* magazine on Cherry Boone—how she'd used laxatives and vomiting to control her weight. I thought: Wow, what a great idea! I was sure that I would never lose control of my habit."

2   Recent media attention to the binge-purge and self-starvation disorders known as bulimia and anorexia—often detailing gruesome particulars of women's eating behavior—may have exacerbated this serious problem on college campuses. But why would a woman who reads an article on eating disorders want to copy what she reads? Ruth Striegel-Moore, Ph.D., director of Yale University's Eating Disorders Clinic, suggests that eating disorders may be a way to be like other "special" women and at the same time strive to outdo them. "The pursuit of thinness is a way for women to compete with each other, a way that avoids being threatening to men," says Striegel-Moore. Eating disorders as a perverse sort of rivalry? In Carol's freshman year at SUNY-Binghamton, a roommate showed her how to make herself throw up. "Barf buddies" are notorious on many college campuses, especially in sororities and among sports teams. Eating disorders as negative bonding? Even self-help groups on campus can degenerate into the kinds of competitiveness and negative reinforcement that are among the roots of eating disorders in the first place.

3   This is not another article on how women do it. It is an article on how and why some women stopped. The decision to get help is not always an easy one. The shame and secrecy surrounding most eating disorders and the fear or being labeled "sick" may keep a woman from admitting even to herself that her behavior is hurting her. "We're not weirdos," says Nancy Gengler, a recovered bulimic and number two U.S. squash champion, who asked that I use her real name because "so much of this illness has to do with secrecy and embarrassment." In the first stages of therapy, says Nancy, much of getting better was a result of building up the strength to (literally) "sweat out" the desire to binge and to endure the discomfort of having overeaten rather than throwing up. "I learned to accept such 'failures' and moreover, that they would not make me fat. . . ."

4   Secret shame or college fad, eating disorders among college women are growing at an alarming rate: in a recent study at Wellesley College, more than half the women on campus felt they needed help to correct destructive eating patterns. These included bingeing, chronic dieting, and "aerobic nervosa," the excessive use of exercise to maintain one's body ideal—in most

women, invariably five to ten pounds less than whatever she currently weighs.

5   Why now? Wasn't the Women's Movement supposed to free women to be any body size, to explore the full range of creative and emotional possibilities? Instead, women in epidemic numbers are developing symptoms that make them feel hopeless about the future, depleting the energy they have for schoolwork and other activities, and if serious enough, send them right back home or into the infantalizing condition of hospitalization. What has gone wrong?

6   For Brenda, college meant the freedom to question her mother's values about sex. But when she abandoned her mother's guidelines, "I went to the other extreme. I couldn't set limits about sex, food, or anything else." The pressure on college women to appear successful and in control, to know what they want among the myriad new choices they are offered, is severe. So much so that many choose internal havoc over external imperfection. Naomi, a bulimic student at Ohio State University, said she would rather be alcoholic like her father than overweight like her mother because "fat is something you can see."

7   One reason college women hesitate to enter therapy, says Stephen Zimmer, director of the Center for the Study of Anorexia and Bulimia in New York City, is that the eating disorder has become a coping mechanism. It allows the person to function when she feels rotten inside. "In the first session," says Zimmer, "I tell my patients: 'I'm not going to try to take your eating behavior away from you. Until you find something that works better, you get to keep it.' Their relief is immense."

8   Brenda at first did not even tell the counselor whom she was seeing that she was bulimic. She started therapy because of a series of affairs with abusive men. As Brenda developed the sense that she had a right to say no to harmful relationships and to make demands on others, her inability to say no to food also disappeared.

9   However, if a woman is vomiting three times a day, she may be unable to concentrate on long-term therapy. Behavioral therapy, which directly addresses the learned habit of bingeing and purging, is a more immediate alternative. For eight years, Marlene Boskind White, Ph.D., and her husband, William White Jr., Ph.D., ran weekend workshops for bulimic women at Cornell University, usually as an adjunct to other forms of therapy. The sessions included nutritional counseling, developing techniques of dealing with binge "triggers," feminist consciousness-raising, and examining the hidden "pay-offs" that keep a woman from changing her eating behavior. Boskind-White and White report that a follow-up of 300 women they had treated one to three years earlier showed that 70 percent had entirely stopped purging and drastically reduced their bingeing.

10   Group therapy (an increasingly popular resource on college campuses) may be the first time a woman realizes she is not alone with her problem. Rebecca Axelrod, who was bulimic throughout college, and now counsels bulimics herself, found that joining the Cornell workshop and meeting other bulimic women defused many of her fears about herself: "I saw ten other women who were not mentally ill, not unable to function," Axelrod says. She remembers the moment when she understood the meaning of her bingeing and purging. "Saturday afternoon, Marlene took the women off alone, and we discussed the 'superwoman syndrome'—that attempt to be the perfect friend, lover, hostess, student . . . and perfect-looking. And bingeing, I saw, was my form of *defiance*. But if you're living life as the perfect woman, you won't cuss, you won't get drunk or laid or drive too fast. No, in the privacy of your own room you'll eat yourself out of house and home. But how dare you be defiant? And so you punish yourself by throwing it up."

11   But "groups can fall into a cycle I call 'bigger and badder,'" says Axelrod. "It starts when one person comes in and says, 'I feel terrible, I binged yesterday.' Somebody else says: 'Oh, that's okay, so did I.' Then a third person says: 'That's nothing, did you know I. . . .' Pretty soon everyone is lending support to the binge instead of to the woman who needs ways of coping with it."

12   However, Axelrod feels that there is much potential for women to help one another. She encourages bulimics to ask for help from their friends, saying that while she herself was initially frightened that being open about her bulimia would alienate her friends, most were very supportive. "The important thing," says Axelrod, "is to be specific about what you need. Don't say: 'Be there for me.' Tell a friend exactly what she can do: for instance, not to urge you to go out for pizza if you tell her you're feeling vulnerable. And rely on three friends, not one."

13   One of the most important strategies in treating eating disorders, says Dr. Lee Combrinck-Graham of the newly opened Renfrew Center for anorectics and bulimics in Philadelphia, is breaking old patterns. Renfrew is a residential center that houses patients for between three weeks and two months, a period that can give women with eating disorders a respite from repetitive and destructive habits that are reinforced by the college environment. But Renfrew is not a "retreat"; its residents work hard. They participate in therapy workshops, take seminars in assertiveness-training and women's issues, and even participate in "new attitude" cooking classes. Dr. Combrinck-Graham stresses that therapy itself has often become a "pattern" for women who come to Renfrew. Many of Renfrew's patients, says Dr. Combrinck-Graham, can say exactly what's "wrong" with them and why, yet are still unable to control their eating habits. Renfrew combines a philosophy that recovery is the patient's responsibility—she sets her own goals and contracts for as much supervision as she needs—with in-

novative art and movement therapy that may bypass some of the rationalizations that block the progress of "talking" therapies.

14   Women who live close to home and whose parents are not separated may want to try family therapy. Family therapy considers the family itself, not the daughter with an eating disorder, to be the "patient." Often, the daughter has taken on the role of diverting attention from unacknowledged conflicts within the family. Family therapists behave somewhat like manic stage managers, interrupting and quizzing various members of a family, orchestrating confrontations in an attempt to expose and demolish old, rigid patterns of relating. Ideally, family therapy benefits all the members of the family. Carol, the student at SUNY-Binghamton, said that family therapy revealed how unhappy her mother was as a homemaker in a traditional Italian family.

15   Situations like Carol's are at the heart of today's epidemic of eating disorders, argues Kim Chernin in her book *The Hungry Self: Women, Eating, and Identity*. Chernin claims that today's college woman is the heir of a particular cultural moment that turns her hunger for identity into an uncontrollable urge for bodily nourishment. Young women of an earlier generation were educated to have children and remain in the home, yet our culture devalued the work they did there. Later, the Women's Movement opened up vast new emotional and career possibilities, and many daughters, on the verge of achieving their mother's suppressed dreams, are struck by panic and guilt.

16   Carol agreed: "I would try to push my mother to take classes, but my father was always against it. I was a good student, but how could I keep on getting smarter than my mother? When I was young, we'd been like one person. I wanted to be a homemaker because she was one. But when I got older, I said to myself: 'This woman has no life. She never leaves the house except to get groceries. And she's miserable.' I wanted to stop growing up, and then she would always be able to lead me and guide me." According to Chernin, an eating disorder may be a way to postpone or put an end to one's development, one's need to choose, the possibility of surpassing one's mother. In a world hostile to the values of closeness and nurturance women learn from and associate with the mother-daughter relationship, an eating disorder can disguise a desire to return to the "nourishment" of that early bond.

17   And why do the daughter's problems focus around food? As Chernin reminds us, originally with her milk, the mother *is* food. Femininity itself has historically been associated with food gathering and preparation. Food—eating it, throwing it up—can become a powerful means of expressing aspects of the mother's life or of traditionally defined femininity that the daughter is trying to ingest or reject. And relationships with other women later in life can replicate this early pattern: food mediates hostility and love.

18   Whatever forms of therapy prove most helpful for women with eating disorders, it is clear that therapy is only half the battle. The Stone Center for Developmental Services and Studies at Wellesley College recognizes the need for early prevention and is preparing a film for adolescents that will feature women and health professionals speaking about the uses and abuses of food in our culture. Janet Surrey, Ph.D., a research associate at the center, stresses the need to educate girls in the 10- to 15-year-old age bracket—66 percent of whom already diet—about the psychological, physical, and reproductive danger of dieting and excessive thinness. Nutritional counseling is another imperative. But to Kim Chernin, our first priority is outreach centers and school programs that will provide developmental counseling and feminist consciousness-raising for this crucial pre-high school group. If women could learn early on to confront their conflicts over their right to development, the use of power, and their place in a still male-dominated world, there might no longer be a need for the "silent language" of eating disorders.

THINKING ABOUT THE TEXT

1. According to Erens, how has popular press coverage of eating disorders exacerbated the problem?

2. What is Erens's purpose in quoting Rebecca Axelrod and others? What do these people and their comments contribute?

3. How can group therapy sessions, frequently joined by people with eating disorders, actually complicate the treatment?

4. What is Kim Chernin's perception of one cause of eating disorders?

5. How effective is Erens's conclusion, a proposal to curtail the number of young women with eating disorders?

WRITING FROM THE TEXT

1. Do you think that women compete with each other by pursuing thinness? Do you think women bond in an effort to achieve thinness? Write an essay in which you describe and analyze the eating patterns of women you know.

2. Argue that the cause of eating disorders is not based in the mother-daughter relationship but in the superthin images in advertising. Cite and *describe* specific examples of advertising to support your view.

CONNECTING WITH OTHER TEXTS

1. Pamela Erens, Jennifer Coleman (p. 198), and Rachel Krell (p. 387) describe the kinds of harm that can be done to women who try to conform

to a standardized concept of beauty. In an analysis essay, examine the problem by connecting the ideas expressed by three of these writers.

2. This article, published in 1985, gives a good review of eating problems, but new information may provide increased or different insights. Use Erens's essay as a model but use more current material to analyze the problem of eating disorders.

Six Rules for Eating Wisely
Michael Pollan

Writer, journalist, educator, editor, columnist, television producer, and natural historian, Michael Pollan (b. 1955) is also a frequent lecturer on food, agriculture, gardening and related topics. Educated at Bennington College, Mansfield College, Oxford, and Columbia University, Pollan has served as a writer in residence at the University of Wisconsin and a visiting writer in non-fiction at the University of Pittsburgh. A prolific writer, Pollan has written for such popular magazines as *Esquire, Vogue, Mother Jones, Gourmet, Travel and Leisure,* and *Smithsonian.* His full-length work includes the best sellers *The Botany of Desire: A Plant's Eye View of the World* (2001), *The Omnivore's Dilemma: A Natural History of Four Meals* (2006), and *In Defense of Food: An Eater's Manifesto* (2008). One reviewer of Pollan's work has observed that the author "isn't preachy" and that he is "funny and adventurous," a tone that seems evident in the *Time Magazine* essay from June 4, 2006 reprinted below.

1   Once upon a time Americans had a culture of food to guide us through the increasingly treacherous landscape of food choices: fat vs. carbs, organic vs. conventional, vegetarian vs. carnivorous. Culture in this case is just a fancy way of saying "your mom." She taught us what to eat, when to eat it, how much of it to eat, even the order in which to eat it. But Mom's influence over the dinner menu has proved no match for the $36 billion in food-marketing dollars ($10 billion directed to kids alone) designed to get us to eat more, eat all manner of dubious neofoods, and create entire new eating occasions, such as in the car. Some food culture.

2   I've spent the past five years exploring this daunting food landscape, following the industrial food chain from the Happy Meal back to the not-so-happy feedlots in Kansas and cornfields in Iowa where it begins and tracing the organic food chain back to the farms. My aim was simply to figure out what—as a nutritional, ethical, political and environmental matter—

I should eat. Along the way, I've collected a few rules of thumb that may be useful in navigating what I call the Omnivore's Dilemma.

3   Don't eat anything your great-great-great grandmother wouldn't recognize as food. Imagine how baffled your ancestors would be in a modern supermarket: the epoxy-like tubes of Go-Gurt, the preternaturally fresh Twinkies, the vaguely pharmaceutical Vitamin Water. Those aren't foods, quite; they're food products. History suggests you might want to wait a few decades or so before adding such novelties to your diet, the substitution of margarine for butter being the classic case in point. My mother used to predict "they" would eventually discover that butter was better for you. She was right: the trans-fatty margarine is killing us. Eat food, not food products.

4   Avoid foods containing high-fructose corn syrup (HFCS). It's not just in cereals and soft drinks but also in ketchup and bologna, baked goods, soups and salad dressings. Though HFCS was not part of the human diet until 1975, each of us now consumes more than 40 lbs. a year, some 200 calories a day. Is HFCS any worse for you than sugar? Probably not, but by avoiding it you'll avoid thousands of empty calories and perhaps even more important, cut out highly processed foods—the ones that contain the most sugar, fat and salt. Besides, what chef uses high-fructose corn syrup? Not one. It's found only in the pantry of the food scientist, and that's not who you want cooking your meals.

5   Spend more, eat less. Americans are as addicted to cheap food as we are to cheap oil. We spend only 9.7% of our income on food, a smaller share than any other nation. Is it a coincidence we spend a larger percentage than any other on health care (16%)? All this "cheap food" is making us fat and sick. It's also bad for the health of the environment. The higher the quality of the food you eat, the more nutritious it is and the less of it you'll need to feel satisfied.

6   Pay no heed to nutritional science or the health claims on packages. It was science that told us margarine made from trans fats is better for us than butter made from cow's milk. The more I learn about the science of nutrition, the less certain I am that we've learned anything important about food that our ancestors didn't know. Consider that the healthiest foods in the supermarket—the fresh produce—are the ones that don't make FDA-approved health claims, which typically festoon the packages of the most highly processed foods. When Whole Grain Lucky Charms show up in the cereal aisle, it's time to stop paying attention to health claims.

7   Shop at the farmers' market. You'll begin to eat foods in season, when they are at the peak of their nutritional value and flavor, and you'll cook, because you won't find anything processed or microwavable. You'll also be supporting farmers in your community, helping defend the countryside from sprawl, saving oil by eating food produced nearby and teaching your children that a carrot is a root, not a machine-lathed orange bullet that comes

in a plastic bag. A lot more is going on at the farmers' market than the exchange of money for food.

8   How you eat is as important as what you eat. Americans are fixated on nutrients, good and bad, while the French and Italians focus on the whole eating experience. The lesson of the "French paradox" is you can eat all kinds of supposedly toxic substances (triple crÃfÂ me cheese, foie gras) as long as you follow your culture's (i.e., mother's) rules: eat moderate portions, don't go for seconds or snacks between meals, never eat alone. But perhaps most important, eat with pleasure, because eating with anxiety leads to poor digestion and bingeing. There is no French paradox, really, only an American paradox: a notably unhealthy people obsessed with the idea of eating healthily. So, relax. Eat Food. And savor it.

THINKING ABOUT THE TEXT

1. Why does Pollan begin his essay acknowledging the controversial food choices that he calls a "treacherous landscape"? How does his citing the conflicting choices attract his reader?

2. After recognizing "Mom's influence" in some of our eating habits, Pollan admits that "Mom" is "no match for the $36 billion in food-marketing dollars" (214). What does Pollan mean?

3. What is the purpose of Pollan's second paragraph, in which he briefly acknowledges his history of food exploration? What has his experience included?

4. Which of Pollan's six rules is most persuasive? Which idea is least convincing or workable for you? Which advice would be easiest for you to incorporate into your life?

5. What *is* the "Omnivore's Dilemma"?

WRITING FROM THE TEXT

1. Write an analysis of a few of your meals in a one-week period to show that Pollan would or would not approve of your choices. Cite specific points in Pollan's essay to show how your eating habits compare or contrast with his advice.

2. Visit a farmers' market in your town with the intention of writing an essay that supports Pollan's view that there is "a lot more . . . going on at the farmers' market than the exchange of money for food" (216). Work for vivid description that *shows* what is going on.

3. With the intention of supporting or refuting Pollan's view that Americans "are fixated on nutrients, good or bad" rather than "the whole eating experience," write an analysis of your eating habits or those of your family or friends.

CONNECTING WITH OTHER TEXTS

1. In "My Son, My Compass" (p. 8), the author shows how her son persuasively influenced his family to profoundly change its eating habits. With Smith's piece as inspiration, write an essay to convince your family or friends that Pollan's advice for eating wisely might be incorporated into your lives.

2. Incorporating information from Jane E. Brody's essay "'Diabesity,' A Crisis in an Expanding Country" (204) and Michael Pollan's advice for eating wisely, argue that Americans, or you and your friends, must make significant changes in eating habits.

Chapter 5

Between
Points of View

In this chapter we present a number of contrasting viewpoints on timely issues and values that influence the choices we make as individuals and as citizens. In our initial pairing, Joe Queenan questions Thomas Friedman's assertion that the Internet has created a threatening transparency that renders us all exposed and vulnerable. The use of the Internet is also a problem for Scott Haig who humorously satirizes the intense Googling of a potential patient while, in contrast, Rahul Parikh argues that physicians should assist their patients' use of the Internet for medical information. Both Clifford Stoll and Don Tapscott also weigh in on opposite sides of the debate on the value of the Internet in the elementary school classroom. Two additional writers who have alternative views—in this case, of reality television—are James Poniewozik, who extols the virtues of reality TV programming, and Jeremy Peters, who perceives that some reality shows are dangerous to participants.

Rather than opposing each other, both Philip Dacey and Andy Warhol see Coke as a symbol of America as much as a popular drink, but they use different media for their creative efforts. In addition, Anne Lamott and Bill McKibben reflect on society's contrasting viewpoints on abortion and global warming. These controversial issues can prompt lively debate, and they can also cause people to pressure others to act—or not act—when responsible decision-making is needed. Carol Tavris urges readers to respond as individuals rather than succumbing to group pressure or, worse, irresponsible lethargy. Two famous works by George Orwell and Martin Luther King Jr. also illustrate the ill effects of group pressure on the decisions we make. As you read these alternate views, you will need to work hard to remain open to ideas that don't immediately appeal to you or seem initially convincing. If you follow Peter Elbow's advice (405–406) and play "the believing game" as you consider each argument, trying to understand it from the inside out, you may find yourself considering fresh views that you would have ridiculed had you only played "the doubting game."

The Whole World Is Watching
Thomas L. Friedman

Having won his third Pulitzer Prize as a foreign affairs writer and columnist for the *New York Times*, Thomas L. Friedman (b. 1953) was elected to the Pulitzer Prize Board in 2005. He earned a Master of Philosophy degree in modern Middle East studies from Oxford University. Working for the *New York Times* since 1981, Friedman has served as bureau chief in both Beirut and Israel as well as the chief economic correspondent in the Washington bureau and the chief Washington correspondent. His book *From Beirut to Jerusalem* (1989) won the National Book Award for non-fiction in 1989, and *The Lexus and the Olive Tree* (2000) won the 2000 Overseas Press Club award for the best non-fiction book on foreign policy and has been published in 27 languages. He also wrote *Longitudes and Attitudes: The World in the Age of Terrorism* (2002) and *The World is Flat: A Brief History of the 21st Century* (2005). In 2004, he was awarded the Overseas Press Club Award for lifetime achievement and the honorary title "Order of the British Empire (OBE)" by Queen Elizabeth. The following column originally appeared in the *New York Times* on June 27, 2007.

1   Three years ago, I was catching a plane at Boston's Logan airport and went to buy some magazines for the flight. As I approached the cash register, a woman coming from another direction got there just behind me—I thought. But when I put my money down to pay, the woman said in a very loud voice: "Excuse me! I was here first!" And then she fixed me with a piercing stare that said: "I know who you are." I said I was very sorry, but I was clearly there first.

2   If that happened today, I would have had a very different reaction. I would have said: "Miss, I'm so sorry. I am entirely in the wrong. Please, go ahead. And can I buy your magazines for you? May I buy your lunch? Can I shine your shoes?"

3   Why? Because I'd be thinking there is some chance this woman has a blog or a camera in her cellphone and could, if she so chose, tell the whole world about our encounter—entirely from her perspective—and my utterly rude, boorish, arrogant, thinks-he-can-butt-in-line behavior. Yikes!

4   When everyone has a blog, a MySpace page or Facebook entry, everyone is a publisher. When everyone has a cellphone with a camera in it, everyone

is a paparazzo. When everyone can upload video on YouTube, everyone is a filmmaker. When everyone is a publisher, paparazzo or filmmaker, everyone else is a public figure. We're all public figures now. The blogosphere has made the global discussion so much richer—and each of us so much more transparent.

5   The implications of all this are the subject of a new book by Dov Seidman, founder and C.E.O. of LRN, a business ethics company. His book is simply called *How*. Seidman's simple thesis is that in this transparent world, "how" you live your life and "how" you conduct your business matters more than ever because so many people can now see into what you do and tell so many other people about it on their own without any editor. To win now, he argues, you have to turn these new conditions to your advantage.

6   For young people, writes Seidman, this means understanding that your reputation in life is going to get set in stone so much earlier. More and more of what you say or do or write will end up as a digital fingerprint that never gets erased. Our generation got to screw up and none of those screw-ups appeared on our first job resumés, which we got to write. For this generation, much of what they say, do or write will be preserved online forever. Before employers even read their résumés, they'll Google them.

7   "The persistence of memory in electronic form makes second chances harder to come by," writes Seidman. "In the information age, life has no chapters or closets; you can leave nothing behind, and you have nowhere to hide your skeletons. Your past is your present." So the only way to get ahead in life will be by getting your "hows" right. Ditto in business. Companies that get their hows wrong won't be able to just hire a P.R. firm to clean up the mess by taking a couple of reporters to lunch—not when everyone is a reporter and can talk back and be heard globally.

8   But this also creates opportunities. Today "what" you make is quickly copied and sold by everyone. But "how" you engage your customers, "how" you keep your promises and "how" you collaborate with partners—that's not so easy to copy, and that is where companies can now really differentiate themselves. "When it comes to human conduct there is tremendous variation, and where a broad spectrum of variation exists, opportunity exists," writes Seidman. "The tapestry of human behavior is so varied, so rich and so global that it presents a rare opportunity, the opportunity to *outbehave the competition*."

9   How can you outbehave your competition? In Michigan, Seidman writes, one hospital taught its doctors to apologize when they make mistakes, and dramatically cut their malpractice claims. In Texas, a large auto dealership allowed every mechanic to spend freely whatever company money was necessary to do the job right, and saw their costs actually decline while customer satisfaction improved. A New York street doughnut-seller trusted his customers

to make their own change and found he could serve more people faster and build the loyalty that keeps them coming back.

10 "We do not live in glass houses (houses have walls); we live on glass microscope slides . . . visible and exposed to all," he writes. So whether you're selling cars or newspapers (or just buying one at the newsstand), get your hows right—how you build trust, how you collaborate, how you lead and how you say you're sorry. More people than ever will know about it when you do—or don't.

THINKING ABOUT THE TEXT

1. What is Friedman's strategy in opening with a personal anecdote about an encounter with another customer? Contrast his response then with the way he would respond today.

2. What does Friedman mean by his claim that we are all "more transparent" now in "this transparent world"? What are the positive and negative aspects of this transparency?

3. Explain the author's summary of the thesis of Dov Seidman's new book *How*. In what ways will a young person's "digital fingerprint" differ from the work resumés of the past?

4. How does Seidman predict that the global blogosphere will provide more "opportunities" for individuals and for companies to *outbehave the competition*"? What examples of "outbehaving" does Seidman provide?

5. Seidman believes that "we don't live in glass houses" but "on glass microscopic slides" (221). What does he mean by this metaphor? And what are the "hows" that people have to get right?

WRITING FROM THE TEXT

1. Using specifics from your own "digital fingerprints" (any blog entries, pages, or spaces that can be traced back to you), write an argument agreeing or disagreeing with Friedman's contention that one's online activity may prejudice an employer even before a work resumé is fully considered. You may want to compare and contrast your digital fingerprint, the persona you have created on your online pages, with your work resumé. You might even write this as a humorous essay, imagining an employer evaluating your online materials instead of ever considering your actual resumé.

2. If you have conducted business transactions online—bought or sold products or services, rented an apartment, posted your performances on YouTube—write an essay explaining whether your encounters with Internet

"transparency" (open access and availability) have been an advantage or disadvantage—or a combination of both. Include specific details from your experiences to support your claims.

3. Write an argument essay supporting or rejecting Friedman's claim that "the blogosphere has made the global discussion so much richer—and each of us so much more transparent" (220). Illustrate specific ways that your life is or isn't richer and more transparent because of online activities.

CONNECTING WITH OTHER TEXTS

1. Read Joe Queenan's "YouTube This!" and write an essay supporting or opposing his criticisms of Friedman's points. Include details from both essays to support your claims.

2. Both Friedman in "The Whole World Is Watching" and Don Tapscott in "Learning as Fun" (p. 255) argue that the Internet has expanded and enriched both commercial and educational opportunities worldwide. Using support from both essays, argue for or against this claim.

YouTube This!

Joe Queenan

A freelance writer since 1990, Joe Queenan (b. 1950) has published a number of popular books "gleefully skewering Hollywood airheads and other hapless patsies," as critic Bruce McCall describes Queenan's stance. Titles of Queenan's books reflect his voice: *Red Lobster, White Trash, and the Blue Lagoon* (1998), *My Goodness: A Cynic's Short-Lived Search for Sainthood* (2000), *Balsamic Dreams: A Short But Self-Important History of the Baby Boomer Generation* (2001), and *True Believers: The Tragic Life of Sports Fans* (2003). Queenan also contributes to such popular periodicals as *Barron's,* the *New York Times Book Review, Gentleman's Quarterly, Rolling Stone,* and *Movieline.* A favorite childhood pastime of going to his Philadelphia neighborhood's local movie theater undoubtedly prompted his decision to review films and write political commentary after his graduation from St. Joseph's University. Although *Twelve Steps to Death* has been described as "atrocious" and a "hyperbolic spoof of moviemaking," Queenan fulfilled his goal, in 1995, of making a film for under $7,000. The essay below appeared originally in the *Los Angeles Times* opinion section on July 8, 2007.

1   In the audaciously predictable style for which he is famous, New York Times columnist Thomas Friedman recently rhapsodized about the many ways in which "transparency" is making our "global discussion . . . so much richer."

2   The theory was that the 24/7 surveillance wrought by camera phones, blogs, YouTube, Facebook and MySpace have turned all of us into public

figures. Because everything we say or do is now apt to turn up on the Internet—potentially with humiliating results—we must now live our lives more judiciously, cognizant that in the new "transparent" age, there is nowhere to hide.

3   Not long ago, such a society would have been deemed an Orwellian nightmare, a living hell where the brain police spied on everyone. But somehow Friedman has gotten it into his head that although surveillance is a bad idea when the government does it, it is just peachy keen when done by amateurs.

4   I'm not so sure. It seems to me that if YouTube had been around when George Washington failed to prevent his Indian allies from butchering unarmed French prisoners (and thereby started the French and Indian War), his career could've been ruined at the start, paving the way for some circumspect scoundrel like Aaron Burr or Benedict Arnold to sabotage the republic before it even got off the ground.

5   If camera phones had been widely available in the 1930s, shots of FDR's wheelchair would have been posted all over the Internet, and Roosevelt might very well have lost the 1936 election to one of the gutless clowns the Republicans regularly ran against him.

6   Friedman's argument that "the whole world is watching"—thereby compelling mankind to be on its best behavior—ignores reality. The Taliban is simply not concerned that some blogger, hammering away at his laptop in his mommy's basement, doesn't approve of its activities. Hamas is not worried about having its latest depredations captured on cellphone cameras.

7   Hugo Chavez doesn't care how many videos poking fun at him are posted on YouTube—he's still going to silence the media, suppress the opposition and wreck Venezuela's economy. By the looks of it, Chavez feels the same way about blogs: Sticks and stones may break his bones, but words will never hurt him.

8   Friedman suggests that the "digital footprint" young people leave on MySpace and Facebook means—and he doesn't seem to think this is necessarily bad—that it will be extremely difficult for them to recover from the mistakes of their youth. Deceitful resumes, compromising photos, ill-advised confessions of sexual predilections could all come back to haunt them. But this assumes that some future version of American society will actually hold people accountable for their bozo-like past behavior. Get real. When the 35-year-old twit who once posted a video of himself mooning Dick Cheney applies for a job with the International Monetary Fund, the 36-year-old interviewing him for the position will be the guy who once blogged about imprisoning George Bush on the planet Alderaan and getting the Death Star to destroy the State Department. That's not a digital foot-print. It's a digital handshake.

9   The one seemingly valid point that Friedman makes is that transparency will force corporations to be on their best behavior. But even this is a flawed

assumption. Camera phones and YouTube videos are useful when depicting pollution or botched surgical procedures. But transparency doesn't work well in the bond market or the private equity field because finance is an abstraction and cellphone cameras cannot capture the invisible. You cannot post a picture of a hyped stock. You cannot post a video of a rigged initial public offering. You cannot depict felonious stock market activity on MySpace unless some white-collar crook agrees to be videotaped.

10   If "the new transparency" could actually deter obnoxious or criminal behavior, it might be worth getting the whole world watching. But YouTube postings are not going to prevent real estate developers from building hideous McMansions, and no amount of blogging is going to keep lunatics in Hummers from plowing into Chevrolet Cavaliers. Muggers, drug dealers, car thieves, ax murderers, hedge fund managers and Antonin Scalia are not afraid of the blogosphere. Especially Scalia.

11   The weapons of transparency may be good at embarrassing people, but this approach only works with people who worry about being embarrassed. The Mafia doesn't. Osama bin Laden doesn't. The guy who's going to key your car tonight just because you stole his parking space doesn't. And the woman who might conceivably confront you with your quasi-pornographic, falsehood-swollen online profile 10 years from now isn't going to because she's the gal who once posted a video of herself puking her guts all over her wedding cake.

12   In a society in which everyone has already decided to immortalize their stupidity, being an idiot isn't going to hurt anyone's career. The new "transparency" is just like the old television: The whole world may be watching, but nobody seems to be paying much attention.

THINKING ABOUT THE TEXT

1. Queenan's essay is a rejoinder to Thomas Friedman's essay "The Whole World Is Watching" (p. 222). If Friedman's thesis is that transparency, being revealed to the public, makes our globe richer and people more cautious, what does Queenan believe?

2. Queenan cites good people whose lives would not have been better with more transparency or public exposure (George Washington, Franklin D. Roosevelt) and some notorious organizations or leaders (the Taliban, Hamas, Hugo Chavez) who aren't affected by YouTube or cellphone cameras. What is the point that Queenan is making?

3. How does Queenan counter the view that young people may risk exposing themselves injudiciously with a youthful "digital footprint"? What is Queenan's point about the "35-year old twit" who posted a shot of

himself mooning Dick Cheney? What does he mean by a "digital handshake"?

4. Why is Queenan not optimistic about YouTube postings having the capacity to curtail corruption?

5. What does Queenan mean when he compares the "new transparency" with the "old television"?

WRITING FROM THE TEXT

1. Write a detailed description of what you or a friend created on YouTube, Facebook, or MySpace and explain why you expressed yourself in this medium.

2. Argue in an essay that a YouTube video is or is not an effective consciousness-raising medium. Analyze two or three short productions to illustrate your point and include specific descriptions of these productions to support your view.

3. Queenan believes that we live in a society in which "everyone has already decided to immortalize their stupidity" (224). Write an analysis of a few MySpace or Facebook postings that seem to support Queenan's view.

4. Describe a time when you observed a change in people's perception because of a YouTube, Facebook, or MySpace posting. Describe the entry and what happened as a result of people viewing it.

CONNECTING WITH OTHER TEXTS

1. After reading both Thomas L. Friedman's "The Whole World Is Watching" (p. 219) and Queenan's work above, write an essay that asserts your own position on the advantages or problems of MySpace, Facebook, or YouTube. Cite the views of both writers as you support your own thesis.

2. Use the strategy of Michael Pollan in "Six Rules for Eating Wisely" (p. 214) and write an essay (not a list) describing and explaining the rules for posting a MySpace entry that is both creative and wise.

When the Patient Is a Googler
Scott Haig

Assistant clinical professor of orthopedic surgery at Columbia University, Scott Haig (b.1958) writes a biweekly medical article for *Time Magazine* in addition to maintaining a private medical practice in Scarsdale, New York. Haig has earned degrees from Yale

University, a B.A. in Physics in 1980 and an M.D. in 1983. A Bronxville High School varsity football player and, at Yale, a member of the Judo Team and an Intramural Football Team Captain, Haig has good writing and eating advice: "Edit, edit, sleep on it and edit again; recast sentences are invariably better. Before every adverb (and donut) ask: 'Do I really need that?' And every word, sentence and paragraph must bring the reader closer to your goal: define that goal as clearly as possible before starting to write." The essay below appeared in *Time Magazine* on May 1, 2006. Can you infer Dr. Haig's goal in writing this essay?

1 We had never met, but as we talked on the phone I knew she was Googling me. The way she drew out her conjunctions, just a little, that was the tip off—stalling for time as new pages loaded. It was barely audible, but the soft click-click of the keyboard in the background confirmed it. Oh, well, it's the information age. Normally, she'd have to go through my staff first, but I gave her an appointment.

2 Susan was well spoken and in good shape, an attractive woman in her mid-40s. She had brought her three-year-old to my office, but was ignoring the little monster as he ripped up magazines, threw fish crackers and Cheerios, and stomped them into my rug. I tried to ignore him too, which was hard as he dribbled chocolate milk from his sippy cup all over my uphol-stered chairs. Eventually his screeching made conversation impossible.

3 "This is not an acceptable form of behavior, not acceptable at all," was Susan's excruciatingly well-enunciated and perfunctory response to Junior's screaming. The toddler's defiant delight signaled that he understood just enough to ignore her back. Meanwhile, Mom launched into me with a barrage of excru-ciatingly well-informed questions. I soon felt like throwing Cheerios at her, too.

4 Susan had chosen me because she had researched my education, read a paper I had written, determined my university affiliation and knew where I lived. It was a little too much—as if she knew how stinky and snorey I was last Sunday morning. Yes, she was simply researching important aspects of her own health care. Yes, who your surgeon is certainly affects what your sur-geon does. But I was unnerved by how she brandished her information, too personal and just too rude on our first meeting.

5 Every doctor knows patients like this. They're called "brainsuckers." By the time they come in, they've visited many other docs already—somehow unable to stick with any of them. They have many complaints, which rarely translate to hard findings on any objective tests. They talk a lot. I often won-der, while waiting for them to pause, if there are patients like this in poor, war-torn countries where the need for doctors is more dire.

6   Susan got me thinking about patients. Nurses are my favorites—they know our language and they're used to putting their trust in doctors. And they laugh at my jokes. But engineers, as a class, are possibly the best patients. They're logical and they're accustomed to the concept of consultation—they're interested in how the doctor thinks about their problem. They know how to use experts. If your orthopedist thinks about arthritis, for instance, in terms of friction between roughened joint surfaces, you should try to think about it, generally, in the same way. There is little use coming to him or her for help if you insist your arthritis is due to an imbalance between yin and yang, an interruption of some imaginary force field or a dietary deficiency of molybdenum. There's so much information (as well as misinformation) in medicine—and, yes, a lot of it can be Googled—that one major responsibility of an expert is to know what to ignore.

7   Susan had neither the trust of a nurse nor the teachability of an engineer. She would ignore no theory of any culture or any quack, regarding her very common brand of knee pain. On and on she went as I retreated further within. I marveled, sitting there silenced by her diatribe. Hers was such a fully orbed and vigorous self-concern that it possessed virtue in its own right. Her complete and utter selfishness was nearly a thing of beauty.

8   When to punt is not a topic taught in medical school. There is but one observation that I can offer: Patients like Susan, as self-absorbed as they are, know it immediately. They can tell when you're about to punt.

9   I knew full well what was wrong with this woman, and I could treat her, probably as well as anyone. But treating her condition, which was chronic patellofemoral pain, would test the mettle of patient and surgeon. What we have doesn't work very well nor very quickly. The swelling takes months to go down, the muscles take even longer to strengthen. Good patients often complain, "It was better before we started," in desperation or anger, before they see improvement. But with plenty of therapy, braces, exercises and one or two operations, this knee does improve. It's often tough going, though, and patients have to stick with you. I like to be straight—"It gets worse before it gets better" is what I tell them. Susan's style, her history and, somehow, most telling, the way she treated her son said she was not going to make it through this. Not with me, anyway.

10   A seasoned doc gets good at sizing up what kind of patient he's got and how to adjust his communicative style accordingly. Some patients are noncompliant Bozos who won't read anything longer than a headline. They don't want to know what's wrong with them, they don't know what medicines they're taking, they don't even seem to care what kind of operation you're planning to do on them. "Just get me better, doc," is all they say.

11   At the other end of our spectrum are patients like Susan: They're often suspicious and distrustful, their pressured sentences burst with misused,

mispronounced words and half-baked ideas. Unfortunately, both types of patients get sick with roughly the same frequency.

12   I knew Susan was a Googler—queen, perhaps, of all Googlers. But I couldn't dance with this one. I couldn't even get a word in edgewise. So, I cut her off. I punted. I told her there was nothing I could do differently than her last three orthopedists, but I could refer her to another who might be able to help. A certain Dr. Brown, whom I'd known as a resident, had been particularly interested in her type of knee problem.

13   Disappointed and annoyed, Susan stopped for a beat.

14   "You mean Larry Brown on Central Avenue?"

15   "Uh, yes—" I started.

16   "I have an appointment with him on Friday. And, Dr. Haig?" she said, pulling Junior by the arm out my office door, "Watch out on your drive home tonight. There was an accident near your exit."

THINKING ABOUT THE TEXT

1. What are Scott Haig's tone and stance in this essay? Cite three specific reasons that explain why he does not want to have Susan as a patient.

2. How do Haig's depictions of Susan's voice in her "excruciatingly well-enunciated and perfunctory response" to her child contribute to his essay and the point that he is making?

3. The title of Dr. Haig's essay suggests that he doesn't like Susan's having researched her knee problem on the Internet. But Haig cites two kinds of intelligent patients he relishes treating. What is the difference that he perceives between them and Susan?

4. Haig's essay has moments of sarcastic humor. Find three or four examples and describe how these droll but humorous lines contribute to the author's intention. What is Haig's intention in this essay?

5. In what specific ways does Haig seem an aloof, arrogant physician? In what ways does he show himself to be an intuitive, reasonable man?

WRITING FROM THE TEXT

1. Describe a time when you had the option of helping or serving someone—a friend, a customer, a neighbor, an employer—but decided "to punt," as Dr. Haig decided. In your description of the event, like Haig, create a vivid portrait of the person whom you declined to assist as you also show your reasons for backing out.

2. Write an evaluative response of Haig's essay to argue that he is right or wrong in his condemnation of Susan and his decision to pass her on to

another physician. Return often to Haig's language to write a convincing essay. You may want to review how to write an evaluative response (pp. 438–444) before you start to draft your work.

CONNECTING WITH OTHER TEXTS

1. After reading "Is There a Doctor in the Mouse?", write a description of an ideal physician using both Haig's and Parikh's positions to inform your analysis.

2. Read "Is There a Doctor in the Mouse?" and write your own response to Scott Haig. You might research a health concern or curiosity that you have using Organized Wisdom, as Dr. Parikh recommends, to write a convincing argument to persuade Dr. Haig that patients have a right to actively investigate their own health problems and treatments.

 ## Is There a Doctor in the Mouse?
Rahul K. Parikh

A physician with a full-time practice, Rahul K. Parikh (b. 1972) serves as Chief of Patient Education for the Kaiser Permanente system in the San Francisco Bay area, working closely with teens. Parikh earned his B.A. from UC Berkeley and his M.D. from Tufts University School of Medicine and has written numerous articles about medicine and society. Parikh's work, archived at www.rahulkparikh.com, has appeared on KQED Radio and in the *Los Angeles Times*, the *San Francisco Chronicle*, the *Contra Costa Times*, and *Slate*. The following essay originally appeared in Salon.com on Jan. 10, 2008, in response to the previous essay, "When the Patient Is a Googler," by Scott Haig on p. 225.

1   In November, Time magazine's medical writer, Dr. Scott Haig, wrote an article, "When the Patient Is a Googler," in which he described a frustrating experience with a patient who had chronic knee pain. Even before he met the woman, Susan, in person, he was frustrated with her because she was Googling information as he talked to her over the phone. Things got worse when she came to his office and told him she had researched his medical background and qualifications, and had read a paper he'd published. "I was unnerved by how she brandished her information, too personal and just too rude on our first meeting," he wrote. He proceeded to call her the "queen, perhaps, of all Googlers," a class of patients he referred to as "brainsuckers."

2   The problem with Haig's article, other than petulance, is that he's ignoring every single Internet trend in healthcare over the past decade. The

medical establishment, in fact, has taken way too much time to understand that the Internet is a disruptive innovation that has overturned the status quo. It has leveled the playing field between expert and novice—in this case, doctor and patient. While some doctors, like Haig, may find that challenge threatening to their status as an expert, the Web is now providing the kind of information doctors need to be aware of if we want to continue to be good at our job and the kind of trends that can help patients be smarter and healthier.

3   According to a 2006 study of online health searches by the Pew Research Center, eight of 10 Internet users, up to 113 million Americans, have gone online looking for health information on behalf of themselves or a loved one. For those with a chronic problem, like Susan, that number rises. People with chronic medical problems are more avid users of the Web and state that their online searches affect treatment decisions, their interactions with doctors, and their ability to cope with their condition. That's not something that any doctor can dismiss.

4   Haig is absolutely right when he says, "There's so much information (as well as misinformation) in medicine—and, yes, a lot of it can be Googled—that one major responsibility of an expert is to know what to ignore." However, in refusing to treat Susan, Haig doesn't seem to have any interest in being that kind of expert. His attitude reflects many doctors' angst about the Internet. A 2004 study showed that almost two-thirds of patients would like to have Internet information provided to them by their doctor. In contrast, a 2001 study of doctors showed that barely half of them encouraged their patients to go online (although the trend has been increasing over time), and 80 percent actually warned them against doing so.

5   In one regard, this is simply bad business. Pew tells us that patients either fire doctors unwilling to help them with the Web or keep going online without telling them. More important, when patients do venture online themselves, they can sink into a swamp of outdated medical studies, confront a lot of misinformation, and risk creating a rift in the doctor-patient relationship.

6   Just ask those of us who are pediatricians. The theory that vaccines cause autism first came onto the scene in the late '90s, just as people were going online en masse. We weren't paying much attention until parents started to refuse vaccines. When we looked, we realized that many parents were exposed to story after story on autism Web sites and in chat rooms about the dangers of vaccines. That echo chamber of opinion became a reality despite our best efforts to prove otherwise. Now we're left with a lingering conspiracy theory that vaccines cause autism, even though the best, unbiased evidence says otherwise.

7   Would things have been different if we had engaged our patients from the get-go by providing them with alternative Web sites, scrutinizing and rebutting anti-vaccine "science," or posting studies demonstrating vaccine safety in the public domain? I would answer, emphatically, yes.

8   Today, there are many accurate, high-quality health sites, and doctors should make it a standard practice to recommend them to each and every patient. Besides reducing the randomness of a Web search, this can reinforce a physician's advice during a visit, which is especially helpful, as studies show that patients typically remember no more than half of what their doctor tells them.

9   Over the past few years, Internet entrepreneurs have realized the vast potential of healthcare information. One example is *Organized Wisdom,* a search engine for medical issues. What gives it an edge over general search engines like Google and Yahoo is that its content is vetted by health professionals. If you type "autism" into *Organized Wisdom,* you'll receive an organized set of links to reliable sites that allow you to look at the symptoms of autism, potential treatments, research studies, and support groups. If you do the same using Google, the first site you'll see is *Autism.org.* If you click the link, you'll be taken to a page sponsored by groups preaching that vaccines are unsafe and favoring "alternative" treatments that are untested and potentially dangerous.

10   Other good sites are linked to academic centers like the renowned Mayo Clinic, private groups like *Kaiser Permanente* (full disclosure: I'm a Kaiser doctor), and the government's *Healthfinder.* These sites feature accurate, up-to-date information that is regularly reviewed and updated. The emergence of personal health records like Microsoft's *Health Vault* has also been beneficial. They allow individuals to store their medical information online and keep it accessible through the usual barrage of job, doctor and insurance changes. All of these ventures, in addition to being potentially lucrative for their creators, help to educate patients. These newer sites have joined traditional health sites like *WebMD,* long a staple of good health information and news.

11   But doctors need to know about them so that along with a prescription for a medication or lab test, they can give patients a prescription for information that informs, empowers and helps patients be smarter and healthier. Patients who, prior to a visit, consult information online can better share in the decision-making process with their doctor. Afterward, they can go online to find information that reinforces their decision or introduces them to viable alternatives.

12   So maybe instead of being sour, Dr. Haig should consider learning a thing or two about Web health himself. I thing it'll only make him a better doctor.

THINKING ABOUT THE TEXT

1. What is Parikh's support for his claim that Haig, in his response to a patient like Susan, is "ignoring every single Internet trend in healthcare over the past decade"?

2. Explain three different benefits of using online searches for people with chronic health problems.

3. Explain Parikh's classic concession-refutation strategy in paragraph 4, where he seems to agree with Haig at first but then opposes him even more adamantly. Why is this strategy so effective?

4. How do the patient studies conducted in 2001 and 2004 support Parikh's claim that many doctors demonstrate an "angst about the Internet"? Why does Parikh contend it "is simply bad business" for doctors to refuse to help patients with Web searches?

5. How does Parikh believe that doctors could have prevented the spreading of the Internet misinformation that vaccines cause autism?

6. Explain why using a medical search engine like *Organized Wisdom* for information on autism is far superior to Googling *autism*. What other medical sites does Parikh highly recommend for good health information and news?

WRITING FROM THE TEXT

1. If you have had physicians guide or help you with Internet searches or criticize and discourage your use of the Web, write an essay analyzing your experience. Use details from Parikh's essay to develop and support your points.

2. If you have used any of the medical sites that Parikh recommends to gather health information, write an essay evaluating Parikh's essay in light of your own experience. (See evaluative response, p. 438.)

CONNECTING WITH OTHER TEXTS

1. After reading "When the Patient Is a Googler" (p. 225), write an essay supporting or countering Parikh's assessment of Haig's attitude and response to Susan.

2. Using Parikh's essay and two other works about the Internet—"Modern Romance" (p. 51), "Virtual Love" (p. 56), "The Whole World Is Watching" (p. 219), "YouTube This!" (p. 222), "When the Patient Is a Googler" (p. 225), "Makes Learning Fun" (p. 247), or "From Learning as Torture" (p. 255)—write an analysis of the strengths and weaknesses of, or cautions for, using the Web.

Why Reality TV Is Good For Us

James Poniewozik

A graduate of the University of Michigan with a B.A. in English, James Poniewozik was the media critic and section editor at Salon.com from 1997 to 1999. He wrote two columns a week on subjects ranging from advertising to the cultural significance of eBay and the Antiques Roadshow. Prior to his jobs at Salon, he contributed to such publications as *Fortune, Rolling Stone*, and *The New York Times Book Review*. He is also a regular commentator on NPR's *On the Media* and *All Things Considered*. Poniewozik joined *Time* as a media and television critic in July 1999 where, in addition to his writing on books, movies, and comic books, and his analyses of such subjects as reality TV, he has also investigated international media coverage of the war in Iraq and the influence of 9/11 on popular culture. The essay reprinted below originally appeared in *Time*, Feb. 17, 2003.

1   For eight single professional women gathered in Dallas, it is holy Wednesday—the night each week that they gather in one of their homes for the Traveling *Bachelorette* Party. Munching snacks and passing a bottle of wine, they cheer, cry, and cackle as their spiritual leader, Trista Rehn, braves heartache, indecision, and the occasional recitation of bad poetry to choose from among her twenty-five swains. Yet something is unsettling Leah Hudson's stomach, and it's not just the wine. "I hate that we've been sucked into the Hoover vac of reality TV," says Hudson, thirty. "Do we not have anything better to do than to live vicariously through a bunch of fifteen-minute-fame seekers?"

2   There you have the essence of reality TV's success: it is the one mass-entertainment category that thrives because of its audience's contempt for it. It makes us feel tawdry, dirty, cheap—if it didn't, we probably wouldn't bother tuning in. And in this, for once, the audience and critics agree. Just listen to the raves for America's hottest TV genre.

3   *"The country is gripped by misanthropy!"—New York Observer*

4   *"Ridiculous and pernicious! Many kinds of cruelty are passed off as entertainment!"—Washington Post*

5   *"So-called reality television just may be killing the medium!"—San Francisco Chronicle*

6   O.K., we added the exclamation points, but you get the idea. Yes, viewers are tuning in to *Joe Millionaire, The Bachelorette*, and *American Idol* by the tens of millions. Yet, to paraphrase Winston Churchill, never have so many watched so much TV with so little good to say about it.

7   Well, that ends here. It may ruin reality producers' marketing plans for a TV critic to say it, but reality TV is, in fact, the best thing to happen to television in several years. It has given the networks water-cooler buzz again; it has reminded viewers jaded by sitcoms and dramas why TV can be exciting; and at its best, it is teaching TV a new way to tell involving human stories.

8   A few concessions up front. First, yes, we all know that there's little reality in reality TV: those "intimate" dates, for instance, are staged in front of banks of cameras and sweltering floodlights. But it's the only phrase we've got, and I'm sticking with it. Second, I don't pretend to defend the indefensible: *Are You Hot? The Search for America's Sexiest People* isn't getting any help from me. And finally, I realize that comparing even a well-made reality show with, say, *The Simpsons* is not merely comparing apples with oranges; it's comparing onions with washing machines—no reality show can match the intelligence and layers of well-constructed fiction.

9   On a sheer ratings level, the latest wave of reality hits has worked a sea change for the networks. And it has put them back on the pop-cultural map, after losing the buzz war to cable for years. Reality shows don't just reach tens of millions of viewers but leave them feeling part of a communal experience—what network TV does best, but sitcoms and dramas haven't done since *Seinfeld* and *Twin Peaks*. (When was the last time *CSI* made you call your best friend or holler back at your TV?) "Reality has proven that network television is still relevant," says Mike Fleiss, creator of the *Bachelor* franchise.

10   This has sitcom and drama writers praying for the reality bust. "The networks only have so much time and resources," says Amy Sherman-Palladino, creator of *Gilmore Girls.* "Rather than solely focusing on convincing the Olsen twins to allow themselves to be eaten by bears in prime time, I wish they would focus on coming up with something that would really last." TV does seem to be in overkill mode, as the networks have signed up dozens of dating shows, talent searches, and other voyeurfests. And like an overheated NASDAQ, the reality market is bound to correct. But unlike earlier TV reality booms, this one is supported by a large, young audience that grew up on MTV's *The Real World* and considers reality as legitimate as dramas and sitcoms—and that, for now, prefers it.

11   And why not? It would be easier to bemoan reality shows' crowding out sitcoms and dramas if the latter weren't in such a rut. But the new network shows of fall 2002 were a creatively timid mass of remakes, bland family comedies, and derivative cop dramas. Network executives dubbed them "comfort"—i.e., familiar and boring—TV. Whereas reality TV—call it "discomfort TV"—lives to rattle viewers' cages. It provokes. It offends. But at least it's trying to do something besides help you get to sleep. Some upcoming reality concepts are idealistic, like FX's *American Candidate*, which aims to field a "people's candidate"

for president in 2004. Others are lowbrow, like ABC's *The Will* (relatives battle for an inheritance), Fox's *Married by America* (viewers vote to help pair up a bride and groom), and NBC's *Around the World in 80 Dates* (American bachelor seeks mates around the world; after all, how better to improve America's image then to send a stud to other countries to defile their women?). But all of them make you sit up and pay attention. "I like to make a show where people say, 'You can't put that on TV,'" says Fleiss. "Then I put it on TV."

12   By and large, reality shows aren't supplanting creative successes like *24* or *Scrubs;* they're filling in for duds like *Presidio Med* and *MDs.* As NBC reality chief Jeff Gaspin says, "There is a little survival-of-the-fittest thing this ends up creating." When sitcoms started cloning goofy suburban dads and quirky, pretty yuppies, we got *The Osbournes.* And now reality TV is becoming our source for involved stories about personal relationships. This used to be the stuff of dramas like the canceled *Once and Again,* until programmers began concentrating on series like *CSI* and *Law & Order,* which have characters as detailed and individuated as checkers pieces. By the time *Survivor* ends, you know its players better than you know *Law & Order's* Detective Briscoe after eleven years. Likewise, the WB's *High School Reunion,* which brings together classmates after ten years, is really asking whether you're doomed to live out your high school role—"the jock," "the nerd," or whatnot—for life. Last fall two scripted shows, *That Was Then* and Do *Over,* asked the same questions but with cardboard characters and silly premises involving time travel. They got canceled. *High School Reunion* got a second season.

13   In Britain, where reality has ruled Britannia's (air)waves for years, TV writers are starting to learn from reality's success. The sitcom *The Office* uses reality-TV techniques (jerky, handheld camera work, "confessional" interviews) to explore the petty politics of white-collar workers. Now airing on BBC America, it's the best comedy to debut here this season because its characters are the kind of hard-to-pigeonhole folks you find in life—or on reality TV. On *Survivor* and *The Amazing Race,* the gay men don't drop Judy Garland references in every scene. MTV's *Making the Band 2*—a kind of hip-top *American Idol*—gave center stage to inner-city kids who would be portrayed as perps or victims on a cop drama.

14   But aesthetics aside, the case against reality TV is mainly moral—and there's a point to it. It's hard to defend the deception of *Joe Millionaire*—which set up twenty women to court construction worker Evan Marriott by telling them he was a multimillionaire—as hilarious as its fool's-gold chase can be. Even the show's Potemkin Croesus contends that producers hid the show's premise from him until the last minute. "The day before I left for France, I signed confidentiality papers which said what the show was about," Marriott tells *Time.* "At that point, could I really back out?" Others are concerned about the message of meanness. "There's a premium on the low-

est common denominator of human relationships," James Steyer, author of *The Other Parent: The Inside Story of the Media's Effect on Our Children.* "It's often women degrading themselves. I don't want my nine-year-old thinking that's the way girls should behave."

15   So *The Bachelorette* is not morally instructive for grade-schoolers. But wallowing in the weaknesses and failings of humanity is a trademark of satire—people accused Jonathan Swift and Mark Twain of being misanthropes too—and much reality TV is really satire boiled down to one extreme gesture. A great reality-TV concept takes some commonplace piety of polite society and gives it a wedgie. Companies value team spirit; *Survivor* says the team will screw you in the end. The cult of self-esteem says everybody is talented; *American Idol*'s Simon Cowell says to sit down and shut your pie hole. Romance and feminism says a man's money shouldn't matter; *Joe Millionaire* wagers $50 million that they're wrong.

16   The social criticisms of reality TV rest on two assumptions: that millions of other people are being taken in by reality TV's deceptions (which the critic himself—or herself—is able to see through) or are being led astray by its unsavory messages (to which the critic is immune). When a reality show depicts bad behavior, it's immoral, misanthropic, sexist, or sick. When *The Sopranos* does the same thing, it's nuanced storytelling. We assume that viewers can empathize with Tony Soprano without wanting to be him; we assume they can maintain critical distance and perceive ironies between his words and the truth. Why? Because we assume that people who like *The Sopranos* are smarter, more mature—better—than people who like *The Bachelorette*.

17   And aren't they? Isn't there something simply wrong with people who enjoy entertainment that depends on ordinary people getting their heart broken, being told they can't sing, or getting played for fools? That's the question behind the protests of CBS's plans to make a real-life version of *The Beverly Hillbillies* with a poor rural family. Says Dee Davis, president of the Center for Rural Strategies, "If somebody had proposed, 'Let's go into the barrio in L. A. and find a family of immigrants and put them in a mansion, and won't it be funny when they interview maids?' then people could see that's a step too far." It's hard to either defend or attack a show that doesn't exist yet, but it's also true that the original sitcom was far harder on Mr. Drysdale than the Clampetts. And on *The Osbournes*, Ozzy—another Beverly Hills fish out of water—was "humiliated" into becoming the most beloved dad in America.

18   Indeed, for all the talk about "humiliation TV," what's striking about most reality shows is how good humored and resilient most of the participants are: the *American Idol* rejectees stubbornly convinced of their own talent, the *Fear Factor* players walking away from vats of insects like Olympic champions. What finally bothers their detractors is, perhaps, not that these

people are humiliated but that they are not. Embarrassment, these shows demonstrate, is survivable, even ignorable, and ignoring embarrassment is a skill we all could use. It is what you risk—like injury in a sport—in order to triumph. "What people are really responding to on these shows is people pursuing their dreams," says *American Candidate* producer R. J. Cutler. A reality show with all humiliation and no triumph would be boring.

19   And at their best, the shows offer something else entirely. One of the most arresting moments this TV season came on *American Idol*, when a single mom and professional boxer from Detroit flunked her audition. The show went with her backstage, with her adorable young son, as she told her life story. Her husband, a corrections officer, was murdered a few years before. She had taken up boxing—her ring name is "Lady Tiger"—because you can't raise a kid on waitress money. Her monologue went from defiance ("You'll see my album. Lady Tiger don't stop") to despair ("You ain't going nowhere in Detroit. Nowhere") to dignified resolve for her son's sake ("We're never going to quit, are we, angel?"). It was a haunting slice of life, more authentic than any *ER* subplot.

20   Was Lady Tiger setting a bad example for her son on national TV? Or setting a good example by dreaming, persevering and being proud? *American Idol* didn't say. It didn't nudge us to laugh at her or prod us to cry for her. In about two minutes, it just told a quintessentially American story of ambition and desperation and shrinking options, and it left the judgment to us. That's unsettling. That's heartbreaking. And the reality is, that's great TV.

THINKING ABOUT THE TEXT

1. Why does Poniewozik believe that reality TV is good for television as a medium as well as for the viewers? Does the author mean that reality TV is actually "good" for us or that it just isn't as "bad" as some people believe?

2. Why is "reality" programming sometimes a deceptive description? What other concessions to his praise of the medium does Poniewozik admit?

3. What does Poniewozik mean by the "communal experience" that reality TV creates that he feels today's sitcoms and dramas miss?

4. What does Poniewozik mean by a "voyeurfest"? How may *voyeurism* describe an audience's interest in reality TV? What else explains the popularity of this programming?

5. What are the moral objections to reality TV that Poniewozik acknowledges? Can you contribute additional objections?

6. What does Poniewozik mean when he defines reality television as satire? Do you agree with this analysis? Is exposing humans' weak-

nesses valid television entertainment if it inadvertently can be seen as "satire"? What does "Potemkin Croesus" (235) allude to?

7. Analyze Poniewozik's description of "Lady Tiger" on *American Idol* to explain in your own words what is "great" about reality TV.

WRITING FROM THE TEXT

1. Using details from Poniewozik's essay as well as examples from your own viewing experiences, write an essay defending reality TV.

2. With the intention of encouraging or discouraging a friend from performing on *American Idol*, write an analysis of that friend's talent and style.

3. Write an analysis of one sitcom or drama that you regularly view to counter Poniewozik's critique that these programs are "derivative," are filled with "cardboard characters and silly premises," and that these shows don't create much "buzz."

4. Pitch a reality TV program that might be seriously adopted or rejected as ridiculous hyperbole—depending on how focused, descriptive, and clever you are at pitching your idea.

"The public's taste in entertainment has certainly changed."

CONNECTING WITH OTHER TEXTS

1. Using points made by Poniewozik and Peters, and your own perceptions of programs that you have watched, write an essay arguing that reality TV has gone too far in humiliating participants or endangering them in physical ways.

2. Write a satirical characterization of a reality TV viewer that uses details from both Poniewozik and Peters as well as amusing or indicting descriptions of your own.

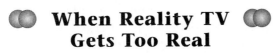

When Reality TV Gets Too Real

Jeremy W. Peters

Beginning his career in journalism as a reporter and, eventually, a news editor for the University of Michigan campus newspaper, Jeremy W. Peters earned degrees in political science and history. He started working for The *New York Times* in 2000 and has worked at their Detroit and New York bureaus covering economic and business news; he is now covering state politics for their Albany bureau. The following essay was published in The *New York Times* on October 8, 2007.

1   On a recent episode of *Intervention,* A&E's documentary series about addiction, no one was stopping Pam, an alcoholic, from driving. As she made her way to the front door—stopping first at the refrigerator to take a swig of vodka for the road—viewers could hear a producer for the show speak up.

2   "You have had a lot to drink," the voice from off camera said. "Do you want one of us to drive?"

3   Pam was indignant. "No, I can drive. I can drive," she mumbled. She then got into her car, managed a three-point turn out of the parking lot and drove off. The camera crew followed, filming her as she tried to keep her turquoise Pontiac Sunfire between the lines.

4   Perhaps more than any other program on television now, *Intervention* highlights the sticky situations that reality-show producers can find themselves in as they document unpredictable and unstable subjects or situations. In recent years, producers and networks have increasingly pushed the boundaries of television voyeurism in search of another ratings hit.

5   At times, this has proved problematic for television networks. There have been several lawsuits related to shows like *Big Brother* and more recently, CBS found itself facing accusations that it had created dangerous working conditions for children in its reality program *Kid Nation,* in which children aged 8 to 15 toiled in the New Mexico desert to build a working society on their own.

6   In the case of reality-TV documentary shows like *Intervention* and the various incarnations of *The Real World* and *Road Rules* on MTV, producers can be witnesses to crimes, raising the question of when they are obligated to step out from behind the camera and intervene. Sometimes the crimes they film are relatively minor, like underage drinking or firsticuffs. But in other cases, like on *Intervention* and VH1's *Breaking Bonaduce,* in which the star, the former child actor Danny Bonaduce, got behind the wheel after he had been drinking and bragged how a car crash would make great television, the program's subjects can put themselves and innocent bystanders at great risk.

7   And legally, producers are treated like witnesses: they bear no responsibility to intervene. "The law in the United States doesn't require you to step in and save people," said David Sternbach, counsel for litigation and intellectual property matters for A&E Television Networks. "And it doesn't require you to stop a crime that's in the works." Often, of course, they have good business reasons not to: people on the edge make for good television. *Intervention* is one of A&E's top shows. This year it has drawn up to two million viewers on its best nights. The premiere of *Kid Nation* attracted 9.1 million viewers but slipped the next week to 7.6 million. The first season of *Breaking Bonaduce* helped VH1 increase its prime-time ratings in 2005, though they faded in the second season. And a wide following for *Cops,* Fox's police ride-along reality show, has kept it on the air since 1989.

8   A&E said *Intervention* has never been sued. And legal experts said that making a case against it or other documentary programs like it would be difficult because the subjects were being filmed in their own homes, engaging in activities that they would be pursuing regardless of whether a camera crew was there. "This is their life with me or without me," said Sam Mettler, "Intervention's" creator and executive producer. The program takes other steps, like requiring potential subjects to undergo psychological evaluations and keeping a family member of the addict on call 24 hours a day during filming, to avoid being negligent.

9   To make a case for negligence, legal experts said, the accusing party would need to prove that the reality program created a situation that put its

subjects in jeopardy. A *Big Brother* cast member sued CBS, for example, in 2002 after another cast member with a criminal record held a knife to her throat. CBS settled the case for an undisclosed amount. When the sister of a woman who appeared on ABC's *Extreme Makeover* committed suicide in 2004, the contestant sued the network for wrongful death and other charges. The contestant, who was competing to win free plastic surgery but lost, claimed that her sister had felt so guilty about mocking her appearance on the program that she killed herself. ABC settled the case for an undisclosed amount last year.

10   But if a subject on a show like *Intervention* or Fox's *Cops* series were to injure someone while engaging in illegal activity, a case for negligence would be more difficult to make because producers are merely observing. "Television producers are not policemen," said Michael J. O'Connor, whose firm, White O'Connor Curry in Los Angeles, Calif., has represented reality shows like *Survivor* and *America's Next Top Model.* He added: "On a moral level, you get to the point where stepping in seems like it would be something you'd want to do. But from a legal standpoint, third parties causing injuries to other third parties is not something a television program is really responsible for."

11   Being absolved of legal responsibility for his documentary subjects, however, does not make shooting the program any easier. "I've had children of alcoholic parents there watching their mother in a drunken stupor, watching their mother pass out, watching their mother throw up," Mr. Mettler said. "Those innocent children as casualties of their mother's addiction was just emotionally heart-wrenching. The trauma of that is horrible, just horrible."

12   *Intervention,* which ends each episode with an actual intervention, has arrangements with substance-abuse rehabilitation centers across the country that provide free in-patient treatment for addicts on the program. "Morally and ethically, none of us can feel good watching someone hurt themselves or hurt someone else. And I'm not going to stand by and have someone who is drunk get behind the wheel of a car and kill someone," Mr. Mettler said. Mr. Mettler himself has had to step out from behind the camera on a number of episodes to prevent someone from driving drunk. In one case, he followed a crack addict named Tim through a swamp. Tim had crawled into a drainage pipe and threatened suicide, so Mr. Mettler had to talk him out.

13   And in another episode, Mr. Mettler's field producers called paramedics after an alcoholic they were filming overdosed on the sedative trazodone. Laney, a wealthy divorced woman who drank half a gallon of rum a day and

traveled long distances in limousines because she did not like putting her cat on commercial jets, swallowed the pills while the cameras were off. She told producers what she had done after they saw her chugging a bottle of juice to wash the pills down.

14　　"Our first position is that this is a documentary series, we are there capturing real people in their real lives," said Robert Sharenow, A&E's senior vice president for nonfiction and alternative programming. "If there was an immediate danger, that was sort of our line. If the person was putting themselves or anyone else in immediate danger, then we'd cross the line." He added: "It's a very, very delicate balance."

Thinking about the Text

1. Summarize the opening scene of this essay and explain why this episode of the reality series *Intervention* is such an effective introduction for this essay. What are some questions that this episode raises?

2. Which incidents does the author include to show how reality television has "pushed the boundaries of television voyeurism in search of another ratings hit"?

3. Although reality television producers, like other witnesses, have no *legal* responsibility to intervene if a crime occurs while they are taping, why might they still be sued—and for what?

4. What are some business reasons why producers might not step in and save people?

5. What are some precautions that the producers of *Intervention* take to avoid being negligent and to help addicts at the end of an episode?

6. What is the line or limit that will cause A&E producers to intervene during filming? Give a few examples of when that has happened.

Writing from the Text

1. Using examples from your own reality television viewing as well as from Peters's essay, write an evaluative response, supporting or refuting the author's concern that reality television may be encouraging participants' poor choices and exploiting their traumas. For help with this assignment, see evaluative response, pp. 438–444.

2. Write an argument to convince readers that reality television programs do not merely observe or document people living "on the edge" but that they often create artificial situations and exploit dangerous choices to enter-

tain viewers. Include examples from Peters's article and from your own viewing to support your claims.

Connecting with Other Texts

1. Using examples from Peters's essay and from "Why Reality TV Is Good for Us" (p. 233), write an analysis of the moral shortcomings of reality TV: the deception of both participants and viewers as well as the exploitation of pain, shame, and risky behavior that fuels reality television programs. Include quotations and details from both essays to support your claims.

2. In "Why Reality TV Is Good for Us" (p. 233), James Poniewozik contends that what ultimately bothers critics of reality TV is not that the participants "are humiliated but that they are not" (237). Write an essay arguing for or against this claim, based on details from both Poniewozik's and Peter's essays. Would both writers agree that participants are not typically humiliated by reality programs or are they both selecting very different programs to support their claims?

3. After reading "The Difference Between Pity and Empathy" (p. 162), write an essay determining the role of pity and empathy in reality television viewing. Does Peters suggest that viewers feel pity, empathy, superiority, or another emotion as they watch individuals choosing extreme and dangerous behaviors? Include direct quotations and examples from both essays as you develop and support your thesis.

Coke

Philip Dacey

Poet Philip Dacey (b. 1939) is widely published in anthologies and poetry journals. His books include *What's Empty Weighs the Most: Twenty-four Sonnets* (1997), *The Deathbed Playboy* (1998), *The Paramour of the Moving Air* (1999), *The Adventures of Alixa Doom, and Other Love Poems* (2003), and *Mystery of Max Schmitt: Poems on the Life and Work of Thomas Eakins* (2004). Dacey has an M.A. in English from Stanford and an M.F.A. in creative writing from Iowa State University. The following poem was first published in *Night Shift at the Crucifix Factory* (1991) and later in *Stand Up Poetry: The Anthology* (1994). Dacey has given numerous poetry readings and has recorded "Coke" and other poems set to music by his sons.

> I was proud of the Coca-Cola stitched in red
> on the pocket of my dad's shirt,
> just above his heart.

Coca-Cola was America
5 and my dad drove its truck.

I loved the way the letters curved,
like handwriting, something personal,
a friendly offer of a drink
to a man in need. Bring me your poor,
10 your thirsty.

And on every road I went, faces
under the sign of Coke smiled down
out of billboards at me. We were all
brothers and sisters in the family
15 of man, our bottles to our lips,
tipping our heads back to the sun.

My dad lifted me up when he came home,
his arms strong from stacking
case after case of Coke all day. A couple of
20 cold ones always waited for us in the kitchen.

I believed our President and my dad
were partners. My dad said someday Coke
would be sold in every country in the world,
and when that happened there would be
25 no more wars. "Who can imagine," he asked,
"two people fighting while they swig their Cokes?"
I couldn't. And each night before sleep,
I thanked God for my favorite drink.

When I did, I imagined him tilting the bottle
30 up to his heavenly lips, a little Coke
dribbling down his great white beard.

And sometimes I even thought of his
son on the cross, getting vinegar
but wanting Coke. I knew that if I
35 had been there, I would have handed a Coke
up to him, who would have figured out

how to take it, even though his hands
were nailed down good, because he was God.
And I would have said when he took it,
40   "That's from America, Jesus. I hope
you like it." And then I'd have watched,
amidst the thunder and lightning
on that terrible hill, Jesus' Adam's apple
bob up and down as he drained that bottle
45   in one long divine swallow
like a sweaty player at a sandlot game
between innings, the crucial ninth
coming up next.

And then the dark, sweet flood
50   of American sleep,
sticky and full of tiny bubbles,
would pour over me.

THINKING ABOUT THE TEXT

1. The narrator's opening words, "I was proud . . . ," characterize his attitude as a young boy. Find phrases throughout the poem that reveal the numerous sources of his pride.

2. List the various characteristics of Coca-Cola in the poem. What does Coke represent?

3. Is the poet writing this as a young boy or as a man looking back to an earlier time? How can you tell? What was his vision of the world then? Find images to support your view.

4. Characterize the poet's tone. Is he innocent and hopeful? Smiling at his past naïveté? Bitter and disillusioned? Support your interpretation.

5. A number of images are ironic or incongruous—they contradict our expectation of what seems appropriate and, in this poem, contribute to its humor. List the images that seem ironic or comical.

6. What is the poet implying about a young boy's view of the world? What does America stand for here? Why does the narrator end the poem with this image: "the dark, sweet flood / of American sleep, / sticky and full of tiny bubbles, / would pour over me"? What do these "tiny bubbles" suggest and why does he emphasize that his "American sleep" was "dark" yet "sweet"?

WRITING FROM THE TEXT

1. Write an essay or poem focusing on a key image or symbol from your own childhood and show how your attitude toward this symbol has changed over the years.

2. Read the section on poetry analysis and write an analysis of the product Coke as a critical symbol in this poem. (See exercise 2 on p. 245 for help in brainstorming this topic.)

3. Write an analysis of what the poet is suggesting about American culture and values. Is he critical or supportive of what America represents? Is this poem to be read as a satire or to be read literally? How can you tell?

4. Compare and contrast the world of the young boy with the world of the adult narrator who seems nostalgic for this earlier time.

CONNECTING WITH OTHER TEXTS

1. Write an essay comparing and contrasting the limited vision of the individuals described in both "Mr. Z" (p. 133) and "Coke." Focus on details from both poems as you contrast the reasons for these distorted perspectives.

2. Read "The Red Convertible" (p. 135) and compare Lyman's criticism of government policies with the implied criticism of American values presented in Dacey's poem.

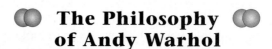

The Philosophy of Andy Warhol

"What's great about this country is that America started the tradition where the richest consumers buy essentially the same things as the poorest. You can be watching TV and see Coca-Cola, and you can know that the president drinks Coke, Liz Taylor drinks Coke, and just think, you can drink Coke, too. A Coke is a Coke, and no amount of money can get you a better Coke than the one that the bum on the corner is drinking. All the Cokes are the same and all the Cokes are good. Liz Taylor knows it, the president knows it, the bum knows it, and you know it."

Makes Learning Fun
Clifford Stoll

An astronomer who is better known for his writings on computer technology, Clifford Stoll (b. 1950) has had the satisfaction of tracking down a computer hacker who constituted a threat to national security, a tale Stoll recounted in *The Cuckoo's Egg: Tracking a Spy Through the Maze of Computer Espionage* (1989). In spite of his expertise and reliance on computers in his own life, Stoll exposes the harmful effects of computers on children in *Silicon Snake Oil* (1995). In *High-Tech Heretic: Why Computers Don't Belong in the Classroom and Other Reflections by a Computer Contrarian* (1999), Stoll deplores the fact that computers take money away from library books and other educational necessities, even as they take time away from young people's social development. The following excerpt is from *High-Tech Heretic*.

1   Technology promises shortcuts to higher grades and painless learning. Today's edutainment software comes shrink-wrapped in computing's magic mantra: "Makes Learning Fun."

2   You'll hear it from IBM: "The latest Aptivas have a superior selection of top-rated educational software titles like Kid's Room, an Aptiva exclusive that gives your kids a fun place to learn." The fluff goes on about "extreme multimedia delivers full-screen action, blazing graphics and front-row-center-seat sound, resulting in maximum impact in any application."

3   Public schools agree. Here's a press release pushing software developed by the Texas Agricultural Extension Service, and aimed at 4-H clubs: "It may sound fishy, but Texas 4th graders now have the opportunity to go fishing for facts on the computer, improve their academic skills, learn how they can conserve water and maintain its quality in the state's lakes and streams and have fun at the same time."

4   The phrase shows up in promotions for college classes, too: The School of Journalism at University of North Carolina at Chapel Hill teaches a core course in Electronic Information Sources. The class motto: Learning is Fun.

5   An Oregon high school student who's spent plenty of time online wrote: "I mean if I had a choice to learn in a fun matter or a tradital [sic] book manner I would choice the fun way of learning."

6   Read the promotion for Western Michigan University software to learn about groundwater: It "uses animation, so learning about Calhoun County is more of a video game than a dry lesson or research project . . ."

7   Learn on your own. Blazing graphics and maximum impact. Go fishing for facts. Learning will be more of a video game than a lesson. Technology makes learning fun. Just one problem.

8   It's a lie.

9   Most learning isn't fun. Learning takes work. Discipline. Commitment, from both teacher and student. Responsibility—you have to do your homework. There's no shortcut to a quality education. And the payoff isn't an adrenaline rush, but a deep satisfaction arriving weeks, months, or years later. Equating learning with fun says that if you don't enjoy yourself, you're not learning.

10   What good are glitzy gadgets to a child who can't pay attention in class, won't read more than a paragraph, and is unable to write analytically? If we want our children to read books, why direct them to computer screens, where it's painful to read more than a few pages? If kids watch too much TV, why bring multimedia video systems into schools?

11   These teaching machines direct students away from reading, away from writing, away from scholarship. They dull questioning minds with graphical games where quick answers take the place of understanding, and the trivial is promoted as educational. They substitute quick answers and fast action for reflection and critical thinking. Thinking, after all, involves originality, concentration, and intention.

12   Computing's instant gratification—built into the learning-is-fun mind-set—encourages intellectual passivity, driven mainly by conditioned amusement. Fed a diet of interactive insta-grat, students develop a distaste for persistence, trial and error, attentiveness, or patience.

13   This obsession with turning the classroom into a funhouse isn't new. Eighty years ago in *Thirteen Lectures,* Austrian educator Rudolf Steiner wrote, "I've often heard that there must be an education which makes learning a game for children; school must become all joy. The children should laugh all the time and learning will be play. This is the best educational principle to ensure that nothing at all is learned."

14   Yep, kids love computers. Indeed, it's mainly adults who are uncomfortable around keyboards and monitors. But just what do children learn from computers?

15   Turning learning into fun denigrates the most important things we can do in life: to learn and to teach. It cheapens both process and product: Dedicated teachers try to entertain, students expect to learn without working, and scholarship becomes a computer game. When in doubt, turn to the electronic mind-crutch.

16   Is the main problem of today's children that they haven't enough fun? Are kids really deprived of excitement? Are schoolchildren exposed to too few media messages—so that we must bring them the Internet with still more? Must every classroom lesson be sugarcoated by dancing animatrons

and singing cartoon characters? Is the job of our schools to provide additional screen time for students who watch three or four hours of television a night?

17   "All schools need high-speed Internet connections and the appropriate computer hardware to deliver the latest educational applications . . . equal resources should be directed to the creation of dynamic, 3-D virtual learning environments," says Linda Hahner, president of Out of the Blue Design Company, who's excited that "Given enough tools, children will be able to build and program their own space missions."

18   Children build their own space missions? I'm impressed when a twelve-year-old carves a balsawood glider.

19   I saw a program for designing Barbie doll clothes . . . it lets kids select styles, colors, and mix outfits. Naturally, it's advertised as a teaching program, though I wonder exactly what it teaches. How to coordinate colors, perhaps, though the kid selects from a most parsimonious palette. You can't mix paints, can't dye cloth, can't stitch things together. At the end of a session, a child has no idea of the tactile difference between calico and corduroy, silk and sailcloth. Can't sew, either.

20   Along with a small group of parents, I visited a kindergarten class near San Francisco. The other visitors were immediately taken by the display of computer graphic printouts hung on the wall . . . clipart, designed by professionals and printed out by the children. The teacher, busy showing several children how to run the computer, didn't notice one frustrated child working at the crafts table.

21   While the visitors chatted about the computers, I watched that six-year-old clumsily fold construction paper into the shape of a house. Struggling with round-nosed scissors, he cut a door, drew windows with a crayon, and pasted the paper onto a base. Near the end of our visit, he completed his project—he called it a firehouse—and proudly showed it to the adults in the room. The teacher gave him a "Go away, I'm busy" nod; none of the other visitors so much as glanced at the boy. You could see his face drop.

22   Well, yes, a six-year-old's crude firehouse hardly compares with a fancy computer printout. But these parents should have recognized the trivial nature of the computer "art."

23   Remember B. F. Skinner? By feeding corn to pigeons whenever they behaved the way he wanted, Skinner showed that he could get animals to learn behavior. In the 1950s, he applied his pigeon experiments to humans, creating a new way for people to learn: programmed instruction.

24   Skinner made machines which would pose questions to students. Correct answers would lead to new topics and further questions; wrong answers caused

a review and more questions to answer. It was a primitive form of hypertext—each answer led to another encapsulated lesson. Widely promoted in its day, programmed instruction was supposed to revolutionize education.

25   Skinner's methods fit well with today's computers. Students peck at their keyboards for dollops of sound and animation; administrators get instant reports; parents hear how their kids now enjoy school. This is supposed to make learning fun, not to mention efficient.

26   Aah, efficiency in education! Get the student to correctly answer questions. Minimize costs and wasted time. Augment teachers with mechanical and electronic aids. Sugarcoat lessons with extreme multimedia and blazing graphics so that student will happily learn on their own, while having fun in the process.

27   But programmed instruction flopped. The machine forced kids to regurgitate whatever answers the programmer wanted. There was no place for innovation, creativity, whimsy, or improvisation. Flashing lights simply couldn't take the place of a live teacher's encouragement. We resent being treated like pigeons.

28   In the wake of Skinner's programmed instruction came even nuttier educational fads—teaching machines, sleep learning, and music-induced hypnotic learning. Anything to make education easy and fun. Despite decades of promotion, they all fizzled.

29   Think Skinner's ideas are dead? Check out the popular children's software program NFL Math. It's designed around professional football and is supposed to teach arithmetic. "Packed with photo-realistic animations," this program "makes hitting a wide receiver with a pass more fun than hitting the books." It promises such "learning skills" as addition, fractions, statistics, and percentages. The kids get to watch short, poorly animated football segments, interrupted by half-baked math questions ("Which is more yards rushed—1,182 or 1,207?"). Result? Your children will "score better grades in math!" Uh, right.

30   The program forces the child to do a math problem in order to be rewarded with two minutes of entertainment. Then the torture begins anew. What a great way to teach hatred of math.

31   NFL Math and its many brethren typically present questions in the format $4 + 3 = ?$ They can accept only the obvious answers. Like Skinner's pigeons, you get rewarded for pressing the right button.

32   A real teacher might well ask, "Seven equals what?" A fascinating question with an infinite number of answers: "Three plus four," "Ten minus three," "Days in a week," "The dwarfs in *Snow White*," "Number of deadly sins," "The Seven Immortals of the Wine Cup," "The Group of Seven revolutionized

Canadian painting," "The number of samurai in Kurosawa's best movie," "The German expression *Siebensachen,* which means the baggage you carry on a trip." These answers, incomprehensible to any computer, make perfect sense to a real teacher . . . and open up whole fields for creative discussion. What began as an arithmetic question blossoms into a lesson on language, art, science, history, or culture.

33   New teachers, fresh out of college, seem to be most affected with the connection between gizmos, classrooms, and fun in learning. Ms. Jennifer Donovan, a student teacher from Stetson University, wrote to me, repeating the standard party line: Lessons must be fun in order to compete with television and to motivate students. "In the 1950s, the job market did not call for computer education. But in a changing world, students are hard pressed to find well-paying jobs that do not involve computer technology."

34   These fit together: Jobs go to those who know computers. Computers motivate students. Students won't learn unless it's fun.

35   Well, many subjects aren't fun. I wonder how the fun-to-learn teacher handles the Holocaust, Rape of Nanking, or American slavery. Perhaps her class creates Web sites about these subjects—and the students concentrate on graphic design instead of history. But scholarship isn't about browsing the Internet—it's about understanding events, appreciating history, and interpreting our world.

36   "But you don't understand," say my techie friends. "Computers are wonderful motivators for students. In this age of television, they won't write or do their homework without one."

37   And so we happily provide computers to students and expect them to suddenly become interested in academic topics. We encourage them to play with the machine . . . any scholastic connection is secondary.

38   Kids do seem to be motivated by computers. But doesn't that multimedia machine mainly motivate kids to play with the computer, in the same way that television motivates kids to watch more videos?

39   Motivation—the will to move—comes from yourself. You choose what puts you in motion and causes you to move. Computers cause you to sit in one place and not to move.

40   Don Tapscott, author of *Growing Up Digital,* sees a new kind of young intellectual explorer who will process information and learn differently than those who came before them. "New media tools offer great promise for a new model of learning—one based on discovery and participation," he says. Thanks to cheap computers, we'll see a shift from teaching to "the creation of learning partnerships and learning cultures. The schools can become a place to learn rather than a place to teach."

41   The field of educational technology is filled with such empty clichés. In this dreamworld, empowered students eagerly learn from one another, encouraged by teachers who act more like coaches than instructors. We'll replace the sage on the stage with a guide on the side. Exciting on-line expeditions will replace outmoded chalk-and-talk lectures. Student-centered learning will be tutor-led and context-based rather than rote plug-and-chug. Child-centered classrooms. Blah, blah, blah.

42   Can't blame students for getting sick of teachers lecturing about how the square of the hypotenuse has something to do with the sum of the squares of the legs of a right triangle. We yearn for depth, narrative, passion, involvement. For experience. Along comes the magic machine promising interactive fun. What kid can resist?

43   And I can't blame teachers for getting sick of students sitting there with mouths agape, not listening but not quite sleeping. Perhaps that's why adults figure that making finger motions on a keyboard is an appropriate activity . . . that something must be happening in the kids' brains. In that sense, computers are parent-pleasing devices: machines to give the appearance of learning and the illusion of interactive, instant information.

44   Seems clear that an inspiring teacher doesn't need computers; a mediocre teacher isn't improved by one. I've never met a teacher who feels there's too much classroom time—they always complain that the periods are too short and there's too much material to cover.

45   Teaching, alas, is a low-paid calling. Some teachers attend college and put up with frustrations for a steady pay and eventual retirement. But I'll bet the best teachers are in it for the feedback: the smile on the kid's face and the "Aha" from the chemistry student. These, of course, are the very things that technology removes. The Internet gets the credit and the teacher gets the blame. And that great promised land of low-cost education—distance learning—essentially eliminates interpersonal interaction. Maybe that's why experienced teachers approach computers with hesitation.

46   In *Teachers and Machines,* Larry Cuban points out that teachers are frequently criticized as Luddites resistant to progress. A century of reformers have blamed the slow introduction of teaching devices on reactionary teaching staff. For instance, Charles Hoban, who worked to introduce instructional radio and TV, said, "The current and historical role of the classroom teacher is highly ritualized." Any change in that ritual is "likely to be resisted as an invasion of the sanctuary by the barbarians . . . Any systematic attempt to scientize and rationalize the intuitively determined interaction patterns of the teacher is likely to elicit at least some teacher hostility and resistance."

47   That hostility is well justified. Teachers need only open a closet door to find stacks of obsolete and unused teaching gizmos: filmstrips, instructional

television systems, Apple II computers, and any number of educational videotapes. Each promised a revolution in the classroom. None delivered.

48   "Oh, but computers are different from old technologies like radio and television" runs the argument. "Computers are interactive. They're fun!"

49   Well, just why is electronic interactivity good for scholarship? With a computer, you're interacting with something, not someone. Doubtless, even the worst teacher is more versatile and adaptable than the finest computer program. Come to think of it, aren't teachers interactive? It's hard to think of a classroom without interaction.

50   The old saw still rings true: What requires the least effort is least cherished. Yet somehow we expect a simple, easy, fun, digital education to be both lasting and valuable.

51   "But the Internet is important to schools," consultants in computer-aided instruction tell me. "It links students straight to famous scientists. They can chat with researchers at observatories and laboratories. And there's instant homework help available online."

52   Well, no. Famous scientists—and obscure ones, too—don't have time to answer e-mail from distant students. Those academics are taking care of their projects, managing post-docs, teaching classes, and writing grant proposals. Astronomers who enjoy working with kids would far prefer to meet the kids, not answer a slew of messages over the Net. That inquiring mind directed to the Net will likely dead-end in some press release or a mountain of indecipherable jargon.

53   Teachers have the difficult job of not just understanding a body of academic facts—they must understand their students. The teaching method that connects for one child won't work with another. The student who's strong in one area will certainly be weak in another. What seems like a game to someone will feel like work to another. The intention should be enlightenment, not entertainment.

54   Learning isn't about acquiring information, maximizing efficiency, or enjoyment. Learning is about developing human capacity. To turn learning into fun is to denigrate the two most important things we can do as humans: To teach. To learn.

Thinking about the Text

1. Clifford Stoll begins his essay by quoting enthusiastic language from computer companies and school administrators extolling the use of technology in classrooms. What is Stoll's strategy in opening his essay with so many positive comments that he then deflates with one short sentence expressing his own view: "It's a lie"?

2. When Stoll writes "Most learning isn't fun" (248), what does he mean? Does his essay reflect the voice of a dreary pedant who wants students' knuckles rapped by a yardstick for giving a wrong answer? How can the reader reconcile the tone of the writer who deplores "glitzy gadgets" but recognizes the creativity in the many possible responses to, for example, what the number seven equals?

3. How true is it to your experience that the "payoff" for learning isn't "an adrenaline rush, but a deep satisfaction arriving weeks, months, or years later" (248)? How does the computer's speed work against true learning?

4. Stoll believes that computers "direct students away from reading, away from writing, away from scholarship" (248). What does he mean? Do you agree?

5. The author relates two experiences in watching students work on a computer: designing doll clothes and printing out graphics made on a computer. What is wrong with both of these "educational" experiences, according to Stoll?

6. How relevant to his argument is Stoll's description of the work of B. F. Skinner, the behavioral scientist who fed corn to pigeons? Besides concluding that human beings resent "being treated like pigeons" (254), what else is wrong with Skinner's approach to educating people, according to Stoll?

7. How do you respond to Stoll's assertion that "scholarship isn't about browsing the Internet—it's about understanding events, appreciating history, and interpreting the world" (251)?

8. In addition to writing about the drawbacks for students using computers for learning, Stoll considers the problems for teachers in computer-filled classrooms. Why might teachers rightly be hostile to technology, according to Stoll?

WRITING FROM THE TEXT

1. In an essay, argue that Stoll is right or wrong in asserting that computers "direct students away from reading, away from writing, away from scholarship" (248). Use specific examples of your habits in using computers— to facilitate assignments or perhaps to distract you from accomplishing assigned work.

2. Describe your precollege learning experiences to show that the best of these were or were not connected to computer use. Use Stoll's essay to show your agreement with his points about creativity and interactions with the teacher or to refute his points by illustrating some good learning experiences you have had using a computer.

3. Write an analysis of the methods of your most memorable teacher. Were the instructor's methods interactive, creative, personal and motivating—a "sage on the stage"—or did other qualities make this professional an important part of your learning experience? Use strong, descriptive details in your essay.

CONNECTING WITH OTHER TEXTS

1. Read the excerpt from Don Tapscott's book *Growing Up Digital* and decide which author makes the stronger point about the use of computers in education. Make your claim and then use the material from both essays to support your point.

2. Compare the role of the teacher as described in Stoll's essay and the essay by Tapscott (below). How does each perceive the instructor's position in the classroom? Write an essay to compare or contrast the authors' perceptions. Review how to organize a comparison-contrast essay (p. 545) for help in organizing your work.

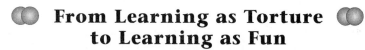

From Learning as Torture to Learning as Fun

Don Tapscott

An expert on the application of technology in business, Don Tapscott (b. 1947) co-founded Digital 4Sight, a company that researches and designs new business models for Global 2000 organizations. He earned a B.S. and B.A. in psychology and statistics from Trent University and an M.Ed. in research methodology and an honorary Doctor of Laws from the University of Alberta. He has authored or coauthored seven books, including *Wikinomics: How Mass Collaboration Changes Everything* (2008), *The Naked Corporation: How the Age of Transparency Will Revolutionize Business* (2003), *Digital Capital: Harnessing the Power of Business Webs* (2000), *The Digital Economy: Promise and Peril in the Age of Networked Intelligence* (1996), and *Paradigm Shift: The New Promise of Information Technology* (1992). The following essay is an excerpt from *Growing Up Digital: The Rise of the New Generation* (1998), which, as Tapscott explains in the initial pages, was written on the Internet: "The research team collaborated with several hundred children and adults located on six continents. The analysis, drafting, and editing were conducted by a core team in five locations using a shared digital workspace, electronic mail, and computer conferencing. The main reference source was the Web." Tapscott welcomes your views and related experiences at *www.growingupdigital.com,* where you can find additional information and links to related topics.

1   Maybe torture is an exaggeration, but for many kids class is not exactly the highlight of their day. Some educators have decried the fact that a generation schooled on *Sesame Street* expects to be entertained at school—to enjoy the learning experience. These educators argue that the learning and entertainment should be clearly separated. As Neil Postman says, ". . . *Sesame Street* does not encourage children to love school or anything about school. It teaches them to love television."

2   But doesn't that say more about today's schools—which are not exactly exciting places for many students—than it does about the integration of learning and entertainment? I'm convinced that one of the design goals of the New School should be to make learning fun! Learning math should be an enjoyable, challenging, and yes, entertaining activity just like learning a video game is. And it can be! Besides, *Sesame Street* let the entertainment horse out of the barn. So did video games, the Web, FreeZone, MaMaMedia, and a thousand others.

3   It is said, however, that if learning is fun it can't be challenging. Wrong! Try getting through the seven levels of Crash Bandicoot or FIFA soccer on your kids' video game if you think entertainment and challenge are opposites. The challenge provides much of the entertainment value and vice versa.

4   Why shouldn't learning be entertaining? *Webster's Ninth College Dictionary* gives the third and fourth definitions of the verb "to entertain" as "to keep, hold, or maintain in the mind," and "to receive and take into consideration." In other words, entertainment has always been a profound part of the learning process and teachers have, throughout history, been asked to convince their students to entertain ideas. From this perspective, the best teachers were entertainers. Using the new media, the teacher becomes the entertainer and in doing so builds enjoyment, motivation, and responsibility for learning.

5   Learning is becoming a social activity facilitated by a new generation of educators.

6   The topic is saltwater fish. The teacher divides the grade 6 class into teams, asking each to prepare a presentation on a fish of its choice covering the topics of history, breathing, propulsion, reproduction, diet, predators, and "cool facts." The students have access to the Web and are allowed to use any resources they want. Questions should be addressed to others in their team or to the others in the class, not the teacher.

7   Two weeks later, Melissa's group is up first. The students in the group have created a shark project home page with hot links for each of the topics. The presentation is projected onto a screen at the front of the class as the girls talk. They have video clips of different types of sharks and also a clip of Jacques Cousteau discussing the shark as an endangered species. They then go live to Aquarius—an underwater Web site located off the Florida Keys. The

class can ask questions of the Aquarius staff, but most inquiries are directed at the project team. One of the big discussions is about the dangers posed to humans by sharks versus the dangers to sharks posed by humans.

8   The class decides to hold an online forum on this and invite kids from their sister classes in other countries to participate. The team invites the classes to browse through its project at any time, from any location, as the site will be "up" for the rest of the school year. In fact, the team decides to maintain the site, adding new links and fresh information throughout the year. It becomes a living project. Other learners from other countries find the shark homepage helpful in their projects and build links to it. The team has to resource the information, tools, and materials it needs.

9   The teacher acts as a resource and consultant to the teams. He is also a youth worker—as one of the students was having considerable problems at home and was not motivated to participate in a team. Although the teacher can't solve such problems, he takes them into account and also refers the student to the guidance counselor. The teacher also facilitates the learning process, among other things participating as a technical consultant on the new media. He learns much from Melissa's group, which actually knows more about sharks than he does (his background is art and literature, not science). The teacher doesn't compete with Jacques Cousteau, but rather is supported by him.

10   This scenario is not science fiction. It is currently occurring in advanced schools in several countries. The teacher is not an instructional transmitter. He is a facilitator to social learning whereby learners construct their own knowledge. The students will remember what they learned about sharks as the topic now interests them. More importantly, they have acquired collaborative, research, analytical, presentation, and resourcing skills. With the assistance of a teacher, they are constructing knowledge and their world.

11   Needless to say, a whole generation of teachers needs to learn new tools, new approaches, and new skills. This will be a challenge—not just because of resistance to change by some teachers, but also because of the current atmosphere of cutbacks, low teacher morale, lack of time due to the pressures of increased workloads, and reduced retraining budgets. . . .

12   What is the new teacher like?

13   Small miracles have been occurring over the last three years at William Lyon Mackenzie Collegiate in North York, Ontario. The Emerging Technologies program mixes grades 10 to 12 to work on projects involving teams and the new media. The students learn by discovery. Through teams they source answers to their questions and resources to conduct their projects—from other students, outside parties, and the Net. The learning model is one of student-centered discovery enabled by emerging technologies.

14   When the program began, teacher Richard Ford told the students on their first day of class that their first project was for each to design their own Web page and present it to the group by Friday. When he asked how many knew how to design a Web page, 6 of the 32 kids in the class indicated they had some experience. Richard then suggested to the class that they should remember those faces, "because they are your mentors."

15   The students learn to cooperate, work in teams, solve problems, and take responsibility for their own learning—by doing. If there's something they don't understand, they must ask everyone else in the class before they can ask the teacher. Right after the first class, one girl asks, "What's a Web page?" Richard shrugs and says, "I don't know." Within a few days the kids have gotten the message. "And who's the last person you ask for help?" says Richard. Everyone replies in unison, "You are."

16   The model is that everyone relies on everyone else, sharing their expertise. Richard told them that if everyone didn't present their Web page on Friday, then everyone would get a zero. On the second day of class some of the kids were going around asking others if they needed help. However, when the learners have exhausted all routes and cannot find a solution to something, they can approach the teacher (called the facilitator). He then will work with them as a team member to find a solution or a resource which can help them.

17   In this class, there were only 15 computers for 30 kids—so they had to share the technology. The class was also very diverse, with children from Korea, India, Pakistan, Sri Lanka, Switzerland, Ukraine, and Russia. There were 15 different languages spoken in the class, with several of the learners having poor English skills.

18   Several kids were petrified to give presentations, but they got a lot of support from the class. One boy who spoke almost no English had to be coaxed by the others to stand up in front of the class. He mustered up the courage to approach the front of the room, then, turning stood there and said, "My Web page. . . . First time. . . . Graphics. . . . See link. Thank you." All the other kids applauded. "It was a very emotional moment for everyone," says Richard. "Everyone knew what an accomplishment it was for this boy to speak in front of everyone else in another language, presenting his first Web page." Afterward, outside the classroom, he approached Richard and said to him, smiling broadly, "I am proud."

19   For Richard, "There is something that happens when you decide for yourself that you're going to learn something and do something. This is much more powerful than when someone else says you have to do this."

20   "The kids not only learned about the new media and developed language and presentation skills, they learned about how to interact with clients and meet deadlines and, most importantly, they learned about how to share

expertise and how to source it as well," says project coordinator Vicki Saunders. "The kids work 10 times longer because they are so excited about their projects."

21 After the first week the learners launched into Web design for real clients. One group built the software for the Canadian Broadcasting Corporation movie Web site. Another did the design for a New York-based artist named Carter Kustera—who came into the class for a week to work with them. IBM hired the group to do a CD-ROM about a conference called "Minds Meeting Media," where 1,900 kids came together in Toronto to present their projects to other kids from across the city. Kids from grade 2 to 13 presented their animation and multimedia projects and all this was captured on a CD.

22 For their midterm "exam," the students had to create a three-page Web site or a three-minute video. They were placed in groups of four, selected intentionally to help them overcome their obstacles to development. For example, all the "blockers" were put in one group. The project had to have a purpose. The students also had to discuss their own individual contributions and to assign marks to each other. The kids really had to wake up and work hard. A lot of buttons were pushed.

23 According to Vicki, "Richard is able to find the hook that turns kids on."

24 Richard has a radical view of the role of the teacher. "I don't teach. If I teach, who knows what they will learn. Teaching's out. I tell kids that there are no limits. You can create whatever you want to create. If it's impossible, it will just take a bit longer. My main function is to get kids excited, to consider things that they haven't done before. I'm working to create citizens in a global society."

25 He also deemphasizes his role as a judge. "We're trying to create a stage for them to present their ideas and their work to others. If a student hands something in to a teacher, she doesn't necessarily learn. The intention of the work becomes to satisfy the teacher's vision. We're not expanding the student's vision.

26 "For example, I whisper to a student who is doing a project on his home country, 'What about if you were to present this project on the Web?' The student realizes people will read it and see it. They might e-mail him back. They might set up a newsgroup. Maybe someone from their home town might join the conference. He may be able to share his ideas with others around the world."

27 Richard acts as a facilitator to set a hook. "If they grab hold, they're off on a voyage of discovery. We both discover. I learn through each of them— I learn about how people carry each other from village to village when he puts a photo on the Web. I learn about his culture when people begin to communicate with him from the other side of the globe.

28   "Everything you do affects others. We're asking kids to create their place in this global society. Whatever you want is possible. There are no limits. You create who you are in your space."

29   Student Aziz Hurzook took Richard literally. Aziz is a real innovator. He learned how to use a music synthesizer for his project and then created an audio CD. For his presentation he told the class to listen to campus radio at midnight. The radio station played the world premier of his music. He later set up a booth advertising Web development services at a conference on the new media. The experience was very positive. People were buzzing all around his booth and he realized there was a big opportunity here: Aziz created a company called "Caught in the Web" and took on his first client. The company had $1.5 million in revenue last year.

30   Says Richard: "If they can't create their own network, then they'll have to go to an authority figure. But if they stop and think about it, they are the authority! They are in charge of their own learning. Only they can decide to do something. And if they choose to do it, there is nobody on this earth who can stop them. Not only will they do something far more creative than you can imagine, they will probably break new ground while doing so."

Thinking about the Text

1. Although Tapscott admits that "learning as torture" may be an exaggeration, what might be his reason for opening with this simile and how does it contrast with his view of learning?

2. Specify the key features of the learning "teams" that Tapscott describes.

3. What does Tapscott mean when he claims that "in advanced schools . . . the teacher is not an instructional transmitter. He is a facilitator to social learning whereby learners construct their own knowledge" (257)? Do you see any problems with this concept?

4. What are the most important aspects of Richard's new type of teaching? Evaluate its strengths and flaws.

Writing from the Text

1. Using details from this essay, write a paper defining the ideal teacher, according to Tapscott. Include specific examples from his essay and analyze each.

2. In an essay, compare and contrast your favorite class in high school with the example that Tapscott provides of Richard's teaching. Your thesis should assert your view of these classes.

3. Write an evaluative response of Tapscott's thesis and of the key components of these "advanced classes" and teachers that he describes.

CONNECTING WITH OTHER TEXTS

1. Read "Makes Learning Fun" (p. 247) and write an essay contrasting Stoll's views with Tapscott's. Your thesis should clarify which view seems more reasonable and compelling to you.

2. After reading "Is There a Doctor in the Mouse?" (p. 229), write an essay comparing Tapscott's view of the role of the Internet in learning with what Parikh sees as advantageous for people researching their medical conditions.

 **In Groups We Shrink**

Carol Tavris

After studying sociology and comparative literature at Brandeis, Carol Tavris (b. 1944) earned her Ph.D. in social psychology at the University of Michigan. Tavris has worked as a freelance writer, taught in UCLA's psychology department, written for *Vogue, Harper's,* and *G.Q.,* and served as an editor for *Psychology Today.* She has published extensively in the field of psychology, with emphasis on emotions, anger, sexuality, and gender issues. She has taught at the New School for Social Research in New York City since 1983. Her works include *The Mismeasure of Woman* (1992), *Psychobabble & Biobunk: Using Psychology to Think Critically About Issues in the News: Opinions, Essays and Book Reviews* (2001), *Mistakes Were Made (But Not by Me): Why We Justify Foolish Beliefs, Bad Decisions, and Hurtful Acts* (2007). The essay printed here appeared in the *Los Angeles Times* in 1991.

1   The ghost of Kitty Genovese would sympathize with Rodney King. Genovese, you may remember, is the symbol of bystander apathy in America. Screaming for help, she was stabbed repeatedly and killed in front of her New York apartment, and not one of the 38 neighbors who heard her, including those who came to their windows to watch, even called for help.

2   One of the things we find appalling in the videotape of King's assault is the image of at least 11 police officers watching four of their colleagues administer the savage beating and doing nothing to intervene. Whatever is the matter with them, we wonder.

3   Something happens to individuals when they collect in a group. They think and act differently than they would on their own. Most people, if they observe some disaster or danger on their own—a woman being stabbed, a pedestrian slammed by a hit-and-run driver—will at least call for help; many will even risk their own safety to intervene. But if they are in a group

observing the same danger, they hold back. The reason is not necessarily that they are lazy, cowardly or have 50 other personality deficiencies; it has more to do with the nature of groups than the nature of individuals.

4   In one experiment in behavioral psychology, students were seated in a room, either alone or in groups of three, as a staged emergency occurred: Smoke began pouring through the vents. Students who were on their own usually hesitated a minute, got up, checked the vents and then went out to report what certainly seemed like fire. But the students who were sitting in groups of three did not move. They sat there for six minutes, with smoke so thick they could barely see, rubbing their eyes and coughing.

5   In another experiment, psychologists staged a situation in which people overheard a loud crash, a scream and a woman in pain, moaning that her ankle was broken. Seventy percent of those who were alone when the "accident" occurred went to her aid, compared with only 40 percent of those who heard her in the presence of another person.

6   For victims, obviously, there is no safety in numbers. Why? One reason is that if other people aren't doing anything, the individual assumes that nothing needs to be done. In the smoke-filled room study, the students in groups said they thought that the smoke was caused by "steam pipes," "truth gas" or "leaks in the air conditioning"; not one said what the students on their own did: "I thought it was fire." In the lady-in-distress study, some of those who failed to offer help said, "I didn't want to embarrass her."

7   Often, observers think nothing needs to be done because someone else has already taken care of it, and the more observers there are, the less likely any one person is to call for help. In Albuquerque, New Mexico, 30 people watched for an hour and a half as a building burned to the ground before they realized that no one had called the fire department. Psychologists call this process "diffusion of responsibility" or "social loafing": The more people in a group, the lazier each individual in it becomes.

8   But there was no mistaking what those officers were doing to Rodney King. There was no way for those observers to discount the severity of the beating King was getting. What kept them silent?

9   One explanation, of course, is that they approved. They may have identified with the abusers, vicariously participating in a beating they rationalized as justified. The widespread racism in the Los Angeles Police Department and the unprovoked abuse of black people is now undeniable. A friend who runs a trucking company told me recently that one of her drivers, a 50-year-old black man, is routinely pulled over by Los Angeles cops for the flimsiest of reasons "and made to lie down on the street like a dog." None of her white drivers has been treated this way.

10   Or the observers may have hated what was happening and been caught in the oldest of human dilemmas: Do the moral thing and be disliked, humiliated, embarrassed and rejected. Our nation, for all its celebration of the Lone Ranger and the independent pioneer, does not really value the individual—at least not when the person is behaving individually and standing up to the group. (We like dissenters, but only when they are dissenting in Russia or China.) Again and again, countless studies have shown that people will go along rather than risk the embarrassment of being disobedient, rude or disloyal.

11   And so the banality of evil is once again confirmed. Most people do not behave badly because they are inherently bad. They behave badly because they aren't paying attention, or they leave it to Harry, or they don't want to rock the boat, or they don't want to embarrass themselves or others if they're wrong.

12   Every time the news reports another story of a group that has behaved mindlessly, violently and stupidly, including the inevitable members who are just "going along," many people shake their heads in shock and anger at the failings of "human nature." But the findings of behavioral research can direct us instead to appreciate the conditions under which individuals in groups will behave morally or not. Once we know the conditions, we can begin to prescribe antidotes. By understanding the impulse to diffuse responsibility, perhaps as individuals we will be more likely to act. By understanding the social pressures that reward groupthink, loyalty and obedience, we can foster those that reward whistle-blowing and moral courage. And, as a society, we can reinforce the belief that they also sin who only stand and watch.

THINKING ABOUT THE TEXT

1. What is Tavris's thesis? How does she support her position?

2. How does the psychologist's term for the behavior Tavris describes explain what actually happens?

3. How does Tavris imagine this condition will right itself?

WRITING FROM THE TEXT

1. Write about an incident that you observed or were a part of that confirms Carol Tavris's point.

2. Write about an incident that you observed or were a part of that shows an exception to Tavris's point.

CONNECTING WITH OTHER TEXTS

1. Read "Discrimination at Large" (p. 198) and argue that people's ridicule of fat people is often part of a group dynamic. Use Tavris's reasoning to show how people in groups sanction such ridicule. As part of your essay, consider Coleman's suggestion that the group can work as a whole to exert pressure on those who discriminate against the fat.

2. Research the Rodney King incident of 1991 to find interviews and court testimony from the police officers involved as participants or observers of the beating. Do their own words and feelings confirm or refute Tavris's thesis?

3. Read "Shooting an Elephant" (below) and write an essay analyzing Orwell's behavior in light of the insights provided by Carol Tavris.

Shooting an Elephant
George Orwell

Renowned writer of prose and fiction, George Orwell (1903–1950) was the pen name of Eric Blair. After graduating from Eton College, Orwell joined the British police in Burma and grew to distrust the methods of the British government there. For years he struggled to support himself with various odd jobs; this experience is described in *Down and Out in Paris and London* (1933). Eventually working as shopkeeper, correspondent, teacher, editor, and radio producer, Orwell tended to empathize with the disenfranchised of society. In *Animal Farm* (1945), Orwell satirizes the Soviet bureaucracy and warns people of the dangers of a totalitarian state. In *1984* (1949), he depicts a rigid government—represented by "Big Brother"—that twists truth and spies on its citizens via two-way television. The following piece is from *Shooting an Elephant and Other Essays* (1950).

1   In Moulmein, in lower Burma, I was hated by large numbers of people—the only time in my life that I have been important enough for this to happen to me. I was sub-divisional police officer of the town, and in an aimless, petty kind of way anti-European feeling was very bitter. No one had the guts to raise a riot, but if a European woman went through the bazaars alone somebody would probably spit betel juice over her dress. As a police officer I was an obvious target and was baited whenever it seemed safe to do so. When a nimble Burman tripped me up on the football field and the referee (another Burman) looked the other way, the crowd yelled with hideous laughter. This happened more than once. In the end the sneering yellow faces of young men that met me everywhere, the insults hooted after me

when I was at a safe distance, got badly on my nerves. The young Buddhist priests were the worst of all. There were several thousands of them in the town and none of them seemed to have anything to do except stand on street corners and jeer at Europeans.

2   All this was perplexing and upsetting. For at that time I had already made up my mind that imperialism was an evil thing and the sooner I chucked up my job and got out of it the better. Theoretically—and secretly, of course—I was all for the Burmese and all against their oppressors, the British. As for the job I was doing, I hated it more bitterly than I can perhaps make clear. In a job like that, you see the dirty work of Empire at close quarters. The wretched prisoners huddling in the stinking cages of the lock-ups, the grey, cowed faces of the long-term convicts, the scarred buttocks of the men who had been flogged with bamboos—all these oppressed me with an intolerable sense of guilt. But I could get nothing into perspective. I was young and ill-educated and I had had to think out my problems in the utter silence that is imposed on every Englishman in the East. I did not even know that the British Empire is dying, still less did I know that it is a great deal better than the younger empires that are going to supplant it. All I knew was that I was stuck between my hatred of the empire I served and my rage against the evil-spirited little beasts who tried to make my job impossible. With one part of my mind I thought of the British as an unbreakable tyranny, as something clamped down, *in saecula saeculorum,* upon the will of prostrate peoples; with another part I thought that the greatest joy in the world would be to drive a bayonet into a Buddhist priest's guts. Feelings like these are the normal by-products of imperialism; ask any Anglo-Indian official, if you can catch him off duty.

3   One day something happened which in a roundabout way was enlightening. It was a tiny incident in itself, but it gave me a better glimpse than I had had before of the real nature of imperialism—the real motive for which despotic governments act. Early one morning the sub-inspector at a police station the other end of the town rang me up on the phone and said that an elephant was ravaging the bazaar. Would I please come and do something about it? I did not know what I could do, but I wanted to see what was happening and I got onto a pony and started out. I took my rifle, an old .44 Winchester and much too small to kill an elephant, but I thought the noise might be useful *in terrorem.* Various Burmans stopped me on the way and told me about the elephant's doings. It was not, of course, a wild elephant, but a tame one which had gone "must." It had been chained up, as tame elephants always are when their attack of "must" is due, but on the previous night it had broken its chain and escaped. Its mahout, the only person who could manage it when it was in that state, had set out in pursuit, but had

taken the wrong direction and was now twelve hours' journey away, and in the morning the elephant had suddenly reappeared in the town. The Burmese population had no weapons and were quite helpless against it. It had already destroyed somebody's bamboo hut, killed a cow and raided some fruit-stalls and devoured the stock; also it had met the municipal rubbish van and, when the driver jumped out and took to his heels, had turned the van over and inflicted violences upon it.

4   The Burmese sub-inspector and some Indian constables were waiting for me in the quarter where the elephant had been seen. It was a very poor quarter, a labyrinth of squalid bamboo huts, thatched with palm-leaf, winding all over a steep hillside. I remember that it was a cloudy, stuffy morning at the beginning of the rains. We began questioning the people as to where the elephant had gone and, as usual, failed to get any definite information. That is invariably the case in the East; a story always sounds clear enough at a distance, but the nearer you get to the scene of events the vaguer it becomes. Some of the people said that the elephant had gone in one direction, some said that he had gone in another, some professed not even to have heard of any elephant. I had almost made up my mind that the whole story was a pack of lies, when we heard yells a little distance away. There was a loud, scandalized cry of "Go away, child! Go away this instant!" and an old woman with a switch in her hand came round the corner of a hut, violently shooing away a crowd of naked children. Some more women followed, clicking their tongues and exclaiming: evidently there was something that the children ought not to have seen. I rounded the hut and saw a man's dead body sprawling in the mud. He was an Indian, a black Dravidian coolie, almost naked, and he could not have been dead many minutes. The people said that the elephant had come suddenly upon him round the corner of the hut, caught him with its trunk, put its foot on his back and ground him into the earth. This was the rainy season and the ground was soft, and his face had scored a trench a foot deep and a couple of yards long. He was lying on his belly with arms crucified and head sharply twisted to one side. His face was coated with mud, the eyes wide open, the teeth bared and grinning with an expression of unendurable agony. (Never tell me, by the way, that the dead look peaceful. Most of the corpses I have seen look devilish.) The friction of the great beast's foot had stripped the skin from his back as neatly as one skins a rabbit. As soon as I saw the dead man I sent an orderly to a friend's house nearby to borrow an elephant rifle. I had already sent back the pony, not wanting it to go mad with fright and throw me if it smelt the elephant.

5   The orderly came back in a few minutes with a rifle and five cartridges, and meanwhile some Burmans had arrived and told us that the elephant was in the paddy fields below, only a few hundred yards away. As I started

forward practically the whole population of the quarter flocked out of the houses and followed me. They had seen the rifle and were all shouting excitedly that I was going to shoot the elephant. They had not shown much interest in the elephant when he was merely ravaging their homes, but it was different now that he was going to be shot. It was a bit of fun to them, as it would be to an English crowd; besides they wanted the meat. It made me vaguely uneasy. I had no intention of shooting the elephant—I had merely sent for the rifle to defend myself if necessary—and it is always unnerving to have a crowd following you. I marched down the hill, looking and feeling a fool, with the rifle over my shoulders and an ever-growing army of people jostling at my heels. At the bottom, when you got away from the huts, there was a metalled road and beyond that a miry waste of paddy fields a thousand yards across, not yet ploughed but soggy from the first rains and dotted with coarse grass. The elephant was standing eight yards from the road, his left side towards us. He took not the slightest notice of the crowd's approach. He was tearing up branches of grass, beating them against his knees to clean them and stuffing them into his mouth.

6   I had halted on the road. As soon as I saw the elephant I knew with perfect certainty that I ought not to shoot him. It is a serious matter to shoot a working elephant—it is comparable to destroying a huge and costly piece of machinery—and obviously one ought not to do it if it can possibly be avoided. And at that distance, peacefully eating, the elephant looked no more dangerous than a cow. I thought then and I think now that his attack of "must" was already passing off; in which case he would merely wander harmlessly about until the mahout came back and caught him. Moreover, I did not in the least want to shoot him. I decided that I would watch him for a little while to make sure that he did not turn savage again, and then go home.

7   But at that moment, I glanced round at the crowd that had followed me. It was an immense crowd, two thousand at the least and growing every minute. It blocked the road for a long distance on either side. I looked at the sea of yellow faces above the garish clothes—faces all happy and excited over this bit of fun, all certain that the elephant was going to be shot. They were watching me as they would watch a conjurer about to perform a trick. They did not like me, but with the magical rifle in my hands I was momentarily worth watching. And suddenly I realized that I should have to shoot the elephant after all. The people expected it of me and I had got to do it; I could feel their two thousand wills pressing me forward, irresistibly. And it was at this moment, as I stood there with the rifle in my hands, that I first grasped the hollowness, the futility of the white man's dominion in the East. Here was I, the white man with his gun, standing in front of the unarmed native crowd—seemingly the leading actor of the piece; but in reality I was

only an absurd puppet pushed to and fro by the will of those yellow faces behind. I perceived in this moment that when the white man turns tyrant it is his own freedoms that he destroys. He becomes a sort of hollow, posing dummy, the conventionalized figure of a sahib. For it is the condition of his rule that he shall spend his life in trying to impress the "natives," and so in every crisis he has got to do what the "natives" expect of him. He wears a mask, and his face grows to fit it. I had got to shoot the elephant. I had committed myself to doing it when I sent for the rifle. A sahib has got to act like a sahib; he has got to appear resolute, to know his own mind and do definite things. To come all that way, rifle in hand, with two thousand people marching at my heels, and then to trail feebly away, having done nothing—no, that was impossible. The crowd would laugh at me. And my whole life, every white man's life in the East, was one long struggle not to be laughed at.

8   But I did not want to shoot the elephant. I watched him beating his bunch of grass against his knees, with that preoccupied grandmotherly air that elephants have. It seemed to me that it would be murder to shoot him. At that age I was not squeamish about killing animals, but I had never shot an elephant and never wanted to. (Somehow it always seems worse to kill a *large* animal.) Besides, there was the beast's owner to be considered. Alive, the elephant was worth at least a hundred pounds; dead, he would only be worth the value of his tusks, five pounds, possibly. But I had to act quickly. I turned to some experienced-looking Burmans who had been there when we arrived, and asked them how the elephant had been behaving. They all said the same thing: he took no notice of you if you left him alone, but he might charge if you went too close to him.

9   It was perfectly clear to me what I ought to do. I ought to walk up to within, say, twenty-five yards of the elephant and test his behavior. If he charged, I could shoot; if he took no notice of me, it would be safe to leave him until the mahout came back. But also I knew that I was going to do no such thing. I was a poor shot with a rifle and the ground was soft mud into which one would sink at every step. If the elephant charged and I missed him, I should have about as much chance as a toad under a steam-roller. But even then I was not thinking particularly of my own skin, only of the watchful yellow faces behind. For at that moment, with the crowd watching me, I was not afraid in the ordinary sense, as I would have been if I had been alone. A white man mustn't be frightened in front of "natives"; and so, in general, he isn't frightened. The sole thought in my mind was that if anything went wrong, those two thousand Burmans would see me pursued, caught, trampled on and reduced to a grinning corpse like that Indian up the hill. And if that happened it was quite probable that some of them would

laugh. That would never do. There was only one alternative. I shoved the cartridges into the magazine and lay down on the road to get a better aim.

10   The crowd grew very still, and a deep, low, happy sigh, as of people who see the theatre curtain go up at last, breathed from innumerable throats. They were going to have their bit of fun after all. The rifle was a beautiful German thing with cross-hair sights. I did not then know that in shooting an elephant one would shoot to cut an imaginary bar running from ear-hole to ear-hole. I ought, therefore, as the elephant was sideways on, to have aimed straight at his ear-hole; actually I aimed several inches in front of this, thinking the brain would be further forward.

11   When I pulled the trigger I did not hear the bang or feel the kick—one never does when a shot goes home—but I heard the devilish roar of glee that went up from the crowd. In that instant, in too short a time, one would have thought, even for the bullet to get there, a mysterious, terrible change had come over the elephant. He neither stirred nor fell, but every line of his body had altered. He looked suddenly stricken, shrunken, immensely old, as though the frightful impact of the bullet had paralysed him without knocking him down. At last, after what seemed a long time—it might have been five seconds, I dare say—he sagged flabbily to his knees. His mouth slobbered. An enormous senility seemed to have settled upon him. One could have imagined him thousands of years old. I fired again into the same spot. At the second shot he did not collapse but climbed with desperate slowness to his feet and stood weakly upright, with legs sagging and head drooping. I fired a third time. That was the shot that did for him. You could see the agony of it jolt his whole body and knock the last remnant of strength from his legs. But in falling he seemed for a moment to rise, for as his hind legs collapsed beneath him he seemed to tower upward like a huge rock toppling, his trunk reaching skywards like a tree. He trumpeted, for the first and only time. And then down he came, his belly towards me, with a crash that seemed to shake the ground even where I lay.

12   I got up. The Burmans were already racing past me across the mud. It was obvious that the elephant would never rise again, but he was not dead. He was breathing very rhythmically with long rattling gasps, his great-mound of a side painfully rising and falling. His mouth was wide open—I could see far down into caverns of pale pink throat. I waited a long time for him to die, but his breathing did not weaken. Finally I fired my two remaining shots into the spot where I thought his heart must be. The thick blood welled out of him like red velvet, but still he did not die. His body did not even jerk when the shots hit him, the tortured breathing continued without a pause. He was dying, very slowly and in great agony, but in some world remote from me where not even a bullet could damage him further. I

felt that I had got to put an end to that dreadful noise. It seemed dreadful to see the great beast lying there, powerless to move and yet powerless to die, and not even to be able to finish him. I sent back for my small rifle and poured shot after shot into his heart and down his throat. They seemed to make no impression. The tortured gasps continued as steadily as the ticking of a clock.

13   In the end I could not stand it any longer and went away. I heard later that it took him half an hour to die. Burmans were bringing dahs and baskets even before I left, and I was told they had stripped his body almost to the bones by the afternoon.

14   Afterwards, of course, there were endless discussions about the shooting of the elephant. The owner was furious, but he was only an Indian and could do nothing. Besides, legally I had done the right thing, for a mad elephant has to be killed, like a mad dog, if its owner fails to control it. Among the Europeans opinion was divided. The older men said I was right, the younger men said it was a damn shame to shoot an elephant for killing a coolie, because an elephant was worth more than any damn Coringhee coolie. And afterwards I was very glad that the coolie had been killed; it put me legally in the right and it gave me a sufficient pretext for shooting the elephant. I often wondered whether any of the others grasped that I had done it solely to avoid looking a fool.

THINKING ABOUT THE TEXT

1. Why was the narrator "hated by large numbers of people" when he lived in Burma? Cite specific examples that reveal how the narrator was truly trapped between worlds.

2. Describe the elephant's destruction and its death. What might the elephant represent here?

3. What do the responses to the shooting of the elephant reveal about the narrator (in his younger days)? About the older Europeans? The younger Europeans? The Burmans?

4. What is significant about the responses to the death of the coolie?

5. What is Orwell suggesting about the effect of imperialism on humanity? Support your response.

6. What different insights can be drawn from this story?

7. Although Orwell's thesis isn't articulated specifically, what do you think it might be?

Writing from the Text

1. Citing specific examples from the text, compare and contrast Orwell as character (in his younger days) with Orwell as interpreter of this incident.

2. Dramatize a time in your life when you felt pressured to do something in order to save face. Parallel Orwell's vivid details. Focus on a strong thesis that shows what you learned from this experience.

Connecting with Other Texts

1. Compare Orwell's experience of living between worlds in India with Marcus Mabry's experience of "Living in Two Worlds" (p. 109). In what ways are their experiences similar? Write an essay from a well-formulated thesis.

2. Write an analysis of George Orwell's behavior in a crowd in light of Carol Tavris's explanations from "In Groups We Shrink" (p. 261). Include specific statements from both essays.

 # The Rights of the Born

Anne Lamott

Known for her lively narrative voice, self-effacing humor, and unconventional Christian views, Anne Lamott (b. 1954) is a captivating speaker and writer. Her favorite subjects range from alcoholism and single motherhood to Jesus. Lamott's best-selling works of non-fiction include *Operating Instructions: A Journal of My Son's First Year* (1993), *Bird by Bird: Some Instructions on Writing and Life* (1994), *Traveling Mercies: Some Thoughts on Faith* (1999), *Plan B: Further Thoughts on Faith* (2005), and a collection of essays entitled *Grace (Eventually): Thoughts on Faith* (2007). Among her novels are *Hard Laughter* (1980), *Rosie* (1983), *Joe Jones* (1985), *All New People* (1989), and *Crooked Little Heart* (1997). She has been honored with a Guggenheim Fellowship, has taught at UC Davis, and writes "Word by Word," a biweekly *Salon Magazine* "online diary," which was voted The Best of the Web by *Time Magazine*. Lamott's ability to be funny while instructive is demonstrated in "Short Assignments" on p. 329, but she also can be outspoken and reflective as in the following essay, which appeared in the *Los Angeles Times* in 2006.

1   Everything was going swimmingly on the panel. The subject was politics and faith, and I was on stage with two clergymen with progressive spiritual leanings, and a moderator who is liberal and Catholic. We were having a discussion with the audience of 1,300 people in Washington about many of the social justice topics on which we agree—the immorality of the federal budget,

the wrongness of the president's war in Iraq. Then an older man came to the mike and raised the issue of abortion, and everyone just lost his or her mind.

2   Or, at any rate, I did.

3   Maybe it was the way in which the man couched the question, which was about how we should reconcile our progressive stances on peace and justice with the "murder of a million babies every year in America." The man who asked the question was soft-spoken, neatly and casually dressed.

4   First Richard, a Franciscan priest, answered that this is indeed a painful issue but that it is not the only "pro-life" issue that progressives—even Catholics—should concern themselves with during elections. There are also the matters of capital punishment and the war in Iraq, and of HIV. Then Jim, an evangelical, spoke about the need to reduce the number of unwanted pregnancies, and the need to diffuse abortion as a political issue, by welcoming pro-choice and pro-life supporters to the discussion, with equal respect for their positions. He spoke gently about how "morally ambiguous" the issue is.

5   I sat there simmering, like a samovar; nice Jesusy me. The moderator turned to me and asked quietly if I would like to respond. I did: I wanted to respond by pushing over our table.

6   Instead, I shook my head. I love and respect the Franciscan and the evangelical, and agree with them 90-plus percent of the time. So I did not say anything, at first.

7   Then, when I was asked to answer the next question, I paused, and returned to the topic of abortion. There was a loud buzzing in my head, the voice of reason that says, "You have the right to remain silent," but the voice of my conscience was insistent. I wanted to express calmly, eloquently, that pro-choice people understand that there are two lives involved in an abortion—one born (the pregnant woman) and one not (the fetus)—but that the born person must be allowed to decide what is right.

8   Also, I wanted to wave a gun around, to show what a real murder looks like. This tipped me off that I should hold my tongue, until further notice. And I tried.

9   But then I announced that I needed to speak out on behalf of the many women present in the crowd, including myself, who had had abortions, and the women whose daughters might need one in the not-too-distant future—people who must know that teenage girls will have abortions, whether in clinics or dirty backrooms. Women whose lives had been righted and redeemed by Roe vs. Wade. My answer was met with some applause but mostly a shocked silence.

10   Pall is a good word. And it did not feel good to be the cause of that pall. I knew what I was *supposed* to have said, as a progressive Christian: that it's

all very complicated and painful, and that Jim was right in saying that the abortion rate in America is way too high for a caring and compassionate society.

11 But I did the only thing I could think to do: plunge on, and tell my truth. I said that this is the most intimate decision a woman makes, and she makes it all alone, in her deepest heart of hearts, sometimes with the man by whom she is pregnant, with her dearest friends or with her doctor—but without the personal opinion of say, Tom DeLay or Karl Rove.

12 I said I could not believe that men committed to equality and civil rights were still challenging the basic rights of women. I thought about all the photo-ops at which President Bush had signed legislation limiting abortion rights, surrounded by 10 or so white, self-righteous married men, who have forced God knows how many girlfriends into doing God knows what. I thought of the time Bush appeared on stage with children born from frozen embryos, children he calls "snowflake babies," and of the embryos themselves, which he calls the youngest and most vulnerable Americans.

13 And somehow, as I was answering, I got louder and maybe even more emphatic than I actually felt, and said it was not a morally ambiguous issue for me at *all*. I said that fetuses are not babies yet; that there was actually a real difference between pro-abortion people, like me, and Klaus Barbie.

14 Then I said that a woman's right to choose was nobody else's goddamn business. This got their attention.

15 A cloud of misery fell over room, and the stage. Finally, Jim said something unifying enough for us to proceed—that liberals must not treat people with opposing opinions on abortion with contempt and exclusion, partly because it's tough material, and partly because it is so critical that we win these next big elections.

16 It was not until the reception that I finally realized part of the problem—no one had told me that the crowd was made up largely of Catholics.

17 I had flown in at dawn on a red-eye, and, in my exhaustion, had somehow missed this one tiny bit of information. I was mortified: I had to eat my body weight in chocolate just to calm myself.

18 But then I asked myself: Would I, should I, have given a calmer answer? Wouldn't it have been more useful and harder to dismiss me if I had sounded more reasonable, less—what is the word—spewy?

19 Maybe I could have presented my position in a less strident, divisive manner. But the questioner's use of the words "murder" and "babies" had put me on the defensive. Plus I am so confused about why we are still having to argue with patriarchal sentimentality about teeny weenie so-called babies—some microscopic, some no bigger than the sea monkeys we used to

send away for—when real, live, already born women, many of them desperately poor, get such short shrift from the current administration.

20   Most women like me would *much* rather use our time and energy fighting to make the world safe and just and fair for the children we do have, and do love—and for the children of New Orleans and the children of Darfur. I am old and tired and menopausal and would mostly like to be left alone: I have had my abortions, and I have a child.

21   But as a Christian and a feminist, the most important message I can carry and fight for is the sacredness of each human life, and reproductive rights for all women is a crucial part of that: It is a moral necessity that we not be forced to bring children into the world for whom we cannot be responsible and adoring and present. We must not inflict life on children who will be resented; we must not inflict unwanted children on society.

22   During the reception, an old woman came up to me, and said, "If you hadn't spoken out, I would have spit," and then she raised her fist in the power salute. We huddled together for awhile, and ate M&Ms to give us strength. It was a kind of communion, for those of us who still believe that civil rights and equality and even common sense will somehow be sovereign, some day.

THINKING ABOUT THE TEXT

1. Describe the panel members, their points of agreement, and what caused Lamott to want "to respond by pushing over our table" (272).

2. How does Lamott describe the struggle between her voice of reason and her voice of conscience? What is the resulting claim or thesis that she longs "to express calmly, eloquently" (272)?

3. Lamott announces that she is speaking out on behalf of whom? Who does Lamott claim should be involved in the decision to have an abortion and who shouldn't? How does she justify this view?

4. Explain why Lamott includes references to Tom DeLay and Karl Rove, two powerful Republicans who later resigned in disgrace. Why also does she refer to Nazi Officer Klaus Barbie, known as the Butcher of Lyon, who was convicted of personally torturing prisoners and is blamed for the deaths of 4,000 people?

5. What does Lamott reveal that she can't believe about "men committed to equality and civil rights" (273)? Why does she mention the photo-ops "at which President Bush had signed legislation limiting abortion rights, surrounded by 10 or so white, self-righteous married men"(273)?

6. Why is Lamott so troubled by the use of words like "murder" and "babies" in reference to abortion? How does she explain her perspective in paragraph 19?

7. How does Lamott describe the various reactions of her audience? What does she feel finally "got their attention" and how did they respond? What does Lamott later realize about the background of her audience members that helps her understand their responses?

8. Lamott wonders if she should have "given a calmer answer," presented her position "in a less strident, divisive manner" and sounded "more reasonable" and less "spewy" (273). What do you think? And how does your answer compare to the audience member who tells Lamott, "If you hadn't spoken out, I would have spit" (274)?

9. As a Christian and a feminist, what message does Lamott feels she is carrying and fighting for? What does she claim are the moral necessities for both women and children today?

Writing from the Text

1. Write an evaluation of Lamott's argument strategies—her thesis and support, reasoning, diction, appeal to audience (both current readers and live audience), diction, political allusions, use of concessions (to her fellow panelist Jim), and flash-back to the panel discussion. Stay focused on an analysis of Lamott's argument and not on your personal views of abortion.

2. Lamott questions whether her passion might have made it easier for an audience to dismiss her than if she "had sounded more reasonable" (273). Focusing on Lamott's use of emotional appeal, write an argument that her passion enhanced or weakened her position and reasoning. Include specific references to support your claims and analyze them fully.

3. Write an essay about a time that you responded passionately and emotionally to an important issue. As Lamott does, dramatize the encounter, reflect on your feelings and responses, consider anything that you may have neglected or not been aware of, and assess what remains important to you about that experience.

Connecting with Other Texts

1. After reading "In Groups We Shrink" (p. 261), write an essay analyzing Lamott's efforts and difficulties speaking out and adhering to her conscience rather than going along with the other panelists and the audience members. Include quotations from both essays to help you analyze her ability to resist the pressure to conform.

2. Write an essay assessing the use of an extended flashback (recollection of an earlier event) to develop one's thesis. You may use Lamott's essay and any two of these other readings to support your points: "The Color of Love" (p. 16), "Virtual Love" (p. 56), "Watching My Back" (p. 82), "King Curtis's Echo" (p. 191), "The Difference Between Pity and Empathy" (p. 162), and "Shooting an Elephant" (p. 264). Analyze how clearly and effectively the narrators present the past event and then weave it throughout their work.

Tilling A New World
Bill McKibben

A former staff writer for *The New Yorker*, American environmentalist Bill McKibben has influenced many, including Al Gore, who claims that his preoccupation with the environment and his Senate title of "Ozone Man" were because he was so swayed by McKibben's descriptions of the effects of global warming. McKibben is the author of many books; his first on global warming written for a general audience, *The End of Nature*, was published in 1999. More recent publications include *Hamish Fulton: Walking Journey* (2002), *Enough: Staying Human in an Engineered Age* (2003), and *American Earth* (2008), an anthology of American environmental writing. McKibben is a scholar in residence at Middlebury College. The essay below appeared in the *Los Angeles Times* on March 21, 2007.

1   Earlier this month, a draft of a White House report was leaked to news outlets. The report, a year overdue to the United Nations, said that the United States would be producing almost 20% more greenhouse gases in 2020 than it had in 2000 and that our contribution to global warming would be going steadily up, not sharply and steadily down, as scientists have made clear it must.

2   That's a pretty stunning piece of information—a hundred times more important than, say, the jittery Dow Jones industrial average that garnered a hundred times the attention. How is it even possible? How, faced with the largest crisis humans have yet created for themselves, have we simply continued with business as usual?

3   The answer is, in a sense, all in our minds. For the last century, our society's basic drive has been toward more—toward a bigger national economy, toward more stuff for each of us. And it's worked. Our economy is enormous; our houses are enormous. We are (many of us quite literally) living large. All that *more* is created using cheap energy and hence built on carbon dioxide—which makes up 72% of all greenhouse gases.

4   Some pollutants, such as smog, decrease as we get richer and can afford things like catalytic converters for our cars. But carbon dioxide consistently tracks economic growth. As Harvard economist Benjamin Friedman concluded last year, CO_2 is "the one major environmental contaminant for which no study has ever found any indication of improvement as living standards rise." This means that if we're going to cope with global warming, we may also have to cope with the end of infinite, unrestrained economic expansion.

5   That sounds gloomy, but maybe not. New data suggest that we've been flying blind for many decades. We made an assumption—as a society and as individuals—that more was better. It seemed a reasonable bet, and for a while it may have been true. But in recent years economists, sociologists and other researchers have begun to question that link. Indeed, they're finding that at least since the 1950s, more material prosperity has yielded little, if any, increase in humans' satisfaction.

6   In the 1990s, for instance, despite sterling economic growth, researchers reported a steady rise in "negative life events." In the words of one of the study's authors, "The anticipation would have been that problems would have been down." But money, as a few wise people have pointed out over the years, doesn't buy happiness. Meanwhile, growth during the decade increased carbon emissions by about 10%.

7   Further, economists and sociologists suggest that our dissatisfaction is, in fact, linked to economic growth. What did we spend our new wealth on? Bigger houses, ever farther out in the suburbs. And what was the result? We have far fewer friends nearby; we eat fewer meals with family, friends and neighbors. Our network of social connections has shrunk. Do the experiment yourself. Would you rather have a new, bigger television, or a new friend?

8   Rebuilding those communities will be hard work—and it will start by rebuilding local economies, so that we actually need our neighbors again. Consider, for instance, food. Farmers' markets are the fastest-growing part of our food economy as people discover the joys of being a "localvore." Some of those joys are culinary—fresh food tastes better, you eat with the flow of the seasons and so on. But some of those joys are emotional, too. Academics who followed shoppers found that those in farmers' markets had 10 times as many conversations as those in supermarkets.

9   And here's what's interesting. Local food also uses about 10 times less energy than food shipped around the globe.

10   If we're going to do anything about that endless flow of carbon that's breaking our planet, we're also going to have to do something about our broken communities. Not just by preaching about neighborliness but by rebuilding the web of economic relationships that grows from farmers' markets, or

effective public transportation, or an energy grid that relies on your rooftop solar panels and my backyard windmill as much as it relies on some central power station.

11   More and better don't lie in the same direction anymore. And that's good news, at a moment when good news is scarce.

THINKING ABOUT THE TEXT

1. What is McKibben's central argument? What is the relationship between his position and the realization that the United States will be producing 20% more greenhouse gases in the next decade?

2. McKibben cites specific examples of how many Americans are "living large." What are those examples and what additional points can you contribute?

3. Smog, as McKibben observes, may decrease as we "get richer and can afford things like catalytic converters for our cars" (277). What does not decrease as standards of living improve? Why not?

4. What thinking must be reversed if the trend toward producing more carbon dioxide is going to be reversed? What points does McKibben make to illustrate how thinking and actions can be altered? What aspects of his reasoning are most convincing to you?

5. How does the apparently simple act of shopping at a farmers' market exemplify some of McKibben's points for reversing the flow of carbon?

6. Analyze the wordplay in McKibben's title.

WRITING FROM THE TEXT

1. Focusing on an incident from your own experience, write an essay illustrating that the pursuit of more and bigger doesn't guarantee happiness.

2. With the intention of illustrating that some material wealth can create satisfaction, write an essay describing a time when "more" made you or a friend happy.

3. Imagine that you are the head of a government organization created to ban products and curtail buying habits that create or increase carbon flow. Write an essay that argues for the immediate ban on specific products or outlaws certain habits. You will need specific details and analysis of these products and habits to convince your reader. (See argument, pp. 404–421.)

4. Create an ideal community by focusing on four or five specific areas that will improve community well-being and reduce carbon flow. Use ideas from McKibben's work as well as your own imagination to develop your essay.

CONNECTING WITH OTHER TEXTS

1. Read "Six Rules for Eating Wisely" (p. 214) and integrate Michael Pollan's points with McKibben's ideas to argue for the creation or development of farmers' markets in your community. Use the ideas of both writers as well as your own observations to show how going to farmers' markets can contribute to our well-being. A note-taking trip to your local farmers' market will help you write a detailed and persuasive essay.

2. Integrate the specific ideas from "How to Get Better Gas Mileage" (p. 463) and the theories of Bill McKibben to argue that decreasing the carbon flow is in each individual's capacity. In your essay, focus on at least four areas where individuals can make a significant difference, with consciousness and conscientious changes in their habits. Use both essays for specific details but also contribute original material for support.

Three Ways of Meeting Oppression
Martin Luther King Jr.

A graduate of Morehouse College, Crozer Theological Seminary, Boston University, and Chicago Theological Seminary, Martin Luther King Jr. (1929–1968) received numerous awards for his literary work and leadership as well as the Nobel Prize for Peace in 1964. An ordained Baptist minister, King became well known as a national and international spokesperson for civil rights after his organization of the successful Montgomery, Alabama, bus boycott. In spite of threatening phone calls, being arrested, and having his home bombed, King continued to work with nonviolent resistance and to argue eloquently for racial equality. He was assassinated on April 3, 1968. The following selection is excerpted from *Stride Toward Freedom*, published in 1958.

1   Oppressed people deal with their oppression in three characteristic ways. One way is acquiescence: the oppressed resign themselves to their doom. They tacitly adjust themselves to oppression, and thereby become conditioned to it. In every movement toward freedom some of the oppressed prefer to remain oppressed. Almost 2,800 years ago Moses set out to lead the children of Israel from the slavery of Egypt to the freedom of the promised land. He soon discovered that slaves do not always welcome their deliverers. They become accustomed to being slaves. They would rather bear those ills they have, as Shakespeare pointed out, than flee to others that they know not of. They prefer the "fleshpots of Egypt" to the ordeals of emancipation.

2   There is such a thing as the freedom of exhaustion. Some people are so worn down by the yoke of oppression that they give up. A few years ago in the slum areas of Atlanta, a Negro guitarist used to sing almost daily: "Ben

down so long that down don't bother me." This is the type of negative freedom and resignation that often engulfs the life of the oppressed.

3   But this is not the way out. To accept passively an unjust system is to cooperate with that system; thereby the oppressed become as evil as the oppressor. Noncooperation with evil is as much a moral obligation as is cooperation with good. The oppressed must never allow the conscience of the oppressor to slumber. Religion reminds every man that he is his brother's keeper. To accept injustice or segregation passively is to say to the oppressor that his actions are morally right. It is a way of allowing his conscience to fall asleep. At this moment the oppressed fails to be his brother's keeper. So acquiescence—while often the easier way—is not the moral way. It is the way of the coward. The Negro cannot win the respect of his oppressor by acquiescing; he merely increases the oppressor's arrogance and contempt. Acquiescence is interpreted as proof of the Negro's inferiority. The Negro cannot win the respect of the white people of the South or the peoples of the world if he is willing to sell the future of his children for his personal and immediate comfort and safety.

4   A second way that oppressed people sometimes deal with oppression is to resort to physical violence and corroding hatred. Violence often brings about momentary results. Nations have frequently won their independence in battle. But in spite of temporary victories, violence never brings permanent peace. It solves no social problem; it merely creates new and more complicated ones.

5   Violence as a way of achieving racial justice is both impractical and immoral. It is impractical because it is a descending spiral ending in destruction for all. The old law of an eye for an eye leaves everybody blind. It is immoral because it seeks to humiliate the opponent rather than win his understanding; it seeks to annihilate rather than to convert. Violence is immoral because it thrives on hatred rather than love. It destroys a community and makes brotherhood impossible. It leaves society in monologue rather than dialogue. Violence ends by defeating itself. It creates bitterness in the survivors and brutality in the destroyers. A voice echoes through time saying to every potential Peter, "Put up your sword." History is cluttered with the wreckage of nations that failed to follow this command.

6   If the American Negro and other victims of oppression succumb to the temptation of using violence in the struggle for freedom, future generations will be the recipients of a desolate night of bitterness, and our chief legacy to them will be an endless reign of meaningless chaos. Violence is not the way.

7   The third way open to oppressed people in their quest for freedom is the way of nonviolent resistance. Like the synthesis in Hegelian philosophy, the principle of nonviolent resistance seeks to reconcile the truths of two opposites—acquiescence and violence—while avoiding the extremes and immoralities of

both. The nonviolent resister agrees with the person who acquiesces that one should not be physically aggressive toward his opponent but he balances the equation by agreeing with the person of violence that evil must be resisted. He avoids the nonresistance of the former and the violent resistance of the latter. With nonviolent resistance, no individual or group need submit to any wrong, nor need anyone resort to violence in order to right a wrong.

8   It seems to me that this is the method that must guide the actions of the Negro in the present crisis in race relations. Through nonviolent resistance the Negro will be able to rise to the noble height of opposing the unjust system while loving the perpetrators of the system. The Negro must work passionately and unrelentingly for full stature as a citizen, but he must not use inferior methods to gain it. He must never come to terms with falsehood, malice, hate, or destruction.

9   Nonviolent resistance makes it possible for the Negro to remain in the South and struggle for his rights. The Negro's problem will not be solved by running away. He cannot listen to the glib suggestion of those who would urge him to migrate en masse to other sections of the country. By grasping his great opportunity in the South he can make a lasting contribution to the moral strength of the nation and set a sublime example of courage for generations yet unborn.

10   By nonviolent resistance, the Negro can also enlist all men of good will in his struggle for equality. The problem is not a purely racial one, with Negroes set against whites. In the end, it is not a struggle between people at all, but a tension between justice and injustice. Nonviolent resistance is not aimed against oppressors but against oppression. Under its banner consciences, not racial groups, are enlisted.

11   If the Negro is to achieve the goal of integration, he must organize himself into a militant and nonviolent mass movement. All three elements are indispensable. The movement for equality and justice can only be a success if it has both a mass and militant character; the barriers to be overcome require both. Nonviolence is an imperative in order to bring about ultimate community.

THINKING ABOUT THE TEXT

1. What are the three ways that "oppressed people deal with oppression" (279)? Is the first method that King defines actually a way to "deal" with oppression?

2. What does King decide about each of the ways he defines and describes? What are the advantages of the method he prefers? Why does he prefer this method?

3. Cite the ways that King establishes that his argument is not only about "the Negro" struggling for rights.

4. King concludes that for "the Negro" to achieve civil rights and integration, "he must organize himself into a militant and nonviolent mass movement" (281). Because King has ruled out violence as a means of meeting oppression, the word "militant" may seem inappropriate. What does the word actually mean?

5. This excerpt from King's writing functions as an essay but lacks an articulated thesis. What do you infer to be the central assertion of this selection?

6. Study King's exemplary rhetorical devices to be able to answer these questions:

   • How does King organize this section of his writing?

   • What are King's transitional devices?

   • What are the lines that remind the reader that King was a minister who spoke meaningfully and memorably from the pulpit?

   • How does King use the pronoun *it* as an effective connecting device within paragraph 5? (See pp. 393–395 for a discussion of this device.)

WRITING FROM THE TEXT

1. King concludes this section of his writing with the awareness that "nonviolence is an imperative in order to bring about ultimate community" (281). Write an essay that describes an "ultimate community" that King would consider acceptable.

2. Write an essay that shows your own experience or observations of specific moments of acquiescence, violence, or nonviolent resistance in response to oppression. Provide details about what worked and what did not work. Does your experience confirm or refute King's position?

CONNECTING WITH OTHER TEXTS

1. Read "Who Shot Johnny?" (p. 186) and "King Curtis's Echo" (p. 191) and write an essay showing how both essays support King's recommendations for handling oppression. In what ways are the philosophies of the three writers complementary?

2. After reading Brent Staples's "Black Men and Public Space" (p. 181), analyze how Staples's responses and methods are consistent with King's ideas.

Chapter 6

Between
Screens

Visual images have the power to move us in diverse ways. For example, the photograph of Philippe Petit stepping on the taut wire above New York City skyscrapers arrests the viewer, stirring feelings of terror, amazement, and awe, all in a moment of time. Wordless though the image is, it speaks to us, as powerfully as any language. This stunning image may provoke an immediate, impressionistic response: "Wow—That's amazing! Incredible!" or "How could *anybody* do that?" or "Why would he take such a risk?" The image may also evoke more personal feelings, "I can't imagine doing that—I'm afraid of heights," or "Is that guy crazy?" or "Just looking at that photo makes my stomach flip!" Visuals elicit feelings, thoughts, and questions, and often invite us to analyze them further. If we realize how varied our responses and analyses are to a static image, we can begin to understand the overwhelming power of thousands of moving images that captivate us during a two-hour film.

Film as Text

Film is an important part of our lives, beyond mere entertainment. The movies we see find their way into our conversations, passionate debates with friends, and even our classrooms. In fact, as soon as we leave the theater (and sometimes sooner, until viewers around us object), we rush to share our impressions, opinions, and evaluations with anyone who has seen the film.

Dialogues about films, like classroom discussions of other texts, help us to express not only our views but also our uncertainties as we attempt to get our questions answered. Further, we often seek reviews, both before the film, so we know what to anticipate, and after the film, so we can discover what we missed or how someone else might have interpreted a scene. DVD versions have become so popular because they offer those special features—running commentaries, interviews with the actors, director, and writer, and even explanations of deleted scenes. All of this information helps us better understand the moving images. And frequently, we want to express our own ideas about a film, to counter or expand on others' ideas. Writing about film, therefore, becomes an extension of this dialogue and motivates us to analyze and evaluate what we have seen and heard.

Why *Analyze* Films?

A memorable film resonates long after the credits fade; fresh lines linger and striking images take hold. While some viewers may fear that analyzing a film will ruin the enjoyment, most students come away from class discussions of essays, short stories, plays, and poems, realizing that analysis enhances the learning experience. Just as further examination of the parts of a written text can increase our understanding of the whole, writing about the parts of a film can be meaningful and exhilarating. Capturing our ideas in writing lets us relive and recall our impressions of a film before the images flee.

This chapter, then, provides an opportunity to go beyond film as entertainment and to share analyses and evaluations with others. Here we read film as text—just as essays, stories, poems, and plays are read—as catalysts for class discussion and writing assignments.

The section on each film provides a short overview that cites the writer, director, actors, and any awards won. Critical reviews of each film follow. We have included reviews and interviews by well-known and respected film analysts whose commentaries appear in newspapers, magazines, online, and on television and radio. Many moviegoers rely on these critics in selecting the films they see and in evaluating them afterward.

As you read these reviews, notice which writers provide rich details, historical background, facts that viewers might not know, perceptive insights, incisive evaluations, and keen awareness of the strengths and shortcomings of the film. The best critiques should stand as models for your own writing about film, just as the professional and student essays in the rhetoric section model good writing. You also may disagree with the critics, offering your own interpretations and analyses to counter their views. Therefore, the critical reviews provided in this chapter can serve as inspiration for your writing and as resources to help you remember characters' names, recall key scenes, and perceive themes. You will find the critics' analyses provocative and their easy accessibility here advantageous as you write your own critical responses to the films.

"Thinking about the Film" provides questions that you should review before watching the film and then again afterward as preparation for class discussion. "Writing from the Film" provides topics for analytical essays, and "Connecting with Other Texts" offers assignments that encourage you to incorporate the reviewers' ideas with your own. In essence, each section of this chapter provides you with sources for analytical thinking and writing about film.

Between Worlds and Film Choices

The films and documentaries studied in this chapter reflect not only our taste in movies but our sense of what others will also enjoy and find worth analyzing. We limited the choices to films that were easily available at local libraries and rental stores. With stacks of DVDs before us, we searched for films that would reflect the themes of the readings in *Between Worlds*: conflicts between generations, issues between genders, diversity of cultures, problems of self-perception, and the question of values and point of view. Because of the myriad movies to choose from, our selection wasn't easy. Ultimately we chose films that continue to play in our minds—the images stir us, the characters come to life, the dialogues echo in our ears, and the themes and issues resonate long after the film has ended.

American Beauty reminds us that the suburbs aren't always as predictable as they are perceived to be. The film satirizes the story of a middle-aged man infatuated with his daughter's close friend, characterizes the turmoil of teenagers trying to survive their hostile families, and ridicules many of the choices and values of American culture.

Crash captures anxieties about urban life and conflicts exacerbated by racial and ethnic tension. Filmed as a series of vignettes, this intense film exposes the characters' prejudices and, at the same time, compels us to confront our own unconscious stereotyping.

An Inconvenient Truth documents Al Gore's lifelong mission to expose the dangers of global warming. With historical footage, scientific graphs, and inspirational words, Gore convinces viewers that we have a "moral imperative" to change government policies as well as personal habits.

Man on Wire recreates the breath-taking feats of wire-walker Philippe Petit. This gripping documentary combines actual footage, personal interviews, and re-enacted dramatizations of the daring preparations and cunning subterfuge of hauling a ton of equipment into the guarded towers of the World Trade Center prior to Petit's famous 45-minute aerial performance.

Common Film Terms and Concepts

- *Theme:* what the film is about, its overall concerns (loss of innocence, triumph of good over evil, shattered ideals, family endurance).

- *Plot:* what happens from beginning to end of the film, including the order or arrangement of these key events.

- *Characterization:* how the main characters are depicted and how they change; how minor characters may illuminate the main characters' struggles or values.

- *Narration:* the story line or unfolding of the story from beginning to end; some experimental films may be non-narrative and tell no story; some documentaries may focus on a real event without organizing the details into a story.

- *Point of view (POV):* films often use an objective point of view, but the camera can also create a character's more subjective perspective; in addition, the first person ("I") may also be used, often involving *voice-overs*, that is, the narrator speaking off camera in the first person.

- *Flashback:* an image, scene, or sequence that illustrates a past action or event.

- *Flashforward:* an image, scene, or sequence that illustrates a future action or event.

Active Viewing

Just as we initially learned to read a text actively, we need to move beyond passive viewing of a film to "read" it actively. Clearly we cannot underline key points and write notes in the margin as we do when we read printed matter, but we can learn to critically view a film and jot down key details from scenes to analyze later. Your notes on the film will become your text—to use for class discussion and for writing an essay. Learning to take effective notes can save you time and frustration. Even during the first viewing of a film, you should take careful notes. It is ideal to see a film more than once, adding to your preliminary notes as you watch.

Before you begin watching any of the films in this chapter, consider the following questions, so you can anticipate what's coming:

- What is the significance of the *title*?
- What is the *setting*—time and place—of this film?

- Why does the film *open* as it does?
- What is important about the *concluding images*?
- What is the *point of view*? Does it limit or control the viewer's vision?
- Do the main characters *change or develop* during the film? How?
- Which *four to five sequences* seem most striking to you?
- Is there any unusual *camera work*? Mixed genres?
- What were the most important *repetitions*?

If the questions focus on characterization, key scenes, or significant lines, you will be more apt to critically consider the images on the screen and not slip into passive viewing. These questions will help you focus your note taking. Once the film has ended, your notes are the only text you will have. Because watching a film takes about two hours, you will want to make each viewing count.

 Final Tips for Writing about Film

- Review the "Thinking about the Film" questions *before* you begin the film.
- Use *shorthand and abbreviations* so you can jot down quick notes while keeping your eye on the film.
- If not using a bound notebook, *number your pages* as you write.
- *Leave extra lines between scenes* so you can fill in more details when the film ends.
- Try to recognize and record *key narrative facts, shots, and sequences.*
- Jot down *specific details* about the opening sequence, key scenes, and ending.
- Use *quotation marks* to designate dialogue copied exactly as spoken.
- Spend time immediately after a film *adding details* and interpreting your shorthand notes while the film is still fresh.
- See the film a second and third time, if possible, *adding to your notes* each time.
- Return to the "Thinking about the Film" questions *now* and answer them as specifically as you can.

American Beauty

The 1999 Academy Award winner for Best Picture, this insightful dark comedy satirizes suburban families and values even as it entertains with surprising twists. The film stars Kevin Spacey (Best Actor) as Lester Burnham, Annette Bening as Carolyn Burnham, Thora Birch as Jane, Mena Suvari as Angela, Wes Bentley as Ricky Fitts, and Chris Cooper as Colonel Fitts. Additional Academy Awards include Best Director (Sam Mendes), Best Screenwriter (Alan Ball), and Best Cinematographer (Conrad Hall). Running 122 minutes, this startling film was named best film by more than sixty-five critics.

Transcending the Suburbs

David Denby, film critic, *New Yorker*

1   Kevin Spacey, of the malevolent stare and insincere good will, may be too ornery a hipster ever to become a popular movie star, but he's certainly a great actor, and never more viciously and tenderly so than in *American Beauty,* which is by far the strongest American film of the year. After a short prologue, Spacey narrates in his insinuatingly mild voice. "This . . . is my neighborhood," he says as the camera glides over a demi-paradise of suburban trees and houses. "This . . . is my life." He introduces himself: Lester Burnham, forty-two years old, householder, father, husband, and flop. Lester's teen-age daughter, Jane (Thora Birch), whom he neglects, has withdrawn from him; his hyperorganized wife, Carolyn (Annette Bening), whom we see busily cutting roses in the front yard, won't sleep with him; at work, his job as a media-magazine reporter is rapidly being defined out of existence. Lester has become a superfluous man, drifting through life in a nasty funk. He masturbates in the shower, or even while lying in bed next to Carolyn—that's his idea of rebellion, and he won't apologize for it. In the past, Kevin Spacey's manner has been so calculated and fishy that he's made a teasing ironist like Bill Murray look as straight as Al Gore. But in *American Beauty* Spacey, for the first time in movies, tastes the ash of authentic misery. Lester's marriage gets blown apart by squalls of comic contempt, and the movie opens up from his unhappiness and takes in the larger community—the dissatisfactions of the business-mad, image-mad nineties. In the end, *American Beauty* offers Lester and his milieu a kind of redemption: the movie's bitter satirical riffs on suburban conformity and social surfaces give way to an appreciation of the vagrant beauty hidden behind the surfaces. It's a rich, brilliant, and unnerving work—a funny movie that hurts—and perhaps no actor but Spacey could hold its contradictory moods together.

2   The screenplay, an original, was written by Alan Ball, who has worked in Off Broadway and on television (*Cybill*). Ball signed on as a producer of *American Beauty*, to protect his script, which happily fell into the hands of Sam Mendes, the British theatre director who mounted *The Blue Room* and *Cabaret* here in the last two seasons. The matchup works well. Ball writes prickly satirical dialogue—the kind of egotistical rant that exposes the person delivering it—and Mendes is a master of embarrassment and discord. He stages a recurring theatrical tableau of domestic misery—mom, dad, and daughter tearing one another apart at the dinner table—and the crack timing he brings to the little cruelties makes us laugh again and again. *American Beauty* might have been a success even if it were merely a brutal razzing of suburban banality. But the filmmakers were interested in much more, and when Mendes wound up working with the great American cinematographer Conrad L. Hall, a miracle was wrought.

3   Hall, who is seventy-three, shot *Cool Hand Luke*, *In Cold Blood*, *Butch Cassidy and the Sundance Kid*, *Fat City*, and many other famous movies. A dazzling technician, he's never been this witty or moving before, and from the opening shots we are stunned by the troubled beauty of the movie's visual scheme. The compositions are gleaming and hard-edged; the figures, standing before glass doors or in front yards, are posed in cleanly organized suburban spaces. But everything is a little too bright, too clear, and the scenes pass into a mesmerizing hyperreality. As Lester airs his unhappiness, the camera perches high above his bed, or creeps along toward a shower where he is working himself over, and the off-kilter handsomeness of the imagery absolves the moment of squalor—we're freed to enjoy Lester's bitterness as a funny aria of despair. A bit later, at a basketball game, Lester becomes fixated not on his daughter, who is one of the cheerleaders, but on her friend Angela (Mena Suvari), a blonde with pouty lips. We see what's in Lester's mind—Angela all alone on the gym floor, vamping just for him. As she unzips her sweater and is about to expose her breasts, rose petals come pouring out. It is the flower of Lester's virility, which his wife has clipped, and throughout the movie, in a touch worthy of David Lynch or even of Buñuel, Lester will dream of Angela naked and covered with ruby-red petals. Again and again, the dreamy moments are extended deep into fantasy, and then abruptly ended, returning us to reality with a chill. The editing, by Tariq Anwar and Chris Greenbury, is superb. The movie is complexly organized but never rushed; everything has weight, even sequences lasting a single shot, and the editing discovers what goes deeper than satire—the hidden connections among things.

4   Angela really does come on to Lester, and he foolishly inquires of two gay men in the neighborhood how to get himself in shape ("I want to look good

naked"). In a series of savagely written scenes, he misbehaves all over the place, insulting his wife and telling off his boss, while devoting himself with monastic discipline to creating a body that a teenager will desire. In separate ways, husband and wife are representative nineties Americans, whipping themselves into frenzies of narcissistic will. Carolyn, a real-estate agent, arrives at a house that she wants to show, and, as she furiously scrubs and polishes the place, Annette Bening, in a peppy little mantra, says to herself, over and over, "I-will-sell-this-house-today, I-will-sell-this-house-today!" On and on she goes: Mendes makes the sequence as rhythmic and stylized as a musical-comedy number, and Bening, pulling her neck cords tight, produces one classic moment of comic hysteria after another. Her Carolyn receives the roughest treatment of any of the characters. She's a joyless perfectionist and a phony—her politeness could freeze Martha Stewart in her tracks—but she's trying so hard, and so unsuccessfully, to be a success that one can't bring oneself to dislike her. The nineties bite, and they leave marks.

5   *American Beauty* offers an official nineties slogan: when Carolyn has an affair with the local real-estate king, Buddy Kane (Peter Gallagher), a smarmy super-salesman, he tells her, "In order to be successful, one must project an image of success at all times." If the satire has a single target, that prime bit of business wisdom is it. Angela, the teen queen, also believes in projecting success all the time, and she terrorizes Lester's daughter, Jane, with her erotic expertise, insisting that she's pleased that grown men like Lester want to sleep with her, "because it means I have a chance of being a model." In her Valley Girl way—she speaks the bullying, media-wise teen idiom— Angela holds herself to corporate standards of presentability. All these characters know about self-actualization; they believe in the gospel of selfishness, and they love the jargon of personal triumph, but underneath they feel bereft, as if their true selves had gone unrecognized.

6   It turns out that help is on the way—a young man with a camera, who sees what others can't. New neighbors move in next to the Burnhams, including a teen-age boy, Ricky (Wes Bentley), who stands at his window and takes pictures of unhappy Jane Burnham with his video camera. At first, the spying Ricky seems like a creep. Solemn, and hooded in manner, with an unsettling direct stare, he's a drug dealer who keeps his life hidden from his Marine-colonel father (Chris Cooper). Ricky's silence is a dodge; he truckles to his authoritarian dad, even takes a beating from him now and then, in order to preserve his secrets. But Ricky is the one who has the courage to go beyond appearances. Using his camera, he discovers the beauty in Jane that she never knew was there. A drug-dealing voyeur as liberator! Ricky is the movie's biggest risk: We are meant to accept him as an artist figure in disguise, the redeemer of the suburbs. He meets Lester and turns him on; the dealer and the

dropout do little more than exchange signals, but they make a kind of informal alliance against that "image of success at all times." The film has a counter-image to propose. It's on Ricky's favorite tape, and it's just a prolonged shot of a small white plastic bag, turning in the wind that arrives before a storm. We hear Ricky speak of "an entire life behind things," and of the unbearable beauty in the world.

7   This is a highly calculated, ironic epiphany—the sublime in a whirling piece of trash—and you may gasp at the oddity of it. But you may also realize, with relief, that there's nothing of sixties cant in Ricky's vision. What he says is free of psychedelic nonsense or political ideology. Instead, he offers a new, rapt way of seeing—the artist's way, the moviemaker's way—and Lester Burnham, the defeated suburban patriarch, picks it up and attains as much happiness as he is capable of. The movies shall lead us out of despair by making us *see*. The story takes a violent and perverse turn at the end— Lester's newly beautiful body disastrously attracts the wrong person—but Lester's narration continues to control the tone, and *American Beauty* ends in peace, even in an affirmation, as Lester blesses the world that has destroyed him. "I'm great," Spacey says, offering the first guileless smile of his career. The filmmakers have been working toward this beatific mood all along, developing it in dreams, in Ricky's video explorations, in the increasingly abstract use of rain, light, and color. *American Beauty* is an impassioned fantasia of misery and release. I can think of no other American movie that sets up tensions with smarty-pants social satire and resolves them with a burst of metaphysics. When the different parts of *American Beauty* come together at last, the movie makes something merely clever like *The Truman Show* or *Happiness* look like child's play.

🔵 Dad's Dead, And He's Still 🔵 a Funny Guy

Janet Maslin, film critic, *New York Times*

1   Lester Burnham, played with heavenly finesse by Kevin Spacey in his wittiest and most agile screen performance yet, is a buttoned-down 42-year-old who desperately needs to stop and smell the roses. But he won't get much joy from the ones in his suburban yard. These fussed-over specimens are the handiwork of Lester's wife, Carolyn (Annette Bening), whom Lester introduces at the start of *American Beauty* with the same devilish acuity that keeps the rest of this satire so scalding. "See the way the handle on those pruning shears matches her gardening clogs? That's not an accident," Lester remarks.

2   That Lester happens to be dead when he says this contributes significantly to the film's darker side. *American Beauty,* directed with terrific visual flair by the English stage director Sam Mendes (*Cabaret*) and replete with the kinds of delicate, eroticized power-playing vignettes found in his production of *The Blue Room,* strikes an unusually successful balance between the mordant and bright. Its vision of curdled suburbia, where Lester's marriage is "a commercial for how normal we are when we're anything but," is also somehow embraced with unlikely affection. And it manages to end on a note of acceptance, even in the wake of its forced yet brilliantly staged, devastating climax.

3   As written crisply by Alan Ball (who, like Mr. Mendes, makes a most attention-getting film debut), *American Beauty* takes aim at targets that are none too fresh. His Lester is not the first super-bland suburban paragon to drop out with a vengeance, nor does Carolyn amount to a new take on the ambitious, frigid wife. But as in bourgeoisie-barbecuing movies from *The Graduate* to *Election,* it's the little things that turn the stereotype into something memorable, from the sugary sound of *Bali H'ai* at an otherwise glum Burnham family dinner to the father-daughter give-and-take between Lester and teenage Jane (Thora Birch, in a veritable Christina Ricci role). "So Janie, how was school?" he asks, to which the sarcastic reply is: "It was spectacular, Dad."

4   The film is set in motion when Lester, also none too originally, goes ape for a nubile blond cheerleader (Mena Suvari, lately seen in *American Pie*). That she happens to be Jane's friend doesn't stop Lester from imagining red rose petals floating out of her open sweater. (Mr. Mendes's rueful, cleanly minimalist camera style often gives way to such eloquent flights of fancy.) She is stimulus enough for him to wake up out of a marriage-long coma and start considering life's livelier possibilities.

5   "Red 1970 Firebird, the car I always wanted and now I have it," says Lester of his new vehicle, the one that suits his new career at a fast food restaurant. "I rule!" Mr. Spacey's way of wringing every bit of nasty hilarity out of a line like that is itself worth the price of admission. (His enunciation of "Don't interrupt me, honey" is on an evil par with Jack Nicholson "Heeere's Johnny!") But *American Beauty* is also loaded with equally colorful supporting characters who seem to drift casually through the film until all their fates converge.

6   The teenage voyeur next door is Ricky Fitts (Wes Bentley), whose mother (Allison Janney) is as wordlessly miserable as Carolyn is pert. (Ms. Bening is scathingly funny, and also quite graceful, as a walking monument to despicable values.) Meanwhile, Ricky's ramrod father (Chris Cooper, doing a

wonderful deadpan) is a military man notably out of touch with everyone around him. When two neighbors who cohabit and are both named Jim describe themselves as partners, Ricky's father wants to know what business they're in. (Tax attorney and anesthesiologist.)

7 *American Beauty* hammers heavily on the notion that nonconformity is needed here. That thought is repeated frequently and never carries a whit of surprise. But scene by scene, the film is full of its own brand of corrosive novelty, from the way Lester transforms himself in hopes of attracting the cheerleader to the revitalizing effects of Carolyn's acrobatic affair with a fellow real estate agent (a very smooth Peter Gallagher). As these characters struggle viciously—and hilariously—to escape the middle-class doldrums, the film also evinces a real and ever more stirring compassion. As it detects increasingly vital signs of life behind the absurd surfaces that Mr. Mendes presents so beautifully, the film takes on a gravity to match its evil zest. There's a haunting power to Lester's last narrative note to the viewer: that if you don't share the film's piercing vision of what really matters, someday you will.

The Rose's Thorns
Kenneth Turan, film critic, *Los Angeles Times*

1   Unsettling, unnerving, undefinable, *American Beauty* avoids quick and easy categorization. A quirky and disturbing take on modern American life energized by bravura performances from Kevin Spacey and Annette Bening, *Beauty* is a blood-chilling dark comedy with unexpected moments of both fury and warmth, a strange, brooding and very accomplished film that sets us back on our heels from its opening frames.

2   "This is my neighborhood, this is my street, this is my life," Lester Burnham (Spacey) says in neutral voice-over as the camera narrows in from an aerial perspective to his red suburban front door as he delivers shock No. 1: "I'm 42 years old. In less than a year, I'll be dead. Of course, I don't know that yet. In a way, I'm dead already."

3   To inform us that, as in *Sunset Boulevard*, we're watching a film narrated by a corpse is a quick way to get everyone's attention, but *Beauty*, the provocative debut for director Sam Mendes, goes further. Layered with surprises, at home in unfamiliar territory, this film more than doesn't let on what it's thinking or where it's going; it intentionally misleads with dramatic dodges and feints calculated to throw everyone off balance and keep them there.

4   Whenever a film is this distinctive, it invariably starts with the writing. *Beauty* is the first feature by veteran TV writer Alan Ball (*Cybill* and the upcoming *Oh Grow Up*), and in its ability to make us uncomfortable by changing emotional colors as subtly and gradually as a kaleidoscope, it bears the hallmarks of someone pouring everything he felt constrained from doing in one medium into an extremely personal piece of work in another.

5   *American Beauty*'s subject is the hollow space behind the American dream, the frustrations that hide under the perfectly mannered surfaces of our lives. "Never underestimate the power of denial," one character says, but in some ways what we're shown is not the power but the price of denial, how a world without moorings, without honesty, without human connections turns everyone into a lost soul on the verge of a self-centered psychotic breakdown.

6   Lester certainly fits that description when he takes us on a voice-over tour of his life. The first stop (and, he coolly informs us, the high point of his day) is Lester masturbating in his morning shower before putting in his time at a trade magazine called *Media Monthly*. His wife and daughter, Lester says, consider him "this gigantic loser," and, not really disagreeing, he tells people who've forgotten they've met him, "I wouldn't remember me either."

Anthony played by Ludacris and Graham's brother played by Larenz Tate. This film was written by Paul Haggis and Robert Moresco and directed by Haggis (who also wrote *Million Dollar Baby*). *Crash* runs 100 minutes.

◖◗ **Angry People** ◖◗
David Denby, film critic, *The New Yorker*

1   If there's an ill-tempered remark that has ever been uttered in the city of Los Angeles that hasn't found its way into Paul Haggis's *Crash,* I can't imagine what it is. *Crash* (opening May 6th) is about the rage and foolishness produced by intolerance, the mutual abrasions of white, black, Latino, Middle Eastern, and Asian citizens in an urban pot in which nothing melts. The characters run afoul of each other, say things better left unsaid, and get into terrible trouble. And yet the movie isn't exasperating in the way that movies about steam-heated people often are. *Crash* is hyper-articulate and often breathtakingly intelligent and always brazenly alive. I think it's easily the strongest American film since Clint Eastwood's *Mystic River,* though it is not for the fainthearted. In the first twenty minutes or so, the racial comments are so blunt and the dialogue so incisive that you may want to shield yourself from the daggers flying across the screen by getting up and leaving. That would be a mistake. *Crash* stretches the boundaries: after the cantankerous early scenes, it pulls us into the multiple stories it has to tell and becomes intensely moving.

2   Like other recent movies set in Los Angeles (*Grand Canyon, Short Cuts, Magnolia*), the picture is structured in vignette form, a natural dramatic outgrowth of a strange automotive paradise in which people live in separate racial and class enclaves, drive to work, and stick with their own. "We're always behind this metal and glass," a melancholy police detective, Graham (Don Cheadle), says as he sits in his car with his partner and girlfriend, Ria (Jennifer Esposito). "It's the sense of touch. I think we miss that touch so much that we crash into each other just so we can feel something." This may seem a fancy conceit until one realizes that Haggis is pushing the word "crash" beyond the literal: he means any kind of rough contact between folks from different ethnic groups. But after the collision, what then? The stories, which begin on separate paths, slowly mesh; the characters are thrown together in bizarre ways, and they go past their initial distaste for each other and at least admit that they live in the same city, and are touched by the same fatality and magic.

3   Paul Haggis, who is fifty-two, was born in Canada; he crossed the border into the land of dreams and folly in his early twenties. For many years, he

worked successfully in American television, and was responsible for, among other things, the short-lived but much-appreciated series *EZ Streets*. A few years ago, Haggis, working with his friend Bobby Moresco, wrote the screenplay for *Crash* on spec. Most writers who have been around as long as Haggis wouldn't write anything—not even a thank-you note—on spec, but the virtues of working this way are obvious enough: *Crash* was created freely, without the usual anxieties that shape big-budget films. The screenplay then attracted a number of people eager to take some chances, including the star, Don Cheadle, who helped raise a production budget of $6.5 million, which is roughly one-tenth the budget of the average Hollywood studio feature. Yet *Crash* doesn't look small. Haggis, in his first outing as director, has put together an extraordinary cast, and the stories are set high and low, in Brentwood and the ghetto, among cops and civilians, the young and the decrepit elderly.

4   *Crash* begins with out-of-focus lights, moving in the dark, as if a stunned post-collision consciousness were slowly coming back into focus. The time is Christmas, a very cold Christmas for Los Angeles, with dreamy flakes of snow in the air. At the side of the road the police are investigating a shooting; a young black man has been killed. Cheadle's detective examines the crime scene and stares at something in horror. The movie then goes back to the previous afternoon and fills in the events leading up to Cheadle's unhappy moment. Two young African-Americans, Anthony (the rapper Chris "Ludacris" Bridges) and Peter (Larenz Tate), argue merrily on the street. Anthony is convinced that everything in his life, including the large windows on Los Angeles buses, is part of a white plot to humiliate blacks. His friend tries to tease him out of it. The real joke, however, is that Anthony, who rants that whites assume that all young black men are thugs, actually is a thug, and when he and Peter spy a prosperous white couple walking down the street to their Lincoln Navigator, they jump them, at gunpoint, and take off in the car.

5   The couple, it turns out, are the Los Angeles district attorney (Brendan Fraser) and his spoiled-bitch Brentwood wife (Sandra Bullock). At home after the incident, the young D.A. complains hysterically that the incident, which is sure to become public, may lose him either the black vote or the law-and-order vote, and his wife, who saw trouble coming, is mad because people might think she's a racist. Later the same evening, a prosperous black couple, Cameron (Terrence Howard) and Christine (Thandie Newton), are out on the town. A little drunk, Christine performs a companionable sex act on her husband as he drives their own Lincoln Navigator. A white cop, Officer Ryan (Matt Dillon), who's got a heavy case of L.A.P.D. malaise—he knows he's a racist but can't suppress it—pulls them over, even though it's obvious that their Navigator isn't the stolen one. As his partner (Ryan Phillippe) looks on in disgust, Ryan humiliates the couple, reaching up between Christine's thighs in a mock weapons

search. Christine, shaken, taunts her husband for not standing up to the cops, a fight that sickens both of them, because it seems so old: the black manhood issue again. But also that night we see that Ryan's father is in terrible pain from a misdiagnosed prostate problem, and Ryan can't get a straight answer about his father's condition from the black supervisor at their H.M.O. What Ryan does to the black couple is not justified by his problems, but, as we later find out, a racist can also be a good son and a good cop.

6   I give so much detail about a single plot thread because the entire movie is as intricately worked as this one piece of it. Haggis's complex take on each furious encounter makes previous movie treatments of prejudice seem like easy and self-congratulatory liberalizing. Apart from a few brave scenes in Spike Lee's work, *Crash* is the first movie I know of to acknowledge not only that the intolerant are also human but, further, that something like white fear of black street crime, or black fear of white cops, isn't always irrational. In another strand, an Iranian shopkeeper named Farhad (Shaun Toub) has become a quarrelsome fool; he's sure that everyone is out to cheat him. But this incensed man's neighbors think that he and his family are Arabs, and trash his store. In Haggis's Los Angeles, the tangle of mistrust, misunderstanding, and foul temper envelops everyone; no one is entirely innocent or entirely guilty.

7   *Crash* could have turned into an exploding nebula, the superheated pieces flying off into dramatic irrelevance (as they do in many of Lee's movies), but Haggis has imposed a tight formal organization on his narrative. He has set up parallel events and characters (two wealthy couples, two daughters who save their fathers, and so on), and also multiple echoes and variations, all of which deepen the thematic lines. Haggis sustains the temporal fiction—a long day's journey into night, then day, and then back to the film's opening moment at night—with shrewdly timed cutting among the stories and with many silent moments in which a single character, staring at the city's moving lights, falls into a brooding funk similar to Cheadle's melancholy in the first scene. The moments of rest, deepened and prolonged by Mark Isham's gentle electronic score, serve as caesuras between the high-tension scenes. There are plenty of angry people in movies and on television, but Haggis has an intimate feeling for the way rage fuels itself and redoubles—the demotic eloquence of the street, the marital quarrel, the police-station tirade. I can't think of a single flat or dramatically pointless scene, and some of the big moments play out at the edge of insanity, where contentiousness spills over into tragedy or farce.

8   The actors grab at their roles as if their careers depended on it. Thandie Newton and Terrence Howard expose the kind of torment and shame that could drive this educated, privileged couple apart. Cheadle's soft-spoken intelligence has become one of the most expressive elements in American

cinema, and, as the man who sees the most, understands the most, and pays for his knowledge in suffering, he holds this movie together. But everyone steps up, including Matt Dillon, Sandra Bullock, and the angel-faced Ryan Phillippe, who pulls off a moment of near-calamity with character and force. The heart-swelling resolutions of the different stories will, I know, strike some viewers as overwrought. But hasn't Haggis earned the tears? He has laid the groundwork for emotional release by writing some of the toughest talk ever heard in American movies. Some things may be better left unsaid, but the exuberant frankness of this movie burns through embarrassment and chagrin and produces its own kind of exhilaration.

Crash

Roger Ebert, film critic, *Chicago Sun-Times*

1   *Crash* tells interlocking stories of whites, blacks, Latinos, Koreans, Iranians, cops and criminals, the rich and the poor, the powerful and powerless, all defined in one way or another by racism. All are victims of it, and all are guilty [of] it. Sometimes, yes, they rise above it, although it is never that simple. Their negative impulses may be instinctive, their positive impulses may be dangerous, and who knows what the other person is thinking?

2   The result is a movie of intense fascination; we understand quickly enough who the characters are and what their lives are like, but we have no idea how they will behave, because so much depends on accident. Most movies enact rituals; we know the form and watch for variations. *Crash* is a movie with free will, and anything can happen. Because we care about the characters, the movie is uncanny in its ability to rope us in and get us involved.

3   *Crash* was directed by Paul Haggis, whose screenplay for *Million Dollar Baby* led to Academy Awards. It connects stories based on coincidence, serendipity, and luck, as the lives of the characters crash against one another other like pinballs. The movie presumes that most people feel prejudice and resentment against members of other groups, and observes the consequences of those feelings.

4   One thing that happens, again and again, is that peoples' [*sic*] assumptions prevent them from seeing the actual person standing before them. An Iranian (Shaun Toub) is thought to be an Arab, although Iranians are Persian. Both the Iranian and the white wife of the district attorney (Sandra Bullock) believe a Mexican-American locksmith (Michael Pena) is a gang member and a crook, but he is a family man.

5   A black cop (Don Cheadle) is having an affair with his Latina partner (Jennifer Esposito), but never gets it straight which country she's from. A cop (Matt Dillon) thinks a light-skinned black woman (Thandie Newton) is white. When a white producer tells a black TV director (Terrence Dashon Howard) that a black character "doesn't sound black enough," it never occurs to him that the director doesn't "sound black," either. For that matter, neither do two young black men (Larenz Tate and Ludacris), who dress and act like college students, but have a surprise for us.

6   You see how it goes. Along the way, these people say exactly what they are thinking, without the filters of political correctness. The district attorney's wife is so frightened by a street encounter that she has the locks changed, then assumes the locksmith will be back with his "homies" to attack them. The white cop can't get medical care for his dying father, and accuses a black woman at his HMO with taking advantage of preferential racial treatment. The Iranian can't understand what the locksmith is trying to tell him, freaks out, and buys a gun to protect himself. The gun dealer and the Iranian get into a shouting match.

7   I make this sound almost like episodic TV, but Haggis writes with such directness and such a good ear for everyday speech that the characters seem real and plausible after only a few words. His cast is uniformly strong; the actors sidestep cliches and make their characters particular.

8   For me, the strongest performance is by Matt Dillon, as the racist cop in anguish over his father. He makes an unnecessary traffic stop when he thinks he sees the black TV director and his light-skinned wife doing something they really shouldn't be doing at the same time they're driving. True enough, but he wouldn't have stopped a black couple or a white couple. He humiliates the woman with an invasive body search, while her husband is forced to stand by powerless, because the cops have the guns—Dillon, and also a liberal young cop (Ryan Phillippe), who hates what he's seeing but has to back up his partner.

9   That traffic stop shows Dillon's cop as vile and hateful. But later we see him trying to care for his sick father, and we understand why he explodes at the HMO worker (whose race is only an excuse for his anger). He victimizes others by exercising his power, and is impotent when it comes to helping his father. Then the plot turns ironically on itself, and both of the cops find themselves, in very different ways, saving the lives of the very same TV director and his wife. Is this just manipulative storytelling? It didn't feel that way to me, because it serves a deeper purpose than mere irony: Haggis is telling parables, in which the characters learn the lessons they have earned by their behavior.

10   Other cross-cutting Los Angeles stories come to mind, especially Lawrence Kasden's more optimistic *Grand Canyon* and Robert Altman's more humanistic *Short Cuts*. But *Crash* finds a way of its own. It shows the way we all leap

to conclusions based on race—yes, all of us, of all races, and however fair-minded we may try to be—and we pay a price for that. If there is hope in the story, it comes because as the characters crash into one another, they learn things, mostly about themselves. Almost all of them are still alive at the end, and are better people because of what has happened to them. Not happier, not calmer, not even wiser, but better. Then there are those few who kill or get killed; racism has tragedy built in.

11   Not many films have the possibility of making their audiences better people. I don't expect *Crash* to work any miracles, but I believe anyone seeing it is likely to be moved to have a little more sympathy for people not like themselves. The movie contains hurt, coldness and cruelty, but is it without hope? Not at all. Stand back and consider. All of these people, superficially so different, share the city and learn that they share similar fears and hopes. Until several hundred years ago, most people everywhere on earth never saw anybody who didn't look like them. They were not racist because, as far as they knew, there was only one race. You may have to look hard to see it, but *Crash* is a film about progress.

◖◗ Bigotry as the Outer Side ◖◗
of Inner Angst
A. O. Scott, film critic, *The New York Times*

1   What kind of movie is *Crash*? It belongs to a genre that has been flourishing in recent years—at least in the esteem of critics—but that still lacks a name. A provisional list of examples might include *Monster's Ball, House of Sand and Fog* and *21 Grams.* In each of these films, as in *Crash,* Americans from radically different backgrounds are brought together by a grim serendipity that forces them, or at least the audience, to acknowledge their essential connectedness.

2   The look of these movies and the rough authenticity of their locations create an atmosphere of naturalism that is meant to give force to their rigorously pessimistic view of American life. The performances, often by some of the finest screen actors working today, have the dense texture and sober discipline that we associate with realism. But to classify these movies as realistic would be misleading, as the stories they tell are, in nearly every respect, preposterous, and they tend to be governed less by the spirit of observation than by superstition.

3   This is not necessarily bad, and some of these movies are very good indeed. But in approaching *Crash,* we should be more than usually cautious about mistaking its inhabitants—residents of Los Angeles of various hues,

temperaments and occupations—for actual human beings. This may not be easy, for they are played by people of such graven, complex individuality as Matt Dillon, Don Cheadle and Terrence Howard, as well as by less established but equally gifted actors like Michael Pena and Chris Bridges (better known to the world by his rap name, Ludacris).

4   Their characters—and the dozen or so others whose lives intersect in the course of an exceedingly eventful day and a half—may have names, addresses, families and jobs, but they are, at bottom, ciphers in an allegorical scheme dreamed up by Paul Haggis, the screenwriter (most recently of Clint Eastwood's *Million Dollar Baby*), here making his directorial debut.

5   As he demonstrated to galvanizing effect in the *Million Dollar Baby* script, Mr. Haggis is not unduly concerned with subtlety. At a time when ambitious movies are dominated by knowing cleverness and showy sensation, he makes a case for blunt, earnest emotion, and shows an admirable willingness to risk sentimentality and cliché in the pursuit of genuine feeling. Many of the scenes in *Crash* unfold with great dramatic power, even when they lack a credible narrative or psychological motive.

6   Mr. Haggis's evident sincerity and intelligence are reflected in the conviction of the cast, and may also leave an impression on the audience. So much feeling, so much skill, so much seriousness, such an urgent moral agenda—all of this must surely answer our collective hunger for a good movie, or even a great one, about race and class in a modern American city.

7   Not even close. *Crash* writes its themes in capital letters—Race, Class, Life, Fate—and then makes them the subjects of a series of speeches and the pivot points for a succession of clumsy reversals. The first speech, which doubles as introductory voice-over narration, is by Mr. Cheadle's character, a detective named Graham, addressing his partner (and lover), Ria (Jennifer Esposito), after their car has been in a minor accident. He takes the event as a metaphor for the disjunctive, isolated character of life in Los Angeles, while she insists that it is merely a literal, physical occurrence that requires a practical response.

8   It does not take long to figure out whose side Mr. Haggis is on. Metaphor hangs in the California air like smog (or like the snow that is incongruously falling on the Hollywood Hills). The other major element in the atmosphere is intolerance. Ria, who is Hispanic, climbs out of the car and confronts the other driver, an Asian-American woman, and before long their argument has descended into racial name-calling. This sets the pattern for just about every other conversation in the movie.

9   In the next scene, which takes place earlier on the previous day, a hot-tempered Iranian shopkeeper is insulted by the owner of a gun store, who calls him "Osama." And so it goes, slur by slur, until we come full circle, to the original accident, after which a few lingering questions are resolved.

10   In the meantime, quite a lot happens. Guns are pulled, cars are stolen, children are endangered, cars flip over, and many angry, hurtful words are exchanged, all of it threaded together by Mr. Haggis's quick, emphatic direction and Mark Isham's maundering electronic score.

11   Mr. Haggis is eager to show the complexities of his many characters, which means that each one will show exactly two sides. A racist white police officer will turn out to be physically courageous and devoted to his ailing father; his sensitive white partner will engage in some deadly racial profiling; a young black man who sees racial profiling everywhere will turn out to be a carjacker; a wealthy, mild-mannered black man will pull out a gun and start screaming. No one is innocent. There's good and bad in everyone. (The exception is Mr. Pena's character, a Mexican-American locksmith who is an island of quiet decency in a sea of howling prejudice and hypocrisy).

12   That these bromides count as insights may say more about the state of the American civic conversation than about Mr. Haggis's limitations as a storyteller, and there is no doubt that he is trying to dig into the unhappiness and antagonism that often simmer below the placid surface of everyday life. "I'm angry all the time, and I don't know why," says Jean (Sandra Bullock), the wife of the city's district attorney (Brendan Fraser), the day after their S.U.V. has been stolen at gunpoint.

13   Her condition is all but universal in Mr. Haggis's city, but its avenues of expression are overwrought and implausible. The idea that bigotry is the public face of private unhappiness—the notion that we lash out at people we don't know as a form of displaced revenge against the more familiar sources of our misery—is an interesting one, but the failure of *Crash* is that it states its ideas, again and again, without realizing them in coherent dramatic form.

14   It is at once tangled and threadbare; at times you have trouble keeping track of all the characters, but they run into one another with such frequency that, by the end, you start to think that the population of Los Angeles County must number in the mid-two figures—all of it strangers who hate one another on sight.

15   So what kind of a movie is *Crash*? A frustrating movie: full of heart and devoid of life; crudely manipulative when it tries hardest to be subtle; and profoundly complacent in spite of its intention to unsettle and disturb.

Works Cited

Crash. Dir. Paul Haggis. Perf. Sandra Bullock, Don Cheadle, Matt Dillon, Jennifer Esposito, Brendan Fraser, Terrance Howard, Chris (Ludacris) Bridges, Thandie Newton, and Michael Peña. Lions Gate, 2004. Film.

Denby, David. "Angry People." Rev. of *Crash*. Dir. Paul Haggis. *The New Yorker*. 2 May 2005: 110–111. Print.

Ebert, Roger. *"Crash."* Rev. of *Crash.* Dir. Paul Haggis. *rogerebert.com.* *Chicago Sun-Times*, 5 May 2005. Web. 19 July 2005.

Scott, A. O. "Bigotry as the Outer Side of Inner Angst." Rev. of *Crash.* Dir. Paul Haggis. *newyorktimes.com*, The *New York Times*, 6 May 2005. Web. 29 June 2004.

THINKING ABOUT THE FILM

1. Our first impression of every character changes as the film progresses. Describe how you see each of these characters initially and then at the end of the film:

   - Anthony, the car thief
   - Peter, Graham's brother and Anthony's accomplice
   - Officer Ryan
   - Jean, the district attorney's wife
   - Cameron, the television director
   - Graham, the detective
   - Tommy, the rookie cop

2. In addition to the audience's altered impressions of the characters, how do the characters' impressions of each other change as the film progresses?

3. Identify the social conditions that put pressure on well-intentioned individuals like Graham (the detective), Tommy (the rookie cop), and Cameron (the TV director).

4. What insights about stereotyping does the film ultimately offer the viewer?

WRITING FROM THE FILM

1. Write a paper contrasting your initial impressions of several main characters with your perceptions of them by the end of the film. Use specific details to illustrate your points.

2. In the opening of the film, the detective, Graham, claims that people in the city miss a sense of touch so much that "we crash into each other just so we can feel something." Write an essay evaluating this statement as a reflection of the film and include specific scenes to support your views.

3. Write an essay that analyzes how racism and cultural stereotypes function as an insidious force in this film.

4. After Cameron, the television director, hides Anthony from the police, Cameron tells the young car thief, "You embarrass me; you embarrass yourself." Write an essay showing how this line might be delivered by a family member to Jean, to Graham's mother, and to the Iranian father.

CONNECTING WITH OTHER TEXTS

1. David Denby calls *Crash* a strong film, "hyper-articulate and often breath-takingly intelligent and always brazenly alive" (299). In contrast, A. O. Scott claims that *Crash* is "a frustrating movie: full of heart and devoid of life; crudely manipulative when it tries hardest to be subtle; and profoundly complacent in spite of its intention to unsettle and disturb" (306). Write an essay supporting or refuting either critic.

2. In his review, Roger Ebert observes that the characters "learn things, mostly about themselves. Almost all of them are still alive at the end, and are better people because of what has happened to them" (304). Focusing on any three characters, write an analysis of what they have learned and in what specific ways they are better people.

3. After reading "Don't Let Stereotypes Warp Your Judgments" (p. 470), show how specific points in Heilbroner's essay help us understand what happens in particular scenes in *Crash*.

4. Read "Black Men and Public Space" (p. 181) and especially Staples's description of his boyhood friends who were "seduced by the perception of themselves as tough guys" (183). In an essay, illustrate how *Crash* dramatizes the "bravado" that Staples describes and condemns.

An Inconvenient Truth

This compelling 2006 documentary based on Al Gore's campaign against global warming won the 2007 Academy Award for Best Documentary, accepted by Director Davis Guggenheim, and for the Best Original Song, "I Need to Wake Up," by Melissa Etheridge. With a running time of 94 minutes, the film uses graphs, animation, footage of disasters caused by climate change, and documentation of disappearing glaciers, ice shelves, plants and animals. Al Gore and the U.N.'s Intergovernmental Panel on Climate Change won the 2007 Nobel Peace Prize. In his acceptance of the award, Gore stated, "The climate crisis is not a political issue; it is a moral and spiritual challenge to all of humanity."

Al Gore Warms Up to a Very Hot Topic
Kevin Crust, staff writer, Los Angeles Times

1   Critics have labeled Al Gore and his decades-long crusade to curb global warming as "alarmist." But if you've been warning people that the sky is falling for more than 20 years and it really *is* falling (or at least heating up), don't you have an obligation to sound an alarm?

2   The highly persuasive documentary "An Inconvenient Truth" captures Gore delivering a multimedia presentation he has given an estimated 1,000 times since 1989. The talk is augmented with an impressive array of graphs, animation, anecdotes and statistics that convey a flurry of facts, projections and conjecture, all pointing to the ill effects the present rate of emissions has on the environment. A film with a clear point of view (and little room for others'), it is the inspiration of producers Laurie David and Lawrence Bender, who attended Gore's lecture, decided it had to be made into a film to broaden the reach of its message and recruited director Davis Guggenheim to shoot it.

3   Guggenheim intercuts the lecture with footage of Gore on the road, studiously working out his presentation on his ubiquitous laptop, and segments that effectively show the crucible moments in his life that led him to continually rededicate himself to this topic. There's the college professor who first taught him about climate change in the late 1960s, the death of Gore's sister Nancy from cancer and the 1989 accident that nearly claimed the life of his son. While the vignettes establish Gore's long-term commitment, unfortunately there's a slickness to them that plays like a campaign film that might be shown at a political convention.

4   Gore might not be anybody's idea of a pitchman, but here he's matched with the right topic, one for which he demonstrates real passion. He's charming, intelligent, professorial and one might even say . . . presidential. In fact, more than one observer has commented that if this Al Gore had been more visible during the 2000 election there may have been a different outcome.

5   Rather than alarmed, Gore comes off as poised, relaxed and confident. Guggenheim sets up Citizen Al as part rock star, part eco-Buddha. He introduces himself to a small audience saying, "I'm Al Gore, and I used to be the next president of the United States." The line gets a laugh and quickly addresses the considerable baggage that comes with being on the losing end of one of the most divisive political outcomes in U.S. history.

6   This position has its pros and cons for the film. On the plus side, Gore stands tall as an insider pushed to the fringe, a man on a mission with nothing to lose. He's able to attack the issue without equivocation. On the minus side, it's easy for naysayers to claim that the digs he makes at conservatives are sour grapes and he's merely positioning himself to run again in 2008— though this would appear to be a longshot issue on which to do so.

7   The environment has not resonated much with voters or politicians in the past, though the increasing popularity of hybrid cars and eco-friendly products and services might indicate a shift in attitudes. That something so important could be largely ignored for so long is almost inconceivable, and among the things the film does well is an analysis as to why that is. A 2004 *Science* magazine survey of more than 900 peer-reviewed academic papers on the subject of global warming found that all supported the reality while none

contested it. However, a like sampling of mainstream media found that 53% of the stories portrayed global warming as something that was in doubt in the scientific community. The mixed message has kept the automobile and oil industries in the driver's seat and the issue out of political debates.

8   Gore also does an excellent job of explaining the basic science behind climate change and the accelerated rise in temperatures since the 1970s. What could be very dry material is enlivened by Gore's geniality and desire to share the information. The potential for dreaded heaviosity is leavened at times by his dry wit and humorous moments, such as a clip from Matt Groening's animated series "Futurama."

9   Real and projected catastrophes reveal what is at stake. Glacier erosion, the threat to wildlife and the spread of deadly viruses make for some terrifying scenarios. Hurricane Katrina and other weather-related disasters that occurred in late 2005 are included, giving the film a sense of timeliness and a powerful visual element, which Gore compares to "a nature hike through the Book of Revelations."

10   The other strong point that Gore makes is to dispute the "either/or" argument presented by big business when it comes to making the necessary changes. He uses Upton Sinclair's quote, "It is difficult to get a man to understand something when his salary depends upon his not understanding it," to not-so-subtly stress the motivation behind this line of thinking.

11   The film's title refers to politicians' apprehensiveness in addressing the problem. Attempts at strict environmental reform have long been met with gloomy projections from the right—of economic disaster in the form of lost jobs and factory closures—and Gore rebuts this by suggesting that green business can be good business.

12   Although the message of the film sounds bleak, it is actually quite rousing. Gore offers measures that can be taken on personal and community levels but also stresses that major changes require a larger response. The film's ultimate significance is that this requires political will—which Gore labels a "renewable resource"—and that if our present representatives are not up to the challenge, we elect men and women who are.

◖◗ Did Al Get the Science Right? ◖◗
Katharine Mieszkowski, senior writer, *Salon.com*

1   To the tune of the Allman Brothers Band's "Ramblin Man," Al Gore's face rides a cartoon airplane across a map of the United States. As he zips from

coast to coast in a Web video clip titled "Al Gore: An Inconvenient Story," a ticker at the bottom of the screen displays his rapidly rising CO_2 emissions next to the comparatively modest emissions of everyday folk. The climate-change Paul Revere's steed is an airplane, powered by fossil fuels. The implication: Gore's sure spewing a lot of carbon dioxide as he travels the land spreading the word about global warming.

2   Produced by the industry flacks at the Competitive Enterprise Institute, which is funded in part by Exxon-Mobil, the clip dismisses Gore as a hypocrite, leading a carbon-intensive lifestyle while scolding us plebes that we should strive to reduce our own carbon footprints. Of course, nowhere does this oil-industry-funded propaganda mention that Gore used carbon offsets to mitigate the global warming impact of his travel for *An Inconvenient Truth*, that Gore pledged to make the documentary carbon-neutral.

3   The Web clip is just one bit of the skeptic zaniness that has greeted the release of Gore's film. On Fox News, another Exxon-Mobil-funded pundit, Sterling Burnett, compared watching *An Inconvenient Truth* to learn about global warming to watching Joseph Goebbels' Nazi propaganda to learn about Nazi Germany. Over at the *New York Post,* a reviewer baldly asserted that "there is widespread disagreement about whether humans are causing global warming," a false statement that even oilman-in-chief President Bush doesn't accept anymore. Meanwhile, the College Republican National Committee encouraged skeptical students to throw global warming beach parties. Global warming? Break out the bikinis!

4   Ideological blowback or no, *An Inconvenient Truth* is drowning plenty of competition at the box office. Last weekend, playing at only 77 theaters around the country, it was the ninth most popular film, and took in more money per screen than any other film showing, with many screenings in liberal cities like San Francisco and Boston sold out. The film opens more widely this weekend.

5   Yet global warming skeptics continue to infiltrate media outlets as mainstream and reputable as PBS *The NewsHour* with Jim Lehrer, which failed to acknowledge the industry ties of the Competitive Enterprise Institute, while giving the group a free pass to call Gore's film "alarmist." One of the most widely read critiques of the science in the film has come from longtime climate-change skeptic Robert C. Balling Jr., a professor of climatology at Arizona State University, who has received more than $400,000 from the coal and oil industries, according to the Center for Media and Democracy. On the industry-backed Web site *Tech Central Station,* Balling posted a purported fact-check of the film titled "Inconvenient Truths Indeed," which charges that the movie is "not the most accurate depiction of the state of global warming science," casting doubts on its claims about

melting glaciers and intensifying hurricanes. The article has made the rounds of the right-wing blogosphere as a takedown of Gore, and the *Philadelphia Daily News* published it as an Op-Ed without any acknowledgement of Balling's well-documented ties to industry.

6   Balling's critique inspired this dismissive reaction from one climate scientist: "Some people believe the earth is flat, too." That's Eric Steig, an isotope geochemist at the University of Washington, who is one of the co-founders of the *Real Climate* Web site, where working climate scientists provide commentary and context about the news in their now-hot field. Steig e-mailed his reaction from Greenland, where he's conducting field research on the ice. He'd posted his own largely favorable review of *An Inconvenient Truth* on the *Real Climate* site before he left.

7   Judd Legum, research director at the Center for American Progress, a liberal think tank, has rebutted each of Balling's claims on the *Think Progress* Web site. For instance, some of the most dramatic images in the film show the rapid retreat of glaciers all over the world, including the melting snows of Mt. Kilimanjaro. Balling contends the snowpack retreat on Kilimanjaro is caused by declining atmospheric moisture, which has been going on for more than 100 years, not global warming. Legum counters that scientists have shown that the Kilimanjaro glacier previously survived a 300-year drought and its retreat cannot be fully accounted for by changes in atmospheric moisture, especially the shrinking that has occurred in recent decades. Besides, focusing on that one example overshadows the larger point that glaciers all over the world are disappearing.

8   Steig confirmed the facts in Legum's rebuttal. "All those points are accurate," he wrote in an e-mail. "Some of them could probably have been stronger; that is, Balling is even more wrong that Legum indicates."

9   Climate scientists who have seen Gore's film say on the whole it presents a scientifically valid view of global warming and does a good job of presenting what's likely to occur if human-induced greenhouse gas emissions continue unabated. Dr. Gavin Schmidt, a climate modeler for NASA, was pleased the film didn't say: "You're all going to die, woo-hoo." Schmidt, who stressed that his views are his own, not NASA's, says the movie plays it relatively safe by saying, "These are the things that have happened so far. These are the things that are likely to happen should we continue on the trajectory we're on, and these are the moral consequences of it."

10   Scientists express surprise that Gore could present the science in an accurate way without putting everyone in the audience to sleep. "Such an amount of relatively hard science could have been extremely dull, and I've been to a lot of presentations on similar stuff that were very dull," says Schmidt. "Where there was solid science, he presented it solidly without going into nuts and

bolts, and where there were issues that are still a matter of some debate, he was careful not to go down definitively on one side or the other."

11   Lonnie Thompson, a professor at Ohio University, whose work on retreating glaciers from the Andes to Kilimanjaro and Tibet is featured in the film, was happy with the result. "It's so hard given the breadth of this topic to be factually correct, and make sure you don't lose your audience," he says. "As scientists, we publish our papers in *Science* and *Nature*, but very few people read those. Here's another way to get this message out. To me, it's an excellent overview for an introductory class at a university. What are the issues and what are the possible consequences of not doing anything about those changes? To me, it has tremendous value. It will reach people that scientists will never reach." John Wallace, a climate scientist at the University of Washington, agreed. "I think that he's gone to great lengths to make the science comprehensible to the layman," he says. "Given the fact that this was a film intended to bring the message to the lay public, I think it was excellent."

12   Yet some scientists who are enthusiastic about the film had their own critiques of how the science is presented. One of the biggest challenges in the film is visually portraying the likely consequences of global warming in the future. For instance, invasive species, both plants and insects, are a growing scourge, which will likely be exacerbated by global warming. Yet, the film, while not saying anything technically wrong about invasive species, could leave the erroneous impression that the dandelion in your backyard was planted there by climate change, simply by omitting other contributing factors. "Anybody having to fight kudzu in their garden knows it has nothing to do with global warming. It has to do with the fact that we introduced the species from Europe," says Steig. At the same time, he says, invasive species are opportunistic, thriving in many different environments, so they're likely to thrive under climate change. "The ecological niche for certain species are changing quite rapidly," says Schmidt. "You have situations where only a small amount of climate change can make a big difference."

13   The deadly aftermath of Hurricane Katrina is featured prominently in the film, and may lead viewers to conclude global warming is to blame for the disaster. But the truth is not that simple. As global temperatures rise, hurricane scientists predict that we'll see stronger storms as rising sea temperatures feed their fury. Yet it's hotly debated among hurricane specialists whether the intensity of tropical cyclones seen around the world over the past few years already show the impacts of global warming. Sketchy data from past decades makes nailing down that proof difficult, amplifying the debate. "There is a difference between saying 'we are confident that they will increase' and 'we are confident that they have increased due to this effect,'" explains Steig.

14 Also, any one event—like Hurricane Katrina—cannot be definitively linked to an overall global trend of more powerful storms, just as any specific car accident on a highway cannot be blamed on the raising of the speed limit, even if statistics show a higher speed limit makes accidents more likely to happen. Yet any one storm and its aftermath can be presented—as "An Inconvenient Truth" does—as an example of what we're likely to experience in the future because of climate change. In Gore's defense, says Steig, "Never in the movie does he say: 'This particular event is caused by global warming.'"

15 Schmidt agrees. "Gore talked about 2005 and 2004 being very strong seasons, and if you weren't paying attention, you could be left with the impression that there was a direct cause and effect, but he was very careful to not say there's a direct correlation," he says.

16 There is one example in the film that Steig says is simply a technical error. Climate scientists use ice cores from Antarctica and the Arctic to study temperature and other climatic conditions of the past. Gore says it's possible to see the influence of the Clean Air Act by observing the ice core changes in pollution concentrations over two years. In the film, the happy implication is that the ice cores show that human actions, notably political legislation, can have a quick, measurable impact, even in the ice at the ends of the earth. If we acted decisively, Gore suggests, we could do the same to stem greenhouse gases. Yet Steig, who specializes in studying ice cores by doing chemical measurements on them, says it would be impossible to isolate the years the Clean Air Act took effect. It is possible, he says, to observe the decline over the years in certain substances that have been regulated, such as lead. But he's skeptical that pinpointing the Clean Air Act in the ice can be done.

17 David Battisti, a professor of atmospheric sciences, also at the University of Washington, thinks the science in the film is well represented, yet worries about one of the most dramatic moments in the film. "There is only one place in the film I struggled," he says. "It makes a powerful theatrical point, but it leaves open the criticism that you're stretching the truth."

18 Gore notes the relationship between CO_2 and temperature, as revealed in ice cores. He then shows a graph correlating the amount of CO_2 in the atmosphere with temperature over hundreds of thousands of years. The lines closely follow each other up and down. Literally for millenniums, the amount of CO_2 has hovered between 200 and 300 parts per million. But since the industrial revolution, when humans started pumping more CO_2 into the atmosphere with all our machines, it's risen to the current amount of 380 parts per million. Economists and climate scientists believe it will continue to rise as dramatically over the course of this century. To demonstrate the skyrocketing increase, Gore rides a mechanical lift to rise as high as the

CO_2 is likely to go. While the temperature line does not jump up that high in the film, the audience is left to assume—with horror—that it will follow.

19   Scientists predict the jump in temperatures will be serious, but more modest than the graph implies. "The graph shows CO_2 going through the roof, and the thing is the temperature doesn't follow that line with the same amount of jump," says Battisti. "The good thinking person who knew nothing about the science would come away with the wrong interpretation. The world Gore paints in the future is an appropriate representation of the science. It's just that graph that is misleading."

20   "Gore is correct to link temperature and CO_2 in ice core records," concurs Steig. "That's very sound science. But he is incorrect to imply that you can take the one curve and use it to predict where the other curve will go in the future. It ain't so simple."

21   Steig notes that other factors, such as the earth wobbling on its axis as it revolves around the sun, have influenced temperatures in the past hundreds of thousands of years. Now, as humans continue dumping more greenhouse gases into the atmosphere—scientists predict the CO_2 level will rise to 1,000 parts per million by early next century—CO_2 will have more impact. "In the past, the oscillation between temperature and CO_2 were driven by the sun," says Battisti. "The CO_2 was a positive feedback. It wasn't the driver. The CO_2 is going to be the driver."

22   Yet while objecting to the way the graph is presented, Battisti agrees with the qualitative point that temperatures are rising, and will continue to do so, thanks to human-induced global warming, which is a serious problem. "Wherever you live, this is a huge change, and it dwarfs anything that we've seen in the last 150 years, or the last 1,000, or the last 10,000 years. If you want to see a change that big, you have to go back to the Ice Ages."

23   The scene that has inspired the most charges that the film is alarmist is the depiction of what would happen if the sea level rose 20 feet, with the World Trade Center Memorial site underwater, and landscapes where millions of people live, from Shanghai to San Francisco, swamped. Audiences might be left with the impression that the deluge is just around the corner, lapping at our feet.

24   Schmidt says a 20-foot rise in sea level is not unrealistic in the long run— the very long run. "The 20 feet number comes from an analog with the last time the planet was a degree warmer than it is now—120,000 years ago. Sea levels were about 20 feet higher. Where did that water come from? Half from Greenland, and half from Antarctica." How long would it take for that rise to happen again? "Maybe 1,000 years," says Schmidt. "There's some uncertainty about how quickly that could happen, but Gore was very careful not to say this is something that is going to happen tomorrow."

25   If in fact there's 800 to 1,000 parts per million of CO_2 in the atmosphere, Battisti says, it's going to be a very different world. Twenty feet of additional sea-level rise could occur if Greenland melts. "That's most likely if we get to 800 parts per million by the end of the century; within 500 years Greenland will be gone," he says. In fact, there was a time when there were 1,000 parts per million of CO_2 in the atmosphere. That was during the Eocene, about 50 million years ago, when there were crocodiles in the Arctic and palm trees in Wyoming, which was then 10 degrees farther north than it is today. "This was a time when the planet was so warm that you had amazing hot swamp-like conditions," says Battisti. "You had a lot of plant life dying that was actually forming the oil and coal we're now burning."

◖◗ **Warning of Calamities** ◖◗ **and Hoping for a Change**
A. O. Scott, film critic, *The New York Times*

1   *An Inconvenient Truth*, Davis Guggenheim's new documentary about the dangers of climate change, is a film that should never have been made. It is, after all, the job of political leaders and policymakers to protect against possible future calamities, to respond to the findings of science and to persuade the public that action must be taken to protect the common interest.

2   But when this does not happen—and it is hardly a partisan statement to observe that, in the case of global warming, it hasn't—others must take up the responsibility: filmmakers, activists, scientists, even retired politicians. That *An Inconvenient Truth* should not have to exist is a reason to be grateful that it does.

3   Appearances to the contrary, Mr. Guggenheim's movie is not really about Al Gore. It consists mainly of a multimedia presentation on climate change that Mr. Gore has given many times over the last few years, interspersed with interviews and Mr. Gore's voice-over reflections on his life in and out of politics. His presence is, in some ways, a distraction, since it guarantees that *An Inconvenient Truth* will become fodder for the cynical, ideologically facile sniping that often passes for political discourse these days. But really, the idea that worrying about the effect of carbon-dioxide emissions on the world's climate makes you some kind of liberal kook is as tired as the image of Mr. Gore as a stiff, humorless speaker, someone to make fun of rather than take seriously.

4   In any case, Mr. Gore has long since proven to be a deft self-satirist. (He recently told a moderator at a Cannes Film Festival news conference to

address him as "your Adequacy.") He makes a few jokes to leaven the grim gist of *An Inconvenient Truth,* and some of them are funny, in the style of a college lecturer's attempts to keep the attention of his captive audience. Indeed, his onstage manner—pacing back and forth, fiddling with gadgets, gesturing for emphasis—is more a professor's than a politician's. If he were not the man who, in his own formulation "used to be the next president of the United States of America," he might have settled down to tenure and a Volvo (or maybe a Prius) in some leafy academic grove.

5   But as I said, the movie is not about him. He is, rather, the surprisingly engaging vehicle for some very disturbing information. His explanations of complex environmental phenomena—the jet stream has always been a particularly tough one for me to grasp—are clear, and while some of the visual aids are a little corny, most of the images are stark, illuminating and powerful.

6   I can't think of another movie in which the display of a graph elicited gasps of horror, but when the red lines showing the increasing rates of carbon-dioxide emissions and the corresponding rise in temperatures come on screen, the effect is jolting and chilling. Photographs of receding ice fields and glaciers—consequences of climate change that have already taken place—are as disturbing as speculative maps of submerged coastlines. The news of increased hurricane activity and warming oceans is all the more alarming for being delivered in Mr. Gore's matter-of-fact, scholarly tone.

7   He speaks of the need to reduce carbon-dioxide emissions as a "moral imperative," and most people who see this movie will do so out of a sense of duty, which seems to me entirely appropriate. Luckily, it happens to be a well-made documentary, edited crisply enough to keep it from feeling like 90 minutes of C-Span and shaped to give Mr. Gore's argument a real sense of drama. As unsettling as it can be, it is also intellectually exhilarating, and, like any good piece of pedagogy, whets the appetite for further study. This is not everything you need to know about global warming: that's the point. But it is a good place to start, and to continue, a process of education that could hardly be more urgent. *An Inconvenient Truth* is a necessary film.

Works Cited

An Inconvenient Truth. Dir. Davis Guggenheim. Perf. Al Gore. Paramount Classics, 2006. Film.

Crust, Kevin. "Al Gore Warms Up to a Very Hot Topic." Rev. of *An Inconvenient Truth.* Dir. Davis Guggenheim. *calendarlive.com. Los Angeles Times,* 24 May 2006. Web. 12 Aug. 2008.

Mieszkowski, Katharine. "Did Al Get the Science Right?" *salon.com.* Salon Media Group, Inc. 10 June 2006. Web. 28 July 2008.

Scott, A. O. "Warning of Calamities and Hoping for a Change in *An Inconvenient Truth." nytimes.com.* The *New York Times.* 24 May 2006. Web. 12 Aug. 2008.

THINKING ABOUT THE TEXT

1. Why does the film open and close with serene images of nature: lush green leaves and a gently flowing river on a sunny day, followed by Al Gore's voice-over about this peaceful place?

2. What is the intention of showing Gore delivering his slide show at town-hall-style meetings? How does Gore come across to the viewers as the camera follows him behind the scenes and on his tours?

3. What is the effect of Gore opening his presentation on a serious subject with self-irony: "I used to be the next president of the United States"? And after the audience laughs, Gore quips, "I don't find that particularly funny." Where else in this discussion of an environmental crisis do we see Gore's humor?

4. In this film, Gore narrates a moment in 1989 when his six-year-old son dropped his father's hand, ran into the street, and was severely injured. How does this personal story relate to Gore's mission?

5. Gore also tells a story of his father's tobacco farm and business and of his older sister Nancy who died of lung cancer. How is Gore's personal history relevant to this film?

6. Because so much of the film consists of scientific facts and charts, you may have been challenged to record sufficient notes. Work with class-mates to answer as many of the following questions as you can:

   • Why do we have global warming?
   • What is the relationship between carbon dioxide and temperature?
   • How does global warming (the increase in worldwide temperatures) contribute to an increase in the number and severity of storms, hurricanes, tornadoes, and typhoons?
   • How can global warming cause both violent precipitation as well as droughts?

7. Explain the significance of each of these references from the film:

   • the findings of core drills
   • the thawing of the permafrost, the splitting of the Ward Hunt ice shelf, and the disappearance of the Larson ice shelf
   • the Arctic ice cap disappearing
   • the image of a canary in a coal mine
   • the image of the frog in the cooking pot

8. Cite five ecological consequences of global warming in the animal and plant communities.

9. Explain the three factors that are causing "a collision between our civilization and the earth."

10. Gore includes several resonant quotations from important authors and creates his own memorable claims as well. Explain how each of these is illustrated in the film:

   • from Mark Twain: "What gets us into trouble is not what we don't know; it's what we know that just ain't so."
   • from Winston Churchill in 1936: "The era of procrastination, of half-measure, of soothing and baffling expedients, of delays is coming to its close. In its place, we are entering a period of consequences."
   • from Upton Sinclair: "It is difficult to get a man to understand something when his salary depends upon his not understanding it." Cite specific ways that this statement is illustrated throughout this film.
   • from Stephen Pacala and Robert Socolow in *Science* magazine: "Humanity *already* possesses the fundamental scientific, technical, and industrial know-how to solve the carbon and climate problems."
   • from Al Gore: "We have everything we need save, perhaps, political will but in America, political will *is* a renewable resource."

11. How does Gore counter the myth that scientists disagree with the fact that we are causing global warming and that it is a serious problem?

12. How does Gore expose the misconception that we have to choose between the economy and the environment?

13. What historical facts about the United States does Gore cite to oppose those who claim that global warming is too big of a problem to solve?

14. When Gore took his scientific evidence of global warming to Congress, he expected that this compelling information would "cause a real sea change" in the government. He saw global warming as a moral issue that needed to be acted on and not a political issue to be derided and dismissed. What specific evidence in the film demonstrates that special interests, political corruption, and denial have prevented some necessary reforms?

15. Explain the significance of the film's title *An Inconvenient Truth*.

WRITING FROM THE TEXT

1. Write a focused character study of Al Gore, analyzing details from the film to support the inferences established in your thesis. See pp. 485–493 for help in writing a character analysis.

2. Using one of the specific quotations in question 10 above, write an essay explaining its meaning and illustrating its significance in the film.

3. Using specific support from the film, write an argument convincing a skeptic that global warming is a serious problem that we are causing and that we must change our habits and behavior.

4. To reflect your understanding of specific concerns in the film, write an analysis of changes that you have made or intend to make in your life.

5. Film critic Roger Ebert has written that in his entire career of reviewing movies, he has never before claimed that viewers "owe it" to themselves to see a film, as he does for *An Inconvenient Truth*. Write an argument that supports the necessity for seeing this film.

CONNECTING WITH OTHER TEXTS

1. Write an essay that first explains and then analyzes three or four of the negative criticisms of Al Gore's film represented in Mieszkowski's essay. Decide if these criticisms are reasonable or if they weaken the documentary for you or any viewer.

2. In his review, A. O. Scott remarks on the "jolting and chilling" effects of graphs shown in this film (317). Write an analysis of the "jolting and chilling" elements of this film, in addition to the graphs, that most affected you. Consider Gore's personal narrations and images, the animations, the photographs of glaciers taken years ago and more recently, film footage of storms, and any other material in the film that moved you.

3. After reading Kevin Crust's critique of *An Inconvenient Truth*, write an analysis that supports your perception that Crust's review of both the film and of Gore is generally positive, negative, or a combination of both. Analyze specific details from the review and film to support your claim.

4. Read Al Gore's book *An Inconvenient Truth: The Planetary Emergency of Global Warming and What We Can Do About It*. Write an essay arguing that either the book or the documentary makes a more convincing mandate for change. Include support from both works to explain your stance.

Man on Wire

This riveting documentary records Philippe Petit's astounding high-wire walk between the Twin Towers of the World Trade Center on August 7, 1974. Released on the 34th anniversary of this enthralling event, the film shows the often hilarious yet stealthy preparations leading up to what has been called "the artistic crime of the century." The film uses actual footage, personal interviews, and re-enacted dramatizations of the daring preparations and cunning subterfuge of hauling a ton of equipment into the guarded towers of the World Trade Center prior to Petit's famous 45-minute aerial performance. This documentary was masterfully directed by James Marsh whose artistic decisions create the tension and suspense of this fast-paced, 96-minute story. A fact missed by some viewers—and even professional reviewers—is that this documentary has actors: Paul McGill plays the young Philippe in the re-enactments; Petit's girlfriend Annie Allix appears in the earlier footage but in the present-day interviews, she is played by Ardis Campbell; similarly, Jean Louis Blondeau appears in the earlier footage, but David Demato plays him in the later interviews.

 Walking on Air  Between the Towers

A. O. Scott, film critic, *The New York Times*

1   On the morning of Aug. 7, 1974, after months of preparation and years of dreaming, a French daredevil named Philippe Petit stepped into the sky above Lower Manhattan. For almost 45 minutes he ambled back and forth on a metal cable strung between the towers of the World Trade Center, a feat of illegal tightrope walking that, according to a New York Police Department sergeant who recounted Mr. Petit's act of physical poetry in dry press-conference prose, would more aptly be described as dancing.

2   For many years after, Mr. Petit's stunt was a cherished footnote in the annals of New York history, one of the touchstones of a crazy, awful, glittering era in the life of the city. The destruction of the twin towers, in the terrorist

attacks of Sept. 11, 2001, revived the memory of that earlier aesthetic assault on the buildings, which is now the subject of *Man on Wire,* James Marsh's thorough, understated and altogether enthralling documentary. Wisely, Mr. Marsh, who based his film on a book Mr. Petit published in 2002, never alludes to Sept. 11. That would have been both distracting and redundant, since it's impossible, while watching a movie so intimate in its attention to the towers, not to be haunted by thoughts of their fate.

3   But it is also worth recalling that the trade center inspired more love posthumously than while it stood. Mr. Petit was an exception. A zealous, daring wire walker—the French word *funambule* is a more lyrical, as well as a somewhat more ridiculous-sounding term—he conceived a passion for the structures even before they were built.

4   As he recalls it (and as Mr. Marsh imagines the scene in one of many witty, unobtrusive re-enactments), the young Mr. Petit was flipping through a magazine at a doctor's office when he saw an article about plans to construct the two tallest skyscrapers in the world side by side at the bottom of Manhattan. In his mind, and then in a series of sketches and diagrams, he drew a simple line connecting the buildings and imagined himself perched atop it.

5   What kind of person would think of such a thing? How would he go about accomplishing it? Why? Those are the questions that preoccupy Mr. Marsh, whose earlier films include the semidocumentary *Wisconsin Death Trip* and the fictional feature *The King.*

6   The first question is answered largely by Mr. Petit's own testimony. In his 50s, he is elfin and energetic, a beguiling combination of showboat, idealist and con man. And in his early, outlaw years, before the twin towers walk brought him fame and a measure of legitimacy, he combined an exalted sense of artistic mission with a street criminal's sense of serious mischief.

7   Accordingly, *Man on Wire* is constructed like a heist movie, in the manner of *Rififi* or the revived *Ocean's Eleven* franchise. Though Mr. Petit was alone on the cable that August morning, his walk in the sky was the result of a conspiracy of true believers and casual adventures. In his two previous acts of guerrilla funambulism—at the Cathedral of Notre-Dame in Paris and on the Harbor Bridge in Sydney—he relied on the logistical and moral support of several friends, including his lover, Annie Allix, and his faithful sidekick, Jean-Louis Blondeau.

8   In interviews, they and some of Mr. Petit's other confederates—including two American goofballs and Barry Greenhouse, a flamboyant insurance executive who served as the all-important inside man—reconstruct their project, which they referred to at the time as "the coup," in fascinating detail. There were engineering problems and also challenges that seem to belong to

the world of espionage, as well as the inevitable tensions that arise when a group of people pursue a dangerous goal.

9 Why did they do it? Rather than risking banality by addressing this question head-on, Mr. Marsh allows the answer to be at once self-evident and profoundly mysterious. A work of art is its own explanation, and *Man on Wire* leaves no doubt that Mr. Petit's coup deserves to be called art. Mr. Blondeau, a sensitive and cerebral foil to the impish Mr. Petit, chokes up when he recalls watching his friend step out over the abyss. "The important thing is that we did it," he says.

10 And without making any grandiose claims, this lovely, touching film demonstrates that the World Trade Center sky walk was an important event. The proof is in the emotions—amusement, amazement, awe—evoked by those images of a tiny human figure balancing above a void. Also gratitude. It is easy to imagine that, in contemplating the scale and solidity of those brand-new towers, Mr. Petit saw them at least partly as the vehicle of his own immortality (whether or not he survived the crossing). No one looking up at the New York sky on a hazy morning 34 years ago and seeing a man on a wire could have suspected that the reverse would turn out to be true.

Man on Wire
Kenneth Turan, film critic, *Los Angeles Times*

1 They say that seeing is believing, but *Man on Wire* will make you doubt what your eyes are telling you—it really will—as you shake your head in amazement and awe.

2 A rare double winner of both Sundance's jury prize and its audience award for world documentary, this exhilarating film treats French aerialist Philippe Petit's Aug. 7, 1974, walk between the twin towers of New York's 110-story World Trade Center as if it were a daring bank robbery. This is a police procedural, if you will, about what's been called the artistic crime of the century.

3 Made by director James Marsh with the human interest of a psychological drama and the "You Are There" factor of a classic doc as well as the pace of a thriller, *Man on Wire* underlines the fact that often the events most worth investigating are the ones we think we already know everything about.

4 That would be Petit's 45-minute frolic on a cable stretched the 200 feet between those looming towers, which stood 1,350 feet above the ground. The 24-year-old Frenchman crossed the distance eight times and enjoyed himself so thoroughly up there that the New York City policeman who eventually

arrested him called him a "tightrope dancer" and accurately noted: "I personally figured I was watching something somebody else would never see again in the world."

5   Though the hubbub and good will around Petit's exploit was immense—President Nixon resigned two days later and when he boarded his helicopter he said, "I wish I had the publicity that Frenchman had"—it turns out that the story behind the walk is much more complicated and involving than anyone knew at the time.

6   British-born filmmaker Marsh, impressively assisted by editor Jinx Godfrey, has deftly woven several strands of material together. There is heart-stopping documentary footage of Petit's earlier walks in Paris and Sydney, astonishing photographs of his unfilmed jaunt across the towers, deftly done dramatic recreations of behind-the-scenes events as well as interviews with the aerialist's support team, an unlikely group of individuals who are flabbergasted to this day at what they pulled off.

7   Best of all is Petit himself, who turns out to be a dream subject for a documentary. Intensely dramatic and formidably articulate, he vividly relives every aspect of his moment in history as if it were yesterday. "My story is a fairy tale," he baldly announces, and then proceeds to prove it.

8   Cutting back and forth between a blow-by-blow detailing of the 1974 WTC event and Petit's earlier life, *Man on Wire* reveals that the Frenchman was obsessed with the twin towers before they were even built. Seeing a plan for them in a newspaper in a dentist's office when he was 17 and deciding that "I must acquire my dream," Petit brazenly ripped out the article and walked out the door.

9   A self-taught wire walker, Petit dreamed not of wealth or publicity but of "conquering beautiful stages," of doing things that were, in the words of a collaborator, "against the law but not wicked or mean," like walking between the towers of Paris' Notre Dame Cathedral. As Annie Alix, his girlfriend at the time, says, "Every day was a work of art for him."

10 Above all else, literally and metaphorically, New York's World Trade Center towers were on his mind.

11 "He felt the towers were constructed just for him," says childhood best friend and collaborator Jean-Louis Blondeau. "He could not live without trying."

12 *Man on Wire* shows the months of intense planning and false starts that went into the famous walk (including the fecklessness of random American helpers) as well as near misses on the day of the event that nearly ruined everything. When Petit remembers thinking "Death is very close," he's not being hyperbolic.

13 Named after what was written on the NYPD arrest complaint handed to Petit when he returned to the building, *Man on Wire* has made the bold

and quite correct decision not to so much as hint at the ultimate fate of the twin towers. What Petit did was so exceptional it deserves to be given space of its own.

14   Marsh's fine documentary also emphasizes how much a work of art wire-walking is for Petit, who tried unsuccessfully to explain to American reporters that there was no "why" to what he did. He's refused to commercialize his feat and continues to live by the philosophy that "Life should be lived on the edge of life." *Man on Wire* is a primer on just what that means.

Works Cited

Man on Wire. Dir. James Marsh. Perf. Philippe Petit, Paul McGill, Annie Allix, Ardis Campbell, Jean-Louis Blondeau, and David Demato. Magnolia, 2008. Film.

Scott, A. O. "Walking on Air Between the Towers." Rev. of *Man on Wire*. Dir. James Marsh. *nytimes.com*. The *New York Times*. 25 July 2008. Web. 13 Aug. 2008.

Turan, Kenneth. "*Man on Wire*." Rev. of *Man on Wire*. Dir. James Marsh. *calendarlive.com*. Los Angeles Times. 8 Aug. 2008. Web. 13 Aug. 2008.

THINKING ABOUT THE FILM

1. What is the effect of opening the film, in rain, with Philippe Petit's nightmare, his fear that some crates have not been nailed shut? How does he interpret his own dream?

2. Why does the film show a television set turned on with Richard Nixon's denial of using surveillance equipment? What is the effect on the audience of the characters in the film busily packing up equipment we can't identify, with voices describing fear of arrest? How does the fact that some of the film was photographed in black and white contribute to the effect of the film?

3. When does Philippe Petit get the idea for what he calls his "great dream"? How does his action of stealing the photograph from the magazine foreshadow what the audience will come to understand as his methods and his values?

4. Early in the film's old footage of Philippe Petit, he describes himself as a "20 year old shy guy." What specific details of his personal and professional life, recorded in the film, contrast with his self-description?

5. Describe what the camera shows of Philippe Petit and his friends' practice sessions. How do these sessions of twenty-somethings romping in fields belie what we see of their characters during the preparations for the WTC aerial walk?

6. Before his 45-minute event—8 walks between the twin towers of New York's 110-story World Trade Center—what other Petit feats does the film record? What do these daring events have in common?

7. Cite specific examples of how the film maintains the exhilarating pace of a thriller, a "nail-biting" suspense even though the audience knows from the beginning that the central character is going to succeed in his goal. What specific events and scenes contribute to the suspense?

8. What specific artistic decisions did James Marsh, the documentary director, make to create such a successful film? Consider the director's juxtaposition of old footage, interviews, and re-created scenes; Michael Nyman's music (Petit's practice-session music also used in the film); personal statements made by Petit; and your own observations to analyze why the film is effective.

9. The title of the film comes from the description on the police report at the World Trade Center, where Petit is arrested, handcuffed, and charged with trespassing and disorderly conduct. In what other ways is *Man on Wire* an appropriate title?

10. The director decided to exclude all mention of the September 11, 2001, fate of the World Trade Center Towers. Why do you think Marsh made this decision? What is your response to his decision?

WRITING FROM THE FILM

1. Using specific details from the film, and the multiple voices recorded, write an essay that supports the statement made by one of the collaborators, that what Philippe Petit did, "the artistic crime of the century," was "against the law, illegal, but not wicked or mean."

2. Using details recorded and perhaps discussed in question 7 above, write an essay analyzing the artistic decisions of director James Marsh. Support your forecasting thesis with specific details from the film that you describe and analyze.

3. Petit has said, "Life is short, and an artist or poet should not lose [his or her] time and energy asking permission." Petit also says: "Exercise rebellion," and "Refuse to repeat yourself," and "Live your life on a tight rope." Compare something daring you have done with Petit's achieving his fairy tale, or "conquering beautiful stages." In your narration, use some of Petit's statements to describe your own story.

4. Write a character analysis of Philippe Petit. Analyze details from the film to support a strongly focused thesis. (See character analysis, pp. 485–493 for a reminder of prewriting and development strategies.)

Connecting with Other Texts

1. In Leselle Norville's focused biography of Amelia Earhart (p. 497), Leselle infers that complacency and other character flaws contributed to Earhart's death. Write an essay showing the similarities and contrasts between the characters of Earhart and Petit. Include specific details about their skills, preparations, awareness of risks, and other key contrasts, drawing a conclusion about the significance of their character differences.

2. Kenneth Turan claims that the film has the "human interest of a psychological drama and the 'You Are There' factor of a classic doc as well as the pace of a thriller" (323). Write an essay supporting Turan's claim by analyzing specific scenes in the film.

3. A. O. Scott asserts that "A work of art is its own explanation, and *Man on Wire* leaves no doubt that Mr. Petit's coup deserves to be called art" (323). Evaluate Scott's statement in an essay that uses specific details from the film, and perhaps other claims that Scott makes in his review, to support your position.

4. Read Petit's 2002 memoir *To Reach the Clouds* and write a focused biography of Philippe Petit. See focused biography (pp. 493–508) for help in writing this essay.

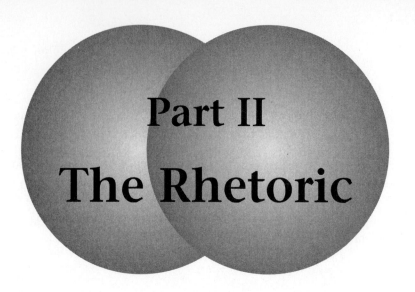

Part II
The Rhetoric

Part II—the rhetoric—is designed for you to use as an easy and constant reference, not only in class with your instructor but also at home when you are on your own. The instruction is deliberately focused and practical. We are convinced that you will only learn to write better by actually writing, and our prewriting exercises prompt you to do just that. We guide you through the entire process, from discovering a topic and writing a draft to supporting a thesis and revising the essay.

Throughout this rhetoric, you will gain skills to craft the varied types of papers that you will need to write. We provide instruction, examples, and discussions of particular methods for developing essays, and we show you how to draft these essays, too. We offer opportunities for you to practice active reading, taking notes, incorporating quotations, and interviewing—all important skills to help you write successful papers. We show how important it is to consider audience and style. In addition to the many shorter assignments, we provide instructions for all stages of a longer research paper, with guides to the most current Modern Language Association (MLA) and American Psychological Association (APA) documentation forms.

Chapter 7

Getting Started . . . Now!

B efore you become anxious about your next writing assignment or bored from merely *reading* about writing, we would like to introduce you to Anne Lamott—a writer who understands anxiety and is never boring. You may have read her forceful argument in the "Points of View" chapter. In that essay she defends "The Rights of the Born" (p. 271), clearly a controversial position. In the following essay about starting a writing assignment, Lamott's argument is less hard-hitting but nevertheless persuasive. She urges writers to bite off just a bit of the assignment at a time, keeping it manageable and appetizing. As you read her essay, highlight key points and vivid wordings. What do you like about her voice, tone, and attitude? What keeps you reading? What does she have to share? How persuasive is she? The following essay is from *Bird by Bird: Some Instructions on Writing and Life* (1994).

Short Assignments

Anne Lamott

1   The first useful concept is the idea of short assignments. Often when you sit down to write, what you have in mind is an autobiographical novel about your childhood, or a play about the immigrant experience, or a history of—oh, say—women. But this is like trying to scale a glacier. It's hard to get your footing, and your fingertips get all red and frozen and torn up. Then your mental illnesses arrive at the desk like your sickest, most secretive

relatives. And they pull up chairs in a semicircle around the computer, and they try to be quiet but you know they are there with their weird coppery breath, leering at you behind your back.

2   What I do at this point, as the panic mounts and the jungle drums begin beating and I realize that the well has run dry and that my future is behind me and I'm going to have to get a job only I'm completely unemployable, is to stop. First I try to breathe, because I'm either sitting there panting like a lap-dog or I'm unintentionally making slow asthmatic death rattles. So I just sit there for a minute, breathing slowly, quietly. I let my mind wander. After a moment I may notice that I'm trying to decide whether or not I am too old for orthodontia and whether right now would be a good time to make a few calls, and then I start to think about learning to use makeup and how maybe I could find some boyfriend who is not a total and complete fixer-upper and then my life would be totally great and I'd be happy all the time, and then I think about all the people I should have called back before I sat down to work, and how I should probably at least check in with my agent and tell him this great idea I have and see if he thinks it's a good idea, and see if *he* thinks I need orthodontia—if that is what he is actually thinking whenever we have lunch together. Then I think about someone I'm really annoyed with, or some financial problem that is driving me crazy, and decide that I must resolve this before I get down to today's work. So I become a dog with a chew toy, worrying it for a while, wrestling it to the ground, flinging it over my shoulder, chasing it, licking it, chewing it, flinging it back over my shoulder. I stop just short of actually barking. But all of this only takes somewhere between one and two minutes, so I haven't actually wasted that much time. Still, it leaves me winded. I go back to trying to breathe, slowly and calmly, and I finally notice the one-inch picture frame that I put on my desk to remind me of short assignments.

3   It reminds me that all I have to do is to write down as much as I can see through a one-inch picture frame. This is all I have to bite off for the time being. All I am going to do right now, for example, is write that one paragraph that sets the story in my hometown, in the late fifties, when the trains were still running. I am going to paint a picture of it, in words, on my word processor. Or all I am going to do is to describe the main character the very first time we meet her, when she first walks out the front door and onto the porch. I am not even going to describe the expression on her face when she first notices the blind dog sitting behind the wheel of her car—just what I can see through the one-inch picture frame, just one paragraph describing this woman, in the town where I grew up, the first time we encounter her.

4   E. L. Doctorow once said that "writing a novel is like driving a car at night. You can see only as far as your headlights, but you can make the whole trip that way." You don't have to see where you're going, you don't

have to see your destination or everything you will pass along the way. You just have to see two or three feet ahead of you. This is right up there with the best advice about writing, or life, I have ever heard.

5   So after I've completely exhausted myself thinking about the people I most resent in the world, and my more arresting financial problems, and, of course, the orthodontia, I remember to pick up the one-inch picture frame and to figure out a one-inch piece of my story to tell, one small scene, one memory, one exchange. I also remember a story that I know I've told elsewhere but that over and over helps me to get a grip; thirty years ago my older brother, who was ten years old at the time, was trying to get a report on birds written that he'd had three months to write, which was due the next day. We were out at our family cabin in Bolinas, and he was at the kitchen table close to tears, surrounded by binder paper and pencils and unopened books on birds, immobilized by the hugeness of the task ahead. Then my father sat down beside him, put his arm around my brother's shoulder, and said, "Bird by bird, buddy. Just take it bird by bird."

6   I tell this story again because it usually makes a dent in the tremendous sense of being overwhelmed that my students experience. Sometimes it actually gives them hope, and hope, as Chesterton said, is the power of being cheerful in circumstances that we know to be desperate. Writing can be a pretty desperate endeavor, because it is about some of our deepest needs: our need to be visible, to be heard, our need to make sense of our lives, to wake up and grow and belong. It is no wonder if we sometimes tend to take ourselves perhaps a bit too seriously. So here is another story I tell often.

7   In the Bill Murray movie *Stripes,* in which he joins the army, there is a scene that takes place the first night of boot camp, where Murray's platoon is assembled in the barracks. They are supposed to be getting to know their sergeant, played by Warren Oates, and one another. So each man takes a few moments to say a few things about who he is and where he is from. Finally it is the turn of this incredibly intense, angry guy named Francis. "My name is Francis," he says. "No one calls me Francis—anyone here calls me Francis and I'll kill them. And another thing. I don't like to be touched. Anyone here ever tries to touch me, I'll kill them," at which point Warren Oates jumps in and says, "Hey—lighten up, Francis."

8   This is not a bad line to have taped to the wall of your office.

9   Say to yourself in the kindest possible way, Look, honey, all we're going to do for now is to write a description of the river at sunrise, or the young child swimming in the pool at the club, or the first time the man sees the woman he will marry. That is all we are going to do for now. We are just going to take this bird by bird. But we are going to finish this *one* short assignment.

Analyzing Lamott's Purpose

Because Lamott's style is so informal and amusing, it is easy to overlook her argument. Despite her relaxed manner, her writing is focused and unified around her purpose for writing and her central points. After we read an essay, and before we write one, it helps to clarify the aim and the claim.

What's the Aim?...What's the Claim?

Anne Lamott's *aim* (or purpose) seems clear—to convince writers not to become overwhelmed by the writing task or assignment. She provides suggestions, personal anecdotes, and encouragement, all chosen to propel the writer to start and to finish one short assignment.

Anne Lamott's *claim* (or point) is that even large projects and tasks may get started sooner and be done better if we tackle them step by step or "bird by bird" rather than feeling paralyzed by the task at hand.

Analyzing Lamott's Strategy

From the beginning, Lamott speaks in her own voice and shares her real experiences: she wonders if she could "find some boyfriend who is not a total and complete fixer-upper," she tries to decide if she is "too old for orthodontia," and she fears that she has run out of writing ideas and is "completely unemployable." These are all problems that we can identify with. Her strategy is to use a voice that sounds authentic—the voice of a friend sharing anxieties, not a professional writer offering advice from on high. Further, to engage us, she amuses us with fresh and zany images. She refers to those "mental illnesses"—an overstated image of insecurities—that arrive at your desk like "your sickest, most secretive relatives" who inhibit your writing as they "form a semicircle around the computer," condemning, criticizing, and censoring your efforts. And she depicts herself as a "dog with a chew toy" as she wrestles with the problems that keep her from getting down to work. Who hasn't had these same experiences, such as putting off an assignment or fearing the censure of a peer reader or instructor? Thus, Lamott's strategy of personal stories and self-deprecation make her credible and compelling.

Part of her strategy also involves the use of effective language. The absence of clichés and stale language create our perception of her as a lively, spirited individual, without pretension or airs. In fact, her diction (word choice) is far from pretentious. She admits to having financial problems that are "driving me crazy" and to worrying about daily concerns that "leave me winded." Because her strategy is to make her advice accessible to the reader, she uses words that would not be appropriate in all types of assignments. Like the film character in *Stripes* who advises his fellow platoon member to "lighten up," she tries to relax her reader. "Say to yourself in the kindest possible way, Look, honey. . . ."

"Lighten up" may be just the advice you need to get started on a class assignment so that you don't start to censor yourself before you can get your ideas down on the page. In the following section, we will demonstrate prewriting techniques that may help you warm up to your writing assignments.

Prewriting as Discovery

As soon as you are assigned a paper, begin thinking about the topic and what you already know about it. You might discover that you already have feelings about the subject or have had experiences that relate to it. These can be valuable resources for you and can help you avoid procrastinating.

Individual Brainstorming

As soon as you let yourself think freely about the topic, your brain will both consciously and subconsciously consider anything that relates to it. You will have moments of insight or inspiration that can be exciting *and* useful. During this brainstorming stage, certain recollections can help you generate material and can trigger a chain reaction of associated ideas. Soon you will want to jot these ideas down on paper so that you don't forget them or overlook what you can learn from them.

It seems paradoxical to suggest that you will discover what you want to write by writing. But students frequently tell us—and our own writing habits confirm—that the very act of working with words, ideas, or feelings on a page or computer screen helps writers learn what they want to express about a topic.

Sometimes a spirited exchange with a friend or roommate will help you "get going" on a writing topic because you start to reconsider and refine your ideas as you discuss them, and you start to care whether your ideas have been communicated or accepted. Actually, the best thing you can do when you are assigned a writing task is immediately to jot down any responses and ideas. Consider this initial, quick writing as a conversation with yourself, because that is what it is.

To help you get moving, here are some prewriting strategies that come from the reading and writing topics in this book. Try these different methods; you may find a few that help you get beyond the blank page or screen.

Freewriting

As the term implies, *freewriting* involves jotting down uncensored thoughts as quickly as you can. Don't concern yourself with form or correctness. Write whatever comes into your mind without rejecting ideas that may seem silly or irrelevant. In freewriting, one thought might trigger a more intriguing or significant one, so anything that comes into your head may be valuable. Here is one student's freewriting response to the topic of stereotyping:

> Stereotyping? I don't think I stereotype—maybe I do. But I sure have had it done to me. When people see my tatoo they seem to think I'm in Hell's Angels or a skinhead. Talk about prejudgements! It's as if the snake coiling up my arm is going to get them, the way they look at it and pull back from me. I remember once, in a campground in Alaska, a bunch of us campers were stranded when the road washed out. As food and supplies dwindled, people started borrowing from each other. In the john one morning I asked this guy if I could borrow a razor blade and he jumped back. Not till he looked away from my arm and into my eyes did he relax. He gave me a blade, we talked, later shared some campfires together. . . . I could write about that experience, a good story. I wonder if people with tatooes have always been connected with trouble—pirates maybe, sailors, bikers and gang members today anyhow. It could be interesting to find out if the negative stereotypes about tatooes have always been there even though I just read they estimate about 20 million people have tatts now. That's some research I could get into.

Pete's response to the topic of stereotyping starts with his personal feeling that the subject doesn't really relate to him. But then he thinks about the fact that he has been stereotyped by others. As he considers how people react to his tattoo, he recalls an incident he thinks he could write as a narrative. As he thinks more about the nature of tattoos, he finds an aspect of stereotyping that concerns him and that he might like to research. If he had not written down his feelings about stereotyping, he might have settled for a more pre-dictable response to the assignment.

Notice that Pete's freewriting starts with a question that he asks himself about the topic—a perfect way to get himself warmed up and moving. He's not worried about checking his spelling. He can consult a dictionary when he is drafting his paper to learn that *tattoos* and *prejudgments* are the correct spellings. Pete also uses language in his prewriting that might not be appropriate in his essays: "guy," "bunch," "john," "anyhow," and "get into." Most important is that Pete got started on his assignment and explored his own unique thoughts and feelings. He found a personal experience he might relate and discovered research that he would like to do.

 PRACTICING FREEWRITING

To help you see how freewriting can lead to discovery, write for fifteen minutes, without stopping, on one of the following topics. Do not worry about form and do not censor any idea, fact, picture, or feeling that comes to you. Freewrite about the following:

1. Something that one of your parents neglected to teach you.

2. A grandparent's unexpected revelation

3. A family gathering when you learned something.

4. Your response to "Are Families Dangerous?" (p. 37).

5. For young people, "piercing or tattoos may be seen as personal and beautifying statements" (Martin, 25). With this quotation at the top of your page, respond freely.

Your freewriting may be written on a sheet of paper, composed at a computer, or jotted down in your journal.

Journal Writing

Journal writing may be looked on as a conversation with yourself to sort out your views or ideas about a work that you've read or a movie that you've seen. A journal entry also may be a way to warm up before writing a paper or to discover your own perspective; in fact, many professional writers rely on journals to store ideas for future stories, articles, editorials, and poems.

Your professor may ask you to keep a journal while you are in a composition course. Nearly all of the "Thinking about the Text" questions and many of the "Writing from the Text" assignments in Part I make ideal topics for a journal. Using your journal to write responses to assigned readings provides many benefits:

- You will be better prepared for class discussions.
- You will retain more material from the readings.
- You will gain more writing practice.
- You will sharpen your evaluations of the readings.

For your journal entries, you can use a notebook of any size, but many students prefer to compose directly on the computer and find that they write considerably more than they would in longhand.

Using a Journal for Pre-Reading

A journal is an ideal place to figure out how you feel about a subject *before* you have read an essay about it. If you have done some thinking about the subject, you will be more engaged and read more attentively to learn someone else's view on the subject. If an instructor assigns "Pigskin, Patriarchy, and Pain" (p. 85), your journal is a place to record your views of what high school and college football players experience on and off the field. If your instructor assigns "Why Reality TV Is Good For Us" (p. 233), you could use your journal to vent feelings about reality TV programs that you like or loathe before reading the author's argument. And if your instructor assigns "The Good Daughter" (p. 12), you may use your journal to explore your own opinions about what characterizes a "good" daughter or son.

In the Table of Contents (pp. iii–xv), we provide blurbs or brief summaries as pre-reading help to stimulate your thoughts and interest even before you begin reading the essay. These blurbs can also prompt pre-reading responses in your journal. For example, the brief comment for "The Good Daughter" states: "These immigrant parents make many sacrifices for their daughter. Is she then 'indentured' to her parents, forced to 'straddle two cultures?'" Here is how one student might respond to this summary even before reading the essay itself:

> My own parents left their family and friends behind to make a better life for them-selves and their future children. When my dad arrived in the U.S., he had to take a job that he didn't like, just to pay the bills, and then had to take on another part-time job after my brother and sisters were born. It makes me feel that I need to pay them back, not only by earning money but by not dropping out of school. Almost every pay day my dad complains that he's worn out and there's never enough money. So even now while I'm in school, I'm expected to hold a job to help buy clothes for my younger brothers and sis-ters. The hours I have to work are hurting my grades, but I feel that I owe my parents so much for what they went through so we could grow up here.

By reading the blurb in the Table of Contents as well as the author's brief biography preceding each reading, you can stimulate your thoughts on the topic before reading each work.

Using a Journal for Active Reading

One type of assigned active reading is a *dialectical journal.* In this kind of jour-nal you write down specific phrases or meaningful lines from your readings and then record your thoughts about these phrases; in effect, you have a con-versation with your reading material. Include specific details that you want to interpret or analyze. Record your responses to those lines and phrases; those responses may he valuable if you later decide to write a paper on the topic.

Imagine Pete, the student who did freewriting about stereotypes, respond-ing specifically to the essay "Don't Let Stereotypes Warp Your Judgments" (p. 470). His journal response to the essay might look like this:

> "Are criminals more likely to be dark than blond?" That's a provocative question the author asks. It makes me think about all the bad guys in movies. Aren't they always dark? You never see Robert Redford playing a villain—or do you? I think some of our

stereotyping comes from films, which is Heilbroner's point when he writes about "type-casts." Maybe only bad films use "types." I like what the author says about stereotypes making us "mentally lazy." I can see what he means when he says there are two people hurt in stereotyping—the person who is unjustly lumped into some category and the person who is "impoverished" by his laziness. Heilbroner says that a person can't "see the world in his own absolutely unique, inimitable and independent fashion." That makes sense about being independent. But I wonder what "inimitable" means.

Notice that Pete begins his journal entry with a question from the essay itself; he also might have started with his own question about the work. Pete jots down ideas that come to him as he responds to the reading. Note that he puts quotation marks around any words, phrases, or sentences from the text; in case he uses these later, Pete wants to remember that the ideas and language belong to the author of the essay.

In addition to moving Pete into his assigned topic, his journal writing lets him record his responses to parts of Heilbroner's essay. He is practicing finding the essence of the essay, as well as parts that he might want to quote in his own work. Further, if Pete reads "The Myth of the Latin Woman" (p. 172) and "Black Men and Public Space" (p. 181), he will have relevant material in his journal that he can connect to these other readings, either for his own interest or for writing assignments. In addition, as Pete begins reflecting on his journal entries, he may choose to develop his material in vastly different ways. On pp. 353–354, you can find some of Pete's choices.

 ### Practicing Journal Writing

Respond to any of the following quoted lines by conversing with yourself and thinking critically about these memorable quotations:

1. "I wanted my ego not merely massaged but kneaded. I wanted unfettered affection, soul-mating, true romance..." (Daum 59).

2. "Winning at sports meant winning friends and carving a place for myself within the male pecking order" (Sabo 85).

3. "We don't have to achieve to be accepted by our families. We just have to be" (Goodman 4).

Clustering

Clustering is a more visual grouping of ideas on a page. Many students use clustering for in-class writing assignments, including essay exams, where the object is not to discover a topic but to organize information that they already have.

A student named Rachel started with the assigned question of how she was "between worlds" and used that as a center or starting point for her personal inquiry into areas where she experienced "betweenness."

She wrote the assignment as a question in the middle of the page, then she drew lines from the topics to several subtopics, which she placed in boxes. As you can see in the illustration, her subtopics are based on the chapter titles in Part I of this book. She placed "perceptions" and "genders" in the same box because, for her, these areas were closely related. Next to each subtopic, she then wrote down a brief phrase or reference to experiences and concerns that related to it. By clustering her responses, Rachel discovered topics that were important to her.

She was also able to group related issues—an immediate advantage of clustering. You may want to read the paper (p. 387) that came from this prewriting discovery work. But first look at Rachel's clustering exercise, which is reproduced below.

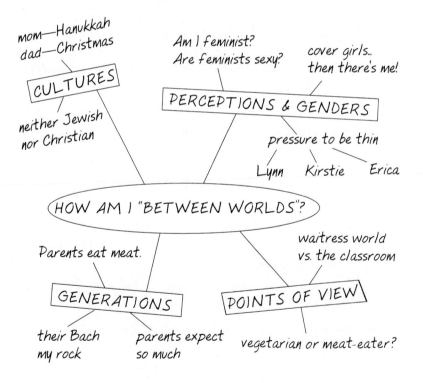

PRACTICING CLUSTERING

1. Center "self and family" in a box on a page. As you cluster, consider how you are "a part of" your family and how you are "apart from" your family.

Listing **339**

2. Center "incidents that united my family" in a box on a page. Draw lines to other boxes that will include specific outings, celebrations, crises, customs, and events that have united your family. Don't forget the surprising or unlikely incidents that no one expected would draw you together.

Clustering may help you in the process of discovering topics that interest you as well as finding relationships between ideas that you have written on your page.

Listing

Listing is a way of making a quick inventory of thoughts, ideas, feelings, or facts about a topic. The object is to list everything, again without censoring any notion that comes to you. In addition to clustering her "between-worlds" experiences, Rachel listed her ideas after she discovered a topic for her paper. (You can see her list on p. 360–361.)

Another student, who was assigned to read the two essays on reality TV (pp. 233–243), decided to consider this topic beforehand to sharpen his attention as he read the assigned pages. He realized that this topic is controversial so he decided to make two lists, one with the positive features and another with the negative traits of reality TV:

The positive aspects of reality TV:	The negative aspects of reality TV:
—unknowns have a chance at fame	—untalented and undeserving can end up as stars
—seems real: anything can happen	—it's fake; so much is edited and even scripted
—the programs are varied, fresh, limitless	—the contests and games are like gladiator sports
—viewers are excited and engaged	—many of the shows bring out the worst in people
—daring subject matter, shocking revelations	—dumbed-down subject matter, shock-value only
—an alternative to predictable sitcoms	—talented writing and creative content are missing
—make-overs change lives, make a difference	—only extreme behavior & spectacles are valued
—demonstrates how resilient people can be even when they lose	—exploits people's failings & encourages fantasies

By jotting down these two lists, this student has started to focus his own thoughts about reality television even before he has read the assigned essays: "Why Reality TV Is Good For Us" (p. 233) and "When Reality TV Gets Too Real" (p. 239). With these prewriting lists of his own ideas and with the views and illustrations from both readings, the student will have plenty of material to formulate an argument and to group and organize ideas according to related topics. In addition, the writer can easily add specific TV programs and episodes as he starts to draft his essay.

In addition to using listing for a pre-reading warmup, you can also use listing *after* you read. If you are answering a specific question or know what your topic is, you can list data from the readings. Listing will also help you see ways to group and to arrange the material that you have found.

For example, a student who is assigned a character analysis based on a particular reading may list details from the text that indicate the character's traits. In order to write a character analysis of Connie, the central character in the short story "Where Are You Going, Where Have You Been?" (p. 92), student Marianela Enriquez wrote the list shown on p. 486. Notice how Marianela's list helps her find important details and then organize those details for her essay.

 ## Practicing Pre-Reading Listing

1. Write a list of the positive and negative consequences of online encounters.

2. List the advantages and disadvantages of playing football.

3. List the complications that can occur when you realize that you have romantic feelings for a friend.

Practicing Post-Reading Listing

4. List the reasons for getting or not getting a tattoo ("On Teenagers and Tattoos," p. 24, and "Under My Skin," p. 29).

5. List the advantages and disadvantages of computer-centered classrooms ("Makes Learning Fun," p. 247, and "From Learning as Torture to Learning as Fun," p. 255).

6. List the behavior traits of Marcus in "Peaches" (p. 71).

After you have made pre-reading lists for 1–3 in the previous exercise, you may want to read the essays related to each topic:

1. "Modern Romance," p. 51, and "Virtual Love," p. 56

2. "Pigskin, Patriarchy, and Pain," p. 85

3. "Boy Friend: Between Those Two Words, A Boy Can Get Crushed," p. 44.

Active Reading

Active reading can help you focus on, retain, and perceive the organizational scheme of a work you are reading and assessing. Active reading is also an appropriate prewriting strategy when you are asked to write a specific response to something that you have read, or when you know that your own experience and knowledge provide insufficient information for a meaningful essay.

We find active reading such an imperative skill that we chose to begin the reading section of this book (pp. 2–6) with the guidelines repeated here, so you may already be familiar with this method—and we hope that you are using it! Reading with a pen in your hand—and using it to interact with the material— will save you time and frustration. As you read your own text or the photocopied pages of a library book, do the following:

- *Underline* the thesis (if it is explicitly stated), key points or topic sentence, and supporting details.
- *Mark* meaningful or quotable language.
- *Place checkmarks and asterisks* next to important lines.
- *Jot* brief summary or commentary notes in the margins. Infer the thesis and write it in the margin if it is not explicitly stated.
- *Circle* unfamiliar words and references to look up later.
- *Ask* questions as you read.
- *Seek* answers to those questions.
- *Question* the writer's assumptions and assertions as well as your own.

Reading actively will allow you to examine and challenge the ideas of an author. It will also help you find important lines more easily so that you don't have to reread the entire work each time that you refer to it during class discussions or in your essays. Don't underline or highlight *everything*, however, or you will defeat your purpose of finding just the important points.

Rachel, the student who used clustering to discover her concern about the pressure among her friends to be thin, decided to do some reading about eating disorders. The excerpt presented here from "Bodily Harm" (p. 208) illustrates her active reading.

Recent media attention to the binge-purge and self-starvation disorders known as <u>bulimia</u> and <u>anorexia</u>—often detailing gruesome particulars of women's eating behaviors—may have exacerbated this serious problem on college campuses. But why would a woman who reads an article on eating disorders want to copy what she reads? Ruth Striegel-Moore, Ph.D., director of Yale University's Eating Disorders Clinic, suggests that <u>eating disorders</u> may be a way to be like other "<u>special</u>" <u>women</u> and at the same time strive to

[margin notes:]

...k specific -finitions

Media may exacerbate the problem

ecial" = v to be nique?

general term

thinness as competition— without threatening men.

outdo them. "The pursuit of thinness is a way for women to compete with each other, a way that avoids being threatening to men," says Striegel-Moore. Eating disorders as a perverse sort of rivalry? In Carol's freshman year at SUNY-Binghamton, a roommate showed her how to make herself throw up. "Barf buddies" are notorious on many college campuses, especially in sororities and among sports teams. Eating disorders as negative bonding? Even self-help groups on campus can degenerate into the kinds of competitiveness and negative reinforcement that are among the roots of eating disorders in the first place.

How ironic

Self-help groups as negative reinforcement

Key focus:

    This is not another article on how women do it. It is an article on how and why some women stopped. The decision to get help is not always an easy one. The shame and secrecy surrounding most eating disorders and the fear of being labeled "sick" may keep a woman from admitting even to herself that her behavior is hurting her. "We're not weirdos," says Nancy Gengler, a recovered bulimic and number two U.S. squash champion, who asked that I use her real name because "so much of this illness has to do with secrecy and embarrassment." In the first stages of therapy, says Nancy, much of getting better was a result of building up the strength to (literally) "sweat out" the desire to binge and to endure the discomfort of having overeaten rather than throwing up. "I learned to accept such 'failures' and moreover, that they would not make me fat."

labeled "sick"

secrecy is part of the problem.

Need to accept our "failures"

    Writing notes in the margins helped Rachel to stay involved as she read and to remember details from the essay.

⬤ PRACTICING ACTIVE READING AND CRITICAL THINKING

1. Practice the steps listed on p. 3 and actively read the next work that you have been assigned in this course. Do you feel better prepared for class discussion? Did you find the central point or thesis of the essay as a result of your active reading? Was the author's organization scheme apparent to you?

2. Actively read "My Son, My Compass?" (p. 8), "The Good Daughter" (p. 12), or "The Only Child" (p. 34). After you have actively read one of these essays, join a small group of other students who have read the same essay. Compare your active-reading notes with those of others in your group.

Group Brainstorming—Collaborative Learning and Critical Thinking

Writing doesn't have to be an isolated, lonely activity. In fact, much professional writing is a collaborative effort in which writers work together or consult editors. Corporations, educational institutions, and governmental organizations hold regular "brainstorming" sessions so that everyone can offer ideas, consider options, and exchange opinions. Reporters often work together on a story, business experts pool ideas to draft a proposal, and lawyers work as a team on a brief. Many of your textbooks—including this one—are the result of extensive collaboration.

Your college writing classes may offer you opportunities to work together in small groups, brainstorm for topics or supporting details, and critique and edit your classmates' writing. These small groups can stimulate new thoughts, multiple perspectives, and critical questions. Small-group discussion should prompt you to consider the ideas of others and help alleviate the fear that you have nothing to say.

In the classroom, groups of four or five work well, with each person recording the group's comments and key ideas for an assigned question. Students in the group can alternate explaining each response, so that the burden of reporting the discussion does not fall on any one group member. Your instructor, however, may ask that someone from each group serve as "group secretary," recording responses and then reading them. Either way, the goal is to generate as many different responses as possible to a given topic or question. As in all of the prewriting activities, no idea or comment should be censored.

Let's assume you have been assigned a paper about growing up with or without siblings. Each group can take a different aspect of this topic:

- The advantages of growing up with siblings
- The advantages of growing up as an only child
- The ways that only children find "substitutes" for siblings
- The reasons for sibling rivalry and competition, and the solutions to these problems
- The unexpected bonds that develop between siblings
- The reasons that sibling friendships fail

After ten to fifteen minutes of discussion, each group shares its key points with the class. After each group's report, all students should be invited to add comments or insights on that topic.

Group brainstorming is an ideal way to discuss reading assignments, and most of the "Thinking about the Text" questions in Part I are designed for collaborative work. Next you will find brainstorming exercises for both general topics and specific readings.

PRACTICING BRAINSTORMING IN SMALL GROUPS

1. Brainstorm about the positive and negative aspects of online forums like Facebook, MySpace, chatrooms, or YouTube.

2. Discuss the complications that arise in a friendship when one of the friends develops romantic feelings for the other.

3. Discuss the various types of families currently portrayed on television. Topics:
   - Analyze the impact of the media on the family.
   - Compare sitcoms with family dramas, family reality programs, or PBS specials on the family.
   - Contrast portraits of more conventional families with those of less conventional ones.
   - Suggest programs that could help or support the family.
   - Evaluate programs for their level of violence.

4. Read "Living in Two Worlds" (p. 109) and "The Only Child" (p. 34) and discuss specific ways that family members develop different values and habits. You may add your own experiences to this discussion.

5. Read "The Good Daughter" (p. 12) and discuss how parents' expectations can affect their children's lives.

Why Brainstorm?

Brainstorming lets you see the perspectives of others and consider their views in relation to your own—an awareness you will need when you are writing for an audience other than yourself. Collaborative work gets you away from the isolation of your own desk or computer screen and into a social context.

Incubation

After you have tried one or more of the prewriting strategies to get started on an assignment, allow yourself an incubation period—time to think about your topic before you begin to draft the paper. Students often comment on experiencing flashes of insight about their papers while in the shower, falling asleep, or doing some physical activity.

You, too, will find that your brain will continue to "work" on your paper if you are preoccupied with it when you are away from it, and thus it is a good idea to leave time for incubation at each point in the writing process. For example, if you do some prewriting on your paper when it is first assigned, your early thoughts and ideas may develop during incubation. Later, you may also be able to refine the purpose of your essay, which in turn will help you hone your topic, improve the support of your main points, discover connections among ideas in your paper, and recall words that will sharpen your meaning.

Considering Audience

Identifying Your Audience

All writing is intended for readers—that is, for an audience. But who *is* the audience?

In some situations, you can easily define the audience: for example, your reader may be a friend or family member who will receive your letter. You are surely aware that your writing tone—the voice that you use that affects your word choice and emphasis—will differ if you are writing to your friend, lover, brother, elderly aunt, or mother. However, you may be less able to define the audience for other writing situations.

In general, you should not assume that your only reader is your composition instructor, for that conclusion will prompt you to write for a very small audience. Furthermore, your English teacher may be your easiest audience, because he or she is *required* to read what you have written, comment on your thinking and writing skills, and then perhaps place a grade on your work.

Academic Audiences. Academic readers (your instructors and classmates) expect a certain depth of response, even in a short paper. The reader expects to learn specific facts, find actual examples, discover important insights, or see particular relationships that she or he was not aware of prior to reading your paper.

An academic audience also expects you to have worked with integrity when incorporating the ideas, facts, or words of another writer. (See the discussions of plagiarism on p. 372 and on p. 519.) An academic audience expects you to make some point and to support that point logically, with sufficient details (of description, fact, or example) to be convincing.

Academic readers expect your material to be presented in an orderly way. Finally, they expect the language of your work to be appropriate: standard English and well-chosen words without slang, jargon, or text message codes. For example, most instructors will prefer that you use "children or son and daughter" rather than "kids" and won't be pleased to see "BFF" in an essay about friendship. Academic readers will also expect that you have edited your essays to remove errors in grammar, spelling, and mechanics.

Nonacademic Audiences. For writing outside the classroom—for example, a letter to a newspaper, a report for your boss, or an analysis for a community project—you must engage an audience that is not required to read your writing. What are the expectations of this audience? For the most part, nonacademic audiences also expect good organization, no errors or plagiarism, and logically supported points.

In addition, you may need to convince nonacademic readers that your subject and the way you have treated it are worth their time. You may have to establish the value of your subject and the quality of your writing in the first few sentences. Developing an engaging style will help keep your reader interested.

Voice. Most instructors will tell you to "write in your own voice." This means that they want you to write using the vocabulary, sentence structure, and style that you use for communicating as an adult. You do not want to use pretentious words or artificial language, nor do you want to use diction that is more appropriate for rap lyrics or text-messaging a friend.

Style, Stance and Tone. To engage your audience quickly, you will want to consider style, the conscious use of language. Word choice is a key part of style; precisely chosen words, wordplay, and level of diction should be considered. (See also pp. 603–606 on word choice.) The structures of sentences—length, types, and variety—contribute to your style. You should also assume a stance and tone that is positive for all readers, even those who are disinterested in your topic. You may want to anticipate possible objections, doubts, or lack of interest by writing in a tone that does not put off any reader. Consider the style, stance, and tone of these opening sentences from two different essays on tattoos:

> Tattoos and piercing have become a part of our everyday landscape. They are ubiquitous, having entered the circles of glamour and the mainstream of fashion, and they have even become an increasingly common feature of our urban youth. (Martin 25)

> Every tattoo tells a story. Mine tells a story about a story. I got it to commemorate my first fiction publication in a literary magazine—a minor milestone that, at the time, seemed so epic and momentous I wanted the occasion memorialized in my flesh for all eternity. (Bowen 29)

The tone of Martin's opening is informational and assertive. He is leading toward his argument: to convince readers that tattoos are common and fashionable today. His stance is positive, authoritative, and knowledgeable. It is not surprising that he is writing to persuade psychiatrists, whose patients may be decorated with tattoos, that they should be "interested and nonjudgmental" (25). His use of the word "ubiquitous" and, later, concepts like "self-mutilation," "family matrix," and "unambiguously demarcated" reflect his position as an academic professional.

In contrast, the tone of Bowen's opening is personal and conversational. He is sharing his own experience and providing information rather than presenting a formal argument—although he may be convincing his readers, as well as himself, to consider the pain in removing a tattoo. His stance is upbeat, narrative, and informative. His intended audience is anyone considering getting or removing a tattoo. His language is colloquial rather than professional or technical: "the tube-shaped thingamajig," techniques that "hurt like the devil," and "ditching your tattoo" reflect his role as an informed and amusing story-teller.

You need to choose the tone for your particular writing assignment. The subject matter of your work, the audience for whom you are writing, and your stance on the subject will help you determine the appropriate tone for your essay.

 ## Practicing Style

1. Write two letters—one to your best friend, and one to your parents or children—describing a party that you recently attended. Your letters probably will vary in vocabulary, kinds of details, sentence structure, and tone.

2. Draft two lists describing the same television show or movie—one directed to a friend and the other for an academic essay. Use language appropriate to each audience.

Analyzing Audience Awareness

We can profit from the study of the techniques that writers use to hold their particular audience. The following essay by William F. Harrison has been published in a number of places, including the *Los Angeles Times* on July 7, 1996. Harrison is an obstetrician and gynecologist who practices in Fayetteville, Arkansas. A smoker of twenty years, Harrison saw the effects of cigarette addiction on his own body. For ten years he tried to stop smoking and, because he limited himself to a single cigarette a day, he thought he was not harming himself. Nevertheless, he had chronic bronchitis and laryngitis. After consulting with pulmonologists and pathologists, he learned that even one cigarette a day harms the body irreparably. He knew that he needed to stop entirely, and he did. He also knew that he needed to convince his patients to stop smoking. This essay reports the results of Harrison's research. Does the writer convince his reader?

Example: Convincing an Audience

 # Why Stop Smoking?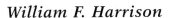
Let's Get Clinical
William F. Harrison

1   Most of us in medicine now accept that tobacco is associated with major health consequences and constitutes the No. 1 health problem in this country.

2   What smokers have not yet come to terms with is that if they continue smoking, the probability of developing one or more of the major complications

of smoking is 100 percent. It absolutely will happen. They will develop chronic bronchitis, laryngitis, pharyngitis, sinusitis and some degree of emphysema. It is also highly probable that they will develop serious disease in the arteries of all vital organs, including the brain and heart, markedly increasing their risk of heart attack and stroke. If they continue, they increase the probability of developing cancer of the lips, gums, tongue, pharynx, larynx, trachea, bronchi and lungs, of the bladder, cervix, gallbladder and other organs. Smoking contributes to rapid aging of the skin and connective tissues—women and men who smoke usually have the skin age of a person ten to twenty years older than one who doesn't smoke, given the same degree of exposure to the sun.

3   About 415,000 people die prematurely each year in the United States as a result of smoking—the equivalent of eighteen 747s crashing every week with no survivors. Many of these victims die after long and excruciating illnesses, burdens to themselves, their families and society. The cost of this misery is incalculable, but we do know that the tobacco industry grosses about $50 billion a year from the agonies it inflicts.

4   How does all this damage come about?

5   In normal lungs, the trachea and bronchi—the large and small tubes leading to the alveoli (the tiny sacs that do the actual work of the lungs)—are lined with a film of tissue that is one cell layer thick. The surface of these cells is covered with tiny, finger-like structures called cilia. These cilia beat constantly in a waving motion, which moves small particles and toxic substances out of the lung and into the back of the throat where they are swallowed. In a smoker or someone like a coal miner, who constantly breathes in large amounts of toxic substances, many of the cilia soon disappear. If exposure continues, some ciliated cells die and are replaced by squamous cells, the same type that form the skin. Without the cleansing function of the ciliated cells, toxic materials and particles are breathed further into the lungs, staying longer in contact with all the tissue. Each group of ciliated cells killed and replaced by squamous cells decreases by a certain fraction the lungs' ability to cleanse themselves. As this occurs, the amount of damage done by each cigarette increases to a greater and greater degree. By the time one has been a pack-a-day smoker for ten years or so, extensive damage has already been done. By twenty years, much of the damage is irreversible and progresses more rapidly. After ten years of smoking, each cigarette may do as much damage to the body as three or more packs did when a smoker first started.

6   The longer one smokes, the harder it gets to quit. Smoking is one of the most addictive of human habits, perhaps as addicting as crack cocaine or heroin. One has to quit every day, and there are no magic pills or crutches that make stopping easy. It is tough to do. Only those who keep trying ever quit. And even those who have smoked for only a short time or a few

cigarettes a day will probably find it difficult to stop. But the sooner a smoker makes this self-commitment, the more probable it is that he or she will quit before having done major damage to the body.

Analyzing the Essay

Clearly, William Harrison's purpose in writing is to convince readers who are smokers to stop smoking. His obligation as a writer is to produce plenty of research to answer the question: "Why Stop Smoking?" His intention also may be to prevent people from starting and to arm nonsmokers with specific evidence to help persuade a family member or a friend who smokes to stop.

His opening engages the reader because he is straightforward in his presentation of facts. Harrison specifically cites those diseases that all smokers definitely will get and those diseases that smokers probably will get. No organ of the body remains untouched, and Harrison might have written just that statement. But by actually citing the organs, the reader is almost overwhelmed by the catalog of specific details. In addition, to catch the interest of the person indifferent to health, Harrison appeals to the reader's vanity by stating that smokers' skin is aged ten to twenty years beyond that of nonsmokers.

When Harrison provides the number of smokers who die prematurely— 415,000 per year—he also gives a disturbing equivalent for this figure: "eighteen 747s crashing every week with no survivors." The writer's purpose here is to shock us. We may be complacent about the number of smokers who die each year, but we all know the effect of a newspaper headline announcing the crash of a single plane. Imagine reading that eighteen planes crashed each week all year! Cleverly, Harrison admits he doesn't know the cost of the "excruciating illnesses"—and the misery—that precede death from smoking-related diseases. But he knows and gives the profits of the tobacco industry—"$50 billion a year."

Harrison might have generalized what happens to the lungs when people smoke, but instead he credits his readers' intelligence by providing a highly specific and scientific account of how the cilia cells that normally cleanse the lungs disappear. In fact his word choice is that the "ciliated cells die," a far more emphatic way to show that toxic material is no longer filtered out. By showing the human body as a mechanical organism, he convinces the reader that the smoker's body has no more chance to continue running well than a car would if it were deprived of oil or gasoline.

To drive home his point about the toxicity of smoking, Harrison equates the smoker with "a coal miner"; both breathe in "large amounts of toxic substances." He notes that after ten years of smoking the lungs are so vulnerable that "each cigarette may do as much damage to the body as three or more packs did when a smoker first started." He uses this startling research to convince both the smoker who planned to stop after a few years and the smoker of ten years who cuts down to an occasional cigarette, that profound harm is done to the body regardless of the smoker's intention.

Harrison's conclusion has to do with nicotine addiction, and he compares the addiction to quitting cocaine or heroin. In his frightening comparison, he provides any young person considering smoking ample reason not to start, and he gives any person who loves a smoker the impetus to seek professional help to rid the smoker of this powerful and deadly addiction.

Finally, Harrison's title is an effective play on words. He's relying on the reader to hear "Let's Get Physical," a lyric from a popular song, in "Let's Get Clinical." His essay provides vivid clinical evidence of the physical damage the smoker will do to his body, information as far from a popular tune as it can be.

 ### PRACTICING AUDIENCE AWARENESS

1. Write a letter to your college president or dean of student affairs to convince the administrator that your college needs more stringently enforced "no smoking" regulations in outdoor areas.

2. Write a letter to a friend who smokes to convince that person to stop. Use the data in Harrison's essay for your letter.

A Final Word about Audience

Good style—achieved with deliberately chosen vocabulary, sentence structure, and tone—can engage your reader immediately. Providing solid support will sustain that reader. With a realistic understanding of your audience in mind, you are ready to begin organizing and drafting your essay.

Chapter 8

Organizing and Drafting an Essay

From Prewriting to Purpose

The prewriting exercises presented in the previous chapter should have helped you discover focus points and different ways that you might respond to your writing assignment. You were also given some ideas about considering the audience for your writing, to help you select an appropriate stance and tone. The stance or position that you take will be influenced by your aim in writing and the assignment you have been given.

Purpose in Writing

Clearly your purpose or aim in writing is to satisfy your instructor's assignment—and to get a good grade on your paper! Your primary purpose—assigned by your instructor or discovered on your own—may be to express, inform, analyze, or persuade. For example, if your instructor assigns an evaluative, analytic, or persuasive essay, your aim has been delineated for you. But if you have been given a more open-ended assignment—to write on a topic or respond to readings—you need to discover your aim for yourself.

What's Your Aim?

Before you can articulate your aim, you need to make sure that your subject is manageable and not too general. During your prewriting, you have probably written about a variety of general subjects—and these may include *Between Worlds* subjects as varied as anger, reality television programs, and stereotyping. Clearly, these subjects are too broad to write about in a college essay. Freewriting, clustering, and listing will help you hone your general subject to discover a more limited subject, one that can be handled in an essay rather than an entire book. Once you have discovered your limited subject, you will need to determine your particular purpose or aim for writing. Do you want to persuade, inform, express, or analyze? Knowing your aim, you will be able to express your point or claim.

What's Your Claim?

Every essay requires a **thesis—an assertion or claim about a limited subject that the writer of the essay will support, prove, or describe**. Often, but not always, the view of the writer shows in the language of the thesis. Sometimes the writer constructs a thesis to forecast the plan or organization of the paper. The thesis should reflect the aim or intention of the paper and should clarify the focus of the essay for both the writer and the reader. Throughout your writing, it will help to hear your reader asking, *"What's your aim? What's your claim?"*—two questions that will ensure that you are staying focused. Remember also that your claim or thesis may change a number of times as you draft and revise your paper.

Finding a Focus

Finding a focus often results from a prewriting exercise. After freewriting in your journal and perhaps responding to the readings, you may discover your feelings about a subject. For example, you may have been intrigued by the Table of Contents blurb for "King Curtis's Echo": "Do I want to live in a world where my response to a personal affront is going to land me in jail, an emergency room, or in the morgue?" (Thayer 193). This quotation from the essay may prompt you to write in your journal about a time when you were angered by a rude driver, an insulting customer, or an aggressive sports fan. As you prewrite on this subject, you will start to move from the general topic of anger or responses to anger to a more focused position, clarifying your aim and claim.

Or perhaps you are assigned to write about reality television programs. In your freewriting, you may discover that you have strong feelings about reality TV—that you enjoy it, find it a waste of time, or a little of both. As you express your ideas, you may start listing your positive and negative feelings as the writer does on p. 339. You may have been assigned to read "Don't Let Stereotypes Warp Your Judgment" (p. 470), and like the student Pete, you may have written about stereotyping—whether you have prejudged others or feel that they have preconceived ideas about you. In prewriting about stereotyping, you may discover, like Pete, that you have a number of potential paper topics embedded in the broader subject of stereotyping. Your prewriting has helped you discover a subject that you are interested in and your thoughts and feelings about that topic. Working from the general ideas in your journal, you are ready to discover your purpose in writing—your aim—and to craft a good thesis—your claim. The chart below will illustrate how writers move from a general subject to a supportable claim.

Discovering the Claim—From General to Specific

General Subject	Limited Subject	Aim	Claim
anger	responses to anger	to analyze the danger of impulsive responses	A moment of reflection can often prevent unnecessary violence.
reality TV	negative aspects	to convince readers that reality TV can endanger participants	Reality TV sacrifices participants' safety to boost ratings.
stereotyping	harmful effect	to persuade readers to resist stereotyping	Stereotyping can create unnecessary anxiety and deprive us of worthwhile experiences.

Varying the Thesis

The compact nature of this chart may suggest that the wording of each thesis is inevitable and predictable, but actually the possibilities are limitless, even for the same subject matter. Let's return again to our student Pete who did the earlier journal writing (p. 336) to discover this thesis: "Stereotyping can create unnecessary anxiety and deprive us of worthwhile experiences." His particular interest has to do with his tattoo and how he is stereotyped because of it, an awareness he gained in freewriting (p. 334). Pete realized that he had a good focus for a story he could narrate. He also discovered that he was interested in doing some reading about the history of tattoos to learn whether they were always regarded negatively.

If Pete's assignment had been to write about a personal experience involving stereotyping, he probably would have written about the incident in the Alaskan campground. Had his purpose been to define stereotyping, show its consequences, and persuade his reader that it is wrong, Pete might have recalled his dialectical journal prewriting (pp. 336–337) on the essay "Don't Let Stereotypes Warp Your Judgments" (p. 470), and he would have developed his paper in a different way. Pete may have used any of the following for a working thesis, depending on his aim in writing the paper:

- An experience in Alaska showed me how uncomfortable stereotyping can be for the person stereotyped.
- Because tattoos have been worn by the lower classes and fringe members of various cultures throughout history, prejudice against them still exists.
- Because prominent citizens of the world have started to wear tattoos, earlier prejudice against tattoos has diminished.
- Stereotyping, or prejudgments based on "standardized pictures" in our heads, can create unnecessary anxiety and deprive us of worthwhile experiences. (This is the same thesis as shown in the chart).

Each of these assertions requires Pete to develop his paper in a slightly different way. The first thesis can be supported with his own experience. The second and third thesis statements require Pete to research material in order to support his claims. The fourth statement requires using some appropriately documented material from Heilbroner's essay on stereotyping, as well as personal experience. Like Pete, your personal interests, as well as the aim of the assignment itself, will help you decide on a suitable thesis.

 PRACTICE EXERCISE: RECOGNIZING A THESIS

A thesis is a complete sentence that makes an assertion about a limited subject. Which of the following are supportable thesis statements? Which are not? What can be done to each deficient example to make it a strong thesis?

1. Patients' use of the Internet for medical information.

2. Patients' use of the Internet for medical information should be encouraged by doctors.

3. I think that the school's cafeteria should post a nutritional analysis of every meal it offers.

4. Online romances and conventional dating are similar and different.

5. Is reality television sacrificing participants' safety to boost ratings?

6. A moment of reflection can often prevent unnecessary violence.

7. How to get a friendship to turn romantic.

8. Blogs and YouTube have made the global discussion so much richer—and each of us so much more transparent.

9. In this essay, I plan to show that identifying people according to their race may limit an appreciation of their cultural identity.

10. You shouldn't eat fast food.

Explaining the Errors

Below you will find explanations of each example as well as corrections to modify deficient attempts at a thesis. If your instructor notes that your own thesis statements are weak, you can return to this thesis-revision exercise to remind yourself of what a strong thesis statement looks and sounds like.

1. This first example may be a suitable subject or topic for an essay, but it is not a thesis. As the absence of a verb indicates, the example lacks an assertion that makes a claim about patients using the Internet for medical information. See 2 below.

2. This example does make a claim about patients using the Internet and is a reasonable thesis. It has a limited subject (patients' use of the Internet), and it has an assertion (that this use "should be encouraged by doctors").

3. This statement contains a clear assertion, but "I think" is unnecessary. The thesis should directly express this conviction: *The school's cafeteria should post a nutritional analysis of every meal it offers.*

4. While the plan to compare and contrast may be promising, this is not yet a focused thesis because it is much too general. Nearly everything, in some sense, is "similar and different." By specifying an important way that online and conventional dating are similar and/or a way that they are different, you will have a stronger thesis and may even forecast the direction of your essay:
   - Although both online romances and conventional dating involve some risk, Internet sites offer more opportunities to meet the right person and a better environment for intimate and honest communication than a bar or office can. (See Biever 51.)
   - Online relationships often create and nurture a fantasy that cannot endure the real world of sustained conversations, unexpected obligations, and comfortable routines. (See Daum 56.)

5. A question may be a good way to engage a reader in an introduction, but it is not an assertion, so it is not a suitable thesis. The question encourages an unfocused, disorganized response. Contrast the direction implicit in example 2 with this question, and you will see why it is not effective.

6. This example is a very explicit thesis statement. It includes a clear assertion that reflection "can often prevent" violence and it anticipates that "a moment of reflection" will be described in the essay.

7. This is not a thesis because it isn't a complete sentence and lacks a point. It is a topic or title but not a thesis. We can turn this into a thesis by writing a clear assertion:

    - Getting a friendship to turn romantic may involve unbearable embarrassment and frustration unless there is mutual determination.
    - Moving from friend to boyfriend can often sacrifice both the friendship and the romance.

8. This example is a strong thesis because it contains a clear, two-part assertion—that blogs and YouTube have made our lives more globally connected and "richer" and that they have also made each of us more "transparent" so that we can't hide so easily from public scrutiny. This thesis lends itself to an argument. (See Friedman 219.)

9. A thesis should not be an announcement of what the writer intends to do. Instead, as Nike insists, the writer should "just do it!" The actual assertion is strong and can stand alone: *Identifying people according to their race may limit an appreciation of their cultural identity.*

10. This may be good advice, but it is not a good thesis. Most readers would object to the preachy voice, the direct confrontation implicit in "you," and the simplistic advice. Instead, the writer could forecast reasons for avoiding fast food: *For economic, nutritional, and aesthetic reasons, we would all be better off avoiding fast food.*

The Ideal—A Forecasting or Blueprint Thesis

Often a strong thesis not only clarifies the point of the essay but forecasts or anticipates the development of the paper. Such a thesis is ideal because it can help the writer better organize the material and can help the reader better follow the development. Several of the corrected thesis statements above provide such forecasts:

- **Although both online romances and conventional dating involve some risk, internet sites offer more opportunities to meet the right person and a better environment for intimate and honest communication than a bar or office can.** (See Biever 51.) This thesis is especially strong because of the "although" or "even though" format that allows the writer to make a connection between the two types of dating but then promises to go beyond this link. The writer notes a specific similarity between online and offline dating (both involve risk) so the writer is promising that this will be developed and supported in the paper. But this thesis also offers two specific contrasts, arguing that online dating is preferable because it offers more opportunities to meet the right person *and* a better environment for intimacy and honesty. Both of these claims will need to be developed and supported in the essay, giving the writer plenty to develop but also giving the writer and reader a direction to follow.

- **Online relationships often create and nurture a fantasy that cannot endure the real world of sustained conversations, unexpected obligations, and comfortable routines.** (See Daum 56.) This thesis requires the writer to illustrate how online relationships both create and nurture a fantasy world. Then the writer also will need to show how such fantasies may be fed by the clever, clipped communication of the computer but not be able to sustain deeper, prolonged conversations of everyday life. The writer will also need to illustrate how unexpected obligations can disrupt the fantasy as much as someone's comfortable routines can destroy the mystique of online romance.

- **Getting a friendship to turn romantic may involve unbearable embarrassment and frustration unless there is mutual determination.** Such a thesis specifies some obstacles to the goal of turning a friendship into a romance so these difficulties can be illustrated and developed. But the thesis also suggests that if both people share the attraction, a romance may be possible, again inviting the writer to support and prove this claim.

- **Moving from friend to boyfriend can often sacrifice both the friendship and the romance.** This thesis anticipates a direction that could be serious and cynical or lighthearted and ironic—or a little of both. But the assertion is clear and it promises that the writer will show how both the friendship and the romance can often be threatened by efforts to fire up the friendship.

Changing the Thesis

A thesis statement can undergo many changes in the course of drafting and rewriting a paper. All writers have had the experience of finishing a draft only to discover that their feelings about the subject have changed. In order to reflect that new awareness in the paper, the writer will want to return to the thesis, revise it, and then reshape the points in the paper so they will adequately support the new assertion. Writers find that it is perhaps best to consider any thesis as a working thesis until they are about to edit their final draft. (See Rachel's work on developing a thesis, pp. 361–364.)

The "Missing" Thesis

Some writers do not explicitly state their thesis, and some instructors do not demand one. Sometimes the overt assertion may spoil the sense of discovery that the writer intends for the reader. But even if a thesis is implied rather than stated, in a well-structured essay you should be able to articulate the writer's fundamental assertion.

Positioning the Thesis

For many writers, and for many essays, placing the thesis at the end of the introduction makes sense. The thesis follows logically from the introductory materials used to engage the audience, and the plan or direction of the paper is set forth so that the reader knows not only what is coming but in what order the support will be presented. This forecasting also helps the writer of the essay to stay organized and on target.

Essays that are tightly written, with very well-organized support, may conclude with the thesis—expressed in different words—to bring a necessary sense of closure. The reader will perceive where the writer is headed, so the assertion at the end of the paper will not come as a surprise.

Many writing instructors, tired of wondering and writing "Where is all of this going?" in the margins of student papers, require that you place your thesis within the first few paragraphs of your essay. These instructors favor the clearly stated thesis that forecasts the subtopics and their order of presentation. In any case, a strong focus—whether stated in a thesis or implied—contributes to good writing, and you will want to perfect your ability to focus your work.

The more essays you read, the more you will recognize how a thesis statement sounds. Take, for example, the thesis of Don Sabo's "Pigskin, Patriarchy, and Pain" (p. 85): "Becoming a football player fosters conformity to male-chauvinistic values and self-abusing lifestyles" (88). In his essay he examines the reasons males play football and the detrimental effects of playing this sport. The author wants to show that football conditions men to perpetuate "chauvinistic values," inflict pain on others, and tolerate constant pain themselves. The author asserts his point in a statement, a thesis, that forecasts those areas that he will examine—chauvinistic values and self-abusing lifestyles—two consequences of playing football.

Although reading other writers' thesis statements will help you understand the mechanics of thesis writing, you need to practice writing your own assertions for your own papers. You also need to have readers critique the thesis statements that you have written.

PRACTICING THESIS WRITING

1. Return to one of your prewriting exercises or freewrite for fifteen minutes on the subject of a parent's ability or inability to be open to new and possibly controversial ideas. Then reread what you have written. Find an aspect of that material that interests you. Limit your focus and write two or three different thesis statements that you can support with the ideas in your freewriting. Use a computer to write these assertions on a sheet of paper and print out three copies prior to your next class session.

2. Work in groups of four students to comment on each other's assertions. Let each student in the group make comments about one thesis statement

before you go on to look at each person's second assertion. Determine which statements are true assertions that can be supported. Then predict the type of support that is necessary (narrative of personal experience, definition, or examples from research material) for each thesis.

Critical Thinking and the "So What?" Strategy

After you have a tentative assertion around which to direct your support, ask yourself, "So what?" A sure way to realize that your assumed assertion isn't headed anywhere meaningful is to discover yourself shrugging indifferently at your own claim. As you jot down answers to this question, you will start to see what you are actually claiming. For example, imagine what would happen if you started with this assertion:

Thesis: Many people in the world are victims of stereotyping.

"So what?"

Some people have preconceived ideas about others.

"So what?"

It's unfair. People see them as types, not individuals.

"So what?"

These prejudgments limit the people who are stereotyped *and* the people doing the stereotyping.

As you continue to answer the "So what?" questions, you may discover a way to state your assertion that makes your reader more eager to read your paper. Compare the following assertion with the first one. In what way is it better?

Thesis: Prejudgments limit the lives of the stereotyped individual and the person doing the stereotyping.

Notice how this statement conforms to the requirements of a thesis. It is a complete sentence, not a question or a phrase, and it articulates a definite opinion or assertion. Unlike the first attempt at a thesis, this statement establishes a definite focus on prejudgments (they "limit . . . lives"), and it suggests an order for the analysis ("the stereotyped individual" and "the person doing the stereotyping").

By asking yourself "So what?" *throughout* your writing, you will not only sharpen your thesis but also help yourself discover points and insights worth sharing with readers. If you continue to ask this question, you will prompt yourself to think more critically about each claim as you make it. You also ensure that you are writing from a worthwhile assertion and that you are explaining your points to your reader.

Supporting a Thesis

Drafting

No one writer drafts the same way; in fact, there are as many methods (and "non-methods") for drafting as there are writers. But there are countless strategies and approaches that help writers organize, develop, and support their ideas and assertions.

On the following pages, we trace how one student, Rachel, drafted her paper. Look back to pages 338–339 to see Rachel's clustering exercise, where she discovered a topic related to living "between worlds." From this initial prewriting, she perceived that recurrent topics of interest were related to food: her vegetarianism, her friends' preoccupation with slimness, her awareness that her body does not fit the cover-girl mold, and even her job as a waitress.

Developing Support

Reviewing all of these food-related topics, Rachel realized she was most interested in her friends' eating problems. She started by actively reading "Bodily Harm" (p. 208). You can read an excerpt from this prewriting exercise on pages 341–342. This active reading helped stimulate Rachel's thinking and helped her understand her friends' experiences.

Listing

After her prewriting activities, Rachel started to list more specific ideas and experiences that related to eating disorders:

- My friend, Lynn, hospitalized for anorexia, nearly died.
- Another friend, Kirstie, was proud she could vomit automatically every time she ate.
- My friend, Erica, in a treatment program, was shocked by the number of women over 30 still plagued by eating disorders.
- Binge-and-purge syndrome needs to be explained.
- Ads depict tall models in size 3 bikinis.
- "Bodily Harm" examines psychological motives, "barf buddies," and "aerobic nervosa."
- Jane Fonda, once bulimic, hooked so many on her "Work Out" videos.
- Princess Di—bulimic and suicidal—the myth collapses.
- Kate Moss, Mary Kate Olsen, and Kate Bosworth are skinny superstars.
- My own insecurity involves my weight.
- My cousin spent weeks in a hospital program for anorexics.
- Weight loss—the ultimate "control" mechanism?

- Women's movement trying to free women from such images.
- Young women torn between being feminist or sexy—why either/or?
- Sexy women are always pictured as thin.
- Women competing without threatening men.

Working Thesis

From this list, Rachel linked certain topics: friends' experiences, celebrities with serious eating disorders, advertising images of women, psychological motives, the women's movement, and dieting as a control mechanism. These groupings helped her draft a working thesis so she could start planning her paper.

> **Working Thesis:** Many women suffer from eating disorders.

Using this preliminary thesis as a guide, Rachel started to write.

First Draft

In this day and age many women suffer from eating disorders. Influenced by television commercials and movies, most women have been conditioned to believe they must be thin to be beautiful. Who wouldn't want to hear friends whisper, "What a body! She really knows how to stay in shape!" or "Don't you hate someone who looks that good?" Either way, the sense of envy is clear. A thin girl has something that others don't—and this gives her power and control. She can make herself in the image of the cover girls. "The pursuit of thinness is a way for women to compete with each other, a way that avoids being threatening to men" (Erens 209).

Unfortunately, this competition keeps women from seeking or obtaining the help they might otherwise get from close friends. Many bulimics keep their secret as guarded as they can. For example, my friend Kirstie did this. She waited for years before she told friends (and later, her family) that she was bulimic. At first, only her "barf buddy" (from Erens?) knew.

Kirstie seemed to have a good life with her family and friends. But years later, she revealed to me that her greatest pride was when she discovered that she was now vomiting automatically after eating, without needing to use a finger or spoon.

Erica was another friend who needed help. In fact, her situation was so bad that she needed to go into a hospital. And my friend Lynn would have died had she not entered the hospital when she did. She had to drop out of Berkeley immediately and get prolonged therapy for herself and her family. As Erens notes, "Family therapy considers the family itself, not the daughter with the eating disorder, to be the 'patient.' Often the daughter has taken on the role of diverting attention from unacknowledged conflicts within the family."

One problem Lynn had was conforming to her parents' expectations. Lynn decided to major in art even though her parents wanted her to get a degree in computer science so she would have a job when she graduated. There was so much stress in that house every time Lynn enrolled in another art class. Maybe she felt that the only thing she could control in her life was how thin she could get.

The message to be thin comes from popular celebrities. Magazine covers feature the weight loss of actress and tabloid-favorite Mary-Kate Olsen who was in rehab for bulimia. In the 80s, actress Jane Fonda sold many on the value of her "Work Out" and helped spawn "aerobic nervosa" (Erens 209–210). Many women who admired her shape may not know that Fonda was once bulimic. And no one watching the televised spectacle of Prince Charles and Princess Diana's wedding could have predicted that years later biographers would be discussing "Di's bulimia."

Not just the supermodels like Kate Moss, or the actress Kate Bosworth, but most popular personalities seem incredibly thin today. It seems that many women—celebrities, models, and my friends—have not escaped this curse.

Evaluating the First Draft

As Rachel was writing this draft she found herself crossing out occasional words and adding phrases, but her main concern was getting her ideas down on the page. She remembered relevant ideas from some assigned readings in *Between Worlds,* and she put some of the quoted material in her draft. She did not worry about the form of her quotes, but she was careful to copy the page numbers correctly so she wouldn't have to waste time searching for them later. Once she had written this rough draft, she reread it with a pen in hand, spotting weak areas and making quick notes to herself. Her own critique of her first draft follows.

cliche?   *dull*
(In this day and age) many women suffer from eating disorders. Influenced by television commercials and movies, most women have been conditioned to believe they must be thin to be beautiful. Who wouldn't want to hear friends whisper, "What a body!

She really knows how to stay in shape!" or "Don't you hate someone who looks that
good?" Either way, the sense of envy is clear. A thin girl has something that others don't—
and this gives her power and control. She can make herself in the image of cover girls.
"The pursuit of thinness is a way for women to compete with each other, a way that
avoids being threatening to men" (Erens 209).

maybe save...

*put thesis
here?*

Unfortunately, this competition keeps women from seeking or obtaining the help
they might otherwise get from close friends. Many bulimics keep their secret as guarded
as they can. For example, my friend Kirstie did this. She waited for years before she told
friends (and later, her family) that she was bulimic. At first, only her "barf buddy" (from
page?
Erens) knew.

illustrate

develop Kirstie seemed to have a good life with her family and friends. But years later, she
revealed to me that her greatest pride was when she discovered that she was now
vomiting automatically after eating, without needing to use a finger or spoon.

*too gross?
or OK?
better link
here?*

Erica was another friend who needed help. In fact, her situation was so bad
that she needed to go into a hospital. And my friend Lynn would have died had she not
entered the hospital when she did. She had to drop out of Berkeley immediately and get
prolonged therapy for herself and her family. As Erens notes, "Family therapy considers
the family itself, not the daughter with the eating disorder, to be the 'patient.' Often the
daughter has taken on the role of diverting attention from unacknowledged conflicts
page? within the family." *discuss & link better
to next¶*

develop

One problem Lynn had was conforming to her parents' expectations.
Lynn decided to major in art even though her parents wanted her to get a degree in
computer science so she would have a job when she graduated. There was so much
stress in that house every time Lynn enrolled in another art class. Maybe she felt that
the only thing she could control in her life was how thin she could get.

link?

The message to be thin comes from popular celebrities like Mary-Kate Olsen.
Actress Jane Fonda has sold many on the value of her "Work Out" and has helped
spawn "aerobic nervosa" (Erens 209–210). Many women who admired her shape may
not know that Fonda was once bulimic. And no one watching the televised spectacle of
Prince Charles and Princess Diana's wedding could have predicted that years later
biographers would be discussing "Di's bulimia."

Put earlier

Not just the supermodels like Kate Moss, or actresses like Kate Bosworth, but most
popular personalities seem incredibly thin today. It seems that many women—celebrities,
models, and my friends—have not escaped this curse. *Ok for thesis?*

Revising the Thesis: What's Your Aim? What's Your Claim?

Writing the draft helped Rachel realize the link between her friends' experiences and the influence of the media. Once she had a more defined aim—to criticize the media's influence on women's self-perceptions—she needed to revise her claim to reflect this criticism. Her claim is expressed in her new working thesis.

> **New Working Thesis:** Magazine ads and commercials influence how women see themselves and how they behave.

Rachel felt that her material—both her personal experiences and readings—would support her new thesis. She also realized that this thesis helped her link the influence of the media to women's actions and behavior. Rachel showed her thesis to her instructor, who suggested she apply the "So what?" response to this assertion:

> Ads and commercials influence women's self-perceptions.
>
> "So what?"
>
> Women try to look like the skinny models.
>
> "So what?"
>
> It's dangerous! Women are starving themselves.
>
> "So what?"
>
> The media has to change—they are responsible for programming women this way.

After thinking about this conversation with herself, Rachel now had a stronger claim and she revised her working thesis again:

> **Revised Working Thesis:** The media must be forced to stop programming young women to believe that skeletal models are the ideal.

Rachel's revised thesis more accurately reflected her claim that the media must change what they are doing to women, and her reference to the "skeletal models" would permit her to discuss her friends' experiences.

Writing an Outline

Organizing to Highlight Key Points

Excellent ideas and interesting information can get lost or buried in a paper that is not carefully arranged and organized. If you arrange your thesis to reflect your organization scheme, you can more easily draft your essay. Notice how Rachel's thesis forecasts her essay's key points:

> The media must be forced to stop programming young women to believe skeletal models are the ideal.

Rachel's thesis suggests that she will first look at how the media is "programming" women, and then she will show how specific women become "skeletal" victims of the advertising that they see. Further, her assertion that the media "must be forced to stop" this practice invites her to propose a solution. Although Rachel devised a general scheme for organizing her paper, she knew she needed a more detailed outline.

To Outline or Not to Outline

By helping you arrange your materials effectively, an outline can save you time and frustration. Just as most drivers need a map to direct them through unfamiliar territory, most writers need outlines in order to draft their papers.

However, you probably have had the experience of being in a car without a map, when someone could intuit the right direction and get you where you needed to be. Some writers have that intuition and therefore find detailed outlines unnecessary. But these writers still craft a strong thesis and rely on their intrinsic sense of organization to guide them as they write.

Most of us have also been in cars with drivers who were convinced they could manage without a map, but couldn't. Such indirection or "backtracking" in papers prompts instructors to note in the margins: "Order?" "Repetitious," "Organization needs work," "Relevant?" "Transition needed," or "Where is this going?" If you see these indicators on your papers, you know your sense of direction is failing you. Outline before you write! Unless your instructor requires a particular outline form, your outline may be an informal "map" of key points and ideas in whatever order seems both logical and effective.

Ordering Ideas

You have a number of options for effective organization, and your purpose in writing will help you determine your arrangement. For example, Rachel's purpose was to convince readers that the media must stop promoting thinness as an ideal. Because this was the most important part of her argument, she saved it until the end, building support for it as she wrote. Rachel thus chose an emphatic arrangement scheme.

In an *emphatic* or *dramatic organization,* you arrange your material so that the most important, significant, worthy, or interesting material (for which you generally have the most information) is at the end of the paper. This is the principle that guides Ellen Goodman in her essay, "When a Woman Says No" (p. 89). Goodman presents summaries of three court cases involving charges of rape. She deliberately orders the three cases so that the most controversial one—involving the woman's prior sexual conduct—is last. The virtue of this type of organization is that it permits the writer to end in a dramatic way, using the most vital material or emphatic support for a concluding impression.

Some papers, however, invite a *spatial arrangement.* Often used in description, this kind of arrangement permits you to present your points in a systematic movement through space. In "The Only Child" (p. 34), John Leonard deliberately moves from external descriptions of his brother's shabby boarding house to internal descriptions of his filthy room. From these physical descriptions, he then moves further inward to an analysis of his brother's psychological condition.

In order to narrate a series of events, a *chronological ordering* may be useful. Jeff Z. Klein's essay "Watching My Back" (p. 82) chronicles a time when he and his girlfriend face drunken attackers in Prague. He describes the initial incident, their ensuing discussions of it, and finally his decision to take a self-defense class. A *chronological arrangement* is useful to tell a story, give historical detail, or contrast past and present.

An Informal Outline

Because Rachel found it was difficult to focus her initial draft and order her supporting details, she decided to write an informal outline: a list of points, written in a logical order, that she planned to cover in her essay. She knew this outline would simply be a personal guide to help her include all relevant materials, so she didn't spend hours on the outline or concern herself with its wording.

Rachel wrote her working thesis first and then listed her key points in the order she planned to cover them. She planned to focus on the stories of three friends, and she had to decide how to order their stories. The chronology of these friendships seemed less relevant than the differences in their problems and treatment programs. She decided to begin with Kirstie, who received out-patient treatment but continued to deny her problem. She ended with Lynn, who had the most extreme eating disorder—she came close to death—and the most dramatic recovery. Lynn's experience provided the most emphatic evidence for Rachel's essay, so Rachel knew that she wanted to end her examples with Lynn's experience. Rachel also knew that she would add other points or perhaps modify this order as she wrote the paper, but at least she would have a map to head her in the right direction.

> **Thesis:** The media must be forced to stop programming young women to believe skeletal models are the ideal.

INTRODUCTION

—Typical ad described: model in bikini

—Models as unhealthy and obsessed with being thin

—The horror: skinny models seem "right"

—Thesis

ANOREXIA AND BULIMIA AS EPIDEMICS

—Jane Fonda and her "Work Out"

—Princess Di, reputed bulimic

—Kate Moss, Mary-Kate Olsen, and Kate Bosworth perpetuate the skinny image

—Women competing with each other (use Erens)

MY FRIEND KIRSTIE, BULIMIC

—Kept this secret; only her "barf buddy" and I knew

—Obsessed with food

—Outpatient counseling didn't really work

—I didn't know how to help her

MY FRIEND ERICA, ANOREXIC

—Enrolled in in-hospital program

—Shocked by number of older women in program

—Received nutritional and emotional help

MY FRIEND LYNN, ANOREXIC, ALMOST DIED

—Dropped out of Berkeley, enrolled in hospital

—Family received treatment too (use Erens)

—These friends felt programmed by the media to be thin

—Diet industry undermines women's control

CONCLUSION

—A time for shock *and* action

—Refuse to support products that promote these images

In an informal outline like this, the ideas that you loosely group as "information blocks" may become paragraphs. In some cases, your grouping or block may end up being split into two or more paragraphs. This outline includes supporting details, but the topic sentences are not written out; therefore the outline is still rather sketchy. In Rachel's case, she didn't feel she needed more elaboration because she had already done some prewriting and initial drafting.

Writing a Paragraph

Focusing the Paragraph with a Topic Sentence

Once you have done some prewriting and have written a working thesis, you are ready to draft your essay. Your thesis has made an assertion you need to support, and the body of your essay consists of paragraphs that build this support. Each of those paragraphs may include a *topic sentence*—a sentence that expresses the central idea of that paragraph. The topic sentences emerge naturally from the groupings discovered in prewriting and from the subtopics of the outline.

Not all paragraphs in an essay have a topic sentence, but all paragraphs must have a focus or controlling idea. The value of a topic sentence is analogous to the value of a thesis: both keep the writer and reader on track. Again, like the thesis, the topic sentence should be deliberately placed to help the reader understand the focus of the paragraph.

Let's look at some short paragraphs that lack topic sentences.

 ## PRACTICING TOPIC SENTENCES

Practice writing your own topic sentence (the central idea) for each of the following paragraphs:

1. Lines to see an advisor extend beyond the walls of the counseling department. Because the health service requires proof of insurance, students wait in long lines to argue for exemptions. The financial aid office assigns appointment times, but invariably lines form there, too. At the bookstore, students wait twenty minutes at a register, and I need to have my out-of-state check verified in a separate line. Even before classes begin, I'm exhausted.

2. A great amount of corn is used as feed for cattle, poultry, and hogs. Corn is also distilled into ethanol—a fuel for cars and a component in bourbon. Corn is made into a sweetener used in snacks and soft drinks and a thickener for foods and industrial products. A small amount of corn is consumed at dining tables in kernel or processed form.

Although each paragraph is clearly focused, both would profit from an explicit assertion. Compare your topic sentences with your classmates' assertions before reading the following possibilities. Although topic sentences may be placed anywhere in the paragraph, the topic sentences here seem to be most effective as the first or last sentence in these paragraphs. Here are some possibilities for the first example:

- Going back to school means getting in lines.
- Lines are an inevitability at my college.
- Lines are the worst aspect of returning to school.

Here are some possibilities for the second example:

- Corn is used for extraordinarily diverse purposes.
- Humans, animals, and machines profit from products made of corn.
- Corn is a remarkably useful grain.

In addition to evaluating your classmates' topic sentences, it may be worthwhile to evaluate the relative strengths of the sentences above. Which are stronger, and why?

Analyzing the Use of a Topic Sentence

In the following paragraph, notice how Rachel includes very good supporting details but lacks a topic sentence that expresses the central idea of the paragraph:

> During Kirstie's senior year in high school, she was dating a college guy, was enrolled in college prep classes, jogged religiously every morning and every evening, and loved to ski with her family and beat her brothers down the slope. She seemed to crave the compliments she received from her brothers and their friends because of her good looks, and she received plenty! But years later, she revealed to me that her greatest pride at that time was when she discovered that she could vomit automatically after eating, without needing to use a finger or spoon.

Rachel realized that she had not articulated the focus of her paragraph. She went back to clarify her point—that "Kirstie had it all." But Rachel also realized that her perception of her friend was an illusion. Rachel brought the two ideas together to form a topic sentence:

> Few of us ever suspected that Kirstie was in trouble because she seemed to have it all.

Rachel asserts that Kirstie "seemed to have it all" but was really "in trouble." First Rachel shows specific examples of Kirstie's seemingly happy life: "dating a college guy," being in "college prep classes," jogging "religiously," and skiing with her family. Then Rachel supports the fact that Kirstie was really a troubled young woman.

It is important that you use very specific examples to support your topic sentence. It would not have been enough for Rachel to claim that Kirstie had "everything" without showing specifically what that meant. She doesn't just mention that Kirstie had a boyfriend, but that he was a "college guy." Kirstie doesn't simply have a close family; they go skiing together, and she spends time with her brothers' friends. Rachel's support is vivid, visual, and specific. Her shocking last sentence is graphic and unforgettable because it is so detailed in its description.

Unifying the Paragraph

Rachel's last sentence also contributes to paragraph coherence and unity. Rachel's opening sentence suggests Kirstie was in trouble, even though she did not appear to be. Subtle references to this trouble appear in the paragraph: Kirstie seems obsessed with exercise, and she craves compliments. Finally, after enumerating Kirstie's apparent successes—what she *should* be proud of—Rachel stuns the reader with the irony of Kirstie's "greatest pride," her ability to vomit automatically. Thus the concept of pride unites the paragraph. The key word in the topic sentence, "seemed," predicts the illusions that permeate and unite the paragraph. (For more on paragraph unity and coherence, see pp. 390–397.)

Eliminating Irrelevant Details

In addition to focusing the paragraph with a topic sentence, you will need to make sure that all details in your paragraph relate to your controlling idea. This means that every sentence in your paragraph must support your topic sentence. Often when you are drafting a paragraph, you may include sentences that seem relevant at the time, but in rereading the paragraph, you discover that a certain detail doesn't contribute to that paragraph's focus. You should eliminate the sentence from that paragraph, but you may be able to use it elsewhere in your essay. Make sure that you reread your work with an eye on maintaining focus in each paragraph. Recognizing those sentences that don't fit and removing them during the revision process will strengthen the paragraph and your essay.

 PRACTICING HOW TO RECOGNIZE IRRELEVANT DETAILS

Read the following paragraphs and determine which sentences are irrelevant because they do not support the focus of the paragraph:

1. When it comes time to pay for a date, an awkward pause often threatens to ruin the good vibe and even the entire evening. This discomfort can be prevented if both individuals immediately pay their share, just as they would with a friend or a co-worker, without any hesitation or reluctance. The notion that males should automatically pay or that the person who initiated the date should always pay *is* old-fashioned and outdated. It's getting ridiculous that so many restaurants and clubs charge such inflated prices, and the cost of gas keeps rising. Unless someone has made it clear that he or she is treating the other or that the date is a gift, neither should expect to be paid for or should wait around, pressuring the other into paying. It doesn't matter if the date involves a casual lunch, a costly dinner, or admission to a movie, club, or sporting event, both individuals should pay for themselves, so that neither one feels burdened or resentful.

2. In her study of how men and women communicate, Deborah Tannen claims that even in childhood, males and females socialize differently. Boys base their bonding on active play. Many boys play baseball and football in neighborhood parks. Boys struggle not to be subordinate in a group that is larger and more hierarchical than girls' groups, so physical

play and a desire for dominance, rather than listening to each other, is their way of communicating. In contrast, girls base their relationships on intimate talk and exchanging secrets. Girls see conversation about their thoughts and feelings as an important way to create closeness. Girls can get really close sharing intimacies with each other, especially at pajama parties. The contrasting communication patterns of each gender continue into adulthood and cause serious problems for men and women who may marry and then discover their talking styles are in conflict.

Analyzing the Practice Paragraphs

In the first example, the writer's controlling idea is expressed in the second sentence—that the end-of-the-date "discomfort can be prevented if both individuals immediately pay their share." The writer supports this focus by insisting that it is "old-fashioned and outdated" for males to automatically pay for everything on a date. Unless it has already been established that the date is a "treat" or a "gift," the couple should share the cost. The fourth sentence—"It's getting ridiculous that so many restaurants and clubs charge such inflated prices, and the cost of gas keeps rising"—should be removed from this paragraph. The increasing costs on dates are irrelevant to the focus of this paragraph that argues for gender equality in paying for dates. However, the fact that dates are costly could be developed in a separate paragraph even though that idea distracts the reader from the focus here.

In the second paragraph, the controlling idea is in the first sentence, "That even in childhood, males and females socialize differently." The writer notes Tannen's points that boys bond through active play and respond physically rather than sitting and listening to each other. In contrast, girls connect by talking and sharing feelings and secrets. Two sentences in this paragraph are irrelevant because they don't support the topic of communication: "Many boys play baseball and football in neighborhood parks" (third sentence) and "Girls get really close sharing intimacies with each other, especially at pajama parties" (seventh sentence). Each of these sentences may be true, but each is offering specific details that are irrelevant to the controlling idea that males and females have contrastive communication styles.

Developing a Paragraph

When you have a topic sentence or controlling idea for a paragraph, it is essential to support it with examples and any necessary explanation. Try to anticipate questions or objections your reader may have; you can use the "So what?" response here to make sure the significance of your idea is clear. If you discover irrelevant sentences or details that don't develop your paragraph's focus, remove them. Irrelevant details work against paragraph development. Good support for your topic sentences can be drawn from your own ideas, experiences, and observations, as well as from readings and research.

Using Sources for Support

Giving Credit and Avoiding Plagiarism

Although in a formal research paper you may be required (or prefer) to use notecards or photocopies for recording data, for a short paper with a single source, you might choose to work directly from the margin notes you made during your active reading. No matter how you have recorded your supporting material, you must give the exact source and page number for borrowed ideas and for quoted material. In addition, you need to put quotation marks around the quoted words and around the titles of essays, short stories, or poems that you are using in your essay. The titles of longer works—books, plays, films, magazines, newspapers, Web sites, online databases—any work that can be published independently should be in italics. See p. 397 for more information about titles. By including the author's name and a page number after every idea or quotation that she used, Rachel avoided *plagiarism*—using other writers' words or ideas without giving them credit.

Even if she *paraphrased* the material—put the ideas in her own words—Rachel knew she had to give the author credit for the idea or concept. Had she neglected to do this, she would have inadvertently plagiarized those ideas. (For more discussion of inadvertent plagiarism, see pp. 519–520.)

Rachel's instructor required her to use the documentation form recommended by the Modern Language Association (MLA). Therefore she gave credit by either citing the author's name before the material and then giving the source's page number in parentheses afterward or by including both the author and page citations in parentheses immediately following the quotation. For example, Rachel wrote that Jane Fonda helped spawn "aerobic nervosa" (Erens 209–210). Two popularly used documentation forms (MLA and APA) are described in detail with examples in Chapter 12.

Remember; giving credit means the following:

- Using quotation marks around borrowed words or phrases
- Acknowledging the source and page number of any borrowed words or paraphrased ideas immediately afterward
- Including the complete source—author, title, and publishing information—in the list of works cited at the end of the paper.

Incorporating Quoted Material

Quoted material should support your ideas and may be a vital component of your paper. If the original material is particularly well written or precise, or if the material is bold or controversial, it makes sense to quote the author's words so you can examine them in detail.

All quoted material needs to be introduced in some way. It is a mistake to think that quoted material can stand on its own, no matter how incisive it is.

Often, in fact, it is vital to introduce and also to comment on the quoted material. Let's look at an example from Rachel's paper:

Lynn's family became involved in her therapy, too. Erens emphasizes the importance of the family in any treatment plan: "Often, the daughter has taken on the role of diverting attention from unacknowledged conflicts within the family" (212). In therapy, Lynn and her family gradually learned that her parents' "unacknowledged conflicts" over Lynn's choice of art as a major instead of computer science contributed to Lynn's stress. Therapy involved acknowledging these internalized conflicts as well as seeing a relationship between her eating disorder and that stress.

In this passage, Rachel uses Lynn's experience to lead into the quoted material. The quote provides an explanation of family dynamics that reflects Lynn's situation. Rather than letting the quotation stand by itself, Rachel *uses* it by discussing the connection between the quoted material and her friend's specific experience. In order to understand how Rachel has incorporated quoted material in her essay, let's look at a strategy we call "the sandwich."

The Sandwich as a Development Technique

If you have had instructors comment that your papers need more development, or you have trouble meeting the required length for an assignment, or you find that you are merely "padding" your paper with strings of quotations, you will discover that the "sandwich" strategy is a solution to your problem. Even if your papers seem to satisfy the page requirement but you are earning B's instead of A's on your papers, the problem may be that you have not critically thought about and *used* your supporting material.

Because effective supporting material is often quoted from sources, you need to incorporate direct quotations effectively. The "sandwich" technique helps you write better-developed and more convincing papers. Just as bread holds the contents of a sandwich together, a writer needs to use the introduction to the quotation and the discussion about it to hold the quoted material together.

It may help to visualize the "sandwich":

- **The lead-in or introduction**—the top slice of bread—appeals to the reader and helps by identifying the author or speaker and any necessary background or credentials. The introduction should provide enough of a context or an awareness of the plot for the quoted material to make sense and should anticipate and identify any pronouns used within the quotation. The lead-in may also emphasize the focus point that you intend to support with the quoted material. The introduction needs to be informative without duplicating the material in the quotation.

- **The direct quotation**—the "meat" of the sandwich—comes next.
- **The analysis or commentary**—that essential bottom slice of bread—provides those necessary lines of clarification, interpretation, analysis, or discussion after the quotation. You need to explain or define the author's terms or discuss the significance of the quotation to the work as a whole. Most importantly, your analysis demonstrates the necessity of that quoted material for the point you are making.

In the previous example from Rachel's paper, Rachel introduces the quotation by identifying the author's last name so that she needs to give only the page number in parentheses after the quote. In her lead-in, Rachel also anticipates Erens's focus point about "the importance of the family in any treatment plan" without repeating Erens's exact words. Her analytic comment after the quotation is a good example of how to use the author's words. When Rachel returns to Erens's observation about the family's "unacknowledged conflicts," she works with the quotation and underscores Erens's meaning.

 ## PRACTICING THE SANDWICH

The following passage appears in Brent Staples's essay "Black Men and Public Space" (p. 181):

> I often witness that "hunch posture," from women after dark on the warrenlike streets of Brooklyn where I live. They seem to set their faces on neutral and, with their purse straps strung across their chests bandolier style, they forge ahead as though bracing themselves against being tackled.

Because the passage that begins "They seem to set their faces on neutral" has such memorable language to describe the women that Staples sees walking at night, students often choose to incorporate his description. In your notebook, try writing a lead-in and then your analysis of that one line.

LEAD-IN:

_____

_____

_____

_____

_____

"They seem to set their faces on neutral and, with their purse straps strung across their chests bandolier style, they forge ahead as though bracing themselves against being tackled" (183).

ANALYSIS:

_____

_____

_____

_____

You might want to compare your sandwich with a classmate's. See if you both managed to avoid the following problems in your lead-in. Can you identify the reasons that these lead-ins are weak?

1. *Brent Staples says,* "They seem to set their faces on neutral and, with their purse straps strung across their chests bandolier style, they forge ahead as though bracing themselves against being tackled" (183).

2. *In paragraph 6, Brent Staples quotes,* "They seem to set their faces on neutral and, with their purse straps strung across their chests bandolier style, they forge ahead as though bracing themselves against being tackled" (183).

3. *Brent Staples feels like a criminal:* "They seem to set their faces on neutral and, with their purse straps strung across their chests bandolier style, they forge ahead as though bracing themselves against being tackled" (183).

4. *Recent statistics show that urban violence is epidemic:* "They seem to set their faces on neutral and, with their purse straps strung across their chests bandolier style, they forge ahead as though bracing themselves against being tackled" (183).

5. *Staples's essay shows that women who walk at night* "They seem to set their faces on neutral and, with their purse straps strung across their chests bandolier style, they forge ahead as though bracing themselves against being tackled" (183).

Explanation of the Errors

1. This lead-in effectively identifies the author, but it doesn't give a context for the quotation that follows. The reader cannot know who "they" are. (See pronoun reference, p. 574, for an explanation of this error.) Further, the writer needs to prepare the reader for what is important in the quotation so that it makes sense to the reader.

2. This lead-in also identifies the author, but there is nothing gained by starting with the paragraph number and in fact this pointless information is distracting. Furthermore, the writer does not prepare the reader for this quotation. It is also not accurate to write that "Brent Staples quotes" because Staples is not quoting anyone; he is the writer who is being quoted.

3. The writer seems to understand the discomfort that Brent Staples feels—"like a criminal"—but he has not shown how this feeling is a consequence of the women's posture. Moreover, there is no referent for "they."

4. This lead-in doesn't accurately anticipate the quotation. It may be true that "urban violence is epidemic," but this lead-in does not prepare the reader for the description of the women's posture.

5. This lead-in is effective because it identifies, before the reader is confused, that "they" are the "women who walk at night." However, the writer has a grammar error in the double subject—"women" and "they"—which prompts the reader to stumble between the lead-in and the quotation. The writer could easily correct this by starting the quotation with "seem" to avoid the double subject and moving smoothly from lead-in to quotation: *Staples's essay shows that women who walk at night "seem to set their faces on neutral."*

Here is one example of an effective sandwich—good lead-in *and* analysis—using this same quotation. If the title and author's full name have already been included in the essay, only the last name of the author is needed here:

Staples describes the posture of women who walk at night: "They seem to set their faces on neutral and, with their purse straps strung across their chests bandolier style, they forge ahead as though bracing themselves against being tackled" (183). **Staples suggests that these women need to play multiple roles. They must appear to be indifferent to their environment and not make eye contact as they "set their faces on neutral." Further, they become soldiers with bandoliers and defensive football players guarding themselves against being attacked.**

Analyzing the Example. Notice that the lead-in identifies the author so that only a page reference will be necessary in the parenthetical citation. Further, the referent for the pronoun "they," which begins the quotation, is clarified in the lead-in—"women who walk at night."

Students often neglect the analysis portion of the sandwich, assuming that the quotation is self-explanatory. However, the only way to convince your reader of your interpretation of the quoted material is to analyze it—to work with it.

Notice that the analysis is quite complete. The first statement—"These women need to play multiple roles"—is a general assertion drawn from the specific images of women as soldiers with their bandoliers and as football players guarding "against being tackled." Because the women are on the defensive, the student explains that they don't make eye contact and they "appear to be indifferent" as they "set their faces on neutral." The student has analyzed the word choice and imagery so that he can convince the reader of his interpretation of Staples's description.

Paraphrasing

Paraphrasing a writer's ideas makes that information available to the reader in a condensed form. Sometimes you will want to put the essence of an entire piece that you have read into your own words; other times you will want to paraphrase just one section of the work. If the author's idea is useful but the material is wordy, filled with jargon, or contains information you do not need, you will paraphrase rather than quote the text.

Illustrating Paraphrasing

Assume that you are writing an essay on failure—and how individuals might actually gain strength from surviving a painful failure. You might decide to include ideas from J.K. Rowling's commencement address: "The Fringe Benefits of Failure, and the Importance of Imagination" (p. 165).

Original from "The Fringe Benefits of Failure, and the Importance of Imagination"

The knowledge that you have emerged wiser and stronger from setbacks means that you are, ever after, secure in your ability to survive. You will never truly know yourself, or the strength of your relationships, until both have been tested by adversity. Such knowledge is a true gift, for all that it is painfully won (168).

Paraphrase

Failure is necessary because when people survive adversity, they often gain wisdom and strength from their ability to endure. Such testing brings deeper self-knowledge and a truer understanding of relationships with others (Rowling 168).

The important point that Rowling makes about failure is retained while her wording is condensed. Most importantly, note that her name and the page number are given in parenthesis because the ideas are Rowling's. *To fail to cite her name and a page number would be plagiarism.*

 PRACTICING PARAPHRASING

Practice paraphrasing the following paragraph—a challenging one—before you read the paraphrase that follows it.

Original from "Why Stop Smoking? Let's Get Clinical" (p. 347)

In normal lungs, the trachea and bronchi—the large and small tubes leading to the alveoli (the tiny sacs that do the actual work of the lungs)—are lined with a film of tissue that is one cell layer thick. The surface of these cells is covered with tiny, finger-like structures called cilia. These cilia beat constantly in a waving motion, which moves small particles and toxic substances out of the lung and into the back of the throat where they are swallowed. In a smoker or someone like a coal miner, who constantly breathes in large amounts of toxic substances, many of the cilia soon disappear. If exposure continues, some ciliated cells die and are replaced by squamous cells, the same type that form the skin. Without the cleansing function of the ciliated cells, toxic materials and particles are breathed into the lungs, staying longer in contact with all the tissue. Each group of ciliated cells killed and replaced by squamous cells decreases by a certain fraction the lungs' ability to cleanse themselves. As this occurs, the amount of damage done by each cigarette increases to a greater and greater degree (348).

Paraphrase

Healthy lungs contain tiny sacs that are lined with cilia, hair-like fingers that move poisons out of the lungs. In coal miners or smokers, these cilia are destroyed and are replaced by cells that can't do the cleansing so the toxics touch more tissue longer. With the cleansing cells gone, the damage continues to increase each time smoke is inhaled (Harrison 348).

This paraphrase condenses complicated scientific information while stressing Harrison's key point. Again, because the ideas are Harrison's, his name and the page source must be included in the citation. *To fail to cite his name and a page number would be plagiarism.*

Combining Paraphrase and Quotation

Most often, the material you use to support your points will be a blend of paraphrase and direct quotation. You can capture the essence of an author's idea by paraphrasing it, but there will be well-crafted phrases and key ideas that need to be quoted to convey the flavor of the original work. When you combine paraphrase and direct quotation, you still need to be careful to give credit for both.

Original from "Is There A Doctor in the Mouse?" (p. 229)

The theory that vaccines cause autism first came onto the scene in the late '90's, just as people were going online en masse. We weren't paying much attention until parents started to refuse vaccines. When we looked, we realized that many parents were exposed to story after story on autism Web sites and in chat rooms about the dangers of vaccines.

That echo chamber of opinion became a reality despite our best efforts to prove otherwise. Now we're left with a lingering conspiracy theory that vaccines cause autism, even though the best, unbiased evidence says otherwise (230).

Paraphrase with Quotation

In "Is There A Doctor in the Mouse?" Rahul K. Parikh regrets the popularization of the idea that vaccines cause autism—a false notion perpetuated by poor Web sites and chat rooms, which left "the echo chamber of opinion" to become entrenched reality and "conspiracy theory" (230).

If you are paraphrasing an expert, you will gain credibility by introducing the title and author of the work prior to your paraphrase as illustrated here. Because the author's original words are particularly strong—"echo chamber of opinion" and "conspiracy theory"—they are purposefully incorporated into paraphrase, and the quotation marks need to be retained and the entire reference cited. Because Parikh's name appears in the lead-in to the quotation, only the page number is needed in the parenthetical citation. (See p. 540.)

 ## Practicing Combining Paraphrase and Quotation

Practice incorporating choice quotations into your paraphrased versions of the following passages. In your lead-in, you may want to include the author's name and the source of the material. Compare your paraphrases with those written by your classmates. The page numbers given are from the essays as they appear in this textbook.

1. From "King Curtis's Echo": "Now, long after the anger over the driveway affront has dissipated, it's something I strive to remember when some idiot swerves into my lane without signaling or an eager shopper jostles me in the grocery store. The obscene waste of King Curtis's life and my memory of his jubilant horn give me pause and, on a good day, a touch of grace. I have to thank the Russian deli customer for that" (Thayer 193–194).

2. From "Why Stop Smoking? Let's Get Clinical": "By the time one has been a pack-a-day smoker for ten years or so, extensive damage has already been done. By twenty years, much of the damage is irreversible and progresses more rapidly. After ten years of smoking, each cigarette may do as much damage to the body as three or more packs did when a smoker first started" (Harrison 379).

3. From "Makes Learning Fun": "Computing's instant gratification—built into the learning-is-fun mind-set—encourages intellectual passivity, driven mainly by conditioned amusement. Fed a diet of interactive

insta-grat, students develop a distaste for persistence, trial and error, attentiveness, or patience" (248).

As you work on refining your incorporation of paraphrased and quoted material, you also will be revising your essay. Rewriting is such a critical activity in preparing an essay that we have devoted the entire next chapter to various aspects of revision.

Final Tips for Organizing and Drafting an Essay

- Review your prewriting to discover your **aim** or purpose in writing.

- Formulate a tentative thesis—your **claim**—by using the "So What?" strategy.

- Make sure that your **thesis** is an assertion and not a question, phrase, or announcement.

- Consider placing your **thesis at the end of your introduction** to guide both writer and reader.

- Use the **forecasted elements** of your thesis to organize and outline your essay.

- Examine paragraphs for **sufficient focus** (topic sentences) and **support** (examples, facts, and illustrations).

- If using sources, give credit for ideas and words to **avoid plagiarism**.

- If you are including direct quotations, use the **sandwich technique** so that you have an informative lead-in before your quote and adequate analysis after it.

Chapter 9

Revising an Essay

Rewriting and Rewriting

It is essential that you give yourself ample time to reconsider your rough draft in its entirety and revise it before handing it in as your final paper. Usually this revision involves sharpening the thesis, reorganizing ideas, developing sketchy points, adding new material for support, removing irrelevant material, improving transitions between ideas, strengthening the introduction and conclusion, and editing for word choice, mechanics, and spelling.

Thinking Critically for an Audience

Every phase of the writing process involves thinking critically—reasoning, analyzing, and assessing—so that your points are clear and understandable to your audience. The act of revision calls on these same skills.

As you begin to organize your prewriting notes into a coherent essay, ask yourself: Can a reader follow my logic? Do the examples support my main point? What, if any, examples should I cut? Your decision to remove irrelevant details reflects your awareness that irrelevant points not only weaken your support but also confuse your readers.

The need for clarity and precision continues throughout drafting and revision. As you revise, continue to question whether the depth of your analysis and support for your assertions are sufficient. You need to reconsider your focus, the logic of your organization, and the strength of your conclusion. As you edit, scrutinize your word choice, sentence structure, grammar, and mechanics so that surface flaws do not frustrate your reader.

Thinking critically requires you to recognize that your audience does not necessarily share your views. Thus the writing process forces you to challenge your own assertions and consider your readers' perspectives. Although it may appear that these stages of writing a paper involve a step-by-step process, all of these writing activities occur concurrently.

You may revise while you are drafting your paper, and possibly edit from the early drafts until the moment you hand the paper to your instructor. As noted in the previous chapter, Rachel started revising her draft as soon as she had a printout from her computer. Thinking critically about her aim in writing this essay—to persuade readers of the media's role in fostering eating disorders—Rachel made substantial changes as she revised her rough draft.

Revising a Rough Draft

Working from her own evaluation of her rough draft (see pp. 361–362), Rachel rewrote her draft and, as required by the assignment, showed it to her instructor for comments. Rachel's paper had started out very rough, as most first drafts do, but she continued to develop her ideas and rearrange them. She felt that her second draft was stronger than the first but still could be improved. Her instructor helped her by identifying weak areas and suggesting improvements.

Example: Draft With Instructor's Comments

Eating Disorders and the Media ⟩ *more striking or*
suggestive title

except for?
Bare, (with the exception of) a bikini, the deep-tanned model poses at a beach.

Tighten—avoid repeating "she is" She is surrounded by five adoring guys. She is sipping a frothy soda and inviting all of us to do the same . . . if we want to get the guys . . . if we want to be the envy of our friends. *How thin? How tall?* She is thin but tall. Viewers don't notice the bony ribs, (how hungry she is,) *not //* *very graphic* and all the "diet pills" she popped to stay that thin. A picture doesn't reveal the vomit on her breath or the spearmint gum used to mask it. In fact, our magazines and T.V. *stronger verb?* commercials present us with such ads until such girls don't seem skinny anymore— they seem right. ✓*clear point*

It doesn't seem to matter that, for some years now, the media has been reporting the epidemic among college "coeds" of eating disorders, anorexia and bulimia. It *diction (old-fashioned?)* *briefly distinguish* doesn't seem to matter that the Women's Movement has tried to free women from being so caught up on the way they look. Despite the varied opportunities now available to women, many women say they would rather lose pounds than achieve academic or career goals. In the early years of aerobics, actress Jane Fonda has sold many *What is?* on the value of her "Work Out" and has helped spawn "aerobic nervosa" (Erens 209–210).

Many women who admire Jane Fonda's shape may not know that Fonda was once a bulimic. And no one watching the televised spectacle of Prince Charles and Princess Diana's wedding could have predicted that years later, biographers would be discussing "Di's bulimia." *transition? More current examples?*

Who wouldn't want to hear friends whisper, "What a body! She really knows how to stay in shape!" or "Don't you hate someone who looks that good?" *necessary?* Either way, the sense of admiration and affirmation is clear. A thin girl has something that others don't—and this gives her power and control. She can make herself in the image of the cover girls. In "Bodily Harm," the author quotes Ruth Striegel-Moore: "The pursuit of thinness is a way for women to compete with each other, a way that avoids being threatening to men" (209). *specify what is wrong with this* *You need Erens's name here or in your ( ) at end of this line*

Unfortunately, this competition keeps women from seeking or obtaining the help they might otherwise get from close friends. Many bulimics keep their secret as guarded as their mothers might have kept their sex life. My friend Kirstie did this. She waited for years before she told her friends (and later, her family) that she was bulimic. At first, only her "barf buddy" (Erens 209)—a cousin who had initially introduced her to this "great diet plan"—knew. Gradually, their friendship revolved exclusively around this dark secret and was eroded by their unacknowledged rivalry. *Ref?* *wk split of subj/verb*

Few of us ever suspected Kirstie was in trouble: she seemed to have it all. But years later, she revealed to me that her greatest pride at that time was when she discovered that she was now vomiting automatically after eating, without needing to use a finger or spoon. *illustrate* *develop*

Even when Kirstie received out-patient counseling and her family thought she was "cured," she wasn't. For her it was either fasting or bingeing—there was no in-between. As her friend, I often felt trapped between either respecting her confidence or letting some adult know, so she might get the help she needed. While encouraging her to find other interests and to be open with her therapist, I felt quite helpless. I didn't want to betray her confidence and tell her parents, but I worried that my silence was betraying our friendship. *How could you tell?* *transition?*

According to another friend, many young women continue to have obsessions with food for years afterwards. My friend Erica was shocked by the number of women who where over thirty in her hospital treatment program for anorexics. She admitted

Ref?   that (this) is what made her decide she needed help while she was still in college. Unlike Kirstie, Erica decided she needed an in-hospital treatment program that cut her off from her old habits and helped her deal with her emotions and learn better nutritional habits. Erica managed to enter the program as soon as her finals were

good transition   over and therefore she didn't jeopardize her schooling.

But some don't have that choice. My friend Lynn would have died had she not entered the hospital when she did. She had to drop out of Berkeley immediately and get prolonged therapy before she could be released to her parents and begin her recovery. Her family became involved in her therapy, too. As Erens notes, "Family therapy considers the family itself, not the daughter with the eating disorder, to be the 'patient.' Often, the daughter has taken on the role of diverting attention from unacknowledged conflicts within the family" (212). In therapy, Lynn and her family

tighten this discussion?   gradually learned that her parents' "unacknowledged conflicts" over her mother's return to work and over Lynn's choice of art instead of computer science as a major contributed to Lynn's stress. Therapy involved acknowledging these internalized conflicts as well as examining the pressure to be thin.

effective link between personal experience & reading   In addition to absorbing family conflicts, each of these friends felt that they were programmed by advertisers to accept and seek a lean look as the ideal. Fashion magazines often use underweight preteen models who are made up and dressed to seem older than they are. This makes women with real hips and breasts feel overweight. In fact, the fashion world does not seem to view large bodies, strength, or maturity as attractive features for women.

It is ironic that this should happen at a time when women have more freedom to control their lives and their bodies. Unfortunately, women still spend much of their

develop or combine these short paragraphs   earnings on the cosmetic and diet industries. Our generation has witnessed the weight of fashion models drop way down and the number of eating disorders go way up.

It is time to let ourselves become shocked again. And then we need to move beyond shock and take action. Those who make the images will only change when those of us who support them stop buying products and tuning in on shows that continue to impose "bodily harm" on us.   *Return to your opening image, if you can, and sharpen your thesis. Don't forget "Works Cited."*

Revising Can Make the Difference

Every paper can benefit from careful revision and editing, but many students do not have their instructors' comments on their drafts to use as they revise. Occasionally students can find trained tutors at the college writing center, for example, or peers who will offer feedback and suggestions. These students' comments may not be as thorough as those Rachel received, but they can help the writer see the essay from another perspective.

 ### A Checklist for Revising and Editing Papers

Whether you are revising your own essay or commenting on a classmate's, the following checklist should help:

- **Aim:** What is the purpose or aim of the essay? Are there any sections that seem to stray from this aim?
- **Claim:** What is the thesis? How can you make it clearer or more convincing?
- **Support:** Which points could be better illustrated and supported?
- **Organization:** Does the paper reflect the order of ideas forecast in the thesis?
- **Paragraphs:** Could any paragraph be better focused or developed? How?
- **Sentences:** Is there any sentence that is not clear or grammatical? Are the sentences varied?
- **Wording:** Circle any unnecessary or confusing words.
- **Transitions:** Locate any gaps in logic or any missing information.
- **Introduction:** How could the opening be more captivating? Does it set the right tone? Does the introduction move smoothly into the thesis?
- **Conclusion:** Is there a sense of closure or resolution? Does the conclusion return to the thesis?
- **Style:** Is the diction consistent with the purpose of the essay? Are there any words that need to be replaced?
- **Mechanics:** Correct punctuation? Grammar? Spelling?
- **Title:** Is the title fresh and enticing? Can you improve it with wordplay or by deleting unnecessary words?

Some instructors may spend time helping students work in small groups as "peer editors" who critique each other's papers. A good peer editor need not excel at grammar nor be an excellent writer. An effective editor needs to be a careful *reader,* one who is sensitive to the writer's main point and supporting details.

If you are editing a classmate's essay, you do not have to be able to correct the errors. A peer editor needs only to point out areas that seem flawed or confusing; it is then the writer's responsibility to use a handbook (like the one in this book) and correct the errors.

After studying the instructor's comments and corrections, Rachel continued modifying her draft. She rewrote certain phrases and paragraphs a number of times, shifted words and sentences, and found ways to "tighten" her prose by eliminating unnecessary words. Most of all, she tried to replace sluggish words with more precise and specific details. Notice below how her title gained more punch and how the opening is tighter and less repetitive. She also took the time to develop certain thoughts and paragraphs and to clarify her points. The following version is her final essay.

STUDENT EXAMPLE: FINAL ESSAY

Rachel Krell

Professor Ansite

English 1A

7 October 2008

Dieting Daze: No In-Between

Bare, except for a bikini, the deep-tanned model poses at a beach surrounded by five adoring and adorable guys. She is sipping a frothy diet drink and inviting us to do the same, if we want to get the guys and be the envy of our friends. She stands 5′ 10″ and wears a size 3. Viewers don't notice the bony ribs, the hunger pangs, and the "diet pills" she popped to stay that thin. A picture doesn't reveal the vomit on her breath or the spearmint gum used to mask it. In fact, our magazines and TV commercials bombard us with such ads until these girls don't seem skinny anymore—they seem right.

It doesn't seem to matter that, for years now, the media has been reporting the epidemic among college women of eating disorders, anorexia (self-starvation) and bulimia (binge and purge). It doesn't seem to matter that the women's movement has tried to free women from bondage to their bodies. Despite the varied opportunities now available to women, many women say they would rather lose pounds than achieve academic or career goals. In the early years of aerobics, actress Jane Fonda sold many on the value of her "Work Out" and helped spawn "aerobic nervosa"—the excessive use of exercise to maintain an ideal weight (Erens 209). Many women who admired Jane Fonda's shape may not know that Fonda was once bulimic. And no one watching the televised spectacle of Prince Charles and Princess Diana's wedding could have predicted that years later, biographers would be discussing "Di's bulimia." Current super models such as Kate Moss and popular young celebrities like actresses Mary Kate Olsen and Kate Bosworth perpetuate the concept that to be successful, one must be thin.

Such celebrities, and those females in the ads, are held up as models for all of us to mirror. A thin girl has something that others don't—and this gives her power and control. She can make her body resemble a cover girl's. In "Bodily Harm," Pamela Erens quotes Ruth Striegel-Moore, Ph.D., director of Yale University's Eating Disorders Clinic: "The pursuit of thinness is a way for women to compete with each other, a way that avoids being threatening to men" (209). But this competition threatens and endangers the women's well-being because it keeps women from seeking the help they might otherwise get from close friends.

In fact, many bulimics—models and celebrities included—keep their secret as guarded as their mothers might have kept their sex life. My friend Kirstie waited for years before she told friends (and later, her family) that she was bulimic. At first the only one who knew about her bulimia was her cousin who had initially introduced her to "this great diet plan." This cousin became Kirstie's "barf buddy" (Erens 209). Gradually, their friendship revolved exclusively around this dark secret and was eroded by their unacknowledged rivalry.

Few of us ever suspected Kirstie was in trouble because she seemed to have it all. During her senior year in high school, she was dating a college guy, was enrolled in college prep classes, jogged religiously every morning and every evening, and loved to ski with her family and beat her brothers down the slope. She seemed to crave the compliments she received from her brothers and their friends because of her good looks—and she received plenty! But years later, she revealed to me that her greatest pride at that time was when she discovered she could vomit automatically after eating, without needing to use a finger or spoon.

Even when Kirstie received out-patient counseling and her family thought she was "cured," she would still binge and purge at will. Every conversation with Kirstie inevitably returned to the subject of food—fasting or bingeing—there was no in-between. As her close friend, I often felt helpless, trapped between either respecting her confidence and keeping her dark secret or letting an adult know and perhaps getting her more help. I didn't want to betray her confidence and tell her parents, but I worried that my silence was betraying our friendship. Even though we each went to different colleges and gradually lost touch, I find myself wondering if Kirstie ever got the help she needed.

According to another friend, even mature women continue to have obsessions with food. My friend Erica was shocked by the number of women over thirty in her hospital treatment program for anorexics. She admitted that seeing these older women is what convinced her she needed help while she was still in college. Unlike Kirstie, Erica decided she needed an in-hospital treatment program that cut her off from her old habits and helped her deal with her emotions and learn better nutritional habits. Erica managed to enter the program as soon as her finals were over, and therefore she didn't jeopardize her schooling.

But some don't have that choice. My friend Lynn would have died had she not entered the hospital when she did. She had to drop out of Berkeley immediately and get prolonged therapy before she could be released to her parents and begin her recovery. Lynn's family became involved in her therapy, too. Erens emphasizes the importance of the family in any treatment plan: "Often, the daughter has taken on the role of diverting attention from unacknowledged conflicts within the family" (212). In therapy Lynn and her family gradually learned that her parents' "unacknowledged conflicts" over Lynn's choice of art as a major instead of computer science contributed to her stress. Therapy involved acknowledging these internalized conflicts as well as seeing a relationship between her eating disorder and that stress.

In addition to absorbing family conflicts, each of these friends felt that she was programmed by advertisers to accept a lean look as the ideal. Fashion magazines often use underweight, preteen models who are made up and dressed to seem older than they are. This makes women with normal hips and breasts feel overweight. In fact, the fashion world does not seem to view large bodies, strength, or maturity as attractive features for women.

It is ironic that this should happen at a time when women have more freedom to control their lives and their bodies. Unfortunately, women still spend much of their earnings on cosmetic and diet products. Our generation has witnessed the weight of fashion models decline and the number of eating disorders increase while women often feel powerless. Stripped of control, many women feel compelled to diet constantly; images of emaciated models that were once so shocking have now become commonplace.

It is time to let ourselves become shocked again—shocked by an epidemic that is destroying women's lives. And then we need to move beyond shock—and beyond the stories of Kirstie, Erica, and Lynn—and take action against the media's manipulation of

---

Krell 4

the female form. Insisting that our television sponsors, magazines, and video artists stop perpetrating such deadly images of women is something we can all do. A letter from one viewer carries clout because stations often assume that each letter represents many who didn't take the time to write. Ten letters from ten viewers wield even more power. It is time to protest the images of bikini-clad models parading before us and demand images that reflect the emotional and intellectual scope and diversity among women in our society. With some of our best and brightest dying among us, there is no in-between position anymore. Those who make the images will only change when those of us who support them stop buying products and stop tuning in on programs that continue to impose "bodily harm" on us.

Krell 5

Work Cited

Erens, Pamela. "Bodily Harm." *Between Worlds: A Reader, Rhetoric, and Handbook*. Ed. Susan Bachmann and Melinda Barth. 6th ed. New York: Pearson Longman, 2010. 208–213. Print.

Rewriting for Coherence

As you may have noticed, Rachel devoted considerable attention to the way she linked information and ideas within and between her paragraphs. The goal, of course, is to ensure that all parts of the paper cohere (that is, that they hold together).

To sustain your readers' interest and ensure their comprehension of your work, you will want to examine the drafts of your essays to see if your ideas hold together. Each idea should follow logically from the one before, and all of your points must support your focus. That logical connection must be clear to the reader—not just to you, the writer of the essay, who may gloss over a link that is not obvious. All readers value clear connections between phrases, sentences, and paragraphs.

A Paragraph That Lacks Coherence

If writing is carefully organized, the reader will not stumble over irrelevant chunks of material or hesitate at unbridged gaps. Let's examine an incoherent paragraph:

> Students who commute to campus suffer indignities that dorm students can't imagine. Parking is expensive and lots are jammed. It is embarrassing to walk into class late. Often it takes over a half hour to find a spot. Commuters feel cut off from students who can return to the dorm to eat or rest. Commuters seldom have a telephone number to get missed lecture notes. Study groups readily form in dorms. Dorm students have a sense of independence and freedom. Commuters need to conform to old family rules and schedules, to say nothing of the need to baby-sit or cook for younger siblings and drive grandparents to the bank.

Although this paragraph has a clear focus and the ideas are all relevant, its coherence needs to be improved. You may sense that the information is out of order, the logic of the writer is not always obvious to the reader, sentences do not flow together, words are repeated, and emphasis is lost.

In the pages that follow, you will learn how to correct paragraphs like this and to avoid these problems in your own writing. You will also have the opportunity to correct this paragraph.

Using Transitions

Even when material is carefully organized, well-chosen transition words and devices help you connect sentences and paragraphs and cohere your points. You are familiar with most of these words and expressions. But if you have been trying for more than five minutes to find a specific word to connect two ideas or sentences in your essay, the following list of transition terms will enable you to gain unity in your essay.

Transition Terms

- *Time relationship:* first, second, before, then, next, meantime, meanwhile, finally, at last, eventually, later, afterward, frequently, often, occasionally, during, now, subsequently, concurrently
- *Spatial relationship:* above, below, inside, outside, across, along, in front of, behind, beyond, there, here, in the distance, alongside, near, next to, close to, adjacent, within
- *Contrast:* in contrast, on the contrary, on the other hand, still, however, yet, but, nevertheless, despite, even so, even though, whereas
- *Comparison:* similarly, in the same way

- *Examples or illustrations:* for example, for instance, to illustrate, to show, in particular, specifically, that is, in addition, moreover
- *Causes or effects:* as a result, accordingly, therefore, then, because, so, thus, consequently, hence, since
- *Conclusions or summaries:* in conclusion, finally, in summary, evidently, clearly, of course, to sum up, therefore

Noticing Transitions

If you are writing a narrative, some part of your essay—if not the entire work—probably will be arranged chronologically. See if you can spot the *time signals* in the following excerpt from Judith Ortiz Cofer's "The Myth of the Latin Woman" and underline them.

> It is surprising to my professional friends that even today some people, including those who should know better, still put others "in their place." It happened to me most recently during a stay at a classy metropolitan hotel favored by young professional couples for weddings. Late one evening after the theater, as I walked toward my room with a colleague (a woman with whom I was coordinating an arts program), a middle-aged man in a tuxedo, with a young girl in satin and lace on his arm, stepped directly into our path. With his champagne glass extended toward me, he exclaimed "Evita!" (175).

Can you see how "even today," "still," "most recently," "late one evening," and "as I walked" are transitions used to help the reader connect the actions in the narrative?

With three or four of your classmates, read the next paragraph of this essay (which starts on p. 172) and underline the transition words that have to do with the essay's chronological connections.

Chronological concepts may also be important for gaining transition and coherence in non-narrative essays. Look at this paragraph from "Discrimination at Large" (p. 198) to see if you can identify the time concepts around which this paragraph is structured.

> Since the time I first ventured out to play with the neighborhood kids, I was told over and over that I was lazy and disgusting. Strangers, adults, classmates offered gratuitous comments with such frequency and urgency that I started to believe them. Much later I needed to prove it wasn't so. I began a regimen of swimming, cycling, and jogging that put all but the most compulsive to shame. I ate only cottage cheese, brown rice, fake butter, and steamed everything. I really believed I could infiltrate the ranks of the nonfat and thereby establish my worth.

You may rightly perceive that "since the time I first," "I began," and "much later" are the three terms that denote the passage of time within this paragraph. But you may also note that the writer uses the past tense, as if what Jennifer Coleman "really believed" at one time is different from what she believes now. The chronological ordering of the essay emphasizes this fact. Read the rest of the essay to observe how Coleman uses these time-relationship transitions—"along the way," "for a while," "still," "until," "until then," and "now" and "finally"—to emphasize the history that led to her change in self-perception.

Essays that include description often require terms that connect sentences or paragraphs in a *spatial relationship*. Notice the spatial concepts that connect the descriptions in this paragraph from "The Only Child" (the complete essay starts on p. 34).

> The room is a slum, and it stinks. It is wall-to-wall beer cans, hundreds of them, under a film of ash. He lights cigarettes and leaves them burning on the windowsill or the edge of the dresser or the lip of the sink, while he thinks of something else—Gupta sculpture, maybe, or the Sephiroth Tree of the Kabbalah. The sink is filthy, and so is the toilet. Holes have been burnt in the sheet on the bed, where he sits. He likes to crush the beer cans after he has emptied them, then toss them aside.

Do you see this paragraph, as we do, as a movement from the periphery to the interior? We sense that the author moves from broad description—"wall-to-wall beer cans" around the room—to smaller, interior descriptions—"holes [that] have been burnt in the sheet on the bed, where he sits." The outside-to-inside movement of this description parallels the author's description of elements outside of his brother (in his room) to his observation of what is closer and more central to him (his thoughts, his talk, his gestures). The arrangement also complements the author's argument that his brother's life and mind were destroyed by drugs—the external environment destroying the interior.

The use of the transition words will seem contrived if you rely on them too often in any one essay, or if you use the same ones in every essay you write. You also have other, more subtle ways to gain connections between sentences and paragraphs in your essays.

Key Word Repetition

In some cases you will want to repeat a word that emphasizes an important point that you are making. Such repetition reinforces the focus of your paragraph and essay.

In another paragraph from "The Only Child" (p. 34), the author emphasizes his disdain for his brother's living conditions by repeating his brother's explanation. Can you hear the irony or sarcasm in the author's repetition?

> He tells me that he is making a statement, that this room is a statement, that the landlord will understand the meaning of his statement. In a

week or so, according to the pattern, they will evict him, and someone will find him another room, which he will turn into another statement, with the help of the welfare checks he receives on account of his disability, which is the static in his head.

Notice that the repetition of "statement" is very deliberate and strategic, rather than boring for the reader, because it emphasizes the nonreasoning to which the brother's mind has been reduced.

Synonyms or Key Word Substitutions

You can connect the ideas or concepts within a paragraph and throughout your essay by skillfully using synonyms or key word substitutions—words that have the same or similar meanings—to emphasize your focus. Notice how Jennifer Coleman in "Discrimination at Large" (p. 198) piles word substitutions into her sentences to simulate for her reader the effect of being assaulted, as fat people are, by denigrating words:

It was confusing for awhile. How was it I was still lazy, weak, despised, a slug, and a cow if I exercised every waking minute? This confusion persisted until I finally realized: it didn't matter what I did. I was and always would be the object of sport, derision, antipathy and hostility so long as I stayed in my body. I immediately signed up for a body transplant. I am still waiting for a donor.

How many substitutions for "lazy" did you find? How many implied substitutions for "contempt"? Coleman cites many specific terms for how she has been perceived and treated to make clear to the reader that these attacks come under many names, but the intention to denigrate is always the same.

Pronouns

Pronouns, words substituting for nouns that clearly precede or follow them, can effectively connect parts of a paragraph. By prompting the reader to mentally supply the missing noun or see the relationship the pronouns imply, the writer also has a way to engage the reader. To emphasize the contrast between people who are fat and those who are not, Coleman uses pronoun substitutions to unite her paragraphs:

Things are less confusing now that I know that the nonfat are superior to me regardless of their personal habits, health, personalities, cholesterol levels, or the time they log on the couch. And, as obviously superior to me as they are, it is their destiny to remark on my inferiority regardless of who I'm with, whether they know me, whether it hurts my feelings. I finally understand that the thin have a divine mandate to steal self-esteem from fat people, who have no right to it in the first place.

> Fat people aren't really jolly. Sometimes we act that way so you will leave us alone. We pay a price for this. But at least we get to hang on to what self-respect we smuggled out of grade school and adolescence.

In the first paragraph, *I* and *me* contrast with *they* and *their* to emphasize the separation between the author and the "nonfat" and "superior" other people. In the second paragraph the author unites herself with "fat people," repeatedly saying "we" to emphasize their unity. Coleman's entire essay coheres because she skillfully employs numerous unifying devices within and between her paragraphs. Read the essay in its entirety (pp. 524–538) to see how key word repetition, synonyms, and transitions between sentences and paragraphs create coherence within an essay.

Transitions between Paragraphs

Key word repetition is also an important way to achieve the important goal of *connection between paragraphs*. While your reader may be able to follow your movement and sustain your ideas within a paragraph, coherence within your essay as a whole requires transition sentences and, in longer essays, entire paragraphs of transitions.

One device that works well is to offer a specific example to illustrate a general point that concludes the previous paragraph and use it toward the beginning of the new paragraph. Notice the following excerpts from Shannon Paaske's research paper, which begins on page 524. What moves the reader between paragraphs?

> According to Jan Gavlin, director of assistive technology at the National Rehabilitation Hospital in Washington, "If you can move one muscle in your body, wiggle a pinkie or twitch an eyebrow, we can design a switch to allow you to operate in your environment" (qtd. in Blackman 71).
>
> An example of one such device is the Eyegaze Response Interface Computer Aid (ERICA), developed by biomedical engineer Thomas Hutchinson at the University of Virginia. . . .

By giving a specific example of "assistive technology" introduced in theory in the previous paragraph, the author is able to connect the two paragraphs.

In another section of her research paper, Shannon uses a question to help her reader move from one paragraph to another:

> Rebecca Acuirre, 16, who has cerebral palsy, says that she recently asked a stranger what time it was and he kept walking as though he didn't hear her. "Some people are prejudiced and ignore us. That makes me angry," she says.
>
> How can these prejudices be abolished? "We need more exposure," says DeVries.

The repetition of the word "prejudice" helps these paragraphs cohere. The question engages the reader because most of us feel obliged to think about answers to questions. This rhetorical question does not merely repeat the word. Instead, it moves the reader beyond the previous aspect of prejudice to the solution Paaske will discuss in the next section.

Although all paragraphs in your essay should hold together, the device of repeating key words should not be overused or strained. You may irritate your readers if they perceive your technique as a formula. For example, let's imagine you have written a paragraph that ended with the sentence "These are rationalizations, not reasons." Avoid merely repeating the exact phrasing, like "Although these are rationalizations, not reasons," at the start of your next paragraph. Instead, you might want to begin with something like this: "Such rationalizations are understandable if one considers the. . . ." With conscious practice of the technique, you'll improve your skills.

Avoiding Gaps

Transition terms and devices help you achieve coherence in your work, but they can't fill in for gaps in logic—sentences or paragraphs that just don't go together, or that are out of order. You can't expect your readers to move from one point to another if you have failed to put your reasoning into words. For example, in the incoherent paragraph on page 391, the writer places the following two sentences together:

> Parking is expensive and lots are jammed. It is embarrassing to walk into class late.

In the writer's mind, these two thoughts are logically connected. That link is not at all apparent to readers, and a transition term like *and* or *therefore* will not bridge that gap. The writer must write something to express the connection between the two sentences so there is no gap and no need for the readers to invent their own bridge. The writer needs to explain the relationship between "jammed" and "expensive" parking lots and the embarrassment of "walking into class late." You can work on this skill in the next exercise.

 ### Practicing Coherence

In small groups, return to the incoherent paragraph on page and discuss its problems. As a group, rewrite the paragraph so that all information is included, but also so that the ideas are logically linked. As you fill in the gaps in logic, practice using the transition terms and devices that ensure coherence in this paragraph. Here is one solution to improve the coherence of the paragraph.

> Students who commute to campus suffer indignities that dorm students can't imagine. Even before commuting students get to classes they have a problem. Parking on campus is expensive and hard to find

because the lots are jammed. Often it takes over half an hour to find a spot. By then class has started, and it is embarrassing to walk into class late. Commuters also feel cut off from those students who can return to the dorm to eat or rest. And while study groups readily form in dorms, commuting students seldom have even a telephone number to get missed lecture notes. Dorm students have a sense of independence and freedom from their families, but commuters need to conform to old family rules and schedules. Often the indignities of living at home include doing those tasks the students did through high school, like baby-sitting or cooking for younger siblings, or driving grandparents to the bank.

Writing Titles

A good title sets up an expectation for readers, allowing them to anticipate the subject and tone for the essay. A captivating title is brief, suggestive, and witty. Often wordplay, imagery, alliteration—the tools of the poet—are employed to draw readers in. Notice the intriguing titles and techniques of several works in this text:

"On Teenagers and Tattoos": alliteration; articulates the specific topic

"Under My Skin": wordplay that twists the common idiom for an irritation

"Pigskin, Patriarchy, and Pain": alliteration that forecasts the focus points of the essay

"Race Is a Four-Letter Word": suggests the author's anger and yet appeals with humor

"Hidden in Plain Sight": an oxymoron that attracts with a deliberate contradiction

"If the Genes Fit": a pun on "jeans"

"Discrimination at Large": a pun and wordplay

"Is There a Doctor in the Mouse?": wordplay

Notice how these titles are clever *phrases*, not wordy explanations or dry announcements. In fact, focused, appropriate humor is a plus and goes a long way to captivating readers. Moreover, you should not use another writer's exact title, even if you are analyzing that work in your essay. You may decide to play with the original title or allude to it as Robert Sakatani refers to "Breaking Tradition" in his title "Breaking the Ties that Bind." Honing such a resonant title may require some thought, but if you have started the essay early enough, you will be ready for flashes of inspiration. Your title might come to you at any time: during a brainstorming session, while revising a draft, or during the incubation stage, when you are not physically working on the paper. A choice title, like an effective introduction, draws the reader to your work.

Writing Introductions

Introductions and Audience

Typically, a strong introduction "hooks" the reader and then expands on the hook while building to the thesis statement, which often concludes the introduction. The introduction to an essay—the aim—has two obligations: (1) to attract the reader to the subject of the essay and (2) to establish for the reader the particular purpose and focus of the writer—the claim. The focus of the writer—the claim he or she is making about a limited subject—is contained in the thesis statement. The thesis statement does not have to be at the end of the introduction, but that is often a natural place for it because both the writer and reader are then immediately aware of the key assertion that will be supported in the essay. The concept of the thesis is discussed in more detail on pages 352–359.

If you have not discovered in your prewriting activities a useful way to lead to your thesis, you may find the ideas below helpful. Some subjects will seem best introduced by one type of introduction rather than another, and it's a good idea to keep your audience in mind as you draft possible "hooks" to your topic.

Types of Introductions

You may find that if you deliberately vary your introductions, perhaps trying each of the methods suggested here, you will not be intimidated by that blank sheet of paper or empty computer screen each time you start to write.

Direct Quotation. An essay that begins with the words of another person, especially a well-known person, should help convince your reader that you are a prepared writer who has researched the views of others on the subject and found relevance in their words. For example, when we were preparing Part I of this book, we discovered that Ellen Goodman had incorporated into her essay a particularly compelling comment by André Malraux, which we decided to use in our chapter introduction. André Malraux—a French novelist, political activist, and art critic—is not a noted authority on the sociology or psychology of family life. Nevertheless, his mildly philosophical statements about the family interested us, and we found his thoughts relevant for our introduction. Notice how we use Malraux's words throughout our introduction.

> In the essay that we used to demonstrate active reading (p. 3), author Ellen Goodman quotes André Malraux that "without a family" the individual "alone in the world, trembles with the cold" (qtd. in Goodman 4).

The family often nurtures its members and tolerates differences and failings that friends and lovers cannot accept. But as you may realize from your own experiences and observations, people also tremble with fear or anxiety even within the family unit. The writers in this chapter show the family as a source of both nurturing and anxiety.

Description. An introduction using description—whether it is a vivid picture of nature or of a person—can appeal to the imagination and the senses simultaneously. The power of the opening can be enhanced if the writer also postpones specific identification of the subject, place, or person until the reader is engaged. In the following paragraph from "The Only Child" (p. 34), notice that John Leonard does not reveal his subject. In fact, the reader does not know that he or she is reading about Leonard's brother until the last line of the essay.

> He is big. He always has been, over six feet, with that slump of the shoulders and tuck in the neck big men in this country often affect, as if to apologize for being above the democratic norm in size. (In high school and at college he played varsity basketball. In high school he was senior class president.) And he looks healthy enough, blue-eyed behind his beard, like a trapper or a mountain man, acquainted with silences. He also grins a lot.

Question. The psychology behind asking a reader a question probably lies in the fact that most of us feel obliged to at least *consider* answering a writer who has asked us something. If we don't have an immediate answer, we consider the subject and then continue with the reading—exactly what the writer wants us to do. But readers may find questions irritating if they seem silly or contrived, like "What is capital punishment?" Notice your own interest as you read the questions in the introduction to Robert Heilbroner's essay "Don't Let Stereotypes Warp Your Judgments" (p. 470).

> Is a girl called Gloria apt to be better-looking than one called Bertha? Are criminals more likely to be dark than blond? Can you tell a good deal about someone's personality from hearing his voice briefly over the phone? Can a person's nationality be pretty accurately guessed from his photograph? Does the fact that someone wears glasses imply that he is intelligent?

Anecdote or Illustration. Just as listeners look up attentively when a speaker begins a speech with a story, all readers are engaged by an anecdote. If the story opens dramatically, the involvement of the reader is assured. In the following example, from Brent Staples's essay "Black Men and Public Space" (p. 181), the author initially misleads the reader into thinking the writer has malicious intentions—exactly the misconception that is the subject matter of his essay.

> My first victim was a woman—white, well dressed, probably in her early twenties. I came upon her late one evening on a deserted street in Hyde Park, a relatively affluent neighborhood in an otherwise mean, impoverished section of Chicago. As I swung onto the avenue behind her, there seemed to be a discreet, uninflammatory distance between us. Not so. She cast back a worried glance. To her, the youngish black man—a broad six feet two inches with a beard and billowing hair, both hands shoved into the pockets of a bulky military jacket—seemed menacingly close. After a few more quick glimpses, she picked up her pace and was soon running in earnest. Within seconds she disappeared into a cross street.

Definition.   Often the definition of a term is a necessary element of an essay, and a definition may interest the reader in the subject (if the writer does not resort to that boring and cliché opener, "According to the dictionary . . ."). Sometimes the term may be unfamiliar, but often the term might be well known but the meanings may vary according to each reader. Recognizing these multiple meanings in "O.K., So I'm Fat" (p. 201), Neil Steinberg clarifies *his* definition of "fat" by using humor and by negation—explaining what "fat" does not mean.

> Some people are no doubt fat because of glandular disorders or the wrath of an angry God. I am not one of those people. I am fat because I eat a lot. Since fat people are held in such low regard, I should immediately point out that I am not that fat. Not fat in the Chinese Buddha, spilling-out-of-the-airplane-seat sense. The neighborhood kids don't skip behind me in the street, banging tin cans together and singing derisive songs. Not yet, anyway.

Deliberate Contradiction.   Sometimes a writer may start a paper with a view or statement that will be contradicted or contrasted with the subject matter of the essay. In his essay "Makes Learning Fun" (p. 247), Clifford Stoll does just that in an introduction that starts:

> Technology promises shortcuts to higher grades and painless learning. Today's edutainment software comes shrink-wrapped in computing's magic mantra: "Makes Learning Fun." . . . Just one problem. It's a lie.

Statistic or Startling Fact or Idea.   An essay that starts with a dramatic statistic or idea engages the reader at once. Notice how the following introduction from William F. Harrison's "Why Stop Smoking? Let's Get Clinical" (p. 347) uses statistics to engage (or frighten) the reader.

> Most of us in medicine now accept that tobacco is associated with major health consequences and constitutes the No. 1 health problem in this country.

What smokers have not yet come to terms with is that if they continue smoking, the probability of developing one or more of the major complications of smoking is 100 percent. It absolutely will happen. They will develop chronic bronchitis, laryngitis, pharyngitis, sinusitis and some degree of emphysema.

Mixture of Methods. Many well-crafted introductions combine the approaches described above. For example, in the introductory paragraph of "The Color of Love" (p. 16), Danzy Senna employs narration, description, comparison-contrast, illustration, allusion, definition, a startling idea, and deliberate contradiction to dramatize the differences between the writer and her grandmother.

We had this much in common: We were both women, and we were both writers. But we were as different as two people can be and still exist in the same family. She was ancient—as white and dusty as chalk—and spent her days seated in a velvet armchair, passing judgments on the world below. She still believed in noble bloodlines; my blood had been mixed at conception. I believed there was no such thing as nobility or class or lineage, only systems designed to keep some people up in the big house and others outside, in the cold.

Writing Conclusions

The conclusion of an essay should give the reader a feeling of completion or satisfaction. Ideally, the conclusion will fit like the lid on a box. You might return to your introduction and thesis, select key images or phrases that you used, and reflect them in your conclusion. This return to the start of the paper assures your reader that all aspects of your assertion have been met in the essay. Furthermore, the purpose of your paper—to express, inform, analyze, or persuade—should be consistent with the tone and stance of your conclusion. If your aim has been to persuade your reader, your conclusion needs to be more forceful than if you only had intended to inform your reader. An effective conclusion echoes the tone of the introduction without merely repeating the exact words of the thesis (a type of conclusion that is contrived and dull). Although your ending may be weakened by "tacking on" a new topic or concept without sufficient explanation and development, you may want to suggest that there is some broader issue to think about, or some additional goal that might be achieved if the situation you have discussed were satisfied.

For his conclusion to the essay "Don't Let Stereotypes Warp Your Judgments" (p. 470), Robert Heilbroner returns to the images of the pictures in our mind, the ideas stirred by the questions he had asked earlier in his introduction:

Most of the time, when we type-cast the world, we are not in fact generalizing about people at all. We are only revealing the embarrassing facts about the pictures that hang in the gallery of stereotypes in our own heads.

Another effective conclusion appears in Marcus Mabry's "Living in Two Worlds" (p. 109). Mabry refers to his opening line describing the sign that proclaims "We built a proud new feeling." Throughout his essay, he contrasts the "two universes" of his home and school environments. Now in his conclusion, he creates the phrase that will also be the title of his essay:

> Somewhere in the midst of all that misery, my family has built, within me, "a proud feeling." As I travel between the two worlds, it becomes harder to remember just how proud I should be—not just because of where I have come from and where I am going, but because of where they are. The fact that they survive in the world in which they live is something to be very proud of, indeed. It inspires within me a sense of tenacity and accomplishment that I hope every college graduate will someday possess.

Mabry's conclusion also reflects his broader thoughts about pride, not only about his pride in where he is headed but also his pride in his family's ability to survive. He brings his reader a sense of hope and inspiration and gives his essay closure.

The student papers in this book also show effective techniques in their conclusions. Rachel, who wrote the paper on eating disorders (pp. 387–390), was advised by her instructor to strengthen the conclusion of her rough draft (pp. 361–362) by returning to the images and key words of her introduction. Rachel did this in her final paper. She was also able to echo the title of a source that she used in her essay. The following part of her conclusion mirrors her introduction:

> It is time to protest the images of bikini-clad models parading before us and demand images that reflect the emotional and intellectual scope and diversity among women in our society. With some of our best and brightest dying among us, there is no in-between position anymore. Those who make the images will only change when those of us who support them stop buying products and stop tuning in on programs that continue to impose "bodily harm" on us.

Shannon Paaske also returned to her introduction to conclude her research paper on the disabled, "From Access to Acceptance: Enabling America's Largest Minority." Her thesis and conclusion are printed here, but you can read her entire essay on pages 524–538. Notice that the title of Shannon's essay also is echoed in her conclusion.

Thesis

Although combinations of technological advances, equality-promoting legislation, and increasing media exposure have worked as a collective force in bringing about improvements in the lives of the people who make up what is sometimes termed

"America's largest minority" (Davidson 61), ignorance and prejudice continue to plague the disabled.

Conclusion

The legislation and technology that were developed at the end of the twentieth century will continue to make new worlds accessible to the disabled. Ideally, these developments will permit the disabled to be viewed in terms of their capabilities rather than their disabilities. In that climate, the disabled can gain acceptance in the worlds to which they have access. With the steps being taken by government, science, and the media, individuals alone are needed to make the dream of acceptance a reality for the disabled.

Final Tips for Revising

- Give yourself ample time to revise.
- Return to the checklist on p. 385 and reread your draft with each question in mind. Enlist the help of a peer, if you can.
- Reread your essay to see if your essay has or needs appropriate transitions.
- Reconsider your title to see if you can lighten and tighten it with humor, wordplay, and brevity.
- Revise the opening of your introduction by employing one of these hooks: a relevant quotation, vivid description, startling fact or idea, deliberate contradiction, compelling question, anecdote, definition, or a mixture of these methods.
- Develop your introduction so it flows smoothly from your opening hook to your thesis.
- Revise your conclusion to reflect a key word, image, or answer to a question posed in your introduction.
- Edit your conclusion to echo but not repeat the exact wording of your thesis.
- Consider your reader. Have you brought a sense of significant closure to your paper? Proofread carefully for grammar, punctuation, and spelling errors. Don't rely only on spellcheck.

You have been considering your reader and the aim of your paper throughout as you have rewritten your rough drafts, verified the logic of your organization, strengthened the introduction and conclusion, and edited for surface errors. These essential revision strategies can help you convince your readers that your essays are worth their time and consideration—and may inspire them, too.

Chapter 10

Writing to Persuade

Prevalence of Persuasion

Nearly all essays aim to persuade readers of the writer's view. Whether the writing is humorous, serious, personal, informative, or expressive, all essays have a point to make and a reader to convince. Essays that deal with issues and controversies are deliberately designed to sway readers to one view or another. In this textbook, many authors aim to persuade readers—for example, whether computer-centered classrooms are an advantage or disadvantage or whether reality TV benefits or harms the participants. Writers focusing on these topics intend to demonstrate that their views are sound, and they may even want to promote change.

But even writing that does not appear issue-driven—for example, a first-person account—often aims to convince readers. For example, in this text one author shows that online romances can seldom hold up in real time. Another writer demonstrates that even a migrant farm worker can become a neurosurgeon; a third illustrates how group pressure can cause us to respond differently than we would if we were alone. These accounts may not have an explicit thesis, but they often have an implicit aim—to prompt the reader to reconsider choices or expectations, to help people realize their potential, or to be wary of social pressure.

In fact, any type of essay may have an argument embedded within. When you write a narrative, for example, your aim may be to promote a change of thinking or behavior in your reader. You may be assigned to write an evaluative response to an essay, but you will inevitably need to persuade readers that the author's conclusions do or do not reflect your own observations.

When analyzing a person's life story, you may also be persuading readers that the individual made wise or flawed decisions. In a research-based essay, you may find yourself convincing your reader, for example, that the government should increase funding for research on autism. Even when you write an analysis of a poem, you will be convincing readers that your perceptions and interpretations are correct. All of these persuasive papers, to one degree or another, involve argument.

Persuasion as Argument

The term "argument" often conjures up images of people shouting at each other, disagreeing and disputing others' views, but a written argument does not need to be contentious and certainly not combative. In fact, an aggressive attack and tone *may* persuade the reader—to actually stop reading! A good argument depends on sound reasoning and support to persuade readers to renew their commitment to a certain perspective, to reconsider their views, or to change their course of action. Before any readers will be convinced, they will require sufficient evidence—support that the writer needs to provide and analyze.

Convincing others that your beliefs and perspectives are worth understanding, and perhaps even supporting, can be a definite challenge. Sometimes you will need to anticipate your readers' preconceptions and to counter their convictions in order to get them to modify their beliefs or change their behavior. Persuasion is a part of many writing situations, and convincing readers that a certain assertion or opinion is supportable is the heart of argument.

The Doubting and Believing Games

Peter Elbow, respected professor and writer on composition and rhetoric, encourages writers to reconsider their understanding of the process of argument. In his paper "The Believing Game—Methodological Believing," delivered at a college composition and communication conference (CCCC) in 2008, Elbow contends that it is unfortunate that skepticism and doubt have been synonymous with critical thinking. Writers and readers assume that by doubting others' ideas, "we can discover hidden contradictions, bad reasoning, or other weaknesses" (Elbow 1). Indeed, finding weaknesses in an argument is a skill often emphasized in writing classrooms because poor reasoning creates flawed and unconvincing papers. Elbow acknowledges that the "doubting game . . . develops an indispensable dimension of intelligence or rationality" (7) needed to evaluate arguments. But while Elbow recognizes the value of "the doubting game," he feels that "the believing game," a more positive approach to considering arguments, has been nearly ignored in the teaching of critical thinking. He argues that we also need to value "the believing game—the disciplined practice of trying to be as welcoming or accepting as possible to every idea we encounter" (1). This acceptance does not mean that Elbow doesn't want students to think critically and write well-reasoned, convincing papers. But Elbow asserts that "we cannot see what's good in someone else's idea (or in our own!) till we work at believing it" (2). He urges students to strive to embrace unfamiliar ideas, silence skepticism, and try to get *inside* someone else's view. We find that Peter Elbow raises important questions about the nature of critical thinking and verifies that both doubting *and* believing are valuable tools in understanding arguments. Throughout *Between Worlds*, our readings, questions, and assignments have encouraged you to play the believing game—to value "what's good in someone else's ideas" even if the ideas seem unfashionable or alien to your own views. Elbow's point is clear: "The believing game suggests modes of writing persuasively and analytically that are nonadversarial" (9)—that is, not combative or hostile. We support Elbow's advice while we also encourage you to develop sound arguments and to avoid fallacious reasoning. And we urge you to play the believing game as energetically as you play the doubting game.

When to Use Argument

Argument is frequently a part of all types of essay writing. Even when a particular method or mode of development is assigned, you may still be writing persuasively even if you are not writing an actual argument. For example, if you are attempting to convince a reader that one course of action is superior to another, you may be developing your essay using comparison-contrast, but you are, nevertheless, writing an argument. If you are assigned a cause-and-effect essay, you may be arguing that a particular behavior or event caused a certain consequence. When you are assigned an analysis of a poem or of a character in a story, you will be trying to convince readers of the validity of your interpretations. In all cases, your thinking and writing will be stronger if you remain open to multiple perspectives—play the believing game—even as you analyze and critique the reasoning in your own and others' work—play the doubting game.

Brainstorming for an Argument

When you are assigned a topic and begin brainstorming for ideas and feelings, record your uncensored responses as you freewrite, list, or cluster ideas. This unrestricted prewriting—embracing the believing game—should help you discover what you know about your subject and what you will need to find out. Here are some specific questions to consider as you prepare a persuasive essay:

- What do you already know about this issue? List everything that comes to mind.
- What are your feelings about this subject and why do you feel this way? Freewriting in your journal may help here.
- Do you have any biases about this subject that block you, even tentatively, from embracing another's views—and playing the believing game?

- What questions do you have about this subject? Read for answers in your textbook and online.

- How has this reading affected your opinions or perceptions of this issue? Jot down meaningful lines and respond to these quotations in your journal.

- What is your view or position on the controversy? How might your stance inform your aim or purpose in the paper?

- Given this aim, what is a possible claim or point that you can support? Write down this working thesis.

- Determine if your goal is to persuade your readers to agree with your position—or to both agree and to act. Will you have an implied or a clearly expressed argument?

- Would it help you to compare and contrast opposing points? Will you need to define a concept as a key part of your argument? Should you focus on the causes and effects of a certain problem? (If your brainstorming shows that any of these methods of development would be helpful, see Chapter 11, pp. 444–460.)

Explicit and Implicit Arguments

If, in your brainstorming, you have discovered a clear aim—to overtly alter your readers' view—and if your claim is directly stated, you have an explicit argument and a thesis that you will need to support. On the other hand, if convincing your reader is secondary to your aim to express, entertain, inform, or analyze, then you are probably developing an implicit argument. An analysis of two essays in this text may help you see this distinction between an explicit and implicit argument

If you have not yet read these two essays, you will want to read Jennifer Coleman's "Discrimination at Large" (p. 198) and Neil Steinberg's "O.K., So I'm Fat" (p. 201). Although these writers address the same topic—what it means to be heavy in a culture that reveres thinness—their essays are quite different.

An Explicit Argument

Coleman's argument is explicit: Her aim is to convince readers that discrimination because of weight is unjust and cannot be tolerated. This claim or thesis is explicitly stated at the end of her essay. In "O.K., So I'm Fat," Neil Steinberg's argument is implicit: His aim is to express his annoyance and his claim is that some thin people have superior attitudes that make him feel uncomfortable. His stance is softer because his argument is implicit; he is not expecting people to reform. However, Coleman *is* demanding such a change.

In "Discrimination at Large," Jennifer Coleman asserts that discrimination against heavy people, in jokes and attitudes, is as "damaging as any racial or ethnic slur" (200). In this essay, her aim is to persuade the reader that attitudes and actions against "fat people" need to be changed so that ridicule is not acceptable. She argues that people who would not tolerate jibes about someone's race, culture, disability, or sexual orientation often do mock fat people.

Coleman expresses her feelings about being harassed for simply ordering food at a restaurant or appearing on a beach, but her main purpose extends beyond expressing herself. She wants to persuade her reader that discrimination because of weight is as unfair and unacceptable as discrimination because of race and ethnicity. As in any argument, she must present evidence of how she has been harassed. She does this by reporting hostile attacks like "Move your fat ass" and unsolicited comments like "You would really be pretty if you lost weight."

Her aim, to persuade her reader, also requires her to anticipate an opponent who might argue that this harassment is not the same as racial and ethnic slurs because weight, unlike race or ethnicity, can be controlled. The average reader might contend that she should diet and exercise. Coleman anticipates this objection by delineating the details of her acute exercise and dietary phase. She reveals that her pulse, cholesterol level, and respiration were excellent; she was fit but still fat. Finally, she exposes the poor reasoning of those who want her to exercise but still attack her for riding a bike ("Hey lady, where's the seat") or denigrate her by trumpeting like elephants while she is jogging. While she exercises, she has heard people shout, "Lose some weight, you pig." She demands that her reader "go figure," emphasizing how irrational some people are, perhaps even some readers. We think that her primary goal is achieved—to persuade readers with her explicit argument that such harassment should not be tolerated or perpetuated by anyone who is sensitive and reasonable.

An Implicit Argument

In "O.K., So I'm Fat," Neil Steinberg's argument is implicit rather than explicit. What is his aim? We see this as an expressive essay that still persuades readers because Steinberg is revealing how he feels about the "smug superiority" of some thin people (202). He probably does not aim to reform people's behavior, but readers may be persuaded to be more sensitive. He acknowledges that there is "a social stigma" in being fat as well as "medical peril" and some discomfort in "dragging all that excess weight around."

But what he wants to express is that the "ignominy" for fat people is "thin people." This is his implied argument. He cites as evidence "overly familiar office mates" and "wiry panhandlers" who address him as "big guy," and those who slyly refer to fad diets or offer him a Diet Coke, hoping to elevate him to the "sainted ranks of the thin." He cites the "wisp of a woman" hostess with "legs like beef jerky" who prepared "an intensely fattening dessert—Bananas Foster, thick slices of ripe bananas awash in butter and sugar and cinnamon and liqueur accompanied by ice cream" but who didn't have any herself. He notes the smug superiority in her refusal as she "gazes down" on him. Steinberg also mentions that he is not bothered by thin people who don't need to watch what they eat; he is "comfortable, happy, never put off" by them.

Steinberg's purpose is to express his perceptions about the superior attitude of thin people—not to reform his readers' opinions or behavior. Steinberg makes it clear that thin people's attitude toward the obese is not, dare we say, a weighty subject. In both Coleman's and Steinberg's essays, each writer's purpose or aim is evident in the explicit or implied thesis or central claim of the essay.

Arguments and Proposals

A distinction can be made between two types of writing that attempt to convince readers to reconsider their views and beliefs:

An *argument* employs logic to reason a point and get the reader to think.

A *proposal* employs logic to influence others and get the reader to think and act.

Although these types of writing often overlap, some assignments seem to fit more in one category than the other. If you are asked to analyze an essay and argue for or against the writer's views, your essay will involve *argumentation*. You will be expected to focus on a thesis that can provoke the reader's thoughts and to use supporting evidence that is logically presented and carefully analyzed.

If you are asked to offer a solution to a problem or to persuade others to modify or change their behavior, your essay will need to include a *proposal* in addition to argumentation. You will be expected to create a thesis that elicits a response. Therefore you will also need to suggest a reasonable plan of action or activities for your reader.

Sound Reasoning: Balancing Logos, Pathos, and Ethos

Sound reasoning is the backbone of all convincing arguments. The ancient Greeks, whose theories of rhetoric and argument continue to influence writers today, understood that arguments have three main components: *logos, pathos,* and *ethos*. A good essay is based on the logic or *logos* of the argument. The *logos* is the reasoning, the work done with the supporting evidence—the facts, data, and statistics collected for support. However, readers often initially respond to an emotional appeal, the *pathos,* of an argument. This emotional appeal is created by stirring the readers' feelings and recognizing their needs and concerns. Finally, the ethics or *ethos* of an argument is the credibility or authority that convinces readers that the writer and his or her ideas and views are reliable and trustworthy. Ideally, the writer's ethos should ensure that the logos is sound and that the pathos is not excessive or manipulative.

Sound reasoning governs and strengthens the entire body of the essay, from the opening to the conclusion. Readers will expect all claims to be carefully explained and supported with evidence and illustrations so that the material is not distorted or misrepresented. Good critical thinkers need to be self-defense experts—on guard against attempts to manipulate their emotions or deceive them with false information or fallacious reasoning. However, good critical thinkers also need to be open to new and often unfashionable ideas, playing the believing game as they read material alien to their own way of thinking.

Audience and Argument

It is critical to identify one's *audience* and to find an approach that would best appeal to that audience. Identification of your readers may include asking these questions:

- Are your readers aware that the problem exists?
- Will your readers find the problem sufficiently important?
- Are your readers affected by the problem?
- Do your readers have special interests or biases that will cause them to resist the information? The argument? The essay?

If the writer can determine whether the readers are likely to be sympathetic, neutral, or hostile, the approach can then be designed to reach that audience.

Argument Introductions

Once you have identified your audience—college comp classmates, film goers, history majors—you will be able to design your introduction to appeal to those readers. If you know their interests and backgrounds, you can write your opening with this background in mind. If you realize that your readers may be hostile or indifferent to your views, you know that you need to work hard to appeal to them and convince them of your perspective. They will not overlook your flawed logic, irrelevant or insufficient examples, or sweeping generalizations and assumptions. In fact, they will be seeking reasons to dismiss your views, so you don't want to make it easy for them to reject your argument.

In fact, even if you suspect that your audience may be sympathetic to your aim and may agree with you, it is wise to write your essay with your most adamant opponent in mind so that your argument is as strong as you can make it. You will want to reason clearly, support claims fully, and anticipate any objections so you can counter these concerns before your reader even raises the issues.

Because you are attempting to convince readers of a view that may be different from their own, it often helps to begin by illustrating the problem and showing what is wrong with the current thinking or practice on this issue. If there are any myths, misconceptions, or misinformation about your subject, it may help to acknowledge them in your opening as you set out to question or disprove them.

For example, if a writer is arguing that female students in the early grades need greater encouragement to succeed in math and science classes, then it would make sense to first establish the need. The introduction and part of the body of the essay might demonstrate how females are discouraged from pursuing math and science majors and how few women today excel in these fields, even though studies indicate females are no less capable of succeeding in science and math than males are. Providing your readers with the statistical data to verify these findings will help convince both genders. However, the writer needs to be aware that females may be more interested in this topic than males or that readers in non-science fields may need to be persuaded that this subject is relevant.

Organizing and Developing an Argument

An outline can be critical for keeping the argument focused and organized. The outline can be informal, merely an ordered list of points that the writer plans to cover. The outline may also help an instructor follow the argument and detect any flaws or gaps before the essay is actually written. In such cases, a more formal outline may be required. (For an illustration of an informal outline for an argument, see pp. 366–367.)

Preparing Your Argument

Earlier in this chapter we provided questions for use as you brainstorm for an argument (p. 406). We also have previously demonstrated freewriting, listing, and clustering, using students Rachel and Pete (pp. 333–340). These prewriting exercises can be used for all types of essays, and certainly as you prepare for an argument. In fact, Rachel's essay on eating disorders *is* an argument, using her own experiences and a reading from this text for support (pp. 387–390).

These additional suggestions for writing an argument will help to get you started after you have finished prewriting and brainstorming for a topic:

- **Identify your aim** or purpose in writing the essay and determine your stance.
- Search the library databases for articles and books or use reputable internet sites to **increase your knowledge** and understanding of the subject. The more evidence you have, the more convincing your argument will be.
- Focus your topic into a **claim** or **working thesis** that reflects your position on the issue.
- Decide if your argument will contain a **proposal** for a solution to the problem and reflect that in your thesis.
- **Briefly outline** your ideas to correspond with your aim and claim. Consider some possible methods of developing your points: narration, comparison-contrast, cause and effect, and extended definition. See pp. 429–460 for help using these methods.
- **Consider your audience** and determine their biases or lack of information. Experiment with the most effective way to appeal to your readers.

Strategies for Writing an Argument Essay

Once you have brainstormed to discover your specific topic and your position on it, you are ready to draft your essay. As you write to persuade your reader, certain strategies can help strengthen your essay and convince readers to consider your view. Although these points are listed in order, we do not mean to suggest that there is a correct chronology. We know from our own experience and from our students' efforts that writing is a recursive process: We return to many of these strategies again and again before we move ahead to others.

Illustrations from the Text

Each strategy here is illustrated with an example from arguments in this text:

- **In your introduction, help the readers see that there *is* a problem, issue, or need that has prompted your argument.** If your tone is inviting and your wording is clear and accessible, readers may already be open to your views and ready to be persuaded.

  In "Terra Firma: A Journey from Migrant Farm Labor to Neurosurgery" (p. 116), Alfredo Quiñones-Hinojosa knows that his subtitle may intrigue readers because it seems so implausible. His opening lines make the problem clear: "'You will spend the rest of your life working in the fields,' my cousin told me when I arrived in the United States in the mid-1980s. This fate indeed appeared likely: a 19-year-old illegal migrant farm worker, I had no English language skills and no dependable means of support. I had grown up in a small Mexican farming community, where I began working at my father's gas station at the age of 5. Our family was poor and we were subject to the diseases of poverty: my earliest memory is of my infant sister's death from diarrhea when I was 3 years old" (117). Opening with a haunting quotation and then a vivid personal narrative, Quiñones-Hinojosa depicts himself and his family as hard-working and still poor. He is careful to avoid manipulating the reader or appealing only to pity by presenting the facts and showing that he and his family didn't want or expect charity.

- **Make sure that you support your claims with plenty of evidence that you analyze fully.**

  An illustration of this technique is clear in Andres Martin's essay "On Teenagers and Tattoos" (p. 24). Throughout his essay, he uses several case studies of his patients with tattoos to specifically support his thesis: that parents and psychiatrists should not harshly judge teens' tattoos but should see them as a way to better understand teenagers (26–27). Martin includes detailed descriptions and analyses of the symbolism of each patient's tattoos to convince his readers who may only see teenage tattoos as self-mutilation.

- **Anticipate your opponents' objections and counter them.**

In "Why Reality TV Is Good for Us," James Poniewozik not only antici-pates his opponents' objections, but he also spotlights the most adamant complaints against reality programs as he vividly quotes their charges: "Ridiculous and pernicious! Many kinds of cruelty are passed off as enter-tainment!" and "So-called reality television just may be killing the medium!" The author even quotes a self-critical comment of a viewer who watches "The Bachelorette" weekly: "Do we not have anything better to do than to live vicariously through a bunch of fifteen-minute-fame seekers?" (213). He deliberately uses the charges of both critics and fans to underscore his claim that reality TV is a success "because of its audience's contempt for it" (213) and because "it makes us feel tawdry, dirty, cheap" (233). After Poniewozik devotes several paragraphs anticipating and articulating some viewers' con-tempt for reality TV, he asserts his thesis that "reality TV . . . is the best thing to happen to television in several years" (234).

After jolting his readers with this brazen thesis, the author even acknowl-edges his own objections to reality TV. He admits that everyone knows that "there is little reality in reality TV," that some programs are "indefensible," and that "no reality show can match the intelligence and layers of well-constructed fiction" (234). However, even after quoting critics' disdain for reality TV programming and admitting his own objections, Poniewozik argues that reality shows have re-vived interest in network television; created a communal experience for viewers; demonstrated how good humored and resilient most participants are; and influ-enced the creation, techniques, and scripts of successful sitcoms.

- **Clarify your view as you provide reasons and analysis.**

In "Six Rules For Eating Wisely" (p. 214), Michael Pollen presents "a few rules of thumb" to help readers make decisions about food choices. For each rule, he makes a bold assertion—like "Don't eat anything your great-great-great grandmother wouldn't recognize as food" (215), or "Pay no heed to nutritional science or the health claims on packages" (215). He clarifies each view by pro-viding many specific examples to reason his points. He argues that the "epoxy-like tubes of Go-Gurt," or the "preternaturally fresh Twinkies," aren't foods that your great-grandmother would recognize as food—and they aren't. And he pro-vides reasons for ignoring health claims on packages of food by illustrating that science has made mistakes, and the healthiest foods in the supermarket, the produce, come without FDA-approved health claims—unlike some highly processed foods that come replete with suspicious claims.

- **Offer a concession to your opponent that doesn't undermine your argument and then use it as a way to strengthen your position.**

In "Is There a Doctor in the Mouse?" (p. 229), physician Rahul K. Parikh argues that patients should be encouraged to use reliable Internet resources for medical information. Although he opposes physician Scott Haig's criticism of patient Susan's use of the Internet, Parikh concedes that in one regard, "Haig is absolutely right." Parikh agrees with Haig that there is "so much medical information (as well as misinformation) in medicine—and, yes, a lot of it can be Googled—that one major responsibility of an expert is to know what to ignore" (230). But then Parikh argues, "However, in refusing to treat Susan, Haig doesn't seem to have any interest in being that kind of expert" (230). Here Parikh refutes Haig's refusal to guide Susan to good medical Web sites and reasserts his own view that doctors should not only tolerate but direct and encourage a patient's Internet search rather than ignoring or condemning it.

- **Use sound reasoning and avoid logical fallacies.**

  In "My Favorite School Class: Involuntary Servitude" (p. 416), Joe Goodwin writes a convincing argument even though it contains logical fallacies. One fallacy, a hasty generalization, occurs when Goodwin doesn't support his sweeping claim that values are no longer taught in the home. Goodwin adds that the values of respect, patience, and compassion must be "learned elsewhere, since we live in a world in which many families have two parents working long hours every day and many more have just a single parent" (416). Goodwin implies that single parents or families with two working parents are too busy to foster values in their children so the schools need to fulfill this obligation. However, Goodwin ignores the fact that there are plenty of families that disprove his claim. Such a fallacy may weaken Goodwin's argument, but it does not necessarily invalidate the essay if the rest of his support is convincing. You can read Joe Goodwin's complete essay and our analysis of his argument on pp. 416–419.

Conceding and Refuting

Rather than twisting facts or attacking an opponent, it is best to anticipate objections and refute them, logically and directly, before the reader can utter "But . . .". Overlooking or ignoring potential holes in an argument can render it vulnerable to attack. Your argument will not necessarily be weakened if you recognize what may appear to be a weakness in your plan—provided you can show that it doesn't really undermine your argument.

Another effective strategy is to acknowledge conflicting viewpoints and perhaps even admit they have merit, but then show how your solution or viewpoint is still superior. Such a strategy suggests that you are informed, open-minded, and reasonable—qualities that make the reader more receptive to your argument.

Arguments and proposals written by students can be more than mere classroom exercises. They can be sent to newspapers, television stations, corporations, and government boards. Several of the argument assignments in the "Writing from the Text" and "Connecting with Other Texts" sections in Part I involve college-related issues and may be appropriate for the editorial or opinion page of your campus or local newspaper.

Evaluating an Argument

As you read an argument, consider these questions to evaluate its effectiveness:

- Who is the targeted audience, and how does the writer appeal to this audience?
- What is the problem? What is the thesis?
- What are the supporting points?
- What are the strengths of the argument?
- Does the writer anticipate and refute objections?
- What are the weaknesses? Are there any logical fallacies?
- How does the ending bring satisfying closure to the essay?

EXAMPLE: AN ARGUMENT ESSAY

The following argument was written by Joe Goodwin, who was in high school when he published this essay in the "Campus Correspondence" section of the *Los Angeles Times* on August 9, 1992. Goodwin responds to the controversy surrounding a policy mandating community service for junior high through high school students in Maryland schools. In 1997, Maryland made it a graduation requirement that students need to complete seventy-five hours of community service. The numbers in the margin of this essay correspond to the numbers of the explanatory notes on the facing page.

My Favorite School Class: Involuntary Servitude

1 2

3

4

Like most teen-agers, I hate to be told what to do. I chafe at curfews, refuse to patronize restaurants that tell me what to wear, and complain daily about the braces my parents and dentist want me to have. Yet, I look forward to the "forced opportunity" for community service my high school requires. While criticism mounts against Maryland's action in becoming the first state to mandate students to perform 75 hours of community service over seven years, it is well to look at the experience of local school districts that have instituted similar programs.

5a

For five years, every student at the Concord-Carlisle Regional High School in Massachusetts has been required to perform 40 hours of community service in order to graduate. Conventional wisdom would have us believe that this would be an especially burdensome task, perhaps an impossible one, for students who hold outside paying jobs. But the graduation requirement may be satisfied within the school by working as teacher's aides, library assistants, or tutors. Outside school, the requirement may be met by working at hospitals, nursing homes, senior citizens' centers, soup kitchens, or for the town's park service or recreational department.

5b

To be sure, it would be wonderful if students volunteered such service. But the great benefit of the mandated program is the responsibility it places on the school to work with community leaders to locate the places where students can best make a solid contribution. It is unrealistic to expect students to roam from place to place in search of service opportunities. Once the arrangements for those opportunities are made, the student needs only to decide which kind of service best fits his or her personality.

5c

6

Those who oppose the community-service mandate fear it will interfere with the regular school curriculum. But what more important class can a student take than one that teaches values and responsibility? Clearly it is better to be helping the elderly and homeless rather than listening to long lectures about their plight.

5d

7

Some say that schools should not be in the business of fostering civic concerns among its youth. But what more important role can a school play than in shaping values—respect for the elderly, patience for those younger, compassion for those less fortunate—among its young? These and related values used to be taught in the home. Now, they must be learned elsewhere, since we live in a world in which many families have two parents working long hours every day and many more have just a single parent.

Explanatory Notes for the Argument Essay

The numbers on these explanatory notes correspond to the numbers in the margin of the argument essay.

1. *Audience:* Goodwin's audience is students who might resist community service, or their parents who might not want the school day lengthened with extra work, or taxpayers or school boards who might be voting on whether to institute the compulsory service requirement in their communities.

2. *Appeal:* Goodwin appeals to his audience by identifying himself as a typical teenager who "hate[s] to be told what to do." He creates an image of himself as a teen who resents curfews, dress codes, and wearing braces.

3. *Thesis:* Goodwin's thesis is that in spite of his resistance to being told what to do, he sees a program of mandatory community service as a valuable "forced opportunity" for students.

4. *Problem:* Goodwin identifies the problem as those who resist mandatory community service.

5. *Objections/refutations:* Goodwin anticipates objections and refutes them:

    a. Doing community service is a burden for students who hold outside paying jobs. (Students can choose to work on campus or off.)

    b. Students should volunteer for such service. (He concedes that they should volunteer but believes that it is unrealistic to expect students to search for such opportunities on their own.)

    c. Community service will interfere with regular curriculum. (He believes that community service is as important as any class and that it teaches students to apply what they are learning in the classroom.)

    d. Schools should not be in the business of fostering civic concerns among students. (He argues that schools must help shape values, especially since many children do not get such training at home.)

    Logical fallacy: Goodwin's point about values is a good one, but he has a logical fallacy: *hasty generalization.* He claims that values "used to be taught in the home" and that homes with two parents working or with single parents are not teaching values. These are assumptions Goodwin can't support. He could have written "now values *may* need to be learned elsewhere" because *some* working or single parents *aren't always* available to teach values or reinforce the ones they have taught. (See pp. 419–420)

6. *Support:* Goodwin supports his argument by insisting that it is better to be working directly with the elderly rather than reading about or hearing lectures about their "plight."

7. *Support:* Goodwin supports his argument by asserting that the school should do what many homes are not doing—teaching and reinforcing the

8   Sociologists and journalists decry the decline of American society and the disintegration of the American family. Yet, when those who find pleasure in lecturing about this decline are faced with a solution that would help strengthen society, they fall back on the past. It is this negative attitude toward change that has caused the country to reach the point of such neglect.

9   Today, the passion and commitment that marked my parents' generation—the 1960s—is gone, replaced by an ominous silence. I listen to my parents talk of their experiences with the civil-rights movement, the sit-ins, the war on poverty, and I am impatient for the time when my own generation is similarly involved in the great public events of our day. Although 40 hours of community service is not very much, it is a beginning.

My interest in community service was heightened last spring. While on a class trip to the Science Museum in Boston, a group of students in my 8th-grade class were involved in an altercation with another group of students from a largely black school in Roxbury, a neighborhood near downtown. Taunts were exchanged, a fight broke out. It was unsettling.

10   The following week, teachers from both schools arranged a daylong meeting of a representative sampling of students at each school. The discussion that resulted was an extraordinary experience. As I listened to black students describe their stereotypes of whites in the suburbs, as I heard one black girl say she cried herself to sleep the night of the fight in fear and frustration that racial relations would never improve, I realized how far America was from the ideals of equality and justice. If community service could help to bridge the gap between ideal and reality, I will feel happy indeed.

Explanatory Notes *(continued)*

values "of respect for the elderly, patience for those younger, compassion for those less fortunate."

8. *Clarification:* Goodwin clarifies the problem: Weak values contribute to the "decline of American society" and "the disintegration of the American family" and yet many people resist a program that could strengthen values.

9. *Support:* Goodwin supports his argument by arguing that the "passion and commitment" of his parents' generation, sadly lacking in youth today, might be reinvigorated by community service.

10. *Logical fallacy:* Goodwin attempts to support his argument with a personal anecdote about a class trip to an inner-city museum. In his mind, his discovery on the trip supports the need for community service programs. However, his reasoning is not clear to the reader. Goodwin makes a leap that the reader can't comprehend. Goodwin may have meant that "community service could move students into worlds they don't routinely inhabit and could bridge communication gaps." If he had articulated the connection between the racial tension on the class trip and community service, he would have had a stronger conclusion to his argument. (See below.)

Throughout his essay, Goodwin's tone is restrained and reasonable. His writing reflects a healthy balance between idealism (free choice) and realism (mandatory service). He might have been tempted to resort to name-calling or offensive attacks, but instead he relies on examples and explanations to support his case.

Avoiding Logical Fallacies

Often an argument may be persuasive but still illogical. If a claim has no basis or foundation in reason, a *logical fallacy* will result, discrediting the argument and eroding the reader's trust. By recognizing these fallacies in others' arguments and avoiding them in your own writing, you can become a more effective critical thinker. Let's look at some of the most common types of logical fallacies, listed in alphabetical order:

- *Appeal to false authority:* Uses a person or celebrity who does not have expertise in that area to try and sway the reader. ("Brad Pitt wears Gap jeans so they must be well made.")

- *Appeal to fear:* Attempts to convince by implicitly threatening the audience but not offering any logical support for the fear. ("Unless you major in business, you will end up unemployed.")

- *Appeal to pity:* Occurs when an argument appeals solely to our emotions rather than our intellect or reasoning. ("If I don't receive an 'A' in your course, professor, I won't get into law school.")

- *Bandwagon appeal:* Suggests that "everyone is doing this—why don't you?" This pressures the reader to conform whether or not the view or action seems logical or right. ("All good teachers are using PowerPoint presentations.")

- *Begging the question (circular reasoning):* Does not prove anything because it simply restates the assertion. ("Instructors who teach writing are better teachers because good instructors teach writing.")

- *False analogy:* Compares two things that aren't really comparable and therefore results in a false conclusion. ("If developmental math classes can be taught effectively in a large lecture hall, developmental English classes can be, too.")

- *False cause:* Assumes a cause-effect relationship between two events just because one precedes another. It claims a causal relationship solely on the basis of a chronological relationship. ("Because Joe got a new laptop this semester, he earned an "A" in both his English and math classes.")

- *False dilemma (either/or argument):* Sets up a false black-and-white dilemma, assuming that a particular viewpoint or course of action can have only two diametrically opposed outcomes. ("College professors either require writing assignments or they are poor teachers.")

- *Hasty generalization:* Consists of drawing a broad conclusion from a few unrepresentative generalizations ("Math teachers use Scantron tests; math teachers don't teach students to think critically.")

- *Personal or "ad hominem" ("against the man") attacks; name-calling:* Whether intentional or not, these slurs are often associated with advertisers and politicians, whose careers may depend on their power to manipulate and mislead the public. Calling someone a "leftist radical" or a "warmonger" is intended to get the audience to respond emotionally to a prejudice rather than to think rationally about an issue. Often these attacks are designed to divert attention from the issue to the opponent's personal traits or associations that may be irrelevant. ("Why should we even consider an opinion from The *New York Times*? All *Times* writers are liberals.")

- *Unqualified generalization:* Makes too broad a claim that cannot be proven but requires qualifiers such as words like "often," "seldom," "most," "may," and "could." ("All college freshmen are overwhelmed by the heavy reading assignments.")

- *Slippery slope or the domino theory (or ripple effect):* Purports that if a certain action is taken, it will necessarily cause other extreme results, whether or not the evidence supports these conclusions. ("If students use the Internet for research, they will be tempted to plagiarize and will end up failing all of their classes.")

PRACTICING WRITING ARGUMENT ESSAYS

Write an essay to convince your reader of one of the following assertions. The page numbers in parenthesis refer to readings in the text.

1. The lyrics in contemporary music reflect (or incite) societal tension.

2. Reality television is or is not compelling programming (p. 233 and p. 239).

3. Football should or should not be played in high school (p. 85).

4. The burka does or does not limit the world's perception of the woman who wears it (p. 129).

5. Rita should (or should not) continue her relationship with Marc (p. 71).

6. Internet dating is or is not a reliable way to meet a mate (p. 51).

 ## Final Tips for Argument Essays

- **Brainstorm for a topic** and freewrite or list what you already know about this subject.

- Read more about your subject. As you **gather information**, stay open to new ideas—play the believing game. By suspending judgment, you will be able to understand, and perhaps value alternative views.

- Recognize your **purpose**: argument or proposal for action.

- **Identify your readers**, consider their perspective, and prepare your appeal. Avoid insulting or attacking them.

- Word your **thesis** carefully to provoke thought or action.

- **Outline** your argument so it is focused and organized.

- **Support all claims** with convincing evidence and reasoned analysis.

- **Anticipate objections** and differing viewpoints, and show why your argument is stronger even if the others have some merit.

- Guard against **logical fallacies**; they weaken any argument.

- Make sure your conclusion brings satisfying **closure** to your argument. Avoid tacking on any new points.

Chapter 11

Methods for Developing Essays

Your instructor may ask you to write a paper using a particular method of development for presenting your support, such as a narrative or a comparison-contrast study. You may be assigned an argument essay, which is fully covered in Chapter 10, but you may find yourself using one of the following methods to structure your argument. If your instructor doesn't assign a particular type of paper, then your purpose for writing will influence the methods of development you choose. To help you better understand how these types of support differ from one another, we have identified the following models for discussion: summary, narration, evaluative response, definition, cause and effect, comparison-contrast, and, in Chapter 12, analysis. By examining these methods in isolation, we do not mean to suggest that all paper topics will fit precisely into one of these categories. Nothing could be further from our experience as students, teachers, and writers.

You may recall that Rachel's essay "Dieting Daze" (p. 387) incorporates narrative, definition, description, and comparison-contrast in a problem analysis paper that argues for a change. These multiple approaches are ideal complements, and together they helped Rachel meet her goal. Her purpose was to convince her reader that advertisers need to be more responsible for the body images they promote.

Combining Multiple Methods

Because you may be asked to develop a paper with a single and particular strategy, we have included in this chapter models of the methods most often assigned. But because we believe that most essays are developed with combined methods, we start our discussion with Dan Neil's "If the Genes Fit" (p. 178), an essay that combines multiple development techniques.

Neil's intention is to argue that homosexuality is inborn and not a choice and that those who resist this reality are fighting a battle that they "cannot hope to win." Neil's argument relies on his use of multiple methods of development: narration, summary, comparison-contrast, definition, analysis, and cause and effect. Let's now look at how each method contributes to his argument.

Analyzing Mixed Methods

Narration: To engage his reader, Neil opens his essay with his personal history that he "did not decide to be straight, never came to a sexually-oriented fork in the road to choose the road more traveled" (178). His account of his firsthand experience is heightened by his humorous quip that he was "never indoctrinated by anyone advancing a heterosexual agenda. Talk about coals to Newcastle" (178). In this final allusion, Neil acknowledges that heterosexuals walk "the road more traveled" and that it is as unnecessary to be "indoctrinated" to this sexual orientation as it would be to bring coal to an area that mines it. His use of narration is also evident when he recounts the retort of his good friend Brad. Neil wonders if Brad's sexual orientation might be "something environmental, something learned," to which Brad replies, "Yeah, right . . . I read a book on it when I was 3 years old" (178). The use of narration and humor engages readers before the author details scientific information that might otherwise turn off the general reader.

Summary: Neil succinctly summarizes the "vignettes of self-discovery and disclosure" that fill the book *When I Knew,* a collection of stories from gays and lesbians who describe their epiphanies, when they realized that "they belonged in the same-sex sandbox" (178). These summarized accounts are funny ("No you're not [lesbian], you're Romanian") and poignant (the boy playing hopscotch and overhearing his father's friend say, "I think you got a problem"). To support his argument, Neil also summarizes three articles from scientific journals: one describing how gene modification alters sexual orientation in fruit flies; another illustrating that gay men respond to the scent of males just as heterosexual women do; and another documenting "hundreds of examples of homosexual behavior in the animal kingdom" (179). These succinct summaries of scientific studies substantiate Neil's claim that homosexuality is genetic, not learned behavior.

Definition: Neil not only uses definition to explain scientific terms but, more fundamentally, to drive home his argument. Because he is reporting on scientific information, Neil does need to define certain terms for the average reader. For example, he reports the study of brain scans that demonstrate "that gay males react to male sweat pheromones the same way heterosexual women do" (179). Then he defines the word "pheromones—scent chemicals that govern sexual behavior in many species" (179). Neil also defines "gay gene," a term that he attributes to geneticist Dean Hamer and journalist Peter Copeland, as shorthand for the evidence that sexual orientation is inborn. However, Neil's use of definition is not limited to scientific terms but is an integral part of his argument. When he defines "the campaign to marginalize and criminalize gays" as "the bigoted pogrom that it is" (180), he is clearly opposing the "rabidly anti-gay Focus on the Family" organization (180). Ultimately, the entire piece relies on definition to argue for the understanding and acceptance of homosexuality as innate and natural behavior.

Comparison-contrast: Although "If the Genes Fit" does not reflect characteristic comparison-contrast form (see pp. 454–460), Neil's argument is based on the initial *contrast* between heterosexuals' and homosexuals' awareness of their sexual orientation and the deeper *comparison* that all humans are genetically wired for sexual preference. Neil contends that for a heterosexual there is no moment of discovery: "It never dawned on me that I was straight. I just was" (179). Although heterosexuals don't have "Eureka! moments" but simply intuit that they are part of a statistical majority, Neil observes, "For gays and lesbians, it seems, there is always a moment when they realize that what they want isn't officially sanctioned" (179). But more significantly, the heart of Neil's argument is based on comparison—that both heterosexuals and homosexuals inherently "know, at the core of their self-conception that they were born straight or gay" (180). Because sexual orientation has a genetic foundation, Neil emphasizes the commonality, the comparison, of all humans' response to their genetic wiring.

Analysis: In addition to providing numerous anecdotal and scientific examples, Neil analyzes the material he incorporates. For example, when he cites the realization of sexual self-awareness that gays and lesbians have, he refers to that "cognitive moment that marks a cleaving away from the larger heterosexual world," and he describes that cleaving away as "the opening of an otherness, like jets peeling off in the missing-man formation" (179). In this striking simile, Neil captures the experience of homosexuals and helps the reader understand the separation and "otherness" that homosexuals may feel as they move away from the traditional pattern.

Cause and Effect: The support for Neil's thesis is dependent on cause and effect reasoning. Neil summarizes scientific studies revealing that "homosexuality is a natural variation in the human genome" and that homosexuality is genetically based. These are the causes that lead him to the effect—his conclusion that "homosexuals are not guilty of anything except being human" (180). Further, Neil contends that because homosexuality is natural, then the appropriate effect should be social acceptance not repudiation. Therefore, "the campaign to marginalize and criminalize gays is revealed as the bigoted pogrom that it is" (180). His argument relies on cause and effect reasoning: The condemnation of homosexuality is irrational and denies scientific evidence.

Why This Analysis?

The purpose of this analysis of "If the Genes Fit" (178) is to encourage you to recognize the multiple modes and devices that professional writers use to engage and inform their readers. Employing these devices will improve your writing. By practicing the single-development assignments given in the "Writing from the Text" topics described in Part I, you will learn to employ multiple methods confidently to write an appealing and convincing paper. Let's now look at each strategy in greater detail.

SUMMARY

Summarizing is an important skill that demonstrates your ability to understand both the content of the reading and the way the material is arranged. A summary demonstrates your ability to read, comprehend, and write. Summaries of assigned readings in any class can become particularly useful personal learning tools, serving as study guides for examinations. But you may be asked in some classes—from undergraduate through graduate studies—to submit summaries to show that you have read and understood journal articles, essays, or books. Your purpose in writing a summary is to give your audience a condensed but complete view of the original work. In a sense, you are saving your reader the time and effort of reading the original—if your summary is accurate!

Organizing and Developing a Summary

The following steps can be used to summarize assignments in any class—from psychology, education, and philosophy to political science and English. These same steps may also be the first you take if you are asked to summarize an essay and then evaluate it, an assignment frequently given in college courses.

1. Read the work actively, marking directly on the copy (if possible) the obvious divisions or sections within the text. Underline the thesis, if one is explicitly stated, as well as any key points or examples you see as you read.

2. Reread the text. On a separate sheet of paper, write a few sentences of summary (combining paraphrased and quoted material) for each section of the work that you have marked in the margins of the original.

3. Write the author's thesis or what you infer to be the central assertion of the entire essay. You may write a general thesis or one that forecasts the points the writer will use to support the assertion.

4. Write a draft that starts with the thesis, even if the writer delayed the central assertion of the work. Continue the draft with the sentence summaries that you wrote for each of the sections of the text. Use the full name of the author of the work once, then use only his or her last name in other places in your summary. It is important to use the writer's name so that your reader is reminded who had the ideas in the original text.

5. Reread your draft to be sure of the following:
   • Your thesis reflects the author's *full* point.
   • Each section of your summary has its own assertion (or topic sentence) and sufficient support from the original.
   • Your summary parallels the original in tone and order.
   • Your summary is both objective and complete. *Objective* means that none of your feelings about the text are reflected in statements or tone. *Complete* means that you have not left out any sections of the original.

6. Reread your summary to be certain that you used quotation marks around any key words or phrases that you have taken from the text. Most of the summary should be in your own words, but a particularly memorable phrase or expression will resist paraphrasing. You will want to include this memorable language in your summary within quotation marks. Be certain that the title of the work that you are summarizing is either in quotation marks (for short works) or italics (for longer works). See p. 595. Check for spelling, mechanical errors, and sentence correctness. Insert necessary transition words and phrases prior to your final writing.

7. Unlike an essay that you have written, a summary of someone else's work does not need a conclusion. End your summary with the author's final point.

STUDENT EXAMPLE: A SUMMARY

The following is an example of one student's summary of Martin Luther King Jr's essay "Three Ways of Meeting Oppression" (p. 279).

Chris Thomas

Professor Blake

English 1A

3 February 2008

A Summary of "Three Ways of Meeting Oppression"

In an excerpt from his book *Stride Toward Freedom,* Dr. Martin Luther King Jr. shows that oppressed people deal with their oppression in three characteristic ways: with acquiescence, violence, or nonviolent resistance. King shows that only a mass movement committed to nonviolent resistance will bring a permanent peace and unite all people.

Although acquiescence—passive acceptance of an unjust system—is the easiest method of dealing with injustice, King insists that it is both morally wrong and the way of the coward. To acquiesce to unfair treatment is to passively condone the behavior of one's oppressors. King says, "Noncooperation with evil is as much a moral obligation as is cooperation with good. The oppressed must never allow the conscience of the oppressor to slumber" (280). King maintains that respect for Negroes and their children will never be won if they do not actively stand against the system.

However, King contends that violence is no solution because it never concerns itself with changing the belief system of oppressors. "In spite of temporary victories, violence never brings permanent peace" (280). Thus King insists that violence is impractical as well as immoral: "The old law of an eye for an eye leaves everybody blind" (280). King states that bitterness and corruption become the legacy of this destructive method that "annihilates" rather than "converts." Thus violence destroys any possibility of brotherhood.

King's principle of nonviolent resistance is his answer to how one must deal with oppression. It is confrontational without resorting to physical aggression. Nonviolent resistance avoids "the extremes and immoralities" of the other two methods while integrating the positive aspects of each. The nonviolent resister, like the person who acquiesces, agrees that violence is wrong, but like the violent resister, he believes that "evil

Thomas 2

must be resisted" (281). King insists that this is the method that oppressed people must use to oppose oppression. It allows neither cowardice nor hatred. "Through nonviolent resistance the Negro will be able to rise to the noble height of opposing the unjust system while loving the perpetrators of the system" (281).

King states that by using nonviolent resistance, the American Negro and other oppressed people can "enlist all men of good will in [the] struggle for equality" (281). He maintains that the struggle is not between people or races but is "a tension between justice and injustice" (281). Only a mass movement of nonviolent resistance will unite people in a community.

Thomas 3

Work Cited

King, Martin Luther, Jr. "Three Ways of Meeting Oppression." *Between Worlds: A Reader, Rhetoric, and Handbook.* Ed. Susan Bachmann and Melinda Barth. 6th ed. New York: Pearson Longman, 2010. 279–281. Print.

Analyzing the Writer's Strategy

Chris begins his summary of the excerpt by identifying its source and the author's complete name. Notice that Chris has the title of the excerpt from King's book in quotation marks while the title of the book is in italics. (See p. 540 for more information about indicating titles.) Although King does not state his thesis explicitly, Chris infers it from King's writing and then states it in the first paragraph. Chris's thesis and paragraphs reflect the three main points of King's essay, so Chris has organized his summary to parallel the original. This is a tremendous help to his readers, who immediately gain an overview of the entire work. The quoted material that he chooses from King's essay reflects what Chris finds most significant in language and specificity to support King's points. Although a different summary writer might choose other quotations to define and illustrate those points, the points and thesis would be nearly the same in each summary.

Summary as Part of a Larger Assignment

Chris's assignment was to write a complete and objective summary of another writer's work. Other assignments might require a response or evaluation of the content in addition to the summary. A character analysis might have an introduction that summarizes the plot of the story in a few sentences. An even more abbreviated use of summary occurs when writers incorporate direct quotation into their essays and need to briefly summarize the context as they introduce the quotation. An argument essay might progress from a short summary of an experiment or survey. Even poetry analysis, which must go beyond summary to be effective, will, nevertheless, employ limited summary of plot or context. The act of summarizing helps you see what you do and do not understand about a reading. Your effective summary then can convince your reader that you comprehend the original well enough to incorporate it into your own points.

 Final Tips for a Summary

- Begin with a statement of the author's complete thesis; include the author's full name.
- Focus each paragraph of your summary to reflect the sections of the original.
- Parallel the original in tone and order.
- Summarize all parts of the essay and be objective.
- Paraphrase most of the essay but incorporate memorable language in quotation marks.
- End with the author's final point; no conclusion is necessary in your summary.

NARRATION

Everyone loves a good story, and most people enjoy telling one. The process of narration—telling a single story or several related ones—is often associated with myths, fairy tales, short stories, and novels, but writers of all types of essays use narrative strategies. The purpose of narration is to use firsthand experiences to engage or entertain, inform, or persuade an audience.

When to Use Narration

Narration can be used to argue a point, define a concept, or reveal a truth. Writers in all disciplines have discovered the power of the narrative. Journalists, historians, sociologists, and essayists often "hook" their readers by opening with a personal anecdote or a human interest story to capture the reader and illustrate points. In fact, many writers use narration to persuade their audiences about a course of action. For example, George Orwell's famous narrative "Shooting an Elephant" (p. 264) is a compelling indictment of imperialism.

Personal narratives can be powerful if they focus on a provocative insight and if details are carefully selected and shaped. Therefore narratives are more than mere diary entries because certain details may be omitted while others may be altered. Narratives may help the writer better understand the significance of an experience, and they help readers "see for themselves." Typically narratives require no library research (our lives are rich with resources for this type of essay), but often writers may choose to supplement personal narration with research and outside sources to move beyond their own experience.

Organizing and Developing a Narrative

Narratives often focus on an incident involving a conflict, whether it is between opposing people, values, or perceptions. The writer then dramatizes the incident so the reader can picture what happened and can hear what was said. Such incidents often involve some aspect of change—a contrast between "before" and "after"—even though the change may be internal (a change in awareness) rather than external or physical.

Narratives do not have to feature life-shattering incidents or have a somber tone. In fact, some superb narratives may be humorous or have a witty or ironic outcome. Many of the best narratives involve profound changes that are not always obvious to others. In the essay "Virtual Love" (p. 56), Meghan Daum relates the story of her romantic email courtship with PFSlider, who penetrates her cynicism and captivates her before she ever meets him in person. Although her essay involves little action, it is memorable because of her self-revelations and her ability to capture real-life disappointments, which, when rendered skillfully, make compelling narratives.

Brainstorming for a Subject

Writers usually need to dig deep to find those buried experiences that have changed their attitudes and views. To help generate ideas, you will find specific narrative assignments at the end of many essays, poems, and stories in the "Writing from the Text" sections in Part I. If your assignment is more general— to write about any significant moment or change in your life—it will help to consider these questions.

- What are my most vivid memories of
    Kindergarten? First grade? Second? Third? Fourth? Fifth?
    Middle school? High school? College?

Team sports?

Learning to laugh at myself?

Overcoming a challenge?

Dealing with failure or illness?

Living in another culture?

Staying with friends or relatives?

Getting a job or working?

Making a costly mistake?

- When did I first

   Try too hard to impress others?

   Feel ashamed (or proud) of myself?

   Stand up to my parents?

   Realize teachers make mistakes?

   Give in to peer pressure?

   Pressure another to go against authority?

   Wish I had different parents?

   Wish someone would disappear from my life?

   Want to change who I am?

- How did one incident show me

   What living between two worlds really means?

   How foolish we can be?

   How it feels to be alone?

   Why conformity isn't always best?

   How stereotyping has affected me?

   How different I am from my sister/brother/friend?

   Why we have a certain law?

   How it feels to live with a physical disability?

   How little I know myself?

Additional Prewriting

If you prefer a visual strategy, you might try clustering or mapping your ideas. One method is to write your topic—for example, "significant changes"—in a circle in the center of your page and then draw spokes outward from it. At the end of each spoke, write down a specific incident that triggered important changes in your life. Write the incident in a box and then use more spokes, radiating from the box, to specify all the changes that resulted. (For an illustration of clustering, see p. 338.)

After you have brainstormed about all possible changes, choose the incident that seems most vivid and worth narrating. Then use another sheet of paper and write about a specific change in a circle at the center and write down all the details that relate to it. After you have recorded all relevant details, you are ready to focus these thoughts and draft your paper.

From Brainstorming to Drafting a Paper

In a narrative essay, the thesis is not always articulated in the essay itself because it can ruin the sense of surprise or discovery often associated with narratives. In fact, an explicit thesis can slow the momentum of the story or spoil the ending. Whether it is articulated or implied, however, a thesis is still essential in order to keep the writer focused and to ensure that the story has a point or insight to share.

Beginning with a Working Thesis. For example, in the student essay that follows, Rebekah Hall-Nakanuma focuses on a time when her sister's illness prompted her own discoveries about family and self. When she began writing about her sister's unexpected illness, Rebekah probably did not begin with a thesis because the insight, focus, or assertion is seldom clear at first. Rebekah had only a topic, her sister's hospitalization. But after she clustered or listed some details, she probably wrote a *working* thesis—a preliminary assertion that could be changed and refined as the narrative took shape.

> **Working Thesis:** My sister's hospitalization took us all by surprise.

Discovering the Real Thesis. Most writers aren't lucky enough to identify a thesis immediately. Often, particularly in a narrative, it takes considerable writing before the best thesis is discovered. Therefore writers typically continue sharpening their thesis throughout the writing process as they, too, discover the point of their story. As Rebekah narrated this experience, it developed as a genuine "between worlds" experience.

> **Discovered Thesis:** The pressure to be perfect can ultimately cause family members to bury or deny very real fears and needs.

Once the thesis becomes clear to the writer, the rough draft needs to be revised so that all the details relate to this new thesis. Notice, however, that the thesis statement does not need to be specified in the actual essay.

The following essay written by student Rebekah Hall-Naganuma describes a family's discovery that "crept in through the cracks" when least expected.

STUDENT EXAMPLE: A NARRATIVE

Rebekah Hall-Naganuma

Professor Anderson

English 1A

20 January 2008

Through the Cracks

It was late at night as I listened to my father's low rumble, his face buried in the phone receiver that was nearly resting on his chest. I sat on the edge of the coffee table, straining to understand the words he used. Dad was not easily disturbed. He took the unexpected in stride, so his now hushed tone scared me. I looked around, trying to clarify the moment. Craig's ears were plugged with headphones; his thoughts seemed inside the computer directly in front of him. Mom moved about the kitchen, her lips spread in the thin line that told me she was troubled. Normally voluble, her silence was foreboding.

Finally, Dad ended the conversation. I leaned forward, reaching for some kind of explanation. I watched his face, hoping for a revelation. His face was pale and closed. He didn't return my look but stood up and walked into the kitchen. I followed and stared at Mom's straightened back.

"Heather is in the hospital," Dad said, his voice raspy, as he told us about my older sister. I noticed his Adam's apple dip and heard him swallow. Mom turned around, her posture unnatural. She tilted her head in question. Dad continued, "She had a blackout and checked herself into the hospital. They're running some tests." He watched my mother's face as if to relay a secret message. She didn't get the message.

"What do you mean by 'blackout'?" she asked, with a look of confusion on her face.

"She ended up in Houston somehow and then couldn't remember how she got there." Dad began to sound matter-of-fact, as if this were secondhand local news.

We didn't say anything. I could imagine all sorts of scenarios—disease, drugs, brain tumor. I did not want to believe any of these. Mom began to bustle around the tidy kitchen, smiling and singing. Her cheerfulness, her way of pretending that everything was under control, irritated me.

Naganuma 2

But she had taught us well. We all had an uncanny ability to hide our flaws. Our unconscious goal was to be perfect. We were perfectionists stranded in the never-ending desert of dysfunctionalism. Owning up to the defects in our family would mean giving up on our ideals. It would mean sacrificing the commendation of others. People would always comment on how close we all were and how happy we always looked together. We had developed our skills well in fabricating happiness.

The next day one result was in; it turned out that Heather would be in a psychiatric ward for awhile. Her doctor didn't know for how long. "Craig . . . Rebekah . . . I don't want you talking about your sister's condition with anyone. I think this should stay in the family," Dad cautioned, after sitting us down one day. His eyes were serious, and his hands were folded in front of him, almost as if he were praying.

Mom had decided to fly to Texas, where Heather lived with her husband and children. She was going there, "to straighten things out," she said, as if it were merely a miscommunication that needed clarification. They had both told the church, where dad pastored, that Heather needed help with her kids. I wanted to laugh aloud at them; at the same time, I wanted to pound my fists against them.

My parents had a way of being silent when matters required questions, confessions, and tears. I tried to understand it—they came from the era of church picnics, nice homes and nice cars. They dreamed of a nice family that would fit into their plans. They had us instead: Heather with her drug problems, Duane with his alcoholism, Kim with her bartending career, and me with my loud music and cigarettes. Craig was really the only one who went along with their scheme. My mother's camaraderie with him had always angered me as though he proved her point of motherhood.

The front that they kept up was like water just beginning to boil, but I knew it would someday. My dad had been the counselor and the mentor to the lost and the troubled; he had kept our image pure. We weren't allowed to listen to rock music at home, yet somehow mental illness had crept in through the cracks in our family. We could see the signs beneath the surface and behind closed doors.

Heather's problems set free a flood of dark emotion in our family. We had to admit that no matter how hard we tried, sadness and tragedy could not be avoided. It could not be covered up. Heather's honesty began to open up the doors that we had never been allowed to walk through. We gradually discovered our own humanity through the questions prompted by Heather's illness. The pictures of blood and gore that Heather drew in art therapy, the shock treatment, the crazy hairstyles that Heather flaunted at 35 years of age gave us a glimpse outside the wonderland of daisies and rainbows. And it let out the dogs that had been howling inside of me.

I hadn't been able to sleep well for weeks. I started having the most frightening nightmares. Images were in my subconscious that I never would have guessed were there: people attacking me, wars raging, fires out of control. Then the panic attacks began—the sleepless nights, the senseless roaming with friends at night. I needed someone to explain it all to me. I searched for someone to tell me what to do. Dad was never good at opening up his mind to these things. I knew what his answer would be: "It's because you're listening to that rock music" or "because you are so rebellious." And somehow, no matter how much I disliked my mother's incessant optimism, I had become like her. I could not explain my problems to anyone; I could not show my sorrows. Maybe that is part of the reason why I decided to tell Mom about my anxiety.

Her response surprised me. We were talking on the phone, and I started telling her about the nightmares and the craziness of my life. "Rebekah," she said slowly. "The time that I have been spending here with Heather has helped me to understand some things." She paused as if she were lifting a veil and not sure what she would find underneath. "I always thought that simply being a kind person would make everything okay. I thought I could be a good mother by just being thoughtful."

And she told me how, in this latest phase of her life, she had learned that people deserved more than just an occasional "please" and "thank you." People were filled with anger, sorrow, frustration, silliness, hate, exhaustion, deceit, and fear. And all of those emotions did not make a person weak, wrong, or mistaken. Those emotions made a person human. The anger turned the forgiveness into a beautiful act of love. The sorrow made the laughter more joyous. All of those years she had thought that her duty as a mother was to protect us from our dark sides, to wash away our tears with cake or promises or smiles. But instead of just letting us cry, she had made us stop.

> After Heather's breakdown, we all began to talk—and cry—and to heal. It wasn't painless or automatic. But we found ways to express fears, and to listen, and to kid each other rather than to hold feelings in and stay silent. I could feel us turning onto a new road, one that would be bumpier and more cracked, but where the scenery would be fresh and often exhilarating at times.

Analyzing the Writer's Strategy

When writers narrate a story, they try to recreate scenes—to show rather than tell—so that the reader can experience the moment as they did. Rather than simply telling us what they felt, they try to *show* us. For example, in the student model, Rebekah could have simply told us of her sister's "blackout" and subsequent hospitalization. Instead, she lets us observe and hear as her father discloses this unexpected news to her and her family:

> I watched his face, hoping for a revelation. His face was pale and closed. He didn't return my look but stood up and walked into the kitchen. I followed and stared at Mom's straightened back.
>
> "Heather is in the hospital," Dad said, his voice raspy, as he told us about my older sister. I noticed his Adam's apple dip and heard him swallow. Mom turned around, her posture unnatural. She tilted her head in question. Dad continued, "She had a blackout and checked herself into the hospital. They're running some tests." He watched my mother's face as if to relay a secret message. She didn't get the message.
>
> "What do you mean by 'blackout'?" she asked, with a look of confusion on her face.

Such a scene draws the reader in because each of us can sense the confusion and concern that the family members feel. The writer doesn't need to write, "My entire family was worried" because she has *shown* this more vividly than any claim she could make. Rebekah's use of dialogue, action, and vivid details (her father's "pale and closed" face and "raspy voice," her mother's "straightened back" and "unnatural" posture) makes us sense their anxiety.

Selecting Telling Details. The key to describing scenes and characters is to make sure each detail is revealing. It is not important to know the narrator's hair color or height, so such details would not be relevant or "telling." But the fact that she listens to rock music even though it wasn't allowed at home reveals that she is not willing to conform totally to the family's standards and rules. Such details help us to understand better the narrator's character as well as the dynamics within her family.

Similarly, the setting can be revealing. Although the time of day is not always important in a story, here it seems fitting that it is "late at night" when the father hears that Heather has been hospitalized and that it is during the night that the narrator roams senselessly with friends and also is awakened by panic attacks and nightmares. All of these nighttime activities underscore the inability to avoid or deny the darker reality of their lives.

 ## PRACTICING WRITING ESSAYS WITH NARRATION

Many of the topics in the "Writing from the Text" sections in Part I invite you to relate your own experience to the particular readings and to respond with a narrative. Here are some additional assignments:

1. Write an essay describing one home or school experience that taught you an unexpected lesson. Show us the incident as it happened, and describe what you learned and why it was unexpected.

2. Write an essay focusing on a time when you bullied or were bullied or embarrassed by someone else. Let us see what happened and what you discovered about yourself and others.

3. Write about an incident when you felt that your cultural or family background was incorrectly prejudged. Describe what happened so that your reader can understand the event and your response to it. Did you make any discoveries as a result of this experience?

 ## Final Tips for a Narrative

- Focus on a **provocative insight** so that your story reflects some real thought.
- Continue **sharpening your thesis** as your narrative develops. Remember, the thesis does not need to be explicitly stated in the essay.
- **Dramatize** a scene or two, using action and dialogue. Don't just tell the reader; show the scene.
- Include **telling details** that reveal relevant character traits. Have your characters interact with each other.
- **Rewrite sentences** and revise paragraphs to eliminate wordiness and generalizations.
- **Study other narratives** in the text, looking for techniques and strategies. Experiment!

EVALUATIVE RESPONSE

Each day when you appraise or assess the value or quality of something—a movie, editorial, song lyric, college course—you are evaluating it. Informally, a friend may ask how you liked a particular film, and you offer your evaluation, without defining your criteria. Sometimes, however, you need to give a written evaluation. You may be asked to fill out an evaluation form on a course you are taking or on the instructor. You may be asked to write a movie or book review for a newspaper or a course. In some cases, you will need to evaluate something using specific criteria—established by you or someone else. In most cases, you will support your evaluation with examples from a text—a film, an essay, a book, or an editorial. The purpose of an evaluative response essay is to give your judgment of a work based on both your experience and a careful reading of the text.

When to Write an Evaluative Response Essay

Throughout your college writing, you will be asked to respond to assigned readings and texts. You will be expected to summarize passages, analyze key points, incorporate direct quotations, and evaluate assertions and evidence. In English classes, such an assignment may involve your relating your own observations or experiences to the readings.

Organizing and Developing an Evaluative Response Essay

To write an evaluative response essay, you need to present the author's thesis and key points, and then respond to them in terms of your own views, experiences, and judgments. Your essay must show that you have read the text closely, and it should include quotations from the text and a discussion of each quotation. Overall, your essay should both analyze and evaluate the text: What are the author's central points? Do you agree or disagree with them?

You may find that you agree with some of the author's points but not with others, and you will need to explain and support your stance on each. Most importantly, your thesis should articulate your main focus as well as your view of the author's key claims. For example, in the student essay that follows, Marin Kheng briefly summarizes Ellen Goodman's position in "Thanksgiving" (p. 3) but shows how she disagrees with it:

> While Goodman's essay is a suitable guide to how a family should function, it is es-
> sentially an idealistic portrayal of the family, and thus it ignores the harsher realities
> that are present in many American households.

Marin's essay will be a treatment of "the harsher realities" that she has observed in families she knows. She includes meaningful passages from the original text and uses her own observations to counter them. For example, Marin writes: "Goodman assures us that 'while the world may abandon us, the family promises . . . to protect us'" (5). She then uses this quotation as a departure point to describe a contrasting case of her friend Brahim, whose family deserted him. In your own essays, you will want to show how the original concurs—or doesn't concur—with your own experiences or observations. Whether you agree or disagree with the author, you will be evaluating the original and supporting your stance.

In any case, you will want to make sure that you have sufficiently understood and represented the text. It is not enough in an evaluative essay to simply give the title and author and then progress with your own story. Instead, you want to *use* the material that you have read. You might think of your response essay as a kind of conversation with the writer: You will be listening to, reflecting on, and evaluating the writer's many points and then inserting your own examples that parallel, extend, or counter the author's perspective.

STUDENT EXAMPLE: AN EVALUATIVE RESPONSE ESSAY

To satisfy an assignment for her composition class, Marin Kheng was asked to respond to and evaluate one of the essays in *Between Worlds*. She chose Ellen Goodman's "Thanksgiving" (p. 4) because she found that her observations of friends' experiences countered the world that Goodman describes, and Marin thought that this contrast would create a compelling essay.

Kheng 1

Marin Kheng

Professor Barth

English 1A

11 March 2008

Thanksgiving Beyond the Cleaver Family

The boy sits alone in the darkness of the family room, his eyes wide and yearning, hungry for the images that flash across his TV set. A family—mothers, fathers, siblings, uncles, aunts, cousins, grandparents—all sit down at the dining table to share their Thanksgiving dinner and a part of their lives. They are smiling, talking,

---

laughing, at times bickering, as cranberry sauce and slices of turkey meat are passed around from person to person. The images play across the boy's face, inviting him to join in the warmth and the camaraderie before cruelly slipping away from his grasp and back into the dark black haven of the TV screen. The commercial has ended, and the boy is left alone in his family room with his 2-for-3-dollars TV dinner before him and the muffled sounds of screaming adult voices seeping through from his parents' bedroom. This is his Thanksgiving.

This is not, however, the Thanksgiving depicted in Ellen Goodman's essay, "Thanksgiving" (3). According to Goodman, Thanksgiving is a time for individuals in all parts of the United States to reconvene with their families in remembrance of and appreciation for the warmth, love, and support that the family structure provides. Goodman also contends that Americans are constantly struggling between the freedom and loneliness that the world of the individual brings and the selflessness and support that the world of the family brings. They cannot deny themselves either world because both the family and the individual are intrinsically connected and dependent upon each other. While Goodman's essay is a suitable guide to how a family should function, it is essentially an idealistic portrayal of the family, and thus it ignores the harsher realities that are present in many American households. The truth is that for many Americans like the boy, the workings of the ideal family described in Goodman's essay are in sharp contrast with what actually goes on in their own families.

Goodman believes that a contradiction exists in being "raised in families . . . to be individuals" (4) because individualism must arise from a structure promoting togetherness. For my friend Nicole, there is no dilemma in being an individual within a family because there is no threat of the loss of individualism in her family. With a father who spends the little spare time he has at the neighborhood bar and a negligent mother who constantly eats to escape her marital problems, Nicole has had to be independent for most of her life, doing for herself the things most children have taken for granted. She has had to work parttime jobs to pay for basic expenses such as food and clothing, walk down to the free clinic by herself when she is ill, and spend family-oriented holidays by herself or with friends. For Nicole there will not be

Kheng 3

"a ritual of belonging" around a dining table (4). To Nicole, the idea of togetherness and unity do not align themselves with family. Instead, the only words that correspond with family are independence, maturity, and adult responsibilities forced onto a girl far from grown up.

Other families, like that of my cousin Jana's, do not force their children to raise themselves, but instead require them to earn the privilege of being accepted by the family. Contrary to Goodman's assertion that "we don't have to achieve to be accepted by our families. We just have to be" (4), Jana has to be everything that her parents desire in order to be given praise and affection, and more importantly to Jana, to stop the criticism inflicted on her by her parents. The pressure is increased when her older sister Heny, who at 21 is getting her Ph.D. in chemistry at Harvard University, comes to visit. This demand for perfection placed on Jana has led her to become an AP student with a 4.2 GPA, co-captain of the varsity swimming team and a star tennis player, president of various campus clubs, treasurer for her student council, an intern at a prestigious law firm, and a manic-depressive neurotic. In September, two weeks after the start of her senior year, she suffered a nervous breakdown and attempted suicide. When she survived, her parents stood beside her hospital bed and told her, "We are very disappointed in you. Heny would never have done something like this." While Goodman asserts that the family is "not the place where people ruthlessly compete with each other," Jana's parents clearly cultivate sibling rivalry and don't seem to understand that the family is "not for the survival of the fittest but for the weakest" (5). Although Jana's parents have given her every material comfort a teen could desire, the demands they make in return for these comforts threaten her physical, mental, and emotional well-being. But they have never given her the one thing she needs most, which ironically no amount of money could ever buy. They have never given her their acceptance.

Complete abandonment, however, is perhaps the worst thing parents can do to one of their own. Goodman assures us that "while the world may abandon us, the family promises . . . to protect us" (5). In the case of my friend Brahim, his family left one day and never came back. A straight-A student who grew up in a neighborhood infamous for its drugs and its hookers, he had been the filial son, patiently dragging his drunken brother up the stairs to their motel room, selling cheap marijuana to pay the rent when his father had spent a month's wages on a night at the Bicycle Club Casino, and assuring his teachers his black eye and the welts on his arm were caused in a fist fight with another boy when, in fact, they were caused by his own mother. Yet, despite all his efforts at holding his family together, he was abandoned in the end. At 13, he was homeless on the streets of North Hollywood with pocket change and a trash bag full of clothes. The ideal of a family that supports and protects its members and measures "their common legacy . . . the children" (4) means nothing to him because he realized at that young age the ridiculousness and cruelty of this ideal.

   If Nicole, Jana, Brahim, the boy eating his TV dinner alone, or any of the countless number of Americans with dysfunctional families were to read "Thanksgiving," they would not be able to understand the ideals of family that Goodman espouses or the people she gathers around her dining table. It is not that they do not know what a family should be like, or that they do not want a family, but for them Goodman's family belongs in another world, a world that no amount of wishing and desiring could ever realize. Their eyes will linger at André Malraux's statement that "Without a family, man, alone in the world, trembles with the cold" (qtd. in Goodman 4). Some may become angry, some may snort in lonely contempt, or some may simply be perplexed, because the sad irony in their reality is that although they have families, they, too, are trembling alone in the cold.

Work Cited

Goodman, Ellen. "Thanksgiving." *Between Worlds: A Reader, Rhetoric, and Handbook.* Ed.
   Susan Bachmann and Melinda Barth. 6th ed. New York: Pearson Longman, 2008.
   3–5. Print.

Analyzing the Writer's Strategy

Marin's purpose is to show that while Goodman's essay is a suitable guide to how a family should function, it is an idealistic portrayal of the family, and thus ignores the harsher realities of many American households. In her opening, her strategy is to use narration to dramatize an anonymous character who could be anyone her reader might know.

Marin's thesis is clear. She states that "the truth is that for many Americans like the boy, the workings of the ideal family described in Goodman's essay are in sharp contrast with what actually goes on in their own families." She builds her support by incorporating direct quotations, and she contrasts these with her own experiences. For example, Marin writes: "Goodman assures us that "while the world may abandon us, the family promises . . . to protect us." She then shows how her friend Brahim's family deserted, rather than protected, him. In Marin's conclusion, she returns to the notion that "Goodman's family belongs in another world, a world that no amount of wishing and desiring could ever bring" to the friends she describes.

Notice that Marin puts quotation marks around Goodman's essay title when she first refers to it in paragraph 2, and then in her conclusion, when she returns to Goodman's title "Thanksgiving." Remember that titles of essays, short stories, and poems are indicated by quotation marks. See p. 540 for more information on titles.

In your own evaluative essays, you will assess the original essay in light of your own views and experiences. You may find that you agree with some points that the author makes but not with all of them. Regardless of your stance, you need to examine specific quotations from the original work.

PRACTICING WRITING AN EVALUATIVE RESPONSE ESSAY

1. Write an evaluative response to "Makes Learning Fun" (p. 247) that takes a stand on the use of computers in education. After fully explaining Stoll's position, use examples from your own academic experience to support or oppose his thesis and key points.

2. After reading "The Whole World Is Watching" (p. 219), write an evaluative response of Thomas Friedman's concern about the prevalence of cell phone cameras and online blogs.

3. Evaluate and respond to the ideas in "The Good Daughter" (p. 12) in terms of your parents' expectations and your responses to them.

4. Respond to and evaluate any of the essays in *Between Worlds*, perhaps one that has not been discussed in class.

5. After viewing the film *Crash* and reading the reviews (pp. 298–304), write an evaluative response of one of the following essays: "Don't Let Stereotypes Warp Your Judgments" (p. 470), "Black Men and Public Space" (p. 181), "Who Shot Johnny?" (p. 186), or "Bigotry as the Outer Side of Inner Angst" (p. 304). Focus your essay on key quotations from the essay and use examples from the film *Crash* to illustrate and support your claims about the author's main points.

Final Tips for an Evaluative Response Essay

- **Read carefully** the essay you intend to evaluate, underlining or recording in a journal any language that you find interesting.
- Determine whether you **agree with or oppose** the author's main point and shape this view into your thesis.
- Find good material in the text, especially **choice language**, as well as examples from your own experience to support your position.
- **Reread the original essay** after you have written your evaluative response to see whether there is additional material you should pull into your paper.
- Refine your conclusion to insure that you have **restated your thesis in different words** and that your conclusion offers important insights.

DEFINITION

Whether your entire essay is a definition or you have incorporated a definition into your essay to clarify a term or concept for your reader, explaining what a term means is an integral part of writing. Knowing your intended audience and purpose in writing will help you determine which words you need to define.

When to Use Definition

In a paper for a psychology class, for example, you would not need to define terms generally used in that field. But when you write for a general reader and use language unfamiliar to most people—a technical or foreign term, or a word peculiar to an academic discipline—you will need to define the term so your reader can understand it. Even if you are using a familiar word, you need to explain its meaning if you or an author you are quoting use it in a unique way.

Sometimes a brief definition is all that you need. In that case, a few words of clarification, or even a synonym, may be incorporated into your text quite easily:

Los Vendidos, or "The Sellouts," is the Spanish-language title of Luis Valdez's play (144).

Achondroplasia—a type of dwarfism—may affect overall bone structure and cause arms and legs to be disproportionately smaller than the rest of the body.

Eating disorders include "bingeing, chronic dieting, and 'aerobic nervosa,' the excessive use of exercise to remain one's body ideal" (Erens 209).

As these examples show, incorporating definition into your text is unobtrusive and superior to writing a separate sentence to define the term.

Organizing and Developing a Definition Essay

When an assignment calls for an extended definition of a concept or term, the following methods may be used alone or in combination:

- *Dictionary definition:* Including a formal definition of a word from a dictionary before developing your point. Even common words may require you to take this route so that you and your reader have the same sphere of reference.
- *Expert's definition:* Presenting an expert's definition of a term to show that you have sound support for your understanding of a word.
- *Comparison-contrast:* Contrasting your definition of a word with the way it is typically used or with the actual dictionary definition of the term. If the term is unfamiliar, you might show how it is similar to another concept.
- *Description:* Defining a term by describing its characteristics: size, shape, texture, color, noise, and other telling traits.
- *Exemplification:* Giving examples and illustrations of a concept to enable your reader to understand it better. Because such examples are rather specific, they should only help supplement a definition rather than be used by themselves.
- *Negation:* Explaining what something is *not* in order to help limit the definition and eliminate misconceptions.

The Purpose of Defining

You may be asked to write a "definition essay"—a paper that develops with the primary intention of increasing the reader's understanding of a term—in a psychology, sociology, history, philosophy, or English course. Usually, however, your goal will be something else. You may be attempting to convince your reader to consider the explained term in a positive light, or to compare it—even to prefer it—to something else. Sometimes the persuasive aspect of the essay relies on the reader's willingness to reconsider the definition of a word, as occurs in the next essay.

EXAMPLE: AN ESSAY BASED ON DEFINITION

The following essay was written by Jon Winokur, a freelance writer and author of twenty reference books and anthologies, including *Zen to Go* (1988), *True Confessions* (1992), *The Rich Are Different* (1996), and *How to Win at Golf Without Actually Playing Well* (2000). In "You Call That Irony?," published in the *Los Angeles Times* in 2007, Winokur defines irony and shows how this word is often incorrectly used.

You Call That Irony?
Jon Winokur

1   When it was revealed in 2003 that William J. Bennett, author of "The Book of Virtues," had a secret gambling habit, more than one commentator termed it a delicious irony, and it was indeed a pleasure to see a sanctimonious scold get his comeuppance. But it wasn't irony, just hypocrisy.

2   It was ironic when, on "The Daily Show," Jon Stewart commended Bennett for his indignation, and for "standing up to the William Bennetts of the world."

3   Here's another example of irony: the 1959 episode of "The Twilight Zone" titled "Time Enough at Last," in which Burgess Meredith plays Henry Bemis, a bookish bank teller with thick glasses and an insatiable appetite for reading. One day, knocked unconscious by a giant explosion, he awakens to find that he's the last man on Earth.

4   Wandering the desolate city, overwhelmed with loneliness, he is about to kill himself when he notices the ruins of . . . a library! Cut to: stacks of books piled high on the library's steps and Henry, giddy with joy. But as he settles down on the curb with the first book, his glasses fall off and shatter on the ground, trapping him forever in a blurry world.

5   Now that's irony.

6   Irony is one of the most misused words in the English language. Much of the confusion comes from the existence of several distinct forms of irony. Verbal irony is the act of saying one thing but meaning the opposite with the intent of being understood as meaning the opposite, as in, "Nice weather we're having" on a rainy day.

7   Cosmic irony involves quirks of fate, as when a UPS driver on his way to deliver parts to a hospital has a serious accident, is taken to the same hospital by ambulance, but the hospital can't perform necessary tests because one of its machines is down and the parts to fix it are in the driver's wrecked van.

8   Socratic irony is a strategy for refuting dogma. In the Platonic dialogues, Socrates assumes the role of the *eiron*, a sly dissembler who feigns naivete by asking seemingly foolish questions that gradually hang his opponents by their own admissions. A modern practitioner is Sacha Baron Cohen, whose characters Borat and Ali G expose pomposity by pretending to be stupid.

9   Irony is about the interplay of opposites, not the random proximity of events. It's ironic that Beethoven was deaf, but merely coincidental that Brad Pitt tore his Achilles tendon while playing Achilles in Troy. People miss the distinction and say "ironic" when they mean "coincidental," an abuse encouraged by Alanis Morissette's 1996 hit single, "Ironic," in which situations purporting to be ironic are merely annoying ("a traffic jam when you're already late, a no-smoking sign on your cigarette break").

10   It is ironic that "Ironic" is an unironic song about irony. Is that perfectly clear?

11   In case you're confused, here are some more examples of irony:

12   •   Brewing heir Adolph Coors III was allergic to beer.

13   •   County supervisors in Pima County, Ariz., held a closed meeting to discuss Arizona's open meeting law.

14   •   U.S. Border Patrol uniforms are manufactured in Mexico.

15   •   When the Berlin Wall came down in 1989, so many visitors were taking souvenir pieces that a protective fence was installed, so that, yes, the Berlin Wall was guarded by a wall.

16   •   Zimbabwean President Robert Mugabe's 2005 state of the nation address, in which he promised to remedy his country's chronic electricity shortages, was blacked out by a power failure.

17   •   A 17-year-old Amish boy was electrocuted by a downed power line that became tangled in the wheels of his horse-drawn buggy.

18   •   The "Marlboro Man" died of lung cancer.

19   •   A 2001 Father's Day tribute on ESPN featured "How Sweet It Is (to be Loved by You)," sung by Marvin Gaye, who was shot and killed by his father in 1984.

20   •   Entries for the Florida Press Club's 2005 Excellence in Journalism Award for hurricane coverage were lost in Hurricane Katrina.

Analyzing the Writer's Strategy

The purpose of this essay is to convince readers that there is a wide misuse of the word "irony" and that speakers and writers need to be more definitive in their word choice. Winokur uses the following methods to explain "irony":

- *Dictionary Definition:*   Winokur doesn't resort to the predictable "according to Webster's dictionary . . ." to define "irony." But he does provide distinct definitions of two different types of irony: verbal irony—the act of saying one thing but intentionally meaning the opposite—and cosmic irony—the quirks of fate that afflict all human beings when the opposite of what is deserved or expected occurs. Further, he informs his reader that the word "irony" is derived from the Platonic dialogues of Socrates in which he "assumes the role of the *eiron,* a sly dissembler who feigns naivete by asking seemingly foolish questions that gradually hang his opponents by their own admissions" (447). Winokur needs to clarify the dictionary meanings of "irony" in order to support his view of its misuse.

- *Comparison-contrast:* Winokur shows what irony is and contrasts it with what irony is not: "Irony is about the interplay of opposites, not the random proximity of events" (447). The author notes that it is ironic that the composer Beethoven was deaf because he could not hear his own musical compositions, but it is merely a coincidence, or random proximity of events, that Brad Pitt tore his Achilles tendon while playing the role of Achilles.

- *Description:* In order to show what irony is, Winokur describes in great detail a *Twilight Zone* plot in which a bank teller with "an insatiable appetite for reading" is rendered unconscious by an explosion. He awakes to discover that he is alone on earth and is lonely and depressed until he discovers a pile of books at a library. Just as he is about to start reading, his glasses fall off and shatter, leaving him "forever in a blurry world" (446). Winokur's description supports his perception that this episode is ironic. The episode's title, "Time Enough At Last" is itself ironic.

- *Exemplification:* Even though this is a short essay, Winokur packs it with 14 specific illustrations of irony. Some of our favorite examples include: "Brewing heir Adolph Coors III was allergic to beer"; "County supervisors in Pima County, Ariz., held a closed meeting to discuss Arizona's open meeting law"; and "The 'Marlboro Man' died of lung cancer" (447). After studying each example, the reader gets a clearer sense of this often-misused term. Although bulleted lists are typically avoided in essays, Winokur's use here seems effective because such a misuse needs thorough exemplification.

- *Negation:* Because Winokur believes that the word "irony" is so often misused, he opens his essay with an example of a situation that many would claim is ironic. However, he insists that it isn't. Winokur contends that William Bennett's authorship of *The Book of Virtues*—despite Bennett's own gambling addiction—is an example of hypocrisy, not irony. Further, Winokur claims that the examples from Alanis Morissette's song "Ironic" are wrong: "a traffic jam when you're already late, a no-smoking sign on

your cigarette break" are annoyances, not illustrations of irony. Ultimately, readers who have too often exclaimed, "That's ironic!" may rethink
their word choice because of Winokur's use of negative illustrations.

 PRACTICING WRITING DEFINITION ESSAYS

1. In your college papers, you will frequently use short definitions to clarify
   terms. In small groups, armed with dictionaries, practice writing one-
   sentence definitions of the following terms:

   a. satire   c. boyfriend

   b. environmentalist   d. empathy

2. Although you will use definition most often as a component of your papers, it is useful to practice writing short definition essays. In small
   groups, collaborate with your classmates to write a short essay that defines one of the following:

   a. green movement   d. unconditional love

   b. "between worlds"   e. disabled

   c. a cheap date

 Final Tips for a Definition Essay

- Is your **purpose** for defining to inform? To analyze? To persuade?
- Identify the needs of your audience; **determine which words**
  your readers cannot be expected to know or may misunder-
  stand.
- Whenever possible, incorporate into your text the **necessary
  clarification** of a term. Avoid writing a separate sentence to
  define the term.
- Remember that **definitions can also be developed** by comparing and contrasting that word with other terms, by describing
  the characteristics of a term, by presenting examples, and by
  illustrating what the term is not.

CAUSE AND EFFECT

Throughout your life you have been made aware of the consequences of your
behavior: not getting your allowance because you didn't keep your room
clean; winning a class election because you ran a vigorous campaign; getting

a C on an exam because you didn't review all of the material. In all of these cases, a particular behavior seems to *cause* or result in a certain *effect*. In the case of the denied allowance, for example, your parents may have identified the cause: not keeping your room clean.

Causes are not always so easy to identify, however, for there may be a number of indirect causes of an action or inaction. For example, you may have won an election because of your reputation as a leader, your popularity, your opponent's inadequacies, your vigorous campaign, or even a cause that you may not have known about or been able to control. Effects usually are more evident: homeless families, few jobs for college graduates, small businesses failing, and houses remaining on the market for years are all obvious effects of a recession. What has caused the recession typically is more difficult to discern, but good critical thinking involves speculating about possible causes and their effects.

When to Use Cause-and-Effect Development

Cause-and-effect development can be used in diverse writing situations. For example, you would use this strategy to trace the reasons for a historical event, such as the causes and results of the American entry into World War II. You perceive cause-and-effect relationships when you analyze and write about broad social problems (like runaway teens) or more personal concerns (such as why you and your siblings are risk takers). All of these thinking and writing tasks invite you to examine the apparent effects and to question what has caused them. This questioning inevitably involves speculation about causes rather than absolute answers, but this speculation can lead to fruitful analysis and provocative papers.

Organizing and Developing a Cause-and-Effect Essay

To get started, you may want to brainstorm and let all of your hunches emerge. In fact, a lively prewriting session is the key to a lively cause-and-effect paper. To produce a paper that goes beyond predictable or obvious discussion, take time to think about diverse causes for an effect you have observed and to contemplate the most dramatic effects of causes that you perceive.

You may find that you want to focus more on the causes or on the effects rather than trying to spend equal time on both. The wording of your thesis will be critical to forecast your emphasis and clarify your stance to your reader. For example, the following essay focuses on the effects of the writer's experience as a soldier in an unpopular war. Notice how he analyzes his feelings of shame, anger, envy, and pain—all effects of a single cause, serving in the Marines during the Vietnam War.

EXAMPLE: A CAUSE-AND-EFFECT ESSAY

Robert McKelvey's goal in "I Confess Some Envy" is to present an analysis of a social issue. McKelvey, a Bronze Star recipient for his service in Vietnam and now a child psychiatrist and professor at Baylor, analyzes the causes of the envy he felt while watching the Desert Storm troops receive public acclaim. He cites the reasons that his generation of soldiers failed to gain support and the effects of this failure on him and his peers. Veterans who have returned more recently from Afghanistan or Iraq might compare their experiences with McKelvey's. His essay first appeared in the *Los Angeles Times* on June 16, 1991, shortly after the return of American troops from the Persian Gulf.

I Confess Some Envy
Robert McKelvey

1   Every year on the Marine Corps' birthday, the commandant sends a message to all Marine units worldwide commemorating the event. On November 10, 1969, I was stationed with the 11th Marine Regiment northwest of Da Nang in Vietnam. It was my task to read the commandant's message to the Marines of our unit.

2   One sentence, in particular, caught my attention: "Here's to our wives and loved ones supporting us at home." Ironically, that week my wife had joined tens of thousands of others marching on the nation's capital to protest U.S. involvement in Vietnam.

3   It was a divisive, unhappy time. Few people believed the war could be won or that we had any right to interfere in Vietnam's internal affairs. However, for those of us "in country," there was a more pressing issue. Our lives were on the line. Even though our family and friends meant us no harm by protesting our efforts, and probably believed they were speeding our return, their actions had a demoralizing effect.

4   Couldn't they at least wait until we were safely home before expressing their distaste for what we were doing? But by then, the military had become scapegoats for the nation's loathing of its war, a war where draft dodgers were cast as heroes and soldiers as villains.

5   Watching the Desert Storm victory parades on television, I was struck by the contrast between this grand and glorious homecoming and the sad, silent and shameful return of so many of us 20-odd years ago. Disembarking from a troop ship in Long Beach, my contingent of Marines was greeted at the pier by a general and a brass band. There were no family, friends, well-wishers, representatives of the Veterans of Foreign Wars, or children waving American flags.

6   We were bused to Camp Pendleton, quickly processed and sent our separate ways. After a two-week wait for my orders to be cut, during which time I spent most days at the San Diego Zoo, I was discharged from active duty. I packed up and flew home to begin premedical studies.

7   As the plane landed in Detroit, the on-board classical music channel happened to be playing Charles Ives's "America." The piece's ironic, teasing variations on the theme, "My Country 'Tis of Thee," seemed a fitting end to my military service.

8   My wife met me at the airport and drove me directly to Ann Arbor for a job interview. We were candidates for a job as house parents for the Religious Society of Friends (Quakers) International Co-op. Face to face with these sincere, fervent pacifists, I felt almost ashamed of the uniform I was still wearing with its ribbons and insignia.

9   I recalled stories of comrades who had been spat upon in airports and called "baby killers." The Friends, however, were exceptionally gentle and kind. They, at least, seemed able to see beyond the symbols of the war they hated to the individual human being beneath the paraphernalia. Much to my surprise, we got the job.

10   I took off my uniform that day, put it away and tried to resume the camouflage of student life. I seldom spoke of my service in Vietnam. It was somehow not a topic for polite conversation, and when it did come up the discussion seemed always to become angry and polarized.

11   Like many other Vietnam veterans, I began to feel as if I had done something terribly wrong in serving my country in Vietnam, and that I had better try to hush it up. I joined no veterans' organizations and, on those rare times when I encountered men who had served with me in Vietnam, I felt embarrassed and eager to get away. We never made plans to get together and reminisce. The past was buried deep within us, and that is where we wanted it to stay.

12   The feelings aroused in me by the sight of our victorious troops marching across the television screen are mixed and unsettling. There is pride, of course, at their stunning achievement. Certainly they deserve their victory parade. But there is also envy. Were we so much different from them?

13   Soldiers do not choose the wars they fight. Theirs happened to be short and sweet, ours long and bitter. Yet we were all young men and women doing what our country had asked us. Seeing my fellow Vietnam veterans marching with the Desert Storm troops, watching them try, at last, to be recognized and applauded for their now-distant sacrifices, is poignant and sad.

14   We have come out of hiding in recent years as the war's pain has receded. It has become almost fashionable to be a veteran and sport one's jungle fatigues. Still, a sense of hurt lingers and, with it, a touch of anger. Anger that

the country we loved, and continue to love, could use us, abuse us, discard and then try to forget us, as if we were the authors of her misery rather than her loyal sons and daughters. It was our curious, sad fate to be blamed for the war we had not chosen to fight, when in reality we were among its victims.

Analyzing the Writer's Strategy

McKelvey's purpose is to express his pain and sorrow as he reviews his history as a veteran of the Vietnam War. He analyzes the causes of his personal frustrations and the effects of American response to that war in contrast to the response to the Persian Gulf War twenty years later.

McKelvey's strategy is to dramatize moments in his personal history and to lead his reader to discover the irony implicit in these events. For example, while he was reading to his unit the commandant's message applauding the support of "wives and loved ones" at home, his own wife had joined a massive demonstration in Washington protesting U.S. involvement in Vietnam. McKelvey contrasts the "grand and glorious homecoming" of the Desert Storm troops with his own "sad, silent and shameful return." He shows himself "almost ashamed" of his uniform with its ribbons and insignia when he applied to be a house parent for the Quakers. He notes that "soldiers do not choose the wars they fight," and yet the Desert Storm troops were celebrated as heroes while he and his fellow vets from Vietnam were called "baby killers" and spat upon when they returned.

Through irony, McKelvey helps his reader understand the effects of the anti–Vietnam War sentiment on one individual who articulates for many suffering but silent soldiers, also the "victims" of that war. He avoids using the terms "cause" and "effect" or the predictable "cause and effect" paragraph structure, favoring instead subtle juxtaposition of causes and their profound effects.

 ## PRACTICING WRITING ESSAYS ABOUT CAUSES AND EFFECTS

Write an essay that focuses on the causes or effects of one of the following:

1. Your having revealed an important truth about yourself to a member of your family

2. Your moving away from home

3. Your family combining cultural customs for a holiday occasion

4. Your sense of being caught living between two worlds, as described by Marcus Mabry (p. 109), Caroline Hwang (p. 12), and Judith Ortiz Cofer (p. 172)

5. Your discovery that you are unwillingly intimidating others, as Brent Staples describes (p. 181)

6. Your feeling of being manipulated by the media's depiction of ideal female body shapes as discussed by Rachel Krell (p. 387).

Final Tips for Cause-and-Effect Development

- **Brainstorm** to come up with every possible cause or effect for your particular topic.
- Review your list of causes and effects to **determine whether each point is reasonable** and supportable. Eliminate any that are illogical or for which you lack data. Do research if additional evidence is needed.
- Apply the **"So what?" standard** (see pp. 359 and 364). Will this cause-and-effect analysis make worthwhile reading?
- Group ideas that belong together and **order your evidence** to conclude with your most emphatic and well-developed support.
- **Develop your explanations** fully so that your reader doesn't need to guess your assumptions.

COMPARISON AND CONTRAST

Whether you are examining your own experiences or responding to texts, you will inevitably rely on comparison and contrast thinking. To realize how two people, places, works of art, films, economic plans, laboratory procedures, or aspects of literature—or anything else—may be alike or different is to perceive important distinctions between them.

While we may start an analysis process believing that two subjects are remarkably different (how they *contrast*), after thoughtful scrutiny we may see important similarities between them. Conversely, although we may have detected clear similarities in two subjects (how they *compare*), the complete analysis may reveal surprising differences. Therefore, while comparison implies similarity and contrast implies difference, these two thinking processes work together to enhance perception.

When to Use Comparison-Contrast Development

Subtle comparison-contrast cues are embedded in writing assignments, both in-class exams and out-of-class papers. For example, an economics instructor may ask for a study of prewar and postwar inflation; a philosophy instructor may ask for examples showing how one philosophical system departs from another; a psychology instructor may require an explanation of how two different psychologists interpret dreams; or a literature instructor may assign an analysis of how a character changes within a certain novel.

The prevalence of such assignments in all disciplines underscores the importance of comparison and contrast in many experiences and learning situations. Assignments that ask writers to explain the unfamiliar, evaluate certain choices, analyze how someone or something has changed, establish distinction, discover similarities, and propose a compromise all require some degree of comparison and contrast.

For example, a writer may initially believe that women and men have quite different complaints about their lives. Women feel that they need to be attractive; they feel limited in their choice of career and restricted by the career heights and pay they may attain; and they feel obligated to be domestic (good mothers, cooks, and housekeepers). Men feel they need to be successful at work to be attractive to women; they feel burdened to select high-status, high-paying jobs regardless of their real interests; and they must work continuously. Many feel precluded from domestic life—cut off from their children and home life.

At first, the complaints of each gender appear to be quite different. But the writer examining these complaints may perceive that they have something in common: that women *and* men suffer from "an invisible curriculum," a series of social expectations that deprive human beings of choice. A thesis for this study might look like this:

Thesis: Although women and men seem to have different problems, both genders feel hampered by an "invisible curriculum" that affects their self-esteem and limits their choices at work and in their families.

Organizing and Developing a Comparison-Contrast Essay

There are two basic methods for organizing data to compare or contrast. In the *block* method, the writer would organize the material for a study of conflicts affecting gender like this:

BLOCK 1. WOMEN

1. Need to feel attractive to be successful

2. Feel limited in workplace choices, level, pay

3. Feel obligated to be mothers, domestic successes

BLOCK 2. MEN

1. Need to feel successful at work to feel attractive

2. Feel burdened to achieve high position, work continuously

3. Feel cut off from children and domestic choices

In the *point-by-point* method, the writer would organize the material like this:

POINT 1. FACTORS THAT GOVERN SELF-ESTEEM

a. Women need to feel attractive

b. Men need to feel successful at work

POINT 2. RELATIONSHIP TO WORK

a. Women feel restricted in choice, level, pay

b. Men feel burdened to achieve high position, work continuously

Which Method to Use: Block or Point by Point?

Although the block method may seem easier, it tends to allow the writer to ramble vaguely about each subject without concentrating on specific points of comparison or contrast. The resulting essay may resemble two separate discussions that could be cut apart with scissors. The advantage of the point-by-point method is that it keeps the writer focused on the relationship between both works and on the similarities or differences between them. Writers are less likely to digress and wander off topic in a point-by-point arrangement and are more likely to emphasize the points that they are making. Moreover, the summary statement that appears at the end of each paragraph in point-by-point organization tends to unify the essay more emphatically than the summary statement at the end of each block.

EXAMPLE: A COMPARISON-CONTRAST ESSAY

Writers do not always announce their intention to compare and contrast in their thesis, even though comparison and contrast elements predominate in the development of their thinking and writing. The following essay, published in the *Los Angeles Times* on June 16, 1999, was written by Alex Garcia, a staff photographer who lived in Cuba for several months. Although Garcia does not articulate his contrast plan in a thesis, from the first sentence of his essay he makes clear his intention to contrast the worlds of the United States and Cuba.

Reality Check
Alex Garcia

1   It appears Uncle Sam and El Comandante, while not quite seeing eye to eye, are exchanging curious glances. On baseball fields, in concert halls and

in schoolyards, the citizens of Cuba and the United States have recently been getting a glimpse of cultures that have been closed to one another for four decades. The United States says it hopes these exchanges will make it easier to export cultural values to Fidel Castro's Cuba. But it's worth underscoring that such exchanges go both ways.

2   I recently spent several months in Havana and the Cuban countryside as part of a language and cultural program hosted by San Francisco–based Global Exchange, one of the few organizations in the United States that legally sponsors trips to the island. As someone of Cuban origin, I stepped into such waters cautiously.

3   I have a cousin now living in the United States who risked his life swimming to the naval base at Guantánamo Bay to escape what he considers a prison. I also have a cousin who became president of his neighborhood block committee in Havana out of loyalty to what he believes is a worker's paradise. Both have made tremendous sacrifices to stay true to the values they hold dear. That I would find some of my values in conflict with those I found in Cuba came as no surprise. But I was uncomfortable with how even my most basic assumptions would be challenged.

4   For example, as one of our core values, U.S. citizens presume the inherent goodness of individualism, of being ruggedly independent, John Wayne-style. So it came as a surprise when one of my tutors said, "I would never want to think of myself as independent." "Me neither," another said coldly.

5   Come again? As a program participant, I was paired with University of Havana students who served as language tutors and cultural assistants. We had been talking about their future hopes, and I had asked what they were going to do once they were independent.

6   "Being independent means being selfish, cold, unwilling to help other people," my tutor told me. After years of struggling to be independent myself, I was at first uneasy with that idea. But I recalled the communal spirit of the many Cubans I met: the ubiquitous hitchhikers getting free rides from passing motorists; neighbors borrowing the car and the telephone as if they were family; hotel workers trading shifts and bicycles in a spirit of *compañerismo,* or camaraderie.

7   And there was the pedestrian who jumped into my cab to mooch a ride, defending his appropriation of my fare by saying to the driver, "Hey we're Cuban, aren't we?" I can't imagine hitchhiking in downtown Los Angeles, or even calling my neighbor "cousin," much less sharing with him a roll of toilet paper—a commodity rationed in Cuba. The U.S. model encourages people to value individual effort over shared sacrifice. But to many Cubans, it can seem a lonely path to take.

8   Expressing the values I believe the United States stands for was not simple either, in large part because Cuban television shows the flip side of them, through news and entertainment. For instance, if I cite civil liberties, the state-run television network Cubavision will air a Hollywood movie about the Ku Klux Klan, hate crimes or out-of-control gangbangers in Los Angeles. If I advocate multi-party democracy, a Cubavision documentary will point to a two-party system in the United States tainted by special-interest money and embarrassed by a 30% voter turnout. If I stress the benefits of upward mobility, the government-controlled national newspaper *Granma* will remark that the majority of people who are born in poverty in the United States die in poverty.

9   Fair or not, the contrarian views fostered in the Cuban media take away the shine with which we like to present ourselves.

10   Wastefulness isn't exactly one of my core values, but it certainly revealed itself as a personal trait while I was in Cuba. Given the choice between buying a new backpack, or repairing an old one by hand—sewing it with used dental floss—which do you think I chose? Or using my family's old kerosene lantern during blackouts versus pulling out my fancy flashlight that, oops, used expensive and rare batteries? Or tossing plastic bottles without considering their secondary storage value? I guess seeing thousands of commercials by age 10 has pushed me to think: "Where can I go to get or buy what I need?"

11   By contrast, most Cubans first ask, "What do I already have that I could use?" Some even bragged about such *resolver,* or resourcefulness. My relatives, not terribly amused with my lack of *resolver,* were quite patient. Their frugality is probably borne of necessity rather than virtue, but my lack of it was embarrassing to me. Perhaps I've been too busy shopping for values instead of cultivating them.

12   More embarrassing was a discussion about personal hygiene and what it seems to say about one's priorities. I was blindsided when asked, "Why do you all have the habit of showering in the morning before work instead of after work? You mean to tell me you come home to be with your family or friends, and you don't shower then? You go to bed with your wife after a full day of sweat? Eeeeeyyyyewww!"

13   It was surprising for me, as an American photojournalist, to see how images in our media that seem clear-cut can have quite another meaning for a Cuban. In Havana, I met a Cuban photographer working for an international news agency who showed me a picture he'd taken that day. It was of Castro, excitedly raising his fists in the air as he stood behind a lectern. "Ha? Ha? Isn't that great?" the photographer said proudly. "This will show the exiles in Miami that Fidel is still going strong!" I looked at him, incredulous. From a certain U.S. perspective, the gray-haired leader waving his fists appeared as the stereotypical crazed pariah.

14   Becoming aware of our own preconceptions or biases, and accepting them, may well be the ultimate value of any culture exchange. Staging a sing-along, a ballgame or other cultural encounter might have great symbolic value and surface appeal. But if the two nations are to make a genuine connection and resolve the decades' old conflict, we need to look deeper and not get lost on an island of assumptions.

Analyzing the Writer's Strategy

Garcia's stance is established in his first sentence, when he shows his footing in two worlds, the United States and Cuba. He creates the image of "Uncle Sam and El Comandante . . . not quite seeing eye to eye . . . exchanging curious glances" to establish the *differences* in the two cultures he observed during his stay in Cuba. Using these informal nicknames, he establishes a light-hearted tone that softens the negative aspects of American values as viewed through the eyes of his Cuban hosts.

Garcia notes that while the goal of the language and cultural program is that it "will make it easier to export cultural values to Fidel Castro's Cuba," ironically he returned questioning his own values. Irony abounds in his family background and in the discoveries he makes. He has family on both sides of the political spectrum: one cousin escaped Cuba, calling it "a prison," and another cousin serves as a leader in Cuba, believing it to be "a worker's paradise." Therefore, Garcia expected to find some of his values in conflict with those he found in Cuba, but he did not expect to have his "most basic assumptions" challenged. Rather than promoting American values to the Cubans, Garcia came to question them.

Garcia's sense of irony comes through in his examples of American life that don't make sense to Cubans: that American individualism is won at the expense of greater good for the group, that American civil liberties allow the existence of racist groups such as the Ku Klux Klan, that Americans enjoy the right to vote but turn out in embarrassingly low numbers, that America is praised as the land of opportunity yet most of its citizens who are born poor also die poor. As he says, "The contrarian views fostered in the Cuban media take away the shine with which we like to present ourselves."

After exposing the ironies of public and political life, Garcia moves to personal observations on his wastefulness, indifference to environmental protection, and consumerism, and he concludes that perhaps he has been "too busy shopping for values instead of cultivating them." His carefully worked out irony and well-chosen words earn him the empathy rather than the antagonism of his American readers.

To illustrate how far apart cultural perceptions can be, Garcia juxtaposes two responses to the same photo of Castro, with his fists raised. The Cuban's view is that the photo shows Fidel is "still going strong," but the American is more likely to see the gray-haired leader as "the stereotypical crazed pariah."

Garcia concludes his essay by admitting that the highest value of a cultural exchange program might be that we become "aware of our own preconceptions or biases." By acknowledging that his stay in Cuba forced him to confront his own assumptions, he creates the same opportunity for his reader. He finally hopes that both nations will "make a genuine connection" and "not get lost on an island of assumptions," a final well-crafted allusion to the isolation of cultural boundaries.

 ### PRACTICING WRITING ESSAYS THAT USE COMPARISON AND CONTRAST

Select one topic to write an essay that uses comparison or contrast.

1. A family member's response to an important decision; how you expected that person to respond

2. A perception of a family member that you held in your youth; a view of that person that you have today

3. Your understanding or interpretation of a particular movie, song, or event; a friend's view of the same thing

4. Your concept of ideal employment; a job you have held or hold now

5. The role of computers in education as described in "Makes Learning Fun" (p. 247) and "From Learning as Torture to Learning as Fun" (p. 255)

6. The authors' attitudes about being fat in "Discrimination at Large" (p. 198) and in "O.K., So I'm Fat" (p. 201)

 ## Final Tips for Comparison and Contrast Essays

- Make sure that your **thesis includes both subjects** that are being compared and contrasted, and that the wording is specific. Avoid a thesis that simply claims they are both alike and different.

- Consider using the **point-by-point** method of comparison-contrast for a more emphatic delivery of information.

- Continue **interrelating the two subjects** so that you never make a point about one without showing how it relates to the other.

- Search for **subtle links and distinctions** as well as for the obvious ones. Then analyze the reasons for those differences.

Chapter 12

Analysis

ANALYSIS OF A PROCESS, PROBLEM, OR SUBJECT

All essays involve analysis. Whether the method of development is comparison-contrast, cause and effect, or any other strategy, all college writing requires analysis—a close examination of the parts in order to better understand the whole. The "parts" may include a scrutiny of a particular author's key points, supporting examples, word choice, and organizational strategy. The purpose of any analysis is not merely to take the process, problem, or subject apart, but to see the value of the individual parts and to appreciate their interaction in creating the whole.

When to Use Analysis

Written analysis is assigned in every academic discipline. Whether you are writing a lab report on the dissection of a frog in biology, interpreting a painting in art history, examining a short story in English, reviewing curriculum in education, exploring a management problem in business, or studying a discrimination problem in law, you will be expected to write analytical papers.

These papers will be specifically targeted to the subject you are studying, but three basic types of analytical assignments predominate: analysis of (1) a process, (2) a problem, or (3) a subject. Sometimes these distinctions blur, depending on the writer's purpose and audience. However, all papers involve breaking the whole into parts and examining the parts to show a reader their importance to the whole.

Analysis of a Process

A paper that examines a process explains how to do something or how the process itself is done. Examples might include performing a swimming pool rescue, getting a classmate to ask you out, cooking in a wok, paying car insurance while earning minimum wage, or getting a roommate's friend to move out.

Brainstorming for a Topic

If a topic has not been assigned, brainstorm for possibilities. Consider what you know how to do that others don't or what you would like to learn in order to explain that process to a reader. Don't overlook the unusual: how to get your parents to start a compost pile or how to get your roommate to shower daily. Your essay can, in fact, be quite lively if you use ingenuity and a little prewriting energy.

Organizing and Developing a Process Analysis

If you are writing a paper that tells your reader how to do something, or one that describes how something happens, these tips will help:

1. Determine whether chronology is important. For some processes, the sequence of the steps is critical (performing a swimming pool rescue), while for others it isn't as important (getting a classmate to ask you out). If chronology is important, list the steps and reexamine your list to make sure any reader can follow the logic of your arrangement.

2. If the steps in your process resist chronological ordering, determine an arrangement that makes sense. For example, in the model below, the writer first dismisses the most efficient but least probable method to save gas before she offers gas-saving steps that everyone can achieve.

3. Write each point completely, with supporting details and analysis of each. Include all of the necessary information and remove confusing or irrelevant details. Imagine yourself in your readers' position, trying to follow your instructions for something they have never done.

4. Write a thesis that clearly asserts your point:

   Thesis: Success in small-group discussions requires awareness, participation, and cooperation.

   Thesis: Following the proper sequence of steps will facilitate a swimming pool rescue.

5. Draft your essay by linking each step or point with appropriate transitions to move your reader smoothly through this process.

6. Rewrite and edit your essay so that the language is vivid, the directions are precise, and the analysis is complete.

 ## PRACTICING PROCESS ANALYSIS IN SMALL GROUPS

In small groups, write down the steps explaining how to do the following:

1. Find summer employment.

2. Balance a diet to achieve good nutrition.

3. Prepare a three-year-old for a romp in the snow.

4. Stay awake in a dull lecture.

5. Convince an unwilling landlord to make a repair.

6. Use library computers to find a book or an article on immigrants seeking political asylum.

Spend time reaching accord within your group to ensure that all steps follow logically and that no necessary steps are left out. Aim for clarity and precision; remove words that obscure your directions. Any one of these analyses could be drafted into a collaborative paper.

Sections throughout this book explain various processes—for example, how to conduct an interview; how to cluster, list, and read actively; how to incorporate quoted material. These sections may be useful to you as models of process analysis, and they also underscore how important process analysis is to both teaching and learning.

EXAMPLE: A PROCESS ANALYSIS ESSAY

In the following essay, "How to Get Better Gas Mileage," Katharine Mieszkowski, a senior writer at *Salon.com,* provides tips from auto experts and "obsessive hypermilers" on how to go farther on a gallon of gas. Mieszkowski's essay was first posted in 2007, and gas prices have continued to fluctuate wildly. Her advice for conserving gas remains relevant.

How to Get Better Gas Mileage
Katharine Mieszkowski

1 Drink less, give up sweets—the clean calender of a new year inspires many earnest vows of self-improvement. With oil flirting with $100 a barrel, and $3 gas looking like the new normal, perhaps instead of resolving to curb your gluttony in the new year, you should pledge to train your car to be a

fuel sipper. "Every time you get into your car and turn on your ignition you can save money," says Bradlee Fons of Pewaukee, Wis., who teaches seminars on efficient driving. "It helps the country with national security and oil dependence, and it helps the world with global warming."

2   The most efficient way to save gas, as any "one-less-car" transportation activist will attest, is to leave your car in the garage. Walk, ride your bike, take the bus or train, or carpool whenever you can. When you're in the market for a car, choose the most fuel-efficient model. That should get easier to do in the coming years as automakers comply with the just-passed law to move America's fleet from an average fuel economy of 25 miles per gallon to 35 by 2020, a 40 percent increase. It means there should be more fuel-efficient models of all vehicle types from compact to minivan to choose from soon.

3   Yet there are also simple steps that every driver can take with an existing car, truck or SUV to save fuel simply by improving driving habits. "If you're an aggressive driver, and many, many people are, you should become a moderate driver," says Philip Reed, senior consumer advice editor for *Edmunds.com.* Unfortunately, most people who drive aggressively don't realize it. "Driving for most people is a completely unconscious act. Just a little bit of self-awareness about how you drive can make a huge difference," says Bradley Berman, founder of *Hybridcars.com,* which offers both easy and advanced tips for driving more efficiently. Adopting a mellower approach on the road not only will ameliorate your road rage but could save you the equivalent of $1 a gallon, according to the U.S. Department of Energy, by improving your fuel efficiency as much as 33 percent.

4   "We all learned how to drive when gas was cheap, and we have to relearn how to drive," says Fons. To chill out behind the wheel, first curb rapid acceleration and excessive braking. Start by avoiding so-called jack rabbit starts—aggressively accelerating from a standstill at a stop sign or a stoplight. But remember, midrange acceleration also gobbles fuel, according to Reed from Edmunds. "You're going 50, and there's an opening in traffic, and you need to accelerate to 75, and you hammer it—that requires a lot of energy." Learn to accelerate smoothly and gradually. Press down on the pedal with the light touch of a feather.

5   Adopting a lower cruising speed can also help your car go farther with less gasoline. The efficiency of most cars rapidly declines at speeds over 60. In fact, every 5 miles per hour over 60 you drive is like paying an extra 20 cents a gallon for gas, according to the Department of Energy. So the next time you're tempted to pull ahead of the guy in the Ferrari on the freeway, think of the Saudis and keep out of the fast lane.

6   Just as hammering the gas is a bad idea, so is slamming on the brakes. Instead, anticipate stoplights and stop signs so that you can back off the

accelerator, whenever possible, to slow down, and then gently apply the brakes. "If your vehicle weighs 4,000 pounds, it takes a lot of energy to get that going from a dead stop," explains Fons, who drives a 2000 Honda Insight, and through his driving habits manages to wring as much as 100 mpg out of the car, which is rated at 66 mpg by the Environmental Protection Agency. In stop-and-go traffic, strive to maintain one consistent low speed instead of accelerating and braking, accelerating and braking. To do this, drive in the slow lane, and maintain a long buffer zone in front of you, so you won't have to slam on the brakes to avoid rear-ending the next car.

7   Drivers are often unconsciously influenced by the speed of the other cars around them, which can lead to speed creep. "When a faster car passes you, you have a tendency to speed up. Soon, even though you were committed to going 70, you're going 80," says Reed. "In some cases, cars are so well insulated it's easy to go fast without realizing it." A good way to avoid that pitfall: Use the cruise control on the freeway, which will also help you avoid the temptation to constantly dart forward when you see an opening in traffic up ahead.

8   Any time you hear the engine revving high, you're gulping fuel. If you drive a stick shift, and you're cruising along in third, shift to fourth, and hear the revs of the engine drop. Your car is the most inefficient when the engine is still warming up, so taking fewer trips by combining errands into one trip will save gas. Drive to your farthest destination, and then do the errands closer to home on the way back. When choosing your route, avoid hills if possible, so you won't be wasting energy hauling thousands of pounds of steel up an incline.

9   If you've got 57 books in your trunk that you keep meaning to donate to the library, but never get around to doing, try this experiment: "Take all that stuff out, and put it in a wheelbarrow, and push it up and down the driveway once, and you'll see how much energy it takes," says Wayne Gerdes. Gerdes invented the term "hypermiler" to describe the obsessive drivers like him who strive to wring every last mile out of a gallon of gas, exceeding the EPA's estimate of how far a car can go per gallon.

10   The more weight your car has to carry the harder it works, even though the overall gas savings are small, about 1 to 2 percent per 100 excess pounds eliminated, according to the U.S. Department of Energy. Reed at Edmunds doesn't worry too much about excess weight in the trunk, since he believes this tip was crafted back in the 1970s when New Englanders would keep 150-pound bags of sand in their trunks in hopes of getting better traction in the ice and snow in winter.

11   Avoiding excessive idling is also a must. Anytime you're idling for more than 15 seconds, such as at a railroad crossing or when waiting curbside to pick up your child from school, turn off your engine, advises Fons, who cofounded the Milwaukee Hybrid Group, which gives tips on what he calls

eco-driving. The bigger your engine, the more fuel you typically waste idling. But whatever car you have, when it's idling it gets—duh!—zero miles per gallon. Idling is one of those bad habits that die hard. "Cars used to be hard to start. Oil was cheap, and we didn't care about global warming," says Reed. "These days cars are fuel injected."

12   Keeping your car tuned up can also bring some gas mileage improvements. Keeping tires properly inflated and frequently changing the air filter are the two biggies. "Gasoline is only one of the fuels the car burns," explains Reed. "The other is oxygen, so feeding it with clean oxygen is very important."

13   If you really get into saving gas, you can invest in a scan gauge, which costs about $170. It will inform you in real time what miles per gallon your car is getting. (Hybrids already come equipped with them.) Gerdes, who says he once got 127 mpg (over the course of 90 miles) in a 2004 Toyota Prius, believes drivers can realize a 15 percent savings on fuel overnight by buying and heeding a gauge.

14   It used to be said that driving with the air conditioner on was a big fuel waster. But in all but the oldest jalopies with primitive air conditioners, that turns out to be an old wives' tale. "The air conditioners that we have now are highly efficient," says Reed from Edmunds. "Yes, they do take more power from the engine, but we're talking about 1 or 2 percent." The alternative of driving with the air conditioner off and the windows open doesn't offer a significant gain in gas mileage. On the contrary, when Edmunds conducted road tests to measure whether the altered aerodynamics of driving with the windows open impacted gas mileage, they noticed a decline in fuel economy if all the windows and the sunroof were open.

15   Driving experts say there's no need to wait for years to benefit from the new fuel-efficiency law. We can see major gas savings now simply by backing off the accelerator and brakes. "Everybody and anybody can do this no matter what they own and drive," says Gerdes. With practice, you, too, can become a hypermiler, and soon be shaming your lead-foot neighbors with your superior miles per gallon.

Analyzing the Writer's Strategy

Katharine Mieszkowski's highly useful process analysis begins with an allusion to New Year's resolutions because she is writing at the end of a calendar year. She appeals to readers who annually commit to "earnest vows of self-improvement." For this year, she suggests that instead of curbing their own gluttony, readers should train their car "to be a fuel sipper" (464–465). This vivid image is striking and a lively contrast to the predictable tradition of New Year's resolutions. Mieszkowski's voice is reader-friendly even while she incorporates the research of many experts who provide technical data and statistical evidence on how to improve fuel efficiency.

Mieszkowski begins with the most obvious gas-saver, "to leave your car in the garage," but then provides "simple steps that every driver can take with an existing car, truck or SUV to save fuel" (464). She realizes that most readers can't stop driving altogether or even replace their existing vehicle for a more fuel efficient one. Her tips promise to be realistic and workable.

By including advice from experts, she strengthens her argument with technological information about how "jackrabbit starts," hammering the accelerator, and "slamming on the brakes" use excessive fuel. She reports that "adopting a mellower approach on the road not only will ameliorate your road rage but could save you the equivalent of $1 a gallon . . . improving your fuel efficiency as much as 33 percent" (464). These noteworthy statistics should influence any driver.

In addition to convincing her readers with statistics, she also addresses controversies that readers may have heard debated. For example, she notes that extra weight in the trunk is significant to some experts but not to others, but that all seem to agree that an air conditioner does not guzzle fuel, as was once believed. In fact, closed windows improve the car's aerodynamics and gas mileage. By addressing experts' opposed views and by dispelling "an old wives' tale," she anticipates and answers readers' questions.

Without resorting to a bulleted list, Mieszkowski nevertheless quickly provides numerous tips for all drivers willing to change their habits: adopt a lower cruising speed ("every 5 miles per hour over 60 you drive is like paying an extra 20 cents per gallon for gas"); avoid "speed creep," unconsciously increasing your speed to match the drivers around you (use cruise control); avoid idling the car for over 15 seconds (turn off the engine instead of waiting with the engine running).

The author's conclusion affirms her universal appeal that all drivers, regardless of their vehicles, can change habits in order to save fuel: "With practice, you, too, can become a hypermiler, and soon be shaming your lead-foot neighbors with you superior miles per gallon" (466). Mieszkowski is encouraging readers to not only change habits but to change priorities and even values to respond to a pressing need.

⬤ PRACTICING WRITING A PROCESS ANALYSIS ESSAY

Select and describe a process that you know well from the following list:

1. How to get a hot guy or girl to hang out with you

2. How to convince an instructor that you shouldn't lose points on your late paper

3. How to benefit from small-group discussions

4. How to organize for a backpacking or camping trip

Write your description as precisely as you can so that a reader can learn the process. Does your interest in the topic show in your description?

Final Tips for a Process Analysis Essay

- Review the order of the steps you have written to determine that your reader can follow your instructions or description. Consider your tone. Would humor help you engage your reader?
- Examine the details you have given to remove any confusing instructions or irrelevant details.
- Put yourself in your reader's position to see whether you have defined necessary terms, provided relevant details, and analyzed all key points.
- Reread your work to see whether appropriate transitions link the steps or the parts of your analysis.
- Reread to strengthen your language and enliven your essay.

Analysis of a Problem

Another kind of analysis paper describes a problem; it may or may not offer a solution. The writer may trace the history of the problem, but chronology is not as vital to this type of analysis as it is in a step-by-step process analysis. It is critical that the writer establishes the problem, examines its parts, and shows how the parts are related to the problem as a whole.

When to Use Problem Analysis

More than any other single type of writing, problem analysis appears in every academic field and profession. Our daily newspapers and monthly newsmagazines as well as the readings in this textbook all feature essays analyzing a variety of problems: drug abuse, irresponsible parenting, stereotyping, isolation of the disabled, group conformity, and racial, ethnic, and gender discrimination. In spite of the wide range of issues, writers of problem analysis share similar strategies when they examine an issue.

Organizing and Developing a Problem Analysis Essay

Engaging your readers is critical in problem analysis. Why should your readers care about stereotypes, ethnic bias, the rights of the disabled, or any other subject that doesn't directly relate to them? It is your job to create reader interest, and you can do this in a number of ways. Sometimes startling statistics or a bold anecdote will jar complacent readers out of apathy. Sometimes posing a direct question to readers prompts them to consider their responses and become involved in the topic—at least enough to read the work. After you have engaged your readers, decide how much background information they require in order to understand the problem. For example, if you are writing an analysis of changing interest rates, you will include less background material if you are writing the paper for your business class than for your English class.

Then, as in all analysis papers, you will need to choose which parts of the problem you want to examine. You must describe the problem so that any reader can understand it. This might include a discussion of the severity of the problem, the numbers affected by it, which population is most affected, and the consequences if this problem is uncorrected. A detailed study of each aspect of the problem and how it relates to the other parts will constitute the body of your paper. If it is relevant to your analysis, you might speculate about the barriers to solving this problem (such as cost, social bias, frustration with earlier failures, indifference, or denial).

It is important that this analysis has a focus and a clear point or assertion. For example, if you are concerned about the fact that Americans are on the job more than workers in other countries, it is not enough merely to identify the number of hours that American employees work each week. Nor is it enough to show that they work more hours per week and more weeks per year than their European counterparts, or that they are not routinely given flexible work schedules so they can coordinate their family's needs with their work responsibilities. All of these important facts could support a point, but the point must be made.

You will need to clarify, in the form of a thesis or assertion, why the analysis of these facts is important: that American workers are overworked, that Americans have insufficient leisure time, that American children grow up deprived of their parents, or any other point that you deem significant as a result of your analysis. But without a point, you have no paper.

Once you have determined your assertion, you are ready to outline, draft, and revise your paper. Specific suggestions about outlining, drafting, and revising can be found in the student example of a problem analysis on eating disorders (pp. 387–390).

EXAMPLE: A PROBLEM ANALYSIS ESSAY

The following analysis was written by a Harvard-educated economist, Robert L. Heilbroner, who has written extensively on economics and business. This essay, originally published in *Reader's Digest,* contains a unique perception of a common problem.

Don't Let Stereotypes Warp Your Judgments

Robert L. Heilbroner

1 Is a girl called Gloria apt to be better-looking than one called Bertha? Are criminals more likely to be dark than blond? Can you tell a good deal about someone's personality from hearing his voice briefly over the phone? Can a person's nationality be pretty accurately guessed from his photograph? Does the fact that someone wears glasses imply that he is intelligent?

2 The answer to all these questions is obviously, "No."

3 Yet, from all the evidence at hand, most of us believe these things. Ask any college boy if he'd rather take his chances with a Gloria or a Bertha, or ask a college girl if she'd rather blind-date a Richard or a Cuthbert. In fact, you don't have to ask: college students in questionnaires have revealed that names conjure up the same images in their minds as they do in yours—and for as little reason.

4 Look into the favorite suspects of persons who report "suspicious characters" and you will find a large percentage of them to be "swarthy" or "dark and foreign-looking"—despite the testimony of criminologists that criminals do not tend to be dark, foreign, or "wild-eyed." Delve into the main asset of a telephone stock swindler and you will find it to be a marvelously confidence-inspiring telephone "personality." And whereas we all think we know what an Italian or a Swede looks like, it is the sad fact that when a group of Nebraska students sought to match faces and nationalities of fifteen European countries, they were scored wrong in 93 percent of their identifications. Finally, for although horn-rimmed glasses have now become the standard television sign of an "intellectual," optometrists know that the main thing that distinguishes people with glasses is just bad eyes.

5 Stereotypes are a kind of gossip about the world, a gossip that makes us prejudge people before we ever lay eyes on them. Hence it is not surprising that stereotypes have something to do with the dark world of prejudice. Explore most prejudices (note that the word means prejudgment) and you will find a cruel stereotype at the core of each one.

6 For it is the extraordinary fact that once we have typecast the world, we tend to see people in terms of our standardized pictures. In another demonstration of the power of stereotypes to affect our vision, a number of Columbia and Barnard students were shown thirty photographs of pretty but unidentified girls, and asked to rate each in terms of "general liking," "intelligence," "beauty," and so on. Two months later, the same group were shown

the same photographs, this time with fictitious Irish, Italian, Jewish, and "American" names attached to the pictures. Right away the ratings changed. Faces which were now seen as representing a national group went down in looks and still farther down in likability, while the "American" girls suddenly looked decidedly prettier and nicer.

7   Why is it that we stereotype the world in such irrational and harmful fashion? In part, we begin to type-cast people in our childhood years. Early in life, as every parent whose child has watched a TV Western knows, we learn to spot the Good Guys from the Bad Guys. Some years ago, a social psychologist showed very clearly how powerful these stereotypes of childhood vision are. He secretly asked the most popular youngsters in an elementary school to make errors in their morning gym exercises. Afterwards, he asked the class if anyone had noticed any mistakes during gym period. Oh, yes, said the children. But it was the unpopular members of the class—the "bad guys"—they remembered as being out of step.

8   We not only grow up with standardized pictures forming inside of us, but as grown-ups we are constantly having them thrust upon us. Some of them, like the half-joking, half-serious stereotypes of mothers-in-law, or country yokels, or psychiatrists, are dinned into us by the stock jokes we hear and repeat. In fact, without such stereotypes, there would be a lot fewer jokes. Still other stereotypes are perpetuated by the advertisements we read, the movies we see, the books we read.

9   And finally, we tend to stereotype because it helps us make sense out of a highly confusing world, a world which William James once described as "one great, blooming, buzzing confusion." It is a curious fact that if we don't know what we're looking at, we are often quite literally unable to see what we're looking at. People who recover their sight after a lifetime of blindness actually cannot at first tell a triangle from a square. A visitor to a factory sees only noisy chaos where the superintendent sees a perfectly synchronized flow of work. As Walter Lippmann has said, "For the most part we do not first see, and then define; we define first, and then we see."

10   Stereotypes are one way in which we "define" the world in order to see it. They classify the infinite variety of human beings into a convenient handful of "types" toward whom we learn to act in stereotyped fashion. Life would be a wearing process if we had to start from scratch with each and every human contact. Stereotypes economize on our mental effort by covering up the blooming, buzzing confusion with big recognizable cut-outs. They save us the "trouble" of finding out what the world is like—they give it its accustomed look.

11 Thus the trouble is that stereotypes make us mentally lazy. As S. I. Hayakawa, the authority on semantics, has written: "The danger of stereotypes lies not in their existence, but in the fact that they become for all people some of the time, and for some people all the time, substitutes for observation." Worse yet, stereotypes get in the way of our judgment, even when we do observe the world. Someone who has formed rigid preconceptions of all Latins as "excitable," or all teenagers as "wild," doesn't alter his point of view when he meets a calm and deliberate Genoese, or a serious-minded high school student. He brushes them aside as "exceptions that prove the rule." And, of course, if he meets someone true to type, he stands triumphantly vindicated. "They're all like that," he proclaims, having encountered an excited Latin, an ill-behaved adolescent.

12 Hence, quite aside from the injustice which stereotypes do to others, they impoverish ourselves. A person who lumps the world into simple categories, who type-casts all labor leaders as "racketeers," all businessmen as "reactionaries," all Harvard men as "snobs," and all Frenchmen as "sexy," is in danger of becoming a stereotype himself. He loses his capacity to be himself—which is to say, to see the world in his own absolutely unique, inimitable and independent fashion.

13 Instead, he votes for the man who fits his standardized picture of what a candidate "should" look like or sound like, buys the goods that someone in his "situation" in life "should" own, lives the life that others define for him. The mark of the stereotyped person is that he never surprises us, that we do indeed have him "typed." And no one fits this straitjacket so perfectly as someone whose opinions about other people are fixed and inflexible.

14 Impoverishing as they are, stereotypes are not easy to get rid of. The world we type-cast may be no better than a Grade B movie, but at least we know what to expect of our stock characters. When we let them act for themselves in the strangely unpredictable way that people do act, who knows but that many of our fondest convictions will be proved wrong?

15 Nor do we suddenly drop our standardized pictures for a blinding vision of the Truth. Sharp swings of ideas about people often just substitute one stereotype for another. The true process of change is a slow one that adds bits and pieces of reality to the pictures in our heads, until gradually they take on some of the blurriness of life itself. Little by little, we learn not that Jews and Negroes and Catholics and Puerto Ricans are "just like everybody else"—for that, too, is a stereotype—but that each and every one of them is unique, special, different and individual. Often we do not even know that we have let a stereotype lapse until we hear someone saying, "all so-and-so's are like such-and-such," and we hear ourselves saying, "Well—maybe."

16 Can we speed the process along? Of course we can.

17   First, we can become aware of the standardized pictures in our heads, in other people's heads, in the world around us.

18   Second, we can become suspicious of all judgments that we allow exceptions to "prove." There is no more chastening thought than that in the vast intellectual adventure of science, it takes but one tiny exception to topple a whole edifice of ideas.

19   Third, we can learn to be chary of generalizations about people. As F. Scott Fitzgerald once wrote: "Begin with an individual, and before you know it you have created a type; begin with a type, and you find you have created—nothing."

20   Most of the time, when we type-cast the world, we are not in fact generalizing about people at all. We are only revealing the embarrassing facts about the pictures that hang in the gallery of stereotypes in our own heads.

Analyzing the Writer's Strategy

Heilbroner's immediate goal is to convince his readers that they stereotype, even though they may think that they do not. Throughout his essay, Heilbroner's tone is light and not accusatory because most people intellectually know that stereotyping is unfair—and would even deny that they do it. His strategy is to engage his readers by asking an entire paragraph of carefully chosen questions that he knows everybody answers in the same predictable way—evidence of the pervasiveness of stereotyping. Using statistical evidence from tests that have been given to college students (seemingly people of above average intelligence), Heilbroner then shows that all people "typecast the world." The author incorporates quoted statements about stereotyping from famous thinkers and philosophers to illustrate his own views.

Ultimately Heilbroner's strategy is to convince his readers that stereotyping "impoverishes" the person who does the stereotyping because it makes that person "mentally lazy." He can accomplish this only by giving many specific examples of how people substitute stereotypes for true observation. His strategy is further to convince his readers that a slow process of conscious awareness can reduce the tendency to stereotype.

PRACTICING WRITING A PROBLEM ANALYSIS ESSAY

Problem analysis assignments appear after many of the readings in this text. In addition to those that reflect the theme of being "between worlds," you might write an analysis of any of these problems:

1. Limited inexpensive housing available for college students

2. Policies at work or school that seem poorly conceived

3. A family's inability to communicate

4. Athletes' use of drugs

5. Unnecessary packaging of products

6. Overdrinking and overeating in American society

 Final Tips for a Problem Analysis Essay

- Engage your readers to convince them of the importance of the problem.
- Provide sufficient background information for your intended audience.
- Make sure that your thesis expresses why your analysis of the problem is important.
- Reread and revise to ascertain that you have adequately discussed the parts of the problem that require analysis and that you have related those parts to the problem as a whole.

Analysis of a Subject

Another type of analysis paper examines a subject—a painting, short story, or budget—or a particular aspect of the subject—the composition of a painting, a character in a short story, or an entertainment allowance in a budget. These papers, like problem and process analysis, involve breaking the subject into parts and closely examining its parts to show the reader their importance to the subject as a whole.

Brainstorming for a Topic

If a topic has not been assigned, brainstorm to find a subject that interests you or for which you have some information, but don't select a subject that is too familiar. The purpose of any writing assignment is discovery, and nothing will help you understand a subject better than careful analysis.

When to Use Subject Analysis

Instructors expect analysis when their assignments and exam questions contain words like *explain, interpret, describe, explore why, show how, explicate, discuss, relate,* or *trace.* If you have been asked to examine an art object, interpret a poem, explore the ramifications of affirmative action in college admissions, or describe a community's recycling plan, you are required to examine the parts—or a part that has been assigned—and show how that part or those parts relate to the whole.

Organizing and Developing a Subject Analysis

Examine carefully the subject that you have selected or that has been assigned. Question the significance of the work, responding to it freshly. Determine for yourself why the subject is worth the time that you will devote to examining it.

If you have not been assigned a particular part to analyze, make a list of as many aspects or parts of the subject as you can. Then consider which parts are most significant and which you can most productively examine. In some cases, the success of your paper and how you will be evaluated will be determined by your ability to limit your selection to particularly provocative or relevant aspects. Ultimately, your job will be to show the significance of the parts or a particular part in relation to the entire work.

As introductory material, before you begin your analysis of the parts, describe the whole subject *briefly*. Remember that description is not the same thing as analysis, but realize also that your reader can't care about the parts without knowing something about the whole. Depending on the subject of your analysis, this introductory description might involve a historical context, an overall physical description, or a summary.

Write your minute description and detailed perception of the parts that you perceive to be the most significant for an understanding of the work. As you write an analysis of each part, keep your eye on the whole. You will need to return to your subject repeatedly to be sure that you are seeing or reading it thoroughly and carefully. You will not be able to write an analysis of a painting quickly glimpsed or a poem read only once.

Focus your paper with an assertion that shows your perception of the parts in relation to the subject that you are analyzing. Expressing your perception in the form of a thesis will keep both you and your reader on target.

ESSAY ASSIGNMENTS FOR SUBJECT ANALYSIS

Practice writing an analysis of one of the following subjects:

1. A favorite painting or a photo from a magazine

2. The lyrics to a piece of music

3. A controversial campus policy

4. The setting or music in a particular film

5. Rita or Marc in "Peaches" (p. 71)

6. The images in "Coke" (p. 243)

7. The grandfather in "Blue Spruce" (p. 79)

POETRY AND CHARACTER ANALYSIS
What Is Poetry Analysis?

When you are asked to write an essay about a poem, you will be expected to analyze it—that is, to study its parts and explain how they relate to the whole. This examination involves a closer scrutiny than an overview or summary. In a summary, you tell what the poem is about or what happens in the poem. In an analysis, you explain how certain elements function in the poem and why the poem is written as it is. Although summary cannot take the place of analysis, you might need to summarize as a part of analysis. But poetry analysis requires a close look at the poem's elements—key words, images, and figures of speech.

An exploration of *key words* is a productive way to analyze a poem. Even though you may feel you know what a word means, the poet may be using a less-known meaning of the word. Because most of us don't know the origin or obscure meanings of all words, a dictionary is indispensable when reading a poem. In addition to the *denotation,* or dictionary definition of a word, you may be aware of the *connotation* or emotional association that the word conveys, and the poet may be counting on your feelings about the word. Knowing the connotations, unusual definitions, or multiple meanings of a word is critical to understanding the poem.

For example, in "Facing It" (p. 195), Yusef Komanyakaa clearly is working with at least two different meanings of the verb "to face": "to look toward or in the direction of," as the speaker is looking in the direction of the Vietnam Veterans Memorial, and also "to confront courageously," as the narrator must "confront" or come to terms with his experiences in the Vietnam War. There are additional meanings of "facing" as both a verb and noun and those meanings should be considered to see if any contribute to an understanding of the poem. Because words are the most basic element of any poem, the dictionary is a useful first step in analyzing poetry and helping you understand the other elements. Your knowledge of the multiple meanings of words can provide the focus for your analytic essay.

All poems consist of *images*—words that stir the senses: sight, sound, smell, touch, and taste. Because images are such vital elements of a poem, a productive analysis of a poem often involves examining particular images or patterns of images that seem to work together. In "Blue Spruce" (p. 79), Stephen Perry weaves a pattern of musical images throughout his poem: his grandfather's sousaphone, bandstand "with instruments—alto sax, tenor sax, tuba or sousaphone," congregation singing, the "oompah-pahs" of the sousaphone, and musical "notes."

In addition, he appeals to multiple senses: our sense of sight as a baby is raised "into the bell of his sousaphone," our sense of smell with the "barbershop / smelling of lotions," our sense of touch with the "smooth-rough hide" of the black razor strop, and our sense of sound "as the horses clip-clopped on ice" (80).

Images used suggestively rather than literally are called *figures of speech*, and a study of these figures can enhance your discussion of imagery. Of the many kinds of figures of speech, the most common are metaphor, simile, and personification. A *metaphor* is an implied comparison between two unlike things. Poets aren't the only ones who use metaphors; you probably use them daily without realizing it. For example, when you say, "My boyfriend is a gem," you are comparing him to something that is valuable, dazzling, impressive! In Stephen Perry's poem, he makes a direct comparison when he pictures how "the tiny hairs would gather / on the blade, a congregation singing" (79). The tiny hairs become a "congregation singing."

In contrast with metaphor, a *simile* is an explicit comparison between unlike things, using the words "like" or "as." In Perry's poem, the speaker describes how his grandfather lifted him high into the bell of his sousaphone "as if I were a note / he'd play into light—" (80). The baby is not literally a musical note but is compared to a lively, "light" sound that the grandfather would "play." The baby is "light" in contrast to the adults who judge the grandfather's affair darkly.

Perry also uses *personification*—giving human characteristics to an inanimate object, animal, or abstraction. In this poem, the speaker describes the town fountain in winter as one that had "frozen into a coiffure / of curly glass" (80). In addition to the coiffeur being a metaphor (an implied comparison) for the frozen water, the fountain is given human characteristics because it has styled hair, a "coiffure."

You may hear people refer to a *symbol* or to *symbolism* when they are discussing poetry. A symbol is something concrete used to represent or suggest something more abstract. In Perry's poem, the "sousaphone"—a large commanding instrument with a deep, forceful sound—represents the grandfather who is bold and impossible to ignore.

How to Actively Read a Poem

When you are assigned a poem to read, you need to read it through without worrying about what you don't understand. In a second or third reading, read the poem aloud, so that your ear catches connections that the poet intends. Then, just as you have been reading the essays in this book—actively—with a pen in hand, read the poem again and circle unfamiliar words, underline key words or lines, mark important ideas, and jot down comments in the margin. This is the time to use the dictionary to look up not only the words that may be new to you but words that the poet may have used differently than you

would expect. You need to write down, on the page with the poem or on a separate piece of paper, the multiple meanings of each word as well as relevant
origins of the word.

As you read, mark the examples of simile, metaphor, and personification,
as well as images that relate to each other by similarity or contrast. Ask questions as you read: Why does the poet use a particular word, or how do two images relate? Your responses to these questions provide notes that will help you
choose the focus for your analysis.

Here is an example of active reading that a student, Robert Sakatani,
did to prepare for class discussion of Janice Mirikitani's poem "Breaking
Tradition" (p. 21).

EXAMPLE: ACTIVE READING OF A POEM

Breaking Tradition
Janice Mirikitani

dedication ➔ for my daughter

    ✓   My daughter denies she is like me,
         Her <u>secretive</u> eyes avoid mine.   *daughter: "secretive," "veiled"*
            She reveals the hatreds of womanhood
            already <u>veiled</u> behind music and smoke and telephones.
    5   I want to tell her about the empty room
         of myself.
            This room we lock ourselves in   *repeats "room" = key metaphor?*
            where whispers live like fungus,
            giggles about small breasts and cellulite,
    10   where we confine ourselves to jealousies,
            bedridden by menstruation.
            This waiting room where we feel our <u>hands</u>
            are useless, dead <u>speechless clamps</u>   *striking metaphor*
            that need hospitals and forceps and kitchens
    15   and plugs and ironing boards to make them useful.
    ✓   I <u>deny I am like my mother</u>, I remember why:
            She kept her room neat with silence, —— *grandmother's room: "neat with silence"*
            defiance smothered in requirements to be (otonashii,)
            passion and loudness wrapped in an (obi) —— *meanings?*

20   her steps confined to ceremony,
the weight of her sacrifice she carried like
a foetus. Guilt passed on in our bones.
I want to break tradition—unlock this room
25   where women dress in the dark.
Discover the lies my mother told me.
The lies that we are small and powerless.
that our possibilities must be compressed
to the size of pearls, displayed only as
passive chokers, charms around our neck.

30   Break Tradition.
I want to tell my daughter of this room
of myself
filled with tears of violins,
the light in my hands,
35   poems about madness,
the music of yellow guitars
sounds shaken from barbed wire and
goodbyes and miracles of survival.
This room of open window where daring ones escape.
40   My daughter denies she is like me
her secretive eyes are walls of smoke
and music and telephones,
her pouting ruby lips, her skirts
swaying to salsa, teena marie and the stones,
45   her thighs displayed in carnivals of color.
I do not know the contents of her room.
She mirrors my aging.
She is breaking tradition.

Margin annotations:
- *ts title:*
- *mother's "lies"*
- *ts title:*
- *narrator wants to escape: "unlock this room"*
- *narrator's room*
- *ator esses otions ively*
- *meaning?*
- *relocation camps?*
- *repeats opening images*
- *aughter is Westernized*
- *daughter's room—unknown*
- *eats title:*
- *like mother, like daughter—each in her own way*

Active Reading Discussed

Student Robert Sakatani underlined key words and circled words he needed to look up because he didn't know the meanings or thought the word might have an unusual meaning. He also blocked off words that were repeated, and he underlined significant metaphors. He noted repeated images of "rooms" and apparently discovered a pattern: daughter, mother, and grandmother, each with her own room. His active reading not only prepared him for class discussion but also for the essay that he later wrote.

Although Robert and his classmates went through the poem line by line, questioning meanings and making observations about Mirikitani's word choices and imagery, Robert's instructor had warned the students that a written line-by-line explication could easily slip into mere summary. Therefore, the instructor required that the students write an analysis that stems from a thesis. In a thesis-driven analysis, the writer controls the organization of ideas rather than just following the lines of the poem.

The instructor also reminded students of the value of using the "sandwich" when incorporating quoted lines from the poem. (You may want to review this technique on pp. 373–376). You will notice in Robert's paper, which follows, how skillfully he introduces the line he is quoting and how deliberately he explains and analyzes the words and images in each line that he includes. Notice that poetry lines are documented by line number in parentheses and that a break between two lines of a poem is indicated by a slash with a space on each side. (See p. 600 for discussion of the slash.)

When Robert refers to the "narrator" of the poem, he means the speaker or "I" of the poem. In poetry analysis it is important not to assume that the poet and speaker in a poem are always the same person. Although Janice Mirikitani may seem to be the speaker of this poem because she is an Asian woman, Robert avoids an unprovable assumption by using the word "narrator" or "mother."

Robert used his active reading notes and ideas from class discussion to prepare the following analysis. Notice that he found the focus for his paper in the parallels and contrasts that he perceived among the three generations of "rooms."

Student Example: Poetry Analysis

Robert Sakatani

Professor Waterworth

English 1A

3 October 2008

Breaking the Ties that Bind

Adolescence is a stage in human development filled with physical and emotional changes that a child often finds difficult, frustrating, and at times, painful. It is a journey all individuals must travel as they forge their own identity. Mirroring the growing pains of their child, a mother and father experience changes in the dynamics of their role as parents. Feelings of alienation and rejection are common as the parents witness their son or daughter seeking outside role models to emulate. The mother who narrates Janice Mirikitani's poem "Breaking Tradition" (p. 21) feels this estrangement from her daughter and shares with the reader what she cannot share with her daughter. Through this process, the mother not only traces her own rebellious nature and desire to "break tradition," but she also recognizes a parallel between her daughter's life and her own past.

"Breaking Tradition" is both a poem and a letter. Mirikitani structures her poem in this manner to reveal the indirect way the mother has to express her emotions because she can't communicate this directly to her daughter. It begins with a dedication: "for my daughter" (1). The isolation and larger typeface of this line reveals the significance of the daughter in the mother's life. This is the mother's way of telling her child that she is so important to her. In contrast, a plaintive statement of truth follows it: "My daughter denies she is like me / Her secretive eyes avoid mine" (2–3). The mother loves her daughter unconditionally, yet she feels the sting of her daughter's rejection. She is shut out of her child's world, "veiled behind music and smoke and telephones" (5). The daughter's tactics are typical of most adolescents who develop a need for privacy. Shutting the world out by slipping on headphones and listening to loud music, or talking endlessly on the telephone are smoke screens that the daughter uses to avoid communicating and revealing what is metamorphosing within her.

The narrator observes "the hatreds of womanhood" as her daughter experiences not only the physical changes of adolescence but also the changing role she will have as a woman in society. The mother empathizes with her daughter's frustration, and she yearns to have that mother/daughter relationship where she can confide in her and "tell her about the empty room / of myself" (5–6). This may be a metaphor for her soul—empty only because there is no one with whom to share her innermost thoughts about womanhood. Mirikitani uses vivid imagery to illustrate the mother's frustration with gender roles that imprison the spirit of a woman. The mother makes an acute observation that the submissive nature of women allows the cycle of male dominance to continue in their lives. The author uses the metaphor of women's hands as "useless, dead speechless clamps" (13) to illustrate how women have been reduced to objects "that need hospital and forceps and kitchens / and plugs and ironing boards to make them useful" (14–15). This further implies that many women define themselves by the gender roles established by society—those of child bearers, cooks, and housekeepers. The suppression of women by other women is just as detrimental. In the simile "whispers live like fungus" (8), Mirikitani implies that being critical of one another will "confine ourselves to jealousies" (10), allowing repressed feelings to multiply and spread.

In her attempt to understand her child, the mother begins processing her own experience as a daughter, revealing that she too denied her own mother. While her daughter resists sharing her inner thoughts with her mother, the narrator recalls her own mother's mandate to be "otanashi"—a Japanese word meaning to be mild, submissive, or docile. To be a woman in her mother's time was to be "smothered" (18) and "confined to ceremony" (20). It was a culture where a woman spoke with an indirect gaze and walked behind the man softly. The narrator exposes her contempt for her mother who "kept her room neat with silence" (17) and surrendered herself to manipulation by her family and society, keeping her "passion and loudness wrapped in an obi" (19). Through her recollections, she discovers her own suppressed anger towards this legacy that has left her with an "empty room" for a soul: "I want to break tradition—unlock this room / where women dress in the dark" (23–24) and "discover the lies my mother told me" (25). The mother realizes that in order to emancipate herself from her inherited guilt and shame about her body and social mandates, she needs to understand the truth about her mother.

In turn, the mother knows very little about her maturing daughter. All that the mother knows of her daughter is what she discovers through observation—that the daughter's sense of style, "pouting ruby lips, her skirts / swaying to salsa, teena marie and the stones" (43–44) celebrates her freedom to express herself openly, free from the confinements of Asian tradition. The mother wants the opportunity to bond with her daughter and let her know that she, too, has hidden desires to be self-expressive. Mirikitani uses vivid imagery of "tears of violins," "light in my hands," and "music of yellow guitars" perhaps to convey how much she values self-expression, in tears,

Sakatani 4

music, and poetry—the "light" in her hands. While the daughter keeps her true feelings within the fortress of her room, the mother is ready to set herself free.

Through the mother's observations of her daughter's "secretive eyes," the mother has also discovered herself. She now understands the nature of her daughter's rebellion, for it is not unlike her own. Everything that she has wished for her daughter has been the same thing that she wished her own mother could have provided her. In the mother's confession that her daughter "mirrors my aging" (47), there is a realization that she too has been undergoing life-altering changes. As she sees her child in a new perspective, she celebrates that she now can identify with her daughter in pursuit of "breaking tradition."

Sakatani 5

Work Cited

Mirikitani, Janice. "Breaking Tradition." *Between Worlds: A Reader, Rhetoric, and Handbook.* Ed. Susan Bachmann and Melinda Barth. 6th ed. New York: Longman, 2010. 21–23. Print.

Analyzing the Writer's Strategy

To engage the reader, Robert begins with a universal statement about adolescence, noting that both children and parents suffer during this time. Preparing the reader for the subject matter of this poem, he discusses how parents often find themselves "mirroring the growing pains of their child" and experiencing parallel feelings of alienation and rejection. Robert then gives the title and author and clarifies the context of the poem—a mother's lament about her daughter's secrecy and detachment. Now he builds to his thesis, which concludes his introduction: "Through this process, the mother not only traces her own rebellious nature and desire to 'break tradition,' but she also recognizes a parallel between her daughter's life and her own past." The rest of his paper needs to support this thesis, by illustrating the mother's own rebellion in the past but also her understanding of her daughter's distance.

Robert's frequent use of quotations from the poem as well as his careful analysis of each not only supports his thesis but works to convince readers that his interpretations are sound. Notice how each quotation is always preceded by a smooth lead-in and then followed by careful explanation of the images and language. These "sandwiches" provide development for Robert's ideas and support for his claims. He not only incorporates the line smoothly but also works with the language of the image.

Robert never expects the quoted line to stand on its own without him analyzing it. He also is careful to make sure that his interpretations of certain lines make sense in the context of the poem as a whole. Often there is intentional ambiguity in a poem and it is worthwhile to address it. For example, Robert speculates, using "may" and "perhaps," when he interprets that "the empty room may be a metaphor" for the mother's soul and that she refers to the "'music of yellow guitars' perhaps to convey how much she values self-expression." Another reader of the poem might infer different meanings from this metaphor. If you aren't sure about the poet's intention, you can soften your assertion with "may," "perhaps," or "probably" without resorting to "I think" or "I feel." This "I" voice is unnecessary and can be avoided in analytic writing.

In his conclusion, Robert returns to his opening ideas about both the mother's and the daughter's parallel feelings of alienation and rejection, but he does not repeat his exact words. He expresses what he has gained through his analysis of the poem—a deeper awareness of the poem's theme. He now perceives that both the mother and daughter are "undergoing life-altering changes . . . in pursuit of 'breaking tradition.'" In concluding with this insight, he returns to the title of the poem and gains a succinct final sentence.

 PRACTICING WRITING POETRY ANALYSIS

In small groups, select one of the following poems and write a list of images that would be interesting to analyze: "The Lanyard" (p. 41), "Blue Spruce" (p. 79), "Mr. Z" (p. 133), "Facing It" (p. 195), "Coke" (p. 243). Group the images that belong together, arrange the images in an order that makes sense, and write an assertion—a thesis—that would be workable for an analysis of the poem.

Final Tips for Poetry Analysis

- Actively read the poem several times, marking key words, images, figures of speech, and your impressions.
- Note repetitions and image patterns that might help you find a focus for your analysis.
- Decide which elements provide the most productive approach to the poem and formulate a thesis based on that decision.
- Analyze the quoted words or lines you have chosen to support your thesis. Remember to use the "sandwich."
- In your introduction, engage your audience and then briefly prepare your reader for your thesis. Briefly summarize the poem so that your reader has some context for your study.
- In the conclusion, return to your opening idea and thesis without repeating yourself.

WHAT IS CHARACTER ANALYSIS?

Because narratives, short stories, novels, and biographies are often read in freshman composition classes, we include here a character analysis to demonstrate the process of analyzing a subject—a fictitious character or an actual person. Whether you are examining a subject from life or print, you want to observe and record telling details—those that reveal something significant about the person. As you study a character, you will accumulate lots of facts, some that you will discard as irrelevant and others that you will decide are indicative of the person's character. From these facts you will make assumptions about your subject's personality and character. In fact, the heart of your analysis will depend on inference—that is, a hypothesis that you formulate about the character based on the facts that you have observed.

Character Analysis: Short Story

As you actively read the narrative or short story, list specific examples of speech, behavior, and thought that reveal the character. Mix facts and your responses or inferences about them as you go along. Simply write your list; you will sort, eliminate, and reword examples later.

Prewriting: Listing Information from a Short Story

If you are taking notes from a short story for a character analysis, you need to record telling descriptions, behaviors, and speech that will help you determine what kind of person that character is. It helps to list all revealing observations in the left column and leave room between observations so you can group similar details. As you list and group related ideas, jot down in the right column an inference about that character. An inference is a hypothesis or supposition about a character that you will later prove or refute from the data collected. Here is a list of observations and inferences about Connie in Joyce Carol Oates's short story, "Where Are You Going, Where Have You Been?" (p. 92):

Observations about Connie	Inferences about Connie
"quick nervous giggling habit"	self-conscious
cranes neck to glance into mirrors	vain
ignores a boy from the high school	callous
leaves her friend to go off with Eddie	callous, self-absorbed
checks "other people's faces to make sure her own was all right"	self-conscious, insecure
"she knew she was pretty and that was everything"	self-assured, superficial
thought her mother preferred her to June because Connie was prettier	self-assured, superficial
checks her hair and worries about how bad she looks when a strange car pulls in driveway	insecure, self-conscious
"wished her mother were dead and she herself were dead and it were all over"	depressed

"everything about her had two sides to it, one for home and one for anywhere that was not home"
    jersey
    her walk
    lipstick
    laughter
	two-sided, sneaky? rebellious?

says she is going to the movies but goes to drive-in restaurant	deceitful
avoids conversation with family about "movie" and "Pettinger girl"	sneaky, evasive

doesn't go to family barbecue—rolls her eyes at mother	indifferent, evasive, rebellious?
goes to Eddie's car	likes being with boys
"her mind slipped over into thoughts of the boy she had been with the night before"	daydreamer, romantic
daydreams about the boys she hangs out with, "how sweet it always was . . . the way it was in movies and promised in songs"	romanticizes about love, naive
"her eyes wander over the windshields and faces all around her"	always on lookout for cute guys
"smirked and let her hair fall loose over one shoulder"	flirtatious
couldn't decide if Arnold Friend is attractive or a jerk	naive
doesn't realize at first that Friend is so much older	naive
flattered by Friend's interest in her	naive
amazed by all Friend knows about her:	naive, vulnerable
her name	
friends' names	
description of June	
family at barbecue	
fat woman at barbecue	
neighbor with chickens	
appalled by Friend's graphic talk of sex	intimidated, innocent
cries out for mother	childlike, needy
can't phone police	inexperienced, terrified, paralyzed
realizes she will never see mother or sleep in her bed again	childlike

Arranging and Thesis Construction

Consider how you will arrange your character traits and the specific examples that support the traits. What do you want to emphasize in your analysis? Consider ending your character analysis with the trait that you find most significant or most indicative of character. By using your most emphatic point in the terminal spot in your paper, you will have a natural conclusion—one that gets at both the heart of your subject and the theme of the short story.

Perhaps the place to start is with the most obvious feature of the subject for analysis because it will take less effort to convince your audience of your perception if your reader shares your perception. In the case of Connie, the writer might address her preoccupation with her looks or her apparent self-assuredness. The writer might also want to look at her flawed family relationships or her boy-craziness. Depending on how you perceive Connie, you may want to order the inferences in your thesis to reflect the reasons for her behavior. Your final character inference should lead naturally to the conclusion of your paper, and you will want to keep this in mind as you order the inferences in your thesis.

Determining a Thesis. You need to have a thesis for your character study, whether or not you include it in your paper. You can determine one by using the character traits that you perceived during grouping. Remember that your thesis expresses a view about a limited subject, such as Connie's character. If you have many observations on your prewriting list, you know you have good support ready.

Possible Thesis Statements. Here are some possibilities for thesis statements for the character analysis of Connie. Remember, each writer's perceptions and preferences will determine the thesis and the order in which the information will be presented.

1. Although Connie appears to be a self-assured teenager, she is actually an insecure, sexually innocent, two-sided girl whose inexperience does not prepare her for the encounter with Arnold Friend.

2. Connie seeks male attention, hangs out with older kids, and affects a sexy exterior, but she is no match for someone with criminal intentions.

3. Connie's life is filled with paradoxes. She is a gregarious girl without a true friend; she lives in a traditional family but has no real bonds with family members; she craves the attention of boys but does not know how to protect herself. Ultimately, these paradoxes render her vulnerable to an attack by someone like Arnold Friend.

4. Because Connie's home life is deficient, Connie develops survival mechanisms. She daydreams, evades interaction with her family, and deceives

her family and friends—behavior that could not help her withstand Arnold Friend.

5. Connie projects a brazen, rebellious exterior that masks the naive, insecure girl within.

STUDENT EXAMPLE: CHARACTER ANALYSIS ESSAY

As you read the following character analysis by student writer **Marianela Enriquez**, notice that in addition to an examination of the separate qualities of Connie's character, Marianela returns to the essence of the entire work to bring closure to her study.

Marianela Enriquez

Professor Hackner

English 1A

16 April 2008

Who Were You, Connie, and Why Did You Go?

Readers of "Where Are You Going, Where Have You Been?" (92) may be tempted to condemn the protagonist, Connie, as a self-absorbed and superficial 15-year-old and to reduce the story to a simple warning against risky behavior. But it would be a mistake to do so. Throughout the work, author Joyce Carol Oates takes great care to illustrate situations and describe feelings and a personality all survivors of teenage angst have experienced and can recognize. In this way, her chilling short story about a rapist and his teenage victim becomes much more than a tale of fear. It becomes a tragedy of a teenage girl struggling with adolescence on her own and dealing with all the insecurities of her age. Although Connie appears to be a self-assured teenager, she is actually an insecure, sexually innocent, two-sided, and naive girl whose inexperience cannot prepare her for the encounter with Arnold Friend.

Connie herself is pretty, with long, dark blonde hair and brown eyes, and like most girls her age, she is preoccupied with her looks. But even in realizing that this is a typical teenage trait, one can see that Connie's preoccupation is a sign of her insecurity. She has habits of always looking at herself in mirrors and "checking other people's faces to make sure her own was all right," two practices that reveal her insecurity and contradict the self-assuredness of her belief that "she was pretty and that was everything"(93). Even when a "car she didn't know" pulls into her driveway, Connie's first concern is to check her hair and wonder "how bad she looked" (96). She feels that her physical attractiveness is at the root of everything. She reasons that the tension existing between herself and her mother is because her mother is jealous that her own looks are gone. But, in spite of that thinking, she also reasons that her mother preferred her to her sister June because Connie is the prettier of the two. Connie's beauty seems to be the only asset recognized by other people, so in her insecurity, Connie clings to people's compliments. When seen in this light, one can start to understand Connie not as a conceited person, but as a confused girl who attempts to work the one good quality she thinks she has.

Because Connie believes that beauty is everything, she naturally moves toward people who will appreciate her beauty—boys. Whether she is at the shopping plaza or a drive-in restaurant "where older kids hung out" (94), Connie always has her eye out for someone to fulfill her dreams of romance. While she does enter cars with boys she barely knows, there is no evidence that Connie actually has intercourse with any of them. According to Connie, her experiences are always sweet, "not the way someone like [her sister] June would suppose but sweet, gentle, the way it was in movies and promised in songs" (96). Connie doesn't have one special boyfriend about whom she dreams. In fact, "all the boys fell back and dissolved into a face that was not even a face, but an idea, a feeling" of romance. Even Arnold Friend recognizes Connie as sexually innocent when he claims he will be her "lover" but adds, "You don't know what that is, but you will" (102). Her shock at his graphic language and her insistence that "people don't talk like that" (102) confirm her innocence as well.

Perhaps the greatest key to understanding Connie's character is to understand her duality. Oates specifies that "everything about her had two sides to it, one for home and one for anywhere that was not home" (94). Connie is full of contrasts: "She wore a pullover jersey blouse that looked one way when she was at home and another when she was away from home" (93). In addition to rearranging her clothing to look older, she changes her walk "that could be childlike and bobbing" when she is at home or "languid" when she is out. "Her mouth that is pale and smirking

Enriquez 3

most of the time, but bright and pink on evenings out" suggests that Connie is re-belling against her parents' make-up rules, and deliberately making herself look older when she leaves her house. Connie's laughter "was cynical and drawling at home," probably in response to family jokes, but is "high pitched and nervous anywhere else" (94). This duality includes deceit. For example, while her family thinks that she and a friend are going to the movies, they often "went across the highway, ducking fast across the busy road" (94). And when her mother bluntly asks, "What's this about the Pettinger girl?" Connie dismisses the question, refusing to let her mother into her world. Whether consciously or unconsciously, Connie builds walls around herself and doesn't talk to anyone with any sort of depth. She can't relate to her older sister, June, who is praised by their mother, and her father ignores the family to "read the newspaper at supper" (93). The indifference of her family is damaging to Connie who is, in actuality, a lonely girl desperate for some kind of positive attention.

Her desire for attention and her teenage naivete makes her the perfect victim for Arnold Friend. It is ironic that Connie's killer should be the only one in the story who has any kind of understanding into her character. Apparently, the man has been watching Connie for some time and knows of her love for music, of her innocent encounters with boys, and of her family situation so that he can intimidate Connie with what he knows or can guess. Friend is able to create an image of himself that Connie finds appealing. She is interested that they are listening to the same radio station, and she finds his car impressive. She "liked the way he was dressed, which was the way all of them dressed" (98) and at first she is so blinded by the familiarity of his looks that she can't tell if "she liked him or if he was just a jerk" (97). Because of her naivete, Connie at first doesn't notice that Arnold and his friend are much older than the boys Connie knows. Because Connie craves attention, she is easily flattered by Arnold Friend even though her intuition tells her that something is wrong with these two older men.

Taking advantage of Connie's insecurity and naivete, Friend manipulates her responses and plays upon her existing insecurities. Armed with facts about Connie's life, Friend plays upon the rivalry between June and Connie by calling her sister "fat" and a "poor, sad bitch" (101), and he plays on Connie's feelings of abandonment, created by her father's disinterest, by repeating that her father isn't coming back for her.

Enriquez 4

Arnold lets her know that locking the door will not keep him out. Connie's vulnerability is evident in the story's most disturbing scene when Connie tries to telephone the police. Arnold's abuse puts Connie in such a hysterical state that she botches her one chance to escape. Oates's description of "her breath jerking back and forth in her lungs as if it were something Arnold Friend were stabbing her with again and again" (105) is powerful with its sexual implications, and we realize that Connie is raped emotionally before she is physically raped. He let her know that she is hopelessly trapped.

Connie becomes paralyzed by the knowledge that she is alone and vulnerable and that if she doesn't go along with Friend, her family will be murdered. She must feel guilty remembering "how she sucked in her breath just at the moment she passed him" and "how she must have looked at him" at the restaurant (98). In the end, Connie breaks and resigns herself to a sure death. No longer the teenager, Connie is a little girl who can only think, "I'm not going to see my mother again . . . I'm not going to sleep in my bed again" (105).

In creating a character so recognizable in her insecurities, duality, and naivete, Joyce Carol Oates also creates a character we can pity. Oates creates a sense that the difference in where Connie is going and where we may have gone at the tender age of 15 may not be so much the result of differences in action but the result of differences in fate. This awareness completely destroys the security that comes with thinking that through the avoidance of certain behaviors, we can prevent negative outcomes, and this realization heightens the horror of Connie's story. We are forced to reckon with the uncontrollable nature of chance, a chance that doesn't shrink away from giving a 15-year-old innocent girl a Friend who may take her life.

Enriquez 5

Work Cited

Oates, Joyce Carol. "Where Are You Going, Where Have You Been?" *Between Worlds: A Reader, Rhetoric, and Handbook.* Ed. Susan Bachmann and Melinda Barth. 6th ed. New York: Longman, 2010. 92–106. Print.

Analyzing the Writer's Strategy

Marienela begins her analysis by acknowledging that some readers will find Connie merely a "self-absorbed and superficial" teenager and will "reduce the story to a simple warning against risky behavior," but Marienela cautions that "it would be a mistake to do so." In fact, she defends Connie to the point of saying that Connie is not to be blamed for what happens to her, and throughout her analysis of Connie's character, Marienela illustrates the forces that contribute to Connie's personality, values, and vulnerability. Marienela supports her inferences about Connie's character with well-integrated and analyzed quoted material from the story, recognizing the importance of including and interpreting many specific illustrations to prove her claims about Connie.

 PRACTICING WRITING A CHARACTER ANALYSIS

In small groups, select one of the following individuals and write a list of character traits: Rita or Marc in "Peaches" (p. 71) or Lyman Lamartine in "The Red Convertible" (p. 135). Group the details that belong together, arrange the details, and write an assertion—a thesis—that would be workable for a character analysis.

Character Analysis: Biography

Reading a good biography—the study of a person's life—can be a great pleasure. We learn something intimate, entertaining, and instructive about the subject of the book and the time period in which the person lived. Even readers who would not elect to read a history book discover that a biography vicariously connects them to a culture and time they may not know and permits them to glimpse choices that the subject of the biography made, which perhaps even influenced that epoch. Readers of biography learn about personal conviction as well as about a period of time not their own—discoveries that can be both informative and inspirational. In addition, a longer character analysis written from reading a full-length biography can be a rewarding research project.

Gathering Information from a Book: Inference Cards

If you are taking notes for a paper based on a biographical study and are using a full-length book, keep separate index cards for each character trait that you observe while you are reading. For example, if you find that your subject was "strong-willed," even in childhood, you would head an index card with that inference. As you read the book, every time you see that trait reflected in an action of your subject or a comment made by someone about the character, simply record the page number. When you infer another trait, perhaps "maternal" or "ambitious," start new cards and continue to record page numbers. When you have completed a 400-page or longer biography, you may have twenty or thirty "inference cards," each with a different trait at the top and each with many recorded page numbers. It may seem time-consuming and even awkward to stop reading to record a page number on an existing card or to start a new card with an inferred trait, but you will not need to reread the full-length book in order to write a good paper. You will have page numbers that indicate the support you need for each inference if you keep track of traits from the beginning of your reading. You will be actively reading and inferring traits, focusing your reading from the start.

Grouping Cards

After you have finished reading the biography and writing inference cards, group the cards that seem to belong together. For example, if you have cards with "strong-willed," "determined," and "obsessed," you would be able to combine those cards for one section of your subject analysis. The number of page references that you have noted on the cards will help you decide if the trait that you observed is supportable. In your paper, you would use only those character traits for which you have many page numbers recorded.

A Working Thesis

Write a working thesis featuring those traits that seem to have sufficient support, based on the pages you have recorded on the index cards. You wouldn't want a thesis that features each trait that you have observed, so you'll need to be selective, even if you have grouped two or three different cards that will work together to form one section of your paper. Leselle Norville, in her analysis of Amelia Earhart (p. 497), had inference cards indicating that Earhart was "irresponsible," "indifferent," "complacent," "inept," and "careless." She ultimately selected "complacent" for her thesis, but she returned to the other words, synonyms or near-word equivalents, as she drafted her paper and included examples from each of the cards.

Decide which traits and terms most fairly and completely represent your subject. Write a thesis based on those traits, knowing that you may decide to change the thesis or rearrange it as you draft your paper.

Arranging the Support

Decide what you want to emphasize about your subject. If the traits that you have observed are both negative and positive, determine which predominate. Arrange the traits in your thesis to project the organization of your paper. Do you want your paper to conclude with surprising information about your subject—inferences that you have discovered in reading the full study of your subject's life—or would you rather have your reader be comforted with a conclusion of familiar material about the subject of your paper? Do you want to emphasize the negative by concluding with those traits, or do you want to show that in spite of problems, your character triumphed? Further, you may see consequences that are derived from your character's strengths, weaknesses, or inconsistencies, and you may want to predict a cause-and-effect relationship in your thesis.

Leselle perceives that Amelia Earhart had contradictory character traits, and she structures her paper around these contrasting traits. For example, she sees "reserve" in Earhart but also "charisma." She sees "competence" but also "complacency." These antithetical traits alternate in the arrangement of her support. Further, Leselle deduces that Earhart's "insecurity" was the cause of these inconsistencies and she forecasts that idea in her thesis and concludes her paper with that awareness.

From Inference Cards to Drafted Paper

After you have arranged the inference cards in an order that makes sense for your thesis, return to the note cards and look up the page numbers that support each trait. You will want to select examples of behavior, anecdotes, statements from people about your subject, and statements from your subject that most vividly show your subject's personality and character. Your goal is to render a lively portrait of your subject. Remember that you can "tell" your reader many times that your subject was "charismatic," but even one "showing" illustration or revealing anecdote will do more to create a vivid image in your reader's mind.

As you use the material from the page numbers on your cards, combine paraphrased and quoted material. Use your own words to narrate an example most of the time, but where there is vivid description by the author of your biography, or quoted material from someone about your subject, use direct quotation, too. In Leselle's paper, she uses Amelia Earhart's own voice to help her reader hear the kind of person she was. To show Earhart's restlessness, she quotes Earhart's fear that marriage would be "living the life of a domestic robot" (qtd. in Rich 42) and that her prenuptial agreement insisted she have freedom "from even an attractive cage" (qtd. in Chapman 182). By letting her subject speak in her own voice, Leselle captures the tone of a restless young woman who refuses to be confined.

Be certain as you draft that you note the page number where you derived both the paraphrased and quoted material that supports your inferred trait because you will need to include an in-text citation to inform your reader of the source of your information. Compose directly on the computer, if you can, but if you write in longhand, write on only one side of the lined paper so that if you later want to cut the draft up to rearrange sections, you will be able to do so. If you compose directly on the computer, you will be able to cut and paste to rearrange sections of your draft. Develop each section of the paper and take a break before you go on to another trait. Remember Anne Lamott's suggestion and write your focused biography one trait at a time or "bird by bird" (329). If you recognize the incremental nature of this paper, and work on single sections at a time, you won't be overwhelmed by the project.

Transitions Within and Between Sections

When you have finished drafting each section of the paper, look for ways to create transitions between the sections of analysis. You may decide to rearrange some of your support so that the illustration or quotation that concludes one section can be used as a bridge to the next trait or section of analysis. Leselle finished one section of her analysis of Earhart's restlessness with this sentence:

> Earhart's [prenuptial] requirements of GP were bluntly but honestly stated in [a] letter and reveal that she had a true fear of settling (500).

The next section of Leselle's paper moves from restlessness or "fear of settling" to Earhart's "determination." The new section begins with this sentence:

> Perhaps the only thing to match Earhart's restlessness was her audacious drive. She had an aggressive determination and sheer willpower (500).

As you connect the parts of your paper, check to see that you are returning to the focus points of each section forecast in your thesis. In addition, use key word repetition or synonyms within each section of your paper, perhaps alternative words that were on your inference cards. For example, by showing that Earhart "neglected" to practice, "ignored" safety precautions, was "inept" in necessary skills, and was "apathetic" about equipment that she should have brought on her final flight, Leselle supports her perception that her subject was "complacent" about the realities of aviation. By using substitute words—"neglected," "ignored," "inept," and "apathetic"—to describe Earhart's "complacency," Leselle avoids monotonous repetition of the same word while still supporting her focus. See pages 391–393 for help on transitions.

Writing the Introduction

After you have drafted each section of the paper to support a particular trait, you are ready to write an introduction. See pages 398–401 for suggestions of particular types of introductions. Leselle, for example, uses the concept of contradiction to "hook" her audience: "How fascinating that a woman slow of speech, ordinary-looking, and capable only of piloting a plane held the world spellbound for almost a decade." You may find your "hook" by reexamining any circled page numbers on your inference cards that indicate a lively anecdote or quotation that could be used to precede your thesis. Leselle was impressed by a photograph of Amelia Earhart that shows her as poised and confident, an image that Leselle perceived as "rehearsed." Further, an Earhart poem that Leselle discovered seems to capture Earhart's values. The photograph and poem, and Leselle's interpretation of them, work well to introduce Earhart's character. She decides to write two introductory paragraphs before moving to her thesis in her third paragraph. Notice as you read Leselle's paper how it is structured to support the thesis, based on inferred character traits, and that it is not a mere summary of a biography.

STUDENT EXAMPLE: BIOGRAPHY ESSAY

Leselle Norville

Professor Breckheimer

English 1A

2 June 2008

The Earhart Appeal

How fascinating that a woman slow of speech, ordinary-looking, and capable only of piloting a plane held the world spellbound for almost a decade. She attended parades and banquets given in her honor, she mingled with royalty and celebrities, and she drew enormous crowds when she gave lectures. On March 17, 1937, just twenty-two days before her fortieth birthday, Amelia Earhart embarked with Fred Noonan, her navigator, on what promised to be her greatest adventure—an unprecedented flight around the world's equator (Rich 270). She never returned, and although the government mounted a search and rescue operation, neither the craft nor its occupants were ever recovered. Earhart became a legend and is still unquestionably the most popular aviatrix today.

It is doubtful, however, that the world ever truly saw Amelia Earhart, the person, for it is in one's most unguarded moments that true character emerges. She carried herself poised for a snapshot, and newsreels of her show that events were sometimes restaged in order to portray Earhart in the most confident light. In many of her photographs, she wore a much-rehearsed expression. However, there does exist a photograph of her dressed completely in white, from her unfastened leather flying cap to her flight suit, and, curiously enough, she is encircled by a soft, angelic glow (Lovell, plate 1). This photograph was not candid and shows her lips pressed together as she had been directed to do by her husband (Rich 58). She appeared serene and composed, but also in this photograph is an unmistakable ardor in the eyes that peer out from an otherwise restrained, calm face. That insatiable hunger is discernible in the first line of Earhart's poem, "Courage," printed in Doris L. Rich's *Amelia Earhart—A Biography*. It reads, "Courage is the price that life exacts for granting peace" (48) and is a true reflection of Earhart's belief that contentment is not acquired without risk. In that photograph, because her essence shone through, Earhart was beautiful.

Quite often, the fame achieved by beauty is fleeting; the same is true for fame by riches or by well-placed connections. The Earhart appeal knew no such limits. Earhart was captivating because of her complexity, and the result was enduring celebrity. She was an intriguing blend of reserve and charm, of restlessness and determination, and of competence and complacency; however, it is her insecurity that accounted for her varied shades of character, the sum of which made her the architect of her life as well as her unfortunate demise.

Throughout her life, Earhart was reserved. Her difficult childhood, which was spent in the care of an unreliable father and with unsupportive friends, caused her to be withdrawn because "to depend on those she loved could be disappointing, [and] to confide in others might lead to humiliation" (Rich 12). Consequently, Earhart guarded her innermost thoughts very closely. Even in high school, she alienated herself from her classmates. Mary S. Lovell, in *The Sound of Wings: The Life of Amelia Earhart*, refers to the caption beneath Earhart's yearbook photograph which reads, "the girl in brown who walks alone" (22) and which adequately captures the solitary nature of Earhart that would be a constant throughout her life. She also tended to be reserved because she valued her privacy greatly. At Ogontz, a finishing school in Pennsylvania, she wrote a letter begging her mother not to write her teachers because she would "just shrivel" at the thought of having her personal affairs being discussed with others (qtd. in Rich 15). To Earhart, even her mother's concern was no excuse for divulging private issues.

In her youth, Earhart learned that reserving one's true feelings was necessary to preserve one's confidence. These convictions never left her and eventually made publicity a source of much distress for her. She was often overwhelmed by fans desperate to touch her and get her autograph. Soon after her first transatlantic flight, the first wave of criticism hit. She, herself, felt that her contribution to the flight, on which she was really just a passenger, was only minimal. Nevertheless, Earhart was hurt by comments made in a London newspaper that claimed her presence on the flight was no more significant than that of a sheep on board (Rich 65). Earhart "fibbed," saying that "from first to last [her] contact with the press [was] thoroughly enjoyable" (Rich 66). To say otherwise would have been to betray her injured self-image. Sally Putnam Chapman, in *Whistled Like a Bird*, has recorded the words of empathy for Earhart's situation that Dorothy Putnam entered in her diary. Seeing the erosion of Earhart's privacy, Dorothy Putnam wrote that "there [is] a penalty to being famous and one pays the price by having no privacy whatever!" (111). In light of Earhart's quiet nature, it is amazing that she was able to tactfully handle the press, giving only enough and never too much.

In an interesting twist, the unassuming Earhart seemed destined for great things. It was her reserve that made her remote, but it was her charm that allowed her to win the affection and admiration of others, and she was repeatedly called to leadership by her peers. Jean Adams and Margaret Kimball, in their book, *Heroines of the Sky*, took great pains to emphasize "the gaiety, the humor, and the real kindliness which made the charm of her face" (174). This warm side of Earhart contributed to her magnetism and led to the many leadership posts in her life. Earhart's letters have been compiled by Jean Backus, author of *Letters from Amelia—An Intimate Portrait of Amelia Earhart*, and in one of her letters written from Ogontz, Earhart told her mother that she was "secretary by popular vote" (Backus 37). She quickly elevated to class president status.

In spite of her solitary nature, Earhart was able to create a lighthearted, comfortable atmosphere with her quick wit, refreshing honesty, and gracious manner, causing others to trust and respect her. She was so charming that, according to news articles, "no private party [was] complete without her," and she was "the one essential, apparently, for a successful entertainment" (Rich 171). Her complex character made her both a mysterious loner and a socialite. Fortunately, her quietness, which was sometimes mistaken for aloofness, was offset by her charisma, making it easier to overlook her faults. Placing a distant third in the first Women's Air Derby of 1929 did not blemish her popularity or credibility (Rich 94). The Ninety-Nines, a group of aviatrixes, chose Earhart to be their president, exhibiting great confidence in her ability to represent their interests. Transcontinental Air Transport, a then newly-formed airline, also recognized that charm was an excellent persuader and employed Earhart as their spokesperson (Rich 98).

Amelia's charisma, her ability to hold people's interest and attention, required quite a bit of liveliness, and Earhart had such an abundance of it that she tended to be restless. She lacked focus and became impatient quite quickly. Her cousin, Nancy Morse, in an interview for PBS's *The American Experience*, attributes Earhart's unsettled spirit to her childhood because her family was always moving. It is her belief that "Amelia got easily bored." Earhart's educational and career goals were not concrete. Her interests were widely varied from the sciences to the arts to humanities, and she always made time for sports. She abandoned her plan to graduate from the Ogontz finishing school and decided to aid victims of World War I as a nurse's aid in Canada (Rich 18). She later returned to college to study medicine, dropping out in the end because of financial difficulties. She had as many as twenty-eight jobs including truck driver, fashion designer, social worker, and photographer. When Earhart found flying, her assertion that "[she'd] die if [she] didn't" comes as no surprise (Rich 24). She had been unfulfilled for some time and knew that she could find peace in the freedom of the air.

Earhart could not bear the thought of an uneventful life. Her aversion to settling down accounted for her late marriage. She thought that marriage was "living the life of a domestic robot" (qtd. in Rich 42). She could not bear the thought of being the typical housewife trapped in an unrelenting routine of house tending. "I don't want anything all of the time" she said, and, therefore, just before she married George Palmer Putnam, popularly known as GP, she ensured that she had some freedom "from even an attractive cage" by listing some prenuptial conditions in a letter to him (qtd. in Chapman 182). Earhart, as kindly as possible, informed GP to "let [her] go if [they found] no happiness together" (qtd. in Chapman 182). Earhart's requirements of GP were bluntly but honestly stated in the letter and revealed that she had a true fear of settling.

Perhaps the only thing to match Earhart's restlessness was her audacious drive. She had an aggressive determination and sheer willpower. In childhood, neither admonishment from her grandmother nor risk of injury could deter Earhart. For example, a seven-year-old Earhart decided that "belly-slamming," sleighing downhill in snow while prone, was fun, and she proceeded to do so despite her grandmother's view of the act as unladylike (Rich 3). Young Earhart just barely avoided collision with a horse-drawn wagon because the sleigh, moving too fast for Earhart to control it, sped right under the horse's belly. Relishing the thrill, "the grinning, triumphant speedster" (3) did not consider personal injury or warnings from her grandmother to be a deterrent. This early show of daring and determination was an indication of the resolve she would exhibit later in her life.

Her drive and her restlessness seem incongruent; however, they went hand in hand. Because she tended to be fickle, it was necessary for her to find an activity that could engage her wholly. Rich cites a London newspaper's reference to Earhart as having an "unquenchable determination to go on attempting the hitherto un-achieved" (65). Aviation, because it had just begun to gain popularity, provided Earhart with limitless opportunities to set records and then surpass them. Clearly, glory was not her motivation. Earhart referred to her first unofficial altitude record in 1922 as a mere "calibration of the ceiling" because it was an accomplishment that was personally significant, and with every feat accomplished, there remained a greater one unaccomplished (qtd. in Rich 34). She pushed the ceiling higher throughout her career. In spite of the many records she set and the awards she re-ceived, however, Earhart was never satisfied. Her drive was not for the record but rather for the achieving of it.

It is not surprising, then, that health took second place to aviation in Earhart's life. Nothing consumed her more than flying. Thus, she overworked herself to finance her career. She once said, "No pay, no fly, no work, no pay," indicating her determination to fly regardless of how hard she had to work to support her passion (Rich 37). Earhart always had a hectic monthly schedule of lecturing to earn a living. She believed that illness was an acceptable cost for the privilege of flying, and as a result, she was hospital-ized many times with stress-induced illnesses. Even while she was in college, Earhart never relented. A friend noted that Earhart was exhausted quite often, but "admonitions on the subject were ignored" (Rich 21). She insisted on working and playing hard and found time to study and still play tennis, field hockey, and any other sport that inter-ested her. As long as she felt the activity challenging enough, she was interested.

Earhart's drive to succeed at whatever she attempted outweighed controversy about the motives for her 1935 flight from Honolulu to the mainland. She endured resistance from the Army, from the press, and from the sponsors of her flight (Backus 163). Regardless, she made known her intentions to "make the flight with or without" sponsorship (Backus 163). With renewed confidence in Earhart's success, her sponsors supported her.

One who is driven needs courage, and courage requires remarkable resolve. Earhart was so bent on flying that even though the fumes from the fuel that entered the cockpit sometimes made her nauseous, she preferred to be sick and fly. Earhart, in her poem "Courage," said that "each time we make a choice, we pay with courage" (Rich 49). She knew she could stand the adverse conditions in her plane so long as she could fly.

Although the determination that spawns courage is readily identified with Earhart, competence is seldom attributed to her. She was shrewd, frugal, and responsible, but she is usually portrayed as a victim of GP's fierceness. An interesting fact is that GP's "aggressive action" was excused as "his recipe for success," but Earhart's acquiescence was "less understandable" (Lovell 152). Obviously she was misunderstood. In fact, Earhart's supposed acquiescence belied her astute judgment. Adams and Kimball's *Heroines of the Sky*, even though it contains a highly romanticized account of Earhart's life titled "Amelia Earhart—She Dramatized Flying," fails to acknowledge Earhart's own role in her success. Instead, Adams and Kimball describe GP as being "the real impresario of this prima donna" (162). Earhart knew the value of a resourceful man and used him to her advantage. She valued his "brilliant mind" and "keen insight" (Lovell 117). Gore Vidal, in an interview for *The American Experience*, supported the view that Earhart's partnership with GP was an excellent tactical move because "he made life very easy for her in many ways." She was certainly not a weak person as is commonly perceived.

Furthermore, during her marriage to GP, Earhart ensured that she was responsible for her own finances by keeping them separate. In her prenuptial letter, she required that GP "not interfere with [her] work or play" (qtd. in Chapman 182).

Apparently, she was wise enough to prevent problems and control issues that could arise from shared finances by establishing an unrelenting standard before the marriage. Although GP's former wife Dorothy Putnam saw Earhart as "a brainless puppet who does whatever [George] advises" (qtd. in Chapman 139), it is clear that Earhart was very much the master of her own affairs.

In fact, she had always managed her affairs wisely. In school, she was often able to tell her mother not to send money and not to worry because she had enough money to make do. Earhart "hate[d] to spend money for things [she] would never need or want," and she sometimes sewed, altered, or bought second-hand clothing (Rich 15). She chose to be resourceful, carefully avoiding the wastefulness of her parents. Earhart never wanted to inherit what she called the "family failing" (Backus 119). As a result, she "never dealt sentimentally with money" (155). Later in her life, she often asked that her mother and sister send her bills and statements before she gave out significant sums of money. She said that she needed them "just for records" (qtd. in Backus 117).

Efficient use of time was another aspect of Earhart's competence that is evidenced in her letters to her mother. While she was at Ogontz, she delighted in sharing her schedule with her mother, relishing the idea that "every minute [was] accounted for" (29). Earhart was not the kind to waste time on meaningless activities. She would read a book or spend the afternoon playing a sport rather than staying indoors with nothing to do. Later in her life, she was able to keep her appointments and business arrangements in spite of her hectic lecturing schedule, "often with two lectures booked for the same day" (Rich 148). As taxing as her career must have been, Earhart was able to lecture while designing her own clothing line, representing a major airline, and supporting her mother, sister, and a mentally retarded uncle.

As competent as Earhart was, she could also be complacent. She had many accidents throughout her career, which is understandable because airplanes lacked the technology that exists today. Nevertheless, Earhart failed to take responsibility to prevent accidents. In a television interview, Elinor Smith, who was voted the best woman pilot of 1930, pinpointed Earhart's most crucial flaw: failure to practice.

Smith observed that in a time when flying was not made simple by technology, "you had to fly every single day," but Earhart "never seemed to practice" (*The American Experience*). In order to facilitate the continuation of her career in aviation, Earhart had turned much of her attention to lecturing and other pursuits, but, ironically, these activities left hardly any time for flying. Instead of slowing down the hectic pace at which she was working, Earhart allowed her skills to become dull. She was already neglecting her health, but she showed gross disregard of accidents and risks when she said she "just does not think about crackups" (qtd. in Rich 131). She seemed to be leaving herself at the mercy of fate. Referring to the Women's Derby of 1929, Smith notes that although Earhart had "the fastest and the most powered plane in that race" (*The American Experience*), Earhart still came in a distant third because she simply did not have the skills to do any better.

In addition to neglecting practice, Earhart abandoned any further instruction in the operation of her craft. Consequently, she was inept in many of the skills essential for safe, successful flying. In all her years of flying, Earhart had never learned Morse code or how to properly operate the plane's radio. Throughout the period of preparation for her ill-fated round-the-world adventure, Earhart exhibited inexcusably poor judgment. According to explorer and aerial photographer Brad Washburn, Earhart ignored "fundamentally important things" (*The American Experience*). Washburn was to have been Earhart's navigator for the trip but abandoned the project in the final stages of preparation because he doubted her judgment. He said that just minutes before her final flight, Earhart decided that taking her parachute and life raft would prove too bothersome, so she left them behind just as she had left her Morse code machine and antenna. Ultimately, Earhart's complacency—demonstrated by her failure to bring essential equipment on such a challenging flight—was greatly responsible for her tragic end.

Earhart was complex, having varied and seemingly incongruous character traits; however, the one link between her strengths and failings was her insecurity. Her fear of humiliation caused her to withdraw, while her fear of alienation sparked her charisma. She was restless, which was not only an indication of unfocused energy but revealed her indecisiveness and uncertainty. She was certainly driven but needed to reassure herself of her worth. Earhart's meticulous handling of money and time management was a shield against becoming like her parents, but her complacency revealed a lack of common sense and self-preservation. She was trapped in a vicious cycle of overwork and overplay and, perhaps, she was overwhelmed. In her poem "From an Airplane," Earhart describes darkness as unavoidable, slow, and unrelenting: "Even the watchful purple hills that hold the lake could not see so well as I the stain of evening creeping from its heart" (*The American Experience*). These lines may seem prophetic, considering Earhart's premature death.

In her final desperate communication with the world, possibly just before she fell from the sky into the lonely Pacific, Earhart stumbled over her words, her voice "shrill and breathless, her words tumbling over one another" (Rich 270). Earhart's life was undeniably remarkable, but perhaps unfulfilling. Once again, Earhart's poetry, whether intentionally or inadvertently, describes her life. An excerpt from an unfinished poem reads, "Merciless life laughs in the burning sun and only death, slow, circling down" (qtd. on *The American Experience*). And such was her end.

Works Cited

Adams, Jean, and Margaret Kimball. "Amelia Earhart—She Dramatized Flying." *Heroines of the Sky.* Freeport, NY: Doubleday, 1942. Print.

"Amelia Earhart: The Price of Courage." Narr. Kathy Bates. *The American Experience.* PBS. 1993. Videocassette.

Backus, Jean L. *Letters from Amelia: An Intimate Portrait of Amelia Earhart.* Boston: Beacon Press, 1982. Print.

Chapman, Sally Putnam. *Whistled Like a Bird: The Untold Story of Dorothy Putnam, George Putnam, and Amelia Earhart.* Ed. Stephanie Mansfield. New York: Warner Books, 1997. Print.

Norville 11

Lovell, Mary S. *The Sound of Wings: The Life of Amelia Earhart.* New York: St. Martin's
 Press, 1989. Print.

Rich, Doris L. *Amelia Earhart: A Biography.* Washington, DC: Smithsonian Institution
 Press, 1989. Print.

Analyzing the Writer's Strategy

The purpose of a character analysis of a once-living person is not entirely different from a character analysis of a fictitious character. The goal is to create a vivid portrait of the subject by focusing on inferred traits that can be supported with text. The analysis must be focused around a thesis based on inferences about the person so that the paper does not become a birth-to-death summary of the subject's life, or a mere review of the book read about the subject.

Writing the Thesis

The writer has plenty of creative opportunity to decide which character traits may best represent the subject's life. Most people are complex personalities, whose lives are filled with moments of strength and weakness, failure and triumph. Leselle was most interested in the contradictions within Amelia's character, how her life developed and may have ended because of these inconsistencies. Leselle made the decision to balance these contrasting traits so that her focused biography of Earhart fully represents the woman behind the famous pilot. Further, Leselle is insightful and sees that Earhart's insecurity accounted for the variations in her character, and she focuses her thesis to reflect that cause-and-effect perception:

> Earhart was captivating because of her complexity, and the result was enduring celebrity. She was an intriguing blend of reserve and charm, of restlessness and determination, and of competence and complacency; however, it is her insecurity that accounted for her varied shades of character, the sum of which made her the architect of her life as well as her unfortunate demise (498).

In her opening paragraph, Leselle deliberatelyrefers to Earhart's fatal accident rather than postponing this fact. Her strategy is to show the reader that Earhart's premature death may have been a consequence of certain character traits and not totally unexpected.

Selecting Support to "Show," Not "Tell"

Leselle uses statements from other people as well as Earhart herself to support the points in her paper and to create a vivid portrait of her subject. In order to show that Earhart was "reserved," Leselle includes the line beneath Earhart's high school photograph that reads: "the girl in brown who walks alone." In that quotation, Leselle uses another's voice to show Earhart's solitary nature. To reveal Earhart's character and values, Leselle also includes numerous examples of Earhart's own voice; she documents these appropriately, adding "qtd. in" within the parenthetical reference so the reader knows that the words are from someone other than the biographer. For example, Leselle provides an excerpt from a letter that Earhart wrote to her mother "begging her mother not to write to her teachers because she would 'just shrivel' at the thought of having her personal affairs being discussed with others" (498). By recording Earhart's vivid word choice, "shrivel"—to wither, become helpless and useless—Leselle captures Earhart's extreme fear of having her teachers talk about her. Throughout her analysis, Leselle selects memorable descriptions and anecdotes to show her subject, reveal Earhart's character, and promote the reader's interest.

Conclusions

In her conclusion, Leselle recalls her thesis, that "Earhart was complex, having varied and seemingly incongruous character traits." Leselle underscores the cause-and-effect perception that she forecasts in her thesis by discussing many of the incongruous traits that were the result of Earhart's insecurity. Leselle satisfies readers need for closure, how Earhart's life ended, and she reminds readers' of the drama that she projected in her introduction—that Earhart's plane never returned from her last flight over the Pacific. Finally, Leselle frames her focused character study by incorporating lines from yet another Earhart poem.

 Final Tips for Writing a Focused Biography

- Select a good biography to read, one that has documented sources. When in doubt, get advice from your school librarian or your instructor.

- Find additional biographical sources at the library and online to complement your primary biography.

- Write a thesis based on character inference, using traits you can support.
- Arrange the traits in the thesis thoughtfully to reflect your full perception of the subject.
- Use anecdotes about the character, comments quoted from your subject, and comments made about the subject to support your thesis and to *show* your subject.
- Use a variety of transitional devices between sections of your paper in order to gain unity, coherence, and emphasis.
- Write an enticing introduction to your analysis and conclude meaningfully, perhaps with some insight about your perception of the person's life.
- Use in-text parenthetical references to document the source of ideas, facts, and quotations.
- Title your work to engage your reader.

Chapter 13

Writing the
Research Paper

The research paper—routinely assigned by most freshman composition instructors and universally dreaded by freshman composition students—has a worse reputation than it deserves. Like most tasks that at first seem overwhelming, the research paper needs time and organization. The steps suggested here, and the model of a student paper in this section, should help you handle such an assignment.

Planning the Research Paper

Even if you had outstanding luck in high school and welded a research paper together in a manic weekend session, your college professor certainly won't value the results of such a rushed job, and you will find your course grade threatened. Instead, admit to yourself that the research paper requires your attention through a number of steps, all of which you can handle. The research assignment is not designed to show what you don't know but to confirm what you can do.

In addition, the assignment encourages you to experience the pleasure of discovering new interests and information. If your instructor allows you to choose your topic, take advantage of this opportunity to pursue one that intrigues you, one that is worth the time and energy that you will devote to the investigation. Enjoy the discovery!

New Tools, New Choices

Computers make the process of discovering an intriguing topic more fun than ever. All libraries now have computers that can not only direct you to books but also provide you with immediate feedback about the status of the book—whether it is in the library or when it should be returned. You can also request that the book be held for you or sent from another library. Periodical searches are equally easy and, in some cases, you can print out the full text of an article or print an abstract, a brief summary that will help you determine whether you want to find the original full text.

We encourage you to use your library's superb databases—even from your home computer—to discover alternative topics that you may not have previously considered. It won't take you long to discover that the databases provide organized searches of authored articles that you will need for college writing. Further, you are not restricted to your own library's collection but can "roam the stacks" of the best libraries worldwide.

Time Schedule for the Research Paper

If your instructor does not assign due dates for the various stages of the paper, try dividing the time between the assigned date and the due date into four approximately equal parts. For example, if you have two months for the preparation of a paper, each stage will have two weeks. If you have one month, you can give each stage a week of your time.

STAGE 1—DISCOVERING A TOPIC AND MATERIALS
- Determine the topic that interests you and satisfies the paper assignment. You may want to choose 2–3 alternatives, to make sure that you are interested in the material and that there are plenty of credible sources for your research. Allow a few days, but do not postpone that first decision for longer than a few days.
- Go to the library and begin your search for materials. Locate the computers with your library's catalog of books and the computers with the periodical databases of credible, previously edited and printed articles.
- Meet a reference librarian—the researcher's best friend. Ask the librarian whether your topic has additional subject headings that you should be aware of so that you can do a complete search while you are in the library.
- Gather a few choice books to explore at home. Also begin your periodical search and email yourself any full-text articles that look promising. You then can decide at home which articles will be most useful and print only those that are relevant.

STAGE 2—TAKING NOTES
- Using pen and paper, a laptop or other electronic tool, begin a list of each of your sources, copying down *all* important information: author, title and subtitle, edition or volume number, editor or translator, city of publication

and publisher, and date of publication. If you are using electronic sources, record the complete URL (Web address) in addition to the above information. If you are only using select pages, or a chapter from an anthology, or if the book is a reference text that you can't check out, make sure that you record the exact page numbers of any paraphrased or quoted material. This precise record-keeping will eliminate hours of unnecessary frustration and return trips to the library.

- Read and take notes on the materials that you find. If you take notes in the library on works that you do not intend to photocopy, write direct quotations and paraphrase these later, when you know how much material you want to use. If you are printing from electronic sources, be selective or you will be hauling home piles of paper. Read widely; print rarely!

- As you take notes, think about how you might focus your paper.

STAGE 3—DRAFTING AND REVISING

- Determine a working thesis and write an outline for the paper.

- Use the computer to draft your paper. The extra time you spend preparing your paper electronically will be doubly compensated in revision speed and quality. **Remember to click on *save* often and to save your work not only on your hard drive but also on a backup disk.**

- Make sure that you have put quotation marks around any borrowed phrases or lines from your sources and include the author's last name and page numbers even in your draft. Be sure also to give credit for all paraphrased material—researched ideas that you have put into your own words. (See more on plagiarism, pp. 519–520.)

- Meet with your instructor or writing center staff for feedback before you continue.

- Revise your manuscript, strengthening the thesis, improving the arrangement, using more emphatic support, improving word choice and transitions, and clarifying any writing that your reader finds ambiguous or weak.

STAGE 4—EDITING AND PROOFREADING

- Examine your paper for coherence and unity. Read for effective transitions between paragraphs and within long paragraphs. (See pp. 390–397.) Edit carefully. Realize that spell-check and grammar-check might flag words that are correct as well as miss an incorrectly used word that appears to be spelled correctly (their/there/they're). Make sure that you have used quotation marks at the beginning and the ending of all quotations and that you have parenthetical citations for all ideas and quotations you have incorporated. (See plagiarism, pp. 372 and 519.)

- Print out the revised copy of your paper, the Works Cited page, and, provide a heading on the first page with your name, professor's name, course number, and date in the upper left-hand corner. (See the MLA model on pp. 524–539.)

If you divide the research paper assignment into parts, you will not be overwhelmed by the task. You may also realize that you need longer to draft your paper but less time for revision because the computer has expedited this process.

Gathering Library Material

Getting Started

Shannon Paaske's instructor required a research paper that was more developed, and used more sources, than the shorter documented papers that had been assigned earlier in her composition course. In addition to the length and source requirements, Shannon's assignment was to respond more fully to one of the subjects included in Part I of *Between Worlds*. Shannon decided that she wanted to learn more about the world of the disabled.

Her initial response to the research paper may have been posed in the form of questions: What are the problems the disabled have in attending classes? In working? In their social lives? What technology is available for the disabled on my campus? What kind of legislation exists to help the disabled? How do the disabled feel about their conditions? Are the attitudes of Soyster characteristic of the disabled? (See p. 158.) Has he written any other articles?

With these questions in mind, Shannon went to her college library.

Meeting the Librarian

The reference librarian can show you how to use the various computers, the periodical databases, and the Internet, and can direct you to specialized reference books and indexes that can be particularly helpful as you begin your research. There are more indexes than you can ever imagine, and a little time browsing these resources can open up new worlds of information. For example, if you have been assigned to write a biography research paper (p. 497) and you are just beginning your search for a subject, a general index such as *Encyclopedia of World Biography* or a more selective index such as *Contemporary Black Biography* are helpful shortcuts to learning about people's lives before you head off to find a full-length biography. Reference librarians are waiting to introduce you to these resources. Also, if you are new to research or to using computers and databases to find materials, consult your reference librarian and express your concerns. Most colleges and universities have short courses or workshops to orient students to library and online research.

Finding Information

Each library has its own computer system with particular options for searching (such as "keyword" or "browse"). Ask the librarian to recommend a method for searching for books and periodicals. If you cannot locate articles under a particular topic, ask the reference librarian for the Library of Congress

Subject Headings, which will provide an alternative term. For example, if you are searching for materials on film, the correct subject heading is "motion pictures," not film or movies. Many students leave libraries empty-handed or with few sources because they have not used the correct search method or because they have not entered all the appropriate headings.

Using Both Books and Periodicals

As you collect research materials, you should search for books as well as periodicals. Books provide greater depth and analysis, and they often include a historical overview (of legislative changes, economic patterns, fashion trends, or art or political movements). Because books take longer to publish, the material may be dated for some subjects, but historical perspective and depth are advantages in most fields. For more current information, you should also check periodicals, using the databases. These articles will provide up-to-date information: news events, current legislation, technological or medical data, or recent statistics. In addition to periodicals, books, and Internet materials, don't neglect videos, films, CD-ROMs, and interviews as potential sources of information.

Using Electronic Sources

As you may already realize, electronic sources offer you several advantages: (1) You can locate materials that are in your local libraries and in libraries thousands of miles from your campus; (2) you can read materials on the Internet that may not yet be available in print because they were posted as recently as the day of your search; (3) you can also tap into the knowledge of other researchers by using general search engines such as Google or Yahoo! or more specialized ones (see p. 514); (4) you can subscribe to a *listserv*, a mailing service that will email you up-to-date articles and answer questions on specialized topics; and (5) using certain services, you can obtain maps, pictures, and graphics that will enhance your understanding of your subject.

Your library has information on just about every topic, so if you do not find what you need, realize that you may be using an incorrect heading or misspelling a term. Computers are helpful, but it often takes a human being— a librarian—to show you how to access that help.

Beginning a Periodical Search—Head for the Databases

In addition to helping you search for books, your librarian will help you access essential databases for your particular research assignment. All of the materials in databases have been written by an author, edited for accuracy and style, previously published in respected print media, and are made available without commercial interest. On these pages, no one will try to sell you anything—other than ideas and information. Libraries subscribe to many different databases, and your librarians can tell you which services are available to you and which are appropriate for your assignment. For example, if you are writing on a current topic, databases such as *ProQuest* or *NewspaperSource* will provide articles from major national newspapers. If you need more depth and development, databases such as *Academic Search Premier* or *ERIC* (*Educational Resources Information Center*) provide articles from magazines and journals. If you need information from a particular field of study—history, fine arts, literature, science—specialized databases can help: *Issues and Controversies; CQ Researcher* (*Congressional Quarterly Researcher*); *Gale Literary Databases* (*Contemporary Authors, Dictionary of Literary Biography,* and *Contemporary Literary Criticism*); *LRC* (Literature Research Center); *Health and Wellness Center; CINAHL* (*Cumulate Index to Nursing and Allied Health Literature*); *MedlinePlus* or *Organized Wisdom*. These are just a few of the special databases that are used by students and faculty for academic research. You may be familiar with *EBSCOhost's* general database which includes popular magazines, but don't overlook the academic journals and magazines needed for most college research. For example, see *EBSCOhost's Academic Search Premier* as a better resource for your college papers.

Beginning an Internet Search— Some Cautions

In contrast to using databases for your academic research, general searches on the Web require some cautions. The Internet is a vast information network, but you must remember that *anyone* can post material on the Web. This means that the article that you are reading about vaccinations or greenhouse gases could be a rant or spoof written by someone with no credible information or expertise. In fact, according to the Berkeley guide to *Evaluating Web Pages*, "Most pages found in general search engines for the Web are self-published or published by businesses small and large with motives to get you to buy something or believe a point of view" (8). See www.lib.berkeley.edu/ TeachingLib/Guides/Internet/Evaluate.html and see the evalution guide included below (pp. 517–518).

Further, students may be tempted to begin their research with Wikis—Web pages modified by any Internet users. One of the most popular is the online encyclopedia *Wikipedia* (www.wikipedia.org), which can provide some initial information to get you started. However, keep in mind that, unlike a printed encyclopedia, *Wikipedia* can be modified by any Internet user. Therefore the information may be biased and inaccurate and should not be quoted or paraphrased in college papers. Instead, you should go to your library's home page and, using the periodical databases, search for relevant articles. Nearly all of these articles will have authors who assume responsibility for their research and editors who have checked and verified the information, and perhaps even edited for precision and clarity.

Refining an Internet Search

When Shannon Paaske updated the research paper that we published in the first edition of this textbook, she knew that the databases would provide her with current and useful material. Using *Medline,* she entered the keyword "disability," and then refined her search by adding "AND" and the terms "assistive and technology," to locate articles about the current technology designed to assist the disabled. Shannon also checked the bibliographies of these articles to find additional information for her paper.

Before starting a search, define your research goal and then list on paper the terms associated with that topic. You should enter those terms in the search box of a *search engine.* As you explore each term one at a time, you may sense that your terms are too general. You can then join the key terms with common words like "and," "or," "but not," so that the selections more closely reflect your interest and the number is manageable. If your term is too general, you will have either thousands of "hits" or none—and you will most likely be overwhelmed or discouraged. Athough you won't necessarily want to restrict your search terms in your initial information-gathering phase, eventually you will refine your search to avoid being overwhelmed with sources. Because every search engine has its own system, be sure to click on the "help" icon of the particular search engine to learn the best search strategies.

Keeping Track of Internet Sources

Quickly read the material on the screen and send to your email only those pages that you sense will be useful and will later want to print. If you want to return to an article or database, you can add a bookmark to mark it. Avoid bookmarking too many sites—a mistake similar to highlighting an entire page rather than selective passages of a textbook.

Keep accurate track of all information and addresses of sites that you use, including the access date, so that you have complete information to provide on your list of works cited. Because the reader of your paper may want to learn more about a particular aspect of your topic, your information must be accurate.

The Abuse of Electronic Sources

It may seem a researcher's dream to discover 3,000 hits on a topic with a print button handy and a fresh supply of paper in the printer. However, our own quick searches of Internet materials have produced mixed results. We found some articles that were well written and prepared with exemplary support. We also found too many trivial, unsigned, poorly written pieces—work that no serious college student should consider using. We thus have serious reservations about students who ignore the library and its databases, and we would undoubtedly fail papers that were last-minute patch jobs of poorly reasoned Web material.

"On the Internet, nobody knows you're a dog."

Evaluating Online Sources

Just as student researchers have always needed to consider the quality of their sources, you too will need to evaluate what you have read and printed from the Internet. Students working from books have the clear advantage of knowing that an editorial staff has evaluated the text and verified the data in it. However, no such safeguards exist on the Internet where literally *anybody* can publish *anything*. So while your job as a student researcher may be lightened in the discovery phase, your job in evaluating material from the Net is more challenging. Let's look at criteria for evaluating Web sources, entitled "The Good, the Bad, and the Ugly: or, Why It's a Good Idea to Evaluate Web Sources," distributed on the Internet by Susan E. Beck, Instruction Coordinator, New Mexico State University Library. (You can visit this site at http://lib .nmsu.edu/instruction/evalcrit.html.) Use the following questions to evaluate the authority, accuracy, objectivity, currency, and coverage of the material that you find on the Web.

Evaluation Criteria for Web Sources: "The Good, the Bad, and the Ugly"

Susan E. Beck

I. Authority

- Is there an author? Is the page signed?
- Is the author qualified? An expert?
- Who is the sponsor?
- Is the sponsor of the page reputable? How reputable?
- Is there a link to information about the author or the sponsor?
- If the page includes neither a signature nor indicates a sponsor, is there any other way to determine its origin?

  Look for a header or footer showing affiliation.

  Look at the URL. *http://www.fbi.gov*

  Look at the domain. *.edu, .com, .ac.uk, .org, .net*

Rationale

1. Anyone can publish anything on the Web.
2. It is often hard to determine a Web page's authorship.
3. Even if a page is signed, qualifications are not usually provided.
4. Sponsorship is not always indicated.

II. Accuracy

- Is the information reliable and error-free?
- Is there an editor or someone who verifies/checks the information?

Rationale

1. See number 1 above.
2. Unlike traditional print resources, Web resources rarely have editors or fact-checkers.
3. Currently, no Web standards exist to ensure accuracy.

III. Objectivity

- Does the information show a minimum of bias?
- Is the page designed to sway opinion?
- Is there any advertising on the page?

Rationale

1. Frequently the goals of the sponsors/authors are not clearly stated.

2. Often the Web serves as a virtual "Hyde Park Corner," a soapbox.

IV. Currency

- Is the page dated?
- If so, when was the last update?
- How current are the links? Have some expired or moved?

Rationale

1. Publication or revision dates are not always provided.

2. If a date is provided, it may have various meanings. For example,

   It may indicate when the material was first written

   It may indicate when the material was first placed on the Web

   It may indicate when the material was last revised

V. Coverage

- What topics are covered?
- What does this page offer that is not found elsewhere?
- What is its intrinsic value?
- How in-depth is the material?

Rationale

1. Web coverage often differs from print coverage.

2. Frequently, it's difficult to determine the extent of coverage of a topic from a Web page. The page may or may not include links to other Web pages or print references.

3. Sometimes Web information is "just for fun," a hoax, someone's personal expression that may be of interest to no one, or even outright silliness.

Resisting Temptation

Even after you have evaluated your sources and verified that your authors are credible, there is another trap to avoid. Because you may have actual copies of good articles on your computer, you could easily be tempted to simply cut and paste chunks of others' work into your draft. Resist this temptation! All college papers need to reflect *your* perception, using experts to *support* your views. Most of your essay should be your own thinking and words, with supporting information from experts. This information needs to be carefully analyzed—explained and evaluated in your own words and voice—and then accurately documented.

Plagiarism

Whether you use computer printouts, note cards, or photocopied pages from a book, you must record all of the necessary information so you can give credit and avoid **plagiarism—using someone else's ideas or language as your own**. Whether this is done accidentally or deliberately, it is a serious offense that schools may punish with expulsion. If you are desperate to complete an assigned paper, using somebody else's work, including work published on the Internet, may seem like a good idea to you. *Don't do it.* Failing a course or risking expulsion from school is not worth it. Realize that you are capable of doing the work that you have been assigned and that accomplishing this task with integrity will strengthen your skills and confidence as a writer.

Plagiarism most often occurs inadvertently—often because of sloppy note taking, poor record keeping, or even ignorance. You can avoid this problem by accurately recording, from your earliest notes on, the source of every idea—even in summary or paraphrased form—and of every key word or phrase of another writer that you are using. Furthermore, if you change or omit anything in the text that you are quoting, you need to use brackets (see p. 600) and ellipses (see pp. 598–599) to signify to your reader that you have made a change. It is important that you use quotation marks as soon as you begin using the author's words. Finally, you need to completely and accurately cite the source of material that you have used. Failure to adhere to these conventions may result in a charge of plagiarism, however inadvertent it may be. Examples of inadvertent plagiarism are shown below, so that you can avoid this error in your own work.

Inadvertent Plagiarism. Plagiarism occurs if a quotation is not used or documented correctly. In the following excerpt, read the original, from Marcus Mabry's "Living in Two Worlds" (p. 109) and the incorrect uses of the quotation.

Original

Most students who travel between the universes of poverty and affluence during breaks experience similar conditions, as well as the guilt, the helplessness and, sometimes, the embarrassment associated with them. Our friends are willing to listen, but most of them are unable to imagine the pain of the impoverished lives that we see every six months. Each time I return home I feel further away from the realities of poverty in America and more ashamed that they are allowed to persist. What frightens me most is not that the American socioeconomic system permits poverty to continue, but that by participating in that system I share some of the blame.

 PRACTICE FINDING THE ERRORS

Identify the incorrect uses of the material in each of these examples:

1. Marcus Mabry talks about the student who travels between the universes of poverty and affluence during school breaks.

2. Mabry is frightened by the fact that "the American socioeconomic system permits poverty to continue" and that "by participating in that system" he shares some of the blame (110).

3. One student who was studying at Stanford describes the guilt, helplessness, and embarrassment that he and other students feel when they move between their school lives and their home lives when they return home for vacation.

4. Mabry is concerned not that "the American socioeconomic system permits poverty to continue, but that by participating in that system he shares some of the blame" (110).

Explanation of Errors

1. In his mistaken notion that he has "only paraphrased," this writer has failed to place quotation marks around Mabry's words ("who travel between the universes of poverty and affluence"). Additionally, the student has not documented with parenthetical information the source of the material that he has taken from Marcus Mabry. Even if the student were to use only the image of the "universes of poverty and affluence," the image is Mabry's and must be documented.

2. This writer has misrepresented Mabry. The original expresses the idea that it is *not* America's "socioeconomic system" that frightens him but his fear that "by participating in that system" he "shares some of the blame." The writer has written a combination of paraphrase and quotation that does not correctly express Mabry's point.

3. The writer here has attempted a paraphrase of Mabry's words that stays too close to the original in repeating "guilt," "helplessness," and "embarrassment," without using quotation marks and which fails, in any case, to attribute and document the source of the idea.

4. This writer has made a change in Mabry's quoted material in order to merge his or her text smoothly with Mabry's words. But the writer has failed to use brackets to inform the reader that there is a change in the quoted material. This is how the quotation should look: "'The American socioeconomic system permits poverty to continue, but that by participating in that [he shares] some of the blame.'"

If you carefully copy material from another source, double-check your paraphrases, and inspect your quoted material and compare it with the original to verify that you have been accurate in your sense as well as in the use of quotation marks, brackets, and parentheses, you will avoid the inadvertent plagiarism that threatens your integrity as a writer and flaws the writing that you produce.

Sample Note Cards

Your instructor may require that you prepare note cards from the materials you have gathered for your research paper. These cards may contain direct quotations, paraphrased material, a combination of paraphrase and quotation, or summary. With the goal in mind of paraphrasing and quoting carefully those relevant sections of her collected texts, Shannon began making note cards for her paper.

Original text

People without the use of their arms or legs can now rely on computerized 'sip and puff' machines. With light puffs into a plastic straw, users can switch on the TV and change its channels, telephone a friend and play computer games. (Blackman 70)

Direct Quotation

> Blackman 70
>
> "People without the use of their arms or legs can now rely on computerized 'sip and puff' machines. With light puffs into a plastic straw, users can switch on the TV and change its channels, telephone a friend and play computer games."

Paraphrased Note Card

> Blackman 70
>
> With new developments in technology, quadriplegics can use the phone, operate the television, and even play games on the computer by blowing into a straw.

Combination of Quotation and Paraphrase

> Blackman 70
>
> Other developments include "computerized 'sip and puff' machines" which enable persons "without the use of their arms or legs" to change television channels, talk on the phone, and "play computer games" by inhaling or exhaling into a straw.

Developing a Working Thesis

While Shannon read from her collection of materials and took notes, she began to focus on her subject in a sharper way. She realized that she had a number of ways to approach the subject of the disabled, but that she was especially interested in three: (1) technology that equips the disabled to leave home and enter the outside world, (2) the media's recent interest in depicting the disabled, and (3) the attitudes of the nondisabled person toward the disabled. Her working thesis looked something like this:

> Technology and the media have improved life for the disabled, but they still suffer social isolation and indignities.

Shannon talked with her instructor about her working thesis and the rough outline of the three parts that she planned to write. (For a discussion of outlining and for illustrations, see pp. 364–367.) After discussing her plan and what she had found in her research, Shannon and her instructor concluded that she did not have enough information about the social isolation of the disabled, and that her own casual observations would be insufficient for a well-developed research paper. The instructor suggested that Shannon approach the special resources center on the campus to arrange interviews with disabled students who would be willing to talk about their social situations. Furthermore, both the instructor and Shannon concluded that they knew very little about legislation that gave rights to the disabled, and both realized that any reader would want to know something about this legislation.

Gathering Additional Information: The Interview

Before she started the first draft of her paper, Shannon returned to the library to collect information on the legislation that guarantees the disabled access and ensures their rights. In the process, she discovered some old laws that were so ridiculous that they could provide a dramatic introduction for her paper.

Shannon also contacted the director of her campus special resources center, who gave her names and telephone numbers of students who volunteered to talk with her. These face-to-face interviews proved to be a valuable resource in her paper. Shannon was able to describe the experiences of real individuals and to catch their actual voices in print.

Conducting the Interview

Although you have prepared questions and ordered them, you may find that the answers cause you to skip to another question or to think up a question on the spot. Your ability to respond with follow-up questions and encouragement ("Why do you think that happened?" "How did you respond?") may determine the depth of the interview. Such follow-up questions may prompt the interviewees to move from predictable responses to those that are fresh and candid.

As you take notes, concentrate on getting down key phrases and controversial claims. Shannon recorded this from one of her interviewees: "Some people are prejudiced and ignore us. That makes me angry." Shannon put quotation marks around exact words so she could remember which words were her subject's and which she added or paraphrased. As you interview your subjects, don't hesitate to ask them to clarify points or expand on ideas so you can get the necessary information. Before you leave, remember to ask about additional sources or reference materials (reading materials, brochures, and names of other specialists). Also, check the spelling of each interviewee's name.

Because these people are giving you some valuable time for the interview, it is essential that you offer to meet where and when it is convenient for *them*. Arrive on time, don't overstay your welcome, and prepare your questions before the meeting. Remember to be exceptionally courteous and to show appreciation for their time and help.

Writing up the Interview

Immediately after the interview, write out or type up the questions and answers while the session is still fresh in your mind. If you discover you have missed any important material or may have misunderstood a point, call back your interviewee immediately for a clarification.

When you integrate the interviewees' comments into your paper, be careful to quote exactly and to represent the context of the statement accurately. Misusing quotations or distorting their intended meaning destroys your integrity as a writer. Shannon found that her conversations with the disabled provided insights that her readings could not. The strength of her argument, however, could not rely only on interviews and personal experiences. She used nine printed sources and three electronic sources to develop her argument.

STUDENT EXAMPLE: RESEARCH PAPER

You may be interested to know that our former student, Shannon Paaske, who wrote the research paper that we published in the first edition of *Between Worlds,* has finished her undergraduate work and is now a first-grade teacher in Los Angeles. It is probably every student's nightmare that a former teacher would track her down, but we did. Shannon agreed to update her paper using more current material, including the Internet. The numbers in the margin of the manuscript correspond to the numbers of the explanations on the facing page. These explanations will guide you through both rhetorical and mechanical considerations for your own paper.

Shannon Paaske

Professor Bachmann

English 1A

3 May 2004

From Access to Acceptance:

Enabling America's Largest Minority

    In the early 1900s, a Chicago city ordinance stated that no "unsightly, deformed or maimed person can appear on the public thoroughfares" (Davidson 62). A court case in Wisconsin in 1919 upheld the expulsion from school of a twelve-year-old boy with cerebral palsy because his teachers and fellow students regarded him as "depressing and nauseating" (62). In contrast to these unjust laws of the first half of the twentieth century, the second half drafted legislation and designed equipment to improve life for disabled people. In 1990, the Americans with Disabilities Act was passed by Congress. This enormous piece of legislation, among other things, requires both public buildings and private businesses to provide architectural access for disabled persons and it prohibits discrimination against them in the workplace. Helping to remove even more barriers, the Assistive Technology Act was signed into law eight years later. This act promotes the use of technological devices designed to help disabled persons lead independent lives. A customized, computerized van allows a man paralyzed from the chest down to operate a motor vehicle by himself. And near the end of the twentieth century, major network television shows such as *Life Goes On*, *L.A. Law*, and *Star Trek: The Next Generation* regularly featured people with all types of disabilities.

    Clearly, America's institutions have come a long way in acknowledging the 43 million people in this country with disabilities (Blackman 70). Although combinations of technological advances, equality-promoting legislation, and increasing media exposure have worked as a collective force in bringing about improvements in the lives of the people who make up what is sometimes termed "America's largest minority" (Davidson 61), ignorance and prejudice continue to plague the disabled.

    Technological developments, almost exclusively computer-oriented, have revolutionized the world of the disabled person. Citizens who were once confined to

Explanatory Notes for the Research Paper

The numbers on these explanatory notes correspond to the numbers in the margin of the research paper.

1. *Securing the paper.* When your paper is finished, staple the pages in the upper left corner. Don't use a folder or plastic binder.

2. *Form.* Type your last name and the page number, as Shannon does, in the upper right corner of each page, one-half inch from the top. All other margins will be one inch.

3. *Heading.* Begin your heading one inch from the top of the first page and flush with the left margin. Include your full name, instructor's name, the course number, and the date, double-spacing between lines. Double-space again and center the title, and then double-space between title and first line of the paper.

4. *Title.* Your title should engage your reader and establish an expectation for what the paper is about. It should please your reader's ears and eyes. If your reader stumbles while reading your title, it needs more work. Shannon's focus is unmistakable: the disabled person's wish for "access" and "acceptance." Do not underline or put quotation marks around your title.

5. *Citations.* Shannon's opening sentence includes a quotation, so she must document the source and page number in parentheses. The second time that Shannon quotes material from Davidson's article, she needs only the page number because Davidson's name has just been given.

6. *Introduction.* Shannon's introduction is a dramatic, abbreviated history of the legislation, equipment changes, and social responses to the disabled in this century. She quotes the exact language of the ordinances because the wording jolts the reader.

7. *Statistic.* Shannon notes that there are "43 million" disabled people in the United States and cites Blackman and the page where she located this figure.

8. *Thesis.* Shannon's thesis that begins with "although" forecasts her intention: to look at the technical and legislative changes, and increased media exposure, as improvements for the disabled. She will also examine the problems that plague the disabled and prevent their full "acceptance."

9. *Uncommon knowledge quoted.* It is not common knowledge that the disabled are "America's largest minority," so Shannon documents the source of this statement.

10. *Summarized material.* Noting past limitations, Shannon summarizes the technological developments that now "enable" the disabled.

Paaske 1

home, forbidden to travel by air, and unable to attend classes or hold jobs have been liberated by recent inventions that encourage independence as well as allow for enriching

11

life experiences. Just how extensive is the new technology? According to Jan Gavlin,
director of assistive technology at the National Rehabilitation Hospital in Washington,
"If you can move one muscle in your body, wiggle a pinkie or twitch an eyebrow, we can
design a switch to allow you to operate in your environment" (qtd. in Blackman 71).

An example of one such device is the Eyegaze Response Interface Computer Aid
(ERICA), developed by biomedical engineer Thomas Hutchinson at the University
of Virginia. This eye-controlled computer empowers severely disabled yet bright people
with the ability to learn and communicate. Ten years ago these people would have
been misdiagnosed as mentally retarded by traditional tests that are unable to correctly
measure their intelligence. Originally designed for children who previously might have
been misdiagnosed, ERICA and other systems like it instead "create pathways for kids

12

to express themselves and for teachers to engage their minds" (Rab and Youcha 22).

This technology also allows severely disabled adults to pursue careers, as in the
case of Brian Dickinson. "Mr. Dickinson has amyotrophic lateral sclerosis [better

13

known as Lou Gehrig's disease], which has stripped him of the power to speak, swallow, move his legs or arms, wiggle his fingers or turn his head" (Felton 1). With the
help of an Eyegaze system, Dickinson continues writing his column for *The Providence
Journal-Bulletin* in Rhode Island. He selects certain functions on his computer screen
simply by looking at the appropriate keys.

14

Other developments include computerized "sip and puff" machines, which
enable people without the use of their arms or legs to change television channels,
talk on the phone, and play computer games simply by inhaling or exhaling into a
plastic straw (Blackman 70). A system called DragonDictate is a computer program
that prints dictation onto a monitor when the user speaks into a microphone (70).
This type of program is especially useful to people who are unable to type because of
poor muscle control (a characteristic of cerebral palsy) or who have various types of
paralysis. The system even comes with a spell-check mode that responds to the incorrect word with an "oops."

Explanatory Notes (*continued*)

11. *Quotation within the article.* Shannon credits a knowledgeable source, Jan Gavlin, as he is quoted in Blackman's article. Because she has wisely used Gavlin's name in her lead, Shannon needs only to cite that he is "quoted" in Blackman and give the page number. If she had not used Gavlin's name in her lead, her parenthetical reference would be: (Gavlin qtd. in Blackman 71).

12. *Two-author citation.* The parenthetical reference from an article written by two authors contains the last name of each author, connected with "and," and the page number of the article.

13. *Altering a quotation.* Shannon adds a clarification to her quoted material using brackets so that the reader knows that she has altered the quotation. A quotation should not be altered unless it is essential for clarity and then the alteration should not change the meaning of the original text.

14. *Paraphrased material.* Even though Shannon describes in her own words how the "sip and puff" machine is used, she must document the source of her information. If Shannon had felt there would be any confusion in her reader's mind about the source of her information, she would have repeated Blackman's name as she does in the next paragraph.

Paaske 2

Modern wheelchair designs also reflect the recent advancements that permit the disabled to leave home and enter the world. Robert Cushmac, 16, who was paralyzed from the neck down in a car accident when he was 10, gets from class to class at his Virginia high school, where he is an honors student, in a wheelchair activated by a chin-controlled joystick (Blackman 71). The Hi-Rider is a "standing wheelchair" that was designed by Tom Houston who is paralyzed from the waist down. His design makes it possible for him to perform tasks previously impossible, such as reaching an object on an overhead shelf, or greeting someone face to face (Blackman 70).

As these examples show, the continuous headway being made in adaptive technology has considerably altered the way of life for many disabled people. However, it is highly unlikely that much of this progress could have been accomplished without the help of a sympathetic political climate. Federal Disability Laws passed by Congress since 1968 addressed the environmental needs of the disabled and particularly focused on independent living as a goal. This goal expressed the desire of people with disabilities to view themselves and be viewed "no longer as passive victims deserving of charitable intervention but as self-directed individuals seeking to remove environmental barriers that preclude their full participation in society" (DeJong and Lifchez 45).

Laws such as the Architectural Barriers Act of 1968 required structures built with federal funds or leased by the federal government to be made accessible, and the Urban Mass Transportation Act and Federal Aid Highway Act of 1970 and 1973 worked to make transportation a reality for the disabled (DeJong and Lifchez 42). Later laws were created to achieve the attitudinal changes implicit in the objectives of the independent living movement. One law is The Rehabilitation Act of 1973, which prohibits discrimination against disabled people in programs, services, and benefits that are federally funded. The Rehabilitation Comprehensive Services and Developmental Disability Amendments of 1978 established independent living as a priority for state vocational programs and provided federal funding for independent living centers (DeJong and Lifchez 42). The Social Security Disability Amendments of 1980 gave disabled people more incentives to work by letting them deduct independent-living expenses from

Explanatory Notes (*continued*)

15. *Transition.* Shannon moves from her review of the technological advancements designed to enhance the lives of the disabled to a review of legislation that has given them rights. Notice that her transition establishes that the technological advancements would not have occurred without the legislative changes. This is a more critically perceptive transition, showing a cause-and-effect relationship, than one that suggests merely "another change for the disabled is in the area of legislation."

16. *Paraphrased and quoted material.* Shannon summarizes the various laws and acts and documents her source of information, the *Scientific American* article written by the two authors noted in her parenthetical references throughout this portion of her text. Her review of this legislation is historical, and it is chronologically arranged.

Paaske 4

their taxes (42). The Americans with Disabilities Act, signed in 1990, reinforced the legislation that was not earlier implemented.

More recently, the Assistive Technology Act of 1998 ensures funding for statewide programs to promote the use of technological devices that improve the functional capabilities of disabled persons ("The ATA"). Because of the important role that such devices play to increase the independence of individuals with disabilities, the impact of this legislation is major. The speed and extent to which this impact can be felt is heavily influenced by the advent of the Internet. Through Websites such as ABLEDATA, ATA (Alliance for Technology Access), and RESNA (Rehabilitation Engineering and Assistive Technology Society of North America) users can look up specific information on assistive technology devices, get help with problems or questions, and even make personal connections in chat rooms (ABLEDATA).

It is undeniable that new legislation, together with the flourishing of adaptive technology and Internet-based sources of support, have created greater awareness of the disabled in our communities. The increasing number of disabled characters in movies and television reflects that awareness. Deaf actress Marlee Matlin, for example, enjoyed success starring in the Academy Award-winning *Children of a Lesser God* in 1986, and later in the television series *Reasonable Doubts*. In assessing Matlin's character in *Reasonable Doubts*, Ben Mattlin (no relation), a writer with a muscular dystrophy-related disease, says he "can't say enough good things about working a highly visible disability into a major character" (Mattlin 8). Ben Mattlin also finds it significant that this character is portrayed as both intelligent and sexy. In addition, on ABC's *Life Goes On*, Christopher Burke, an actor who has Down's Syndrome, played Corky, a "competent, high-functioning integral part of his family" (Mattlin 8). Because Matlin and Burke are disabled actors who portray disabled characters—in contrast to the many able-bodied actors who play disabled roles—they have helped mark a path of new acceptance for the disabled.

In addition, retail stores that employ the disabled to model in their advertising create new public acceptance of the disabled. In 1991, retail store Kids R Us hired disabled children from hospital pediatric wards to work as professional models for their

Explanatory Notes (*continued*)

17. *Documenting electronic sources.* Shannon used the Internet to find the most recent legislation affecting the disabled. Because there was no author, she credits the abbreviated *title* of the site in her parenthetical citation. "The ATA" is an abbreviation for "The Assistive Technology Act," found in the Works Cited section with the Web address so that the reader also can locate the information.

18. *Another electronic source.* Here again Shannon does not have an author so she uses the title of the site in her parenthetical reference.

19. *Conclusion to one section and transition to the next.* Shannon concludes her review of the legislation with a statement that the provisions of the most recent act for which she has information have not yet been fully implemented. She believes the impact will be "undeniable" when the act is fully in effect.

20. *New focus point.* Again, Shannon relates the next section of her paper to the previous sections by asserting that technology and legislation have made the disabled visible citizens in our communities. The media have reflected this visibility by increasing the number of disabled employed in film, television, and advertising.

21. *Parenthetical explanation.* Shannon makes a point of noting that the media critic, Ben Mattlin, is no relation to Marlee Matlin. She is then free to use Mattlin's name in parenthetical documentation without concern that her reader will be confused.

22. *Summary and direct quotation.* In a combination of summarized information and direct quotation, Shannon uses Ben Mattlin's article about the depictions of disabled actors in various media. She was tempted to use Mattlin's critical comments about the "distorted images" of the disabled in particular films, but she realized that this digression would change the balance and focus of her paper. From Mattlin's article, she used only what was relevant to her essay—brief references to actual programs and actors, and the appreciation of a disabled writer for positive portrayals of the disabled in film.

Paaske 5

catalogues and circulars. Some of the store's executives got the idea while watching these kids play. Vice President Ernie Speranza reasoned, "They think of themselves as average kids, so we decided we should too" (Speranza qtd. in Yorks 1). Kids R Us was not the first retail store to make this move, and since 1990, Target and Nordstrom's—representing both ends of the economic spectrum—have hired disabled people of all ages as models in an effort to better represent the diversity of its clientele (Yorks 1).

Also helping to bring more exposure through the media is a television news-magazine, a series of programs created by the mother of an autistic child who wanted to create a television show devoted to disabled people. This series provides "profiles of courage and accomplishment and informs viewers of a wide range of issues and opportunities to enhance quality of life through greater self-sufficiency" (*Disabilities and Possibilities*). Winner of many awards, including an Emmy, this program has aired on PBS stations throughout North America and aims to unify abled and disabled people.

The arts community appears to be responding with greater awareness as well. In 1999, a five-day festival in Los Angeles celebrating "the arts, disability, and culture" hosted more than eight international dance companies featuring disabled performers (Haskins 108). Although efforts such as these indicate that the media have "started to get a broader perspective on real life" (Olson), people with disabilities have yet to enjoy full acceptance by American society. Nancy Mairs, a woman with multiple sclerosis who balances a college teaching and lecturing career with the demands of a marriage and motherhood, finds that while her family and the people she works with have accepted her disability, she still has had to endure an end-of-the-semester evaluation by a student who was perturbed by her disability (122).

While no longer blatantly discriminated against, disabled people often continue to suffer the burden of social bias. Even those remarkable individuals who are able to triumph over physical barriers have trouble surmounting social barriers. Post-polio actor Henry Holden relates his own experience with social discrimination:

> A guy with paralyzed legs is not supposed to be able to sell insurance, but I did very well at it in New Jersey before I became an actor. A guy with paralyzed legs is not supposed to climb mountains, but I made the trek up

Explanatory Notes (*continued*)

23. *Quotation within the article.* The vice president of a retail store is quoted within an article that Shannon read about the use of the disabled as models in advertising. She quotes him in her text and notes his name and the page of the quotation in her parenthetical reference.

24. *Quotation from an interview.* Because there are no page numbers associated with interviews, only the last name of the subject interviewed is enclosed in the parentheses. Shannon uses Steve Olson's comment about the value of images of the disabled in advertising as a transition to the final section of her paper. This section focuses on the feelings that disabled people have about nondisabled people's perceptions of them. Shannon gained these insights in interviews as well as readings.

25. *Paraphrased and summarized material.* An experience noted by an author in her essay is summarized and paraphrased by Shannon, and the source of the material is documented.

26. *Long quotations.* Because the experience of the actor Henry Holden is especially revealing, Shannon decided to include the long quotation in her paper. Because the quotation is longer than four typed lines, it cannot be incorporated within the manuscript. Instead, the longer quotation is set off from the rest of the paper with double-spacing at the top and bottom of the quotation, and it is indented ten spaces or one inch from the left margin. The quotation itself is double-spaced, and the final period precedes the parenthetical information. If the first line of the quoted passage begins a new paragraph, it is indented fifteen spaces.

the cliff at Masada in Israel at four o'clock in the morning. A guy with paralyzed legs is not supposed to ride horses, but I rode in an exhibition in
Madison Square Garden. Yet I am not generally accepted by nondisabled
people in social situations. The attitude in the country is that, if you have a
disability, you should stay home. (Holden qtd. in Davidson 63)

Susan Rodde, who has cerebral palsy, confirms that in most social situations,
"we, the physically challenged, have to be the icebreakers." At parties and social gath-
erings, the disabled person is often isolated or ignored. Having used a wheelchair since
a surfing accident, Berkeley student Steve Olson confirms this experience: "Sometimes I

27   meet people at parties who feel uncomfortable about [my disability]. I talk and tell
jokes to break the ice, and soon no one realizes there's a disabled person—me—sitting
in the room with them." Unfortunately, the "ice" does need to be broken because
many people feel uncomfortable around disabled or disfigured people, and so far, the
responsibility of making social contact lies with the disabled person.

But many disabled people report that fully abled people have a hard time "re-

28   specting the fact that we're the same as they are," says Diane DeVries, who was born
with no legs and only partial arms. Perhaps because of ignorance or fear, our disabili-

29   ties "remind people of their own vulnerabilities" (DeVries). As Nancy Mairs says, "Society is no readier to accept crippledness than to accept death, war, sex, sweat, or

30   wrinkles" (119). Because they may feel vulnerable, able-bodied people tend not to
form close relationships with disabled people, and some even refuse casual contact.
Rebecca Acuirre, 16, who has cerebral palsy, says that she recently asked a stranger
what time it was and he kept walking as though he didn't hear her. "Some people
are prejudiced and ignore us. That makes me angry," she says.

31   How can these prejudices be abolished? "We need more exposure," says
DeVries. Acuirre concurs, saying the media should do more to educate the public. On
a personal level, Bill Davidson, in "Our Largest Minority, Americans with Handicaps,"
recommends the nondisabled public "help reverse centuries of discrimination" by
getting to know disabled people "at work, in the marketplace, at school" and by

Explanatory Notes (*continued*)

27. *Brackets.* Shannon has enclosed in brackets a change that she has made in material from an interview. It is possible that her subject used a pronoun that would have been ambiguous to the reader; Shannon substituted the noun and placed the clarifying term in brackets. The reader understands that the brackets are used to clarify or change tense or other language forms to permit easy reading of the quoted material as it is integrated with the writer's text. No changes may be made and put into brackets that would alter the meaning of the material quoted. (See p. 600 for more information about brackets.)

28. *Incorporating short quotations.* Shannon incorporates into her text the specific quoted material from her reading and interviews. When the subject of an interview is named in the text, there is no need for additional documentation.

29. *Interview subject quoted.* Because Shannon does not reuse Diane DeVries's name in her text, she documents the source of the quotation by using DeVries's last name in parentheses.

30. *Documentation from a book.* Nancy Mairs's name is used in Shannon's text, so only the page number of the book is cited in parentheses.

31. *Incorporating summary and quotations.* Shannon introduces the author and title of the article in her text. This attribution within her text facilitates Shannon's documentation; she needs to note only the page number within the parentheses. Her citations document the specific quoted material as well as the paraphrased content of Davidson's article.

making "contact that is real—not just casual" (63). Able-bodied people can help overcome their own preconceived notions and realize that if disabled people seem bitter, "it's not because of their disability . . . but because of society's attitude toward them." Prejudices can be stopped before they start by encouraging children "not to shun and fear" the disabled (63).

32   The legislation and technology that were developed at the end of the twentieth century will continue to make new worlds accessible to disabled people. Ideally, these developments will permit the disabled to be viewed in terms of their capabilities rather than their disabilities. In that climate, disabled people can gain acceptance in the worlds to which they have access. With the steps being taken by government, science, and the media, individuals alone are needed to make the dream of acceptance a reality for people with disabilities.

33   Works Cited

34   ABLEDATA. The National Institute on Disability and Rehabilitation Research. U.S.
            Department of Education. 11 Apr. 1999 <http://www.abledata.com>. Web.

35   Acuirre, Rebecca. Personal interview. 23 Sept. 1992.

36   "The Assistive Technology Act of 1998." *RESNA*. 11 Apr. 1999
            <http://www.resna.org/ata/>. Web.

37   Blackman, Ann. "Machines That Work Miracles." *Time* 18 Feb. 1991: 70–71. Print.

38   Davidson, Bill. "Our Largest Minority: Americans with Handicaps." *McCall's* Sept.
            1987: 61–68. Print.

39   Dejong, Gerben, and Raymond Lifchez. "Physical Disability and Public Policy."
            Scientific American June 1983: 40–49. Print.

40   DeVries, Diane. Telephone interview. 22 Sept. 1992.

41   *Disabilities and Possibilities Television Newsmagazine*. 10 April 1999
            <http://www.disabilities-tv.com/>. Web.

Explanatory Notes (*continued*)

32. *Conclusion.* In her conclusion, Shannon reviews the relationship between the points she has made in her paper. She concludes by asserting that the advancements for the disabled lie in the hands of individuals, not only institutions. She uses the language of her title to bring a more dramatic closure to her analysis.

33. *The form for the list of sources used in the text.* The Works Cited page should always begin on a new numbered page at the end of the paper. The head is centered on the line, one inch from the top of the page. The first cited work is typed two lines beneath the heading. The entire list is double-spaced. The list is alphabetically arranged by the author or speaker's last name or by the first word in the title of an unsigned article. The entry begins at the left margin. If it is longer than one complete line, its second line begins five spaces indented from the left margin. (More complete information on MLA form begins on p. 540.)

34. Entry for an electronic source.

35. Entry for a personal interview. The date of the interview is noted.

36. Entry for an electronic source.

37. Entry for a signed article in a weekly periodical.

38. Entry for a signed article in a monthly periodical.

39. Entry for a magazine article written by two authors.

40. Entry for a telephone interview. The date of the interview is noted.

41. Entry for an electronic source.

Paaske 9

42   Felton, Bruce. "Technologies That Enabled the Disabled: High-tech or Low, Devices
        Enrich Work." *New York Times* 14 Sept. 1997, late ed.: Sec 3, 1+. Print.

43   Haskins, Ann. "Dance Listings." *LA Weekly.* 28 May 1999: 108. Print.

44   Mairs, Nancy. "On Being a Cripple." *With Wings: An Anthology of Literature by and
        about Women with Disabilities.* Ed. Marsha Saxon and Florence Howe. New
        York: Feminist Press, 1987. 118–127. Print.

45   Mattlin, Ben. "Beyond *Reasonable Doubts*: The Media and People with Disabilities."
        Television and Families 13.3 (1991): 4–8. Print.

46   Olson, Steve. Telephone interview. 18 Sept. 1992.

47   Rab, Victoria Y., and Geraldine Youcha. "Body." *Omni* June 1990: 22+. Print.

48   Rodde, Susan. Telephone interview. 20 Sept. 1992.

49   Yorks, Cindy LaFavre. "Challenging Images." *Los Angeles Times.* 22 Nov. 1991: E1–2.
        Print.

Explanatory Notes (*continued*)

42. Entry for a signed daily newspaper article. Notice the plus sign (+) after page 1 to indicate that after the first page the article continues on nonconsecutive pages.

43. Entry for a signed column in a weekly newspaper.

44. Entry for a chapter within an anthology with two editors. Notice that the name of the author of the chapter Shannon used is listed first.

45. Entry for a signed article in a periodical with volume and number.

46. Entry for a telephone interview.

47. Entry for two authors of an article within a monthly periodical. Notice that the article started on page 22 but did not appear on continuous pages. The "+" symbol indicates that the pages were not consecutive.

48. Entry for a telephone interview.

49. Entry for a signed article in a daily newspaper. Notice the "E" prior to the page number to indicate the section of the newspaper in which the article appeared.

Documenting the Research Paper: MLA Style

Whenever you use the words, information, or ideas of another writer—even if in your own words you summarize or paraphrase—you must credit the source. The following forms show you exactly how to provide the necessary information for documenting your sources according to the Modern Language Association (MLA) style guide. You can check the MLA Web site (www.mla.org) for additional documentation information and updating. *The MLA Handbook for Writers of Research Papers* (7th ed., 2009) is the source for this section, and it is certainly the form that your college English instructors will want you to use.

Indicating Titles

Any titles that you refer to within your essay and in the citations at the end of your work need to be appropriately indicated. **The titles of short works**–those works typically included in anthologies or periodicals and not published independently, such as essays, short stories, poems, songs, and articles—**should be in quotation marks. The titles of longer works**—those works published independently, such as books, plays, newspapers, magazines, Web sites, online databases, television and radio broadcasts, CDs, record albums, performances, and works of art—**should be in italics**.

Writing Parenthetical Citations

Your in-text citation should give just enough information so that your reader can find the origin of your material on the works-cited page (your bibliography) at the end of your paper. Here are sample parenthetical citations to illustrate MLA format.

Author Not Named in the Text. When you haven't included the author's name in your text, you must note in parentheses the author's last name and the page or pages of your source.

> "The first steps toward the mechanical measurement of time, the beginnings of the modern clock in Europe, came not from farmers or shepherds, nor from merchants or craftsmen, but from religious persons anxious to perform promptly and regularly their duties to God" (Boorstin 36).

Author Named in the Text. It is often advantageous to introduce your paraphrased or quoted material by noting the author's name within your text, especially if your author is an authority on the subject. If you do include the author's name in the text, your parenthetical citation will be brief and less intrusive, containing only the page number by itself.

According to Daniel Boorstin, the senior historian of the Smithsonian Institute, "the first steps toward the mechanical measurement of time, the beginnings of the modern clock in Europe, came not from farmers or shepherds, nor from merchants or craftsmen, but from religious persons anxious to perform promptly and regularly their duties to God" (36).

Two Books by the Same Author. If your paper contains two different works by the same author, each parenthetical reference should give an abbreviated form of the title, with the page number, so that your reader will know which work you are citing in each section of your paper.

Ben Mattlin deplores the pity for the disabled that Jerry Lewis's yearly telethon evokes ("Open Letter" 6). Mattlin also exposes the hypocrisy in depicting the disabled as superheroes. His point is that "courage and determination are often necessary when living with a disability. But there's nothing special in that, because there's no choice. Flattering appraisals sound patronizing" ("Beyond *Reasonable Doubts*" 5).

A Work with Two or Three Authors. If the work was written by two or three authors, use each of their names in your text or in the parenthetical citations.

In their study of John Irving's *The World According to Garp*, Janice Doane and Devon Hodges analyze the author's attitude toward female authority: "Even novels that contain sympathetic female characters, as Irving's novel does, may still be oppressive to women" (11).

Critics have charged that John Irving's *The World According to Garp* doesn't really support female authority: "Even novels that contain sympathetic female characters, as Irving's does, may still be oppressive to women" (Doane and Hodges 11).

A Work with More Than Three Authors. If more than three authors wrote your source, you may use only the first author's last name, followed by "et al." and the page number in parentheses, or you may list all of the authors' last names in the text or with the page number in parentheses.

In *Women's Ways of Knowing: The Development of Self, Voice, and Mind*, the authors note that there are many women who "believed they were stupid and helpless. They had grown up either in actual physical danger or in such intimidating circumstances that they feared being wrong, revealing their ignorance, being laughed at" (Belenky et al. 57).

In *Women's Ways of Knowing: The Development of Self, Voice, and Mind*, the authors note that many women "believed they were stupid and helpless. They had grown up either in actual physical danger or in such intimidating circumstances that they feared being wrong, revealing their ignorance, being laughed at" (Belenky, Clinchy, Goldberger, and Tarule 57).

In *Women's Ways of Knowing: The Development of Self, Voice, and Mind*, Belenky, Clinchy, Goldberger, and Tarule note that there are many women who "believed they were stupid and helpless. They had grown up either in actual physical danger or in such intimidating circumstances that they feared being wrong, revealing their ignorance, being laughed at" (57).

Author's Name Not Given.   If the author is anonymous, use the complete title in your text or an abbreviated form of the title with the page number in the parentheses.

The obituary for Allan Bloom in *Newsweek* describes him as the man who "ignited a national debate on higher education" and "defended the classics of Western Culture and excoriated what he saw as the intellectual and moral relativism of the modern academy" ("Transition" 73).

Corporate Author or Government Publication.   Either name the corporate author in your text or include an abbreviated form in the parentheses. If the name is long, try to work it into your text to avoid an intrusive citation.

Southern California Edison, in a reminder to customers to "Conserve and Recycle," gives the shocking statistic that "every hour, Americans go through 2.5 million plastic bottles, only a small percentage of which are now recycled" (*Customer Update* 4).

Literature: Novel, Play, Poem.   Because works appear in various editions, it is best to give the chapter number or part in addition to the page number to help your reader find the reference you are citing.

Novel

In the novel *Invisible Man*, Ralph Ellison uses a grotesque comparison to describe eyes: "A pair of eyes peered down through lenses as thick as the bottom of a Coca-Cola bottle, eyes protruding, luminous and veined, like an old biology specimen preserved in alcohol" (230; ch. 11).

Play

The parenthetical citation includes just the arabic numbers for the act, scene, and lines. These numbers are separated by periods: (4.3.89–90).

> In William Shakespeare's *Othello*, Emilia sounds like a twenty-first-century feminist when she claims that "it is their husbands' faults" if their wives have affairs (4.3.89–90).

Poem

The parenthetical citation includes the line or lines of the poem cited: (13–14).

> Poet Robert Hass, in "Misery and Splendor," describes the frustration of lovers longing to be completely united: "They are trying to become one creature,/and something will not have it" (13–14).

Indirect Source. When you use the words of a writer who is quoted in another author's work, begin the citation with the abbreviation "qtd. in" and both writers' last names if you have not used them in your text.

> Women and men both cite increased "freedom" as a benefit of divorce. But Riessman discovered that women meant that they "gained independence and autonomy" while men meant that they felt "less confined," "less claustrophobic," and had "fewer responsibilities" (Kohler Riessman qtd. in Tanner 40–41).

More Than One Work. If you want to show that two works are the sources of your information, separate the references with a semicolon.

> Two recent writers concerned with men's issues observe that many women have options to work full-time or part-time, stay at home, or combine staying at home with a career. On the other hand, men need to stay in the corporate world and provide for the family full-time (Allis 81; Farrell 90).

Online Sources

Online Source—Author Given

When you incorporate online sources, use the same form as you would for a book or periodical: Give the author's name in parentheses followed by the page number if the entry is longer than one page. If it is one page or less, give only the author's name.

> "Making Media a Familiar Scapegoat" concludes with the claim: "Trench coats don't kill, guns and pipe bombs do" (Rosenberg 3–4).

If the Internet material uses paragraph numbers rather than page numbers, give the relevant number or numbers preceded by the abbreviation *par.* or *pars.*

In the study "National and Colonial Education in Shakespeare's *The Tempest*," Prospero's character is not limited to that of a dramatist: "Throughout the play Prospero teaches all the characters, and the teacher role could be seen to fit him better than even the customary playwright" (Carey-Webb par. 11).

If the material is not on numbered pages or lacks numbered paragraphs, identify by screen number, followed by the number of the screen or screens, in parentheses.

Online Source—Author Unknown

Often no author is given for material available on the Internet. In such cases, use the same form you would for an unsigned article in a periodical or reference book: an abbreviated form of the title (first significant word or two).

An advancement such as the Eyegaze System "enables people with severe motor disabilities to do many things with their eyes that they would otherwise do with their hands" ("Unique Products").

If no author or title is available, use the name of the Web site.

Through the Internet, the disabled can look up specific information on assistive technology devices, get help with problems or questions, and even make personal connections in chat rooms (ABLEDATA).

Preparing the Works Cited Page

Whenever you note in parentheses that you have used someone else's material, you will need to explain that source completely in the works-cited list (the bibliography) at the end of your research paper. The Works Cited page always begins on a new and numbered page at the end of the paper. The entries are arranged alphabetically, according to authors' last names. If there are no authors named, then the works are listed according to title. If the title begins with "A" or "The," keep the article in the title but alphabetize according to the second word.

All sources—whether book or journal article—are arranged together on one list. Do not have a list of books and then a list of periodical titles. Readers can identify **book titles** (and the titles of all longer works: movies, magazines, and newspapers) because they are **italicized**. **Titles of short works**—essays, articles, and songs—are put in **quotation marks**. At the end of each entry, specify the medium of publication, followed by a period: Print, Web, CD, Laser disc, Performance, Film, Television, etc. Even if the article originally appeared in another medium, for example, a newspaper or journal, but you retrieved it online, your citation should identify the medium of publication is the Web, followed by a period and then the date of access. Do not number the entries. Double-space between all lines, both within an entry and between entries. Each entry starts at the left margin and extends to the right margin. If additional lines are needed for an entry, indent five spaces or one-half inch. To see how the Works Cited page should look, turn to the student research paper on page 536. To see how each type of entry should look, study the models below.

Because the complete source is listed only in the works cited, it is essential that each entry conform exactly to standard form so that the reader can easily locate your source. Most of the forms that you will need are illustrated here.

Elements of a Citation

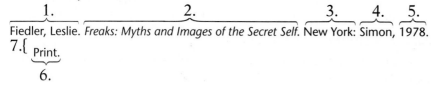

1. Use the author's full name—last name first—followed by a comma and then the first name and any middle name or initial or suffix like Jr. or III. Omit any titles (Dr., Ph.D., Rev.). End with a period and one space.

2. Print the book's full title including any subtitles. Italicize the title and capitalize the first and last words as well as all other important words. If there is a subtitle, separate the main title and the subtitle with a colon and one space. Place a period after the title and leave one space.

3. Type the publication information beginning with the city of publication, followed by a colon and one space.

4. Print the name of the publisher, followed by a comma. Shorten the name by removing "and Co." or "Inc." Abbreviate multiple names to include only the first name. (The "Simon" in the example refers to Simon and Schuster.) If you are citing a university press, abbreviate as "UP." See the Boardman citation below.

5. Include the date of publication and end with a period.

6. Include the medium of publication. For example, the medium of publication for a book would be *Print* while the medium for an online book would be *Web*. Other examples include *CD, Film, DVD, Performance,* etc. *Web* is the medium of publication for any content that you retrieve online, even if it originally appeared in another medium—for example, a newspaper article that you retrieved from a Web site. The medium of publication is generally the last element in your citation. When *Web* is the medium of publication, the last element should be the date of access.

7. Any line after the first line is double-spaced and indented one-half inch or five spaces, a "hanging indent."

Sample MLA Entries

Books

One Author

Fiedler, Leslie. *Freaks: Myths and the Images of the Secret Self*. New York: Simon, 1978. Print.

Two or Three Authors

Doane, Janice, and Devon Hodges. *Nostalgia and Sexual Difference: The Resistance to Contemporary Feminism*. New York: Methuen, 1987. Print.

Notice that any authors' names after the first author are written with the first name before the last name.

More Than Three Authors or Editors

Boardman, John, et al., eds. *The Oxford History of the Classical World*. New York: Oxford UP, 1986. Print.

or

Boardman, John, Jasper Griffin, and Oswyn Murray, eds. *The Oxford History of the Classical World*. New York: Oxford UP, 1986. Print.

With more than three authors, you have the choice of shortening the entry to provide only the first author's name, followed by the Latin abbreviation "et al." (which means "and others"), or you may provide all of the names. Notice that Oxford University Press is abbreviated "Oxford UP."

Author with an Editor or Editors

Shakespeare, William. *King Lear*. Ed. Barbara A. Mowat and Paul Werstine. New York: Washington Square, 1993. Print.

Cite the name of the author first and then, after the title of the work, give the editor's name or names, preceded by "Ed."—an abbreviation for "edited by."

Book with an Editor and No Author Cited

Webb, Charles H., ed. *Stand Up Poetry: The Anthology*. Long Beach: UP California State U, 1994. Print.

If the book does not have an author, cite the editor's name, followed by "ed."

Selection from an Anthology or Collection

Mabry, Marcus. "Living in Two Worlds." *Between Worlds: A Reader, Rhetoric, and Handbook*. Ed. Susan Bachmann and Melinda Barth. 6th ed. New York: Longman, 2010. 109–111. Print.

Mairs, Nancy. "On Being a Cripple." *With Wings: An Anthology of Literature by and about Women with Disabilities*. Ed. Marsha Saxton and Florence Howe. New York: Feminist P at City U NY, 1987. 118–127. Print.

Olds, Sharon. "True Love." *The Wellspring*. New York: Knopf, 1996. 88. Print.

Give the author and title of the selection, using quotation marks around the title. Then give the title of the anthology, in italics. If the anthology has an editor, note the name or names after the "Ed." Give the page numbers for the entire selection as shown.

Two or More Selections from the Same Anthology

Bachmann, Susan, and Melinda Barth, eds. *Between Worlds: A Reader, Rhetoric, and Handbook*. 6th ed. New York: Longman, 2010. Print.

Holman, M. Carl. "Mr. Z." Bachmann 133–134.

Staples, Brent. "Black Men and Public Space." Bachmann 181–185.

To avoid repetition, give the full citation for the book once, under the editor's last name. Then list all articles under the individual authors' names, followed by the title of their work. After each title, put the editor's name as a cross-reference to the complete citation.

Two or More Books by the Same Author(s)

Lamott, Anne. *All New People*. New York: Doubleday, 1991. Print.

—. *Bird by Bird: Some Instruction on Writing and Life*. New York: Doubleday, 1994. Print.

Give the author's name for the first entry only. After that, type three hyphens in place of the name, followed by a period and one space and then the next title. The three hyphens always stand for exactly the same name as in the preceding entry. The titles of the author's works should be listed alphabetically.

Corporate Author

National Council of Teachers of English. *Guidelines for Nonsexist Use of Language in NCTE Publications*. Urbana, Ill.: NCTE, 1975. Print.

Use the name of the institution or corporation as the author even if it is also the name of the publisher. Abbreviate the institution's name if it is repeated: NCTE.

Author Not Named

Webster's New World College Dictionary. 4th ed. New York: Macmillan, 1999. Print.

If a book has no author noted on the title page, begin the entry with the title and alphabetize according to the first word other than "a," "an," or "the."

Other Than First Edition

If you are citing an edition other than the first, place the edition number between the title and the publication information, as in the entry above.

Republication

Melville, Herman. *Billy Budd, Sailor (An Inside Narrative)*. 1924. Chicago: U Chicago P,

1962. Print.

If you are citing a work that has been published by different publishers, place the original date of publication (but not the place or publisher's name) after the title. Then provide the complete information for the source you are using.

Book Title within the Title

Gilbert, Stuart. *James Joyce's* Ulysses. New York: Vintage, 1955. Print.

If the title of the work that you are using contains another book title, do not italicize or place the original book title in quotation marks.

Story or Poem Title within the Title

Cisneros, Sandra. *"Woman Hollering Creek" and Other Stories*. New York: Random House,

1991. Print.

If the title of the work that you are using contains a title that is normally enclosed in quotation marks (a short story or poem), keep the quotation marks and italicize the entire title: *Dare to Eat a Peach: A Study of "The Love Song of J. Alfred Prufrock."* Print.

Multivolume Work

Raine, Kathleen. *Blake and Tradition*. 2 vols. Princeton: Princeton UP, 1968. Print.

If you have used two or more volumes of a multivolume work, state the total number of volumes in the work. Place this information ("2 vols.") between the title and publishing information.

Malone, Dumas. *The Sage of Monticello*. Boston: Little, Brown, 1981. Vol. 6 of *Jefferson and*

His Time. 6 vols. 1943–1981. Print.

If you are using only one volume of a multivolume work, give the title of that volume after the author's name and then give the publishing information. After the publishing date, note the volume number, the title of the book, and the number of volumes in the collection. If the volumes were published over a period of years, indicate the dates.

Translation

Marquez, Gabriel García. *Love in the Time of Cholera*. Trans. Edith Grossman. New York:

Penguin, 1988. Print.

When citing a work that has been translated, give the author's name first. After the title, give the translator's name, preceded by "Trans."

Introduction, Preface, Foreword, or Afterword

Grumbach, Doris. Foreword. *Aquaboogie.* By Susan Straight. Minneapolis: Milkweed,

    1990. Print.

If you are citing material from an introduction, preface, foreword, or afterword written by someone other than the author of the book, give the name of the writer and designate the section she or he wrote. Notice also that "Foreword" is without underlining or quotation marks. After the title of the work, "By" precedes the author's name.

    If the author of the introduction or preface is the same as the author of the book, give only the last name after the title:

Conrad, Joseph. Author's Note. *"Youth: A Narrative" and Two Other Stories.* By Conrad.

    New York: Heinemann, 1917. 3–5. Print.

Article in an Encyclopedia or Other Reference Books

Benet, William Rose. "Courtly Love." *The Reader's Encyclopedia.* 1987 ed. Print.

"Hodgkin's Disease." *The New Columbia Encyclopedia.* 4th ed. 1975. Print.

If there is an author of the edition or article, alphabetize by last name. Otherwise, alphabetize in the works-cited page by the title of the entry.

PERIODICALS: JOURNALS, MAGAZINES, AND NEWSPAPERS

Journal with Continuous Pagination

Cooper, Mary H. "Setting Environmental Priorities." *Congressional Quarterly Researcher*

    9.19 (21 May 1999): 425–428. Print.

Fowler, Rowena. "Moments and Metamorphoses: Virginia Woolf's Greece." *Comparative*

    Literature 51.3 (1999): 217–242. Print.

Journals sometimes paginate consecutively throughout a year. Each issue, after the first one, continues numbering from where the previous issue ended. After the title, give the volume number followed by a period and the issue number, if there is one. (See the first example, "Cooper.") Provide the publication date in parentheses, followed by a colon and the page numbers. Conclude by noting that it is a print medium.

Journal That Paginates Each Issue Separately

Anderson, Maxwell L. "Museums of the Future: The Impact of Technology on Museum

    Practices." *Daedalus* 128.3 (1999): 129–162. Print.

Heilbrun, Carolyn. "Contemporary Memoirs." *The American Scholar* 68.3 (1999): 35–42. Print.

If the journal numbers each issue separately, give the volume number, a period, and the issue number (as in "68.3" above) after the title of the journal.

Monthly or Bimonthly Periodical

Schulhofer, Stephen. "Unwanted Sex." *Atlantic Monthly* Oct. 1998: 55–66. Print.

Notice that in a monthly or bimonthly periodical, the month of publication is abbreviated (except for May, June, and July), and no volume or issue numbers are given.

Weekly or Biweekly Periodical

Anderson, Jan Lee. "The Power of García Marquez." *New Yorker* 27 Sept. 1999: 56–71. Print.

Daily Newspaper, Signed Article

Yee, Amy. "Please Leave Your Stereotypes at the Door." *Christian Science Monitor* 7 July
       1999: 15. Print.

Daily Newspaper, Unsigned Article or Editorial

"Jerusalem and Disney." *Jerusalem Post* 24 Sept. 1999: A26. Print.

If the newspaper is divided into numbered or lettered sections, give the section designation before the page number, as in "A26". If the article continues on a nonconsecutive page, write only the first page number followed immediately (no space) by a + and a period.

Rosenbaum, David E. "Budgetary Posturing." *New York Times*. 2 Mar. 1995, late ed.: A1. Print.

If the newspaper has editions (late ed., natl. ed.) include this item after the date and before the colon.

Titled Review

Friedman, Jane. "An Artist Who Promotes Glass Consciousness." *Washington Post*. 26 Sept.
       1999: G1+. Print.

The page number "G1+" in the citation indicates that the article starts on page G1 but does not continue on consecutive pages.

Untitled Review

Shore, Paul. Rev. of *Backlash: The Undeclared War Against American Women*, by Susan
       Faludi. *The Humanist* Sept.-Oct. 1992: 47–48. Print.

OTHER SOURCES

Interview

Cuff, Ross. Personal interview. 12 Feb. 2006.

Daigh, Sarah. Telephone interview. 18 Mar. 2006.

Film or DVD

In the Line of Fire. Dir. Wolfgang Petersen. Perf. Clint Eastwood, John Malkovich, Rene

    Russo, and Dylan McDermott. Columbia, 1993. DVD.

If you want to refer to a particular individual involved with the film, cite that person's name first:

Malkovich, John, actor. *In the Line of Fire.* Dir. Wolfgang Petersen. Perf. Clint Eastwood,

    Rene Russo, and Dylan McDermott. Columbia, 1993. DVD.

Television or Radio Program

"Inspector Morse: Cherubim and Seraphim." 2 episodes. Mystery. Perf. John Thaw and

    Kevin Whateley. PBS. WNET, New York. 2 Mar. 1995. Television.

As in a film citation, if you wish to refer to a particular person in the program, cite that name first, followed by the rest of the listing. The episode is put in quotation marks; the program name is in italics. A series name (if any) is neither put in quotation marks nor underlined. Except for the comma between the local station and the city, a period follows every item. Narrators, directors, adapters, or performers can be listed if relevant.

Song Lyrics

Coldplay. "Fix You." *X & Y.* Capital, 2005. CD.

Hoobastank. "The Reason." *The Reason.* Island, 2003. CD.

If you are quoting the lyrics of a song, you need to cite the title of the particular song (in quotation marks) followed by the title of the album or CD (in italics), the recording company, the date, and the medium—CD or LP.

A Painting, Sculpture, or Photograph

Wood, Grant. *American Gothic.* 1930. Oil painting. The Art Institute of Chicago.

If you are referring to a painting, begin the entry with the artist's name (last name, first name), the title of the painting (in italics), the date of the work, the medium of the artwork, and the art museum that houses the work. If you are referring to a reproduction of the painting in a book, add the complete publication information for that source and include the medium of presentation: Print.

ELECTRONIC SOURCES

In the spring of 2009, MLA mandated a significant change in the way that electronic sources are documents: **No Web address or URL is required unless the writer feels that readers need the URL to locate the original source.** The updated citation format, described in detail below, is designed to provide the information needed to retrieve an online source in a simpler, more consistent format. Characteristic citations are illustrated here.

An Article in an Online Periodical

A typical entry for an article from a periodical will include the following:

1. Author (if given), director, narrator, performer, editor, compiler, or producer of the work. For works with more than one author or a corporate author, or for anonymous works, follow the guidelines for print sources. If no author is given, begin the entry with item 2, the title of the work.

2. Title of the article. Italicize the title, unless it is part of a larger work. Titles that are part of a larger work should be enclosed in quotation marks.

3. Title of the overall Web site (in italics) if this is distinct from item 2.

4. Version or edition of the site, if relevant.

5. Publisher or sponsor of the site. This information can often be found at the bottom of the Web page. If this information is not available, use N.p. (for no publisher).

6. Date of publication (day, month, and year, if available). If no date is given, use n.d.

7. Medium of publication. For all online sources, the medium of publication is Web.

8. Date of access (day, month, and year) concluded with a period.

If some of the information is not available, cite what is available.

Arieff, Allison. "Grow Your Own." The *New York Times*. The New York Times, 28 July 2008.

> Web. 1 Aug. 2008.

Chao, Loretta. "For Beijing, Etiquette Isn't a Game." The *Wall Street Journal*. The Wall

> Street Journal, 1 Aug. 2008. Web. 1 Aug. 2008.

The first article "Grow Your Own" was accessed on Aug. 1, three days after it was put online.

An Article from a Database or Scholarly Project

For scholarly journal articles accessed through a database, use the format for an article from a print journal. Include Web as the medium of publication, followed by the date of access. If page numbers are not included, use n. pag.

Include the title of the database or Web site from which the content was retrieved, in italics. Do not include the database URL or information about the library system—changes from previous MLA forms.

Tyrell, R. Emmett, Jr. "The Worst Book of the Year." *American Spectator* May 1997.

> *MasterFilePremier. EBSCOhost.* n. pag. Web. 14 Apr. 2000.

"Gabriel (Jose) Garcia Marquez." *Contemporary Authors*. 13 Feb. 2001. *Gale Literary*

> *Databases*. n. pag. Web. 11 Oct. 2001.

An Article in a Scholarly Journal

Carey-Webb, Allen. "National and Colonial Education in Shakespeare's The Tempest."
Early Modern Literary Studies 5.1 (1999): n. pag. Web. 5 Sept. 1999.

An Article in a Magazine

Shenk, Joshua Wolf. "Lincoln's Great Depression." *The Atlantic Monthly* Oct. 2005. Web. 2
Sept. 2005.

An Article in a Newspaper

Gonzalez, David. "From Margins of Society to Center of the Tragedy." The *New York Times*
2 Sept. 2005. Web. 5 Sept. 2005.

A Review in a Newspaper

Ebert, Roger. Rev. of *Eternal Sunshine of the Spotless Mind*, Dir. Michael Gondry. *Chicago
Sun-Times Online*. 19 Mar. 2004. 2 pp. Web. 9 May 2005.

An Online Book Available Independently

Austen, Jane. *Pride and Prejudice*. Ed. Henry Churchyard. 1996. Web. 5 Sept. 1999.

A Professional or Personal Site

Gajewski, Walter. "Oh, What a Web We Weave." California State U, Long Beach. Web. 25
Feb. 2003 <http://www.csulb.edu/~gajewski/web/>.

Perry, Stephen. Poems. Web. 5 Sept. 1999 <http://www.bunnyape.com>.

An Online Government Publication

United States. CIA Publications and Handbooks. *1995 World Factbook*. Washington, D.C.:
Central Intelligence Agency (1995). Web. 3 Jan. 1996 <http://www.odci.gov/cia/
publications/95fact/index.html>.

If no author is given, as in a government publication, cite the institution or publishing agency.

Electronic Conference

Sagady, Alexander. "Mich 'Hands on' Family Law Workshop." 4 June 1996. Newsgroup
alt.dad's-rights. Usenet. Web. 15 July 1996 <asagady@sojournl.sojourn.com>.

Electronic Source Not in Print

Nowviskie, Bethany. "John Keats: A Hypermedia Guide." Wake Forest U. Web. 26 Feb.
2003 <http://www.wfu.edu/~nowvibp4/keats. htm>.

A CD-ROM

Many journals, magazines, newspapers, and periodically published reference works are published both in print and on CD-ROM:

Nehemiah, Marcia. "Nicholas Negroponte." *Digit*. Issue #8. CD-ROM. PC Carullo. 55–60.

The Oxford English Dictionary. 2nd ed. CD-ROM. New York: Oxford UP, 1992.

If you are using only a part of the work, state which part. If the part is a book-length work, underline the title. If you are using a shorter part, such as an article, essay, poem, or short story, enclose the title in quotation marks.

"Artifice." *The Oxford English Dictionary.* 2nd ed. CD-ROM. New York: Oxford UP, 1992.

Documenting the Research Paper: APA Style

Although most English instructors require MLA form for documenting sources, instructors from other disciplines may prefer American Psychological Association (APA) form. Check with your instructors to see which of the two forms they prefer. *These two styles are very different; don't confuse them.*

Writing Parenthetical Citations

The differences between MLA and APA forms are that in APA parenthetical citations, the date of publication, and sometimes the page number of the source are included. The punctuation is also different.

According to APA form, if the sentence preceding quoted material includes the author's name, the date of publication will follow in parentheses. Then, at the end of the quotation, include the page number in parentheses.

In Ben Mattlin's recent study (1991) of the media and people with disabilities, he approves Christopher Burke's role as a "competent, high-functioning, integral part of his family" (p. 8).

Notice that the date of the study is included within the introduction to the quotation, and then the page number is abbreviated as "p." within the final parentheses.

If you do not use the author's name when you introduce the quoted material, place the author's name, the year, and the page number in parentheses at the end of the quoted material. Use commas between the items in the parentheses.

One critic approves Christopher Burke's role as a "competent, high-functioning, integral part of his family" (Mattlin, 1991, p. 8).

If you paraphrase the material rather than quoting it specifically, include the author's last name and the date of publication either in your text or in the parentheses at the end of the summarized material. Do not include the page number.

According to Ben Mattlin (1991), disabled actors are playing important roles in television dramas.

One writer who has examined the media's treatment of the disabled reports some positive changes in television (Mattlin, 1991).

To cite an Internet document in the body of a paper, provide the name of the author, followed by the date. If no author is given, begin with the name of the document. If you use a direct quotation, provide the page number or paragraph number in the parentheses, after the date: (Markels, 1996, p. 6) or (Markels, 1996, para. 4).

Specific Examples of APA Form

Here are specific examples of common situations you may need to document in APA form.

A Work with Two Authors. If your material was written by two authors, name both in the introduction to the material or in the final parentheses each time you cite the work. In the parentheses, use "&" rather than "and."

DeJong and Lifchez (1983) examine state and federal funding for vocational programs and independent living centers provided for disabled citizens.

Two writers have reported on The Rehabilitation Comprehensive Services and Developmental Disability Amendments (DeJong & Lifchez, 1983).

Author's Name Not Given. If the author of the material that you are using is not given, either use the complete title in your introduction to the material or use the first few words of the title in the parenthetical citation with the date.

Retired Supreme Court Justice Thurgood Marshall graduated first in his class at Howard Law School and then sued the University of Maryland Law School, which had rejected him because he was black ("Milestones," 1993).

An obituary from "Milestones" (1993) noted that Thurgood Marshall graduated first in his class at Howard Law School and then sued the University of Maryland Law School, which had rejected him because he was black.

Corporate Author. If you are using a work with a corporate or group author that is particularly long, write out the full name the first time you use it, followed by an abbreviation in brackets. In later citations, use just the abbreviation.

The American Philosophical Association (APA) has prepared "Guidelines for Non-Sexist Use of Language" because philosophers are "attuned to the emotive force of words and to the ways in which language influences thought and behavior" (American Philosophical Association, 1978).

Indirect Source. If you use work that is cited in another source, you need to acknowledge that you did not use the original source.

Actor Henry Holden relates his own experience with social discrimination by noting that he is "not generally accepted by nondisabled people in social situations" (cited in Davidson, 1987).

Preparing the References Page

In APA form, the alphabetical listing of works used in the manuscript is titled "References." (In MLA form, this listing is titled "Works Cited.") Here are some general guidelines for the references page.

- Double-space the entries. The first line should be flush with the left margin, and all subsequent lines should be indented five spaces or one-half inch from the left margin.
- Alphabetize the list by the last name of the author or editor. If the work is anonymous, alphabetize by the first word of the title, excluding "a," "an," or "the."
- All authors' names should be listed last name first, with the parts of names separated with commas. Do not use "et al." unless there are six or more authors. Use initials for first and middle names. Use an ampersand ("&") rather than the word "and."
- In contrast to the way titles normally appear, APA style limits capitalizations of book titles and of articles to the first word of the title and subtitle as well as to all proper nouns. However, all the main words of the titles of journals or magazines are capitalized as they normally appear.
- Italicize the titles of books, journals, and any volume numbers. Do not underline or use quotation marks around the titles of articles.
- Give the full names of publishers, excluding "Inc." and "Co."
- Use the abbreviation "p." or "pp." before page numbers in books, magazines, and newspapers, but not for scholarly journals. For inclusive page numbers, include all figures (365–370, not 365–70).

Sample APA Entries

BOOKS

One Author

Fiedler, L. (1978). *Freaks: Myths and the Images of the Secret Self.* New York: Simon & Schuster.

Two or More Authors

Doane, J., & Hodges, D. (1987). *Nostalgia and sexual difference: The resistance to contemporary feminism.* New York: Methuen.

Editor

Allen, D. M. (Ed.). (1960). *The new American poetry.* New York: Grove Press.

Translator

Ibsen, H. (1965). *A doll's house and other plays* (P. Watts, Trans.). New York: Penguin Books.

Author Not Named

The Oxford dictionary of quotations. (1964). New York: Oxford University Press.

Later Edition

Fowler, R. H., & Aaron, J. E. (1992). *The Little, Brown handbook* (5th ed.). New York: HarperCollins.

Multivolume Work

Raine, K. (1968). *Blake and tradition* (Vol. 2). Princeton, NJ: Princeton University Press.

Malone, D. (1943–1981). *Jefferson and his time* (Vols. 1–6). Boston: Little, Brown.

Work in an Anthology

Mairs, N. On being a cripple. (1987). In M. Saxton & F. Howe (Eds.), *With wings: An anthology of literature by and about women with disabilities* (pp. 118–127). New York: Feminist Press at City University of New York.

Two or More Books by the Same Author

Olsen, T. (1979). *Silences.* New York: Dell Publishing.

Olsen, T. (1985). *Tell me a riddle.* New York: Dell Publishing.

PERIODICALS: JOURNALS, MAGAZINES, AND NEWSPAPERS

Journal with Continuous Pagination

Culp, M. B. (1983). Religion in the poetry of Langston Hughes. *Phylon, 48,* 240–245.

Journal That Paginates Each Issue Separately

Hardwick, J. (1992). Widowhood and patriarchy in seventeenth-century France. *Journal of Social History, 26*(1), 133–148.

Article in a Magazine

Mazzatenta, O. L. (1992, August). A Chinese emperor's army for eternity. *National Geographic*, pp. 114–130.

Article in a Daily Newspaper, Signed

Soto, O. R. (1992, January 28). Putting the tag on graffiti-smearers. *Press Telegram*, sec. B, p. 3.

Article in a Daily Newspaper, Unsigned or Editorial

Back to Future. (1992, May 3). *Los Angeles Times*, p. M–4.

Titled Review

Ansa, T. M. (1992, July 5). Taboo territory [Review of *Possessing the secret of joy*]. *Los Angeles Times Book Review*, pp. 4, 8.

Motion Picture (note: the final period is deleted).

Petersen, W. (Director). (1993). In the line of fire [Motion picture]. United States: Columbia

Personal Interview

Interviews that you conduct yourself are not listed in APA references. Instead, use an in-text parenthetical citation. If the subject's name is in your text, use this form: "(personal communication, February 12, 2003)." If the subject's name is not in your text, use this form: "(S. Daigh, personal communication, March 18, 2003)."

Electronic Sources

The documentation form for electronic sources is still in flux, but the goal is to provide your reader with sufficient information to locate the material you have found. A typical citation includes the conventional APA form for the source, whether it is an article or book, the page numbers if provided, followed by the address (URL). In APA style, writers may divide a URL only after a slash or before a period. There is no end period after a URL (so readers will not think the period is part of the URL). If the online publication exactly duplicates the print version, simply add the description [Electronic version] after the title of the article. If you have reason to believe the text has been changed or updated since the original was published, add the date you retrieved the item and the URL.

Book in Print and Online

Austen, J. (1813). *Pride and prejudice* [Electronic version]. http://uts.cc.utexas.edu/
~churchh/pridprej.html

Article in Print and Online

Markels, A. (1996). MCI unit finds culture shock after relocating to Colorado. *The Wall
Street Journal Interactive Edition.* 7 pp. Retrieved January 23, 2002, from
http://www.wsj.com/

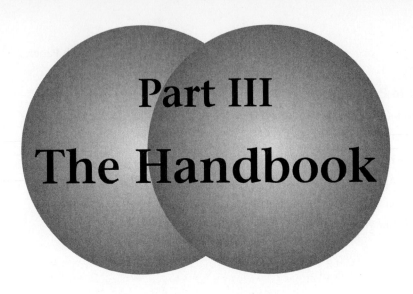

Part III
The Handbook

Part III—the handbook—is designed to help you use words and control sentences in order to write convincing, error-free papers. It will help you in drafting and revising your essays as well as in understanding the comments that your instructors write in the margins of your papers.

We do not believe that you need an extensive background in grammar in order to write clearly and well. But we are convinced that control of grammar and punctuation will give you power over both your ideas *and* your readers.

You may feel discouraged by the numerous mistakes on your papers and by the prevalence of circled words and marginal notes from your instructor. However, if you and your classmates were to examine all of your papers, you would discover that you do not make a great number of *different* errors so much as you repeat the same kind of error many times. For that reason, we have isolated those recurrent errors for discussion and correction. For friendly advice about grammar, visit Grammar Girl at *http://grammar.quickanddirtytips.com.*

This handbook begins with a deliberately succinct Chapter 14, entitled "Understanding How Sentences Work." We try to meet your needs in this chapter without telling you more than you ever wanted (or needed) to know about the elements of a sentence. Chapter 15 precisely identifies and describes the recurrent errors—the "terrible ten"—that typically appear in student papers. Chapter 16 discusses punctuation and helps you eliminate guesswork and punctuate accurately. Chapter 17 focuses on faulty word choice and shows you how well-chosen words can strengthen your essays. To determine quickly whether your word choice is sound, you can use the alphabetical list of commonly confused words in the Glossary of Usage.

Chapter 14

Understanding How Sentences Work

Understanding how sentences work gives you the vocabulary you need to discuss your writing and to correct errors that have been noted in your papers. Such knowledge also increases your power and versatility as a writer. By eliminating some of the guesswork that can hamper student writers, this handbook can help give you the tools and confidence to write with conviction.

As you probably know, every sentence must contain a *subject* and a *verb*. This basic unit is called a *clause*. (For more on clauses, see pp. 566–567.) In key examples throughout this section, we have often underlined the subject once and the verb twice to help you identify them quickly.

Subjects

A *subject* is who or what a clause is about.

Ryan sent his agent an award-winning script.

[Subjects may precede verbs.]

There are several guitars in Adam's apartment.

[Subjects may follow verbs.]

Noun as Subject

The subject of the clause may be a *noun* or a *pronoun*. A *noun* can be a

- *Person:* athlete, Jamie Foxx, veterinarian
- *Place:* Lake Erie, bike path, the Acropolis
- *Thing:* computer, hammock, Harley-Davidson
- *Quality/idea/activity:* wit, peace, dancing

561

Pronoun as Subject

A *pronoun* takes the place of a noun and can also function as the subject of a clause. Pronouns can be

- *Personal:* I, you, he, she, it, we, they

  <u>They</u> reviewed their lecture notes.

- *Indefinite:* all, any, anybody, anything, each, either, everybody, everyone, neither, nobody, none, no one, nothing, one, some, somebody, someone, something

  <u>Everybody</u> needs to recycle.

- *Demonstrative:* that, this, such, these, those

  <u>Those</u> are the sale items.

- *Relative:* who, whom, whoever, whomever, whose, which, whichever, that, what

  The order <u>that</u> is ready is the deluxe pizza.

  [In this example, <u>that</u> is the subject of the dependent or relative clause. The subject of the independent clause is <u>order</u>.] (For more about clauses, see pp. 566–567.)

- *Interrogative:* who, whom, whoever, whomever, whose, which, that, what

  <u>Who</u> recommended this awful film?

Compound Subject

Subjects may be *compound,* as in these sentences:

<u>Julie</u> and <u>Joe</u> restore old automobiles.

<u>Books</u> and <u>papers</u> collected on his desk.

Here are <u>questions</u> and <u>assignments</u> for each reading.

<u>Ashley</u>, <u>Sonja</u>, and <u>Ryan</u> can amuse their families for hours.

Objects

Direct Object

Not all nouns function as the subject of a clause. A noun that receives the action of the verb is called a *direct object*. In the sentence "Julie and Joe restore old automobiles," the noun *automobiles* answers the question, "What do Julie and Joe restore?" *Automobiles* is thus the direct object of the verb *restore*.

Indirect Object

A noun that identifies to or for whom or what the action of the verb is performed is the *indirect object*. In the sentence "The dietician and nurses gave the patients new menus," the noun *patients* answers the question, "To whom were the menus given?"

Object of the Preposition

A noun that follows a preposition (see list on p. 565) is called the *object of the preposition.* In the sentence "Books and papers collected on his desk," the noun *desk* is the object of the preposition *on.*

Objects may provide important information in a sentence, but they are not necessary in order to have a clause. *Verbs,* however, are essential.

Verbs

A *verb* is what the subject does, is, has, or has done to it. The verb may be more than one word (*may be coming*). The verb also changes form to agree with the subject (he *drives; they drive*) and to indicate time (he *drove,* he *has driven*). Regular verbs form their past tense by adding *-ed,* but there are a number of irregular forms like *drive* that have special forms.

Action Verbs

An *action verb* specifies what the subject does, has, or has done to it. The action does not have to be physical in any sense: *meditate* is an action verb. Other action verbs include *dance, think, laugh, provoke, erupt,* and *suggest:*

> Every Christmas Eve, Janine and Tim <u>entertain</u> their relatives with holiday tunes.
>
> Dr. Sanders <u>wrote</u> an insightful study of Oates's work.

State-of-Being Verbs

A *state-of-being* or *linking verb* specifies what the subject is. State-of-being verbs include the following: *is, are, was, were, am, feel, seem, be, being, been, do, does, did, have, has, had.* These can be main verbs or helping verbs. For more on helping verbs, see the following section.

> Evan <u>is</u> interested in engineering with a focus on the environment.

[*is* as main verb]

> Dylan <u>is</u> <u>teaching</u> history at North High.

[*is* as a helping verb]

Note: Words ending in *-ing* need a helping verb in order to function as the main verb of a sentence. The *-ing* form of the verb can also function as a noun: *Playing is a form of <u>learning</u> for small children.* Here *playing* is the subject, and *learning* is the object of the preposition *of.* Thus, just because there is an *-ing* word in a word group, there is not necessarily a verb.

Helping Verbs

The *helping verb* is always used with a main verb. Helping verbs include *can, will, shall, should, could, would, may, might,* and *must.*

The designated driver <u>will get</u> everyone home safely.

Some of the Friedmanns <u>could have camped</u> with the VanValkenburgh family

at Yosemite.

Adjectives and Adverbs

Many sentences contain modifying words that describe the nouns and verbs. *Adjectives* modify nouns (<u>*corroded*</u> *pipes,* <u>*hectic*</u> *schedule*) and pronouns (*the* <u>*curious*</u> *one*). *Adverbs* modify verbs (<u>*cautiously*</u> *responded*), adjectives (<u>*truly*</u> *generous*), adverbs (<u>*very*</u> *slowly*), and word groups (<u>*Eventually,*</u> *he entered the room.*) Adverbs answer the questions *how? when? where?* and *why?* They often end in *-ly,* but not always.

The following sentence contains both adjectives and adverbs. Can you identify each?

According to Barbara Ehrenreich, angry young men often will vent their frustrations

on vulnerable, weaker beings—typically children or women.

The adjectives *angry* and *young* modify the noun *men;* the adjectives *vulnerable* and *weaker* modify the noun *beings.* The adverbs *often* and *typically* modify the verb *will vent.*

Adjectives and adverbs can provide valuable details, but they can be overused. Being descriptive doesn't require a string of adjectives and adverbs. Often a strong verb gives a more precise picture in fewer words:

The drunken man <u>walked</u> unsteadily and unevenly from the bar.

The drunken man <u>staggered</u> from the bar.

The verb *staggered* is vivid and precise. The pile-up of adverbs in the first sentence is wordy and imprecise. Such tightening often improves writing and saves space for more necessary depth and development.

Phrases

A *phrase* is a group of words, typically without the subject and verb of the sentence. Just as clauses do not necessarily have objects, adjectives, and adverbs, clauses also do not necessarily have any phrases. While phrases may provide additional information, they seldom contain the subject and verb in the sentence. Therefore, if you are checking to see that you have a subject and verb, in order to avoid fragments, you can eliminate phrases from your search. There are many types of phrases, but here we discuss two of the most common.

Prepositional Phrases

A *prepositional phrase* always starts with a *preposition*—a word that shows relationships in time and space—and ends with the *object* of the preposition. The most common prepositions are listed here.

about	beside	from	outside	under
above	besides	in	over	underneath
across	between	inside	past	unlike
after	beyond	into	plus	until
against	but	like	regarding	unto
along	by	near	respecting	up
among	concerning	next	round	upon
around	considering	of	since	with
as	despite	off	than	without
at	down	on	through	
before	during	onto	till	
behind	except	opposite	to	
below	for	out	toward	

Some prepositions are more than one word long: *along with, as well as, in addition to, next to,* and *up to* are some examples.

The object of the preposition is always a noun or pronoun:

Elaine <u>assists</u> the dean **of Fine Arts with registration problems.**

On the weekends, <u>Becky</u> and <u>Joey</u> <u>take</u> Kaitlyn **to the park.**

For two weeks in January, <u>Anne</u> <u>vacations</u> **with her daughter's family in Long Beach.**

[In the last sentence, "for two weeks," "in January," "with her daughter's family," and "in Long Beach" are all prepositional phrases. Note how much easier it is to locate the subject and verb when the prepositional phrases are eliminated.]

Verbal Phrases

Verbal phrases resemble verbs, but they do not function as the main verb of the clause. Verbal phrases may serve as subjects, objects, adjectives, and adverbs. Two main types of verbal phrases are *infinitive phrases* and *-ing phrases.*

Infinitive Phrases. If the verb is preceded by *to* (*to ski*), the verb is in the *infinitive* form. It helps to recognize infinitives because they cannot be the main verbs.

Most <u>professors</u> <u>like</u> **to challenge** students.

<u>To think</u> <u>is</u> **to question.**

[Infinitives can function as subjects.]

-ing Phrases. A word ending in *-ing* may look like a verb, but it needs a helping verb or a main verb elsewhere in the sentence. Notice how *working* serves a different function in each of the following sentences (only in the first sentence is it part of the main verb):

Rise Daniels is working as an art instructor.

Working as an art instructor requires overtime hours.

[When *-ing* words function as subjects, they are called **gerunds.**]

The **working** artist exhibited her paintings.

[When *-ing* words function as adjectives, they are called **participles.**]

Words and phrases ending in *-ing* can often lead writers to believe they have a complete sentence—that is, at least one independent clause—when they may have only a fragment. For example, "In the evening after arriving home from work" is not an independent clause; it simply consists of three phrases.

One way to determine if there is an independent clause, and therefore a sentence, is to draw a line through each phrase:

~~In the evening~~ ~~after arriving home~~ ~~from work~~, Bill retreats ~~to his studio~~ ~~for hours~~ ~~to play piano~~ and ~~to compose new songs~~.

Now that you can recognize the most important parts of a sentence, you can better understand how clauses work and how they can be combined.

Clauses

A *clause* is a group of words with a subject and main verb. There are two basic types of clauses: (1) independent and (2) dependent.

Independent Clauses

The *independent (or main) clause* has a subject and main verb and can stand alone:

Rob is a physician's assistant in the New York area.

Alyssa loves performing with Susie.

The band invited Sara and Ryan backstage.

Dependent Clauses

The *dependent (or subordinate) clause* has a subject and main verb but cannot stand alone. Dependent clauses begin with one of these subordinating conjunctions:

after	if, even if	what, whatever
although	in order that	when, whenever
as, as if	since	whether
because	that, so that	which, whichever
before	unless	while
how	until	who, whom, whose

Whenever a clause begins with one of these words (unless it is a question), it is a dependent clause. If we take an independent clause such as

We jogged

and put one of the subordinating conjunctions in front of it, the independent clause becomes dependent (and therefore a fragment):

After we jogged
Because we jogged

To make a complete sentence, we need to add an independent clause (or delete the subordinating conjunction):

After we jogged, we went for a swim.
Because we jogged, we justified eating brownies.

Every sentence must have at least one independent clause in it.

Sentence Variation

If you know how to control and combine clauses, you can vary your sentences for greater emphasis, more clarity, and less monotony. The four basic sentence types are illustrated here.

Simple Sentences

Simple sentences contain *one independent clause:*

Professor Hodges's students submitted fine critical analyses of the textbook.
Despite his busy schedule, Walter edits new podcast selections each night.

Compound Sentences

Compound sentences contain *two independent clauses.* There are only two ways to punctuate a compound sentence:

1. A *comma* followed by a coordinating conjunction (*and, but, for, or, nor, yet, so*):

   We arrived at the cabin, so they left.

2. A *semicolon* by itself (or it may be followed by a word like *nevertheless* or *however*):

   We arrived; they left.
   We arrived; therefore, they left.

Notice that the writer's decision to use a coordinating conjunction or a semicolon is not arbitrary. If the writer wishes to clarify or emphasize the relationship between the two clauses, he or she will use a coordinating conjunction (such as *so*) or a conjunctive adverb (such as *therefore*). If the writer prefers not to define the relationship between the clauses, then the semicolon by itself is more appropriate.

Complex Sentences

Complex sentences contain *one independent clause and one or more dependent clauses.* The following dependent clauses are underscored with a broken underline.

> When the dependent clause comes first in the sentence, a comma is necessary.

> A comma isn't necessary when the dependent clause comes at the end.

Compound-Complex Sentences

Compound-complex sentences contain *two or more independent clauses and one or more dependent clauses.* The dependent clause or clauses may be at the beginning, at the end, or between the independent clauses. Here one dependent clause begins the sentence, and another ends the sentence:

> Although Jane was a senior citizen, she swam competitively, and we were all impressed that she won medals.

In the following sentence, the dependent clause is between the two independent clauses:

> At work Tammy cares for an elderly man who requires constant help, so she enjoys returning home each night to play with Jamie, Paul, and Duane.

 PRACTICING SENTENCE VARIATION

Using details from the last essay that you discussed in class, write your own sentences to illustrate each sentence type: simple, compound, complex, and compound-complex. Then underline all subjects once and all verbs twice to make sure you have the necessary clauses. Manipulating these sentence types will help you vary your sentences and combine your ideas more smoothly.

Chapter 15

Understanding
Common Errors

In the following chapters, we examine the ten errors that appear most frequently in student papers: fragments, run-on or fused sentences, pronoun reference, subject-verb agreement, shifts (in number or person, verb tense, voice, and mood), mixed sentences, misplaced (and dangling) modifiers, faulty parallelism, punctuation (ch 16), and faulty word choice (ch 17). These errors may be noted in the margins of your papers with the symbols that appear in these margins as well as on the inside back cover.

Fragments

Although sentence fragments are used frequently in fiction and advertising copy to simulate spoken English, the sentence fragment is considered nonstandard in formal writing. Fragments may confuse the reader, and they will make your writing seem choppy and your ideas disconnected.

A *fragment* is a group of words that, for some reason, *cannot stand alone*   *frag* as a complete sentence. The reason may be any one of the following:

1. The word group may lack a subject.

   While the students prepared their finals, they sunbathed at the same time.

   <u>Became involved</u> in discussions that distracted them from their studies.   *frag*

   [Add a subject.]

   While the students prepared their finals, they sunbathed at the same time. Soon <u>they became involved</u> in discussions that distracted them from their studies.

2. The word group may lack a complete verb.

frag

Arriving before the concert began, we enjoyed the excitement in the air. The <u>band</u> tuning up before their opening song.

[Add a helping verb.]

Arriving before the concert began, we enjoyed the excitement in the air. The <u>band</u> <u>was tuning</u> up before their opening song.

3. The word group may lack both a subject and a verb.

frag

I value my piano teacher. A bright and patient woman. She encourages perfection even while she tolerates my mistakes.

[Attach the phrase *a bright and patient woman* to the independent clause before or after it.]

I value my piano teacher, a bright and patient woman. She encourages perfection even while she tolerates my mistakes.

or

I value my piano teacher. A bright and patient woman, she encourages perfection even while she tolerates my mistakes.

4. The word group may contain both a subject and a verb but be simply a dependent clause.

frag

Native American music and dances are national treasures. Which is why our dance company performs them regularly.

[Avoid starting any sentence with *which* unless you are asking a question.]

Native American music and dances are national treasures. <u>This</u> <u>is</u> why our dance company performs them regularly.

or

Because Native American music and dances are national treasures, our dance company performs them regularly.

Another example of such a fragment is the following:

frag

Although rap music has been criticized for its violence and harsh language. Rap really reflects the tension in the cities rather than causes it.

Although rap music has been criticized for its violence and harsh language, rap really reflects the tension in the cities rather than causes it.

As noted earlier, writers may deliberately use a fragment for emphasis or to mimic conversation, but these uses are always controlled and planned.

Otherwise, fragments make an essay confusing or choppy. Sometimes the simplest solution is to connect the fragment to an independent clause that is either right before or after it.

Run-on or Fused Sentences

Run-on or *fused sentences,* or sentences flawed with a *comma splice,* occur   *r-o*
when a writer perceives that the thoughts in two complete sentences are related but fails to join the thoughts appropriately. Sometimes the writer makes the mistake of inserting a comma between the independent clauses, creating a comma splice. No punctuation at all between the independent clauses creates a run-on or fused sentence. Both errors occur because the   *fs*
writer sees a relationship between sentences and isn't sure what to do to show the relationship.

The "sentence" that follows is one anyone might say, and a writer might be tempted to write:

It snowed for days the skiers were ecstatic.   *r-o*

The writer has clearly perceived a relationship between the joy of the skiers and the weather conditions. But the word group is incorrectly punctuated and is a run-on or fused sentence.

Comma Splice

The writer may decide to "correct" the error by inserting a comma between the two independent clauses:

It snowed for days, the skiers were ecstatic.   *cs*

The comma is inadequate punctuation, however, for separating the independent clauses. That "correction" results in the sentence fault called a *comma splice,* which is noted as *"CS"* in the margin of a paper.

Correcting Run-on Sentences

The following methods illustrate alternatives for correcting run-on sentences. Notice that the five choices are all grammatically correct, but each places different emphasis on the two clauses and may change the meaning of the sentence.

1. Separate each independent clause with a period.

   It snowed for days. The skiers were ecstatic.

2. Use a comma plus a coordinating conjunction (*and, but, for, or, nor, yet, so*) between the independent clauses.

It snowed for days, and the skiers were ecstatic.

or

It snowed for days, yet the skiers were ecstatic.

or

It snowed for days, so the skiers were ecstatic.

3. Use a semicolon between the independent clauses.

It snowed for days; the skiers were ecstatic.

4. Change one independent clause into a dependent clause.

Because it snowed for days, the skiers were ecstatic.

or

The skiers were ecstatic because it snowed for days.

Notice that when the dependent clause begins the sentence, a comma separates it from the main clause. Conversely, when the independent clause begins the sentence, there is no comma before the dependent clause that concludes the sentence. See page 566 for a list of words that begin dependent clauses.

5. Use a semicolon after the first independent clause, and then a conjunctive adverb (see below) followed by a comma:

It snowed for days; consequently, the skiers were ecstatic.

or

It snowed for days; nevertheless, the skiers were ecstatic.

Conjunctive Adverbs

Conjunctive adverbs include *accordingly, also, anyway, besides, certainly, consequently, conversely, finally, furthermore, hence, however, incidentally, indeed, instead, likewise, meanwhile, moreover, nevertheless, next, nonetheless, otherwise, similarly, specifically, still, subsequently, then, therefore,* and *thus.*

Style and Meaning

Grammatical correction of a run-on sentence is not the only concern of the writer. Style emphasis and meaning also should be considered when you are deciding which conjunction to use. Notice the difference in emphasis in the following examples:

It snowed for days. The skiers were ecstatic.

Because it snowed for days, the skiers were ecstatic.

In the first example, the writer asks the reader to infer the relationship between the skiers' being "ecstatic" and the fact that "it snowed for days." In the second example, the cause-and-effect relationship is defined clearly. Take the following simple sentences, also fused, and notice what happens to the meaning, emphasis, or relationship between the independent clauses when different corrections are employed:

Renée pitched the team won.   *r-o*

1. Renée pitched. The team won.

The writer has not defined a relationship between the facts stated in the two sentences.

2. Renée pitched, and the team won.

A mild relationship is suggested by connecting the two events with *and.*

Renée pitched, so the team won.

The relationship between the team's victory and the person who pitched is defined in this construction using *so.*

Renée pitched, yet the team won.

The use of *yet,* which signals something contrary to expectation, changes the relationship between the independent clauses in this example. The word *yet* tells the reader that in spite of the fact that Renée pitched, the team won.

3. Renée pitched; the team won.

The semicolon does not define the relationship between the two independent clauses although a subtle relationship *is* suggested by the writer's using a semicolon instead of a period. The semicolon is a compromise punctuation symbol. It is stronger than a comma, but it is not as complete a stop as a period.

4. Whenever Renée pitched, the team won.

   The team won because Renée pitched.

   Although Renée pitched, the team won.

   The team won even though Renée pitched.

The dependent clause, whether it begins or ends the sentence, defines the exact relationship between the two clauses in the sentence. Clearly, the subordinate conjunction chosen has everything to do with the meaning of the sentence.

5. Renée pitched; therefore, the team won.

   Renée pitched; nevertheless, the team won.

Again, the conjunctive adverb defines the precise relationship between the two clauses of the sentence. For the purpose of connecting two short independent clauses, most writers would find the combination of semicolon and conjunctive adverb and comma too cumbersome. A coordinating conjunction with a comma would probably be a better method of linking the two clauses.

Pronoun Reference Agreement

Pronouns are words that *take the place of nouns.* In most cases, pronouns are an advantage to the writer because they permit reference to nouns named without the writer having to repeat the noun or finding a clear substitute (or synonym) for it. Ambiguity, vagueness, or confusion can result, however, if the writer has not used pronouns responsibly. The margin symbol *"ref"* indicates a problem with the pronoun reference.

ref

The following chart shows the forms that personal pronouns take.

Singular

Subjective	Possessive	Objective
I	my, mine	me
you	your, yours	you
he	his	him
she	her, hers	her
it	its	it

Plural

we	our, ours	us
you	your, yours	you
they	their, theirs	them

Indefinite pronouns include *all, any, anybody, anything, each, either, everybody, everyone, everything, neither, nobody, none, no one, nothing, one, some, somebody, someone,* and *something.*

Pronoun problems occur when the reader does not know what noun is referred to by the noun substitute, the pronoun.

1. Sometimes the pronoun used could refer to either of two nouns:

ref

When Karen told Pat the news, she burst into tears.

She can refer to either Karen or Pat. The ambiguity must be resolved for the reader:

Pat burst into tears when Karen told her the news.

or

Karen burst into tears when she told Pat the news.

2. Sometimes the subject is implied by the writer but is not stated in the sentence. The pronoun does not clearly refer to any given noun, and confusion results for the reader:

For years, Pete carried rocks from the quarry, and it strained his back.

ref

It cannot refer to the plural *rocks*, and the singular noun *quarry* didn't "strain his back." The writer probably means "this work" or "the constant hauling of heavy rocks." The writer needs to make that clarification in the sentence:

For years, Pete carried rocks from the quarry, and this work strained his back.

3. Indefinite pronouns can also pose a problem for writer and reader if the singular form of the indefinite pronoun is inconsistent with the meaning of the sentence or the gender of the pronoun is assumed by the writer to be a generic *he*. Generally, a singular pronoun should be used with an indefinite pronoun:

<u>Each</u> boy on the football team has <u>his</u> own locker.

<u>Anybody</u> who has <u>her</u> doubts about the safety of breast implants should read Jenny Jones's essay "Body of Evidence."

In the examples above, the gender of the possessive pronoun is clear from the context of the sentence. However, if you are not sure of the gender or number (singular or plural) of your subject, reword your sentence so that the subject pronoun is plural. For example:

Everybody running for class office should report to his counselor.

Everybody is a singular pronoun and requires a singular possessive pronoun: *his* or *her. Their* is plural and can't be used in this sentence. But should the writer assume the generic *his?* A reader might object that the implication of the sentence is that only males may run for class office. A similar misunderstanding would occur if the writer opted for *her* as the singular possessive pronoun. If this were a single-sentence statement, as in a school bulletin, the writer might choose *his or her* for a correct and clear mandate. But the repetitive use of *his or her* (or *his/her*) can be a burden in a lengthy manuscript.

Learn to find alternatives. A plural noun and plural possessive pronoun will take care of the problem:

All of the candidates for class office should report to their counselors.

You may also want to see the discussion of sexist language (p. 606) in Chapter 17.

Pronoun Case

In addition to problems with pronoun referents, writers often have trouble deciding when to use the subjective case pronouns and when to use the objective case pronouns (see chart in the previous section, Pronoun Reference Agreement, p. 574).

Subjective pronouns are used for the subject of the sentence or clause:

We listen to hip-hop music.

Because Dr. Connor is so supportive, he brought the team home for a barbecue.

Subjective pronouns are also used when the pronoun follows a linking verb:

It is I who volunteered.

It was they who chose that route.

Objective pronouns are used for any objects:

Direct object:

Alicia and Mary recognized us at the premiere of their film.

Indirect object:

Tony's band gave him a standing ovation.

Object of the preposition:

Marilyn's energetic water fitness class is ideal for them.

Pronoun pairs such as "you and I" and "you and me" tend to confuse writers, but the same principles apply. Determine whether the pronoun is serving as a subject or object and then choose the correct form (see chart, p. 574). Often it is easier to make this determination if you eliminate the first noun or name in the pair:

Subject:

Garrick and (**I**? **me**?) went to the concert together.

Eliminate "Garrick": *I* went. So choose: Garrick and *I* went to the concert together.

Direct Object:

Josh drove Mike and (**I**? **me**?) to the surfing competition.

Eliminate "Mike": Josh drove *me*. So choose: Josh drove Mike and *me* to the surfing competition.

Indirect Object:

David showed Julia and (**we**? **us**?) his new stallion.

Eliminate "Julia": David showed *us*. So choose: David showed Julia and *us* his new stallion.

Object of a Preposition:

Tiana flew to Paris with her roommate and (**he**? **him**?)

Eliminate "her roommate": Tiana flew to Paris with *him*. So choose: Tiana flew to Paris with her roommate and *him*.

Subject-Verb Agreement

The margin note "*agr*" means that there is an agreement problem; the subject *agr* and the verb do not agree in number. Both subject and verb should be singular or both should be plural. Speakers who are comfortable with standard English usually will not have trouble selecting the correct verb form for the subject of sentences. But some sentences, especially those that have groups of words separating the subject and verb, may offer a temporary problem for any writer. Some conditions to be aware of are listed here.

1. A prepositional phrase does not influence the verb of the sentence:

   The <u>birds</u> in the nest <u>need</u> food from the mother bird.

   Our first five <u>days</u> of vacation <u>are going</u> to be in New Orleans.

   Her <u>secretary</u>, in addition to her staff, <u>prefers</u> the new computer.

   Notice that by removing the prepositional phrases from your consideration, you will use the correct verb form for the subject of the sentence.

2. Subjects connected by *and* usually have a plural verb:

   Alfredo's academic <u>load</u> and work <u>time</u> <u>keep</u> him busy.

   Some exceptions:

   a. When the compound subject (nouns connected by *and*) is regarded as a unit, the subject is regarded as singular and has a singular verb:

      <u>Peanut butter and jelly</u> <u>remains</u> Dalton's favorite lunch.

   b. If the double nouns refer to the same person or thing, the verb is singular:

      Danika's <u>home and studio</u> <u>is</u> 215 Thompson Street.

   c. When *each* or *every* precedes the multiple nouns, use a singular verb:

      <u>Each</u> <u>instructor</u>, <u>student</u>, and <u>staff member</u> <u>prefers</u> the new insurance plan.

    d. When nouns are connected by *or* or *nor,* the verb agrees with the noun closer to it:

Your student ID or room <u>key</u> <u>guarantees</u> the loan of a beach chair.

Your student ID or room <u>keys</u> <u>guarantee</u> the loan of a beach chair.

Neither the police officer nor his <u>cadets</u> <u>were attending</u> the lecture.

Either Arthur or <u>Michael</u> <u>plays</u> the solo tonight.

3. Most indefinite pronouns have a singular verb, even if the pronoun seems to convey a plural sense. Indefinite pronouns include *anybody, anyone, each, either, everybody, everyone, everything, neither, none, no one, someone,* and *something.* Notice how each indefinite pronoun is used in the following sentences:

<u>Each</u> of the band members <u>has</u> two free tickets.

<u>Everybody</u> <u>endures</u> the stress of two finals a day.

<u>Everyone</u> on the school board <u>votes</u> at each meeting.

All, any, or *some,* however, may be singular or plural depending on what the pronoun refers to:

<u>All</u> of the pizza <u>is gone</u>.

<u>All</u> of the books <u>are shelved</u>.

4. Collective nouns (like *band, family, committee, class, jury,* and *audience*) require a singular verb unless the meaning of the noun is plural, or individuality is to be emphasized:

The <u>jury</u> <u>presents</u> its decision today.

The <u>jury</u> <u>are</u> undecided about a verdict.

5. Even when the subject follows the verb, the verb must be in the correct form:

There <u>remains</u> too little <u>time</u> to organize the campaign.

6. Titles require singular verbs:

Roots <u>is</u> the book we will read next.

Jacoby and Associates <u>is</u> the law firm on the corner.

<u>Mysteries</u> <u>is</u> the section of the library Carlos prefers.

7. Nouns describing academic disciplines—like *economics, statistics,* or *physics*—and diseases that end in an *s*—like *mumps* and *measles*—and *news*—are treated as singular nouns:

<u>Physics</u> <u>challenges</u> Maria, but she does well in the course.

<u>Measles</u> usually <u>attacks</u> only the children who have not been inoculated.

Shifts

The margin note *"shift"* marks an inconsistency in the text in person, number, or verb tense.

shift

Shifts in Person and Number

Shifts in person and number sometimes occur because you are not certain from what point of view to write or because you move from one perspective to another without being conscious of the change. You may begin with the idea of addressing a general audience—"someone"—and then decide to address the reader as "you." Or you may begin with a singular reader in mind and switch to a plural sense of "all readers." If you start to write from one perspective and switch to another, a distracting shift occurs:

If <u>someone</u> in the group writes a paper, <u>they</u> may present it.

shift

Corrections:

If a <u>person</u> writes a paper, <u>he or she</u> may present it.

> or, better:

If <u>people</u> write papers, <u>they</u> may present them.

<u>The vegetarian</u> learns to prepare interesting and nutritious meals with vegetables and grains, but then <u>you</u> have to assure <u>your</u> friends that <u>you're</u> getting enough protein.

shift

Corrections:

If <u>you</u> are a vegetarian, <u>you</u> learn to prepare interesting and nutritious meals with vegetables and grains, but then <u>you</u> have to assure your friends that <u>you're</u> getting enough protein.

> or, better:

<u>Vegetarians</u> learn to prepare interesting and nutritious meals with vegetables and grains, but then <u>they</u> have to assure <u>their</u> friends that <u>they</u> are getting enough protein.

Shifts in Verb Tense

Shifts in verb tense confuse a reader about when the action takes place. You have probably heard oral storytellers shift from one tense to another. Eventually you may have figured out the course of the narration, perhaps by asking the speaker to clarify the time of the action. But a shift in tense is particularly distracting in writing because you can't ask a writer for a clarification of the text. Notice how the verb tense in the following example shifts from the past to the present:

Shortly after we <u>arrived</u> at the picnic site, it <u>started</u> to rain. So we <u>pack</u> up the bread, salami, and fruit and <u>rush</u> to the cars.

shift

Correction for verb tense consistency:

Shortly after we <u>arrived</u> at the picnic site, it <u>started</u> to rain. So we <u>packed</u> up the bread, salami, and fruit and <u>rushed</u> to the cars.

Use the present tense throughout to write a summary or a description of a literary work:

shift

Daisy Miller first <u>meets</u> Winterbourne in Geneva, and she later <u>met</u> him in Rome where she <u>is dating</u> the charming Giovanelli. Winterbourne <u>was</u> furious that Daisy <u>does</u>n't <u>realize</u> that Giovanelli <u>was</u>n't a "real" gentleman.

Correction for verb tense consistency:

Daisy Miller first <u>meets</u> Winterbourne in Geneva, and she later <u>meets</u> him in Rome where she <u>is dating</u> the charming Giovanelli. Winterbourne <u>is</u> furious that Daisy <u>does</u>n't <u>realize</u> that Giovanelli <u>is</u>n't a "real" gentleman.

Shifts in Voice

Just as a shift in number or tense can be distracting, a shift from the active to the passive voice can confuse or distract your reader. Use the voice consistently.

When the subject of a sentence does the action, the sentence is in the *active voice:*

<u>Lester</u> <u>brought</u> the tossed salad.

When the subject *receives* the action, the verb is in the *passive voice.* Notice that the passive voice is less effective than the active voice because it is less direct:

The tossed <u>salad</u> <u>was brought</u> by Lester.

When the active and passive voice are combined, the sentence is inconsistent in voice and would be marked with a "shift" in the margin of the paper:

shift

<u>Lester</u> <u>brought</u> the tossed salad, and the soft <u>drinks</u> <u>were</u> <u>brought</u> by Mike.

Correction:

<u>Lester</u> <u>brought</u> the tossed salad, and <u>Mike</u> <u>brought</u> the soft drinks.

In some cases, the passive voice is necessary because what might be the subject of the sentence is unknown or unimportant:

The <u>car</u> <u>was hijacked</u> last week.

Because the hijacker is apparently unknown, the sentence is in the passive voice, with the action being done to the car, the subject of the sentence.

NASA was granted additional funds to complete the study for the space station.

The name of the agency that granted NASA the funds for the study may be unimportant to the writer of this sentence; the important point is that NASA has the funds for the project.

Passive voice constructions may create suspicion that the writer is deliberately hiding information:

> The city council was voted unlimited travel funds.

Clearly, the city resident who reads that sentence in the local paper would want to know *who* did the voting, and why the newspaper failed to name the subject of the verb *voted*. Use the active voice whenever you know and wish to identify the "doer" of a particular act.

Shift in Mood

A shift in mood can also distract the reader. In the English language, there are three moods: **indicative** (to give information), **imperative** (to give commands or advice), and **subjunctive** (to express desires or a condition other than factual). If a writer is using one particular mood, an unexpected shift can be confusing and illogical:

Shift from Indicative to Imperative

> YouTube provides a vehicle for creative expression and entertaining viewing. Don't upload videos that your employer shouldn't see.

shift

The first sentence provides general information (indicative mood). The second sentence shifts to a command (imperative mood). This shift can be confusing to a reader who believes that he is being given information about YouTube and then is suddenly given advice. An improvement would be the following:

Correction:

> YouTube provides a vehicle for creative expression and entertaining viewing, but certain uploads might be too revealing for a prospective employer to see.

Mixed Sentences

The margin note *"mixed"* indicates a mixed construction involving sentence parts that don't go together. The sentence may start with one subject and shift to another, or the verb may not fit the true subject of the sentence. The sentence also may begin with one grammatical construction and end with another. The problem, then, is a misfit in grammar or in logic, so the sentence is confusing to the reader:

mixed

> Although he is active in the men's movement doesn't mean he is a misogynist.

mixed

In this sentence the writer tries to make the dependent clause *Although he is active in the men's movement* the subject of the sentence. The writer probably intends *he* to be the subject of the sentence; rewriting the sentence to show this *and* selecting a correct verb for the subject will eliminate the confusion:

> Although he is active in the men's movement, he is not a misogynist.

Confused Sentence Parts

Each of the mixed sentences below contains a confusion between sentence parts. In some cases, the writer has started with one subject in mind and has ended the sentence with a different or implied subject. In other cases, the grammatical form of the first part of the sentence is inconsistent with the end of the sentence. Most often the revision involves correct identification of the true subject of the sentence and then the selection of an appropriate verb.

mixed   Among those women suffering with eating disorders, they are not always bulimic.

Not all women with eating disorders are bulimic.

mixed   By prewriting, outlining, drafting, and revising is how he wrote good papers.

He wrote good papers by prewriting, outlining, drafting, and revising his work.

mixed   The subject of ecology involves controversy.

Ecology involves controversy.

Faulty Verb Choice

In some sentences with mixed meaning, the fault occurs because the subject is said to do or to be something that is illogical.

mixed   A realization between the academic senate and the dean would be the ideal policy on plagiarism.

The sentence says that "a realization" would be "the ideal policy," which is not exactly what the writer means. Correction of the faulty use of the verb *would be* will clarify the sentence.

> Ideally, a policy on plagiarism would be decided between the academic senate and the dean.

or

> Ideally, the academic senate and the dean would realize the necessity for a policy on plagiarism.

In speech, *is when* and *is where* are common constructions for defining words, but these are mixed constructions and should be corrected in writing.

mixed   Acquiescence is when you give in to your oppressor.

Acquiescence means giving in to an oppressor.

mixed   A final exam is where you show comprehensive knowledge.

On a final exam you show comprehensive knowledge.

Misplaced and Dangling Modifiers

A *modifier* is a word, phrase, or clause used to describe another word in the sentence. The modifier should be as close to that word as possible or it is a *misplaced modifier*, causing confusion or unintentional humor.

mm

> Confused by the assignment, the professor was asked to explain the instructions again to the students.

mm

Written this way, *"confused by the assignment"* appears to describe *the professor* rather than *the students*.

The margin note *"mm"* indicates that this is a *misplaced modifier* because "confused by the assignment" should be close to the word it is modifying, *the students:*

> Confused by the assignment, the students asked the professor to explain the instructions again.

Other examples of misplaced modifiers show that when the modifier is oddly placed, the meaning of the sentence is absurd. Notice how easily the misplaced modifier can be moved so that the sentence makes sense:

> Robert L. Heilbroner insists that prejudging a person hurts not only the one being stereotyped but also the one stereotyping in his essay.

mm

> In his essay, Robert L. Heilbroner insists that prejudging a person hurts not only the one being stereotyped but also the one stereotyping.

> You will value the difficult classes you took semesters from now.

mm

> Semesters from now, you will value the difficult classes you took.

> Yuko's blind date was described as a six-foot-tall musician with a long ponytail weighing only 160 pounds.

mm

> Yuko's blind date was described as a 160-pound, six-foot-tall musician with a long ponytail.

Another kind of problem is a modifier that "dangles" because there may not be a word for the modifier to describe. In this case, the sentence needs to be rewritten:

> At the age of 12, my family hiked into the Grand Canyon.

dm

Here the writer probably does not mean that his or her family was 12 years old, but this sentence does not contain a word for the opening phrase to describe. Therefore, *at the age of 12* is called a *dangling modifier*—a modifier that fails to refer logically to any word in the sentence. Dangling modifiers can be corrected by the following methods:

dm

1. Keep the modifier as it is and add a word for the modifier to describe.

> At the age of 12, I hiked into the Grand Canyon with my family.

2. Turn the modifier into a dependent clause so that the meaning is clear.

When I was 12, my family hiked into the Grand Canyon.

Dangling and misplaced modifiers can turn even the most serious dissertation into a comedy of errors! Occasionally an instructor may write "*awk*" (awkward) or "*confusing*" or "*reword*" in the margins when the problem is that a modifier has been put in the wrong place. Becoming aware of the importance of the *placement* of each word or phrase in a sentence can help you detect and prevent such comical and confusing meanings before you prepare your final draft.

Faulty Parallelism

To achieve clarity, emphasis, and harmony in writing, use *parallel construction* for parts of sentences that you repeat. The "parts" may be single words, phrases, or clauses. Therefore, when you write any kind of list, put the items in similar grammatical form (all *-ing* words, all infinitives, and so on). Instead of writing "He likes hiking and to ski," you should write "He likes hiking and skiing" or "He likes to hike and to ski."

// If faulty parallelism is noted in the margin of your paper, you have not kept the parts of your sentence in the same grammatical form.

Single Words

// The movie entertained and was enlightening.

The movie was **entertaining** and **enlightening**.

Phrases

// Karen enjoys telling complicated jokes, performing the latest dances, and exotic food.

Karen enjoys **telling complicated jokes, performing the latest dances,** and **eating exotic food**.

Dependent Clauses

// Professor Jaffe reminded the students that papers must be submitted on time and to prepare reading assignments before class.

Professor Jaffe reminded the students **that papers must be submitted on time** and **that reading assignments must be prepared before class.**

Independent Clauses

"I came, I did some learning, and I triumphed," announced the jubilant graduate.   *//*

"**I came, I learned**, and **I triumphed**," announced the jubilant graduate.

You can also achieve greater clarity, emphasis, and balance by using parallel constructions with correlative conjunctions (paired terms such as *not only . . . but also; either . . . or;* and *neither . . . nor*):

We discovered that fast walking with a neighbor is good for health and also keeps us   *//*
friendly.

We discovered that fast walking with a neighbor is good <u>not only for health but also</u>
<u>for friendship.</u>

Fran doesn't work as a waitress any longer, and neither does Donna.   *//*

<u>Neither Fran nor Donna</u> works as a waitress any longer.

Chapter 16

Understanding Punctuation

𝒫

A"*P*" in the margin of an essay indicates some sort of error in punctuation. This chapter covers all punctuation symbols. Because the comma is the most frequently used of them, most errors occur in comma use. Commas usually function to separate elements within a sentence, but they also have standard uses in dates, in addresses, and in multiple-digit numbers. Below are models of the standard uses of the comma, with brief explanations to help you avoid comma errors.

The Comma

1. Use a comma before a coordinating conjunction joining independent clauses. (Coordinating conjunctions are *and, but, for, or, nor, yet,* and *so.* See also p. 567.)

   The school board has slashed the budget, so activity fees will increase this year.

   Many men want to take paternity leave when their babies are born, but most companies are not prepared for the requests.

   Short independent clauses may not need a comma with the conjunction, but if there is any doubt about the need or clarity, use a comma.

   He arrived so I left.

   He arrived, so I left.

2. Use a comma to separate introductory elements from the rest of the sentence:

   To register for classes, bring your advisor's signature card.

   If elementary schools continue to close, increased bus service will be necessary.

   Exhilarated, the climber reached the summit.

   By the next century, most college graduates will be in service-related careers.

3. Use a comma to separate items in a series.

   The campus bookstore has been criticized for selling sexist magazines, cigarettes, and greeting cards of questionable taste.

   Triathlons require quick running, swimming, and cycling.

   The requirements for ownership of the condominium include a bank-approved loan, a satisfactory security rating, and a willingness to comply with the homeowners' rules and procedures.

4. Use a comma between coordinate adjectives—adjectives that modify the same word equally—if there is not a conjunction.

   The shady, blooming, fragrant garden welcomed the walkers.

   A shady and fragrant garden welcomed the walkers.

   If the first adjective modifies the second adjective, do not use a comma.

   That mansion's most interesting feature is a white oak staircase.

   Professor Pierce's exams require complicated mathematical computations.

5. Use commas to set off nonrestrictive word groups. Nonrestrictive elements describe nouns or pronouns by giving extra or nonessential information. The nonrestrictive element could be removed from the sentence without sacrificing the meaning of the sentence.

   Walden Pond, which is located outside of Concord, was the site of Thoreau's one-room shelter and bean field.

   Amy Tan's first novel, *The Joy Luck Club*, was written in a few months.

   The Rolls-Royce, its silver hood ornament gleaming in the sun, was completely out of gas.

6. Do *not* use commas with restrictive word groups. Restrictive elements limit the meaning of words or provide vital (or restricting) information.

   The entrees on the left side of the menu are suitable for diners who prefer low-cholesterol diets.

The sentence gives the information that only the entrees on the left side of the menu are low in cholesterol. Presumably, the other items on the menu are not especially suited for clients who prefer low cholesterol.

Our son who lives in Texas teaches anthropology.

For a family with sons residing in different states, the restrictive clause is essential and commas should not be used.

Customers using credit cards collect free airline mileage.

Again, the lack of commas shows that the information is restrictive. Only those customers who use credit cards will collect airline mileage; customers who pay by check or cash do not.

7. Use commas to separate transitional or parenthetical expressions, conjunctive adverbs, contrasting elements, and most phrases from the main part of the sentence.

Silk, for example, can be washed by hand.

Joseph Heller, as the story goes, wanted to call his novel *Catch-18* instead of *Catch-22*.

A medium avocado contains 324 calories; therefore, it is not an ideal fruit for people watching their weight.

Darren, unlike his brother Stephen, can be reasonable.

Her medical studies completed, Nancy started a practice in Fresno.

8. Use commas to set off expressions and questions of direct address, the words *yes* or *no*, and interjections.

Sorry, Professor Hendricks, only two of those books are in the stacks.

You will complete the immigration papers, won't you?

Yes, most readers prefer the new MLA documentation form.

Oh, I can't decide if we really need an attorney.

9. Use commas for dates, addresses, and titles.

James Joyce was born on February 2, 1882, which was St. Bridget's Day and Groundhog Day, too.

The special delivery letter was sent to 10350 Dover Street, Westminster, Colorado.

Will Wood, Ph.D., begins his law practice at Duke University.

10. Use commas to set off direct quotations.

As Richard Ellmann notes, "Stephen Dedalus said the family was a net which he would fly past."

"I too believe in Taos, without having seen it. I also believe in Indians. But they must do *half* the believing: in me as well as in the sun," wrote D. H. Lawrence to Mabel Luhan.

11. Do *not* use a comma to separate a verb from its subject or object. The following examples both show *incorrect* uses of the comma:

Fast walking around a track, can be painless but effective exercise. P

Christine explained to Larry, that practicing law has precedence over going to films. P

12. Do *not* use a comma between compound elements if the word groups are not independent clauses. The following examples show *incorrect* uses of the comma:

Louise can prepare a multi-course meal, and weed her garden on the same day. P

Sara understands that the conference is in June, and that she will need to grade finals while she is attending it. P

13. A comma should not be used to separate an adjective from the noun that follows it. The following examples are *incorrect* uses of the comma:

It was a sunny, warm, and windless, day. P

A massive, polished, ornately carved, buffet stood in the dining room. P

The Apostrophe

The apostrophe is one of the more perplexing punctuation symbols for all writers. In fact, Grammar Girl, a helpful website that we highly recommend, devotes at least two podcasts to answering listeners' questions about how to use the apostrophe. In addition to reading the explanations below, try hearing Grammar Girl's podcasts at <http://grammar.quickanddirtytips.com/apostrophe-plural-grammar-rules.aspx>.

Most frequently, the apostrophe is used to form **contractions** and to show **possession:**

Contractions

When two words are merged into one, the apostrophe takes the place of any missing letters:

does n_ot_	doesn't
it _is_	it's
should _have_	should've
I _would_	I'd

Contractions tend to make writing seem more conversational and informal; therefore, they are often avoided in formal writing and in research papers.

Remember that the apostrophe takes the place of the missing letter and does not ever belong in the break between the two words:

> couldn't [*not* could'nt]

Other instances where apostrophes indicate a missing letter or letters are commonly found in informal writing and speech, particularly in dialogues from narratives and fiction:

around	'round
until	'til
1950s	'50s
playing	playin'

Again, such forms are typically reserved for writing that is intended to sound conversational.

Possession

Possessive nouns indicate belonging or ownership and are typically placed immediately before whatever is owned. Rather than write "the trumpet of Jason" or "the office of his doctor," we eliminate the *of* and move the owner in front of the possession:

> Jason's trumpet
>
> his doctor's office

Sometimes such ownership is loosely implied:

> tonight's party
>
> Thursday's test
>
> one day's sick leave
>
> two weeks' vacation

But, in a sense, the party really does "belong" to tonight (not tomorrow) and the test "belongs" to Thursday (not Friday). Similarly, the sick leave is "of one day" and the vacation is "of two weeks." Clearly, the possessive form here makes the writing smoother and less wordy.

In some cases, the notion of ownership is open to interpretation. For example, you may wonder if you should write *farmers market* or *farmers' market*—or *homeowners association* or *homeowners' association*. It might be argued that the farmers sell at the market but don't own it (hence, *farmers market* seems right and *farmers* is used as an adjective). However, homeowners do own their association because they contribute fees and may manage it (therefore, *homeowners' association* seems reasonable). Ultimately, your sense of whether there is ownership should determine whether or not to use the apostrophe in these situations.

To indicate possession, obey the following guidelines:

1. Add *-'s* if the possessive noun does not end in *s* (whether it is singular or plural):

   Sarah's acting

   Ben's collections

   the men's movement

   the children's enthusiasm

2. Add an apostrophe at the end of the word if the plural possessive noun ends in an *s* (including proper names):

   those actors' salaries

   five students' projects

   two months' salary

   the Knights' generosity

   the Walshes' Super Bowl party

3. If a singular proper name ends in *s*, add an *'* and a second *s*.

   James's routine

   Oates's story

4. There is an exception to the above rule that an *'s* should follow a proper name ending in *s*. If the pronunciation would be awkward with the added *'s*, the writer may use only the apostrophe:

   Billy Collins' poem

   Pamela Erens' essay

Joint Possession. When two or more people possess the same thing, show joint possession by using *-'s* (or *-s'*) with the last noun only:

   We relaxed at Jule and Marsha's home in Colorado Springs.

   Nate and Jess's help is valuable.

Individual Possession. When two or more people possess distinct things, show individual possession by using *-'s* (or *-s'*) with both nouns:

   Andy's and Beth's summer projects aren't completed yet.

   Luis's and Charles's questions were both fascinating.

Compound Nouns. If a noun is compound, use *-'s* (or *-s'*) with the last component of that noun term:

   My brother-in-law's woodworking is very professional.

   Barbara and Julie took their sisters-in-laws' advice.

Indefinite Pronouns. Indefinite pronouns are those that refer to no specific person or thing: *everyone, anyone, no one,* and *something.* These pronouns also need an apostrophe to indicate possession:

> We asked everybody's opinion of the film.

> Is someone's safety in jeopardy?

Possessive Pronouns. Possessive pronouns are already possessive and need no apostrophes:

my, mine	its
you, yours	our, ours
her, hers	their, theirs
his	whose

> *Whose* car should we drive?

> I would prefer to ride in *yours* rather than *theirs.*

Plurals of Letters. Use *-'s* to pluralize the letters of the alphabet:

> He earned three *B's* this term.

> She has two *t's* in her last name.

Plurals of Numbers and Abbreviations. The apostrophe should *not* be used for plurals of numbers or abbreviations:

> They all marched in *twos.*

> By the end of the *1990s,* community recycling was widespread.

> Many students like to purchase used *CDs* at their local music stores.

> All candidates must have earned their *BAs.*

Some reminders:

1. Make sure a noun is possessive (and not merely plural) before you use an apostrophe. The noun *passengers* does not "own" anything in the following sentence; therefore it is a simple plural.

    P   The ~~passenger's~~ *passengers* were not allowed to smoke.

2. Possessive pronouns need no apostrophes.

    P   The crowd expressed ~~it's~~ *its* pleasure.

    P   That responsibility is ~~her's~~ *hers.*

3. Many instructors prefer that their students not use contractions in formal writing and research papers.

The Period, Question Mark, and Exclamation Point

The most obvious use of the period is to mark the end of a sentence—unless the sentence is a direct question or needs an exclamation point:

> Do you remember learning punctuation symbols in elementary school?
>
> Yes, and it all seemed so easy then!

Because the exclamation point is used for strong commands and emphatic statements, it should not be overused. Furthermore, an exclamation mark is never used with a period, a comma, or another exclamation point.

Don't use a question mark for an indirect or implied question:

> I wonder if I ever had trouble with punctuation in elementary school.

Use the period for abbreviations:

> Mr. / Mrs. / Ms.   Dr. / Rev. / Capt.   i.e. / e.g. / etc.
>
> a.m. / p.m.

Notice that no period is used with abbreviations that consist of all capital letters:

> CA   NY   TX   IL   BC   AD   US   CD-ROM

Do not use periods with acronyms (words that are made from the first letters of many words and are pronounced as words):

> NATO   UNICEF   NASA   AIDS   MADD   DARE

Usually no period is used in abbreviations of the names of organizations, schools, and some academic titles:

> NBC   UN   NBA   NYU   BS   MA   PhD   NAACP

The Semicolon

The semicolon is most often used to connect two independent clauses:

> Students with an advisor's signature card register in their division office; students without a signature must register in the gym.

Notice that the semicolon is used in place of a period to show that the two independent ideas—clauses that could stand alone as separate sentences—are *related*. The semicolon suggests the relationship without defining it.

The semicolon is also used after an independent clause and before some transitional phrases (like *on the other hand* or *in contrast*) and after conjunctive adverbs (such as *therefore, however,* and *furthermore;* see the complete list on p. 572).

Newcomers to the United States often enjoy material advantages that they lacked in their native lands; on the other hand, they often feel spiritually deprived in their new country.

Professor Smiley will accept late papers; however, he reduces the grade for each day the paper is late.

The semicolon is used for separating items in a list if the punctuation within the list includes commas. Notice Naomi Wolf's use of the semicolon in this example from *The Beauty Myth:*

In 1984, in the United States, "male lawyers aged 25–34 earn $27,563, but female lawyers the same age, $20,573; retail salesmen earn $13,002 to retail saleswomen's $7,479; male bus drivers make $15,611 and female bus drivers $9,903; female hairdressers earn $7,603 less than male hairdressers" (49).

The Colon

A colon is used to introduce and call attention to a statement, to introduce a list, to introduce a quotation if the quotation is at the end of a sentence, in bibliographic forms, in reporting time, for separating main titles from subtitles, and in distinguishing chapters from verses in the Bible. A colon is usually preceded by a main clause (a word group containing a subject and verb). The main clause does not need to be followed by a complete clause, but if it is a complete clause, capitalize the first word.

The candidates need to realize that women form a significant majority in this country: six million more potential votes.

The application form requires the following: a final transcript, a housing request, a medical report, and the first tuition check.

Women do not expect promotions or high salaries: "Women are often unsure of their intrinsic worth in the marketplace" (Sidel qtd. in Wolf 49).

New York: Longman

Between Worlds: A Reader, Rhetoric, and Handbook

The train departs at 5:30 in the morning.

In some cases, a colon should not be used. For example, do *not* place a colon between a subject and a verb, between a verb and its complements, or between a preposition and its object:

P   The animals in that section of the zoo include: panthers, leopards, lions, and tigers.

P   The courses he needs to take are: biology, chemistry, physics, and calculus.

P   Don't put luggage on: the bed, the desk, or the reading chair.

The Dash

The dash (created by typing two hyphens with no spaces around or between them) is used sparingly for dramatic emphasis, to call attention to material the dash sets off. Sometimes the dash is used in places where a colon could also be used, but the dash is considered more informal. Because the dash indicates a sudden shift in thought and is used for dramatic emphasis, it should not be overused. In formal writing a comma, colon, or period may be more appropriate punctuation symbols.

> We all believe that environmental protection is an obligation of our era—but we still use toxic cleaners in our homes.

Here the dash is used to emphasize the contrast between what "we all believe" and what we do. A comma could also be used in this sentence:

> In the past some successful and even less-successful women had the same goal—to "marry up"—so some men felt a psychological need to be successful at work.

The dash is used here to set off the definitive information, the "same goal" the writer believes women have. A comma could have been used, but the dash achieves more emphasis.

The dash may also be used in the same manner as the colon to announce a dramatic point:

> The candidates need to realize that women form a significant majority in this country—six million more potential votes.

Quotation Marks

Quotation marks are used to enclose direct quotations, some titles, and occasionally words defined or used in a special way. Quotation marks are used in pairs.

Direct Quotations

A *direct quotation* states in exact words what someone has said or written. It is enclosed with quotation marks.

> Brigid Brophy insists, "If modern civilisation has invented methods of education which make it possible for men to feed babies and for women to think logically, we are betraying civilisation itself if we do not set both sexes free to make a free choice."

Notice that Brophy's spelling of *civilisation* is British, and that the writer quoting her is not permitted to change her spelling without indicating the change in brackets: "civili[z]ation." See more on brackets on page 600.

An *indirect quotation* notes what has been said in a paraphrased or indirect way. No quotation marks are needed:

> Brigid Brophy believes that men and women should be free to make the choices that education and technology have made possible.

A *quotation within a quotation* requires the use of standard quotation marks around the outside quotation and single quotation marks around the interior quotation:

> According to Naomi Wolf, "Every generation since about 1830 has had to fight its version of the beauty myth. 'It is very little to me' said the suffragist Lucy Stone in 1855, 'to have the right to vote, to own property, etcetera, if I may not keep my body, and its uses, in my absolute right.'"

Commas and periods are placed inside quotation marks:

> Brigid Brophy thinks that both genders should be "free to make a free choice."
>
> If we do not let men and women make choices, "we are betraying civilisation itself," believes Brigid Brophy.

Semicolons and colons are placed outside quotation marks:

> Brophy says we are all "free to make a free choice"; in fact, we let convention limit our awareness of choice.
>
> Brophy says we are all "free to make a free choice": about our educations, our careers, our domesticity.

Question marks go inside quotation marks if they are part of the quotation but belong outside of quotation marks if the quoted statement is being used as a question by the writer quoting the material:

> The professor asked, "Who agrees with Brigid Brophy's thesis?"
>
> Does Brophy think we "should be free to make a free choice"?

If you are quoting a conversation, begin a new paragraph for each speaker. Notice the punctuation of the quoted conversation in this excerpt from Rebekah Hall-Naganuma's narrative, which begins on page 433.

> "What do you mean by 'blackout?'" she asked, with a look of confusion on her face.
>
> "She ended up in Houston somehow and then couldn't remember how she got there."

If you are quoting poetry, integrate into your own text quoted single lines of poetry. Two or three lines of poetry may be brought into your text and enclosed in quotation marks, or they may be set off from your text, without quotation marks but indented ten spaces (one inch) from the left margin:

> The narrator in Janice Mirikitani's poem "Breaking Tradition" longs to be liberated from her mother's influence:
>
> > I want to break tradition—unlock this room
> > where women dress in the dark.
> > Discover the lies my mother told me.
> > The lies that we are small and powerless. (23–26)

or

The narrator in Janice Mirikitani's poem "Breaking Tradition" longs to be liberated from her mother's influence: "I want to break tradition—unlock this room / where women dress in the dark" (23–24).

The slash (/) is used to indicate the end of a poetry line when poetry lines are incorporated into text. (The use of the slash is described further on pp. 600–601.) Set off poetry quotations of more than three lines and prose quotations of more than four lines.

Titles

Titles of short stories, songs, essays, poems, articles, parts of books, and the titles of episodes on television and radio are enclosed in quotation marks:

"The Red Convertible"

"Imagine"

"Don't Let Stereotypes Warp Your Judgments"

"The Lanyard"

"Tracks" in *Aquaboogie*

Do not use quotation marks around a word that you feel self-conscious about using. Instead, change the word:

The morning meeting is held to give the staff the "rundown" on the advertising goals for the day.

The morning meeting is held to explain that day's advertising goals to the staff.

Italics

Current MLA style requires the use of italics for titles of independently published works—books, plays, periodicals, films, Web sites, online databases, television and radio broadcasts, CDs, record albums, performances, and works of art:

Between Worlds: A Reader, Rhetoric, and Handbook

A Midsummer Night's Dream

Time

Man on Wire

30 Rock

Organized Wisdom

The Animal Years

Nighthawks

Use italics for words and letters referred to as words, foreign words in an English text, and for emphasis.

The silent room is not so much *neat* as it is stifling.

For addresses on envelopes, use the abbreviation for the state, *AZ*, instead of *Arizona*.

Spanish expressions such as *adios* have become common in the United States.

He is *not* the best candidate for the job even though he is qualified.

The Ellipsis

The ellipsis, a set of three spaced periods (. . .), informs the reader that something has been left out of a quotation. For example, a writer quoting material from Naomi Wolf's book *The Beauty Myth* might decide to leave out some material unnecessary to the text he or she is writing. Here Wolf writes about the phenomenon of eating disorders in countries other than the United States:

> It is spreading to other industrialized nations: The United Kingdom now has 3.5 million anorexics or bulimics (95 percent of them female), with 6,000 new cases yearly (183).

Here the passage is revised using an ellipsis:

> It is spreading to other industrialized nations: The United Kingdom now has 3.5 million anorexics or bulimics . . . with 6,000 new cases yearly (183).

The decision to remove material and use the ellipsis must be governed by the writer's intent. But the ellipsis may not be used to remove anything that would change the meaning of the section that the writer is quoting. The fact that 95 percent of the cases of eating disorders in the United Kingdom involve women may not be relevant to the writer of the revised text, so the ellipsis is used as a convenient tool to shorten the quoted material and keep the emphasis where the writer wants it. The missing words in this case do not change the meaning of the original.

If you remove words from the quoted material at the end of the sentence, use a period before the three periods of the ellipsis. Notice this example from "How to Get Better Gas Mileage" (p. 463). Mieszkowski quotes Philip Reed, a consumer advocate, whose full statement might not be entirely relevant to someone using Mieszkowski's material. A writer eliminating a part of the work would use an ellipsis after the period in the first sentence to show that unnecessary material between the two sentences was removed:

> Drivers are often unconsciously influenced by the speed of the other cars around them, which can lead to speed creep. "When a faster car passes you, you have a tendency to speed up. Soon, even though you

were committed to going 70, you're going 80," says Reed. . . . A good way to avoid that pitfall: use the cruise control on the freeway, which will also help you avoid the temptation to constantly dart forward when you see an opening in traffic up ahead. (465)

If a parenthetical reference follows an ellipsis at the end of a sentence, use three spaced periods and then place the period to conclude the sentence after the final parenthesis:

> As Lisa Appignanesi records in her biography *Simone de Beauvoir*, Beauvoir believed that "the genuinely moral person can never have an easy conscience. . ." (79).

To avoid using the ellipsis too often, integrate carefully selected parts of quoted material into your text:

> As Carol Tavris notes, people respond "in shock and anger at the failings of 'human nature.'"

By paraphrasing part of the quotation and integrating the author's text with your own, you can avoid both using lengthy quotations *and* overusing the ellipsis.

Parentheses

Use parentheses to separate a digression or aside from the main sentence:

> Their house number (usually painted on the curb) was on the mailbox.

> Because an increasing number of women (and men) are suffering from eating disorders, we must address the problem at our next NOW conference.

Rules govern the use of punctuation within and outside of parentheses. If a sentence requires a comma in addition to parentheses, use the comma after the second or closing parenthesis:

> During the Civil War (1861–1865), African Americans were trained for active duty and fought in segregated units.

If the information within the parentheses is a complete sentence, the final punctuation is enclosed within the parentheses:

> More information on gardens that require little water appears throughout the book. (See the chapters on cactus and native plants, especially.)

Parentheses also are used in documentation to enclose the source of paraphrased or quoted information. In these cases, the terminal punctuation appears outside the parentheses:

> As Virginia Woolf says in *Orlando*, "Clothes have . . . more important offices than merely to keep us warm. They change our view of the world and the world's view of us" (187).

(For a more complete discussion of how parentheses are used in MLA documentation, see p. 540, and for their use in APA documentation, see p. 554.)

Brackets

Use brackets to enclose words or phrases that you have added to a quotation, to show any changes that you have made in quoted material, or to record your own comments about quoted material:

> Today, more attention is being paid "to the relationship between eating disorders [anorexia and bulimia] and the compulsive eating of many women."

In the preceding example, the writer has clarified a point for the reader by defining within the quotation types of eating disorders. The brackets indicate that the words are not part of the original quotation.

> The Duke of Ferrara, in Robert Browning's poem "My Last Duchess," is disturbed that the Duchess "ranked [his] gift of a nine-hundred-years-old name / With anybody's gift."

In this example, the writer changed the original—"ranked my gift of a nine-hundred-years-old name"—to fit into a text. To show the change from *my* to *his*, the writer placed brackets around the change. The diagonal line (or slash) between "name" and "With" indicates the end of the line in the poem.

> The "Poison Pen Letters" greeting card says, "Everything has it's [sic] price . . . but I didn't know you came so cheap!"

The brackets are used to enclose *sic*, a Latin word meaning "in this manner." The *[sic]* used after *it's* in the above example indicates that the error of not using *its* is in the original, and is not an error made by the person quoting the original.

The Slash

The slash may be used sparingly to show options, like *pass/fail* or *Dean/ Department Head*. Notice that there is no space between the words and the slash when the slash is used to show options.

The slash is also used to define the end of a line of poetry if the line is incorporated into a text. For example, notice how the writer incorporates into a poetry explication some words from Stephen Perry's poem "Blue Spruce":

> The speaker in the poem reveals that his "grandfather had an affair / with the girl who did their nails" (19–20).

The slash indicates where the line ends in the original work (which appears on p. 79). Notice that a space appears on either side of the slash when it is used to indicate the end of a line of poetry.

In bulletins, reports, and some business correspondence, the slash is used in the form *he/she,* as in this sentence:

> The person who lost a ring in the library may claim it after he/she describes
> it to campus police.

In formal writing, you should avoid the form *he/she* by writing *he or she,* as in this sentence:

> The student who aspires to a law degree may attain it if he or she is willing
> to work hard.

Both *he/she* and *he or she* can be avoided by rewriting the sentence:

> The person who lost a ring in the library may claim it by describing it to campus
> police.
> The student who aspires to a law degree may attain it by working hard.

The Hyphen

The hyphen is used to divide a word or to form a compound word. To divide a word that will not fit on the typed or written line, separate the part of the word that will fit on the line with a hyphen at a syllable break, then conclude the word on the next line. The break must occur only between syllables and should not leave fewer than two letters at the end of the line or fewer than three letters at the beginning of the next line. The hyphen appears at the end of the first line, *not* at the beginning of the next line. If you are using a computer, the word processing program automatically moves the full word to the next line (unless directed to hyphenate words).

Notice how each error is corrected:

> Of all of the applicants for the job, she was the best teach-
> er for the class.   *P*
> Of all of the applicants for the job, she was the best
> teacher for the class.

If you choose to hyphenate, a word can be broken between syllables if the break will leave at least two letters at the end of the line and three or more letters at the beginning of the next line. Because the syllables of *teach-* and *-er* will not fit that rule, the entire word must be moved to the next line.

> After his paper was completed, the frustrated student fo-
> und another critical article.   *P*
> After his paper was completed, the frustrated student
> found another critical article.

[A one-syllable word cannot be broken, so *found* must be moved to the next line.]

p

Since the 1993 presidential inauguration, interest in the poetry of Maya Angelou has increased.

Since the 1993 presidential inauguration, interest in the
poetry of Maya Angelou has increased.

[The hyphen is used *only* at the end of the first line.]
Divide compound words only where the hyphen already exists:

p

He gave the family heirloom to his sis-
ter-in-law.

He gave the family heirloom to his sister-
in-law.

p

Histories of popular music describe the heart-throb-
bing gestures of Elvis Presley.

Histories of popular music describe the heart-
throbbing gestures of Elvis Presley.

Hyphens are also used to form compound words that modify a noun:

The grade-conscious students knew the best sequence for the courses.
The award-winning play went on to Broadway.

If the modifiers follow the noun, the hyphens are usually left out.

The students are grade conscious.
The play was award winning and went on to Broadway.

Hyphens are used in spelled-out fractions and compound whole numbers from twenty-one to ninety-nine:

Over one-half of the voters will stay home on election day.
Everyone hates that old school bus song, "Ninety-Nine Bottles of Beer on the Wall."

Hyphens are used to attach some prefixes and suffixes. Usually, prefixes are attached to a word without a hyphen: *preconceived, disinterested, unhappy.* But prefixes such as *ex-, self-,* and *all-,* prefixes that precede a capitalized word, or prefixes that are a capitalized letter usually require a hyphen; for example, *self-supporting, ex-champion, anti-European,* and *U-boat.* Sometimes, to prevent confusion, a hyphen is necessary to separate a prefix ending in a vowel and a main word that starts with a vowel; for example, *de-escalate, re-invent,* and *pre-advise.*

Chapter 17

Understanding Faulty Word Choice

Poor word choice weakens writing, and instructors will note these errors in the margins of your papers. (Specific examples are cited in the alphabetically arranged list of commonly confused words on pages 607–618.) The types of word choice problems are defined and illustrated here.

Clichés

Clichés, or overused words or expressions, should be avoided. Predictable language is stale, and expressions that were once novel and even colorful inevitably lose their descriptive quality through overuse. Like a faded carpet, clichés no longer add color to the space they occupy. If you can complete the following expressions automatically, you know that you have examples of a cliché:

The bread was hard as a _____.

We searched all day, but it was like looking for a needle _____.

Good writing is clear, fresh, and vivid:

The bread was as hard as aged camel dung and about as tasty.

We searched all day, but it was like looking for a button in my mother's tool drawer.

Slang, Jargon, and Colloquial Words

Some of our most vivid language is considered *slang* (highly informal, often coined words used in speaking) or *jargon* (the special vocabulary of people who have the same job, interest, or way of life). In fact, in conversation, if pretentious

language were substituted for some of the commonly used *colloquial* words—
intoxicated for *drunk* or *children* for *kids*—our conversations would sound stuffy
or silly. Slang is often vigorous and colorful, but it is nonstandard and therefore
unacceptable in most formal writing. And the jargon that is acceptable in conversation or memos at work may be unintelligible to the general reader. If you
think your "funky," "laid-back," or "awesome" word choice is going to influence
negatively your reader's feelings about your integrity as a writer, elevate your language and remove the inappropriate word.

Archaic Words, Euphemisms, and Pretentious Words

Some words that appear in literature, especially poetry, may not be appropriate for expository writing:

wd ch

Marcus Mabry was amongst the minority students accepted at Stanford.

Marcus Mabry was among the minority students accepted at Stanford.

The word *amongst,* used in poetry, sounds inflated in expository texts.

Writers sometimes use *euphemisms*—substitutes for words perceived as
offensive—to limit emotional impact. For example, a war report might describe

the results of a bombing mission as "collateral casualties" rather than "civilians killed." A *Newsweek* article states that "the collateral damage of the drug war has been immense"—a euphemism avoiding the recognition that it is human beings who are being incarcerated and homes that are being destroyed in overly aggressive police actions.

Euphemisms are often deliberately used to mask a harsher reality. At best, they are often imprecise, as in this sentence: "We lost our grandmother last week." The reader might wonder if she is still wandering in the parking lot of the local mall. To avoid this confusion and to communicate accurately, use direct and precise language: "Our grandmother died last week."

Pretentious language is used by writers who believe it will make their work appear more refined or elegant. Avoid words like *facilitate* or *utilize* when *help* and *use* are adequate. Some pretentious words have persisted and reached cliché status: *viable* and *parameters,* for example.

Writers who are insecure about their writing may be tempted to overuse a thesaurus or pad their papers with contrived and inflated diction. Readers can usually detect this as a desperate attempt to pump up flat or shallow ideas. Instead of developing their thinking and analysis, pretentious writers try to bluff it. Typically, the end result is wordy, confused, stuffy prose rather than writing that is concise, accurate, and honest. Here are some examples, from student essays, of contrived or inflated diction:

Inflated and Wordy Diction:

The imagery that Baldwin employs engulfs the situation to a reality status. *dic*

Precise:

Baldwin's imagery makes the scene realistic.

Inflated and Wordy Diction:

The story commences with the creation of an atmosphere that posited the couple's *dic* affluency.

Precise:

The setting suggests that the couple is wealthy.

Redundancies

The legal profession has contributed some double-talk, such as *aid and abet,* to our language, and some other redundancies have persisted even though they are bulky or inane: *each and every, revert back, end result, temporary respite,* or *true fact.* You can see that *each* and *every* mean the same thing, so the words should not be used together. To revert means "to go back." And what is a fact if it isn't true? If you regard these redundancies as you would clichés—language that is predictable and imprecise—you will eliminate them from your writing.

Sexist Language

Language that demeans women or men is *sexist*. Most writers would know not to use *chick, broad, stud,* or *hunk* in their work, but more subtle and insidious sexist language also needs to be avoided. If you exclude or offend a portion of your audience, you will lose your reader—even if the rest of your essay is strong—as in the following examples:

> Every professor uses his wisdom to remain objective.
>
> Each nurse is required to store her lunch in a locker.
>
> A clever lawyer parks his car in the free lot.
>
> The competent PTA president uses her gavel rarely.

Even a superficial look at job and lifestyle choices in the last decades would confirm the necessity of unbiased language in print. Nurses and lawyers are both female and male; nowhere is it prescribed that only women will be PTA presidents. Consider the following solutions illustrated below for freeing the above sentences of sexist language:

> A professor uses wisdom to remain objective.
>
> Professors use their wisdom to remain objective.
>
> Nurses are required to store their lunches in lockers.
>
> Each nurse is required to store his or her lunch in a locker.
>
> Clever lawyers park their cars in the free lot.

Avoid the *his/her* construction in formal writing and the *his or her* pattern. You can eliminate both of these bulky and awkward constructions by using the article instead of a possessive pronoun, or by using a plural noun as the subject:

> The competent PTA president uses the gavel rarely.
>
> Competent PTA presidents use their gavels rarely.

Do not assume any job is gender specific. *Fireman* should be *firefighter, clergyman* should be *minister* or *member of the clergy,* and *mailman* should be *letter carrier* or *mail carrier.* Do not add *lady* to job titles; "She is a lady doctor" is as unnecessary a distinction as "He is a male artist."

You can further free your writing from sexism by eliminating the generic use of *man* in examples like the following:

> Mankind is more aware of stereotypes than it was a decade ago.
>
> Humanity is more aware of stereotypes than it was a decade ago.
>
> People are more aware of stereotypes than they were a decade ago.

Glossary of Usage: Commonly Confused Words

a, an: Use *a* before words beginning with consonant sounds, including those spelled with an initial pronounced *h* (*a* horse) and those spelled with vowels that are sounded as consonants (*a* one-hour final, *a* university). Use *an* before words beginning with vowel sounds, including those spelled with an initial *h* (*an* igloo, *an* hour).

a/an, the: *A* and *an* are indefinite articles and are used before nouns that are nonspecific or general (*a* game, *an* acrobat). *The* is a definite article and used before nouns that refer to something specific (*the* game, *the* acrobat).

An avid sports fan, Bill watches a televised football game every weekend.

His favorite team is the Miami Dolphins although his friend always cheers for the Buffalo Bills.

accept, except: *Accept* is a verb meaning "to receive." *Except* is a preposition meaning "excluding" or "but."

I accept your plan to tour all of New York City except for Central Park.

advice, advise: *Advice* is the noun meaning "recommendation about what to do." *Advise* is the verb meaning "to give opinion or counsel."

I advise you to follow your counselor's advice.

affect, effect: *Affect* is usually a verb meaning "to influence." *Effect* is a noun meaning "result." In psychology, *affect* is used as a noun meaning "a feeling or emotion." *Effect* can be used as a verb meaning "to implement, or to bring about."

The eyedrops do not affect his driving.

Candles create a romantic effect in the dining room.

An examination of <u>affect</u> is critical in understanding personality.

Congress must <u>effect</u> a change in the tax laws.

aisle, isle: *Aisle* means a walkway between sections of seats, shelves, or counters. *Isle* means an island.

Deborah and Jeff decided it was time to amble down the <u>aisle</u> together.

The pet food <u>aisle</u> of the supermarket seems to expand each year.

Melanie and Russ were dreaming about snorkeling near some faraway <u>isle</u> in the Pacific.

all ready, already: *All ready* means "completely prepared." *Already* means "by now" or "before now."

We were <u>all ready</u> for the trip, but the bus had <u>already</u> left.

all right: *All right* is typically spelled as two words. (*Alright* appears in some dictionaries, but most readers still consider it a misspelling.)

all together, altogether: *All together* means "in a common location," "in unison," or "as a group." *Altogether* means "completely" or "entirely."

We are <u>altogether</u> certain that caging the rabbits <u>all together</u> is a mistake.

allude/elude: *Allude* means "to refer to"; *elude* means "to escape."

Mimi <u>alluded</u> to the time when Katie studied in France and managed to <u>elude</u> tedious professors.

allusion, illusion: An *allusion* is an "indirect reference"; an *illusion* is "a deceptive appearance" or "a fantasy that may be confused with reality."

Joyce's use of mythological <u>allusions</u> gives the <u>illusion</u> that she is a classicist.

a lot: *A lot* is always two words, never *alot*.

altar, alter: The noun *altar* means "an elevated place or structure where religious rites are performed." *Alter* is a verb that means "to change or modify."

She needed to <u>alter</u> her schedule to allow time to decorate the church <u>altar</u> with fresh daisies for the wedding.

among, between: Use *between* when referring to two; use *among* for three or more.

<u>Between</u> you and me, Alex is <u>among</u> the most creative students in our program.

amount, number: *Amount* refers to a quantity of something that cannot be counted. *Number* refers to items that can be counted.

The <u>amount</u> of flour used depends on the <u>number</u> of cookies you want to bake.

anxious: *Anxious* means "apprehensive" or "worried." Often it is confused with the word *eager,* which means "anticipating" or "looking forward to."

Yumiko was <u>anxious</u> about her performance review because she was <u>eager</u> to be promoted.

a while, awhile: *A while* is an article and a noun; *awhile* is an adverb.

We spoke for <u>a while</u> and then parted.

Wait <u>awhile</u> before you swim.

basically: This word is greatly overused and often unnecessary:

Avoid: Tia and Delaiah are, basically, ideal daughters-in-law.

Better: Tia and Delaiah are ideal daughters-in-law.

being as, being that: These terms should not be used for *because* or *since.*

<u>Because</u> Quarterback Doug Flutie was so popular with fans, the games in Buffalo were always sold out.

<u>Since</u> he signed with the Lakers, Kobe has been a top scorer for the team.

beside, besides: *Beside* is a preposition meaning "next to." *Besides* is a preposition meaning "except," as well as an adverb meaning "in addition to."

The secretary sat <u>beside</u> his dean.

Everyone <u>besides</u> the team rides the school bus to each game.

Leslie's instructional expertise is needed; <u>besides,</u> she knows how to have fun!

brake, break: *Brake* means to slow or stop a vehicle or the device used to stop a vehicle. *Break* means to smash, shatter, become separated, interrupt, or halt.

If that driver doesn't <u>brake</u> soon, he will <u>break</u> the bikes that are in the driveway.

can, may: *Can* means "is able to." *May* indicates permission.

You <u>can</u> talk on the telephone for three hours, but you <u>may</u> not in my house!

capital, capitol: *Capital* refers to the city and is the word to describe an uppercase letter. *Capitol* indicates the building where government meets.

The <u>capital</u> is the destination for the class trip, but a visit to the <u>capitol</u> is impossible because the ceiling is under repair.

censor, censure: *Censor* functions as a verb (meaning "to suppress or remove objectionable material") and as a noun (the person who suppresses the objectionable material). *Censure* is a verb meaning "to criticize severely."

The librarian refused to work with citizens who <u>censor</u> the classics.

The <u>censor</u> of a few decades ago considered *The Adventures of Huckleberry Finn* subversive.

The city council needs to <u>censure</u> neon signs in "Old Town."

cite, site, sight: *Cite* means "to quote by way of example, authority, or proof." *Site* is "the location of." *Sight* is a "spectacle or view."

The tourist <u>sights</u> were on the <u>site</u> of an ancient village <u>cited</u> in the guidebook.

complement, compliment: *Complement* means "to complete" or "something that completes or supplements another." *Compliment* is a noun or verb that means "to praise."

His sensitivity <u>complements</u> her assertiveness.

Most people see through false <u>compliments</u>.

conscience, conscious: *Conscience* is a noun referring to one's sense of right and wrong. *Conscious* is an adjective that means "alert to" or "aware of."

The jury member was <u>conscious</u> of his nagging <u>conscience</u>.

could of, should of, would of: These are incorrect forms for *could have, should have,* and *would have. Of* is a preposition, not a part of a verb.

The trainer <u>should have</u> exercised his horse today.

desert/dessert: *Dessert* (with the double *s*) means the sweet treat at the end of the meal. *Desert* is used for all other meanings: a barren, sandy region; a deserved reward or punishment; to abandon or forsake.

Taylor and Garrett devoured their <u>dessert</u> before they departed for the <u>desert</u>.

Karen had to <u>desert</u> the thief, but she knew he would get his just <u>deserts</u>.

discreet/discrete: *Discreet* means "tactful" or "diplomatic"; *discrete* means "separate" or "distinct."

Dean Lew is always <u>discreet</u> about students' comments on evaluation forms.

Kristi's and Charlotte's duties are <u>discrete</u> from each other.

double negative: Double negatives to emphasize negativity are nonstandard in English.

I didn't see <u>anything</u> [not *nothing*].

The child <u>could hardly control</u> [not *couldn't hardly control*] his tears.

due to: *Due to* is acceptable following a linking verb but is considered less acceptable at the beginning of a sentence.

Most minor injuries during earthquakes are <u>due to</u> panic.

<u>Because of</u> [not *due to*] rain, the beach party was canceled.

due to the fact that: Use *because* to avoid wordiness.

each: *Each* is singular. (See also pp. 574–575.)

effect: See **affect.**

e.g.: This is a Latin abbreviation meaning "for example." It is sometimes confused with *i.e.,* which means "that is." Neither of these abbreviations should be used in the text of a manuscript, but they can be used in parenthetical expressions.

either: *Either* is singular. (See also pp. 574–575.)

Jim and Marti offered to tow the van; <u>either</u> is willing to drive to Coalinga.

elicit, illicit: *Elicit* is a verb meaning "to evoke." *Illicit* is an adjective meaning "illegal or unlawful."

The attorney was unable to <u>elicit</u> any information from her client about <u>illicit</u> drug sales in the neighborhood.

emigrate from, immigrate to: *Emigrate* means "to leave a country or region to settle elsewhere." *Immigrate* means "to enter another country and live there."

When Pano <u>emigrated</u> from Turkey, he missed living near the sea.

After the Revolution, many Cubans <u>immigrated</u> to the United States.

eminent, imminent: *Eminent* means "celebrated" or "exalted." *Imminent* means "about to happen."

The <u>eminent</u> seismologist predicted that an earthquake was <u>imminent</u>.

especially, specially: *Especially* means "particularly" or "more than other things." *Specially* means "for a specific reason."

Ryder <u>especially</u> values working on cabinets. He's known for <u>specially</u> ordered fine pieces of exotic woods.

etc.: Avoid ending a list with the abbreviation *etc.* Writers often overuse it to suggest they have more information than they do. The Latin expression is *et cetera,* which means "and others" or "and other things." The expression is best avoided in your essays because it is vague. It is also often misspelled as *ect.*

everybody, everyone: *Everybody* and *everyone* are singular. (See also pp. 574–575.)

except: See **accept.**

farther, further: *Farther* refers to distance. *Further* implies quantity or degree. *Further* is now widely accepted for both meanings.

Janae swam <u>farther</u> than everyone in her water fitness class.

Jerry is <u>further</u> along on his computer project than he expected.

fewer, less: *Fewer* refers to items that can be counted. *Less* refers to measurable amounts.

Nate has <u>fewer</u> expenses and therefore needs <u>less</u> spending money because he works for the national parks.

firstly: *Firstly* is pretentious. Use *first.*

fun: *Fun* is colloquial when used as an adjective and should be avoided.

Jess and Brian enjoyed the <u>amusing</u> [not *fun*] movie.

further: See **farther.**

good, well: *Good* is an adjective; *well* is usually an adverb.

<u>Good</u> work is almost always <u>well</u> rewarded.

hanged, hung: *Hanged* refers to people. *Hung* refers to pictures and things that can be suspended.

The criminal <u>hanged</u> himself in his prison cell.

The Walshes <u>hung</u> Debbie's recent paintings in the living room.

he, he/she, his/her: The writer should no longer assume that *he* is an acceptable pronoun for all nouns. Furthermore, *he/she* or *his/her* are awkward. To avoid this construction, use the plural or a specific noun instead of the pronoun. (See also p. 606.)

Instead of: When a student works in a small group, <u>he/she</u> participates more.

Write: When <u>students</u> work in small groups, <u>they</u> participate more.

hisself: *Hisself* is nonstandard. Use *himself.*

hung: See **hanged.**

i.e.: This Latin abbreviation for *id est* should be replaced by the English *that is.*

illusion: See **allusion.**

imminent: See **eminent.**

imply, infer: *Imply* means "to state indirectly or to suggest." *Infer* means "to come to a conclusion based on the evidence given."

By covering his ears, he <u>implied</u> that he no longer wanted to listen.

We can <u>infer</u> that the Duke of Ferrara is an arrogant man because he refused to "stoop" to speak to his wife.

irregardless: *Irregardless* is nonstandard. Use *regardless.*

its, it's: *Its* is the possessive form. *It's* is the contraction for *it is* or *it has.* (See also p. 589.)

<u>It's</u> too bad that Dick and Jean's cat has injured <u>its</u> tail.

<u>It's</u> been a bad day for the Jacobys' cat.

later, latter: *Later* refers to time. *Latter* refers to the second of two things named.

Initially many southern European immigrants came to this country, but <u>later</u> the immigration policy restricted the numbers.

Both Diego Rivera and his wife Frida Kahlo painted, but the <u>latter</u> has gained more public recognition in the last few years.

lay, lie: *Lay* means "to place or put" and requires an object. (The past tense is *laid*.) *Lie* means "to rest or recline." (The past tense of *lie* is *lay*, and so the two words are sometimes confused.)

<u>Lay</u> the piano music on the bench where Mrs. Main <u>laid</u> it yesterday.

Twinkle will <u>lie</u> down exactly where she <u>lay</u> yesterday.

lead, led: The present tense of the verb is *lead* and the past tense is *led*. However, *lead* is also used as a noun, meaning a gray metal, and confusion results because it is pronounced the same as "led."

Barbara will <u>lead</u> the tour to Istanbul, and then it will be led by Lexa.

Usually plumbers replace <u>lead</u> pipes with copper.

less: See **fewer.**

lie: See **lay.**

loose, lose: *Loose* is an adjective meaning "unrestrained or unfastened." *Lose* is a verb meaning "to misplace" or "to be defeated."

If his bathing suit is too <u>loose</u>, Lester will <u>lose</u> it in the next wave.

lots, lots of: Avoid these constructions in formal writing. Elevate the diction to *many* or *much*.

mankind: Avoid this term, as its sexism offends many readers. Use *humans, humanity,* or *humankind* instead.

It was one small step for the man who walked on the moon, but it was a giant step for <u>humanity</u>.

maybe, may be: *Maybe* is an adverb meaning "perhaps." *May be* is a verb.

<u>Maybe</u> Vince will open his own restaurant in Oregon, and Sherry <u>may be</u> ready to train their employees again.

may of, might of: These are nonstandard forms of *may have* and *might have.*

media, medium: *Media* is the plural of *medium*, when the word refers to a means of public communication.

The <u>medium</u> most often used by political candidates is television.

Other <u>media</u> such as public radio, newspapers, and documentary films may provide deeper political analysis.

myself: *Myself* is a reflexive or intensive pronoun and, like the other *-self* pronouns, should not be used in place of personal pronouns.

I drove <u>myself</u> to the hospital because no one else was home.

"I can do it <u>myself</u>!" the toddler protested.

Juan ladled the chili for his father and <u>me</u> [not *myself*].

neither: *Neither* is singular. (See also p. 574.)

<u>Neither</u> of us is available to babysit for the Trosts tonight.

nohow: *Nohow* is nonstandard for *in any way*.

none: *None* can be singular or plural depending on meaning.

<u>None</u> of the alternatives seem reasonable.

<u>None</u> of the football players is injured.

nowheres: *Nowheres* is nonstandard for *nowhere*.

number: See **amount.**

of: *Of* is a preposition. It should not be used in place of *have* in constructions like *should have* or *would have*.

off of: *Of* is not necessary with *off*. Use *off* alone or use *from*.

The marbles rolled <u>off</u> the table and continued rolling around Monahan's room.

O.K., OK, okay: All three forms are acceptable, but in formal writing these expressions are inappropriate.

on account of: A wordy way to write *because*.

owing to the fact that: A wordy way to write *because*.

passed, past: *Passed* is the past tense of the verb that means having gone by, having completed a test or course, having transferred a ball or puck to a teammate. *Past* is not a verb. Rather, it is used as a noun, adjective, adverb, or preposition and means a time gone by or having elapsed in time. If you remember to use the form "passed" when you need a verb, you will be correct.

Verb: Julia <u>passed</u> Debra in the hall and told her that Miori had <u>passed</u> the test.

Verb: The Maguires <u>passed</u> around reviews of the film *In the Line of Fire*.

Verb: During the game, Tyler <u>passed</u> the ball to David.

Verb: Jane and Pete <u>passed</u> their summer days at the cabin.

Noun: In the <u>past</u>, Julia and Debra met to discuss the student's progress.

Adjective: The Maguires have collected <u>past</u> reviews of *In the Line of Fire*.

Adverb: Tyler liked to jog <u>past</u> the pier during his morning runs.

Preposition: It was <u>past</u> noon when Jane and Pete arrived at their cabin.

plus: *Plus* is not appropriately used as a conjunction to join independent clauses. Use a standard coordinating or adverbial conjunction such as "moreover" or "in addition."

We celebrated the Fourth of July with hot dogs, corn on the cob, potato salad, and watermelon; <u>in addition</u>, [not *plus*] we enjoyed the firework display at Zaca Lake.

precede, proceed: The verb *precede* means "come before" (note the prefix *pre-*). The verb *proceed* means "go forward" or "move on."

Spanish 4 <u>precedes</u> Spanish 5, "Literature of Mexico."

To <u>proceed</u> without a contract would be foolish.

prejudice, prejudiced: *Prejudice* is a noun; *prejudiced* is an adjective. Do not leave out the -*d* from the adjective.

<u>Prejudice</u> that starts in childhood is difficult to obliterate, and he was distinctly <u>prejudiced</u> against working mothers.

principal, principle: *Principal* is a noun for the "chief official" or, in finance, the "capital sum." As an adjective, principal means "major" or "most important." *Principle* is a noun meaning "a law or truth, rule, or axiom."

The school's <u>principal</u> uses various <u>principles</u> for deciding the graduation speakers; the <u>principal</u> factor seems to be related to academics.

proceed, precede: See **precede.**

quote, quotation: In academic writing, *quote* is a verb; *quotation* is a noun. However, the word *quote* is also used colloquially as a shortened form of the noun *quotation*.

Dennis wanted to <u>quote</u> a line from <u>Macbeth</u>, so he selected a memorable <u>quotation</u>.

raise, rise: *Raise* is a verb meaning "to move or cause to move up," and it takes an object. *Rise* is a verb meaning "to go up," and it does not take a direct object.

The farmers who <u>raise</u> cows are concerned about the disease.

They <u>rise</u> early to attend to the livestock.

reason is because: In speech, this expression is common. In formal writing, it is not appropriate. A clause using *that* is the preferred form:

The <u>reason</u> the Arnolds drove their trailer was <u>that</u> [not *because*] they could transport dune buggies for the Dennis family, too.

reason why: The expression *reason why* is redundant. *Reason* is sufficient.

> The <u>reason</u> [not *reason why*] Jorge attends law school at night is not obvious to anyone but his family.

rise, raise: See **raise, rise.**

should of: *Should of* is nonstandard; use *should have.*

> He <u>should have</u> [not *should of*] known not to build a campfire on that windy hill.

since: *Since* is sometimes used to mean *because,* but it is best to use it only as a conjunction in constructions having to do with time.

> Andy has been waiting <u>since</u> January for his tax forms.

> <u>Since</u> [or *because*] you left, I've been dating others.

sit, set: *Sit* means "to rest the weight of the body" as on a chair. *Set* means "to place."

> Dorothy wants you to <u>sit</u> on the black leather sofa.

> Tom would rather you not <u>set</u> stoneware dishes on his cherrywood table.

site, cite, sight: See **cite, site, sight.**

somebody, someone: *Somebody* and *someone* are singular. (See also p. 574.)

sometime, some time, sometimes: *Sometime* is an adverb meaning "at an indefinite time." *Some time* is the adjective *some* modifying the noun *time.* *Sometimes* means "now and then."

> <u>Sometime</u> we should get together and play tennis.
> Raul devoted <u>some time</u> to perfecting his pronunciation.
> <u>Sometimes</u> Ken discards every yolk from the eggs as he prepares his omelette.

stationary/stationery: *Stationary* is an adjective meaning "immovable, fixed in place." *Stationery* (with an "e" just as in "letter") is a noun meaning "writing material."

> Despite the brisk wind, the sign remained <u>stationary</u>.
> Leslie wrote the letter on <u>stationery</u> from the cruise ship.

supposed to, used to: Don't neglect to use the *-d* ending on these often used and often misspelled words!

> He is <u>supposed to</u> [not *suppose to*] bring the wine for the dinner.

> Ariane became <u>used to</u> [not *use to*] Dee's indifferent housekeeping.

than, then: *Than* is used in comparisons. *Then* is an adverb denoting time.

> There are many more calories in avocados <u>than</u> in apples.

> First Sylvia Plath attended the school, and <u>then</u> she taught there.

their, there, they're: *Their* is a possessive pronoun. *There* is an adverb denoting place. *They're* is a contraction meaning *they are.*

Their plans for hang gliding there in the park are apt to be postponed because they're not ready to pass the safety test.

then, than: See **than, then.**

there is, there are: The verb following the expletive "there" is singular or plural according to the number of the subject that follows the verb. (See also pp. 577 and 578 #5.)

There is a dictionary on the table. There are books and keys on the table.

this here, these here, that there, them there: Nonstandard for *this, these, that,* or *those.*

thru: *Thru* is a nonstandard spelling of *through* that should be avoided in all formal writing.

thusly: Use *thus,* which is less pretentious.

till, until, 'til: *Till* and *until* have the same meaning and both have standard uses. *'Til* is an informal contraction of *until.*

to, too, two: *To* is a preposition meaning "toward" and is part of the infinitive form of the verb (for example, *to run*). *Too* is an adverb meaning "overly." *Two* is a number.

Two trips to the market in one day are not too many for a fine cook like Mike.

toward, towards: Either form is acceptable if used consistently, but *toward* is preferred.

try and: *Try and* is nonstandard; *try to* is preferred.

Try to [not *try and*] meet Mohammed before he locks up his bike.

unique: *Unique* means "distinctively characteristic." It is an absolute adjective that should not be modified by "most" or "very."

A tuxedo shirt and jacket, bow tie, and Bermuda shorts create a unique [not *most unique*] style for a hot-weather prom.

until: See **till, until, 'til.**

usage: The noun *use* should be used whenever possible. *Usage* refers only to convention, as in *language usage.*

The use [not *usage*] of computers has facilitated essay writing, but papers with correct usage have not increased.

used to: See **supposed to, used to.**

weather, whether: *Weather* refers to the atmospheric conditions. *Whether* can be used interchangeably with *if.*

Gail wasn't certain <u>whether</u> the stormy <u>weather</u> would keep John and Mark from jogging to Niagara Falls.

well: See **good, well.**

which, in which: Writers occasionally use *in which* in places where *which* is sufficient. Read work carefully to eliminate the unnecessary preposition.

Salma grabbed the gray cape, <u>which</u> [not *in which*] had been left on the sofa.

which, who: *Which* is used for things, not for people. Use *who* for people.

Martin Luther King, the American <u>who</u> defined civil disobedience for his generation, was a theologian as well as a political figure. His letter from Birmingham, <u>which</u> he wrote in jail, defines his position.

while: Do not use *while* to mean *although* if there is a chance of confusion for the reader. Like *since*, *while* should be reserved for time sense. Unless the point is to show that the actions occur at the same time, *although* is the better word.

Nick begins cooking dinner <u>while</u> Chris drives home from Richmond.

<u>Although</u> [not *while*] Elizabeth continues to invest their savings, Bill never resists a rug sale.

who's, whose: *Who's* is the contraction for *who is* or *who has*. *Whose* is a possessive pronoun.

<u>Who's</u> going to stay at the Sea Bird Motel in Wildwood?
<u>Who's</u> been having dinner with the Grebners every Sunday?
Mike asked Lucy <u>whose</u> design she preferred.

would of: *Would of* is nonstandard for the complete verb *would have*.

Los Vendidos <u>would have</u> [not *would of*] been a perfect theater experience for Cinco de Mayo.

you: The indefinite use of *you*, or even its use to mean "you the reader," can be incongruous or offensive and can be avoided:

A decade ago, the fit hiker [rather than *you*] could camp on the beach with the seals at Pt. Sal, but now even the poor trail has eroded.

It is common practice in some African tribes for prepubescent females [rather than *you*] to be scarified.

your, you're: *Your* is a possessive pronoun. *You're* is the contraction of *you are*.

<u>Your</u> savings will disappear if <u>you're</u> not careful.

Text Credits

Laila Al-Marayati and Semeen Issa, "Muslim Women: An Identity Reduced to a Burka," *Los Angeles Times*, January 20, 2002. Reprinted by permission.

Teja Arboleda, "Race Is a Four-Letter Word" from *In the Shadow of Race: Growing Up as a Multiethnic, Multicultural, and Multiracial American*. Copyright 1998 by Taylor & Francis Group LLC-Books. Reproduced with permission of Taylor & Francis Group-Books in the format textbook via Copyright Clearance Center.

Celeste Biever, "Love Special: Modern Romance," *New Scientist Magazine*, April 29, 2006. © New Scientist Magazine. Reprinted by permission.

Jon Bowen, "Under My Skin," *Salon.com*, June 23, 1999. Reprinted by permission of the author.

Jane E. Brody, "'Diabesity,' a Crisis in an Expanding Country." From The *New York Times*, March 29, 2005. © 2005 The New York Times. All rights reserved. Used by permission and protected by the Copyright Laws of the United States. The printing, copying, redistribution, or retransmission of the material without express written permission is prohibited.

Vincent Canby, "Redford's Ordinary People." From The *New York Times*, September 19, 1980. © 1980, The New York Times. All rights reserved. Used by permission and protected by the Copyright Laws of the United States. The printing, copying, redistribution, or retransmission of the material without express written permission is prohibited.

Judith Ortiz Cofer, "The Myth of the Latin Woman: I Just Met a Girl Named Maria" from *The Latin Deli: Prose and Poetry*. Copyright © by Judith Ortiz Cofer. Reprinted by permission of The University of Georgia Press.

Jennifer A. Coleman, "Discrimination at Large," *Newsweek*, August 2, 1993. Reprinted by permission of the author.

Billy Collins, "The Lanyard," copyright © 2005 by Billy Collins, from *The Trouble with Poetry and Other Poems* by Billy Collins. Used by permission of Random House, Inc.

Libby Copeland, "Boy Friend: Between Those Two Words, a Guy Can Get Crushed." From The *Washington Post*, April 19, 2004. © 2004 The Washington Post. All rights reserved. Used by permission and protected by the Copyright Laws of the United States. The printing, copying, redistribution, or retransmission of the material without express written permission is prohibited.

Kevin Crust, "Movie Review: Al Gore Warms Up to a Very Hot Topic," The *Los Angeles Times*, May 24, 2006. Copyright © 2006 The Los Angeles Times. Reprinted by permission.

Philip Dacey, "Coke" from *Night Shift at the Crucifix Factory*. (Iowa City: University of Iowa Press, 1991). Copyright © 1991 by Philip Dacey. Reprinted by permission of the author.

Meghan Daum, "On the Fringes of the Physical World" from *My Misspent Youth*. (Open City Books, 2001). First published in The *New Yorker*. Reprinted by permission of the author.

David Denby, "Angry People," The *New Yorker*, May 2, 2005. Reprinted by permission of the author.

David Denby, "Transcending the Suburbs," *New Yorker*, September 20, 1999. Reprinted by permission of the author.

Debra J. Dickerson, "Who Shot Johnny?" The *New Republic*, January 1996. Reprinted by permission of the author.

Roger Ebert, review of "Crash" from *Chicago Sun Times*, May 2005. © 2005 The Ebert Company. Distributed by Universal Press Syndicate. Reprinted with permission. All rights reserved.

Barbara Ehrenreich, "Oh, Those Family Values." Copyright © 1994 by Barbara Ehrenreich. First appeared in *TIME Magazine*. Reprinted by permission of International Creative Management, Inc.

Marianela Enriquez, "Who Were You, Connie, and Why Did You Go?" Reprinted by permission of the author.

Louise Erdich, "The Red Convertible" from *Love Medicine*. Copyright © 1984 by Louise Erdich. Reprinted by permission of The Wylie Agency.

Pamela Erens, "Bodily Harm," *Ms.* Magazine, October, 1985. Reprinted by permission of the author.

Alex Garcia, "Reality Check," *Los Angeles Times*, June 16, 1999. Reprinted by permission of the author.

Photo Credits

Author Index

Note: Boldface shows location of readings.

Al-Marayati, Laila, **124–127**
Arboleda, Teja, **120–123**

Beck, Susan E., 516, **517–518**
Biever, Celeste, **51–54**
Bowen, Jon, **29–32**
Brody, Jane E., **204–207**

Cofer, Judith Ortiz, **172–176,** 392, 453
Coleman, Jennifer A., **198–200,** 393–395, 407–408
Collins, Billy, **41–42**
Copeland, Libby, **45–50**
Crust, Kevin, **308–310**

Dacey, Philip, **243–245**
Daum, Meghan, **56–65,** 430
Denby, David, **288–291, 299–302**
Dickerson, Debra J., **186–190**

Ebert, Roger, **302–304**
Ehrenreich, Barbara, **37–39**
Elbow, Peter, 405–406
Enriquez, Marianela, **489–492**
Erdrich, Louise, **135–143**
Erens, Pamela, **208–213**

Friedman, Thomas L., **219–221,** 443

Garcia, Alex, **456–459**
Goodman, Ellen, **3–5, 89–91,** 365, 398, 438–439, 442–443
Goodwin, Joe, 414, **416–418**

Haig, Scott, **225–228,** 414
Hall-Nakanuma, Rebekah, 432, **433–436**
Harrison, William F., **347–349,** 378, 379, 400

Heilbroner, Robert, 354, 399, 401, **470–473**
Holman, M. Carl, **133–134**
Hwang, Caroline, **12–15,** 453

Issa, Semeen, **124–127**

Kheng, Marin, 438, **439–442**
King, Martin Luther, Jr., **279–281,** 428
Klein, Jeff Z., **82–83,** 366
Komanyakaa, Yusef, **195–197,** 476
Krell, Rachel, **387–390,** 422, 453

Lamott, Anne, **271–274, 329–332,** 495
Lara, Adair, **68–69**
Leonard, John, **34–36,** 365, 399

Mabry, Marcus, **109–111,** 402, 453, 519–520
Malik, Zaiba, **129–131**
Malraux, André, 398
Martin, Andres, **24–27,** 412
Maslin, Janet, **291–293**
McKelvey, Robert, **451–453**
McKibben, Bill, **276–278**
McNight, Reginald, **71–77**
Mieszkowski, Katharine, **310–316**
Mirikitani, Janice, **21–23, 478–479**

Neil, Dan, **178–180,** 423–425
Norville, Leselle, 495–496, **497–506,** 507

Oates, Joyce Carol, **92–106,** 486
Orwell, George, **264–270**

Paaske, Shannon, 395–396, 402, 512, 515, 522–523, **524–539**

Parikh, Rahul K., **229–231,** 379, 413–414
Perry, Stephen, **79–80,** 476–477
Peters, Jeremy W., **239–242**
Pollan, Michael, **214–216,** 413
Poniewozik, James, **233–237,** 413

Queenan, Joe, **222–224**
Quiñones-Hinojosa, Alfredo, **112–115,** 412

Rowling, J. K., **165–170,** 377

Sabo, Don, **85–88,** 358
Sakatani, Robert, 478–480, **480–483**
Samuelson, Robert J., **112–115**
Scott, A. O., **304–306, 316–317, 321–323**
Senna, Danzy, **16–20,** 401
Smith, Janna Malamud, **8–11**
Soyster, Matthew, **158–160**
Staples, Brent, **181–185,** 374–376, 399, 453
Steinberg, Neil, **201–203,** 400, 407–408
Stoll, Clifford, **247–253,** 400, 443

Tannen, Deborah, 370–371
Tapscott, Don, **255–260**
Tavris, Carol, **261–263**
Thayer, Max, **191–194,** 379
Thomas, Chris, **427–428**
Turan, Kenneth, **294–297, 323–325**

Valdez, Luis, **144–154**
Vaughn, John A., **162–164**

Warhol, Andy, **246**
Winokur, Jon, **446–447,** 448

Subject and Title Index

Note: Boldface shows location of readings.

a/an/the usage, 607

a/an usage, 607

academic audiences, 345

Academic Search Premier, 514

accept/except usage, 607

action verbs, 563

active reading

  defined, 2

  dialectical journals and, 336–337

  examples, 3–6

  guidelines for, 341–342

  of poetry, 477–480

  as prewriting, 6

active viewing, 286–297. *See also* films

ad hominem attacks, 420

adjectives, 564

adverbs, 564, 572–574

advice/advise usage, 607

affect/effect usage, 607

afterword, introduction, preface, or foreword citations, 549

agreement errors, 577–578

"agr" errors, 577–578

aim/purpose of writing, 332, 351, 380, 385

aisle/isle usage, 608

Al Gore Warms Up to a Very Hot Topic (Crust), **308–310**

alliteration, 397

all ready/already usage, 608

all right/alright usage, 608

all together/altogether usage, 608

allude/elude usage, 608

allusion/illusion usage, 608

a lot/alot usage, 608

altar/alter usage, 608

although/since/while usage, 618

American Beauty (film)

  Dad's Dead, and He's Still a Funny Guy (Maslin), **291–293**

The Rose's Thorns (Turan), **294–297**

Transcending the Suburbs (Denby), **288–291**

American Psychological Association (APA) style guide, 554–559

among/amongst usage, 604

among/between usage, 608

amount/number usage, 608

amusing/fun usage, 612

analysis essays

  biography, 493–496, 506–508

  If the Genes Fit (Neil), 424

  poetry, 476–480, 483–485

  problem, 468–474

  process, 462–463, 466–468

  short story character, 485–493

  subject, 474–476

an/a usage, 607

anecdotes in introductions, 399–400

Angry People (Denby), **299–302**

An Inconvenient Truth (film)

  Al Gore Warms Up to a Very Hot Topic (Crust), **308–310**

  Did Al Get the Science Right? (Mieszkowski), **310–316**

  Warning of Calamities and Hoping for a Change (Scott), **316–317**

anonymous author citations, 542

anxious/eager usage, 609

APA (American Psychological Association) style guide, 554–559

apostrophes, 589–592

appeal to false authority as logical fallacy, 419

appeal to fear as logical fallacy, 420

appeal to pity as logical fallacy, 420

archaic words, 604–605

Are Families Dangerous? (Ehrenreich), **37–39**

argument essays

  aim and stance, 411

  argument *vs.* proposal, 409

  audience identification, 410–411

  brainstorming for, 406

  conceding *vs.* refuting, 414–415

  doubting and believing, 405–406

  evaluating effectiveness, 415

  explicit *vs.* implicit, 407–408

  introductions for, 410–411, 412

  logical fallacies in, 419–420

  logos, pathos, ethos, 409–410

  My Favorite Class: Involuntary Servitude (Goodwin), **416–419**

  outline for, 411

  persuasion, 404–405

  prewriting, 411

  proposals, 409, 411

  research for, 411

  strategies for writing, 412–415

  summary writing in, 429

  thesis for, 411

  when to use, 406

  writing practice, 421

audiences

  identification of, 345–347, 350, 410, 411

  revising for, 381–382

  style, stance and tone, 346

  voice of writing and, 346, 580–581

Why Stop Smoking? Let's Get Clinical (Harrison), **347–349**

author citations, 540–543, 554–555

a while/awhile usage, 609

624

bandwagon appeal as logical
    fallacy, 420
basically usage, 609
because of/due to usage, 610
because/on account of
    usage, 614
because/owing to the fact that
    usage, 614
because/since usage, 609, 616
begging the question as logical
    fallacy, 420
being as/being that usage, 609
The Believing Game—
    Methodological
    Believing (Elbow),
    405–406
beside/besides usage, 609
between/among usage, 608
bibliography for research
    papers, 544–545, 556
Bigotry as the Outer Side of
    Inner Angst (Scott),
    304–306, 443
biography essays
    conclusions, 507
    drafting the paper, 495
    The Earhart Appeal (Norville),
        497–506
    inference cards, 493–495
    introduction, 496
    "show" not "tell," 507
    thesis, 494–495, 506–508
    transitions, 496
    writer's strategy, 506
biography research papers, 512.
        See also biography
        analysis
Black Men and Public Space
    (Staples), **181–185,** 337,
    374–376, 399, 443
block method of organizing
    data, 455–456
blueprint thesis, 356. *See also*
    under thesis of writing
Blue Spruce (Perry), **79–80,** 476,
    484
Bodily Harm (Erens), **208–213,**
    360

Boy Friend: Between Those Two
    Words, a Guy Can Get
    Crushed (Copeland),
    45–50
brackets (punctuation), 519, 600
brainstorming
    argument essays, 406
    cause and effect
        esssays, 450
    group, 342–344
    individual, 333
    narration essays, 430–431
    process analysis essays, 462
    subject analysis essays, 474
brake/break usage, 609
Breaking The Ties that Bind
    (Sakatani), 397
Breaking Tradition
    (Mirikitani), **21–23,**
    478–479, 484

can/may usage, 609
capital/capitol usage, 609
cause and effect essays
    brainstorming for, 450
    critical thinking and, 449–450
    I Confess Some Envy
        (McKelvey), **451–453**
    If the Genes Fit (Neil), 424–425
    organizing and
        developing, 450
    when to use, 450
    writer's strategy, 453–454
    writing practice, 454
cause and effect terms, 392
censor/censure usage, 609
character analysis essays
    biography
        conclusions, 507
        drafting the paper, 495
        The Earhart Appeal
            (Norville), **497–506**
        inference cards, 493–495
        introduction, 496
        "show" not "tell," 507
        thesis, 494–495, 506–508
        transitions, 496
        writer's strategy, 506

short story
    prewriting, 485–487
    thesis construction, 488–489
    Who Were You, Connie and
        Why Did You Go?
        (Enriquez), **489–492**
    writer's strategy, 493
    writing practice, 493
    summary writing for, 429
characterization in films, 286
character traits, 485–486,
    493–494
chronological concepts, 366,
    392–393, 462
CINAHL (Cumulative Index to
    Nursing and
    Allied Health
    Literature), 514
circular reasoning, 420
citations in research papers
    APA style, 554–559
    elements of, 545
    MLA style
        authors, 540–542, 546–547,
            554–555
        corporation or government,
            542, 547
        edition number, 548
        encyclopedia or reference
            book, 549
        film or DVD, 551
        indirect sources, 543
        interviews, 550
        introduction, preface, fore-
            word or afterword, 549
        literature, 542–543, 548
        online sources, 543–544,
            551–554
        painting, sculpture or
            photograph, 551
        periodicals, 549–550
        reviews, 550
        song lyrics, 551
        television or radio program,
            551
        titles, 540, 548, 597
        translations, 548
cite/site/sight usage, 610

claim/intent of writing, 332, 352–359, 380, 385. *See also under* thesis of writing

clauses, 561, 566–568, 584–585

clichés, 603

clustering, 337–339, 431

coherence in essay writing, 369–370, 390–396

Coke (Dacey), **243–245,** 484

colloquial words, 603–604

colons (punctuation), 594

The Color of Love (Senna), **16–20,** 401

commas, 567, 586–589

comma splices, 571

comparison-contrast essays
  block method of organizing information, 455–456
  If the Genes Fit (Neil), 424
  organizing and developing, 455–456
  point-by-point method of organizing information, 456
  Reality Check (Garcia), **456–459**
  thesis in, 456, 460
  when to use, 454–455
  writer's strategy, 459–460
  writing practice, 460

comparison-contrast in definition essays, 445, 448

comparison terms, 391

complement/compliment usage, 610

complex sentences, 568

compound-complex sentences, 568

compound nouns with apostrophes, 591

compound sentences, 567

compound subject of sentences, 562, 577

computer research, 510, 512–514

conceding *vs.* refuting, 414–415

concessions in arguments, 413–414

conclusion writing
  biography, 507
  essays, 401–403
  revising, 385
  terms for, 392

conflict in narrative writing, 430

Congressional Quarterly Researcher (CQ Researcher), 514

conjunctive adverbs, 572–574

connotation, 476

conscience/conscious usage, 610

Conspiracy Against Assimilation (Samuelson), **112–115**

Contemporary Authors, 514

Contemporary Black Biography, 512

Contemporary Literary Criticism, 514

contractions formed by apostrophes, 589–590

contradictions in introductions, 400

contrast terms, 391

corporate author citations, 542

could of/should of/would of usage, 610

countering opponents objections, 413

CQ Researcher (Congressional Quarterly Researcher), 514

Crash (film)
  Angry People (Denby), **298–302,** 443
  Bigotry as the Outer Side of Inner Anguish (Scott), **304–306**
  Crash (Ebert), **302–304**

Crash (film review), **302–304**

critical thinking, 342, 381–382, 449–450

"cs" errors, 571

cultural differences
  An Identity Reduced to a Burka (Issa and Al-Marayati), **124–127**

Conspiracy Against Assimilation (Samuelson), **112–115**

Hidden in Plain Sight (Malik), **129–131**

Living in Two Worlds (Mabry), **109–111**

Los Vendidos (Valdez), **144–154**

Mr. Z (Holman), **133–134**

Race is a Four-Letter Word (Arboleda), **120–123**

The Red Convertible (Erdrich), **135–143**

Terra Firma—A Journey from Migrant Farm Labor to Neurosurgery (Quiñones-Hinojosa), **116–119**

Cumulative Index to Nursing and Allied Health Literature (CINAHL), 514

Dad's Dead, And He's Still a Funny Guy (Maslin), **291–293**

dangling modifiers, 583–584

dashes (punctuation), 595

databases, 510, 513–514

definition essays, 444–449
  If the Genes Fit (Neil), 423
  organizing and developing, 445
  purpose of, 445
  when to use, 444–445
  writer's strategy, 447–449
  writing practice, 449
  You Call That Irony? (Winokur), **446–447**

definitions in introductions, 400

demonstrative pronouns, 562

denotation, 476

dependent clauses, 566, 568, 584

description in definition essays, 445, 448

desert/dessert usage, 610

"Diabesity," A Crisis in an Expanding Country (Brody), **204–207**

dialectical journals, 336–337
dictionary definitions in
definition essays,
445, 448
Dictionary of Literary Biography,
514
Did Al Get the Science Right?
(Mieszkowski), **310–316**
Dieting Daze: No
In-Between (Krell),
387–390, 422
The Difference Between
Pity and Empathy
(Vaughn), **162–164**
differences
cultural, 108–109
gender, 44–45
generational, 7
perceptual, 157–158
in viewpoint, 218–219
direct objects of
sentences, 562
discreet/discrete usage, 610
Discrimination at Large
(Coleman), **198–200,**
392, 394, 407–408, 460
"dm" errors, 583
documenting research papers
APA style guide, 554–559
MLA style guide, 540–544,
546–554
domino theory as logical fallacy,
420
Don't Let Stereotypes Warp Your
Judgments (Heilbroner),
336, 352, 354, 399, 401,
443, **470–473**
double negatives, 610
doubting and believing
arguments, 405–406
drafting a paper, 360–364,
382–384, 432, 495, 511
dramatic organization of
material, 365, 437, 453
due to/because of usage, 610

each as a singular in proper
usage, 438, 610
eager/anxious usage, 609

EBSCOhost's Academic Search
Premier, 514
editing
audience concerns, 381–382,
398–401
checklist for, 385–386
for coherence,
390–391, 396
conclusions, 401–403
critical thinking and, 381–382
Dieting Daze: No
In-Between (Krell),
387–390
essays, 403
gaps, 396
introductions, 398–401
key word repetition, 393–394
key word substitutions, 394
mechanics, 385
pronouns, 394–395
research papers, 511
rewriting, 381
rough drafts, 382–384
style, 385
synonyms, 394
titles, 385, 397–398
transitions, 391–393, 395–396
edition number citations, 548
Educational Resources
Information Center
(ERIC), 514
effect/affect usage, 607
e.g./i.e. usage, 611
either as a singular in proper
usage, 611
either/or argument, 420
electronic sources, 513, 515
elicit/illicit usage, 611
ellipsis (punctuation), 519,
598–599
elude/allude usage, 608
emigrate from/immigrate to
usage, 611
eminent/imminent usage, 611
emotional appeals *(pathos),* 409
emphasizing important points,
393–394
emphatic organization of
material, 365

Encyclopedia of World Biography,
512
encyclopedia or reference book
citations, 549
ERIC (Educational Resources
Information
Center), 514
errors of grammar. *See*
grammar
especially/specially usage, 611
essay writing. *See also* analysis
essays; grammar;
paragraph structure;
research papers; writing
aim/purpose, 332, 351, 380
argument type, 410–415,
419–421
biography analysis, 493–496,
506–508
cause and effect type, 424–425,
449–454
claim/intent, 332,
352–359, 380
coherence in, 369–370,
390–396
comparison-contrast type, 424,
454–460
conclusions, 401–403, 507
definition type, 423, 444–449
evaluative response type,
438–444
freewriting, 333–335
introductions, 398–401,
410–411, 496
mixed methods, 423–425
narration type, 423, 429–437
paraphrasing, 377–380
plagiarism, 372
poetry analysis, 476–480,
483–485
prewriting, 6, 333, 344, 380,
411, 432
problem analysis, 468–474
process analysis, 462–463,
466–468
quoted material in, 372–376
revising, 382–386, 403
short story character analysis,
485–493

subject analysis, 474–476
summary type, 423, 425–429
topic sentences, 367–369
et al usage, 554–555
etc./et cetera usage, 611
ethos, logos, pathos, 409–410
euphemisms, 604–605
Evaluating Web Pages
(Berkeley), 514
*Evaluation Criteria for Web
Sources: "The Good, the
Bad, and the Ugly"*
(Beck), **517–518**
evaluative response essays
defined, 438
organizing and developing,
438–439
*Thanksgiving Beyond the
Cleaver Family* (Kheng),
439–442
when to write, 438
writer's strategy, 442–443
writing practice, 443
everybody/everyone usage, 611
evidence supporting arguments,
412
example terms, 392
except/accept usage, 607
exclamation points, 593
exemplification in definition
essays, 445, 448
expert's definition in definition
essays, 445
explicit *vs.* implicit arguments,
407–408

face-to-face interviews, 522–523
Facing It (Komanyakaa),
195–197, 476, 484
false analogy as logical fallacy,
420
false cause as logical fallacy, 420
false dilemma as logical fallacy,
420
family interactions, 7
farther/further usage, 611
fewer/less usage, 611
figures of speech, 477

film or DVD citations, 551
films
active viewing, 286–287
American Beauty, **288–297**
analysis of, 284–285
*An Inconvenient
Truth,***308–317**
Crash, **298–306,** 443
Man on Wire, **320–325**
terms and concepts, 286
as text, 283
writing about, 287
firstly/first usage, 612
flashback in films, 286
flashforward in films, 286
focus of writing, 352–354, 370,
380
forecasted thesis, 356, 380. *See
also under* thesis of
writing
"frag" errors, 569–571
fragments of sentences, 564,
569–571
freewriting, 333–335
*The Fringe Benefits of Failure,
and the Importance of
Imagination* (Rowling),
165–170, 377
*From Access to Acceptance:
Enabling America's
Largest Minority*
(Paaske), 402, **524–539**
*From Learning as Torture to
Learning as Fun*
(Tapscott), **255–260,** 460
from/off of usage, 614
fun/amusing usage, 612
further/farther usage, 611
fused sentences, 571–574

Gale Literary Databases, 514
gaps in logic, 396
gender differences
Blue Spruce (Perry), **79–80**
*Boy Friend: Between Those Two
Words, a Guy Can Get
Crushed* (Copeland),
45–50

Modern Romance (Biever),
51–54
Peaches (McKnight), **71–77**
Pigskin, Patriarchy, and Pain
(Sabo), **85–88**
Virtual Love (Daum), **56–65**
Watching My Back (Klein),
82–83
When a Woman Says No
(Goodman), **89–91**
*Where Are You Going, Where
Have You Been?* (Oates),
92–106
Who's Cheap? (Lara), **68–69**
gender specific writing, 575, 606
generalizations as logical
fallacies, 420
generational differences
Are Families Dangerous
(Ehrenreich), **37–39**
Breaking Tradition
(Mirikitani), **21–23**
The Color of Love (Senna),
16–20
The Good Daughter (Hwang),
12–15
The Lanyard (Collins), **41–42**
Under My Skin (Bowen),
29–32
My Son, My Compass (Smith),
8–11
The Only Child (Leonard),
34–36
On Teenagers and Tattoos
(Martin), **24–28**
Thanksgiving (Goodman), 3
gerunds, 566
glossary of usage, 607–618
The Good, the Bad, and the
Ugly: or, Why It's a Good
Idea to Evaluate Web
Sources (Beck), 516
The Good Daughter (Hwang),
12–15, 336, 342,
344, 443
good/well usage, 612
Google, 513
government author citations, 542

grammar. *See also* sentences
  adjectives, 564
  adverbs, 564, 572–574
  archaic words, 604–605
  clauses, 561, 566–568, 584–585
  comma splices, 571
  fragments, 569–571
  infinitive phrases, 565
  misplaced modifiers, 583–584
  mixed sentences, 581–582
  parallel construction, 584–585
  prepositions, 563, 565
  pronoun case, 576–577
  pronoun reference
    agreement, 574–576
  pronouns, 562
  run-on sentences, 571
  shifts, 579–581
  subject-verb agreement,
    577–578
  verbs, 563–564

Grammar Girl Online, 560

hanged/hung usage, 612
hasty generalization as logical
  fallacy, 420
have/of usage, 614
he, he/she, his/her usage, 606, 612
Health and Wellness Center, 514
helping verbs, 564
Hidden in Plain Sight (Malik),
  129–131
himself/hisself usage, 612
his/her, he/she usage, 606, 612
hisself/himself usage, 612
humanity/mankind usage, 606,
  613
humor in writing, 397
hung/hanged usage, 612
hyphens (punctuation), 601–602

I Confess Some Envy
  (McKelvey), **451–453**
ideal thesis, 356–357, 380
AnIdentity Reduced to a Burka
  (Issa and Al-Marayati),
  124–127

i.e./e.g. usage, 611
i.e./that is usage, 612
If the Genes Fit (Neil), **178–180,**
  423–425
illicit/elicit usage, 611
illusion/allusion usage, 608
illustration terms, 392
images in poetry, 476
immigrate to/emigrate from
  usage, 611
imminent/eminent usage, 611
imperative mood, 581
implicit *vs.* explicit arguments,
  407–408
implied thesis, 357
imply/infer usage, 612
in addition/plus/moreover
  usage, 615
in any way/nohow usage, 614
An Inconvenient Truth (film)
  *Al Gore Warms Up to a Very Hot
    Topic* (Crust), **308–310**
  Did Al Get the Science Right?
    (Mieszkowski), **310–316**
  *Warning of Calamities and
    Hoping for a Change*
    (Scott), **316–317**
incubation period, 344
indefinite pronouns, 562, 575, 592
independent clauses, 566–568,
  571, 585
indicative mood, 581
indirect objects of
  sentences, 562
indirect source citations, 543
inference cards, 486, 493–495
infer/imply usage, 612
infinitive phrases, 565
In Groups We Shrink (Tavris),
  261–263
Internet research, 511, 514–518
Internet sources in research
  papers, 543–544
interrogative pronouns, 562
interviews, 522–523
introduction, preface, foreword
  or afterword citations,
  549

introduction writing
  anecdotes or illustrations in,
    399–400
  argument essays, 410–411
  biography, 496
  definitions in, 400
  deliberate contradition
    in, 400
  description in, 399
  direct quotations in, 398–399
  mixed methods, 401
  questions in, 399
  revising, 385
  statistic or startling fact or
    idea in, 400
  subject analysis essays, 475
in which/which usage, 618
irony, 453
irregardless/regardless
  usage, 612
irrelevant details, 370–371
isle/aisle usage, 608
Issues and Controversies, 514
Is There a Doctor in the Mouse?
  (Parikh), **229–231,**
  378–379, 413–414
italics (punctuation), 540, 544,
  597–598
its/it's usage, 612

jargon, 603–604
journal citations, 549–550
journal writing, 335–337

key word repetition, 393–396
key words in poems, 476
key word substitutions, 394
King Curtis's Echo (Thayer),
  191–194, 352, 379

The Lanyard (Collins),
  41–42, 484
later/latter usage, 613
latter/later usage, 613
lay/lie usage, 613
lead/led usage, 613
led/lead usage, 613
less/fewer usage, 611

Library of Congress Subject
   Headings, 512–513
library research, 510, 512–514
lie/lay usage, 613
linking verbs, 563
listing, 339–340, 360–361,
   485–487
listservs, 513
literature citations, 542
Literature Research Center
   (LRC), 514
Living in Two Worlds (Mabry),
   109–111, 402, 519
Living Under Circe's Spell
   (Soyster), **158–160**
logical fallacies
   appeal to false
      authority, 419
   appeal to fear, 419
   appeal to pity, 420
   bandwagon appeal, 420
   begging the question (circular
      reasoning), 420
   domino theory, 420
   false analogy, 420
   false cause, 420
   false dilemma (either/or
      argument), 420
   hasty generalization, 420
   name calling, 420
   personal or *"ad hominem"*
      attacks, 420
   ripple effect, 420
   slippery slope, 420
   unqualified
      generalization, 420
logos, pathos, ethos, 409–410
loose/lose usage, 613
Los Vendidos (Valdez), **144–154**
lots/lots of usage, 613
LRC (Literature Research
   Center), 514

magazine citations, 549–550
main clauses, 566
Makes Learning Fun (Stoll),
   247–253, 379, 400, 443,
   460
mankind/humanity usage, 606

Man on Wire (film)
   Man on Wire (Turan), **323–325**
   *Walking on Air Between the
      Towers* (Scott), **321–323**
Man on Wire (film review),
   323–325
many/much usage, 613
mapping ideas, 431
maybe/may be usage, 613
may/can usage, 609
may of/might of usage, 613
media/medium
   usage, 613
MedlinePlus, 514, 515
me/myself usage, 614
metaphors, 477
might of/may of usage, 613
misplaced modifiers, 583
mixed sentences, 581–582
MLA (Modern Language
   Association), 372,
   540–544, 546–554
"mm" errors, 583
Modern Language Association
   (MLA), 372, 540–544,
   546–554
Modern Romance (Biever),
   51–54
modifiers in sentences, 583–584
mood shifts in writing, 581
moreover/plus/in addition
   usage, 615
motion pictures. *see* films
movies. *See* films
Mr. Z (Holman), **133–134,** 484
*My Favorite School Class:
   Involuntary Servitude*
   (Goodwin), 414,
   416–418
myself/me usage, 614
My Son, My Compass (Smith),
   8–11, 342
The Myth of the Latin Woman
   (Cofer), **172–176,**
   337, 392

name-calling as logical
   fallacy, 420
narration essays

brainstorming for,
   430–431
drafting the paper, 432
organizing and developing,
   430–432
prewriting, 431–432
thesis, 432
Through the Cracks (Hall-
   Naganuma), **433–436**
when to use, 429–430, 429–437
writer's strategy, 436–437
writing practice, 437
narration in films, 286
narrator of poems, 480
negation in definition essays,
   445, 448
neither as a singular in proper
   usage, 614
newspaper citations, 550
NewspaperSource, 514
nohow/in any way
   usage, 614
nonacademic audiences, 345
none as singular or plural in
   proper usage, 614
note cards, 493–494, 521
note taking, 486, 510–511
noun as subject of
   sentences, 561
nouns, compound, 591
novel citations, 542, 548
nowhere/nowheres
   usage, 614
number/amount usage, 608

objective pronouns, 576
object of sentences,
   562–563
off of/from usage, 614
of/have usage, 614
O.K., So I'm Fat (Steinberg),
   201–203, 400, 407–408,
   460
O.K./OK/okay usage, 614
on account of/because
   usage, 614
online research, 514–518
online sources in research papers,
   543–544, 551–554

The Only Child (Leonard), **34–36,** 344, 365, 393, 399

On Teenagers and Tattoos (Martin), **24–27,** 412

opinions, 218–219

Organized Wisdom, 514

organizing information
active reading, 341–342
block method, 455–456
chronological arrangement, 366, 392
clustering, 337–339, 431
emphatic/dramatic arrangement, 365
listing, 339–340, 360–361, 485–487
outlining, 364–367, 411
point by point method, 455–456
spatial arrangements, 365, 393

outlining, 364–367, 411

owing to the fact that/because usage, 614

oxymorons, 397

painting citations, **243–245,** 551

paragraph structure
coherence, 369–370, 390–396
irrelevant details, 370–371
revising, 385
topic sentences, 367–369, 380
transitions, 395–396

parallel construction, 584–585

paraphrasing, 377–380, 520–521, 595

parentheses (punctuation), 599–600

parenthetical citations in research papers
APA style, 554–559
elements of, 545
MLA style
authors, 540–542, 546–547, 554–555
corporation or government, 547

edition number, 548

encyclopedia or reference book, 549

film or DVD, 551

indirect sources, 542

interviews, 550

introduction, preface, foreword or afterword, 549

literature, 542–543, 548

online sources, 543–544, 551–554

painting, sculpture or photograph, 551

periodicals, 549–550

reviews, 550

song lyrics, 551

television or radio program, 551

titles, 540, 548, 597

translations, 548

participles, 566

passed/past usage, 614

pathos, ethos, logos, 409–410

Peaches (McKnight), **71–77,** 493

peer editors, 386

perceptual differences
Black Men and Public Space (Staples), **181–185**
Bodily Harm (Erens), **208–213**
"Diabesity," A Crisis in an Expanding Country (Brody), **204–207**
The Difference Between Pity and Empathy (Vaughn), **162–164**
Discrimination at Large (Coleman), **198–200**
Facing It (Komanyakaa), **195–197**
The Fringe Benefits of Failure, and the Importance of Imagination (Rowling), **165–170**
If the Genes Fit (Neil), **178–180**
King Curtis's Echo (Thayer), **191–194**

Living Under Circe's Spell (Soyster), **158–160**

The Myth of the Latin Woman (Cofer), **172–176**

O.K., So I'm Fat (Steinberg), **201–203**

Six Rules for Eating Wisely (Pollan), **214–216**

Who Shot Johnny? (Dickerson), **186–190**

periodicals citations, 549–550

periodicals search, 513

periods (punctuation), 593

"p" errors, 586

personal attacks as logical fallacies, 420

personal pronouns, 562, 574

person and number shifts, 579

personification in poetry, 477

persuasion as argument, 405

The Philosophy of Andy Warhol, **246**

photograph citations, 551

phrases, 564–566, 584

Pigskin, Patriarchy, and Pain (Sabo), **85–88,** 335, 358

plagiarism, 372, 377, 378, 380, 519–520

play citations, 543

plot of films, 286

plural pronouns, 574

plurals and the use of apostrophes, 592

plus/moveover/in addition usage, 615

poem citations, 543, 548

poetry analysis essays
active reading, 477–480
Breaking The Ties that Bind (Sakatani), **480–483**
Breaking Tradition (Mirikitani), **478–479**
defined, 476–477
summary writing in, 429
writer's strategy, 483–484
writing practice, 484

point by point method of organizing data, 455–456

point of view (POV) in films, 286
points of view analysis
  Coke (Dacey), **243–245**
  In Groups We Shrink (Tavris),
    261–263
  Is There a Doctor in the Mouse?
    (Parikh), **229–231**
  *From Learning as Torture to
    Learning as Fun*
    (Tapscott), **255–260**
  Makes Learning Fun (Stoll),
    247–253
  The Rights of the Born
    (Lamott), **271–274**
  Shooting an Elephant
    (Orwell), **264–270**
  *Three Ways of Meeting
    Oppression* (King),
    279–281
  Tilling a New World
    (McKibben), **276–278**
  When Reality TV Gets Too Real
    (Peters), **239–242**
  When the Patient is a Googler
    (Haig), **225–228**
  The Whole World is Watching
    (Friedman), **219–221**
  Why Reality TV is Good for Us
    (Poniewozik), **233–238**
  YouTube This! (Queenan),
    222–224
positioning a thesis, 358–359
possessive nouns and the use of
  apostrophes, 590–592
possessive pronouns, 592
precede/proceed usage, 615
preface, foreword, introduction
  or afterword citations,
  549
prejudice/prejudiced usage, 615
prepositions, 563, 565, 577
pre-reading, 335–336
pretentious words, 604–605
prewriting. *See also* active
  reading; essay writing;
  organizing information
  as active reading, 6
  aim identification, 352

argument essays, 411
claim, 352–353
and critical thinking, 342,
  381–382
as discovery, 333, 380, 432
finding focus, 352
first draft, 361–363
incubation period, 344
narration essays, 431–432
organization of material,
  365–366
outlining, 364–365, 366
purpose in, 351
research papers, 509
revising, 364
short story analysis essays,
  485–487
thesis
  changing of, 357
  claim or aim, 351–352
  developing support, 360
  drafting, 360
  finding focus, 352–353
  forecasting or blueprint,
    356–357
  general to specific claim, 353
  listing, 360
  "missing" or implied, 357
  positioning of, 358
  practice exercise, 354–356
  "so what" strategy, 359
  varying focus, 353–354
  working, 361
  writing practice, 358–359
principal/principle usage, 615
problem analysis essays
  *Don't Let Stereotypes Warp
    Your Judgments*
    (Heilbroner), **470–473**
  organizing and developing,
    468–469
  when to use, 468
  writing practice, 473–474
proceed/precede usage, 615
process analysis essays
  brainstorming for, 462
  How to Get Better Gas Mileage
    (Mieszkowski), **463–466**

organizing and developing,
  462–463
in small groups, 463
writing practice, 467–468
pronouns
  and apostrophe use, 592
  case, 576–577
  pairs, 576
  reference agreement, 574–575
  as subject of sentences, 562
  substitutions, 394–395
proofreading, 511
proposal writing, 409
ProQuest, 514
punctuation
  apostrophes, 589–592
  brackets, 519, 600
  colons, 594
  commas, 586–589
  dashes, 595
  ellipsis, 519, 598–599
  exclamation points, 593
  hyphen, 601–602
  italics, 597–598
  parentheses, 599–600
  periods, 593
  question marks, 593
  quotation marks, 595–597
  semi-colons, 567, 593
  slashes, 597, 600–601
puns, 397
purpose in writing, 351

qtd. in usage, 543
question marks, 593
questions in introductions, 399
quotation marks, 540, 595–597
quoted material. *See also*
  citations in research
  papers
  author credits, 372, 540–542
  corporate or government
    author, 542
  essays and articles, 544
  in evaluative response
    essays, 438
  indirect sources, 543
  in introductions, 398–399

novel, play or poem, 542–543, 596–597

online sources, 543–544

paraphrasing, 377–380, 520–521, 595

plagiarism, 372, 377, 378, 380, 519–520

"sandwich technique" for incorporating, 373–376, 380

songs, 544, 551

titles, 597

quote/quotation usage, 615

Race Is a Four-Letter Word (Arboleda), **120–123**

racial differences, 108–109. *See also* cultural differences

raise/rise usage, 615

reading. *See* active reading

Reality Check (Garcia), **456–459**

reason and analysis in arguments, 413

reason is because/that usage, 615

reason why/reason usage, 616

recognizing a thesis, 354–356, 432

The Red Convertible (Erdrich), **135–143,** 493

redundancies in writing, 605

reference book or encyclopedia citations, 549

references page in research papers, 556. *See also* citations in research papers

"ref" errors, 574–575

refuting *vs.* conceding, 414–415

regardless/irregardless usage, 612

relative pronouns, 562

research papers

APA style guide, 554–559

discovering topic and materials, 510

drafting and revising, 511

Internet research, 514–518

interviews, 522–523

library research, 510, 512–514

MLA style guide, 540–544, 546–554

note cards, 521

note taking, 510–511

plagiarism, 519–520

planning of, 509

references page, 556

thesis development, 522

time schedule for, 510–512

works cited page, 544–545, 556

review citations, 550

revising papers

audience concerns, 381–382, 398–401

checklist for, 385–386

coherence, 390–391, 396

conclusions, 385, 401–403

critical thinking, 381–382

Dieting Daze: No In-Between (Krell), **387–390**

essays, 403

gaps, 396

introductions, 398–401

key word repetition, 393–394

key word substitutions, 394

mechanics, 385

pronouns, 394–395

research papers, 511

rewriting, 381

rough drafts, 382–384

style, 385

synonyms, 394

titles, 385, 397–398

transitions, 391–393, 395–396

The Rights of the Born (Lamott), **271–274**

ripple effect as logical fallacy, 420

rise/raise usage, 615

"r-o" errors, 571, 573

The Rose's Thorns (Turan), **294–297**

run-on sentences, 571–574

"sandwich technique" for incorporating quoted

material, 373–376, 380, 480

scheduling research papers, 510

sculpture citations, 551

search engines, 513, 515

self-perception, 157–158

semi-colons (punctuation), 567, 593

sentences

adjectives and adverbs in, 564

clauses in, 566–568

comma splice, 571

fragments, 569–571

misplaced modifiers, 583–584

mixed, 581–582

modifiers in, 583–584

object of, 562–563

parallel construction, 584–585

phrases in, 564–566

revising, 385

run-on, 571–574

structure of, 561–568

subject of, 561–562

subject-verb agreement, 577–578

topic, 367–369, 380

types of, 567–568

verbs in, 563–564

set/sit usage, 616

sexist language, 575, 606

sexual differences, 44–45

she/he, her/his usage, 612

"shift" errors, 579–581

shifts as grammatical errors

in mood, 581

in person or number, 579

in verb tense, 579–580

in voice, 580–581

Shooting an Elephant (Orwell), **264–270**

Short Assignments, **329–332**

short story character analysis, 485–493

should of/could of/would of usage, 610

should of/should have usage, 616

showing *vs.* telling, 436, 507

sight/site/cite usage, 610
similes, 477
simple sentences, 567
since/because usage, 609, 616
since/while/although
usage, 618
singular pronouns, 574
site/cite/sight usage, 610
sit/set usage, 616
Six Rules for Eating Wisely
(Pollan), **214–216,** 413
skepticism, 405–406
slang, 603–604
slashes (punctuation),
597, 600–601
slippery slope as logical fallacy,
420
small group practice, 463
somebody/someone usage, 616
sometime/some time/sometimes
usage, 616
song lyric citations, 551
"so what?" strategies, 359, 371
spacial relationship terms, 391
spatial arrangement of
material, 365, 393
specially/especially
usage, 611
spell-checking, 511
stance of writing, 346
startling fact or idea in
introductions, 400
state-of-being verbs, 563
stationary/stationery
usage, 616
statistics in introductions, 400
style of writing, 346, 350, 385,
572–573
subject analysis essays, 474–475
subjective pronouns, 576
subject of sentences, 561–562
subject-verb agreement, 577–578
subjunctive mood, 581
subordinate clauses, 566
summary essays
organizing and developing,
425–426

as part of larger assignment,
429
*A Summary of "Three Ways of
Meeting Oppression"*
(Thomas), **427–428**
writer's strategy, 428
*A Summary of "Three Ways of
Meeting Oppression"*
(Thomas), **427–428**
summary terms, 392
supporting a thesis,
360–364, 385
supposed to/used to
usage, 616
symbolism in poetry, 477
synonyms used to emphasize
points, 394

television or radio program
citations, 551
telling *vs.* showing, 436, 507
*Terra Firma—A Journey from
Migrant Farm Labor to
Neurosurgery* (Quiñones-
Hinojosa), **116–119,** 412
Thanksgiving (Goodman), **3–5,**
438–439
*Thanksgiving Beyond the Cleaver
Family* (Kheng),
439–442
than/then usage, 616
that is/i.e. usage, 612
that/reason is because
usage, 616
that there/them there/this
here/these here
usage, 617
their/there/they're usage, 617
theme of films, 286
them there/this here/these
here/that there
usage, 617
there is/there are usage, 617
there/their/they're usage, 617
these here/that there/them
there/this here
usage, 617

thesis of writing
for argument essays, 411
in biography analysis,
494, 506
in character analysis, 488–489
in comparison-contrast essays,
456, 460
drafting, 360–364, 432
in evaluative response
essays, 438
finding focus, 352–354,
370, 380
ideal, 356–357, 380
implied, 357
in narration essays, 432
outlining, 364–367, 411
positioning, 358–359
in problem analysis
essays, 469
recognizing, 354–356, 432
in research papers, 522
"so what?" strategy, 371
in subject analysis
essays, 475
in summary essays, 425–426
supporting, 360–364
they're/there/their usage, 617
this here/these here/that
there/them there
usage, 617
*Three Ways of Meeting
Oppression* (King),
279–281, 428
Through the Cracks
(Hall-Naganuma),
433–436
through/thru usage, 617
thru/through usage, 617
thusly/thus usage, 617
Tilling A New World
(McKibben), **276–278**
till/until/'til usage, 617
time relationship
terms, 391
time signals in essays, 366,
392–393, 462
title citations, 540, 548, 597

titles as clever phrases, 385, 397–398

titles cited in research papers, 540, 597

tone of writing, 346

topic sentences, 367–369, 380

to/too/two usage, 617

toward/towards usage, 617

Transcending the Suburbs (Denby), **288–291**

transition words and devices, 385, 391–393, 395–396, 496

translation citations, 548

try and/try to usage, 617

two/to/too usage, 617

Under My Skin (Bowen), **29–32**

unique/most unique usage, 617

unqualified generalization as logical fallacy, 420

until/till/'til usage, 617

usage glossary, 608–618

usage/use usage, 617

used to/supposed to usage, 616

verbal phrases, 565–566

verbs

  action type, 563

  choice of causing mixed meanings, 582

  defined, 563

  helping type, 564

  infinitive phrases, 565

  -ing phrases, 566

  state-of-being type, 563

  subject-verb agreement, 577–578

  tense shifts, 579–580

viewpoint analysis

  Coke (Dacey), **243–245**

  In Groups We Shrink (Tavris), **261–263**

Is There a Doctor in the Mouse? (Parikh), **229–231**

From Learning as Torture to Learning as Fun (Tapscott), **255–260**

Makes Learning Fun (Stoll), **247–253**

The Rights of the Born (Lamott), **271–274**

Shooting an Elephant (Orwell), **264–270**

Three Ways of Meeting Oppression (King), **279–281**

Tilling a New World (McKibben), **276–278**

When Reality TV Gets Too Real (Peters), **239–242**

When the Patient is a Googler (Haig), **225–228**

The Whole World is Watching (Friedman), **219–221**

Why Reality TV is Good for Us (Poniewozik), **233–238**

YouTube This! (Queenan), **222–224**

Virtual Love (Daum), **56–65,** 430

voice of writing, 346, 580–581

Walking on Air Between the Towers (Scott), **321–323**

Warning of Calamities and Hoping for a Change (Scott), **316–317**

Watching My Back (Klein), **82–83,** 366

weather/whether usage, 617

well/good usage, 612

When a Woman Says No (Goodman), **89–91,** 365

When Reality TV Gets Too Real (Peters), **239–242,** 340

When the Patient is a Googler (Haig), **225–228**

Where Are You Going, Where Have You Been? (Oates), **92–106,** 340, 486

whether/weather usage, 617

which/in which usage, 618

which/who usage, 618

while/although/since usage, 618

The Whole World is Watching (Friedman), **219–221,** 443

Who's Cheap? (Lara), **68–69**

Who Shot Johnny? (Dickerson), **186–190,** 443

who's/whose usage, 618

Who Were You, Connie, and Why Did You Go? (Enriquez), **489–492**

who/which usage, 618

Why Reality TV Is Good For Us (Poniewozik), **233–237,** 336, 340, 413

Why Stop Smoking? Let's Get Clinical (Harrison), **347–349,** 377, 379, 400

Wikipedia, 514

word choice, 385, 603–606, 608–618

wordplay, 397

works cited page in research papers, 544–545, 556

would of/should of/could of usage, 610

would of/would have usage, 618

writing. *See also* argument essays; brainstorming; essay writing; grammar; prewriting; research papers

  aim/purpose, 332, 351, 380

  audience identification, 345–347, 350

  claim/intent, 332, 352–359, 380 (*See also under* thesis of writing)

clichés, 603
conclusions, 385, 401–403, 507
editing, 382–386, 403
euphemisms, 604–605
film reviews, 287
freewriting, 333–335
introductions, 385, 398–401, 410–411, 496
journals, 335–337
key word repetition, 393–396
mood shifts, 581
organizing information, 337–342, 364–367

paragraph structure, 367–371
proposals, 409
quoted material, 372–380
redundancies, 605
revising, 382–386, 403
sexist language, 606
Short Assignments (Anne Lamott), **329–331**
slang, 603–604
style of, 346, 350, 385, 572–573
titles, 385, 397–398
transition words and devices, 385, 391–393, 395–396, 496

vivid language in, 603–606
voice shifts, 580–581

Yahoo!, 513
You Call That Irony? (Winokur), **446–447**
your/you're usage, 618
YouTube This! (Queenan), **222–224**
you/you the reader usage, 618